INSTRUCTORS...

Would you like your **students** to show up for class more **prepared**? *(Let's face it, class is much more fun if everyone is engaged and prepared...)*

Want ready-made application-level **interactive assignments,** student progress reporting, and auto-assignment grading? *(Less time grading means more time teaching...)*

Want an **instant view of student or class performance** relative to learning objectives? *(No more wondering if students understand...)*

Need to **collect data and generate reports** required for administration or accreditation? *(Say goodbye to manually tracking student learning outcomes...)*

Want to **record and post your lectures** for students to view online?

With McGraw-Hill's *Connect*™ *Plus MIS,*

INSTRUCTORS GET:

- Interactive Applications—**book-specific interactive assignments** that require students to APPLY what they've learned.
- Simple **assignment management,** allowing you to spend more time teaching.
- **Auto-graded** assignments, quizzes, and tests.
- **Detailed visual reporting,** where student and section results can be viewed and analyzed.
- Sophisticated **online testing** capability.
- A **filtering and reporting** function that allows you to easily assign and report on materials that are correlated to accreditation standards, learning outcomes, and Bloom's taxonomy.
- An easy-to-use **lecture capture** tool.

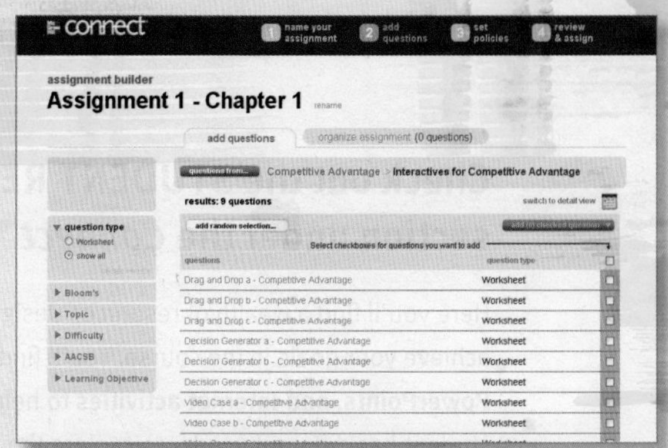

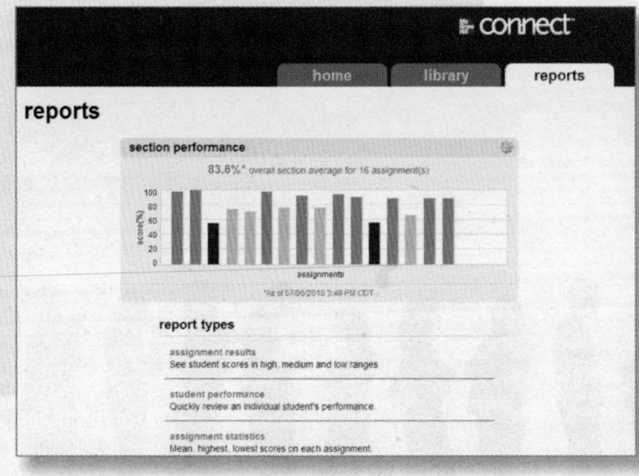

Want an online, **searchable version** of your textbook?

Wish your textbook could be **available online** while you're doing your assignments?

Connect™ Plus MIS eBook

If you choose to use *Connect™ Plus MIS*, you have an affordable and searchable online version of your book integrated with your other online tools.

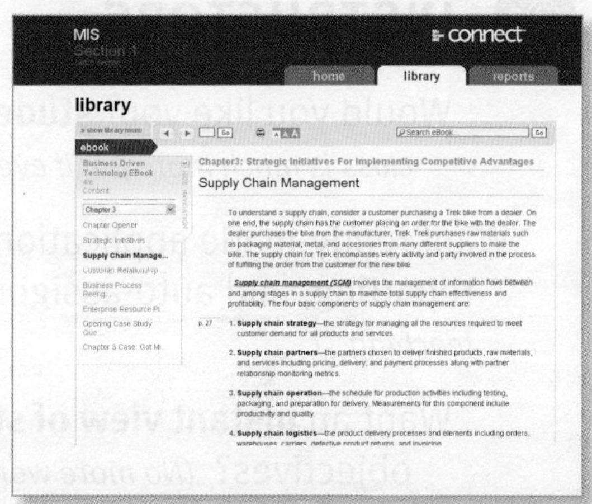

Connect™ Plus MIS eBook offers features like:

- Topic search
- Direct links from assignments
- Adjustable text size
- Jump to page number
- Print by section

Want to get more **value** from your textbook purchase?

Think learning MIS should be a bit more **interesting**?

Check out the STUDENT RESOURCES section under the *Connect™* Library tab.

Here you'll find a wealth of resources designed to help you achieve your goals in the course. You'll find things like **quizzes, PowerPoints, and Internet activities** to help you study. Every student has different needs, so explore the STUDENT RESOURCES to find the materials best suited to you.

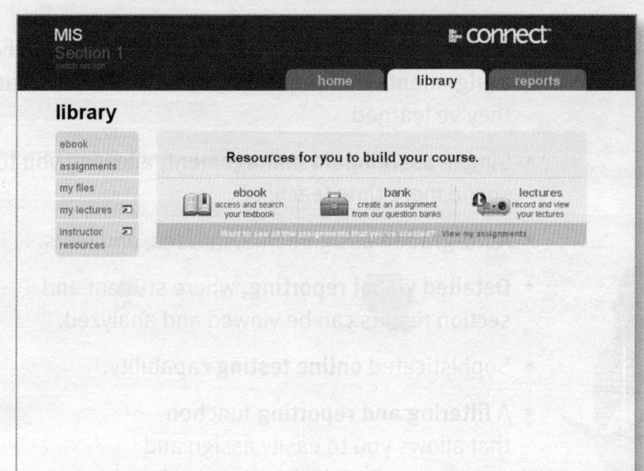

Business Driven Information Systems

Paige Baltzan
Daniels College of Business, University of Denver

Business Driven Information Systems

THIRD EDITION

The McGraw·Hill Companies

BUSINESS DRIVEN INFORMATION SYSTEMS, THIRD EDITION
International Edition 2012

10 09 08 07 06 05 04 03 02 01
20 15 14 13 12 11
CTP COS

When ordering this title, use ISBN 978-1-259-00795-8 or MHID 1-259-00795-2

Printed in Singapore

www.mhhe.com

DEDICATION

To Tony, Hannah, Sophie, and Gus:
What do you always remember?
That I Love You!
That I'm Proud of You!

Paige

BRIEF CONTENTS

CONTENTS

module 1

Business Driven MIS 1

appendices

PREFACE

Business Driven Information Systems discusses various business initiatives first and how technology supports those initiatives second. The premise for this unique approach is that business initiatives should drive technology choices. Every discussion first addresses the business needs and then addresses the technology that supports those needs. This text provides the foundation that will enable students to achieve excellence in business, whether they major in operations management, manufacturing, sales, marketing, finance, human resources, accounting, or virtually any other business discipline. *Business Driven Information Systems* is designed to give students the ability to understand how information technology can be a point of strength for an organization.

Common business goals associated with information technology projects include reducing costs, improving productivity, improving customer satisfaction and loyalty, creating competitive advantages, streamlining supply chains, global expansion, and so on. Achieving these results is not easy. Implementing a new accounting system or marketing plan is not likely to generate long-term growth or reduce costs across an entire organization. Businesses must undertake enterprisewide initiatives to achieve broad general business goals such as reducing costs. Information technology plays a critical role in deploying such initiatives by facilitating communication and increasing business intelligence. Any individual anticipating a successful career in business whether it is in accounting, finance, human resources, or operation management must understand the basics of information technology that can be found in this text.

We have found tremendous success teaching MIS courses by demonstrating the correlation between business and IT. Students who understand the tight correlation between business and IT understand the power of this course. Students learn 10 percent of what they read, 80 percent of what they personally experience, and 90 percent of what they teach others. The business driven approach takes the difficult and often intangible MIS concepts, brings them to the student's level, and applies them using a hands-on approach to reinforce the concepts. Teaching MIS with a business driven focus helps:

- Add credibility to IT.
- Open student's eyes to IT opportunities.
- Attract majors.
- Engage students.

FORMAT, FEATURES, AND HIGHLIGHTS

Business Driven Information Systems is state-of-the-art in its discussions, presents concepts in an easy-to-understand format, and allows students to be active participants in learning. The dynamic nature of information technology requires all students, more specifically business students, to be aware of both current and emerging technologies. Students are facing complex subjects and need a clear, concise explanation to be able to understand and use the concepts throughout their careers. By engaging students with numerous case studies, exercises, projects, and questions that enforce concepts, *Business Driven Information Systems* creates a unique learning experience for both faculty and students.

- **Audience.** *Business Driven Information Systems* is designed for use in undergraduate or introductory MBA courses in Management Information Systems, which are required in many Business Administration or Management programs as part of the common body of knowledge for all business majors.
- **Logical Layout.** Students and faculty will find the text well organized with the topics flowing logically from one chapter to the next. The definition of each term is provided before it is covered in the chapter and an extensive glossary is included at the back of

the text. Each chapter offers a comprehensive opening case study, learning outcomes, closing case studies, key terms, and critical business thinking questions.

- **Thorough Explanations.** Complete coverage is provided for each topic that is introduced. Explanations are written so that students can understand the ideas presented and relate them to other concepts.
- **Solid Theoretical Base.** The text relies on current theory and practice of information systems as they relate to the business environment. Current academic and professional journals cited throughout the text are found in the Notes at the end of the book—a road map for additional, pertinent readings that can be the basis for learning beyond the scope of the chapters or plug-ins.
- **Material to Encourage Discussion.** All chapters contain a diverse selection of case studies and individual and group problem-solving activities as they relate to the use of information technology in business. Two comprehensive cases at the end of each chapter reinforce content. These cases encourage students to consider what concepts have been presented and then apply those concepts to a situation they might find in an organization. Different people in an organization can view the same facts from different points of view and the cases will force students to consider some of those views.
- **Flexibility in Teaching and Learning.** While most textbooks that are "text only" leave faculty on their own when it comes to choosing cases, *Business Driven Information Systems* goes much further. Several options are provided to faculty with case selections from a variety of sources including *CIO, Harvard Business Journal, Wired, Forbes,* and *Time,* to name just a few. Therefore, faculty can use the text alone, the text and a complete selection of cases, or anything in between.
- **Integrative Themes.** Several integrative themes recur throughout the text, which adds integration to the material. Among these themes are value added techniques and methodologies, ethics and social responsibility, globalization, and gaining a competitive advantage. Such topics are essential to gaining a full understanding of the strategies that a business must recognize, formulate, and in turn implement. In addition to addressing these in the chapter material, many illustrations are provided for their relevance to business practice.

WALKTHROUGH

Learning Outcomes

Learning Outcomes. These outcomes focus on what students should learn and be able to answer upon completion of the chapter.

section 3.1 WEB 1.0: EBUSINESS

LEARNING OUTCOMES

3.1 Compare disruptive and sustaining technologies, and explain how the Internet and WWW caused business disruption.

3.2 Describe Web 1.0 along with ebusiness and its associated advantages.

3.3. Compare the four categories of ebusiness models.

3.4. Describe the six ebusiness tools for connecting and communicating.

3.5 Identify the four challenges associated with ebusiness.

Chapter Opening Case Study and Opening Case Questions

Chapter Opening Case Study. To enhance student interest, each chapter begins with an opening case study that highlights an organization that has been time-tested and value-proven in the business world. This feature serves to fortify concepts with relevant examples of outstanding companies. Discussion of the case is threaded throughout the chapter.

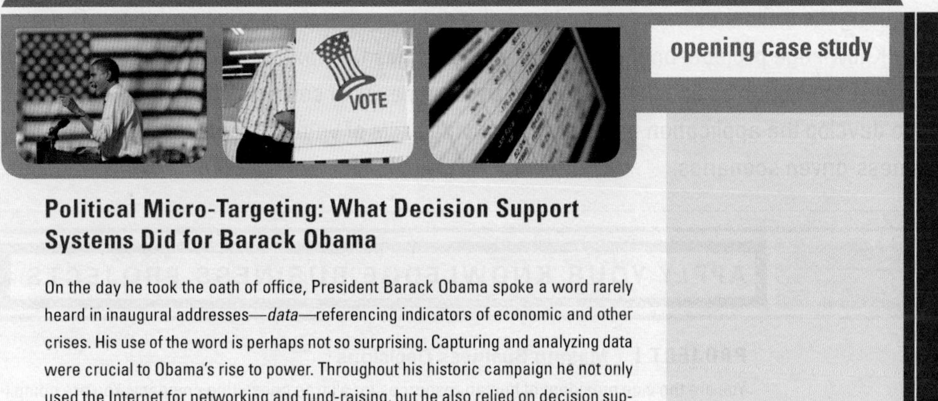

Political Micro-Targeting: What Decision Support Systems Did for Barack Obama

On the day he took the oath of office, President Barack Obama spoke a word rarely heard in inaugural addresses—*data*—referencing indicators of economic and other crises. His use of the word is perhaps not so surprising. Capturing and analyzing data were crucial to Obama's rise to power. Throughout his historic campaign he not only used the Internet for networking and fund-raising, but he also relied on decision support systems to identify potential swing voters. Obama's team carefully monitored contested states and congressional districts, where as few as 2,000 voters could prove decisive—a tiny fraction of the voting public. Both presidential candidates hired technology wizards to help sift through mountains of consumer and demo-

Opening Case Questions. Located at the end of the chapter, poignant questions connect the chapter opening case with important chapter concepts.

OPENING CASE QUESTIONS

1. **Knowledge:** Define the three primary types of decision-making systems, and explain how Obama's campaign team used them to win votes.
2. **Comprehension:** Describe the difference between transactional and analytical information, and determine which types Spotlight Analysis used to identify its 10 tribes.
3. **Application:** Illustrate the business process model used to identify the 10 tribes.
4. **Analysis:** Explain business process reengineering and how Obama's team used it to develop political micro-targeting.
5. **Synthesis:** Formulate different metrics the Obama team used to measure the success of political micro-targeting.

Projects and Case Studies

Case Studies. This text is packed with 27 case studies illustrating how a variety of prominent organizations and businesses have successfully implemented many of this text's concepts. All cases are timely and promote critical thinking. Company profiles are especially appealing and relevant to your students, helping to stir classroom discussion and interest.

Apply Your Knowledge. At the end of each chapter you will find several Apply Your Knowledge projects that challenge students to bring the skills they have learned from the chapter to real business problems. There are also 33 Apply Your Knowledge projects on the OLC that accompanies this text (**www.mhhe.com/baltzan**) that ask students to use IT tools such as Excel, Access, and Dreamweaver to solve business problems. These projects help to develop the application and problem-solving skills of your students through challenging and creative business-driven scenarios.

APPLY YOUR KNOWLEDGE BUSINESS PROJECTS

PROJECT I Making Business Decisions

You are the vice president of human resources for a large consulting company. You are compiling a list of questions that you want each job interviewee to answer. The first question on your list is, "How can MIS enhance your ability to make decisions at our organization?" Prepare a one-page report to answer this question.

PROJECT II DSS and EIS

Dr. Rosen runs a large dental conglomerate—Teeth Doctors—that employs more than 700 dentists in six states. Dr. Rosen is interested in purchasing a competitor called Dentix that has 150 dentists in three additional states. Before deciding whether to purchase Dentix, Dr. Rosen must consider several issues:

- The cost of purchasing Dentix.
- The location of the Dentix offices.
- The current number of customers per dentist, per office, and per state.
- The merger between the two companies.
- The professional reputation of Dentix.
- Other competitors.

End-of-Chapter Elements

Each chapter contains complete pedagogical support in the form of:

Key Terms. With page numbers referencing where they are discussed in the text.

KEY TERMS

Analytical information, 52
Artificial intelligence (AI), 57
As-Is process model, 64
Automation, 69
Benchmarking, 50
Benchmarks, 50
Bottlenecks, 70
Business-facing process, 62
Business process improvement, 69
Business process management (BPM) system, 74
Business process model, 63
Business process modeling (or mapping), 63
Business process reengineering (BPR), 72
Consolidation, 56
Critical success factors (CSFs), 47

Two Closing Case Studies. Reinforcing important concepts with prominent examples from businesses and organizations. Discussion questions follow each case study.

CLOSING CASE TWO

Second Life: Succeeding in Virtual Times

Second Life is a virtual world built and owned by its residents. It opened to the public in 2003, and today it is inhabited by millions of residents from around the world. The three main parts to Second Life are:

- **The World:** The world of Second Life is constantly changing and growing. It is filled with

Critical Business Thinking. The best way to learn MIS is to apply it to scenarios and real-world business dilemmas. These projects require students to apply critical thinking skills and chapter concepts to analyze the problems and make recommended business decisions.

CRITICAL BUSINESS THINKING

1. **Modeling a Business Process**
   Do you hate waiting in line at the grocery store? Do you find it frustrating when you go to the video rental store and cannot find the movie you wanted? Do you get annoyed when the pizza delivery person brings you the wrong order? This is your chance to reengineer the process that drives you crazy. Choose a problem you are currently experienc-

Entrepreneurial Challenge. This unique feature represents a running project that allows students to challenge themselves by applying the MIS concepts to a real business. The flexibility of the case allows each student to choose the type of business he or she would like to operate throughout the case. Each chapter provides hands-on projects your students can work with their real-business scenarios.

ENTREPRENEURIAL CHALLENGE

BUILD YOUR OWN BUSINESS

1. You realize that you need a digital dashboard to help you operate your business. Create a list of all of the components you would want to track in your digital dashboard that would help you run your business. Be sure to justify how each component would help you gain insight into the operations of your business and flag potential issues that could ruin your

About the Plug-Ins

Located on the OLC that accompanies this text (**www.mhhe.com/baltzan**), the overall goal of the plug-ins is to provide an alternative for faculty who find themselves in the situation of having to purchase an extra book to support Microsoft Office. The plug-ins presented here offer integration with the core chapters and provide critical knowledge using essential business applications, such as Microsoft Excel, Microsoft Access, DreamWeaver, and Microsoft Project. Each plug-in uses hands-on tutorials for comprehension and mastery.

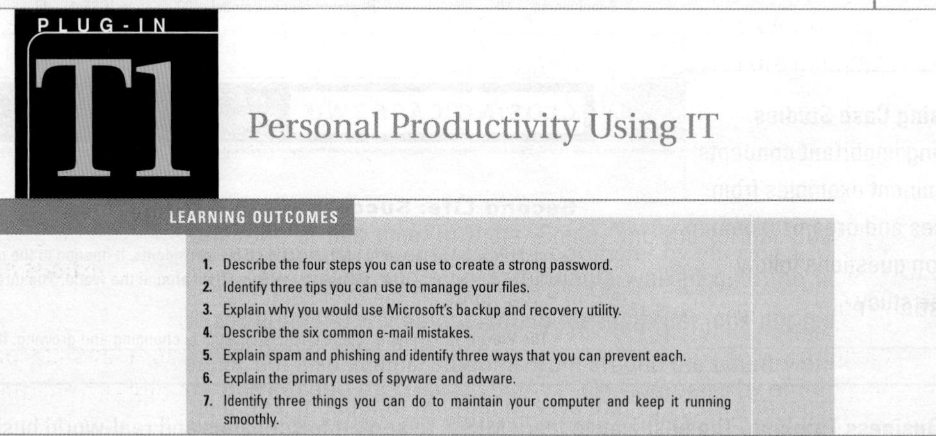

PLUG-IN
T1
Personal Productivity Using IT
LEARNING OUTCOMES
1. Describe the four steps you can use to create a strong password.
2. Identify three tips you can use to manage your files.
3. Explain why you would use Microsoft's backup and recovery utility.
4. Describe the six common e-mail mistakes.
5. Explain spam and phishing and identify three ways that you can prevent each.
6. Explain the primary uses of spyware and adware.
7. Identify three things you can do to maintain your computer and keep it running smoothly.

End-of-Plug-In Elements

Each plug-in contains complete pedagogical support in the form of:
Plug-In Summary. Revisits the plug-in highlights in summary format.
Making Business Decisions. Small scenario-driven projects that help students focus individually on decision making as they relate to the topical elements in the chapters.

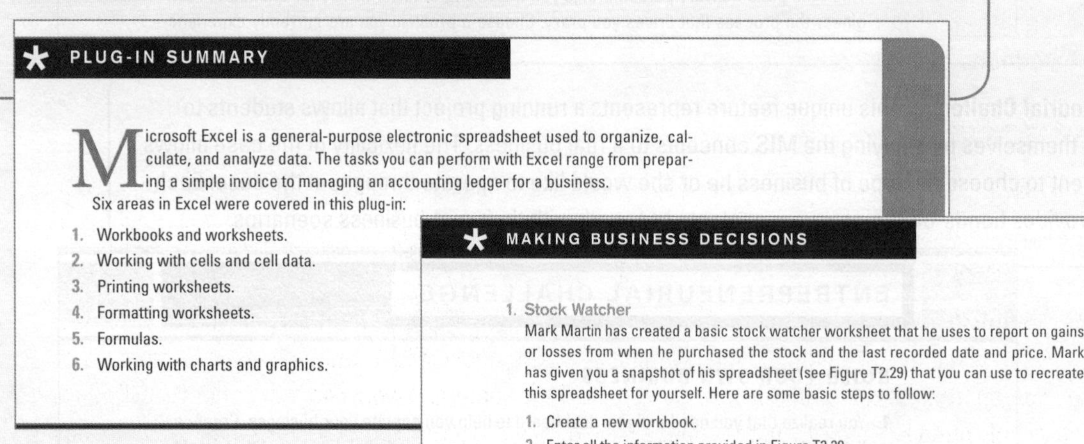

PLUG-IN SUMMARY
Microsoft Excel is a general-purpose electronic spreadsheet used to organize, calculate, and analyze data. The tasks you can perform with Excel range from preparing a simple invoice to managing an accounting ledger for a business.
Six areas in Excel were covered in this plug-in:
1. Workbooks and worksheets.
2. Working with cells and cell data.
3. Printing worksheets.
4. Formatting worksheets.
5. Formulas.
6. Working with charts and graphics.
MAKING BUSINESS DECISIONS
1. Stock Watcher
Mark Martin has created a basic stock watcher worksheet that he uses to report on gains or losses from when he purchased the stock and the last recorded date and price. Mark has given you a snapshot of his spreadsheet (see Figure T2.29) that you can use to recreate this spreadsheet for yourself. Here are some basic steps to follow:
1. Create a new workbook.
2. Enter all the information provided in Figure T2.29.
3. Apply the currency format to the respective columns.

Support and Supplemental Material

All of the supplemental material supporting *Business Driven Information Systems* was developed by the author to ensure you receive accurate, high-quality, and in-depth content. Included is a complete set of materials that will assist students and faculty in accomplishing course objectives.

Online Learning Center (www.mhhe.com/baltzan) The McGraw-Hill website for *Business Driven Information Systems* includes support for students and faculty. All supplements will be available exclusively on the OLC. This will allow the authors to continually update and add to the instructor support materials. The following materials will be available on the OLC:

Video Exercises. Each of the videos that accompany the text is supported by detailed teaching notes on how to turn the videos into classroom exercises where your students can apply the knowledge they are learning after watching the videos.

Test Bank. This computerized package allows instructors to custom design, save, and generate tests. The test program permits instructors to edit, add, or delete questions from the test banks; analyze test results; and organize a database of tests and students' results.

Instructor's Manual (IM). The IM, written by the author, includes suggestions for designing the course and presenting the material. Each chapter is supported by answers to end-of-chapter questions and problems, and suggestions concerning the discussion topics and cases.

PowerPoint Presentations. A set of PowerPoint slides, created by the author, accompanies each chapter and features bulleted items that provide a lecture outline, plus key figures and tables from the text, and detailed teaching notes on each slide.

Image Library. Text figures and tables, as permission allows, are provided in a format by which they can be imported into PowerPoint for class lectures.

Project Files. The author has provided files for all projects that need further support, such as data files.

Cohesion Case. The Broadway Café is a running case instructors can use to reinforce core material such as customer relationship management, supply chain management, business intelligence, and decision making. The case has 15 sections that challenge students to develop and expand their grandfather's coffee shop. Students receive hands-on experience in business and learn technology's true value of enabling business. Please note that the Cohesion Case is not a McGraw-Hill product but a Baltzan direct product. The case can be found at www.cohesioncase.com.

Media Content

Video Content. Twenty videos accompany this text and cover topics from entrepreneurship to disaster recovery. Video content icons are placed throughout the text highlighting where we recommend watching the videos. Video IMs are also available so you can turn the videos into engaging classroom activities.

Use our EZ Test Online to help your students prepare to succeed with Apple iPod® iQuiz. Using our EZ Test Online you can make test and quiz content available for a student's Apple iPod®. Students must purchase the iQuiz game application from Apple for 99¢ in order to use the iQuiz content. It works on fifth generation iPods and better. Instructors only need EZ Test Online to produce iQuiz-ready content. Instructors take their existing tests and quizzes and export them to a file that can then be made available to the student to take as a self-quiz on their iPods.

McGraw-Hill *Connect MIS*

Less Managing. More Teaching. Greater Learning.

McGraw-Hill *Connect MIS* is an online assignment and assessment solution that connects students with the tools and resources they'll need to achieve success.

McGraw-Hill *Connect MIS* helps prepare students for their future by enabling faster learning, more efficient studying, and higher retention of knowledge.

McGraw-Hill *Connect MIS* features

Connect MIS offers a number of powerful tools and features to make managing assignments easier, so faculty can spend more time teaching. With *Connect MIS,* students can engage with their coursework anytime and anywhere, making the learning process more accessible and efficient. *Connect MIS* offers you the features described next.

Simple Assignment Management

With *Connect MIS,* creating assignments is easier than ever, so you can spend more time teaching and less time managing. The assignment management function enables you to:

- Create and deliver assignments easily with selectable end-of-chapter questions and test bank items.
- Streamline lesson planning, student progress reporting, and assignment grading to make classroom management more efficient than ever.
- Go paperless with the eBook and online submission and grading of student assignments.

Smart Grading

When it comes to studying, time is precious. *Connect MIS* helps students learn more efficiently by providing feedback and practice material when they need it, where they need it. When it comes to teaching, your time also is precious. The grading function enables you to:

- Have assignments scored automatically, giving students immediate feedback on their work and side-by-side comparisons with correct answers.
- Access and review each response; manually change grades or leave comments for students to review.
- Reinforce classroom concepts with practice tests and instant quizzes.

Instructor Library

The *Connect MIS* Instructor Library is your repository for additional resources to improve student engagement in and out of class. You can select and use any asset that enhances your lecture.

Student Study Center

The *Connect MIS* Student Study Center is the place for students to access additional resources. The Student Study Center:

- Offers students quick access to lectures, practice materials, eBooks, and more.
- Provides instant practice material and study questions, easily accessible on the go.
- Gives students access to the Personalized Learning Plan described next.

Student Progress Tracking

Connect MIS keeps instructors informed about how each student, section, and class is performing, allowing for more productive use of lecture and office hours. The progress-tracking function enables you to:

- View scored work immediately and track individual or group performance with assignment and grade reports.
- Access an instant view of student or class performance relative to learning objectives.
- Collect data and generate reports required by many accreditation organizations, such as AACSB.

Lecture Capture

Increase the attention paid to lecture discussion by decreasing the attention paid to note taking. For an additional charge, Lecture Capture offers new ways for students to focus on the in-class discussion, knowing they can revisit important topics later. Lecture Capture enables you to:

- Record and distribute your lecture with a click of button.
- Record and index PowerPoint presentations and anything shown on your computer so it is easily searchable, frame by frame.
- Offer access to lectures anytime and anywhere by computer, iPod, or mobile device.
- Increase intent listening and class participation by easing students' concerns about note-taking. Lecture Capture will make it more likely you will see students' faces, not the tops of their heads.

***McGraw-Hill* Connect Plus MIS**

McGraw-Hill reinvents the textbook learning experience for the modern student with *Connect Plus MIS.* A seamless integration of an eBook and *Connect MIS, Connect Plus MIS* provides all of the *Connect MIS* features plus the following:

- An integrated eBook, allowing for anytime, anywhere access to the textbook.
- Dynamic links between the problems or questions you assign to your students and the location in the eBook where that problem or question is covered.
- A powerful search function to pinpoint and connect key concepts in a snap.

In short, *Connect MIS* offers you and your students powerful tools and features that optimize your time and energies, enabling you to focus on course content, teaching, and student learning. *Connect MIS* also offers a wealth of content resources for both instructors and students. This state-of-the-art, thoroughly tested system supports you in preparing students for the world that awaits.

For more information about Connect, go to **www.mcgrawhillconnect.com**, or contact your local McGraw-Hill sales representative.

Tegrity Campus: Lectures 24/7

Tegrity Campus is a service that makes class time available 24/7 by automatically capturing every lecture in a searchable format for students to review when they study and complete assignments. With a simple one-click start-and-stop process, you capture all computer screens and corresponding audio. Students can replay any part of any class with easy-to-use browser-based viewing on a PC or Mac.

Educators know that the more students can see, hear, and experience class resources, the better they learn. In fact, studies prove it. With Tegrity Campus, students quickly recall key moments by using Tegrity Campus's unique search feature. This search helps students efficiently find what they need, when they need it, across an entire semester of class recordings. Help turn all your students' study time into learning moments immediately supported by your lecture.

To learn more about Tegrity watch a 2-minute Flash demo at **http://tegritycampus.mhhe.com.**

Assurance of Learning Ready

Many educational institutions today are focused on the notion of *assurance of learning,* an important element of some accreditation standards. *Business Driven Information Systems* is designed specifically to support your assurance of learning initiatives with a simple, yet powerful solution.

Each test bank question for *Business Driven Information Systems* maps to a specific chapter learning outcome/objective listed in the text. You can use our test bank software, EZ Test and EZ Test Online, or in *Connect MIS* to easily query for learning outcomes/objectives that directly relate to the learning objectives for your course. You can then use the reporting features of EZ Test to aggregate student results in similar fashion, making the collection and presentation of assurance of learning data simple and easy.

AACSB Statement

The McGraw-Hill Companies is a proud corporate member of AACSB International. Understanding the importance and value of AACSB accreditation, *Business Driven Information Systems* 3e recognizes the curricula guidelines detailed in the AACSB standards for business accreditation by connecting selected questions in the test bank to the six general knowledge and skill guidelines in the AACSB standards.

The statements contained in *Business Driven Information Systems* 3e are provided only as a guide for the users of this textbook. The AACSB leaves content coverage and assessment within the purview of individual schools, the mission of the school, and the faculty. While *Business Driven Information Systems* 3e and the teaching package make no claim of any specific AACSB qualification or evaluation, within *Business Driven Information Systems* 3e we have labeled selected questions according to the six general knowledge and skills areas.

McGraw-Hill Customer Care Contact Information

At McGraw-Hill, we understand that getting the most from new technology can be challenging. That's why our services don't stop after you purchase our products. You can e-mail our Product Specialists 24 hours a day to get product-training online. Or you can search our knowledge bank of Frequently Asked Questions on our support website. For Customer Support, call **800-331-5094**, e-mail **hmsupport@mcgraw-hill.com**, or visit **www.mhhe.com/support**. One of our Technical Support Analysts will be able to assist you in a timely fashion.

Apply Your Knowledge

Business Driven Information Systems contains 33 projects that focus on student application of core concepts and tools. These projects can be found on the OLC at **www.mhhe.com/baltzan.**

Project Number	Project Name	Project Type	Plug-In	Focus Area	Project Level	Skill Set	Page Number
1	Financial Destiny	Excel	T2	Personal Budget	Introductory	Formulas	AYK.4
2	Cash Flow	Excel	T2	Cash Flow	Introductory	Formulas	AYK.4
3	Technology Budget	Excel	T1, T2	Hardware and Software	Introductory	Formulas	AYK.4
4	Tracking Donations	Excel	T2	Employee Relationships	Introductory	Formulas	AYK.4
5	Convert Currency	Excel	T2	Global Commerce	Introductory	Formulas	AYK.5
6	Cost Comparison	Excel	T2	Total Cost of Ownership	Introductory	Formulas	AYK.5
7	Time Management	Excel or Project	T12	Project Management	Introductory	Gantt Charts	AYK.6
8	Maximize Profit	Excel	T2, T4	Strategic Analysis	Intermediate	Formulas or Solver	AYK.6
9	Security Analysis	Excel	T3	Filtering Data	Intermediate	Conditional Formatting, Autofilter, Subtotal	AYK.7
10	Gathering Data	Excel	T3	Data Analysis	Intermediate	Conditional Formatting	AYK.8
11	Scanner System	Excel	T2	Strategic Analysis	Intermediate	Formulas	AYK.8
12	Competitive Pricing	Excel	T2	Profit Maximization	Intermediate	Formulas	AYK.9
13	Adequate Acquisitions	Excel	T2	Break-Even Analysis	Intermediate	Formulas	AYK.9
14	Customer Relations	Excel	T3	CRM	Intermediate	PivotTable	AYK.9
15	Assessing the Value of Information	Excel	T3	Data Analysis	Intermediate	PivotTable	AYK.10
16	Growth, Trends, and Forecasts	Excel	T2, T3	Data Forecasting	Advanced	Average, Trend, Growth	AYK.11
17	Shipping Costs	Excel	T4	SCM	Advanced	Solver	AYK.12
18	Formatting Grades	Excel	T3	Data Analysis	Advanced	If, LookUp	AYK.12

(*Continued*)

Project Number	Project Name	Project Type	Plug-In	Focus Area	Project Level	Skill Set	Page Number
19	Moving Dilemma	Excel	T2, T3	SCM	Advanced	Absolute vs. Relative Values	AYK.13
20	Operational Efficiencies	Excel	T3	SCM	Advanced	PivotTable	AYK.14
21	Too Much Information	Excel	T3	CRM	Advanced	PivotTable	AYK.14
22	Turnover Rates	Excel	T3	Data Mining	Advanced	PivotTable	AYK.15
23	Vital Information	Excel	T3	Data Mining	Advanced	PivotTable	AYK.15
24	Breaking Even	Excel	T4	Business Analysis	Advanced	Goal Seek	AYK.16
25	Profit Scenario	Excel	T4	Sales Analysis	Advanced	Scenario Manager	AYK.16
26	Electronic Résumés	HTML	T9, T10, T11	Electronic Personal Marketing	Introductory	Structural Tags	AYK.17
27	Gathering Feedback	Dreamweaver	T9, T10, T11	Data Collection	Intermediate	Organization of Information	AYK.17
28	Daily Invoice	Access	T5, T6, T7, T8	Business Analysis	Introductory	Entities, Relationships, and Databases	AYK.17
29	Billing Data	Access	T5, T6, T7, T8	Business Intelligence	Introductory	Entities, Relationships, and Databases	AYK.19
30	Inventory Data	Access	T5, T6, T7, T8	SCM	Intermediate	Entities, Relationships, and Databases	AYK.20
31	Call Center	Access	T5, T6, T7, T8	CRM	Intermediate Entities, Relationships, and	Databases	AYK.21
32	Sales Pipeline	Access	T5, T6, T7, T8	Business Intelligence	Advanced	Entities, Relationships, and Databases	AYK.23
33	Online Classified Ads	Access	T5, T6, T7, T8	Ecommerce	Advanced	Entities, Relationships, and Databases	AYK.23

MISOURCE

Software Skills and Computer Concepts MISource provides animated tutorials and simulated practice of the core skills in Microsoft Office 2007 Excel, Access, and PowerPoint.

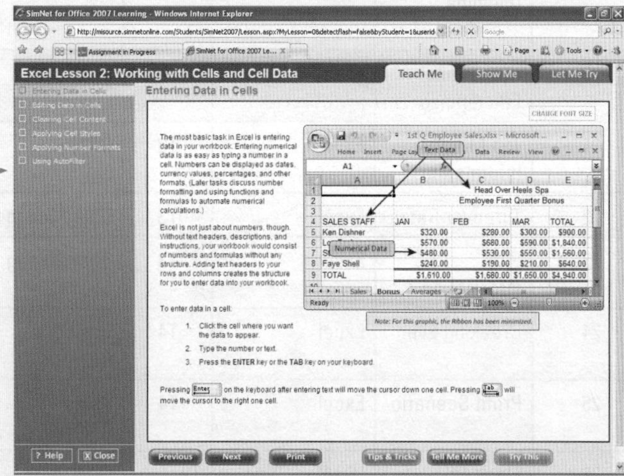

Spend less time reviewing software skills and computer literacy.

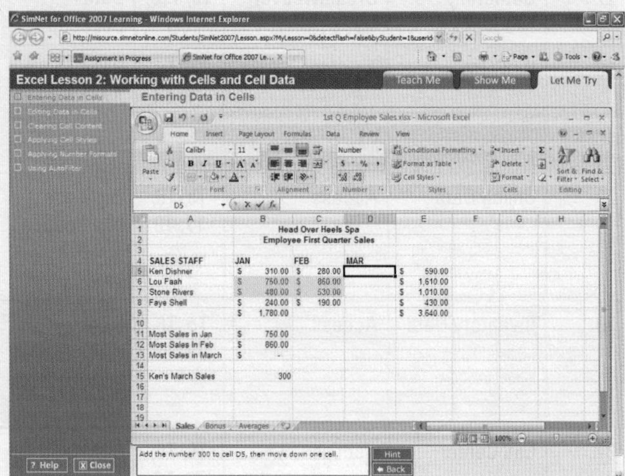

McGraw-Hill Higher Education and Blackboard have teamed up. What does this mean for you?

1. **Your life, simplified.** Now you and your students can access McGraw-Hill's Connect™ and Create™ right from within your Blackboard course—all with one single sign-on. Say goodbye to the days of logging in to multiple applications.
2. **Deep integration of content and tools.** Not only do you get single sign-on with Connect™ and Create™, you also get deep integration of McGraw-Hill content and content engines right in Blackboard. Whether you're choosing a book for your course or building Connect™ assignments, all the tools you need are right where you want them—inside of Blackboard.
3. **Seamless Gradebooks.** Are you tired of keeping multiple gradebooks and manually synchronizing grades into Blackboard? We thought so. When a student completes an integrated Connect™ assignment, the grade for that assignment automatically (and instantly) feeds your Blackboard grade center.
4. **A solution for everyone.** Whether your institution is already using Blackboard or you just want to try Blackboard on your own, we have a solution for you. McGraw-Hill and Blackboard can now offer you easy access to industry leading technology and content, whether your campus hosts it, or we do. Be sure to ask your local McGraw-Hill representative for details.

Craft your teaching resources to match the way you teach! With McGraw-Hill Create, www.mcgrawhill-create.com, you can easily rearrange chapters, combine material from other content sources, and quickly upload content you have written, like your course syllabus or teaching notes. Find the content you need in Create by searching through thousands of leading McGraw-Hill textbooks. Arrange your book to fit your teaching style. Create even allows you to personalize your book's appearance by selecting the cover and adding your name, school, and course information. Order a Create book and you'll receive a complimentary print review copy in 3–5 business days or a complimentary electronic review copy (eComp) via email in about one hour. Go to www.mcgrawhillcreate.com today and register. Experience how McGraw-Hill Create empowers you to teach *your* students *your* way.

ACKNOWLEDGMENTS

Compiling the third edition of *Business Driven Information Systems* has been a tremendous undertaking and there are numerous people whom we want to heartily thank for their hard work, enthusiasm, and dedication.

This text draws from the efforts of a number of people at McGraw-Hill/Irwin. Paul Ducham, our Editorial Director, thank you for your insight, your intellect, and your continuous support and belief in our abilities—we simply could not have succeeded without you! Trina Hauger, our Development Editor, thank you for making all of those lists that keep us on track and focused. Mary Conzachi, our Lead Project Manager, thank you for making the difficult production process smooth and effortless.

In addition we would like to thank Brent Gordon (Editor-in-Chief), Donielle Xu (Marketing Manager), Mary Kazak Sander (Designer), Gregory Bates and Joyce Chappetto (Media Project Managers), Michael McCormick (Production Supervisor), and Keri Johnson (Photo Research Coordinator), for your support and dedication to the success of this text.

Last, but certainly not least, we offer our sincerest gratitude and deepest appreciation to our valuable reviewers whose feedback was instrumental in successfully compiling this text.

Kamal Nayan Agarwal
Howard University

Marvin Albin
University of Southern Indiana

David Bahn
Metropolitan State University

Sunny Baker
California State University—San Bernardino

Cynthia Barnes
Lamar University

Ozden Bayazit
Central Washington University

Jack Becker
University of North Texas

John Benamati
Miami University

Harry Benham
Montana State University

Henry Bojack
Farmingdale State University

Queen Booker
Minnesota State University—Mankato

Timothy Bridges
University of Central Oklahoma

Ralph Caputo
Manhattan College

Judith Carlisle
Dowling College

John Carlson
Baylor University

Jerry Carvalho
Montana State University

Casey Cegielski
Auburn University

Jason Chen
Gonzaga University

Kuan Chen
Purdue University Calumet

Joselina Cheng
University of Central Oklahoma

Robert Chi
California State University—Long Beach

Amita Chin
Virginia Commonwealth University

Richard Christensen
Metropolitan State University

Ta-Tao Chuang
Gonzaga University

Tony Coulson
California State University—San Bernardino

Steven Creason
Metropolitan State University

Jakov Crnkovic
State University of New York—Albany

David Croasdell
University of Nevada—Reno

Peter DeVries
University of Houston—Downtown

David Dulany
Aurora University

Lauren Eder
Rider University

Michael Ekedahl
University of Nevada—Reno

Roger Finnegan
Metropolitan State University

Frederic Fisher
Florida State University—Tallahassee

Linda Fried
University of Colorado—Denver

James Frost
Idaho State University

Jeffrey Gaines
San Jose State University

Norman Garrett
Eastern Illinois University

John Gerdes
University of California—Riverside

Rajni Goel
Howard University

Robert Gordon
Hofstra University

Lorraine Greenwald
SUNY—Farmingdale

John Gudenas
Aurora University

Roslin Hauck
Illinois State University

Rui Huang
State University of Binghamton

Bashorat Ibragimova
University of North Texas

Beata Jones
Texas Christian University

Donald Kalmey
Indiana University Southeast

Rex Karsten
University of Northern Iowa

Chung Kim
Southwest Missouri State

Virginia Kleist
West Virginia University

Mary Beth Klinger
University of Mary Washington

Chang Koh
University of North Texas

Brian Kovar
Kansas State University

Al Lederer
University of Kentucky

Mark Lewis
Regis College

Ying Liu
California State University—
Long Beach

Stephen Loy
Eastern Kentucky University

Joan Lumpkin
Wright State University

Jane Mackay
Texas Christian University

Gary Margot
Ashland University

Don McCubbrey
University of Denver

Nina McGarry
George Washington
University

Alexander McLeod
University of Nevada—Reno

Bernard Merkle
California Lutheran University

Khosrow Moshirvaziri
California State University—
Long Beach

Phillip Musa
University of Alabama—
Birmingham

Bijayananda Naik
University of South Dakota

Thang Nguyen
California State University—
Long Beach

Fred Niederman
Saint Louis University

Michael Pangburn
University of Oregon

Barry Pasternack
California State University—Fullerton

Alan Graham Peace
West Virginia University

Richard Peterson
Montclair State University

Jennifer Pitts
Columbus State University

Floyd Ploeger
Texas State University—
San Marcos

John Powell
University of South Dakota

Leonard Presby
William Patterson University

Mahesh Raisinghani
Texas Women's University

Frederick Rodammer
Michigan State University

I. Michael Romanov
Metropolitan State University

Kirsten Rosacker
University of South Dakota

Bruce Saulnier
Quinnipiac University

Marcos Schniederjans
University of Nebraska—Lincoln

Sheryl Schoenacher
Farmingdale State College

Ken Sears
University of Texas—Arlington

Richard Segall
Arkansas State University

Ravi Sen
Texas A&M University

John Seydel
Arkansas State University

Shanti Shah
Metropolitan State University

Ganesan Shankaranarayanan
Boston University

Stephen Shao
Tennessee State University

K. David Smith
Cameron University

Rafael Solis
California State University—Fresno

Asela Thomason
California State University—
Long Beach

Ray Tsai
St. Cloud State University

Richard Turley
University of Northern Colorado

Robin Wakefield
Baylor University

Shimon Walner
Metropolitan State University

Bin Wang
University of Texas—Pan American

Bruce White
Quinnipiac University

Karen Williams
University of Texas—San Antonio

A. James Wynne
Virginia Commonwealth
University

James Yao
Montclair State University

Myung Yoon
Northeastern Illinois University

Randall Young
University of North Texas

Yue Zhang
California State University—
Northridge

ABOUT THE AUTHOR

Paige Baltzan

Paige Baltzan teaches in the Department of Information Technology and Electronic Commerce at the Daniels College of Business at the University of Denver. She holds a B.S.B.A. specializing in Accounting/MIS from Bowling Green State University and an M.B.A. specializing in MIS from the University of Denver. She is a coauthor of several books, including *Business Driven Technology, Essentials of Business Driven Information Systems, I-Series,* and a contributor to *Management Information Systems for the Information Age.*

Before joining the Daniels College faculty in 1999, Paige spent several years working for a large telecommunications company and an international consulting firm, where she participated in client engagements in the United States as well as South America and Europe. Paige lives in Lakewood, Colorado, with her husband, Tony, and daughters Hannah and Sophie.

Business Driven MIS

module 1

MOST COMPANIES TODAY rely heavily on the use of management information systems (MIS) to run various aspects of their businesses. Whether they need to order and ship goods, interact with customers, or conduct other business functions, management information systems are often the underlying infrastructure performing the activities. Management information systems allow companies to remain competitive in today's fast-paced world and especially when conducting business on the Internet. Organizations must adapt to technological advances and innovations to keep pace with today's rapidly changing environment. Their competitors certainly will!

No matter how exciting technology is, successful companies do not use it simply for its own sake. Companies should have a solid business reason for implementing technology. Using a technological solution just because it is available is not a good business strategy.

The purpose of Module 1 is to raise your awareness of the vast opportunities made possible by the tight correlation between business and technology. Business strategies and processes should always drive your technology choices. Although awareness of an emerging technology can sometimes lead us in new strategic directions, the role of information systems, for the most part, is to support existing business strategies and processes.

MODULE 1: Business Driven MIS

MODULE 2: Technical Foundations of MIS

MODULE 3: Enterprise MIS

Module 1: BUSINESS DRIVEN MIS

1

CHAPTER

Management Information Systems: Business Driven MIS

CHAPTER OUTLINE

SECTION 1.1 Business Driven MIS	SECTION 1.2 Business Strategy
■ Competing in the Information Age ■ The Challenge: Departmental Companies ■ The Solution: Management Information Systems	■ Identifying Competitive Advantages ■ The Five Forces Model—Evaluating Industry Attractiveness ■ The Three Generic Strategies—Choosing a Business Focus ■ Value Chain Analysis—Executing Business Strategies

What's in IT for me?

This chapter sets the stage for the textbook. It starts from ground zero by providing a clear description of what information is and how it fits into business operations, strategies, and systems. It provides an overview of how companies operate in competitive environments and why they must continually define and redefine their business strategies to create competitive advantages. Doing so allows them to survive and thrive. Information systems are key business enablers for successful operations in competitive environments.

You, as a business student, must understand the tight correlation between business and technology. You must first recognize information's role in daily business activities, and then understand how information supports and helps implement global business strategies and competitive advantages. After reading this chapter, you should have a solid understanding of business driven information systems and their role in managerial decision making and problem solving.

opening case study

The World Is Flat: Thomas Friedman

Christopher Columbus proved in 1492 that the world is round. For centuries, sailors maneuvered the seas discovering new lands, new people, and new languages as nations began trading goods around the globe. Then Thomas Friedman, a noted columnist for *The New York Times,* published his book *The World Is Flat.*

Friedman argues that the world has become flat due to technological advances connecting people in China, India, and the United States as if we were all next-door neighbors. Physicians in India are reading X-rays for U.S. hospitals, and JetBlue Airways ticket agents take plane reservations for the company from the comfort of their Utah homes. Technology has eliminated some of the economic and cultural advantages developed countries enjoy, making the world a level playing field for all participants. Friedman calls this Globalization 3.0.

Globalization 1.0 started when Christopher Columbus discovered the world is round and the world shrank from large to medium. For the next several hundred years, countries dominated by white men controlled business. Globalization 2.0 began around 1800, during the Industrial Revolution, when the world went from medium to small. In this era international companies dominated by white men controlled business. Globalization 3.0 began in early 2000, removing distance from the business equation, and the world has gone from small to tiny. In this era, people of all colors from the four corners of the world will dominate business. Farmers in remote villages in Nepal carry an iPhone to access the world's knowledge at, say, Wikipedia or the stock market closing prices at Bloomberg.

Outsourcing, or hiring someone from another country to complete work remotely, will play an enormous role in this era. It has advantages and disadvantages. Outsourcing work to countries where labor is cheap drives down production costs and allows companies to offer lower prices to U.S. consumers. Having an accountant in China complete a U.S. tax return is just as easy as driving to the H&R Block office on the corner, and probably far cheaper. Calling an 800 number for service can connect consumers to an Indian, Canadian, or Chinese worker on the other end of the line. Of course, outsourcing also eliminates some U.S. manufacturing and labor jobs, causing pockets of unemployment. In fact, the United States has outsourced several million service and manufacturing jobs to offshore, low-cost producers.

Figure 1.1 shows Friedman's list of forces that flattened the world. They converged around the year 2000 and "created a flat world: a global, Web-enabled platform for multiple forms of sharing knowledge and work, irrespective of time, distance, geography, and increasingly, language." Three powerful new economies began

FIGURE 1.1

Thomas Friedman's 10 Forces That Flattened the World

Friedman's 10 Forces That Flattened the World	
1. Fall of the Berlin Wall	The events of November 9, 1989, tilted the worldwide balance of power toward democracies and free markets.
2. Netscape IPO	The August 9, 1995, offering sparked massive investment in fiber-optic cables.
3. Work flow software	The rise of applications from PayPal to VPNs enabled faster, closer coordination among far-flung employees.
4. Open sourcing	Self-organizing communities, such as Linux, launched a collaborative revolution.
5. Outsourcing	Migrating business functions to India saved money *and* a Third World economy.
6. Offshoring	Contract manufacturing elevated China to economic prominence.
7. Supply chaining	Robust networks of suppliers, retailers, and customers increased business efficiency.
8. In-sourcing	Logistics giants took control of customer supply chains, helping mom-and-pop shops go global.
9. Informing	Power searching allowed everyone to use the Internet as a "personal supply chain of knowledge."
10. Wireless	Wireless technologies pumped up collaboration, making it mobile and personal.

materializing at this time. In India, China, and the former Soviet Union, more than 3 billion new willing and able participants walked onto the business playing field. Business students will be competing for their first jobs not only against other local students, but also against students from around the country and around the globe.

Bill Gates, founder of Microsoft, says that 20 years ago most people would rather have been a B student in New York than a genius in China, because the opportunities available to students in developed countries were limitless. Today, the opposite is true. It is far easier to succeed as a genius in China because it is so easy to export skills anywhere in the world. A B student in New York is going to have a hard time finding career opportunities.[1]

section 1.1 BUSINESS DRIVEN MIS

LEARNING OUTCOMES

1.1 Describe the information age and the differences among data, information, business intelligence, and knowledge.

1.2 Identify the different departments in a company and why they must work together to achieve success.

1.3 Explain systems thinking and how management information systems enable business communications.

COMPETING IN THE INFORMATION AGE

LO. 1.1: Describe the information age and the differences among data, information, business intelligence, and knowledge.

Did you know that . . .

- The movie *Avatar* took more than four years to create and cost $450 million.
- Lady Gaga's real name is Stefani Joanne Angelina Germanotta.
- Customers pay $2.6 million for a 30-second advertising time slot during the Super Bowl.[2]

A ***fact*** is the confirmation or validation of an event or object. In the past, people primarily learned facts from books. Today, by simply pushing a button people can find out anything, from anywhere, at any time. We live in the ***information age,*** when infinite quantities of facts are widely available to anyone who can use a computer. The impact of information technology on the global business environment is equivalent to the printing press's impact on publishing and electricity's impact on productivity. College student startups were mostly unheard of before the information age. Now, it's not at all unusual to read about a business student starting a multimillion-dollar company from his or her dorm room. Think of Mark Zuckerberg, who started Facebook from his dorm, or Michael Dell (Dell Computers) and Bill Gates (Microsoft), who both founded their legendary companies as college students.

You may think only students well versed in advanced technology can compete in the information age. This is simply not true. Many business leaders have created exceptional opportunities by coupling the power of the information age with traditional business methods. Here are just a few examples:

- Amazon is not a technology company; its original business focus was to sell books, and it now sells nearly everything.
- Netflix is not a technology company; its primary business focus is to rent videos.
- Zappos is not a technology company; its primary business focus is to sell shoes, bags, clothing, and accessories.

Amazon's founder, Jeff Bezos, at first saw an opportunity to change the way people purchase books. Using the power of the information age to tailor offerings to each customer and speed the payment process, he in effect opened millions of tiny virtual bookstores, each with a vastly larger selection and far cheaper product than traditional bookstores. The success of his original business model led him to expand Amazon to carry many other types of products. The founders of Netflix and Zappos have done the same thing for videos and shoes. All these entrepreneurs were business professionals, not technology experts. However, they understood enough about the information age to apply it to a particular business, creating innovative companies that now lead entire industries.

Students who understand business along with the power associated with the information age will create their own opportunities and perhaps even new industries, as co-founders Chris DeWolfe and Tom Anderson did with MySpace and Mark Zuckerberg

APPLY YOUR KNOWLEDGE

BUSINESS DRIVEN DISCUSSION

Pluses and Minuses

The line famously quoted in the film *Spider-Man,* "With great power comes great responsibility," should apply to every type of technology you encounter in business. Technology provides countless opportunities for businesses, but it can also lead to countless pitfalls and traps.

Online trading, for instance, brought many companies profits but cost many individual investors their life savings through fraud. Bernard Madoff, the owner of a high-profile New York investment company, forged investment statements and spent billions of dollars of his client's money. Sites such as Craigslist and eBay allow anyone to become a provider of goods and services and a few unethical individuals have even used it to run online prostitution rings.

A manager must be able to analyze the good and the bad associated with technology. Review some companies that primarily operate on the Internet such as Netflix, Craigslist, or Amazon, and compile a list of the business opportunities and the potential pitfalls associated with doing business online.[3]

did with Facebook. Our primary goal in this course is to arm you with the knowledge you need to compete in the information age. The core drivers of the information age are:

- Data
- Information
- Business intelligence
- Knowledge

Data

Data are raw facts that describe the characteristics of an event or object. Before the information age, managers manually collected and analyzed data, a time-consuming and complicated task without which they would have little insight into how to run their business. Lacking data, managers often found themselves making business decisions about how many products to make, how much material to order, or how many employees to hire based on intuition or gut feelings. In the information age, successful managers compile, analyze, and comprehend massive amounts of data daily, which helps them make more successful business decisions.

Figure 1.2 shows sales data for Tony's Wholesale Company, a fictitious business that supplies snacks to stores. The data highlight characteristics such as order date, customer, sales representative, product, quantity, and profit. The second line in Figure 1.2, for instance, shows that Roberta Cross sold 90 boxes of Ruffles to Walmart for $1,350, resulting in a profit of $450 (note that Profit = Sales − Costs). These data are useful for understanding individual sales; however, they do not provide us much insight into how Tony's business is performing as a whole. Tony needs to answer questions that will help him manage his day-to-day operations such as:

- Who are my best customers?
- Who are my least-profitable customers?
- What is my best-selling product?
- What is my slowest-selling product?
- Who is my strongest sales representative?
- Who is my weakest sales representative?

What Tony needs, in other words, is not data but *information.*

Order Date	Customer	Sales Representative	Product	Qty	Unit Price	Total Sales	Unit Cost	Total Cost	Profit
4-Jan	Walmart	PJ Helgoth	Doritos	41	$24	$ 984	$18	$738	$246
4-Jan	Walmart	Roberta Cross	Ruffles	90	$15	$1,350	$10	$900	$450
5-Jan	Safeway	Craig Schultz	Ruffles	27	$15	$ 405	$10	$270	$135
6-Jan	Walmart	Roberta Cross	Ruffles	67	$15	$1,005	$10	$670	$335
7-Jan	7-Eleven	Craig Schultz	Pringles	79	$12	$ 948	$ 6	$474	$474
7-Jan	Walmart	Roberta Cross	Ruffles	52	$15	$ 780	$10	$520	$260
8-Jan	Kroger	Craig Schultz	Ruffles	39	$15	$ 585	$10	$390	$195
9-Jan	Walmart	Craig Schultz	Ruffles	66	$15	$ 990	$10	$660	$330
10-Jan	Target	Craig Schultz	Ruffles	40	$15	$ 600	$10	$400	$200
11-Jan	Walmart	Craig Schultz	Ruffles	71	$15	$1,065	$10	$710	$355

FIGURE 1.2

Tony's Snack Company Data

FIGURE 1.3

Tony's Data Sorted by Customer "Walmart" and Sales Representative "Roberta Cross"

Order Date	Customer	Sales Representative	Product	Quantity	Unit Price	Total Sales	Unit Cost	Total Cost	Profit
26-Apr	Walmart	Roberta Cross	Fritos	86	$ 19	$ 1,634	$ 17	$ 1,462	$ 172
29-Aug	Walmart	Roberta Cross	Fritos	76	$ 19	$ 1,444	$ 17	$ 1,292	$ 152
7-Sep	Walmart	Roberta Cross	Fritos	20	$ 19	$ 380	$ 17	$ 340	$ 40
22-Nov	Walmart	Roberta Cross	Fritos	39	$ 19	$ 741	$ 17	$ 663	$ 78
30-Dec	Walmart	Roberta Cross	Fritos	68	$ 19	$ 1,292	$ 17	$ 1,156	$ 136
7-Jul	Walmart	Roberta Cross	Pringles	79	$ 18	$ 1,422	$ 8	$ 632	$ 790
6-Aug	Walmart	Roberta Cross	Pringles	21	$ 12	$ 252	$ 6	$ 126	$ 126
2-Oct	Walmart	Roberta Cross	Pringles	60	$ 18	$ 1,080	$ 8	$ 480	$ 600
15-Nov	Walmart	Roberta Cross	Pringles	32	$ 12	$ 384	$ 6	$ 192	$ 192
21-Dec	Walmart	Roberta Cross	Pringles	92	$ 12	$ 1,104	$ 6	$ 552	$ 552
28-Feb	Walmart	Roberta Cross	Ruffles	67	$ 15	$ 1,005	$ 10	$ 670	$ 335
6-Mar	Walmart	Roberta Cross	Ruffles	8	$ 15	$ 120	$ 10	$ 80	$ 40
16-Mar	Walmart	Roberta Cross	Ruffles	68	$ 15	$ 1,020	$ 10	$ 680	$ 340
23-Apr	Walmart	Roberta Cross	Ruffles	34	$ 15	$ 510	$ 10	$ 340	$ 170
4-Aug	Walmart	Roberta Cross	Ruffles	40	$ 15	$ 600	$ 10	$ 400	$ 200
18-Aug	Walmart	Roberta Cross	Ruffles	93	$ 15	$ 1,395	$ 10	$ 930	$ 465
5-Sep	Walmart	Roberta Cross	Ruffles	41	$ 15	$ 615	$ 10	$ 410	$ 205
12-Sep	Walmart	Roberta Cross	Ruffles	8	$ 15	$ 120	$ 10	$ 80	$ 40
28-Oct	Walmart	Roberta Cross	Ruffles	50	$ 15	$ 750	$ 10	$ 500	$ 250
21-Nov	Walmart	Roberta Cross	Ruffles	79	$ 15	$ 1,185	$ 10	$ 790	$ 395
29-Jan	Walmart	Roberta Cross	Sun Chips	5	$ 22	$ 110	$ 18	$ 90	$ 20
12-Apr	Walmart	Roberta Cross	Sun Chips	85	$ 22	$ 1,870	$ 18	$ 1,530	$ 340
16-Jun	Walmart	Roberta Cross	Sun Chips	55	$ 22	$ 1,210	$ 18	$ 990	$ 220
				1,206	**$383**	**$20,243**	**$273**	**$14,385**	**$5,858**

Sorting the data reveals the information that Roberta Cross's total sales to Walmart were $20,243 resulting in a profit of $5,858. (Profit $5,858 = Sales $20,243 − Costs $14,385)

Information

Information is data converted into a meaningful and useful context. Having the right information at the right moment in time can be worth a fortune. Having the wrong information at the right moment; or the right information at the wrong moment can be disastrous. The truth about information is that its value is only as good as the people who use it. People using the same information can make different decisions depending on how they interpret or analyze the information. Thus information has value only insofar as the people using it do as well.

Tony can analyze his sales data and turn them into information to answer all the above questions and understand how his business is operating. Figures 1.3 and 1.4, for instance, show us that Walmart is Roberta Cross's best customer, and that Ruffles is Tony's best product measured in terms of total sales. Armed with this information, Tony can identify and then address such issues as weak products and underperforming sales representatives.

A ***variable*** is a data characteristic that stands for a value that changes or varies over time. For example, in Tony's data, price and quantity ordered can vary. Changing variables allows managers to create hypothetical scenarios to study future possibilities. Tony may find it valuable to anticipate how sales or cost increases affect profitability. To estimate how a 20 percent increase in prices might improve profits, Tony simply changes the price variable for all orders, which automatically calculates the amount of new profits. To estimate how a 10 percent increase in costs hurts profits, Tony changes the cost variable for all orders, which automatically calculates the amount of lost profits. Manipulating variables is an important tool for any business.

Business Intelligence

Business intelligence (BI) is information collected from multiple sources such as suppliers, customers, competitors, partners, and industries that analyzes patterns, trends, and relationships for strategic decision making. BI manipulates multiple variables and in some cases even hundreds of variables including such items as interest rates, weather conditions, and even gas prices. Tony could use BI to analyze internal data such as company sales, along with external data about the environment such as competitors, finances, weather, holidays, and even sporting events. Both internal and external

FIGURE 1.4
Information Gained after Analyzing Tony's Data

Tony's Business Information	Name	Total Profit
Who is Tony's best customer by total sales?	Walmart	$ 560,789
Who is Tony's least-valuable customer by total sales?	Walgreens	$45,673
Who is Tony's best customer by profit?	7-Eleven	$ 324,550
Who is Tony's least-valuable customer by profit?	King Soopers	$ 23,908
What is Tony's best-selling product by total sales?	Ruffles	$ 232,500
What is Tony's weakest-selling product by total sales?	Pringles	$ 54,890
What is Tony's best-selling product by profit?	Tostitos	$ 13,050
What is Tony's weakest-selling product by profit?	Pringles	$ 23,000
Who is Tony's best sales representative by profit?	R. Cross	$1,230,980
Who is Tony's weakest sales representative by profit?	Craig Schultz	$ 98,980
What is the best sales representative's best-selling product by total profit?	Ruffles	$ 98,780
Who is the best sales representative's best customer by total profit?	Walmart	$ 345,900
What is the best sales representative's weakest-selling product by total profit?	Sun Chips	$ 45,600
Who is the best sales representative's weakest customer by total profit?	Krogers	$ 56,050

APPLY YOUR KNOWLEDGE

BUSINESS DRIVEN MIS

Manipulating the Data to Find Your Version of the Truth

How can global warming be real when there is so much snow and cold weather? That's what some people wondered after a couple of massive snowstorms buried Washington, DC, in the winter of 2009–2010. Politicians across the capital made jokes and built igloos as they disputed the existence of climate change. Some concluded the planet simply could not be warming with all the snow on the ground.

These comments frustrated Joseph Romm, a physicist and climate expert with the Center for American Progress. He spent weeks turning data into information and graphs to educate anyone who would listen as to why this reasoning was incorrect. Climate change is all about analyzing data, turning it into information to detect trends. You cannot observe climate change by looking out the window; you have to review decades of weather data with advanced tools to really understand the trends.

Increasingly we see politicians, economists, and newscasters taking tough issues and boiling them down to simplistic arguments over what the data mean, each interpreting the data and spinning the data to support their views and agendas. You need to understand the data and turn them into useful information or else you will not understand when someone is telling the truth and when you are being lied to.

Brainstorm two or three types of data economists use to measure the economy. How do they turn the data into information? What issues do they encounter when attempting to measure the economy? As a manager, what do you need to understand when reading or listening to economic and business reports?[4]

variables affect snack sales, and analyzing these variables will help Tony determine ordering levels and sales forecasts. For instance, BI can predict inventory requirements for Tony's business for the week before the Super Bowl if, say, the home team is playing, average temperature is above 80 degrees, and the stock market is performing well. This is BI at its finest, incorporating all types of internal and external variables to anticipate business performance.

Top managers use BI to define the future of the business, analyzing markets, industries, and economies to determine the strategic direction the company must follow to remain profitable. Tony will set the strategic direction for his firm, which might include introducing new flavors of potato chips or sport drinks as new product lines or schools and hospitals as new market segments.

Knowledge

Knowledge includes the skills, experience, and expertise, coupled with information and intelligence that creates a person's intellectual resources. ***Knowledge workers*** are individuals valued for their ability to interpret and analyze information. Today's workers are commonly referred to as knowledge workers and they use BI along with personal experience to make decisions based on both information and intuition, a valuable resource for any company.

Imagine that Tony analyzes his data and finds his weakest sales representative for this period is Craig Schultz. If Tony considered only this information, he might conclude that firing Craig was a good business decision. However, because Tony has knowledge about how the company operates, he knows Craig has been out on medical leave for several weeks; hence, his sales numbers are low. Without this additional knowledge, Tony

APPLY YOUR KNOWLEDGE

BUSINESS DRIVEN ETHICS AND SECURITY

Information Issues in the Information Age

We live in the information age where the collection, storage, and use of data are hot topics. One example of inappropriate data handling occurred at a college where the monitoring of restrooms occurred every 15 seconds to observe the use of toilets, mirrors, and sinks. Students, faculty, and staff began complaining that the data collection was an invasion of their privacy and a violation of their rights.

Another example of inappropriate data handling occurred when a professor of accounting at a college lost a flash drive containing information for more than 1,800 students, including Social Security numbers, grades, and names. Social Security numbers were included because the data went back to before 1993 when the college used Social Security numbers to identify students.

What types of student data does your college collect? What could happen if your professor lost a thumb drive with all of your personal information? What types of issues could you encounter if someone stole your personal data? What can your college do to ensure this type of data storage violation does not occur?[5]

might have executed a bad business decision, delivered a negative message to the other employees, and sent his best sales representatives out to look for other jobs.

The key point in this scenario is that it is simply impossible to collect all the information about every situation, and yet without that, it can be easy to misunderstand the problem. Using data, information, business intelligence, *and* knowledge to make decisions and solve problems is the key to finding success in business. These core drivers of the information age are the building blocks of business systems.

LO 1.2: Identify the different departments in a company and why they must work together to achieve success.

THE CHALLENGE: DEPARTMENTAL COMPANIES

Companies are typically organized by department or functional area such as:

- **Accounting:** Records, measures, and reports monetary transactions.
- **Finance:** Deals with strategic financial issues including money, banking, credit, investments, and assets.
- **Human resources:** Maintains policies, plans, and procedures for the effective management of employees.
- **Marketing:** Supports sales by planning, pricing, and promoting goods or services.
- **Operations management:** Manages the process of converting or transforming or resources into goods or services.
- **Sales:** Performs the function of selling goods or services (see Figure 1.5).

Each department performs its own activities. Sales and marketing focus on moving goods or services into the hands of consumers; they maintain transactional data. Finance and accounting focus on managing the company's resources and maintain monetary data. Operations management focuses on manufacturing and maintains production data, while human resources focuses on hiring and training people and maintains employee data. Although each department has its own focus and data, none can work independently if the company is to operate as a whole. It is easy to see how a business decision made by one department can affect other departments. Marketing needs to

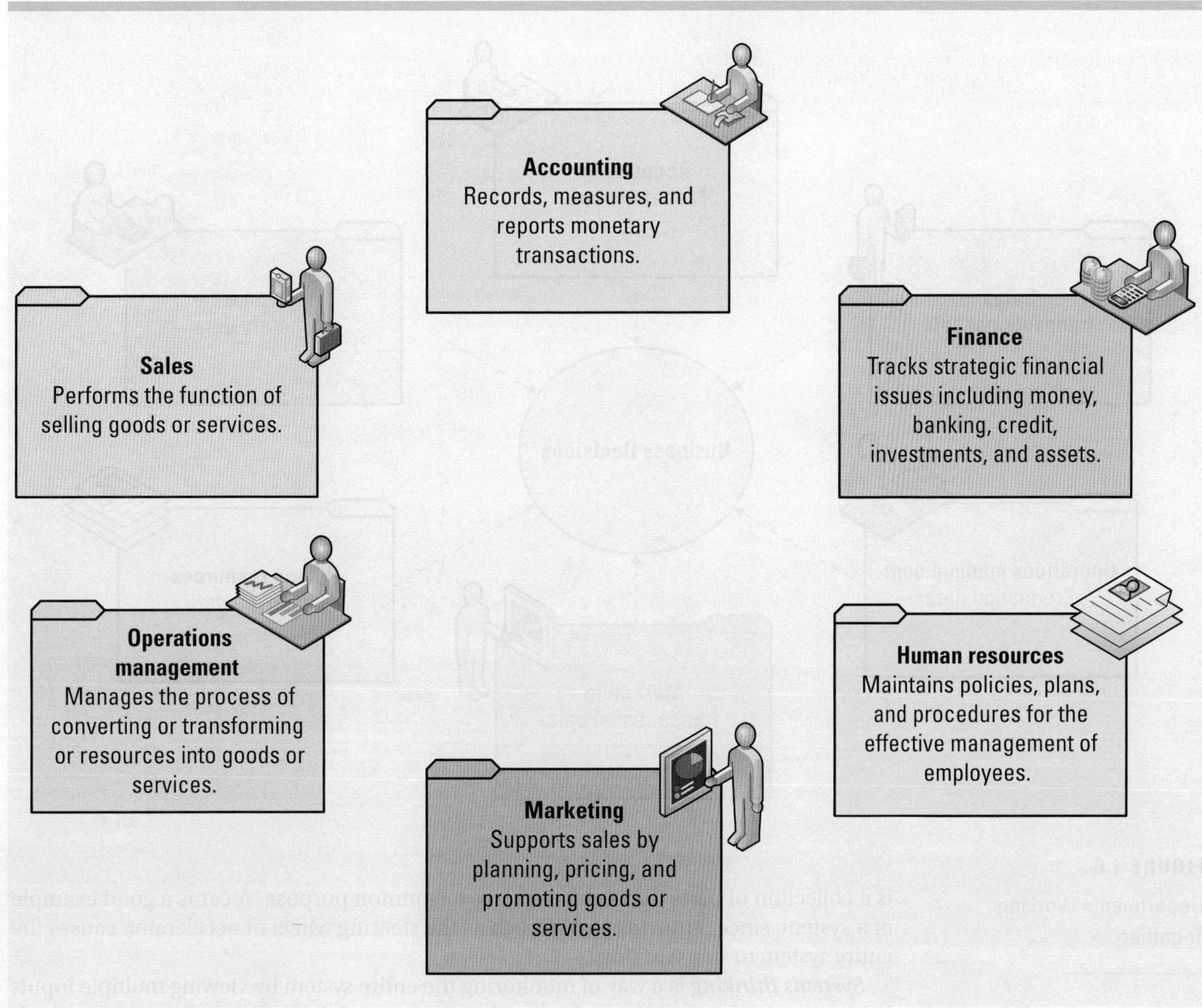
Accounting
Records, measures, and reports monetary transactions.
Sales
Performs the function of selling goods or services.
Finance
Tracks strategic financial issues including money, banking, credit, investments, and assets.
Operations management
Manages the process of converting or transforming or resources into goods or services.
Human resources
Maintains policies, plans, and procedures for the effective management of employees.
Marketing
Supports sales by planning, pricing, and promoting goods or services.

FIGURE 1.5
Departments Working Independently

analyze production and sales data to come up with product promotions and advertising strategies. Production needs to understand sales forecasts to determine the company's manufacturing needs. Sales needs to rely on information from operations to understand inventory, place orders, and forecast consumer demand. All departments need to understand the accounting and finance departments' information for budgeting. For the firm to be successful, all departments must work together as a single unit sharing common information and not operate independently or in a silo (see Figure 1.6).

THE SOLUTION: MANAGEMENT INFORMATION SYSTEMS

LO 1.3: Explain systems thinking and how management information systems enable business communications.

You probably recall the old story of three blind men attempting to describe an elephant. The first man, feeling the elephant's girth, said the elephant seemed very much like a wall. The second, feeling the elephant's trunk, declared the elephant was like a snake. The third man felt the elephant's tusks and said the elephant was like a tree or a cane. Companies that operate departmentally are seeing only one part of the elephant, a critical mistake that hinders successful operation.

Successful companies operate cross-functionally, integrating the operations of all departments. Systems are the primary enabler of cross-functional operations. A ***system***

Accounting
Monetary data

Sales
Transactional data

Finance
Monetary data

Business Decisions

Operations management
Production data

Human resources
Employee data

Marketing
Transactional data

FIGURE 1.6

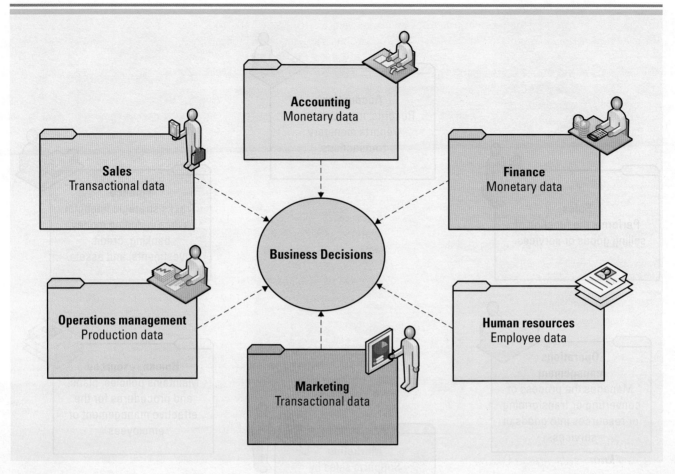

Departments Working Together

is a collection of parts that link to achieve a common purpose. A car is a good example of a system, since removing a part, such as the steering wheel or accelerator, causes the entire system to stop working.

Systems thinking is a way of monitoring the entire system by viewing multiple inputs being processed or transformed to produce outputs while continuously gathering feedback on each part (see Figure 1.7). ***Feedback*** is information that returns to its original transmitter (input, transform, or output) and modifies the transmitter's actions. Feedback helps the system maintain stability. For example, a car's system continuously monitors the fuel level and turns on a warning light if the gas level is too low. Systems thinking provides an end-to-end view of how operations work together to create a product or service. Business students who understand systems thinking are valuable resources because they can implement solutions that consider the entire process, not just a single component.

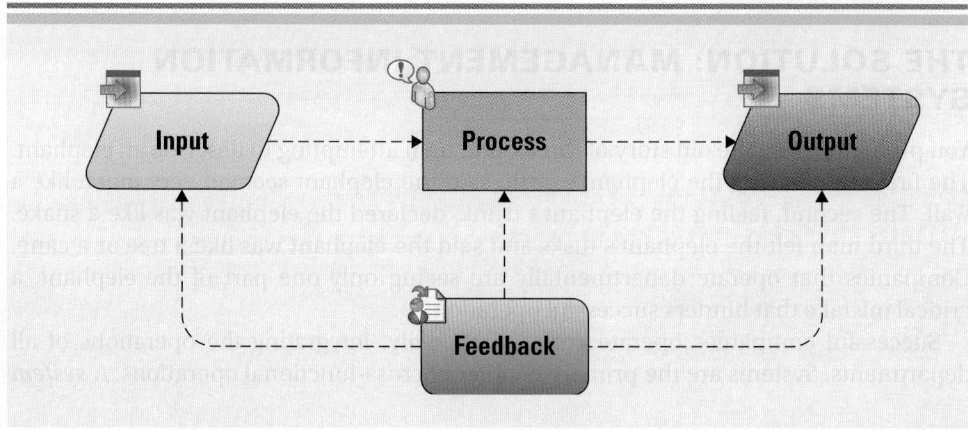

FIGURE 1.7

Overview of Systems Thinking

Management information systems (MIS) is a business function, like accounting and human resources, which moves information about people, products, and processes across the company to facilitate decision making and problem solving. MIS incorporates systems thinking to help companies operate cross-functionally. For example, to fulfill product orders, an MIS for sales moves a single customer order across all functional areas including sales, order fulfillment, shipping, billing, and finally customer service. Although different functional areas handle different parts of the sale, thanks to MIS, to the customer the sale is one continuous process. If one part of the company is experiencing problems, however, then, like the car without a steering wheel, the entire system fails. If order fulfillment packages the wrong product, it will not matter that shipping, billing, and customer service did their jobs right, since the customer will not be satisfied when he or she opens the package.

MIS can be an important enabler of business success and innovation. This is not to say that MIS *equals* business success and innovation, or that MIS *represents* business success and innovation. MIS is a tool that is most valuable when it leverages the talents of people who know how to use and manage it effectively. To perform the MIS function effectively, almost all companies, particularly large and medium-sized ones, have an internal MIS department, often called information technology (IT), information systems (IS), or management information systems (MIS). For the purpose of this text, we will refer to it as MIS.

MIS Department Roles and Responsibilities

MIS as a department is a relatively new functional area, having been around formally for about 40 years. Job titles, roles, and responsibilities often differ from company to company, but the most common are these:

- ***Chief information officer (CIO)*** is responsible for (1) overseeing all uses of MIS and (2) ensuring that MIS strategically aligns with business goals and objectives.
- ***Chief knowledge officer (CKO)*** is responsible for collecting, maintaining, and distributing company knowledge
- ***Chief privacy officer (CPO)*** is responsible for ensuring the ethical and legal use of information within a company.
- ***Chief security officer (CSO)*** is responsible for ensuring the security of business systems and developing strategies and safeguards against attacks by hackers and viruses.
- ***Chief technology officer (CTO)*** is responsible for ensuring the speed, accuracy, availability, and reliability of the MIS.

While many companies may not have a different individual for each of these positions, they must have top managers who take responsibility for all these areas.

section 1.2 BUSINESS STRATEGY

LEARNING OUTCOMES

1.4 Explain why competitive advantages are temporary.

1.5 Describe Porter's Five Forces Model and explain each of the five forces.

1.6 Compare Porter's three generic strategies.

1.7 Demonstrate how a company can add value by using Porter's value chain analysis.

IDENTIFYING COMPETITIVE ADVANTAGES

LO 1.4: Explain why competitive advantages are temporary.

Running a company today is similar to leading an army; the top manager or leader ensures all participants are heading in the right direction and completing their goals and objectives. Companies lacking leadership quickly implode as employees head in different directions attempting to achieve conflicting goals. To combat these challenges, leaders communicate and execute business strategies (from the Greek word *stratus* for army and *ago* for leading). A ***business strategy*** is a leadership plan that achieves a specific set of goals or objectives such as:

- Developing new products or services.
- Entering new markets.
- Increasing customer loyalty.
- Attracting new customers.
- Increasing sales.
- Decreasing costs.

Good leaders also anticipate unexpected misfortunes, from strikes and economic recessions to natural disasters. Their business strategies build in buffers or slack, allowing the company the ability to ride out any storm and defend against competitive or environmental threats. Of course, updating business strategies is a continuous undertaking as internal and external environments rapidly change. Business strategies that match core company competencies to opportunities result in competitive advantages, a key to success!

A ***competitive advantage*** is a feature of a product or service on which customers place a greater value than they do on similar offerings from competitors. Competitive advantages provide the same product or service either at a lower price or with additional value that can fetch premium prices. Unfortunately, competitive advantages are typically temporary, because competitors often quickly seek ways to duplicate them. In turn, organizations must develop a strategy based on a new competitive advantage. Ways that companies duplicate competitive advantages include acquiring the new technology, copying the business operations, and hiring away key employees. The introduction of Apple's iPod and iTunes, a brilliant merger of technology, business, and entertainment, offers an excellent example.

In early 2000, Steve Jobs was fixated on developing video editing software when he suddenly realized that millions of people were using computers to listen to music, a new trend in the industry catapulted by illegal online services such as Napster. Jobs was worried that he was looking in the wrong direction and had missed the opportunity to jump on the online music bandwagon. He moved fast, however, and within four months he had developed the first version of iTunes for the Mac. Jobs' next challenge was to make a portable iTunes player that could hold thousands of songs and be completely transportable. Within nine months the iPod was born. With the combination of iTunes and iPod, Apple created a significant competitive advantage in the marketplace. Many firms began following Apple's lead by creating portable music players to compete with the iPod. In addition, Apple continues to create new and exciting products to gain competitive advantages, such as its recently released iPad, a larger version of the iPod that functions more as a computer than a music player.[6]

When a company is the first to market with a competitive advantage, it gains a particular benefit, such as Apple did with its iPod. This ***first-mover advantage*** occurs when a company can significantly increase its market share by being first with a new competitive advantage. FedEx created a first-mover advantage by developing its customer self-service software, which allows people to request parcel pickups, print mailing slips, and track parcels online. Other parcel delivery companies quickly began creating their own online services. Today, customer self-service on the Internet is a standard feature of the parcel delivery business.

Competitive intelligence is the process of gathering information about the competitive environment, including competitors' plans, activities, and products, to improve a company's ability to succeed. It means understanding and learning as much as possible as soon as possible about what is occurring outside the company to remain competitive. Frito-Lay, a premier provider of snack foods such as Cracker Jacks and Cheetos, does not send its sales representatives into grocery stores just to stock shelves; they carry handheld computers and record the product offerings, inventory, and even product locations

APPLY YOUR KNOWLEDGE

BUSINESS DRIVEN GLOBALIZATION

The Competitive Landscape for Students

According to the Economic Policy Institute, over the past decade the United States has lost an estimated 2.4 million factory jobs to China. Factories in South Korea, Taiwan, and China are producing toys, toothpaste, running shoes, computers, appliances, and cars. For a long time U.S. firms did not recognize these products as competition; they regarded Asia's high-tech products as second-rate knockoffs and believed Asian countries maintained a "factory culture"—they could imitate but not innovate.

In hindsight, it is obvious that once these countries did begin designing and creating high-end products, they would have obvious competitive advantages, with high-value research and development coupled with low-cost manufacturing of unbeatable goods and services. Asia is now on the rise in all industries from wind turbines to high-speed bullet trains. According to *Bloomberg Businessweek*'s 2010 ranking of the most innovative companies, 15 of the top 50 are Asian, up from just 5 in 2006. In fact, for the first time, the majority of the top 25 are based outside the United States.

How do you, as a business student, view these statistics? What type of global business climate will you be competing in when you graduate? If you wanted to gather competitive intelligence about the job market, where would you look and what types of data would you want to analyze? What can you do to create personal competitive advantages to differentiate yourself when searching for a job?[7]

---

of competitors. Frito-Lay uses this information to gain competitive intelligence on everything from how well competing products are selling to the strategic placement of its own products.[8]

Managers use three common tools to analyze competitive intelligence and develop competitive advantages including:

1. The Five Forces Model (for evaluating industry attractiveness).
2. The three generic strategies (for choosing a business focus).
3. Value chain analysis (for executing business strategies).

THE FIVE FORCES MODEL—EVALUATING INDUSTRY ATTRACTIVENESS

LO 1.5: Describe Porter's Five Forces Model and explain each of the five forces.

Michael Porter, a university professor at Harvard Business School, identified the following pressures that can hurt potential sales:

- Knowledgeable customers can force down prices by pitting rivals against each other.
- Influential suppliers can drive down profits by charging higher prices for supplies.
- Competition can steal customers.
- New market entrants can steal potential investment capital.
- Substitute products can steal customers.

Formally defined, ***Porter's Five Forces Model*** analyzes the competitive forces within the environment in which a company operates to assess the potential for profitability in an industry. Its purpose is to combat these competitive forces by identifying opportunities, competitive advantages, and competitive intelligence. If the forces are strong, they increase competition; if the forces are weak, they decrease competition. This section details each of the forces and its associated MIS business strategy (see Figure 1.8).[9]

Buyer Power

Buyer power is the ability of buyers to affect the price they must pay for an item. Factors used to assess buyer power include number of customers, their sensitivity to price, size of orders, differences between competitors, and availability of substitute products. If buyer power is high, customers can force a company and its competitors to compete on price, which typically drives prices down.

One way to reduce buyer power is by manipulating ***switching costs,*** costs that make customers reluctant to switch to another product or service. Switching costs include financial as well as intangible values. The cost of switching doctors, for instance, includes the powerful intangible components of having to build relationships with the new doctor and nurses, as well as transferring all your medical history. With MIS, however, patients can store their medical records on DVDs or thumb drives, allowing easy transferability. The Internet also lets patients review websites for physician referrals, which takes some of the fear out of trying someone new.[10]

Companies can also reduce buyer power with ***loyalty programs,*** which reward customers based on their spending. The airline industry is famous for its frequent-flyer programs, for instance. Because of the rewards travelers receive (free airline tickets, upgrades, or hotel stays), they are more likely to be loyal to or give most of their business to a single company. Keeping track of the activities and accounts of many thousands or millions of customers covered by loyalty programs is not practical without large-scale business systems, however. Loyalty programs are thus a good example of using MIS to reduce buyer power.[11]

Supplier Power

A ***supply chain*** consists of all parties involved, directly or indirectly, in obtaining raw materials or a product. In a typical supply chain, a company will be both a supplier (to customers) and a customer (of other suppliers), as illustrated in Figure 1.9. ***Supplier power*** is the suppliers' ability to influence the prices they charge for supplies (including materials, labor, and services). Factors used to appraise supplier power include number

FIGURE 1.8

Porter's Five Forces Model

Source: Reprinted by permission of Harvard Business School Press. From *The Five Competitive Forces That Shape Strategy*, by Michael Porter. Boston, MA 2008. Copyright © 2008 by the Harvard Business School Publishing Corporation; all rights reserved.

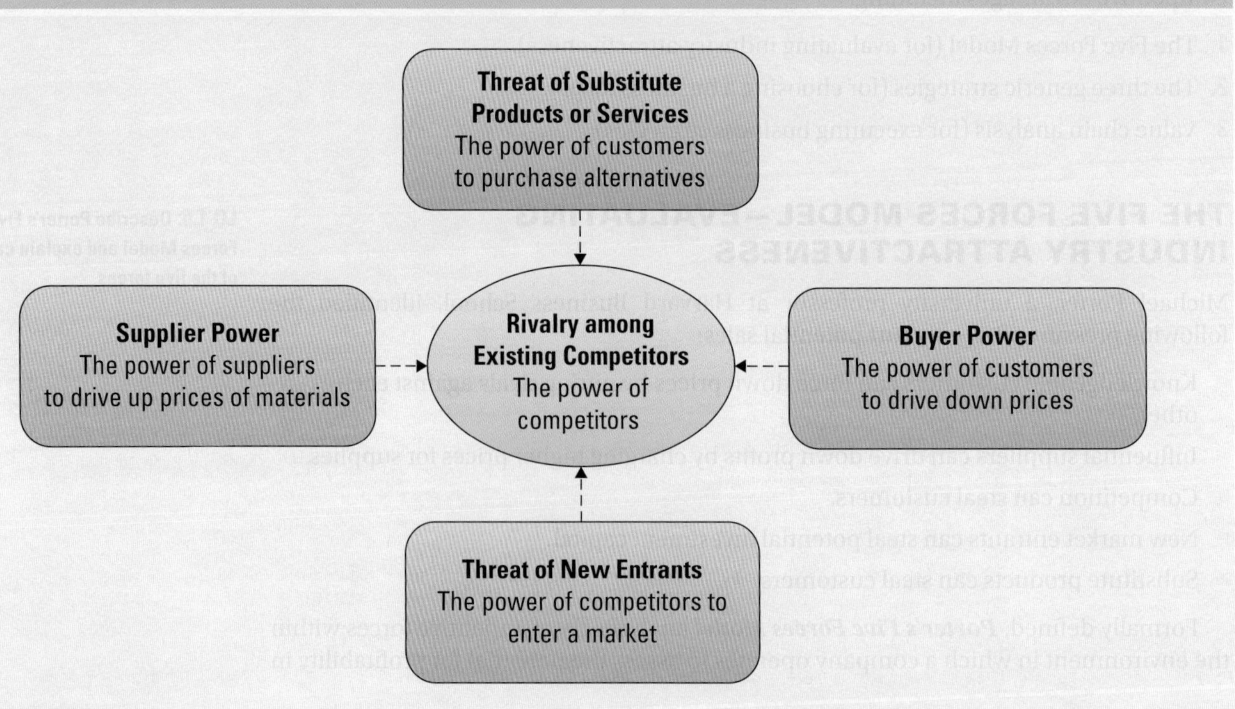

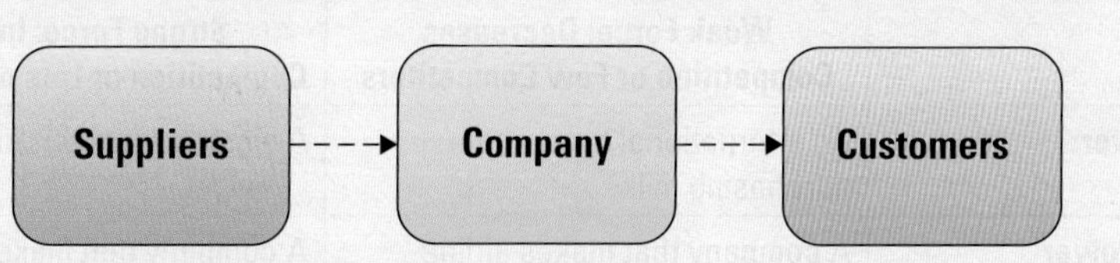

FIGURE 1.9
Traditional Supply Chain

of suppliers, size of suppliers, uniqueness of services, and availability of substitute products. If supplier power is high, the supplier can influence the industry by:

- Charging higher prices.
- Limiting quality or services.
- Shifting costs to industry participants.[12]

Typically, when a supplier raises prices, the buyers will pass on the increase to their customers by raising prices on the end-product. When supplier power is high, buyers lose revenue because they cannot pass on the raw material price increase to their customers. Some powerful suppliers, such as pharmaceutical companies, can exert a threat over an entire industry when substitutes are limited and the product is critical to the buyers. Patient who need to purchase cancer-fighting drugs have no power over price and must pay whatever the drug company asks because there are few available alternatives.

Using MIS to find alternative products is one way of decreasing supplier power. Cancer patients can now use the Internet to research alternative medications and practices, something that was next to impossible just a few decades ago. Buyers can also use MIS to form groups or collaborate with other buyers, increasing the size of the buyer group and reducing supplier power. For a hypothetical example, the collective group of 30,000 students from a university has far more power over price when purchasing laptops than a single student.[13]

Threat of Substitute Products or Services

The ***threat of substitute products or services*** is high when there are many alternatives to a product or service and low when there are few alternatives from which to choose. For example, travelers have numerous substitutes for airline transportation including automobiles, trains, and boats. Technology even makes videoconferencing and virtual meetings possible, eliminating the need for some business travel. Ideally, a company would like to be in a market in which there are few substitutes for the products or services it offers.

Polaroid had this unique competitive advantage for many years until it forgot to observe competitive intelligence. Then the firm went bankrupt when people began taking digital pictures with everything from video cameras to cell phones.

A company can reduce the threat of substitutes by offering additional value through wider product distribution. Soft-drink manufacturers distribute their products through vending machines, gas stations, and convenience stores, increasing the availability of soft drinks relative to other beverages. Companies can also offer various add-on services, making the substitute product less of a threat. For example, iPhones include capabilities for games, videos, and music, making a traditional cell phone less of a substitute.[14]

Threat of New Entrants

The ***threat of new entrants*** is high when it is easy for new competitors to enter a market and low when there are significant entry barriers to joining a market. An ***entry barrier*** is a feature of a product or service that customers have come to expect and entering competitors must offer the same for survival. For example, a new bank must offer its customers an array of MIS-enabled services, including ATMs, online bill paying, and online account monitoring. These are significant barriers to new firms entering the banking market. At one time, the first bank to offer such services gained a valuable first-mover advantage, but only temporarily, as other banking competitors developed their own MIS services.[15]

FIGURE 1.10

Strong and Weak Examples of Porter's Five Forces

	Weak Force: Decreases Competition or Few Competitors	Strong Force: Increases Competition or Lots of Competitors
Buyer Power	An international hotel chain purchasing milk	A single consumer purchasing milk
Supplier Power	A company that makes airline engines	A company that makes pencils
Threat of Substitute Products or Services	Cancer drugs from a pharmaceutical company	Coffee from McDonald's
Threat of New Entrants	A professional hockey team	A dog walking business
Rivalry among Existing Competitors	Department of Motor Vehicles	A coffee shop

Rivalry among Existing Competitors

Rivalry among existing competitors is high when competition is fierce in a market and low when competitors are more complacent. Although competition is always more intense in some industries than in others, the overall trend is toward increased competition in almost every industry. The retail grocery industry is intensively competitive. Kroger, Safeway, and Albertson's in the United States compete in many different ways, essentially trying to beat or match each other on price. Most supermarket chains have implemented loyalty programs to provide customers special discounts while gathering valuable information about their purchasing habits. In the future, expect to see grocery stores using wireless technologies that track customer movements throughout the store to determine purchasing sequences.

Product differentiation occurs when a company develops unique differences in its products or services with the intent to influence demand. Companies can use differentiation to reduce rivalry. For example, while many companies sell books and videos on the Internet, Amazon differentiates itself by using customer profiling. When a customer visits Amazon.com repeatedly, Amazon begins to offer products tailored to that particular customer based on his or her profile. In this way, Amazon has reduced its rivals' power by offering its customers a differentiated service.

To review, the Five Forces Model helps managers set business strategy by identifying the competitive structure and economic environment of an industry. If the forces are strong, they increase competition; if the forces are weak, they decrease it (see Figure 1.10).[16]

Analyzing the Airline Industry

Let us bring Porter's five forces together to look at the competitive forces shaping an industry and highlight business strategies to help it remain competitive. Assume a shipping company is deciding whether to enter the commercial airline industry. If performed correctly, an analysis of the five forces should determine that this is a highly risky business strategy because all five forces are strong. It will thus be difficult to generate a profit.

- **Buyer power:** Buyer power is high because customers have many airlines to choose from and typically make purchases based on price, not carrier.
- **Supplier power:** Supplier power is high since there are limited plane and engine manufacturers to choose from, and unionized workforces (suppliers of labor) restrict airline profits.
- **Threat of substitute products or services:** The threat of substitute products is high from many transportation alternatives including automobiles, trains, and boats, and from transportation substitutes such as videoconferencing and virtual meetings.
- **Threat of new entrants:** The threat of new entrants is high because new airlines are continuously entering the market, including sky taxies offering low-cost on-demand air taxi service.
- **Rivalry among existing competitors:** Rivalry in the airline industry is high, and websites such as Travelocity.com force them to compete on price (see Figure 1.11).[17]

APPLY YOUR KNOWLEDGE

BUSINESS DRIVEN INNOVATION

Fixing the Post Office

Is there anything more frustrating than waiting in line at the post office? Not only are those lines frustrating, but they are also unprofitable. The U.S. Postal Service has faced multibillion-dollar losses every year for the past few years, making for one of the greatest challenges in its history.

What is killing the post office? Perhaps it is Stamps.com, a website that allows you to customize and print your own stamps 24 hours a day. Getting married? Place a photo of the happy couple right on the stamp for the invitations. Starting a business? Place your business logo on your stamps. Stamps.com even keeps track of a customer's postal spending and can recommend optimal delivery methods. Plus, Stamps.com gives you postage discounts you can't get at the post office or with a postage meter.

Evaluate the U.S. Postal Service using Porter's Five Forces Model. How could the Postal Service create new products and services to help grow its business? What types of competitive advantages can you identify for the Postal Service?[18]

FIGURE 1.11

Five Forces Model in the Airline Industry

	Strong (High) Force: Increases Competition or Lots of Competitors
Buyer Power	Many airlines for buyers to choose from forcing competition based on price
Supplier Power	Limited number of plane and engine manufactures to choose from along with unionized workers
Threat of Substitute Products or Services	Many substitutes including cars, trains, and busses. Even substitutes to travel such as video conferencing and virtual meetings.
Threat of New Entrants	Many new airlines entering the market all the time including the latest sky taxis.
Rivalry among Existing Competitors	Intense competition–many rivals.

Source: Reprinted by permission of Harvard Business School Press. From *The Five Competitive Forces That Shape Strategy*, by Michael Porter. Boston, MA 2008. Copyright © 2008 by the Harvard Business School Publishing Corporation; all rights reserved.

THE THREE GENERIC STRATEGIES—CHOOSING A BUSINESS FOCUS

LO 1.6: Compare Porter's three generic strategies.

Once top management has determined the relative attractiveness of an industry and decided to enter it, the firm must formulate a strategy for doing so. If our sample company decided to join the airline industry, it could compete as a low-cost, no-frills airline or as a luxury airline providing outstanding service and first-class comfort. Both options offer different ways of achieving competitive advantages in a crowded marketplace. The low-cost operator saves on expenses and passes the savings along to customers in the form of low prices. The luxury airline spends on high-end service and first-class comforts and passes the costs on to the customer in the form of high prices.

Porter has identified three generic business strategies for entering a new market: (1) broad cost leadership, (2) broad differentiation, and (3) focused strategy. Broad strategies reach a large market segment, while focused strategies target a niche or unique market with either cost leadership or differentiation. Trying to be all things to all people is a recipe for disaster, since doing so makes it difficult to project a consistent image to the entire marketplace. For this reason, Porter suggests adopting only one of the three generic strategies illustrated in Figure 1.12.[19]

FIGURE 1.12

Porter's Three Generic Strategies

Source: Reprinted with the permission of Free Press, a Division of Simon & Schuster, Inc., from *Competitive Strategy: Techniques for Analyzing Industries and Competitors* by Michael E. Porter. Copyright © 1980, 1998 by The Free press. All rights reserved.

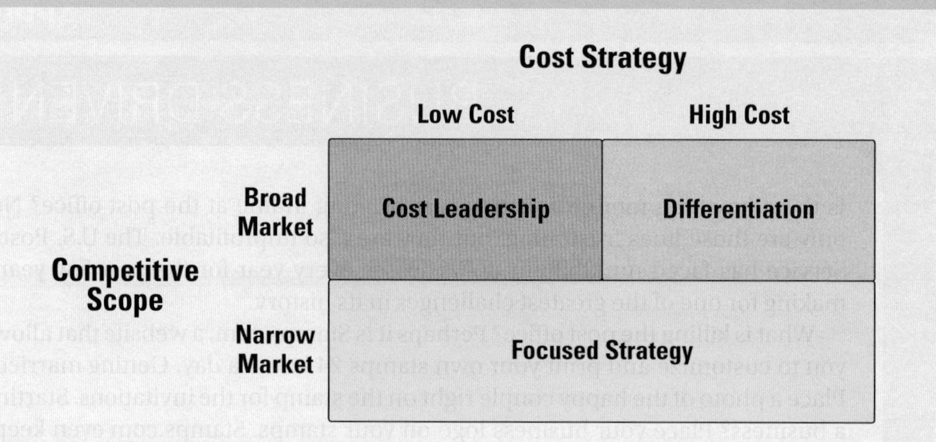

Figure 1.13 applies the three strategies to real companies, demonstrating the relationships among strategies (cost leadership versus differentiation) and market segmentation (broad versus focused).

- **Broad market and low cost:** Walmart competes by offering a broad range of products at low prices. Its business strategy is to be the low-cost provider of goods for the cost-conscious consumer.
- **Broad market and high cost:** Neiman Marcus competes by offering a broad range of differentiated products at high prices. Its business strategy offers a variety of specialty and upscale products to affluent consumers.
- **Narrow market and low cost:** Payless competes by offering a specific product, shoes, at low prices. Its business strategy is to be the low-cost provider of shoes. Payless competes with Walmart, which also sells low-cost shoes, by offering a far bigger selection of sizes and styles.
- **Narrow market and high cost:** Tiffany & Co. competes by offering a differentiated product, jewelry, at high prices. Its business strategy allows it to be a high-cost provider of premier designer jewelry to affluent consumers.

LO 1.7 **Demonstrate how a company can add value by using Porter's value chain analysis.**

VALUE CHAIN ANALYSIS—EXECUTING BUSINESS STRATEGIES

Firms make profits by taking raw inputs and applying business process to turn them into a product or service that customers find valuable. A ***business process*** is a standardized set of activities that accomplish a specific task, such as processing a customer's order.

FIGURE 1.13

Examples of Porter's Three Generic Strategies

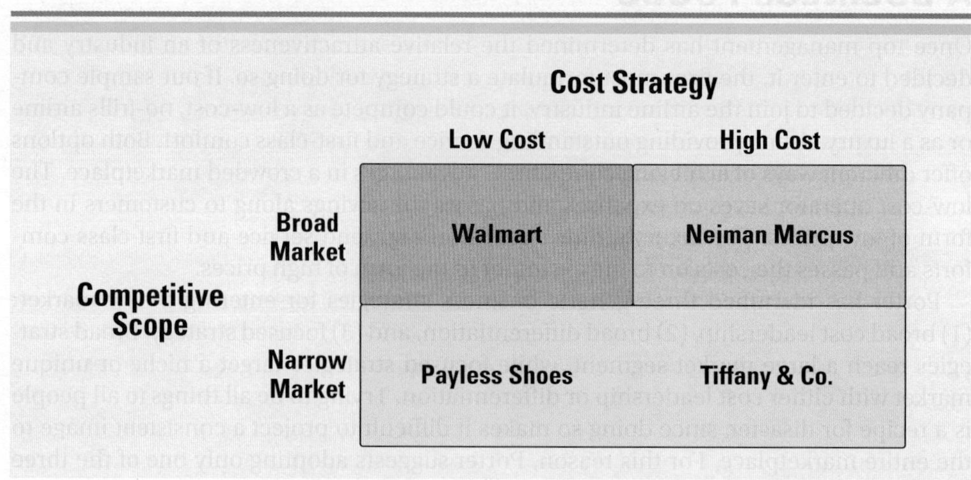

APPLY YOUR KNOWLEDGE

BUSINESS DRIVEN DEBATE

The iPad—Greatest Product in History or Just Another Gadget?

Apple sold 300,000 units of its highly anticipated iPad in the first 15 hours it was available for sale. Hundreds of thousands of Apple devotees flocked to stores during Passover and Easter to be the first to obtain the new device, even though it is neither a phone nor a laptop computer and many people are still wondering what it's for.

The controversy over the usefulness of Apple's portable tablet began as soon as Apple announced the device was heading to market. At first glance, the iPad is little more than a touch screen the size of a slim book, with a few control buttons along the edges and a home button at the bottom. Shrink it, and it would look like an iPod Touch. What is the value of this device? That's the question everyone wants to answer.

The iPad's modest features might represent an entirely new way of consuming media—video, Web pages, music, pictures, and even books. Break into groups and review the current value of the iPad for business. Find three examples of the ways business are using, or could use, the iPad for business. Do you consider it the next revolutionary device or just an overpriced music player?[20]

Once a firm identifies the industry it wants to enter and the generic strategy it will focus on, it must then choose the business processes required to create its products or services. Of course, the firm will want to ensure the processes add value and create competitive advantages. To identify these competitive advantages, Michael Porter created ***value chain analysis,*** which views a firm as a series of business processes that each add value to the product or service.

Value chain analysis is a useful tool for determining how to create the greatest possible value for customers (see Figure 1.14). The goal of value chain analysis is to identify processes in which the firm can add value for the customer and create a competitive advantage for itself, with a cost advantage or product differentiation.

The *value chain* groups a firm's activities into two categories, primary value activities, and support value activities. ***Primary value activities,*** shown at the bottom of the value chain in Figure 1.14, acquire raw materials and manufacture, deliver, market, sell, and provide after-sales services.

1. **Inbound logistics:** acquires raw materials and resources and distributes to manufacturing as required.
2. **Operations:** transforms raw materials or inputs into goods and services.
3. **Outbound logistics:** distributes goods and services to customers.
4. **Marketing and sales:** promotes, prices, and sells products to customers.
5. **Service:** Provides customer support after the sale of goods and services.[21]

Support value activities, along the top of the value chain in Figure 1.14, include firm infrastructure, human resource management, technology development, and procurement. Not surprisingly, these support the primary value activities.

- **Firm infrastructure:** includes the company format or departmental structures, environment, and systems.
- **Human resource management:** provides employee training, hiring, and compensation.

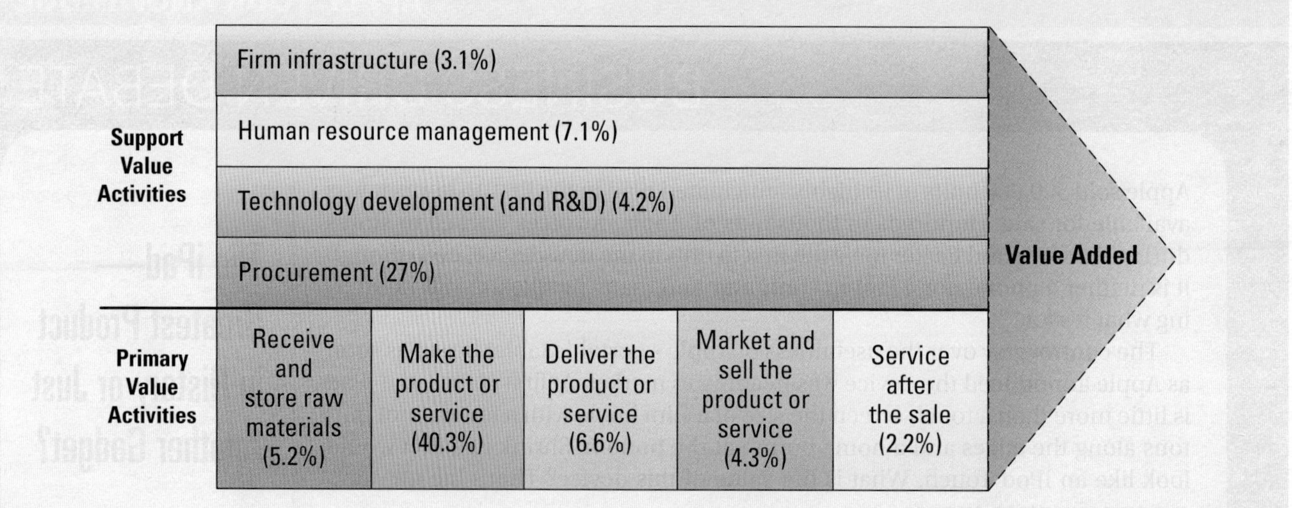

FIGURE 1.14
The Value Chain

Source: Reprinted with the permission of Free Press, a Division of Simon & Schuster, Inc., from *Competitive Advantage: Creating and Sustaining Superior Performance* by Michael E. Porter. Copyright © 1985, 1998 by Michael E. Porter. All rights reserved.

- **Technology development:** applies MIS to processes to add value.
- **Procurement:** purchases inputs such as raw materials, resources, equipment, and supplies.

It is easy to understand how a typical manufacturing firm takes raw materials such as wood pulp and transforms it into paper. Adding value in this example might include using high-quality raw materials or offering next-day free shipping on any order. How, though, might a typical service firm take raw inputs such as time, knowledge, and MIS and transform them into valuable customer service knowledge? A hotel might use MIS to track customer reservations and then inform front-desk employees when a loyal customer is checking in so the employee can call the guest by name and offer additional services, gift baskets, or upgraded rooms. Examining the firm as a value chain allows managers to identify the important business processes that add value for customers and then find MIS solutions that support them.

When performing a value chain analysis, a firm could survey customers about the extent to which they believe each activity adds value to the product or service. This step generates responses the firm can measure, shown as percentages in Figure 1.15, to describe how each activity adds (or reduces) value. Then the competitive advantage decision for the firm is whether to (1) target high value-adding activities to further enhance their value, (2) target low value-adding activities to increase their value, or (3) perform some combination of the two.

MIS adds value to both primary and support value activities. One example of a primary value activity facilitated by MIS is the development of a marketing campaign management system that could target marketing campaigns more efficiently, thereby reducing marketing costs. The system would also help the firm better pinpoint target market needs, thereby increasing sales. One example of a support value activity facilitated by MIS is the development of a human resources system that could more efficiently reward employees based on performance. The system could also identify employees who are at risk of quitting, allowing manager's time to find additional challenges or opportunities that would help retain these employees and thus reduce turnover costs.

Value chain analysis is a highly useful tool that provides hard and fast numbers for evaluating the activities that add value to products and services. Managers can find additional value by analyzing and constructing the value chain in terms of Porter's Five Forces Model (see Figure 1.15). For example, if the goal is to decrease buyer power, a company can construct its value chain activity of "service after the sale" by offering high levels of customer service. This will increase customers' switching costs and reduce their power. Analyzing and constructing support value activities can help decrease the threat of new entrants. Analyzing and constructing primary value activities can help decrease the threat of substitute products or services.[22]

Revising Porter's three business strategies is critical. Firms must continually adapt to their competitive environments, which can cause business strategy to shift. In the

APPLY YOUR KNOWLEDGE

BUSINESS DRIVEN START-UP

Want to Start Your Own Business? Just Find a Problem to Solve

Derek Johnson, a student at the University of Houston, was having lunch with his friend who happened to be the communications director for her sorority. During lunch Derek's friend was telling him how hard it was to communicate with all of her sisters in the sorority. She had to send out important announcements about meetings, charitable events, and even dues. She had tried everything including Facebook, email, and message boards, but so far nothing was working. As Derek pondered his friend's dilemma, he came up with a solution: mass text messaging.

Johnson began researching mass text messaging products and was surprised to find that none existed for the average consumer. Spotting an entrepreneurial opportunity, Derek quickly began working on a product. Within a few months he launched his website, Tatango, and began offering group text messaging at a reasonable price. Now, a few years later, Tatango offers customers subscription plans starting under $20 a month that allows groups to send text messages to all members at once—whether 10 or 10,000—from any device.

In a group, brainstorm a list of problems you are currently experiencing. Decide whether any present potential new business opportunities, and if so, analyze the potential using the tools introduced in this chapter. Be prepared to present your new business to the class.[23]

remainder of this text we discuss how managers can formulate business strategies using MIS to create competitive advantages. Figure 1.16 gives an overview of the remaining chapters, along with the relevant business strategy and associated MIS topics.

FIGURE 1.15

The Value Chain and Porter's Five Forces Model

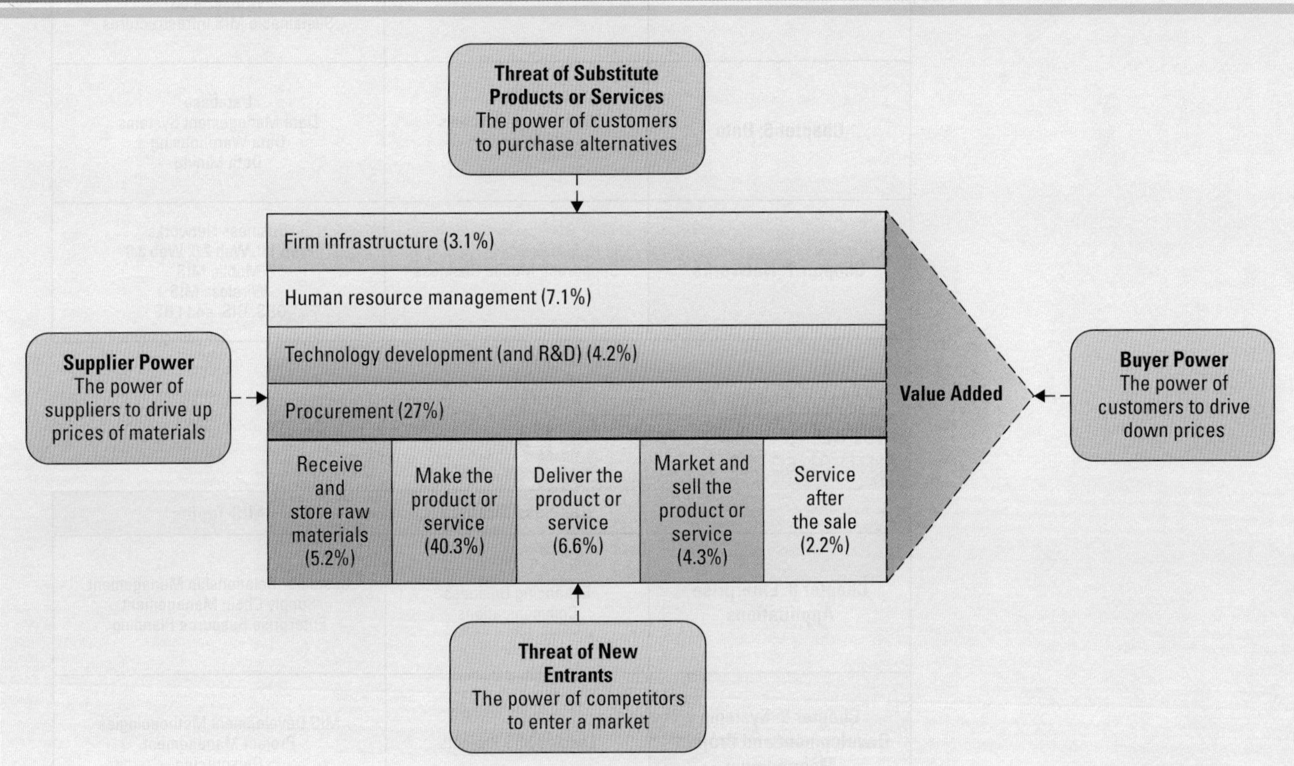

Source: Reprinted with the permission of Free Press, a Division of Simon & Schuster, Inc., from *Competitive Advantage: Creating and Sustaining Superior Performance* by Michael E. Porter.

FIGURE 1.16
Overview of *Business Driven Information Systems*

MODULE 1: BUSINESS DRIVEN MIS

	Business Strategy	MIS Topics
Chapter 1: Management Information Systems	Understanding Business Driven MIS	Data Information Business Intelligence Knowledge Systems Thinking Porter's Business Strategies
Chapter 2: Decisions and Processes	Creating Value Driven Businesses	Transaction Processing Systems Decision support Systems Executive Information Systems Artificial Intelligence Business Process Reengineering
Chapter 3: Ebusiness	Finding Electronic Business Value	eBusiness eBusiness Models Social Networking Knowledge Management Collaboration
Chapter 4: Ethics and Information Security	Identifying MIS Business Concerns	Information Security Policies Authentication and Authorization Prevention and Resistance Detection and Response

MODULE 2: TECHNICAL FOUNDATIONS OF MIS

	Business Strategy	MIS Topics
Chapter 5: Infrastructures	Deploying Organizational MIS	Grid Computing Cloud Computing Virtualization Sustainable MIS Infrastructures
Chapter 6: Data	Uncovering Business Intelligence	Database Data Management Systems Data Warehousing Data Mining
Chapter 7: Networks	Supporting Mobile Business	Business Networks Web 1.0, Web 2.0, Web 3.0 Mobile MIS Wireless MIS GPS, GIS, and LBS

MODULE 3: ENTERPRISE MIS

	Business Strategy	MIS Topics
Chapter 8: Enterprise Applications	Enhancing Business Communications	Customer Relationship Management Supply Chain Management Enterprise Resource Planning
Chapter 9: Systems Development and Project Management	Leading MIS Projects	MIS Development Methodologies Project Management Outsourcing

LEARNING OUTCOME REVIEW

Learning Outcome 1.1: Describe the information age and the differences among data, information, business intelligence, and knowledge.

We live in the information age, when infinite quantities of facts are widely available to anyone who can use a computer. The core drivers of the information age include data, information, business intelligence, and knowledge. Data are raw facts that describe the characteristics of an event or object. Information is data converted into a meaningful and useful context. Business intelligence (BI) is information collected from multiple sources such as suppliers, customers, competitors, partners, and industries that analyzes patterns, trends, and relationships for strategic decision making. Knowledge includes the skills, experience, and expertise, coupled with information and intelligence that creates a person's intellectual resources. As you move from data to knowledge you include more and more variables for analysis resulting in better, more precise support for decision making and problem solving.

Learning Outcome 1.2: Identify the different departments in a company and why they must work together to achieve success.

Companies are typically organized by department or functional area such as accounting, finance, human resources, marketing, operations management, and sales. Although each department has its own focus and its own data, none can work independently if the company is to operate as a whole. It is easy to see how a business decision made by one department can affect other departments. Functional areas are anything but independent in a business. In fact, functional areas are interdependent. Sales must rely on information from operations to understand inventory, place orders, calculate transportation costs, and gain insight into product availability based on production schedules. For an organization to succeed, every department or functional area must work together sharing common information and not be a "silo." Information technology can enable departments to more efficiently and effectively perform their business operations.

Learning Outcome 1.3: Explain systems thinking and how management information systems enable business communications.

A system is a collection of parts that link to achieve a common purpose. Systems thinking is a way of monitoring the entire system by viewing multiple inputs being processed or transformed to produce outputs while continuously gathering feedback on each part. Feedback is information that returns to its original transmitter (input, transform, or output) and modifies the transmitter's actions. Feedback helps the system maintain stability. Management information systems (MIS) is a business function, like accounting and human resources, which moves information about people, products, and processes across the company to facilitate decision making and problem solving. MIS incorporates systems thinking to help companies operate cross-functionally. For example, to fulfill product orders, an MIS for sales moves a single customer order across all functional areas including sales, order fulfillment, shipping, billing, and finally customer service. Although different functional areas handle different parts of the sale, thanks to MIS, to the customer the sale is one continuous process.

Learning Outcome 1.4: Explain why competitive advantages are temporary.

A competitive advantage is a feature of a product or service on which customers place a greater value than they do on similar offerings from competitors. Competitive advantages provide the same product or service either at a lower price or with additional value that can fetch premium prices. Unfortunately, competitive advantages are typically temporary, because competitors often quickly seek ways to duplicate them. In turn, organizations must develop a strategy based on a new competitive advantage. Ways that companies duplicate competitive advantages include acquiring the new technology, copying business processes, and hiring away employees.

Learning Outcome 1.5: Describe Porter's Five Forces Model and explain each of the five forces.

Porter's Five Forces Model analyzes the competitive forces within the environment in which a company operates, to assess the potential for profitability in an industry.

- Buyer power is the ability of buyers to affect the price they must pay for an item.
- Supplier power is the suppliers' ability to influence the prices they charge for supplies (including materials, labor, and services).
- Threat of substitute products or services is high when there are many alternatives to a product or service and low when there are few alternatives from which to choose
- Threat of new entrants is high when it is easy for new competitors to enter a market and low when there are significant entry barriers to entering a market
- Rivalry among existing competitors is high when competition is fierce in a market and low when competition is more complacent

Learning Outcome 1.6: Compare Porter's three generic strategies.

Organizations typically follow one of Porter's three generic strategies when entering a new market: (1) broad cost leadership, (2) broad differentiation, (3) focused strategy. Broad strategies reach a large market segment. Focused strategies target a niche market. Focused strategies concentrate on either cost leadership or differentiation.

Learning Outcome 1.7: Demonstrate how a company can add value by using Porter's value chain analysis.

To identify competitive advantages, Michael Porter created value chain analysis, which views a firm as a series of business processes that each add value to the product or service. The goal of value chain analysis is to identify processes in which the firm can add value for the customer and create a competitive advantage for itself, with a cost advantage or product differentiation. The value chain groups a firm's activities into two categories—primary value activities and support value activities. Primary value activities acquire raw materials and manufacture, deliver, market, sell, and provide after-sales services. Support value activities, along the top of the value chain in the figure, include firm infrastructure, human resource management, technology development, and procurement. Not surprisingly, these support the primary value activities.

OPENING CASE QUESTIONS

1. **Knowledge:** Define Globalization 1.0, 2.0, and 3.0 and provide a sample of the type of business data managers collected during each era.
2. **Comprehension:** Explain Friedman's flat world and the reasons it is important for all businesses, small or large, to understand.
3. **Application:** Demonstrate how students competing for jobs in a "flat world" can create competitive advantages to differentiate themselves in the marketplace.
4. **Analysis:** Analyze the current business environment and identify a new flattener not mentioned on Friedman's list.

5. **Synthesis:** Propose a plan for how a start-up company can use any of Porter's strategies to combat competition in a global world.
6. **Evaluate:** Argue for or against the following statement: "The world is not flat (in Friedman's sense of the term) because many undeveloped countries are not connected electronically."

KEY TERMS

REVIEW QUESTIONS

1. What is data and why is it important to a business?
2. How can a manager turn data into information?
3. What is the relationship between data, information, business intelligence, and knowledge?
4. Why is it important for a company to operate cross-functionally?
5. Why would a company want to have a CIO, CPO, and CSO?
6. Explain MIS and the role it plays in a company and global business.
7. Do you agree that MIS is essential for businesses operating in the information age? Why or why not?
8. Why is it important for a business major to understand MIS?
9. What type of career are you planning to pursue? How will your specific career use data, information, business intelligence, and knowledge?
10. Explain systems thinking and how it supports business operations.
11. What business strategies would you use if you were developing a competitive advantage for a company?
12. Explain Porter's Five Forces Model and the role it plays in decision making.
13. How could a company use loyalty programs to influence buyer power? How could a company use switching costs to lock in customers and suppliers?
14. What are Porter's three generic strategies and why would a company want to follow only one?
15. How can a company use Porter's value chain analysis to measure customer satisfaction?

CLOSING CASE ONE

Apple—Merging Technology, Business, and Entertainment

This might sound hard to believe, but a bit more than a decade ago, Apple was on the brink of bankruptcy. Apple Computer Inc., now back from near oblivion, is blazing a trail through the digital world with innovation and creativity that has been missing from the company for the past 20 years. The unique feature of Apple's competitive advantages is that they come from customers and users, not Apple employees. That's right; the company welcomes products created by consumers to sell to consumers, a trend new to business.

Capitalizing on the iPod

With millions of iPods in the hands of consumers, many people are finding ways to capitalize on the product. John Lin created a prototype of a remote control for the iPod and took his prototype to *Macworld,* where he found success. A few months later, Lin's company had Apple's blessing and a commitment for shelf space in its retail stores. "This is how Apple supports the iPod economy," Lin said.

In the iPod-dominated market, hundreds of companies have been inspired to develop more than 500 accessories—everything from rechargers for the car to $1,500 Fendi bags. Eric Tong, vice president at Belkin, a cable and peripheral manufacturer, believes that 75 percent of all iPod owners purchase at least one accessory—selling over 30 million accessories to date. With most of the products priced between $10 and $200, that puts the iPod economy well over $300 million and perhaps as high as $6 billion. Popular iPod accessories include:

- Altec Lansing Technologies—iPod speakers and recharger dock ($150).
- Belkin—TuneCast mobile FM transmitter ($40).
- Etymotic Research—high-end earphones ($150).
- Griffin Technology—iTrip FM transmitter ($35).
- Kate Spade—Geneva faux-croc mini iPod holder ($55).
- Apple—socks set in six colors: green, purple, blue, orange, pink, and gray ($29).
- Apple—digital camera connector ($29).

Capitalizing on the iPhone

Looking at someone using an iPhone is an interesting experience because there is a good chance they are not making a phone call. They could be doing a number of things from playing a game to trading stocks, watching a TV show, or even conducting business with a mobile version of salesforce.com's customer-management software. In a brilliant strategic move, Apple let outsiders offer software for the iPhone and in less than six months, more than 10,000 applications had been created. In fact, more than 15,000 applications are available at its app store section of iTunes, and they have been downloaded a total of 500 million times. Now, many of the iPhone apps are available for the iPad.

The iPhone and iPad app store market is getting so huge relative to other smart-phone markets that some developers argue there is little point adapting applications for Google's Android or any other iPhone competitor. According to Jeff Holden, CEO of Pelago Inc., when he created his social networking company he fully intended to follow the conventional wisdom for how to build a sizable, fast-growing software company: Get your programs on as many platforms and devices as possible. But when he crunched the numbers he came to an interesting business conclusion: The 13 million iPhone owners had already downloaded more applications than the 1.1 billion other cell phone owners! To entrepreneurs, developing a program for the iPhone automatically provides a significantly larger market—almost 94 times larger than its competitors. "Why would I ever build for anything but the iPhone?" Holden asked.

Capitalizing on the iPad

Apple's latest release, the iPad, is a lightweight, portable, tablet computer, similar to the iPhone, that allows customers to download applications, check email, and play music all at the touch of a button. Both the iPhone and the iPad can multitask, allowing customers to read a Web page while downloading email in the background over wireless networks. The arrival of the iPad brought a simultaneous expansion of the network of accessories. Because the iPad was designed with an exposed screen and without a camera, separate keyboard, memory card slots, or expansion ports, one might say it was specifically built for accessories. Many owners will modify it in some way, whether for mere decoration or hard-core protection. A few of the new accessories include:

- iPad Clear Armor screen protector—$35.
- iPad Antique book case cover—$40.
- iPad wireless keyboard—$99.
- iPad overcoat sleeve—$35.
- iPad Joule luxury stand—$130.[24]

Questions

1. Do you agree or disagree that Apple's iTunes, iPhone apps, and iPad apps give the company a competitive advantage? Be sure to justify your answer.
2. Why are data, information, business intelligence, and knowledge important to Apple? Give an example of each type in relation to the iPad.
3. Analyze Apple using Porter's Five Forces Model.
4. Which of the three generic strategies is Apple following?
5. Which of Porter's five forces did Apple address through its introduction of the iPhone?
6. Which of Porter's five forces did Apple address through its customer-developed applications?

CLOSING CASE TWO

Major League Baseball—The Real Competitive Advantages

The bases are empty and the game is tied as Jayson Werth steps into the batter's box at the end of the eighth inning for the Philadelphia Phillies. Werth, the right fielder, faces Steven Shell, relief pitcher for the Washington Nationals. On Shell's fourth pitch, he leaves a sluggish curveball hanging over the plate. Werth smashes it into the stands for a game-winning home run.

As the stadium goes wild, an incredibly sophisticated information system swings into action and 60 people in a downtown Manhattan office begin slicing and dicing the video of Werth's home run. The clips are sent to thousands of computers and cell phones around the world, and a few minutes after the hit a commuter on the local train to Philadelphia's Main Line watches it for free on his cell phone, while stadium visitors learn that Shell's pitch was a mere 74 miles per hour and broke 14 inches.

The brains behind the business is the Major League Baseball Advanced Media (MLBAM), which generates revenue of about $450 million a year. Fifty percent of MLBAM's revenues come from fans who pay $120 a season to watch games live over the Internet, and the remainder is generated from advertising that runs next to its online content. MLBAM has grown into a significant revenue source for Major League Baseball, which has total revenues of about $6 billion. "They have a passionate base that they went after in a smart way," says Bobby Tulsiani, analyst with the market research firm JupiterResearch.

MLBAM's strategy is enlightening for other sports franchises and, undeniably, for other companies in the online content business. While most leagues limit what they put on the Web and avoid streaming live video online for fear that their television ratings could be hurt, MLB's experience suggests that such concerns might be misplaced. "Rights fees are up, attendance is up, viewership is up," says Bob Bowman, chief executive at MLBAM. "Somehow the strategy of putting [baseball games] on every device that has a plug or a battery has worked for the business partners. Even more important, it's worked for our fans."

Staggering Amount of Stats

The biggest draw for fans to MLBAM's online content is the amount of information the company provides that is unavailable anywhere else or on any other type of device. Without the online content, fans simply would not know that Werth's home run came on Shell's 18th pitch of the evening or that his first and third pitches to Werth were both 89 mph fastballs, while the fateful curveball was 15 mph slower.

One pitfall is that a truly obsessive fan could easily become lost in so much data, including clips of each major event of the season, statistics on how particular players have done against a starting pitcher, and final standings for every season back to 2001. "It's much more than what you can get on television," Jupiter's Tulsiani says. "It taps into the base by offering multiple camera angles, stats, and on-demand video."

MLBAM's New York offices are like an adolescent's idea of a dream job. On one recent summer day, dozens of workers sat at desks watching hour after hour of live baseball. There was a flurry of activity when something important happened in a game, like Werth's homer or a crucial strikeout.

Profitability

MLBAM's primary competitive advantage lies in the unique video editing information system it created that allows employees to produce highlights in just a few minutes, important because the group is sending out about 200 highlights a day during the regular season.

The system works by playing each game on a computer in a small window. As soon as something important happens, an MLBAM employee rewinds the game in the computer and marks the highlight. It is then passed along through two supervisors who send the highlight out over the Internet to thousands of paying customers.

"The program took about two months to make," says MLBAM's Joe Inzerillo, senior vice president for multimedia and distribution. Would MLBAM ever consider licensing its program? "We've had inquiries about people wanting to buy the program, but it is so tethered to our back end that we'd have to address compatibility issues. It's unlikely it would make sense to sell it." Instead, the company uses its technological competitive advantages to work with other sports. This year the NCAA paid between six and seven figures to run its live streaming of the men's college basketball tournament through MLBAM's servers.

Big Sales Opportunity

MLBAM sees mobile phones as the next big revenue opportunity. It is already creating customized applications for a number of phones, including BlackBerries and iPhones, allowing customers to tap into the statistics from the Gameday website. "The one device we all rely on is our cell phone," Bowman says. "It is with us, sadly perhaps, as many as 24 hours a day." As technology continues to improve, and streaming video becomes more portable on all devices, some fear television will disappear. It will be interesting to see how the future for MLBAM unfolds.[25]

Questions

1. Explain competitive advantages and identify any that MLBAM has created. What does MLBAM need to worry about for the future?
2. Using Porter's Five Forces Model, analyze MLBAM's buyer power and supplier power. What could MLBAM do to increase customer loyalty?
3. Which of Porter's three generic strategies is MLBAM following?
4. How could MLBAM use Porter's value chain analysis to detect competitive advantages?
5. Predict what might happen to MLBAM if it failed to secure its subscriber information and all personal information—including credit card numbers—was accidentally posted to an anonymous website.

CRITICAL BUSINESS THINKING

1. Focusing on Friedman

Thomas Friedman's newest book is titled *Hot, Flat, and Crowded: Why We Need a Green Revolution—And How It Can Renew America.* Research the Internet to find out as much information as you can about this text. Why would a business manager be interested in reading this text? How will this text impact global business? Do you think *Hot, Flat, and Crowded* will have as great an impact on society as *The World Is Flat* had on business? Why or why not?[26]

2. Pursuing Porter

There is no doubt that Michael Porter is one of the more influential business strategists of the 21st century. Research Michael Porter on the Internet for interviews, additional articles, and new or updated business strategies. Create a summary of your findings to share with your class. How can learning about people such as Thomas Friedman and Michael Porter help prepare you for a career in business? Name three additional business professionals you should follow to help prepare for your career in business.

3. Renting Movies

The video rental industry is fiercely competitive. Customers have their choice of renting a movie by driving to a store (Blockbuster), ordering through the mail (Netflix), or watching directly from their television (pay-per-view or Netflix). Using Porter's Five Forces Model (buyer power, supplier power, threat of new entrants, threat of substitute products, and competition), evaluate the attractiveness of entering the movie rental business. Be sure to include product differentiation, switching costs, and loyalty programs in your analysis.

4. Working for the Best

Each year, *Fortune* magazine creates a list of the top 100 companies to work for. Find the most recent list. What types of data do you think *Fortune* analyzed to determine the company ranking? What issues could occur if the analysis of the data was inaccurate? What types of information can you gain by analyzing the list? Create five questions a student performing a job search could answer by analyzing this list.

5. Salary Surveys

Salary surveys offer great tools for highlighting the opportunities associated with an MIS major. The starting annual salaries in the MIS field range from $50,000 to $85,000 and many are rising. Figure 1.17 displays a *Computerworld* salary survey. Research the Internet for a current MIS salary survey. Which types of jobs are on the rise? If there are any jobs you are unfamiliar with, research the Internet to determine the job characteristics. List the top three jobs you would want if you were to pursue a career in MIS. What do you find interesting about these jobs? What skills can you build to help you prepare for these jobs?[27]

FIGURE 1.17

Computerworld Salary Survey

Job Description	Compensation
Business intelligence analyst	$ 81,866
Communications specialist	$ 85,938
Database architect	$ 98,995
Ebusiness specialist	$ 71,717
Information security specialist	$ 83,693
IT / IS technology / business systems analyst	$ 78,305
Network architect	$ 96,302
Programmer / analyst	$ 75,995
Project leader	$ 87,922
Senior systems analyst	$ 89,987
Software developer	$ 85,684
Software engineer	$ 93,726
Storage architect / engineer	$111,077
Systems programmer	$ 89,472
Web developer	$ 66,347

6. Starting your own Business

Josh James recently sold his Web analytics company, Omniture, to Adobe for $1.8 billion. Yes, James started Omniture from his dorm room! Have you begun to recognize the unbelievable opportunities available to those students who understand the power of MIS, regardless of their major? Answer the following questions.[28]

a. Why is it so easy today for students to create start-ups while still in college?
b. What would it take for you to start a business from your dorm room?
c. How will this course help you prepare to start your own business?
d. Research the Internet and find three examples of college student start-ups.
e. What's stopping you from starting your own business today? You are living in the information age and with the power of MIS, it is easier than ever to jump into the business game with very little capital investment. Why not start your own business today?

7. The Five Forces Model at Work

Your team is working for a small investment company that specializes in technology investments. A new company, Geyser, has just released an operating system that plans to compete with Microsoft's operating systems. Your company has a significant amount of capital invested in Microsoft. Your boss, Kellee Lazarus, has asked you to compile a Porter's Five Forces analysis for Microsoft to ensure that your company's Microsoft investment is not at risk.

8. Competitive Analysis

Cheryl O'Connell is the owner of a small, high-end retailer of women's clothing called Excelus. Excelus's business has been successful for many years, largely because of O'Connell's ability to anticipate the needs and wants of her loyal customer base and provide them with personalized service. O'Connell does not see any value in IT and does not want to invest any capital in something that will not directly affect her bottom line. Develop a proposal describing the potential IT-enabled competitive opportunities or threats O'Connell might be missing by not embracing IT. Be sure to include a Porter's Five Forces analysis and discuss which one of the three generic strategies O'Connell should pursue.

9. **Applying the Three Generic Strategies**
   This chapter discussed several examples of companies that pursue differentiated strategies so that they are not forced into positions where they must compete solely based on price. In a team, choose an industry and find and compare two companies, one that is competing based on price and another that is pursuing a differentiated strategy enabled by the creative use of IT. Some industries you may want to consider are clothing retailers, grocery stores, airlines, and personal computers. Prepare a presentation for the class on the ways that the company is using IT to help it differentiate and compete against the low-cost provider. Before you begin, spend some class time to make sure each team selects a different industry.

10. **10 Best Things You Will Say to Your Grandchildren**
    Wired magazine recently posted the top 10 things you will say to your grandchildren. For each expression below try to identify what it is referring to and why it will be considered outdated.[29]
    1. Back in my day, we only needed 140 characters.
    2. There used to be so much snow up here, you could strap a board to your feet and slide all the way down.
    3. Televised contests gave cash prizes to whoever could store the most data in their head.
    4. Well, the screens were bigger, but they only showed the movies at certain times of day.
    5. We all had one, but nobody actually used it. Come to think of it, I bet my LinkedIn profile is still out there on the Web somewhere.
    6. Translation: "English used to be the dominant language. Crazy, huh?"
    7. Our bodies were made of meat and supported by little sticks of calcium.
    8. You used to keep files right on your computer, and you had to go back to that same computer to access them!
    9. Is that the new iPhone 27G? Got multitasking yet?
    10. I just can't get used to this darn vat-grown steak. Texture ain't right.

ENTREPRENEURIAL CHALLENGE

BUILD YOUR OWN BUSINESS

You have recently inherited your grandfather's business, which is conveniently located in your city's downtown. The business offers many different kinds of specialized products and services and was first opened in 1952 and was a local hot spot for many years. Unfortunately, business has been steadily declining over the past few years. The business runs without any computers and all ordering takes place manually. Your grandfather had a terrific memory and knew all of his customers and suppliers by name, but unfortunately, none of this information is located anywhere in the store. The operational information required to run the business, such as sales trends, vendor information, promotional information, and so on, is all located in your grandfather's memory. Inventory is tracked in a note pad, along with employee payroll, and marketing coupons. The business does not have a website, uses very little marketing except word of mouth, and essentially still operates the same as it did in 1952.

Throughout this course you will own and operate your grandfather's business, and by taking advantage of business practices discussed in this text, you will attempt to increase profits, decrease expenses, and bring the business into the 21st century. For the purpose of this case, please choose the business you wish to operate and create a name for the business. For example, the business could be a coffee shop called The Broadway Café, an extreme sports store called Cutting Edge Sports, or even a movie store called The Silver Screen. Try to pick a business you are genuinely interested in running and that aligns with your overall career goals.

PROJECT FOCUS: COMPETITIVE ADVANTAGE

1. Identify the business you are going to build throughout this course and choose a name for your business.
2. Write an analysis of buyer power and supplier power for your business using Porter's Five Forces Model. Be sure to discuss how you could combat the competition with strategies such as switching costs and loyalty programs.
3. Write an analysis of rivalry, entry barriers, and the threat of substitute products for your business using Porter's Five Forces Model. Be sure to discuss how you could combat the competition with strategies such as product differentiation.
4. Describe which of Porter's three generic strategies you would use for your business. Be sure to describe the details of how you will implement this strategy and how it will help you create a competitive advantage in your industry.

APPLY YOUR KNOWLEDGE BUSINESS PROJECTS

PROJECT I Capitalizing on Your Career

Business leaders need to be comfortable with management information systems (MIS) for the following (primary) reasons:

- The sheer magnitude of the dollars spent on MIS must be managed to ensure business value.
- Research has consistently shown that when top managers are active in supporting MIS, they realize a number of benefits, such as gaining a competitive advantage, streamlining business processes, and even transforming entire industries.
- When business leaders are not involved in MIS, systems fail, revenue is lost, and entire companies can even fail because of poorly managed systems.

How do companies get managers involved in MIS? One of the biggest positive factors is managers' personal experience with MIS and MIS education, including university classes and executive seminars. Once managers understand MIS through experience and education, they are more likely to lead their companies in achieving business success through MIS.

Project Focus

1. Search the Internet for examples of the types of technologies currently used in the field or industry that you plan to pursue. For example, if you are planning a career in accounting or finance, you should become familiar with financial systems such as Oracle Financials. For a career in logistics or distribution, research supply chain management systems. If marketing appeals to you, research customer relationship management systems, blogs, emarketing, and social networking.

2. As a competitive tool, MIS can differentiate products, services, and prices from competitors' offerings by improving product quality, shortening product development or delivery time, creating new MIS-based products and services, and improving customer service before, during, and after a transaction. Search the Internet for examples of companies in the industry where you plan to work that have achieved a competitive advantage through MIS.
3. Create a brief report of your findings; include an overview of the type of technologies you found and how companies are using them to achieve a competitive advantage.

PROJECT II Achieving Alignment

Most companies would like to be in the market-leading position of JetBlue, Dell, or Walmart, all of which have used management information systems to secure their respective spots in the marketplace. These companies are relentless about keeping the cost of technology down by combining the best of MIS and business leadership.

The future belongs to those organizations perceptive enough to grasp the significance of MIS and resourceful enough to coordinate their business and management information systems.

Project Focus

1. Use any resource to answer the question, "Why is it challenging for businesses to align MIS and their other operations?" Use the following questions to begin your analysis:
   a. How do companies monitor competitive intelligence and create competitive advantages?
   b. What are some of the greatest MIS challenges for most firms?
   c. What drives MIS decisions?
   d. Who or what is the moving force behind MIS decisions for most companies?

PROJECT III Market Dissection

To illustrate the use of the three generic strategies, consider Figure 1.18. The matrix shown demonstrates the relationships among strategies (cost leadership versus differentiation) and market segmentation (broad versus focused).

FIGURE 1.18

Porter's Three Generic Strategies

	Cost leadership strategy	Differentiation strategy
Broad market	Hyundai	Audi
Focused market	Kia	Hummer

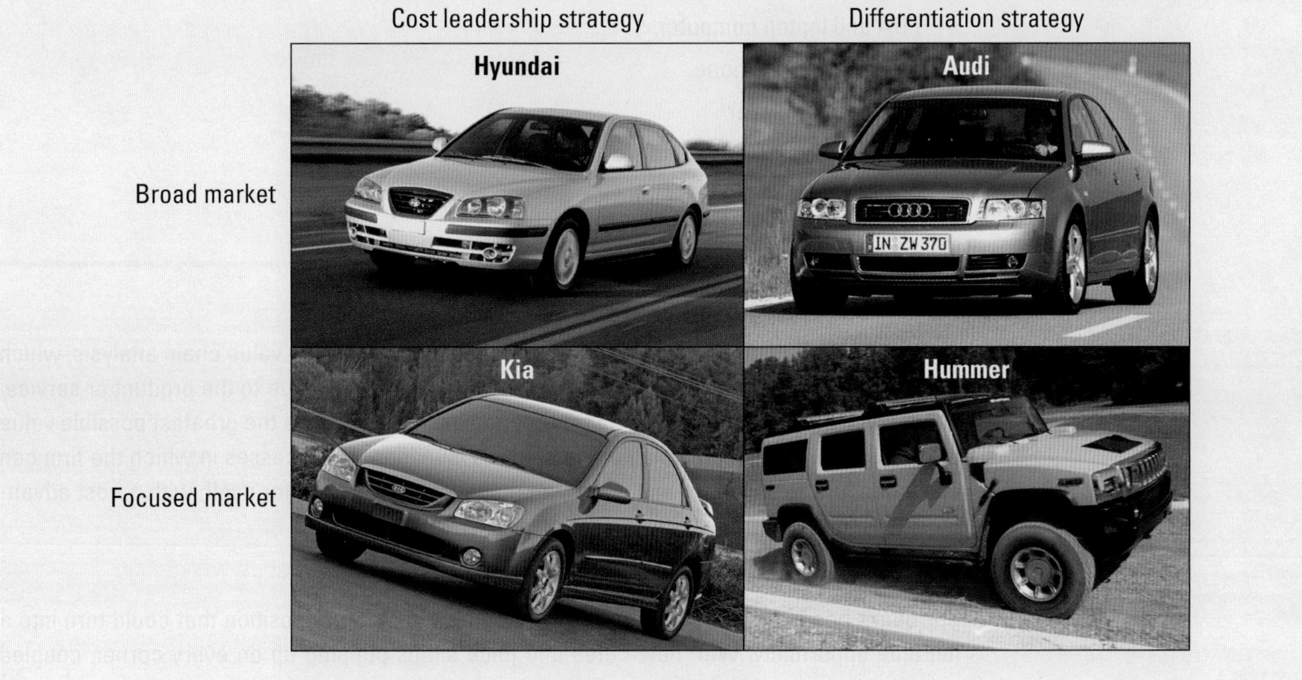

- Hyundai is following a broad cost leadership strategy. It offers low-cost vehicles, in each particular model stratification, that appeal to a large audience.
- Audi is pursuing a broad differentiation strategy with its Quattro models available at several price points. Audi's differentiation is safety, and it prices its models higher than Hyundai's to reach a large, stratified audience.
- Kia has a more focused cost leadership strategy. Kia mainly offers low-cost vehicles in the lower levels of model stratification.
- Hummer offers the most focused differentiation strategy of any in the industry (including Mercedes-Benz).

Project Focus

Create a similar graph displaying each strategy for a product of your choice. The strategy must include an example of the product in each of the following markets: (1) cost leadership, broad market; (2) differentiation, broad market; (3) cost leadership, focused market; and (4) differentiation, focused market. Potential products include cereal, dog food, soft drinks, computers, shampoo, snack foods, jeans, sneakers, sandals, mountain bikes, TV shows, movies.

PROJECT IV Porter's Five Forces

Setting strategic direction for a business is a challenge for even seasoned professionals. The good news is there are many tools available you can use to help you find competitive advantages, including Porter's Five Forces. Porter's Five Forces Model analyzes the competitive forces within the environment in which a company operates to assess the potential for profitability in an industry. Its purpose is to combat these competitive forces by identifying opportunities, competitive advantages, and competitive intelligence. If the forces are strong, they increase competition; if the forces are weak, they decrease competition.

Project Focus

Porter's Five Forces Model is a good framework for understanding market forces. Break into groups and choose a comparison from the list below to perform a Porter's Five Forces analysis.

- Notebook computer and laptop computer.
- PDA and laptop computer.
- iPhone and cell phone.
- iPod and CD player.
- GPS device and a road atlas.
- Digital books and printed books.

PROJECT V Adding Value

To identify these competitive advantages, Michael Porter created value chain analysis, which views a firm as a series of business processes that each add value to the product or service. Value chain analysis is a useful tool for determining how to create the greatest possible value for customers. The goal of value chain analysis is to identify processes in which the firm can add value for the customer and create a competitive advantage for itself, with a cost advantage or product differentiation

Project Focus

Starbucks has hired you after your graduation for a temporary position that could turn into a full-time opportunity. With new cafés and juice shops popping up on every corner, coupled with the global recession, Starbucks is worried about losing market share to competitors. Your boss, Heather Sweitzer, is out of ideas for ways to improve the company's profitability. You decide that one of the most useful tools for identifying competitive advantages is Porter's value chain analysis. Of course, you do not yet have the detailed knowledge to complete all of the elements required, but you know enough to get started and plan to take your draft to Sweitzer next week. Using your knowledge of Starbucks, create a value chain analysis. Feel free to make assumptions about operations; just be sure to list any that you make. Also, be sure to write an overview of the tool and its potential value so Sweitzer can understand how it works.

PROJECT VI Flat Competition

"When I was growing up in Minneapolis, my parents always said, 'Tom, finish your dinner. There are people starving in China and India.' Today I tell my girls, 'Finish your homework, because people in China and India are starving for your jobs.' And in a flat world, they can have them, because there's no such thing as an American job anymore." Thomas Friedman.

Project Focus

In his book, *The World is Flat,* Thomas Friedman describes the unplanned cascade of technological and social shifts that effectively leveled the economic world, and "accidentally made Beijing, Bangalore, and Bethesda next-door neighbors." The video of Thomas Friedman's lecture at MIT discussing the flat world is available at http://mitworld.mit.edu/video/266. If you want to be prepared to compete in a flat world you must watch this video and answer the following questions:

- Do you agree or disagree with Friedman's assessment that the world is flat?
- What are the potential impacts of a flat world for a student performing a job search?
- What can students do to prepare themselves for competing in a flat world?[30]

PROJECT VII Wikiblunders

According to *PC World* these false facts all appeared on Wikipedia:

1. Robbie Williams eats domestic pets in pubs for money.
2. David Beckham was a Chinese goalkeeper in the 18th century.
3. Paul Reiser's dead. (Reiser is an actor)
4. Sinbad's dead. (Sinbad is an actor)
5. Sergey Brin's sexy, dating Jimmy Wales, and dead. (Brin founded Google and Wales founded Wikipedia)
6. Tony Blair worships Hitler. (Blair was the former Prime Minister of the United Kingdom)
7. The Duchess of Cornwall's Christian name is Cow-miller.
8. Robert Byrd's dead. (Byrd is a U.S. Senator from West Virginia)
9. John Seigenthaler helped assassinate John and Robert Kennedy. (Seigenthaler is a journalist)
10. Conan O'Brien assaults sea turtles while canoeing.[31]

Project Focus

We know that people use information technology to work with information. Knowing this, how could these types of errors occur? What could happen if you decided to use Wikipedia to collect business intelligence for a research paper? What could Wikipedia do to help prevent these types of errors?

PROJECT VIII What's Wrong with This Bathroom?

If you were the CEO of a global financial company that was experiencing a financial crisis, would you invest $1 million to renovate your office? Probably not and you are possibly wondering if this is a fabricated story from *The Onion*. Guess what, this is a true story! John Thain, the former CEO of Merrill Lynch, decided to spend $1.2 million refurbishing his office—well after Merrill Lynch posted huge financial losses. Thain personally signed-off all of the following:

- Area Rug: $87,784
- Mahogany Pedestal Table: $25,713
- 19th Century Credenza: $68,179
- Pendant Light Furniture: $19,751
- 4 Pairs of Curtains: $28,091
- Pair of Guest Chairs: $87,784
- George IV Chair: $18,468
- 6 Wall Sconces: $2,741
- Parchment Waste Can: $1,405 (yes, for a trash can!!)
- Roman Shade Fabric: $10,967
- Roman Shades: $7,315
- Coffee Table: $5,852
- Commode on Legs: $35,115[32]

Project Focus

It takes years of education and work experience for people to build the skills necessary to take on the role of CEO. Obviously, a company like Merril Lynch would only hire a highly qualified person for the job. What do you think happened to John Thain? Why would he spend an obscene amount of money redecorating his office when his company was having financial trouble? What happens to a company whose executives are not aligned with company goals? How can you ensure that your company's executives are not making monumental mistakes, such as million dollar bathroom renovations?

PROJECT IX I Love TED!

A small nonprofit started in 1984, TED (Technology, Entertainment, Design) hosts conferences for Ideas Worth Spreading. TED brings people from all over the globe to share award-winning talks covering the most innovative, informative, and exciting speeches ever given in 20 minutes. You can find TED talks by Al Gore, Bill Gates, Steve Jobs, Douglas Adams, Steven Levitt, Seth Godin, Malcolm Gladwell, and so on.[33]

Project Focus

Visit www.ted.com and peruse the thousands of videos that are available then answer the following:

- Review the TED website and find three talks you would want to watch. Why did you pick these three and will you make time outside of class to watch them?
- How can you gain a competitive advantage by watching TED?
- How can you find innovative ideas for a start-up by watching TED?
- How can you find competitive intelligence by watching TED?

AYK APPLICATION PROJECTS

If you are looking for Excel projects to incorporate into your class, try any of the following after reading this chapter.

Project Number	Project Name	Project Type	Plug-In Focus Area	Project Level	Skill Set	Page Number
1	Financial Destiny	Excel	T2	Personal Budget	Introductory Formulas	AYK.4
2	Cash Flow	Excel	T2	Cash Flow	Introductory Formulas	AYK.4
3	Technology Budget	Excel	T1, T2	Hardware and Software	Introductory Formulas	AYK.4
4	Tracking Donations	Excel	T2	Employee Relationships	Introductory Formulas	AYK.4
5	Convert Currency	Excel	T2	Global Commerce	Introductory Formulas	AYK.5
6	Cost Comparison	Excel	T2	Total Cost of Ownership	Introductory Formulas	AYK.5
7	Time Management	Excel or Project	T12 Project Management	Introductory	Gantt Charts	AYK.6

2

CHAPTER

Decisions and Processes: Value Driven Business

CHAPTER OUTLINE

SECTION 2.1
Decision Support Systems

- Making Business Decisions
- Metrics: Measuring Success
- Support: Enhancing Decision Making with MIS
- The Future: Artificial Intelligence

SECTION 2.2
Business Processes

- Evaluating Business Processes
- Models: Measuring Performance
- Support: Enhancing Business Processes with MIS
- The Future: Business Process Management

What's in IT for me?

Working faster and smarter has become a necessity for companies. A firm's value chain is directly affected by how well it designs and coordinates its business processes. Business processes offer competitive advantages if they enable a firm to lower operating costs, differentiate, or compete in a niche market. They can also be huge burdens if they are outdated, which impedes operations, efficiency, and effectiveness. Thus, the ability of management information systems to improve business processes is a key advantage.

The goal of Chapter 2 is to provide an overview of specific MIS tools managers can use to support the strategies discussed in Chapter 1. After reading this chapter, you, the business student, should have detailed knowledge of the types of information systems that exist to support decision making and business process reengineering, which in turn can improve organization efficiency and effectiveness and help an organization create and maintain competitive advantages.

opening case study

Political Micro-Targeting: What Decision Support Systems Did for Barack Obama

On the day he took the oath of office, President Barack Obama spoke a word rarely heard in inaugural addresses—*data*—referencing indicators of economic and other crises. His use of the word is perhaps not so surprising. Capturing and analyzing data were crucial to Obama's rise to power. Throughout his historic campaign he not only used the Internet for networking and fund-raising, but he also relied on decision support systems to identify potential swing voters. Obama's team carefully monitored contested states and congressional districts, where as few as 2,000 voters could prove decisive—a tiny fraction of the voting public. Both presidential candidates hired technology wizards to help sift through mountains of consumer and demographic details to recognize these important voters.

Ten "Tribes"

Spotlight Analysis, a Democratic consultancy, used political micro-targeting to analyze neighborhood details, family sizes, and spending patterns to categorize every person of voting age—all 175 million—into 10 "values" tribes. Individual tribe members do not necessarily share the same race, religion, or income bracket, but they have common mind-sets about political issues: God, community, responsibility, and opportunity. Spotlight Analysis predicted the influence of a particular morally guided (but not necessarily religious) tribe of some 14 million voters, dubbed Barn Raisers. Barn Raisers are of many races, religions, and ethnicities; about 40 percent favor Democrats and 27 percent Republicans. Barn Raisers are slightly less likely to have a college education than Spotlight's other swing groups. They are active in community organizations, ambivalent about government, and deeply concerned about "playing by the rules" and "keeping promises," to use Spotlight's definitions. Spotlight believed the Barn Raisers held the key to the race between Obama and his Republican challenger, Arizona Senator John McCain.

Political micro-targeting, which depends on MIS to support decision making, is turning government segments into sophisticated, intelligent, methodical political machines. In nanoseconds, decision support systems sort 175 million voters into segments and quickly calculate the potential for each individual voter to swing from red or purple to blue.

For some, political micro-targeting signals the dehumanization of politics. For others, this type of sophisticated analysis is a highly efficient way of pinpointing potential voters. For example, the analysis of a voter in Richmond, Virginia, simply identifies the number of his or her school-age children, type of car, zip code, magazine subscriptions, and mortgage balance. Data could even indicate whether the voter has dogs or cats. (Cat owners lean slightly for Democrats, dog owners trend Republican.) After the analysis, the voter is placed into a political tribe, and analysts can draw conclusions about the issues that matter to him or her and make campaign decisions accordingly. Is this a bad thing?

Behavioral Grouping

For generations, governments lacked the means to study individual behaviors and simply placed all citizens into enormous groupings such as Hispanics, Catholics, union members, hunters, soccer moms, and so on. With the use of sophisticated MIS analysis techniques, companies such as Spotlight Analysis can group individuals based more on specific behavior and choices, and less on the names, colors, and clans that mark us from birth.

When Spotlight first embarked on its research, it interviewed thousands of voters the old-fashioned way. The Barn Raisers did not seem significant; the tribe represented about 9 percent of the electorate. However, when Spotlight's analysts drilled down or dug deeper, they discovered that Barn Raisers stood at the epicenter of a political swing. In 2004, 90 percent of them voted for President Bush, but then the group's political leanings shifted, with 64 percent saying they voted for Democrats in the 2006 election. Spotlight surveys showed that Republican political scandals, tax-funded boondoggles such as Alaska's "bridge to nowhere," and the botched recovery job after Hurricane Katrina sent them packing.

Suddenly, Spotlight had identified millions of potential swing voters. The challenge then was to locate them by state. For this, the company analyzed the demographics and buying patterns of the Barn Raisers it had surveyed personally. Then it began correlating its data with commercially available data to match profiles. By Spotlight's count, this approach nailed Barn Raisers three times out of four. So Democrats could bet that at least three-quarters of them would be likely to welcome an election appeal stressing honesty and fair play.

Still Swing Voters

Spotlight has not correlated the Barn Raisers to their actual votes, so it's not clear how well the company's strategy worked. However, it is reasonable to presume that amid that sea of humanity stretched out before the newly inaugurated Obama on the National Mall, at least some were moved by micro-targeted appeals. And if Obama and his team fail to honor their mathematically honed vows, the Barn Raisers may abandon them in droves. They are swing voters, after all.[1]

section 2.1 DECISION SUPPORT SYSTEMS

LEARNING OUTCOMES

2.1 Explain the importance of decision making for managers at each of the three primary organization levels along with the associated decision characteristics.

2.2 Define critical success factors (CSFs) and key performance indicators (KPIs), and explain how managers use them to measure the success of MIS projects.

2.3 Classify the different operational support systems, managerial support systems, and strategic support systems, and explain how managers can use these systems to make decisions and gain competitive advantages.

2.4 Describe artificial intelligence, and identify its five main types.

MAKING BUSINESS DECISIONS

LO 2.1: Explain the importance of decision making for managers at each of the three primary organization levels along with the associated decision characteristics.

Porter's strategies outlined in Chapter 1 suggest entering markets with a competitive advantage in either overall cost leadership, differentiation, or focus. To achieve these results, managers must be able to make decisions and forecast future business needs and requirements. The most important and most challenging question confronting managers today is how to lay the foundation for tomorrow's success while competing to win in today's business environment. A company will not have a future if it is not cultivating strategies for tomorrow. The goal of this section is to expand on Porter's Five Forces Model, three generic strategies, and value chain analysis to demonstrate how managers can learn the concepts and practices of business decision making to add value. It will also highlight how companies heading into the 21st century are taking advantage of advanced MIS capable of generating significant competitive advantages across the value chain.

As we discussed in Chapter 1, decision making is one of the most important and challenging aspects of management. Decisions range from routine choices, such as how many items to order or how many people to hire, to unexpected ones such as what to do if a key employee suddenly quits or needed materials do not arrive. Today, with massive volumes of information available, managers are challenged to make highly complex decisions—some involving far more information than the human brain can comprehend—in increasingly shorter time frames. Figure 2.1 displays the three primary challenges managers face when making decisions.

FIGURE 2.1

Managerial Decision-Making Challenges

MANAGERIAL DECISION-MAKING CHALLENGES
1. Managers need to analyze large amounts of information:
Innovations in communication and globalization have resulted in a dramatic increase in the variables and dimensions people need to consider when making a decision, solving a problem, or appraising an opportunity.
2. Managers must make decisions quickly:
Time is of the essence and people simply do not have time to sift through all the information manually.
3. Managers must apply sophisticated analysis techniques, such as Porter's strategies or forecasting, to make strategic decisions:
Due to the intensely competitive global business environment, companies must offer far more than just a great product to succeed.

The Decision-Making Process

The process of making decisions plays a crucial role in communication and leadership for operational, managerial, and strategic projects. There are numerous academic decision-making models; Figure 2.2 presents just one example.[2]

Decision-Making Essentials

A few key concepts about organizational structure will help our discussion of MIS decision-making tools. The structure of a typical organization is similar to a pyramid, and the different levels require different types of information to assist in decision making, problem solving, and opportunity capturing (see Figure 2.3).

Operational At the operational level, employees develop, control, and maintain core business activities required to run the day-to-day operations. Operational decisions are considered ***structured decisions,*** which arise in situations where established processes offer potential solutions. Structured decisions are made frequently and are almost repetitive in nature; they affect short-term business strategies. Reordering inventory and creating the employee staffing and weekly production schedules are examples of routine structured decisions. Figure 2.4 highlights the essential elements required for operational decision making. All the elements in the figure should be familiar, except metrics which are discussed in detail below.

Managerial At the managerial level, employees are continuously evaluating company operations to hone the firm's abilities to identify, adapt to, and leverage change. A company that has a competitive advantage needs to constantly adjust and revise its strategy to remain ahead of fast-following competitors. Managerial decisions cover short- and medium-range plans, schedules, and budgets along with policies,

FIGURE 2.2

The Six-Step Decision-Making Process

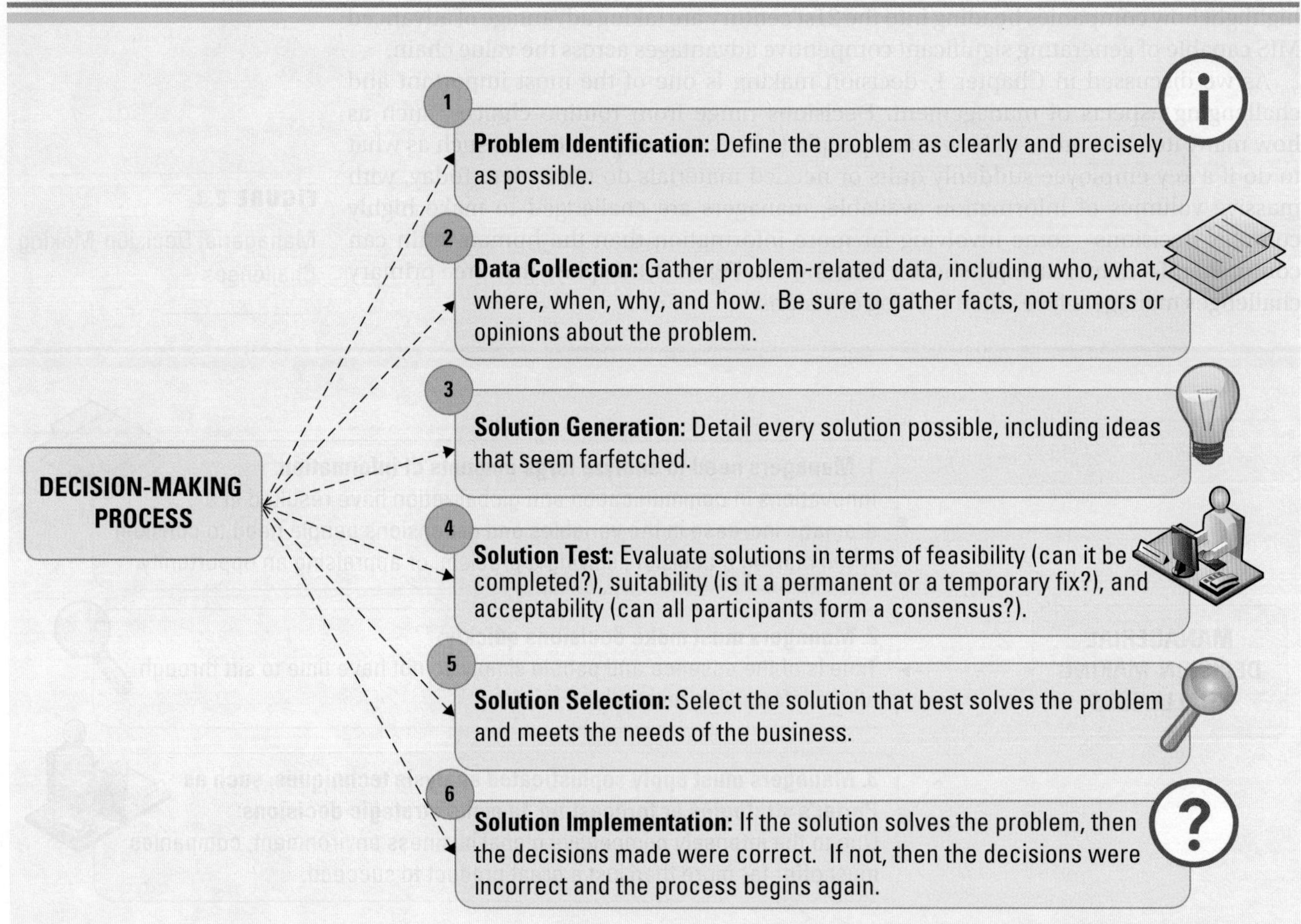

DECISION-MAKING PROCESS
1
Problem Identification: Define the problem as clearly and precisely as possible.
2
Data Collection: Gather problem-related data, including who, what, where, when, why, and how. Be sure to gather facts, not rumors or opinions about the problem.
3
Solution Generation: Detail every solution possible, including ideas that seem farfetched.
4
Solution Test: Evaluate solutions in terms of feasibility (can it be completed?), suitability (is it a permanent or a temporary fix?), and acceptability (can all participants form a consensus?).
5
Solution Selection: Select the solution that best solves the problem and meets the needs of the business.
6
Solution Implementation: If the solution solves the problem, then the decisions made were correct. If not, then the decisions were incorrect and the process begins again.
i
?

STRATEGIC
MANAGERIAL
OPERATIONAL

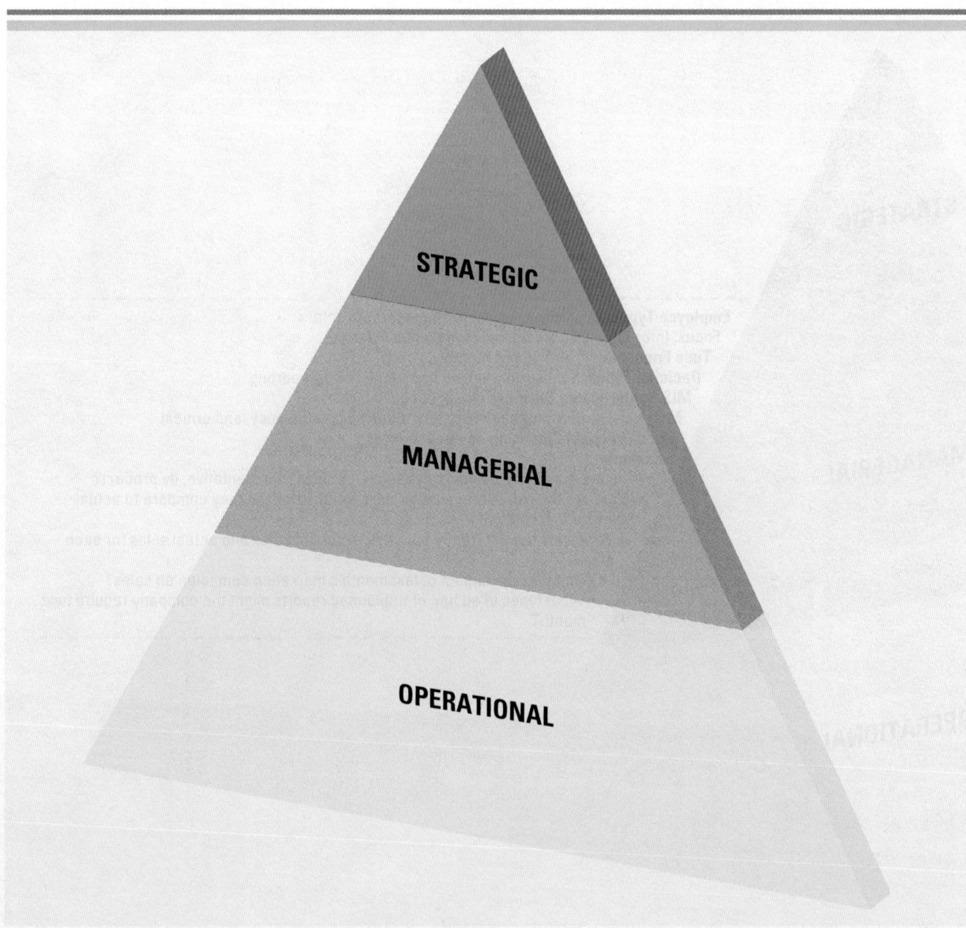

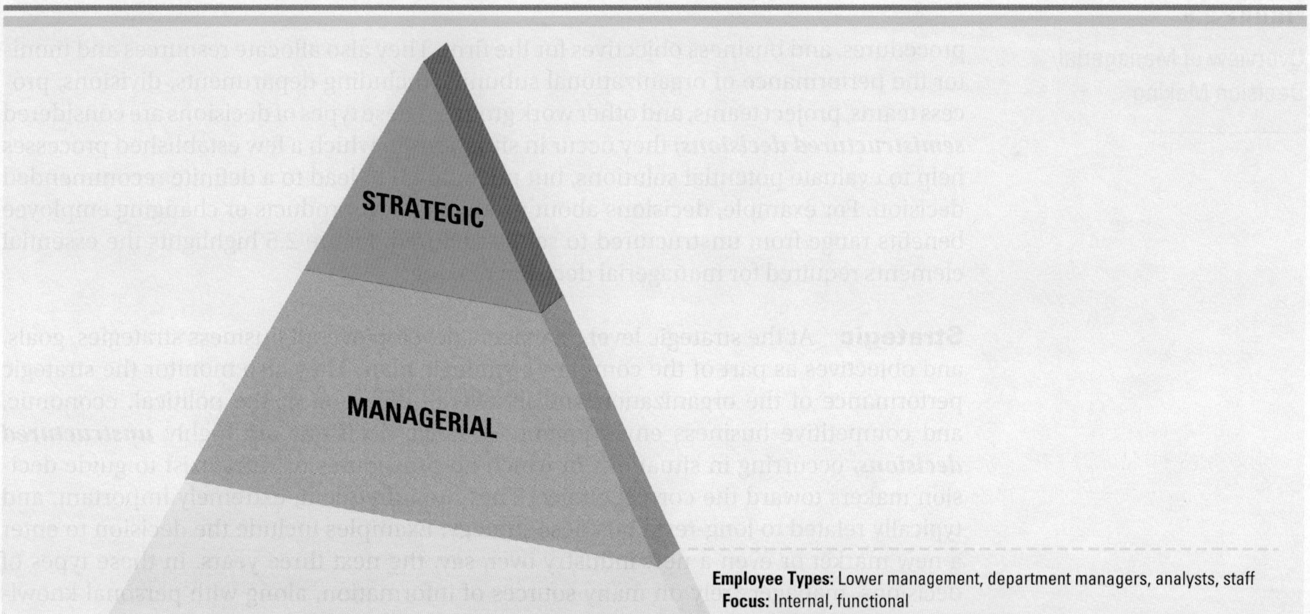

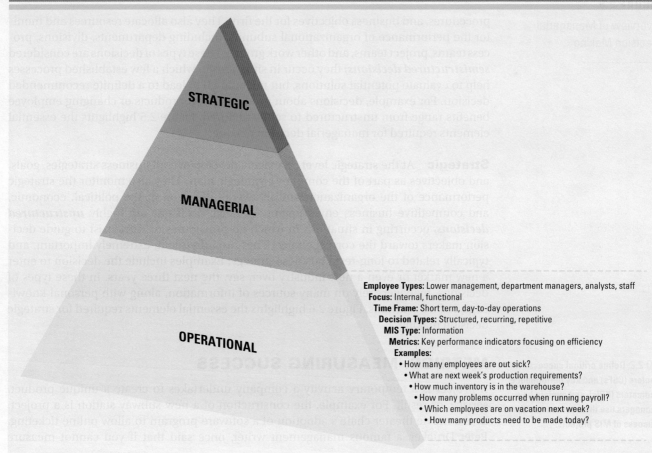

FIGURE 2.3
Common Company Structure

STRATEGIC
MANAGERIAL
OPERATIONAL
Employee Types: Lower management, department managers, analysts, staff
Focus: Internal, functional
Time Frame: Short term, day-to-day operations
Decision Types: Structured, recurring, repetitive
MIS Type: Information
Metrics: Key performance indicators focusing on efficiency
Examples:
• How many employees are out sick?
• What are next week's production requirements?
• How much inventory is in the warehouse?
• How many problems occurred when running payroll?
• Which employees are on vacation next week?
• How many products need to be made today?

FIGURE 2.4
Overview of Operational Decision Making

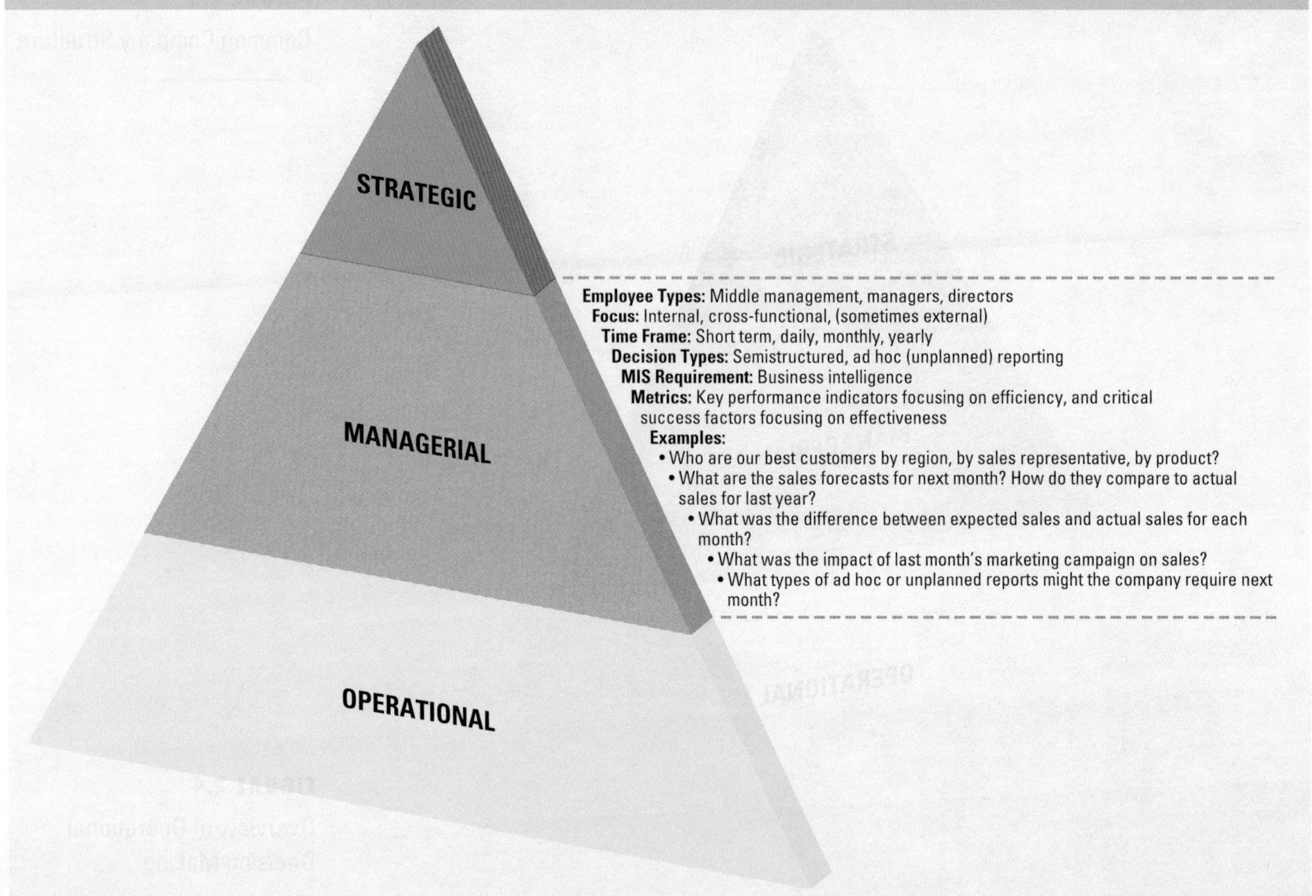

STRATEGIC
MANAGERIAL
OPERATIONAL
Employee Types: Middle management, managers, directors
Focus: Internal, cross-functional, (sometimes external)
Time Frame: Short term, daily, monthly, yearly
Decision Types: Semistructured, ad hoc (unplanned) reporting
MIS Requirement: Business intelligence
Metrics: Key performance indicators focusing on efficiency, and critical success factors focusing on effectiveness
Examples:
• Who are our best customers by region, by sales representative, by product?
• What are the sales forecasts for next month? How do they compare to actual sales for last year?
• What was the difference between expected sales and actual sales for each month?
• What was the impact of last month's marketing campaign on sales?
• What types of ad hoc or unplanned reports might the company require next month?

FIGURE 2.5
Overview of Managerial Decision Making

procedures, and business objectives for the firm. They also allocate resources and monitor the performance of organizational subunits, including departments, divisions, process teams, project teams, and other work groups. These types of decisions are considered ***semistructured decisions;*** they occur in situations in which a few established processes help to evaluate potential solutions, but not enough to lead to a definite recommended decision. For example, decisions about producing new products or changing employee benefits range from unstructured to semistructured. Figure 2.5 highlights the essential elements required for managerial decision making.

Strategic At the strategic level, managers develop overall business strategies, goals, and objectives as part of the company's strategic plan. They also monitor the strategic performance of the organization and its overall direction in the political, economic, and competitive business environment. Strategic decisions are highly ***unstructured decisions,*** occurring in situations in which no procedures or rules exist to guide decision makers toward the correct choice. They are infrequent, extremely important, and typically related to long-term business strategy. Examples include the decision to enter a new market or even a new industry over, say, the next three years. In these types of decisions, managers rely on many sources of information, along with personal knowledge, to find solutions. Figure 2.6 highlights the essential elements required for strategic decision making.

LO 2.2: Define critical success factors (CSFs) and key performance indicators (KPIs), and explain how managers use them to measure the success of MIS projects.

METRICS: MEASURING SUCCESS

A ***project*** is a temporary activity a company undertakes to create a unique product, service, or result. For example, the construction of a new subway station is a project, as is a movie theater chain's adoption of a software program to allow online ticketing. Peter Drucker, a famous management writer, once said that if you cannot measure

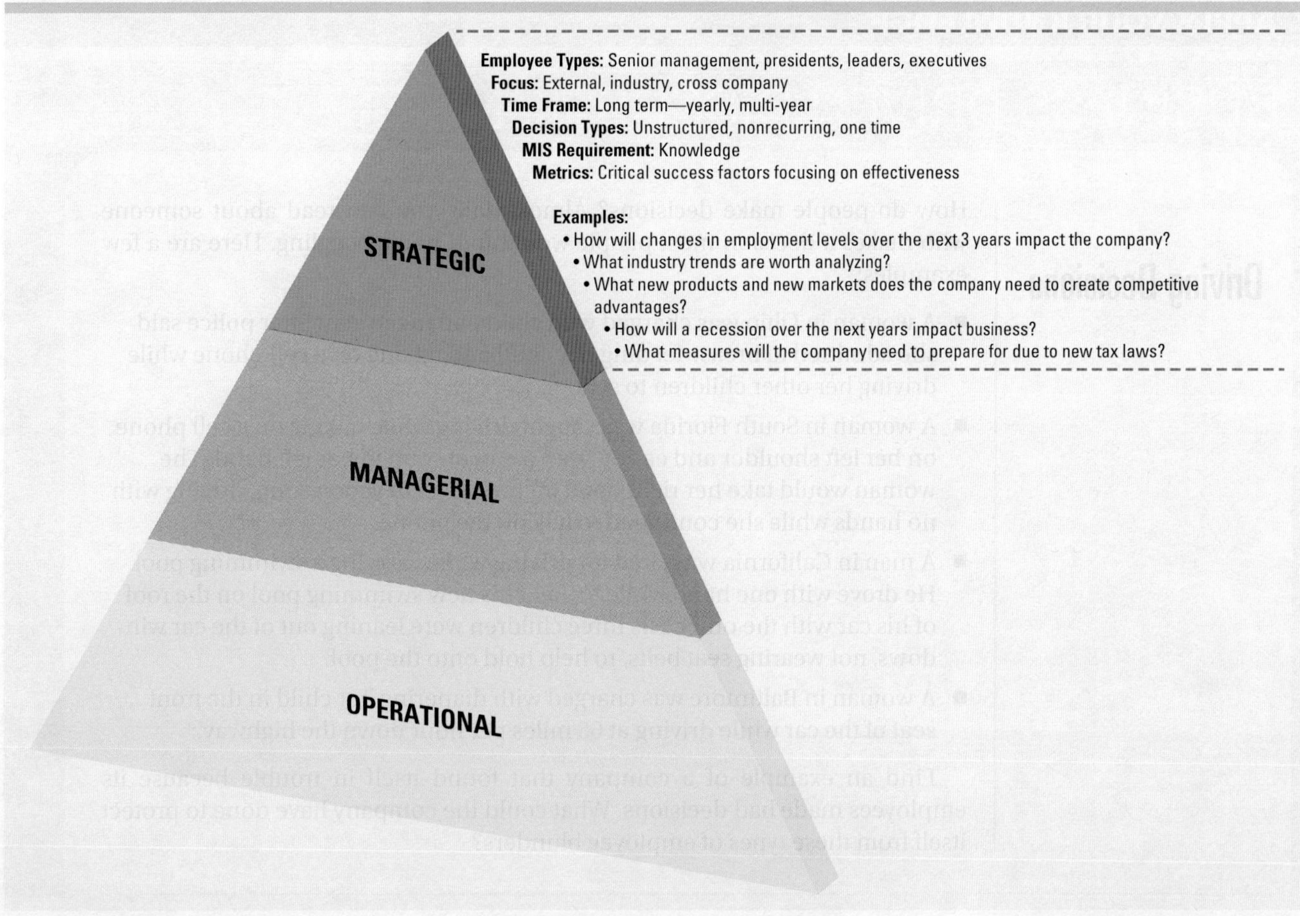

Employee Types: Senior management, presidents, leaders, executives
Focus: External, industry, cross company
Time Frame: Long term—yearly, multi-year
Decision Types: Unstructured, nonrecurring, one time
MIS Requirement: Knowledge
Metrics: Critical success factors focusing on effectiveness
Examples:
• How will changes in employment levels over the next 3 years impact the company?
• What industry trends are worth analyzing?
• What new products and new markets does the company need to create competitive advantages?
• How will a recession over the next years impact business?
• What measures will the company need to prepare for due to new tax laws?
STRATEGIC
MANAGERIAL
OPERATIONAL

FIGURE 2.6

Overview of Strategic Decision Making

something, you cannot manage it. How do managers measure the progress of a complex business project?

Metrics are measurements that evaluate results to determine whether a project is meeting its goals. Two core metrics are critical success factors and key performance indicators. ***Critical success factors (CSFs)*** are the crucial steps companies perform to achieve their goals and objectives and implement their strategies. CSFs include:

- Create high-quality products.
- Retain competitive advantages.
- Reduce product costs.
- Increase customer satisfaction.
- Hire and retain the best business professionals.

Key performance indicators (KPIs) are the quantifiable metrics a company uses to evaluate progress toward critical success factors. KPIs are far more specific than CSFs; examples include:

- Turnover rates of employees.
- Percentage of help desk calls answered in the first minute.
- Number of product returns.
- Number of new customers.
- Average customer spending.

It is important to understand the relationship between critical success factors and key performance indicators. CSFs are elements crucial for a business strategy's success. KPIs measure the progress of CSFs with quantifiable measurements, and one CSF can have several KPIs. Of course, both categories will vary by company and industry.

APPLY YOUR KNOWLEDGE

BUSINESS DRIVEN DISCUSSION

Driving Decisions

How do people make decisions? Almost daily you can read about someone who makes a decision most people would find mind-boggling. Here are a few examples:

- A woman in Ohio was charged with child endangerment after police said she admitted to breast-feeding her child and talking on a cell phone while driving her other children to school.
- A woman in South Florida was caught driving while talking on a cell phone on her left shoulder and eating from a cup of soup in her left hand. The woman would take her right hand off the wheel to spoon soup, driving with no hands while she continued to talk on the phone.
- A man in California was cited for driving while carrying a swimming pool. He drove with one hand while he held his new swimming pool on the roof of his car with the other. His three children were leaning out of the car windows, not wearing seat belts, to help hold onto the pool.
- A woman in Baltimore was charged with diapering her child in the front seat of the car while driving at 65 miles per hour down the highway.[3]

Find an example of a company that found itself in trouble because its employees made bad decisions. What could the company have done to protect itself from these types of employee blunders?

Imagine *improve graduation rates* as a CSF for a college. The KPIs to measure this CSF can include:

- Average grades by course and gender.
- Student dropout rates by gender and major.
- Average graduation rate by gender and major.
- Time spent in tutoring by gender and major.

KPIs can focus on external and internal measurements. A common external KPI is ***market share,*** or the proportion of the market that a firm captures. We calculate it by dividing the firm's sales by the total market sales for the entire industry. Market share measures a firm's external performance relative to that of its competitors. For example, if a firm's total sales (revenues) are $2 million and sales for the entire industry are $10 million, the firm has captured 20 percent of the total market (2/10 = 20%) or a 20 percent market share.

A common internal KPI is ***return on investment (ROI),*** which indicates the earning power of a project. We measure it by dividing the profitability of a project by the costs. This sounds easy, and for many departments where the projects are tangible and self-contained it is; however, for projects that are intangible and cross departmental lines (such as MIS projects), ROI is challenging to measure. Imagine attempting to calculate the ROI of a fire extinguisher. If the fire extinguisher is never used, its ROI is low. If the fire extinguisher puts out a fire that could have destroyed the entire building, its ROI is astronomically high.

Creating KPIs to measure the success of an MIS project offers similar challenges. Think about a firm's email system. How could managers track departmental costs and profits associated with company email? Measuring by volume does not account for profitability, because one sales email could land a million-dollar deal while 300 others might not generate any revenue. Non-revenue-generating departments such as human resources and legal require email but will not be using it to generate profits. For this reason, many managers turn to higher-level metrics, such as efficiency and effectiveness, to measure MIS projects.

Efficiency and Effectiveness Metrics

Efficiency MIS metrics measure the performance of MIS itself, such as throughput, transaction speed, and system availability. ***Effectiveness MIS metrics*** measure the impact MIS has on business processes and activities, including customer satisfaction and customer conversion rates. Efficiency focuses on the extent to which a firm is using its resources in an optimal way, while effectiveness focuses on how well a firm is achieving its goals and objectives. Peter Drucker offers a helpful distinction between efficiency and effectiveness: Doing things right addresses efficiency—getting the most from each resource. Doing the right things addresses effectiveness—setting the right goals and objectives and ensuring they are accomplished. Figure 2.7 describes a few of the common types of efficiency and effectiveness MIS metrics. KPIs that measure MIS projects include both efficiency and effectiveness metrics. Of course, these metrics are not as concrete as market share or ROI, but they do offer valuable insight into project performance.[4]

FIGURE 2.7

Common Types of Efficiency and Effectiveness Metrics

Efficiency Metrics

- **Throughput**—The amount of information that can travel through a system at any point in time.
- **Transaction speed**—The amount of time a system takes to perform a transaction.
- **System availability**—The number of hours a system is available for users.
- **Information accuracy**—The extent to which a system generates the correct results when executing the same transaction numerous times.
- **Response time**—The time it takes to respond to user interactions such as a mouse click.

Effectiveness Metrics

- **Usability**—The ease with which people perform transactions and/or find information.
- **Customer satisfaction**—Measured by satisfaction surveys, percentage of existing customers retained, and increases in revenue dollars per customer.
- **Conversion rates**—The number of customers an organization "touches" for the first time and persuades to purchase its products or services. This is a popular metric for evaluating the effectiveness of banner, pop-up, and pop-under ads on the Internet.
- **Financial**—Such as return on investment (the earning power of an organization's assets), cost-benefit analysis (the comparison of projected revenues and costs including development, maintenance, fixed, and variable), and break-even analysis (the point at which constant revenues equal ongoing costs).

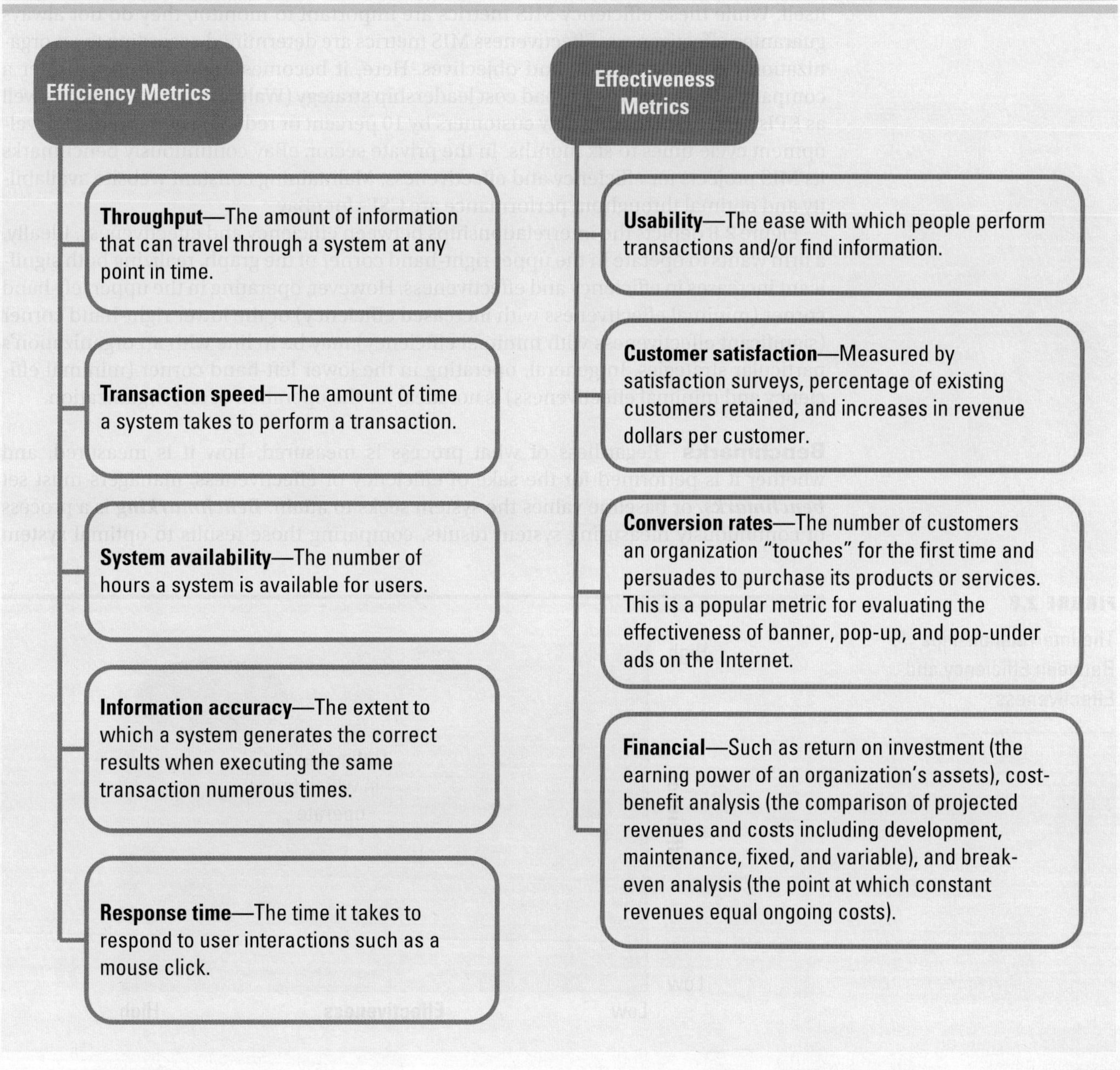

Large increases in productivity typically result from increases in effectiveness, which focus on CSFs. Efficiency MIS metrics are far easier to measure, however, so most managers tend to focus on them, often incorrectly, to measure the success of MIS projects. Consider measuring the success of automated teller machines (ATMs). Thinking in terms of MIS efficiency metrics, a manager would measure the number of daily transactions, the average amount per transaction, and the average speed per transaction to determine the success of the ATM. Although these offer solid metrics on how well the system is performing, they miss many of the intangible or value-added benefits associated with ATM effectiveness. Effectiveness MIS metrics might measure how many new customers joined the bank due to its ATM locations or the ATMs' ease of use. They can also measure increases in customer satisfaction due to reduced ATM fees or additional ATM services such as the sale of stamps and movie tickets, significant time savers and value-added features for customers. Being a great manager means taking the added viewpoint offered by effectiveness MIS metrics to analyze all benefits associated with an MIS project.

The Interrelationship Between Efficiency and Effectiveness MIS Metrics

Efficiency and effectiveness are definitely related. However, success in one area does not necessarily imply success in the other. Efficiency MIS metrics focus on the technology itself. While these efficiency MIS metrics are important to monitor, they do not always guarantee effectiveness. Effectiveness MIS metrics are determined according to an organization's goals, strategies, and objectives. Here, it becomes important to consider a company's CSFs, such as a broad cost leadership strategy (Walmart, for example), as well as KPIs such as increasing new customers by 10 percent or reducing new-product development cycle times to six months. In the private sector, eBay continuously benchmarks its MIS projects for efficiency and effectiveness. Maintaining constant website availability and optimal throughput performance are CSFs for eBay.

Figure 2.8 depicts the interrelationships between efficiency and effectiveness. Ideally, a firm wants to operate in the upper right-hand corner of the graph, realizing both significant increases in efficiency and effectiveness. However, operating in the upper left-hand corner (minimal effectiveness with increased efficiency) or the lower right-hand corner (significant effectiveness with minimal efficiency) may be in line with an organization's particular strategies. In general, operating in the lower left-hand corner (minimal efficiency and minimal effectiveness) is not ideal for the operation of any organization.

Benchmarks Regardless of what process is measured, how it is measured, and whether it is performed for the sake of efficiency or effectiveness, managers must set ***benchmarks,*** or baseline values the system seeks to attain. ***Benchmarking*** is a process of continuously measuring system results, comparing those results to optimal system

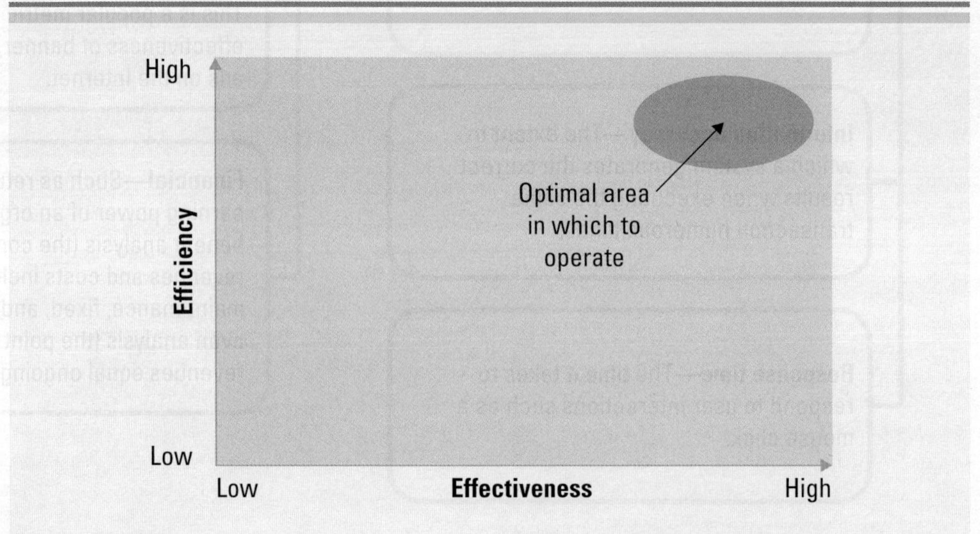

FIGURE 2.8
The Interrelationships Between Efficiency and Effectiveness

APPLY YOUR KNOWLEDGE

BUSINESS DRIVEN GLOBALIZATION

iYogi Help Desk Support

It is late at night and you are working on your final exam when your computer crashes. As your blood pressure climbs and your stress level skyrockets, you call your computer manufacturer's technical support number. Of course that person tells you the problem has nothing to do with the computer and must have a different source. What are you going to do?

iYogi.net is a 24/7 online support service that allows technicians to take remote control of your computer from Gurgaon, India, and try to fix what ails it. iYogi provides technical support for all Walmart computer customers and sells its services through Walmart.com and Amazon.com. If the thought of turning control over to someone you never met half a world away fills you with terror, it shouldn't. All iYogi technicians are Microsoft, Cisco, and Hewlett-Packard certified.[5]

Describe the types of decisions iYogi technicians are required to make when helping a customer with a computer problem. What would potential CSFs and KPIs for iYogi be? What types of metrics would managers track so they could control operations?

---

performance (benchmark values), and identifying steps and procedures to improve system performance. Benchmarks help assess how an MIS project performs over time. For instance, if a system held a benchmark for response time of 15 seconds, the manager would want to ensure response time continued to decrease until it reached that point. If response time suddenly increased to 1 minute, the manager would know the system was not functioning correctly and could start looking into potential problems. Continuously measuring MIS projects against benchmarks provides feedback so managers can control the system.

SUPPORT: ENHANCING DECISION MAKING WITH MIS

LO 2.3: Classify the different operational support systems, managerial support systems, and strategic support systems, and explain how managers can use these systems to make decisions and gain competitive advantages.

Now that we've reviewed the essentials of decision making, we are ready to understand the powerful benefits associated with using MIS to support managers making decisions.

A ***model*** is a simplified representation or abstraction of reality. Models help managers calculate risks, understand uncertainty, change variables, and manipulate time to make decisions. MIS support systems rely on models for computational and analytical routines that mathematically express relationships among variables. For example, a spreadsheet program, such as Microsoft Office Excel, might contain models that calculate market share or ROI. MIS have the capability and functionality to express far more complex modeling relationships that provide information, business intelligence, and knowledge. Figure 2.9 highlights the three primary types of management information systems available to support decision making across the company levels.

Operational Support Systems

Transactional information encompasses all the information contained within a single business process or unit of work, and its primary purpose is to support the performance of daily operational or structured decisions. Transactional information is created, for example, when customers are purchasing stocks, making an airline reservation, or withdrawing cash from an ATM. Managers use transactional information when making structured decisions at the operational level, such as when analyzing daily sales reports to determine how much inventory to carry.

FIGURE 2.9
Primary Types of MIS Systems for Decision Making

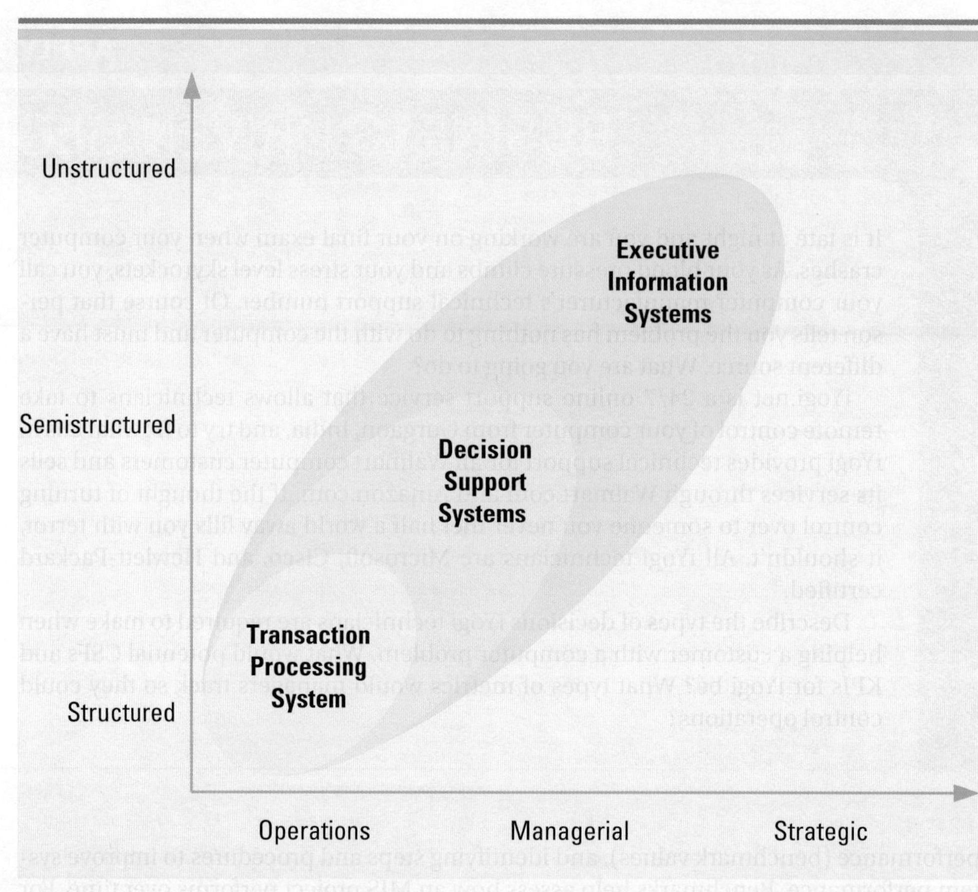

Online transaction processing (OLTP) is the capture of transaction and event information using technology to (1) process the information according to defined business rules, (2) store the information, and (3) update existing information to reflect the new information. During OLTP, the organization must capture every detail of transactions and events. A ***transaction processing system (TPS)*** is the basic business system that serves the operational level (analysts) and assists in making structured decisions. The most common example of a TPS is an operational accounting system such as a payroll system or an order-entry system.

LO 2.1 Classify the different operational support systems, managerial support systems, and strategic support systems, and explain how managers can use these systems to make decisions and gain competitive advantages.

Using systems thinking, we can see that the inputs for a TPS are ***source documents,*** the original transaction record. Source documents for a payroll system can include time sheets, wage rates, and employee benefit reports. Transformation includes common procedures such as creating, reading, updating, and deleting (commonly referred to as CRUD) employee records, along with calculating the payroll and summarizing benefits. The output includes cutting the paychecks and generating payroll reports. Figure 2.10 demonstrates the systems thinking view of a TPS.[6]

Managerial Support Systems

Analytical information encompasses all organizational information, and its primary purpose is to support the performance of managerial analysis or semistructured decisions. Analytical information includes transactional information along with other information such as market and industry information. Examples of analytical information are trends, sales, product statistics, and future growth projections. Managers use analytical information when making important semistructured decisions, such as whether the organization should build a new manufacturing plant or hire additional sales reps.

Online analytical processing (OLAP) is the manipulation of information to create business intelligence in support of strategic decision making. ***Decision support systems (DSSs)*** model information using OLAP, which provides assistance in evaluating and choosing among different courses of action. DSSs enable high-level managers to examine and manipulate large amounts of detailed data from different internal

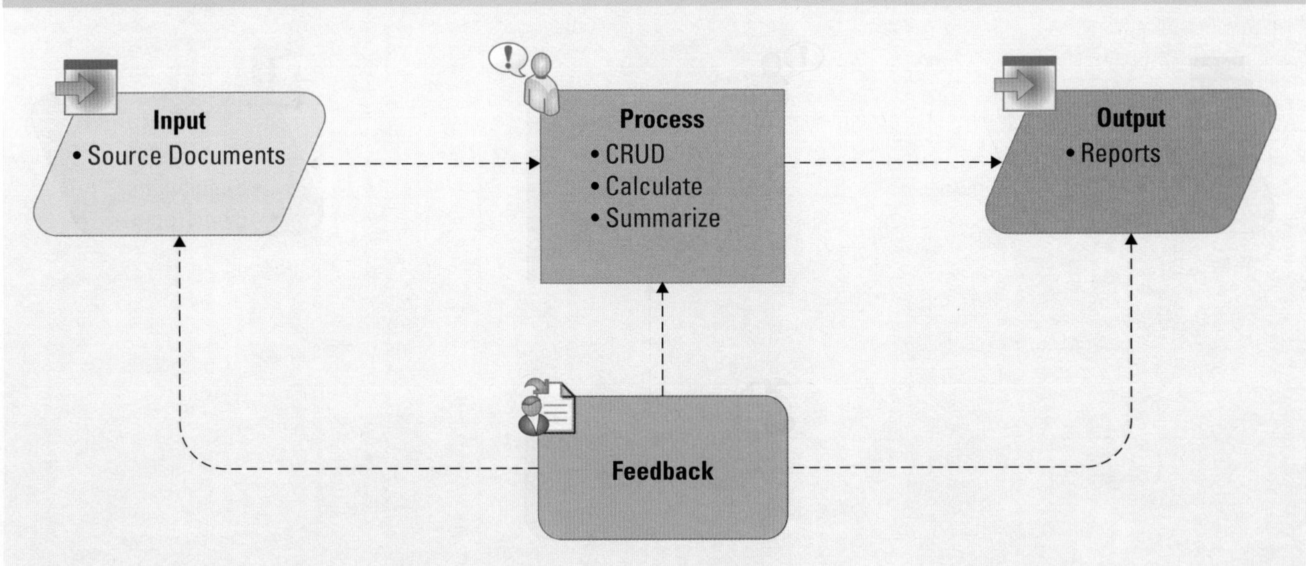

FIGURE 2.10
Systems Thinking Example of a TPS

and external sources. Analyzing complex relationships among thousands or even millions of data items to discover patterns, trends, and exception conditions is one of the key uses associated with a DSS. For example, doctors may enter symptoms into a decision support system so it can help diagnose and treat patients. Insurance companies also use a DSS to gauge the risk of providing insurance to drivers who have imperfect driving records. One company found that married women who are homeowners with one speeding ticket are rarely cited for speeding again. Armed with this business intelligence, the company achieved a cost advantage by lowering insurance rates to this specific group of customers. The following are common DSS analysis techniques.

What-If Analysis ***What-if analysis*** checks the impact of a change in a variable or assumption on the model. For example, "What will happen to the supply chain if a hurricane in South Carolina reduces holding inventory from 30 percent to 10 percent?" A user would be able to observe and evaluate any changes that occurred to the values in the model, especially to a variable such as profits. Users repeat this analysis with different variables until they understand all the effects of various situations.

Sensitivity Analysis ***Sensitivity analysis,*** a special case of what-if analysis, is the study of the impact on other variables when one variable is changed repeatedly. Sensitivity analysis is useful when users are uncertain about the assumptions made in estimating the value of certain key variables. For example, repeatedly changing revenue in small increments to determine its effects on other variables would help a manager understand the impact of various revenue levels on other decision factors.

Goal-Seeking Analysis ***Goal-seeking analysis*** finds the inputs necessary to achieve a goal such as a desired level of output. It is the reverse of what-if and sensitivity analysis. Instead of observing how changes in a variable affect other variables, goal-seeking analysis sets a target value (a goal) for a variable and then repeatedly changes other variables until the target value is achieved. For example, goal-seeking analysis could determine how many customers must purchase a new product to increase gross profits to $5 million.

Optimization Analysis ***Optimization analysis,*** an extension of goal-seeking analysis, finds the optimum value for a target variable by repeatedly changing other variables, subject to specified constraints. By changing revenue and cost variables in an optimization analysis, managers can calculate the highest potential profits. Constraints on revenue and cost variables can be taken into consideration, such as limits on the amount of raw materials the company can afford to purchase and limits on employees available to meet production needs.

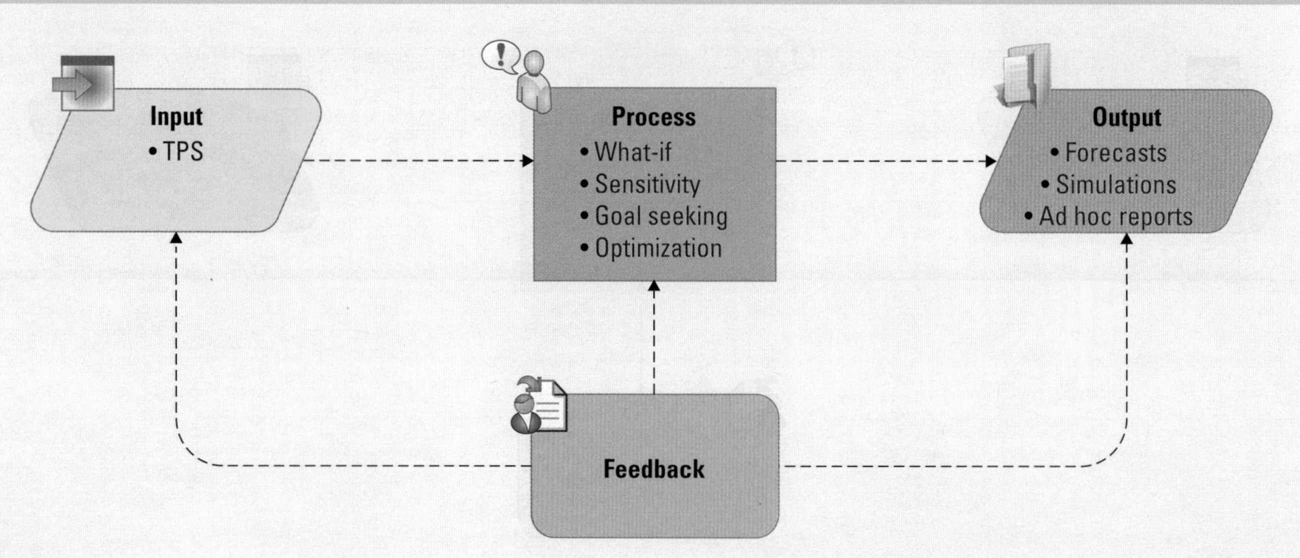

FIGURE 2.11

Systems Thinking Example of a DSS

Figure 2.11 shows the common systems view of a DSS. Figure 2.12 shows how TPSs supply transactional data to a DSS. The DSS then summarizes and aggregates the information from the different TPSs, which assist managers in making semistructured decision.

Strategic Support Systems

Decision making at the strategic level requires both business intelligence and knowledge to support the uncertainty and complexity associated with business strategies. An ***executive information system (EIS)*** is a specialized DSS that supports senior-level executives and unstructured, long-term, nonroutine decisions requiring judgment, evaluation, and insight. These decisions do not have a right or wrong answer, only efficient and effective answers. Moving up through the organizational pyramid, managers deal less with the details ("finer" information) and more with meaningful aggregations of information ("coarser" information). ***Granularity*** refers to the level of detail in the model or the decision-making process. The greater the granularity, the deeper the level of detail or fineness of data (see Figure 2.13).

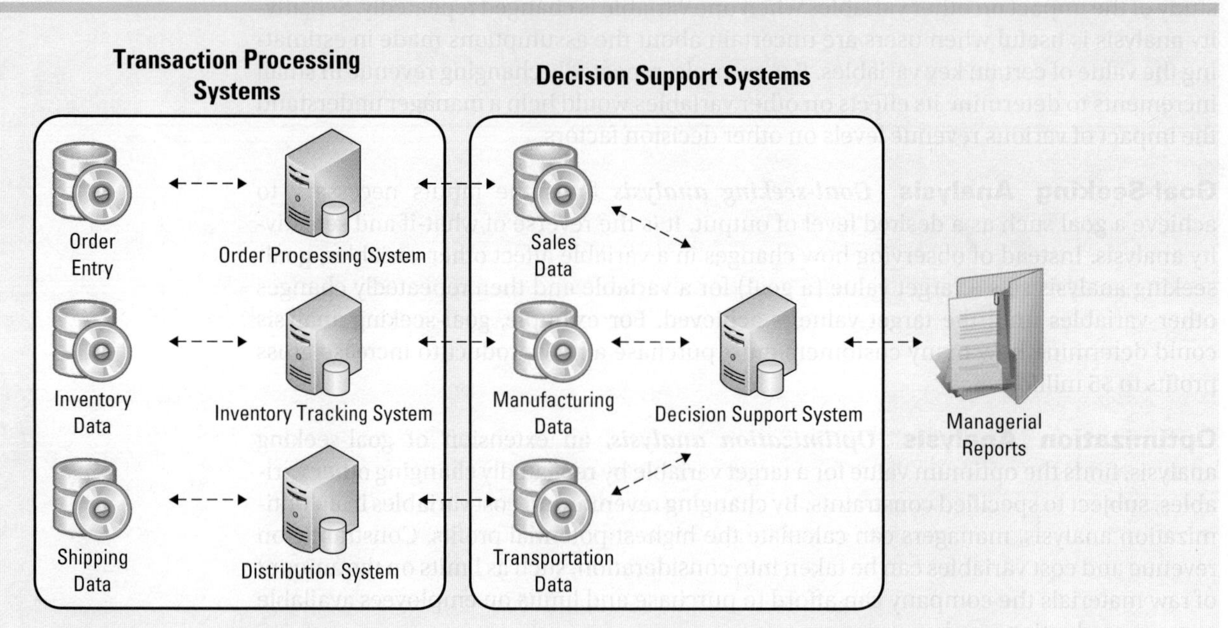

FIGURE 2.12

Interaction Between TPS and DSS to Support Semistructured Decisions

APPLY YOUR KNOWLEDGE

BUSINESS DRIVEN ETHICS AND SECURITY

The Criminal in the Cube Next Door

What if the person sitting in the cubicle next to you was running a scam that cost your company $7 billion? An employee at a French bank allegedly used his inside knowledge of business processes to bypass the system and place roughly $73 billion in bogus trades that cost the bank more than $7 billion to unwind.

Findings from the U.S. Secret Service's examination of 23 incidents conducted by 26 insiders determined that 70 percent of the time, insiders took advantage of failures in business process rules and authorization mechanisms to steal from their company. These insiders were authorized and active computer users 78 percent of the time, and a surprising 43 percent used their own user name and passwords to commit their crimes.[7]

This is a daunting reminder that every employee has the potential to become a knowledgeable insider and, if started on a criminal path, to do tremendous damage to your company. Many DSSs and EISs contain the business intelligence your company needs to operate effectively, and you need to protect these assets. What types of sensitive information is housed in a company's TPS, DSS, and EIS? What problems could you encounter if one of your employees decided to steal the information housed in your DSS? How could you protect your EIS from unethical users? What would you do if you thought the person sharing your cube was a rogue insider?

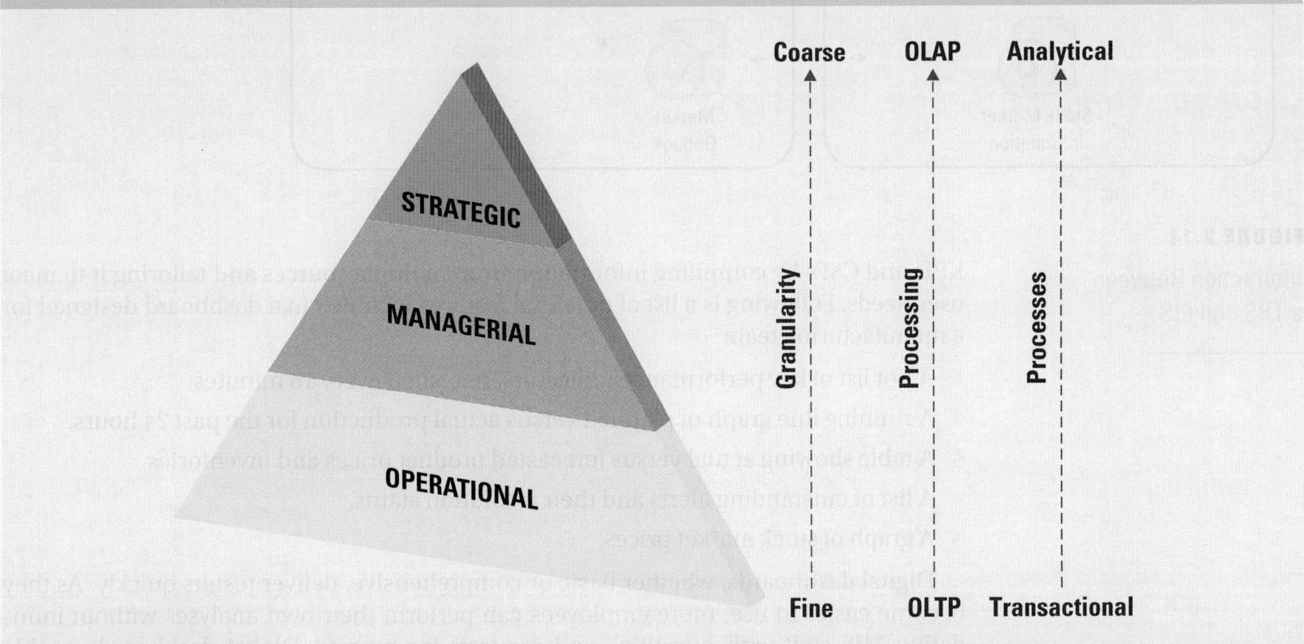

FIGURE 2.13

Information Levels Throughout an Organization

A DSS differs from an EIS in that an EIS requires data from external sources to support unstructured decisions (see Figure 2.14). This is not to say that DSSs never use data from external sources, but typically DSS semistructured decisions rely on internal data only.

Visualization produces graphical displays of patterns and complex relationships in large amounts of data. Executive information systems use visualization to deliver specific key information to top managers at a glance, with little or no interaction with the system. A common tool that supports visualization is a ***digital dashboard,*** which tracks

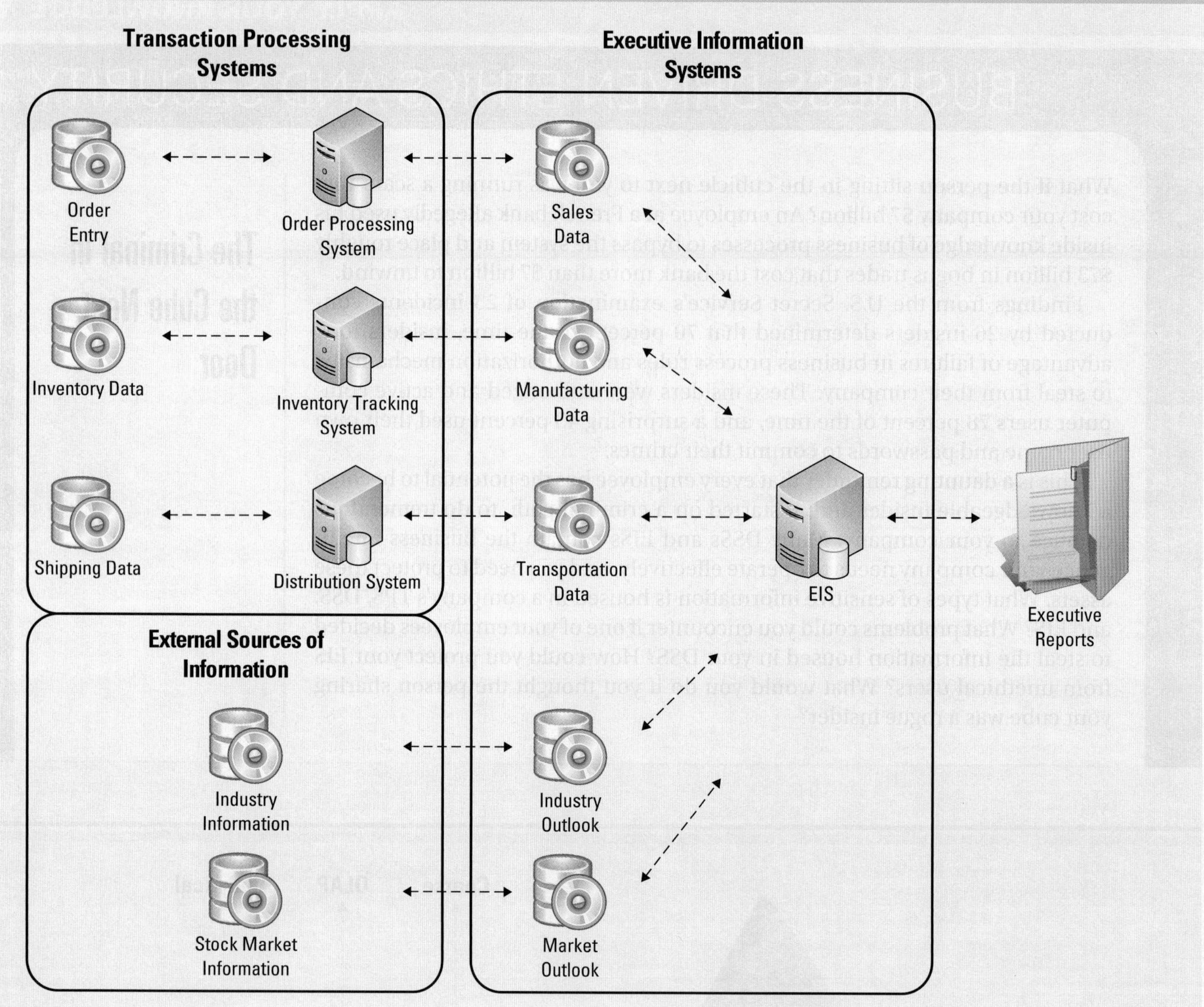

FIGURE 2.14
Interaction Between a TPS and EIS

KPIs and CSFs by compiling information from multiple sources and tailoring it to meet user needs. Following is a list of potential features included in a dashboard designed for a manufacturing team:

- A hot list of key performance indicators, refreshed every 15 minutes.
- A running line graph of planned versus actual production for the past 24 hours.
- A table showing actual versus forecasted product prices and inventories.
- A list of outstanding alerts and their resolution status.
- A graph of stock market prices.

Digital dashboards, whether basic or comprehensive, deliver results quickly. As they become easier to use, more employees can perform their own analyses without inundating MIS staff with questions and requests for reports. Digital dashboards enable employees to move beyond reporting to using information to directly increase business performance. With them, employees can react to information as soon as it becomes available and make decisions, solve problems, and change strategies daily instead of monthly. Digital dashboards offer the following capabilities:

Consolidation *Consolidation* is the aggregation of data from simple roll-ups to complex groupings of interrelated information. For example, data for different sales representatives can then be rolled up to an office level, then a state level, then a regional sales level.

BUSINESS DRIVEN START-UP

Digital Dashboard for Tracking Junk

Do you enjoy kidnapping your rivals' team mascots or toilet-papering their frat houses? If so, you might find your ideal career at College Hunks Hauling Junk. The company hires college students and recent grads to pick up junk and take it away. The founder, Nick Friedman, had a goal of capturing that friendly rivalry so often associated with college life and turn it into profits. When the company launched in 2005, the haulers from Virginia found their truck had been lathered in shaving cream and draped with a University of Maryland flag. The Virginia haulers retaliated, and soon after dead fish were found on the seats of Maryland's truck. Friedman decided to use this energy as an incentive instead of condemning the unorthodox behavior. "We wanted to harness that competitive, prankster enthusiasm and channel it for good," he says.

Freidman made a bold move and decided that instead of tracking typical key performance indicators such as revenue, average job size, and customer loyalty, he would set up his dashboard to track volume of junk collected and amount donated or recycled. The winning team gains such things as bragging rights and banners, modest monetary prizes, and the right to eat first at the annual company meeting. Most employees check the dashboard daily to view their own and rivals' latest standings.[8]

Why do you think competition is helping College Hunks Hauling Junk exceed its revenue goals? If you were to build a team competition dashboard for your school or your work, what types of metrics would you track? What types of motivators would you use to ensure your team is always in the green? What types of external information would you want tracked in your dashboard? Could an unethical person use the information from your dashboard to hurt your team or your organization? What can you do to mitigate these risks?

Drill-Down ***Drill-down*** enables users to view details, and details of details, of information. This is the reverse of consolidation; a user can view regional sales data and then drill down all the way to each sales representative's data at each office. Drill-down capability lets managers view monthly, weekly, daily, or even hourly information.

Slice-and-Dice ***Slice-and-dice*** is the ability to look at information from different perspectives. One slice of information could display all product sales during a given promotion. Another slice could display a single product's sales for all promotions. Slicing and dicing is often performed along a time axis to analyze trends and find time-based patterns in the information.

One thing to remember when making decisions is the old saying, "Garbage in, garbage out." If the transactional data used in the support system are wrong, then the managerial analysis will be wrong and the DSS will simply assist in making a wrong decision faster. Managers should also ask, "What is the DSS *not* telling me before I make my final decision?"

THE FUTURE: ARTIFICIAL INTELLIGENCE

LO 2.4: Describe artificial intelligence, and identify its five main types.

Executive information systems are starting to take advantage of artificial intelligence to facilitate unstructured strategic decision making. ***Artificial intelligence (AI)*** simulates human thinking and behavior, such as the ability to reason and learn. Its ultimate goal is to build a system that can mimic human intelligence.

Intelligent systems are various commercial applications of artificial intelligence. They include sensors, software, and devices that emulate and enhance human capabilities, learn or understand from experience, make sense of ambiguous or contradictory information, and even use reasoning to solve problems and make decisions effectively.

Intelligent systems perform such tasks as boosting productivity in factories by monitoring equipment and signaling when preventive maintenance is required. They are beginning to show up everywhere:

- At Manchester Airport in England, the Hefner AI Robot Cleaner alerts passengers to security and nonsmoking rules while it scrubs up to 65,600 square feet of floor per day. Laser scanners and ultrasonic detectors keep it from colliding with passengers.
- Shell Oil's SmartPump keeps drivers in their cars on cold, wet winter days. It can service any automobile built after 1987 that has been fitted with a special gas cap and a windshield-mounted transponder that tells the robot where to insert the pump.
- Matsushita's courier robot navigates hospital hallways, delivering patient files, X-ray films, and medical supplies.
- The FireFighter AI Robot can extinguish flames at chemical plants and nuclear reactors with water, foam, powder, or inert gas. The robot puts distance between human operators and the fire.[9]

AI systems increase the speed and consistency of decision making, solve problems with incomplete information, and resolve complicated issues that cannot be solved by conventional computing. There are many categories of AI systems; five of the most familiar are (1) expert systems, (2) neural networks, (3) genetic algorithms, (4) intelligent agents, and (5) virtual reality (see Figure 2.15).

Expert Systems

Expert systems are computerized advisory programs that imitate the reasoning processes of experts in solving difficult problems. Typically, they include a knowledge base containing various accumulated experience and a set of rules for applying the knowledge base to each particular situation. Expert systems are the most common form of AI in the business arena because they fill the gap when human experts are difficult to find or retain or are too expensive. The best-known systems play chess and assist in medical diagnosis.

Neural Networks

A ***neural network,*** also called an artificial neural network, is a category of AI that attempts to emulate the way the human brain works. Neural networks analyze large

FIGURE 2.15

Examples of Artificial Intelligence

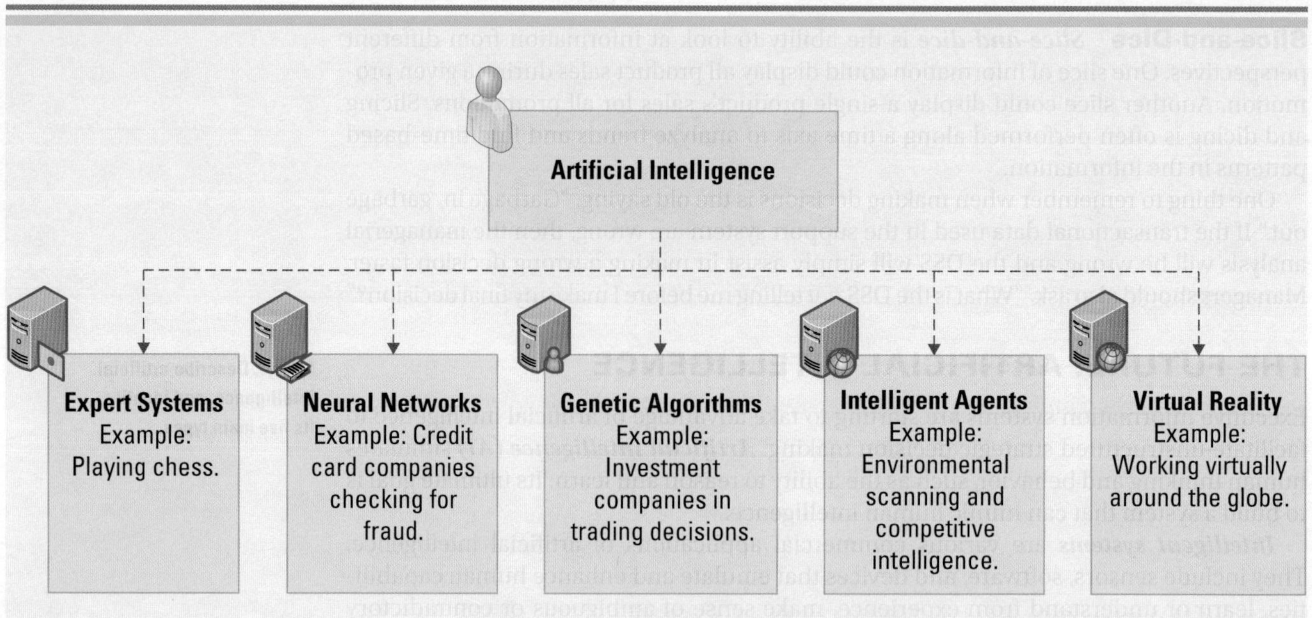

quantities of information to establish patterns and characteristics in situations where the logic or rules are unknown. Neural networks' many features include:

- Learning and adjusting to new circumstances on their own.
- Lending themselves to massive parallel processing.
- Functioning without complete or well-structured information.
- Coping with huge volumes of information with many dependent variables.
- Analyzing nonlinear relationships in information (they have been called fancy regression analysis systems).

The finance industry is a veteran in the use of neural network technology and has been relying on various forms for over two decades. It uses neural networks to review loan applications and create patterns or profiles of applications that fall into two categories—approved or denied. Here are some examples of neural networks in finance:

- Citibank uses neural networks to find opportunities in financial markets. By carefully examining historical stock market data with neural network software, Citibank financial managers learn of interesting coincidences or small anomalies (called market inefficiencies). For example, it could be that whenever IBM stock goes up, so does Unisys stock, or that a U.S. Treasury note is selling for 1 cent less in Japan than in the United States. These snippets of information can make a big difference to Citibank's bottom line in a very competitive financial market.
- Visa, MasterCard, and many other credit card companies use a neural network to spot peculiarities in individual accounts and follow up by checking for fraud. MasterCard estimates neural networks save it $50 million annually.
- Insurance companies along with state compensation funds and other carriers use neural network software to identify fraud. The system searches for patterns in billing charges, laboratory tests, and frequency of office visits. A claim for which the diagnosis was a sprained ankle but treatment included an electrocardiogram would be flagged for the account manager.[10]

Fuzzy logic is a mathematical method of handling imprecise or subjective information. The basic approach is to assign values between 0 and 1 to vague or ambiguous information. Zero represents information not included, while 1 represents inclusion or membership. For example, fuzzy logic is used in washing machines that determine by themselves how much water to use or how long to wash (they continue washing until the water is clean). In accounting and finance, fuzzy logic allows people to analyze information with subjective financial values (intangibles such as goodwill) that are very important considerations in economic analysis. Fuzzy logic and neural networks are often combined to express complicated and subjective concepts in a form that makes it possible to simplify the problem and apply rules that are executed with a level of certainty.

Genetic Algorithms

A ***genetic algorithm*** is an artificial intelligence system that mimics the evolutionary, survival-of-the-fittest process to generate increasingly better solutions to a problem. A genetic algorithm is essentially an optimizing system: It finds the combination of inputs that gives the best outputs.

Genetic algorithms are best suited to decision-making environments in which thousands, or perhaps millions, of solutions are possible. Genetic algorithms can find and evaluate solutions with many more possibilities, faster and more thoroughly than a human. Organizations face decision-making environments for all types of problems that require optimization techniques, such as the following:

- Business executives use genetic algorithms to help them decide which combination of projects a firm should invest in, taking complicated tax considerations into account.
- Investment companies use genetic algorithms to help in trading decisions.

- Telecommunication companies use genetic algorithms to determine the optimal configuration of fiber-optic cable in a network that may include as many as 100,000 connection points. The genetic algorithm evaluates millions of cable configurations and selects the one that uses the least amount of cable.

Intelligent Agents

An ***intelligent agent*** is a special-purpose knowledge-based information system that accomplishes specific tasks on behalf of its users. Intelligent agents usually have a graphical representation, such as "Sherlock Holmes" for an information search agent.

One of the simplest examples of an intelligent agent is a shopping bot. A ***shopping bot*** is software that will search several retailer websites and provide a comparison of each retailer's offerings including price and availability. Increasingly, intelligent agents handle the majority of a company's Internet buying and selling and complete such processes as finding products, bargaining over prices, and executing transactions. Intelligent agents also have the capability to handle all supply chain buying and selling.

Another application for intelligent agents is in environmental scanning and competitive intelligence. For instance, an intelligent agent can learn the types of competitor information users want to track, continuously scan the Web for it, and alert users when a significant event occurs.

Multiagent Systems and Agent-Based Modeling What do cargo transport systems, book distribution centers, the video game market, and a flu epidemic have in common with an ant colony? They are all complex adaptive systems. By observing parts of Earth's ecosystem, like ant colonies, artificial intelligence scientists can use hardware and software models that incorporate insect characteristics and behavior to (1) learn how people-based systems behave, (2) predict how they will behave under a given set of circumstances, and (3) improve human systems to make them more efficient and effective. This process of learning from ecosystems and adapting their characteristics to human and organizational situations is called biomimicry.

In the past few years, AI research has made much progress in modeling complex organizations as a whole with the help of multiagent systems. In a multiagent system, groups of intelligent agents have the ability to work independently and to interact with each other. Agent-based modeling is a way of simulating human organizations using multiple intelligent agents, each of which follows a set of simple rules and can adapt to changing conditions.

Agent-based modeling systems are being used to model stock market fluctuations, predict the escape routes people seek in a burning building, estimate the effects of interest rates on consumers with different types of debt, and anticipate how changes in conditions will affect the supply chain, to name just a few.

Virtual Reality

Virtual reality is a computer-simulated environment that can be a simulation of the real world or an imaginary world. Virtual reality is a fast-growing area of artificial intelligence that had its origins in efforts to build more natural, realistic, multisensory human-computer interfaces. Virtual reality enables telepresence where users can be anywhere in the world and use virtual reality systems to work alone or together at a remote site. Typically, this involves using a virtual reality system to enhance the sight and touch of a human who is remotely manipulating equipment to accomplish a task. Examples range from virtual surgery, where surgeon and patient may be on opposite sides of the globe, to the remote use of equipment in hazardous environments such as chemical plants and nuclear reactors.

Virtual Workforce At Microsoft's headquarters in Redmond, Washington, traffic congestion occurs daily for the 35,000 commuters. To alleviate the congestion Microsoft is offering its employees the ability to work virtually from home. Over 42 percent of IBMs 330,000 employees work virtually saving over $100 million per year in real estate-related expenses. Working virtually offers several advantages such as fewer cars on the road,

APPLY YOUR KNOWLEDGE

BUSINESS DRIVEN INNOVATION

Building Robots

Humans are not permitted inside Staples' Denver distribution center. Who is filling all the orders, you ask? Robots! This 100,000-square-foot space belongs to 150 orange robots that resemble overstuffed ottomans and race around with uncanny accuracy. They're making Staples employees more than twice as productive. The robots, or bots, are built by Kiva Systems, a company with a single critical success factor: Replace the labyrinth of conveyor belts and humans that most distributors rely on to pack items in the online mail-order business. Companies using Kiva bots include Walgreens, Zappos, The Gap, and Amazon.

Robots have captured people's attention for years. From the quirky droids in *Star Wars* to the powerful fighting machines in *Transformers,* they seem to fascinate everyone. Assume your professor has asked you to participate in The Robot Challenge, and you must design a robot that will enhance business operations. It must contain a digital dashboard and provide decision support capabilities for its owners. Be sure to describe your robot, its functions, how the digital dashboard works and supports users, and why customers would purchase your robot. Feel free to include a picture or diagram of how your robot works.[11]

increases in worker productive, and decreasing real estate expenses. Drawbacks include the fear among workers that they will jeopardize their careers by working from home, and some workers need a busy environment to stay productive. Virtual workers also tend to feel alone, secluded, and deprived of vital training and mentoring.

section 2.2 BUSINESS PROCESSES

LEARNING OUTCOMES

2.5 Explain the value of business processes for a company, and differentiate between customer-facing and business-facing processes.

2.6 Demonstrate the value of business process modeling, and compare As-Is and To-Be models.

2.7 Differentiate among business process improvements, streamlining, and reengineering.

2.8 Describe business process management and its value to an organization.

EVALUATING BUSINESS PROCESSES

LO 2.5: Explain the value of business processes for a company, and differentiate between customer-facing and business-facing processes.

Most companies pride themselves on providing breakthrough products and services for customers. But if customers do not receive what they want quickly, accurately, and hassle-free, even fantastic offerings will not prevent a company from annoying customers and ultimately eroding its own financial performance. To avoid this pitfall and protect its competitive advantage, a company must continually evaluate all the business processes in its value chain. Recall from Chapter 1 that a *business process* is a standardized set of activities that accomplish a specific task, such as processing a customer's order. Business processes transform a set of inputs into a set of outputs—goods or services—for another person or process by using people and tools. Understanding business processes helps a manager envision how the entire company operates.

FIGURE 2.16
Sample Business Processes

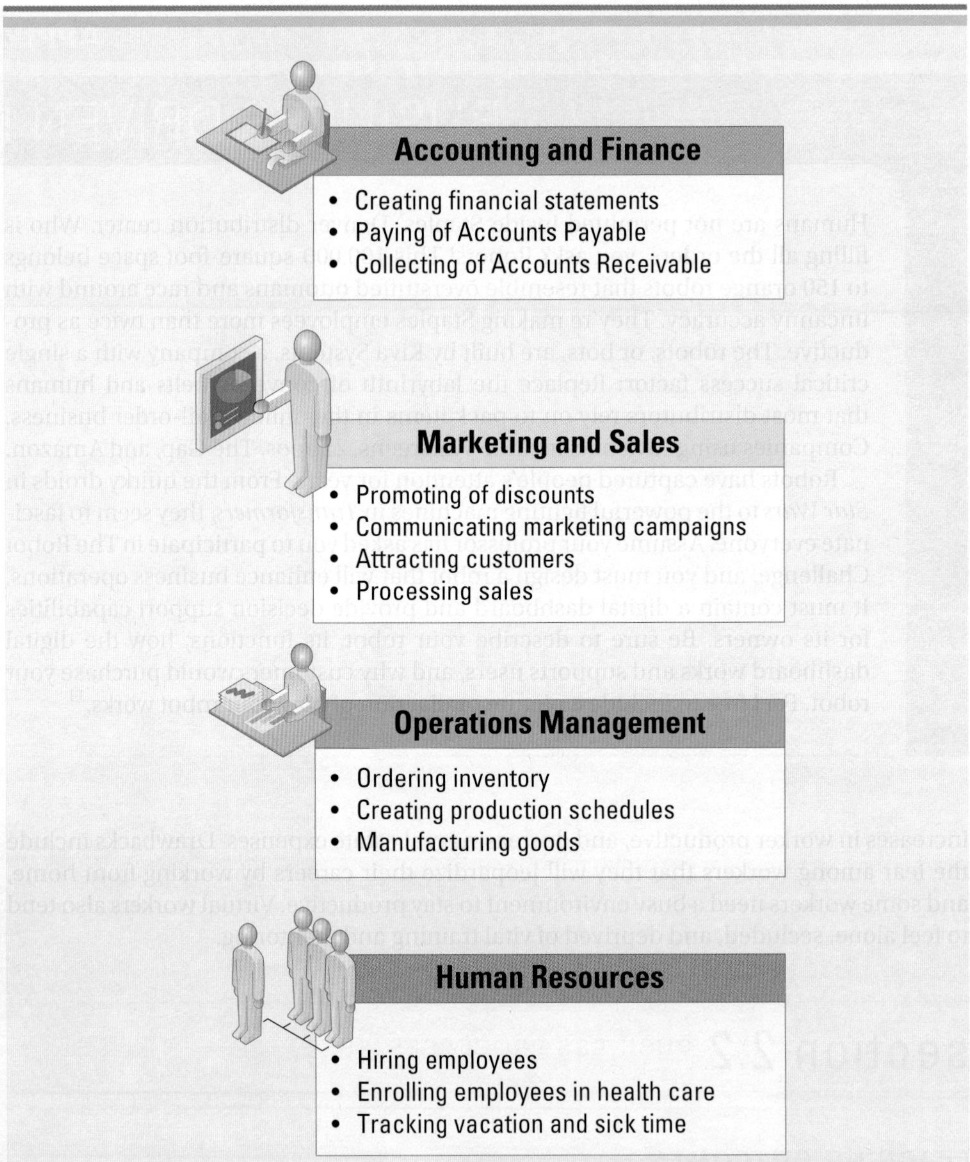

Accounting and Finance

- Creating financial statements
- Paying of Accounts Payable
- Collecting of Accounts Receivable

Marketing and Sales

- Promoting of discounts
- Communicating marketing campaigns
- Attracting customers
- Processing sales

Operations Management

- Ordering inventory
- Creating production schedules
- Manufacturing goods

Human Resources

- Hiring employees
- Enrolling employees in health care
- Tracking vacation and sick time

Improving the efficiency and effectiveness of its business processes will improve the firm's value chain. The goal of this section is to expand on Porter's value chain analysis by detailing the powerful value-adding relationships between business strategies and core business processes. Figure 2.16 illustrates several common business processes.

The processes outlined in Figure 2.16 reflect functional thinking. Some processes, such as a programming process, may be contained wholly within a single department. However, most, such as ordering a product, are cross-functional or cross-departmental processes and span the entire organization. The process of "order to delivery" focuses on the entire customer order process across functional departments (see Figure 2.17). Another example is "product realization," which includes not only the way a product is developed, but also the way it is marketed and serviced. Some other cross-functional business processes are taking a product from concept to market, acquiring customers, loan processing, providing post-sales service, claim processing, and reservation handling.

Customer-facing processes, also called front-office processes, result in a product or service received by an organization's external customer. They include fulfilling orders, communicating with customers, and sending out bills and marketing information. ***Business-facing processes,*** also called back-office processes, are invisible to the external customer but essential to the effective management of the business; they include goal setting, day-to-day planning, giving performance feedback and rewards, and allocating

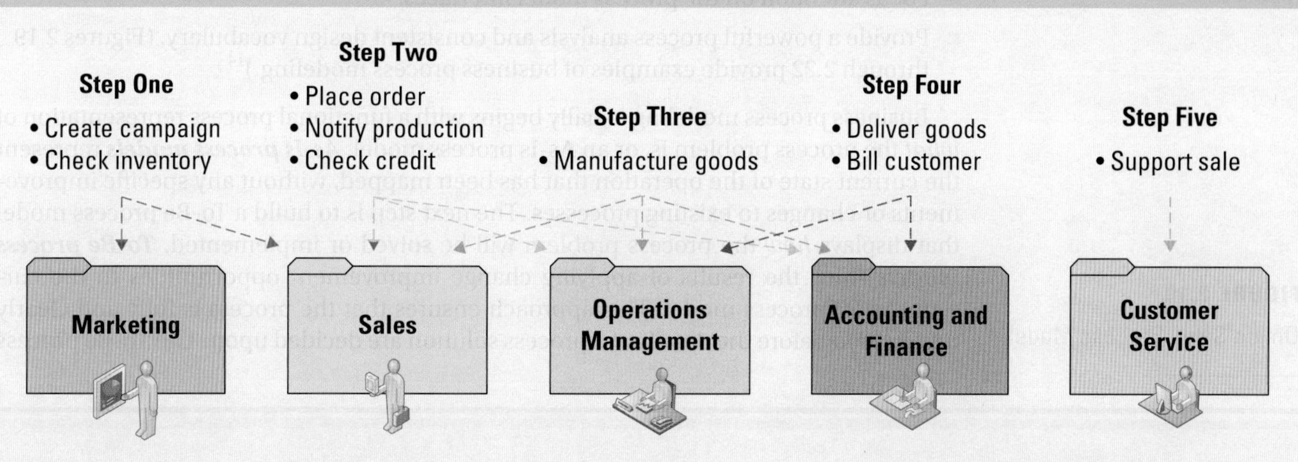

FIGURE 2.17

Five Steps in the Order-to-Delivery Business Process

resources. Figure 2.18 displays the different categories of customer-facing and business-facing processes along with an example of each.[12]

A company's strategic vision should provide guidance on which business processes are core, that is, which are directly linked to the firm's critical success factors. Mapping these core business processes to the value chain reveals where the processes touch the customers and affect their perceptions of value. This type of map conceptualizes the business as a value delivery system, allowing managers to ensure all core business processes are operating as efficiently and effectively as possible.

A firm can even create a value chain map of the entire industry to extend critical success factors and business process views beyond its boundaries. This type of evaluation allowed National Semiconductor to identify the core business processes required to move assembly plants to Southeast Asia. The map identified logistics and distribution as critical to the success of the move. Thus, to ensure reliable delivery of its products, National Semiconductor contracted with Federal Express, combining its outstanding manufacturing process and Federal Express's exceptional distribution processes. The move allowed National Semiconductor to save money by closing nine warehouses while maintaining excellence in logistics and distribution. As this example demonstrates, changing business processes can generate significant competitive advantages across the value chain.[13]

MODELS: MEASURING PERFORMANCE

LO 2.6: Demonstrate the value of business process modeling, and compare As-Is and To-Be models.

Business process modeling, or ***mapping,*** is the activity of creating a detailed flowchart or process map of a work process that shows its inputs, tasks, and activities in a structured sequence. A ***business process model*** is a graphic description of a process, showing the sequence of process tasks, which is developed for a specific purpose and from a selected viewpoint. A set of one or more process models details the many functions of a system or subject area with graphics and text, and its purpose is to:

- Expose process detail gradually and in a controlled manner.
- Encourage conciseness and accuracy in describing the process model.

Customer-Facing Processes	Industry-Specific Customer Facing Processes	Business-Facing Processes
Order processing	Banking—Loan processing	Strategic planning
Customer service	Insurance—Claims processing	Tactical planning
Sales process	Government—Grant allocation	Budget forecasting
Customer billing	Hotel—Reservation handling	Training
Order shipping	Airline—Baggage handling	Purchasing raw materials

FIGURE 2.18

Customer-Facing, Industry-Specific, and Business-Facing Processes

- Focus attention on the process model interfaces.
- Provide a powerful process analysis and consistent design vocabulary. (Figures 2.19 through 2.22 provide examples of business process modeling.)[14]

Business process modeling usually begins with a functional process representation of *what* the process problem is, or an As-Is process model. ***As-Is process models*** represent the current state of the operation that has been mapped, without any specific improvements or changes to existing processes. The next step is to build a To-Be process model that displays *how* the process problem will be solved or implemented. ***To-Be process models*** show the results of applying change improvement opportunities to the current (As-Is) process model. This approach ensures that the process is fully and clearly understood before the details of a process solution are decided upon. The To-Be process

FIGURE 2.19
Online Sales Process Model

FIGURE 2.20
Online Banking Process Model

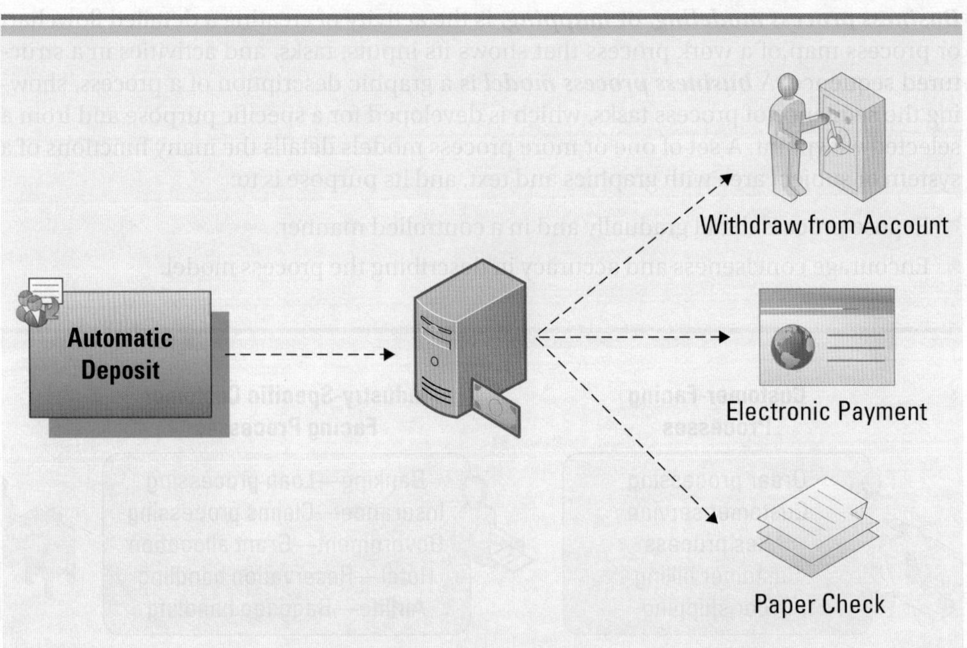

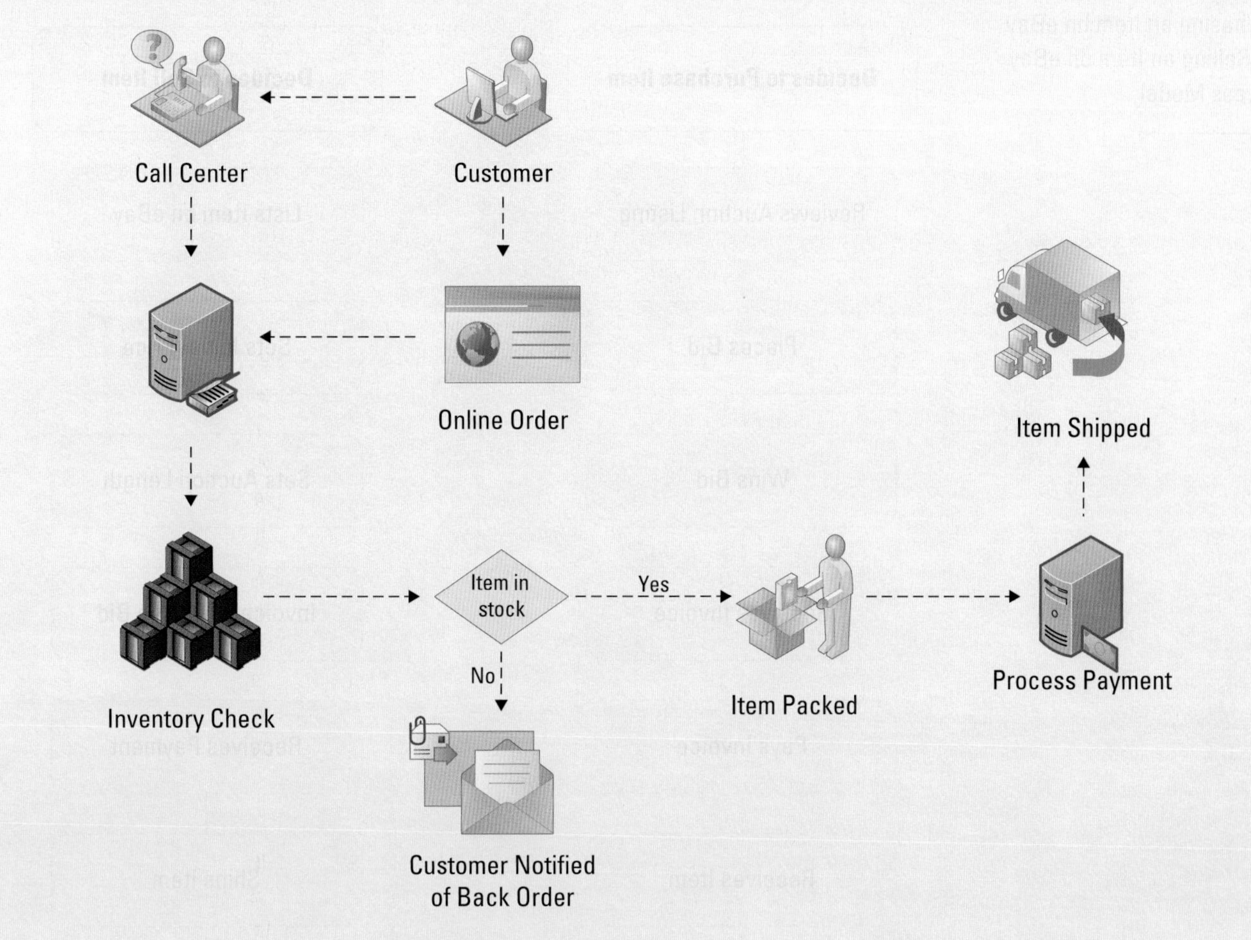

FIGURE 2.21
Order Fulfillment Process Model

model shows *how* the *what* is to be realized. Figure 2.23 displays the As-Is and To-Be process models for ordering a hamburger.

As-Is and To-Be process models are both integral in business process reengineering projects, since these diagrams are very powerful in visualizing the activities, processes, and data flow of an organization. Figure 2.24 illustrates an As-Is process model of the order to delivery process using swim lanes to represent the relevant departments. The ***swim lane*** layout arranges the steps of a business process into a set of rows depicting the various elements.

You need to be careful not to become inundated in excessive detail when creating an As-Is process model. The primary goal is to simplify, eliminate, and improve the To-Be processes. Process improvement efforts focus on defining the most efficient and effective process identifying all of the illogical, missing, or irrelevant processes.

Investigating business processes can help an organization find bottlenecks, remove redundant tasks, and recognize smooth-running processes. For example, a florist might have a key success factor of reducing delivery time. A florist that has an inefficient ordering process or a difficult distribution process will be unable to achieve this goal. Taking down inaccurate orders, incorrect addresses, or shipping delays can cause errors in the delivery process. Improving order entry, production, or scheduling processes can improve the delivery process.

Business processes should drive MIS choices and should be based on business strategies and goals (see Figure 2.25A). Only after determining the most efficient and effective business process should an organization choose the MIS that supports that business process. Of course, this does not always happen, and managers may find themselves in the difficult position of changing a business process because the system cannot support the ideal solution (see Figure 2.25B). Managers who make MIS choices and only then determine how their business processes should perform typically fail.

FIGURE 2.22

Purchasing an Item on eBay and Selling an Item on eBay Process Model

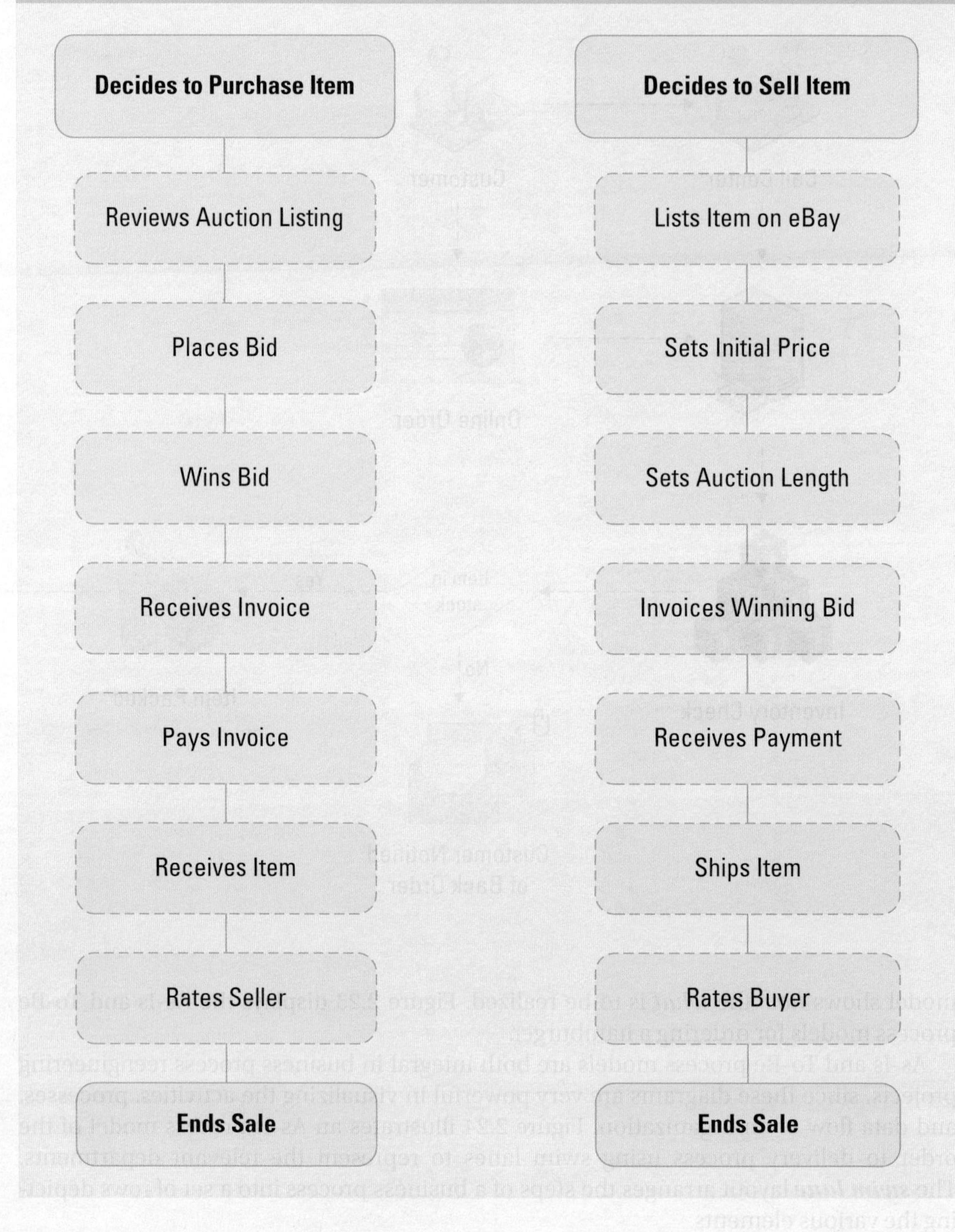

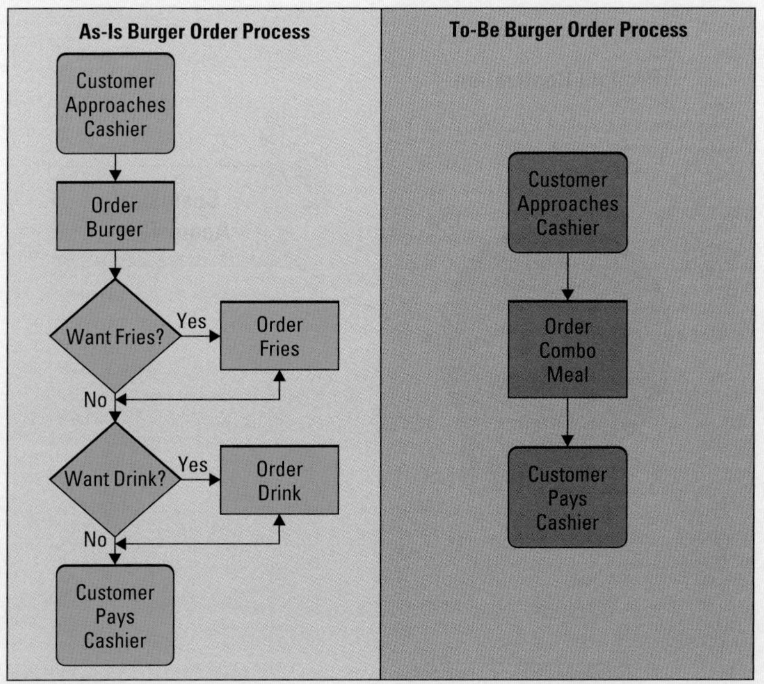

FIGURE 2.23

As-Is and To-Be Process Model for Ordering a Hamburger

FIGURE 2.24

As-Is Process Model for Order Fulfillment

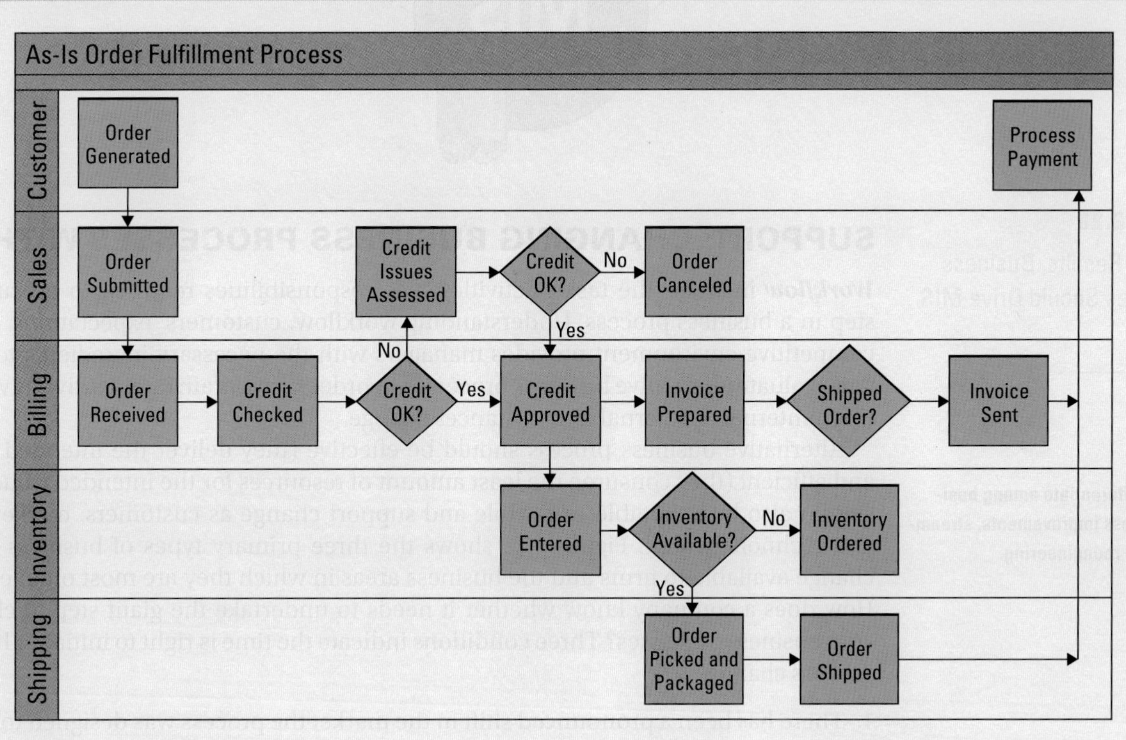

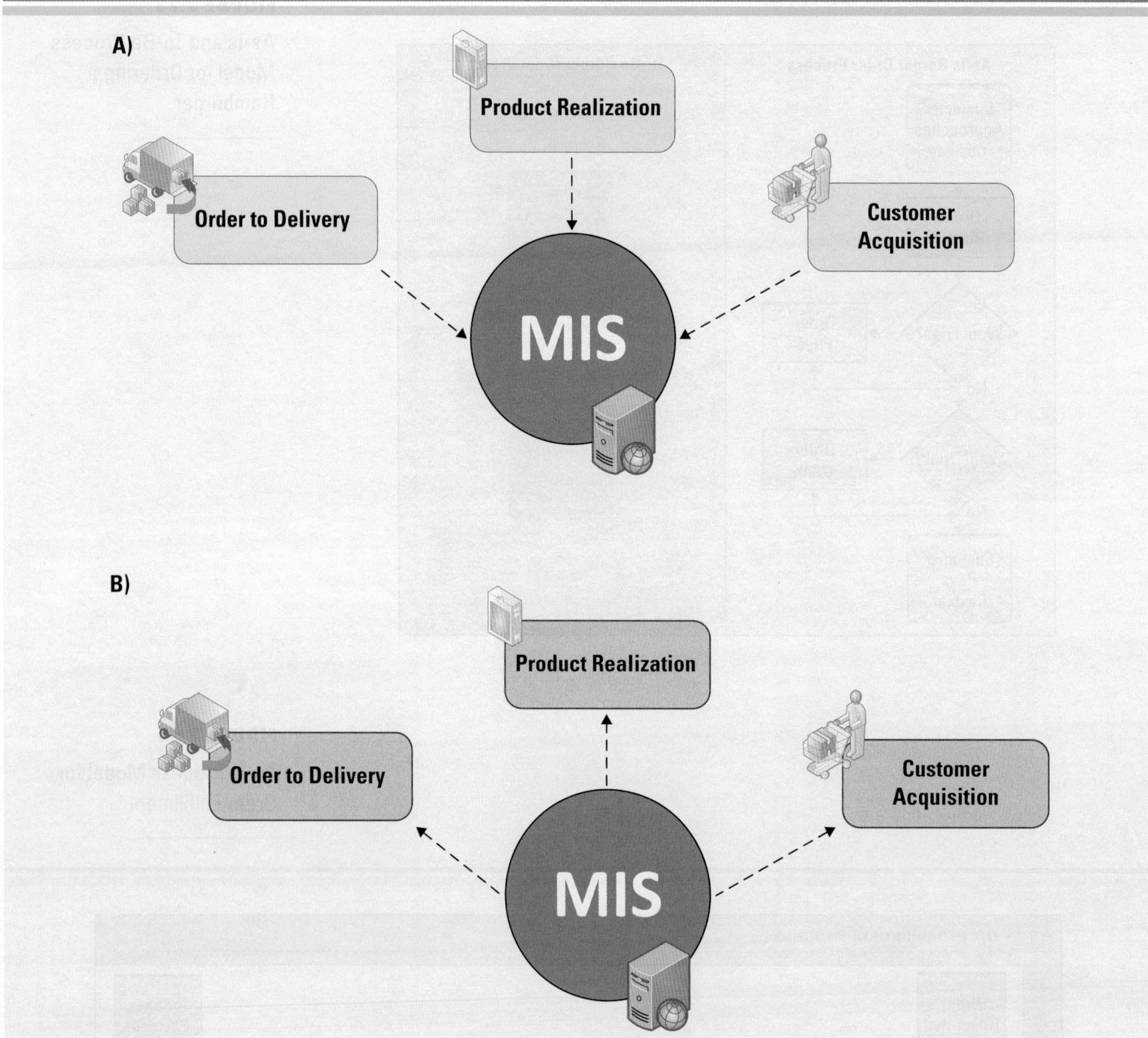

FIGURE 2.25

For Best Results, Business Processes Should Drive MIS Choices

LO 2.7: **Differentiate among business process improvements, streamlining, and reengineering.**

SUPPORT: CHANGING BUSINESS PROCESSES WITH MIS

Workflow includes the tasks, activities, and responsibilities required to execute each step in a business process. Understanding workflow, customers' expectations, and the competitive environment provides managers with the necessary ingredients to design and evaluate alternative business processes in order to maintain competitive advantages when internal or external circumstances change.

Alternative business process should be effective (they deliver the intended results) and efficient (they consume the least amount of resources for the intended value). They should also be adaptable or flexible and support change as customers, market forces, and technology shift. Figure 2.26 shows the three primary types of business process change available to firms and the business areas in which they are most often effective. How does a company know whether it needs to undertake the giant step of changing core business processes? Three conditions indicate the time is right to initiate a business process change:

1. There has been a pronounced shift in the market the process was designed to serve.
2. The company is markedly below industry benchmarks on its core processes.
3. To regain competitive advantage, the company must leapfrog competition on key dimensions.[15]

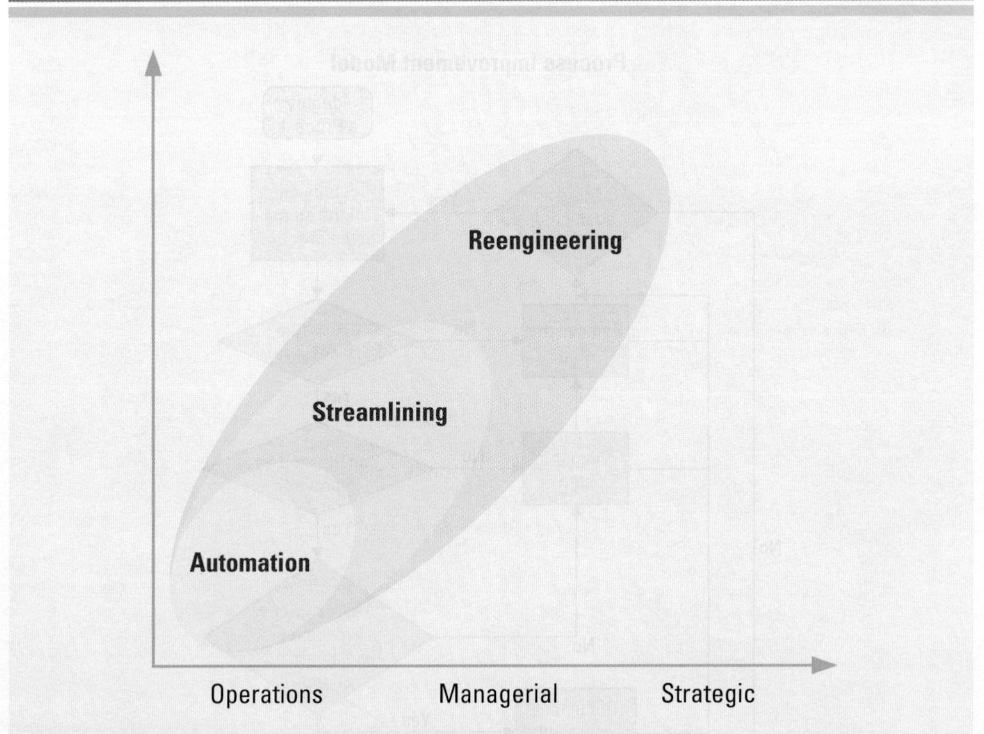

FIGURE 2.26
Primary Types of Business Process Change

Improving Operational Business Processes—Automation

Improving business processes is critical to staying competitive in today's electronic marketplace. Organizations must improve their business processes because customers are demanding better products and services; if customers do not receive what they want from one supplier, often they can simply click a mouse to find many other choices. ***Business process improvement*** attempts to understand and measure the current process and make performance improvements accordingly. Figure 2.27 displays a typical business process improvement model.[16]

Early adopters of MIS recognized that they could enhance their value chain through automation, which reduces costs and increases the speed of performing activities. ***Automation*** is the process of computerizing manual tasks, making them more efficient and effective and dramatically lowering operational costs. Payroll offers an excellent example. Calculating and tracking payroll for 5,000 employees is a highly labor-intensive process requiring 30 full-time employees. Every two weeks accounting employees must gather everyone's hours worked, cross-check with wage rates, and then calculate the amount due, minus taxes and other withholding such as pension contributions and insurance premiums, to create the paychecks. They also track benefits, sick time, and vacation time. If the payroll process is automated, however, one employee can easily calculate payroll, track withholding and deductions, and create paychecks for 5,000 people in a few hours, since everything is performed by the system. Automation improves efficiency and effectiveness and reduces head count, lowering overall operational costs. Transaction processing systems (TPS) are primarily used to automate business processes.

Figure 2.28 illustrates the basic steps for business process improvement. Organizations begin by documenting what they currently do, then they establish a way to measure the process, follow the process, measure the performance, and finally identify improvement opportunities based on the collected information. The next step is to implement process improvements and measure the performance of the new improved process. The loop repeats over and over again as it is continuously improved.[17]

This method of improving business processes is effective for obtaining gradual, incremental improvement. However, several factors have accelerated the need to radically improve business processes. The most obvious is technology. New technologies (such as wireless Internet access) rapidly bring new capabilities to businesses, thereby raising the

FIGURE 2.27
Business Process Improvement Model

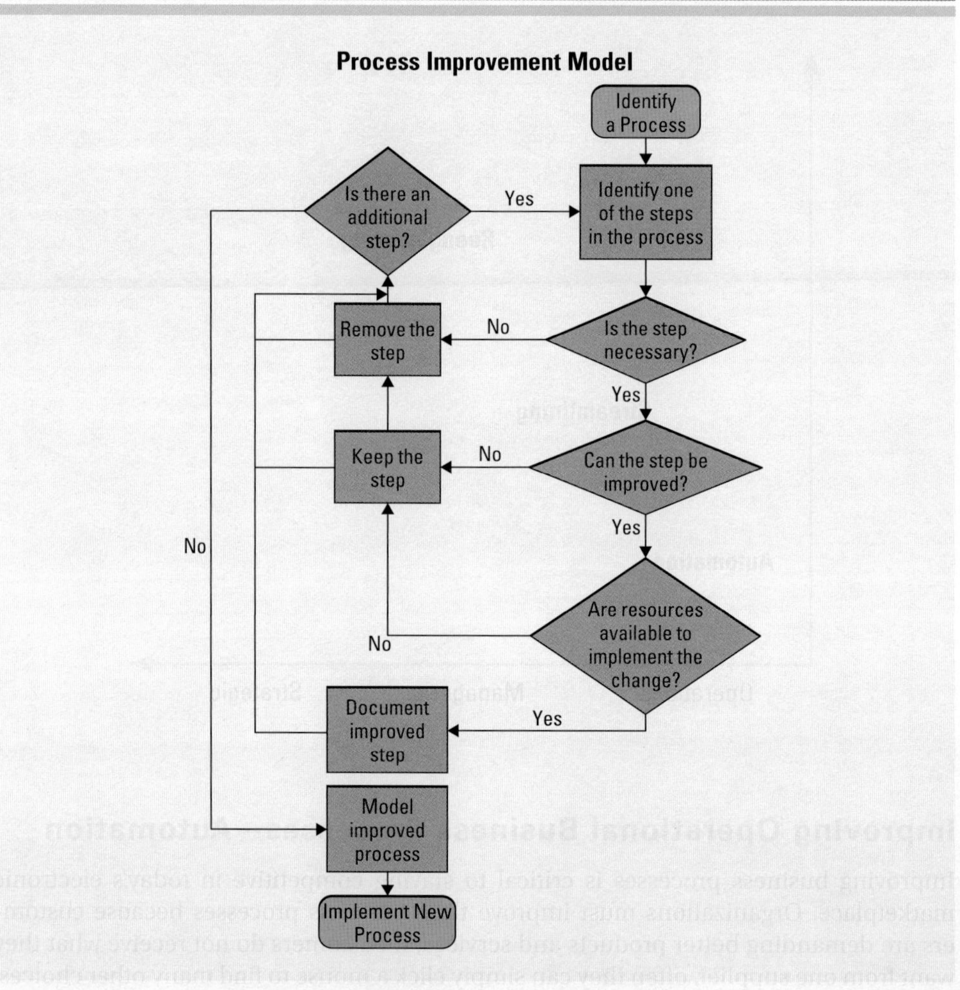

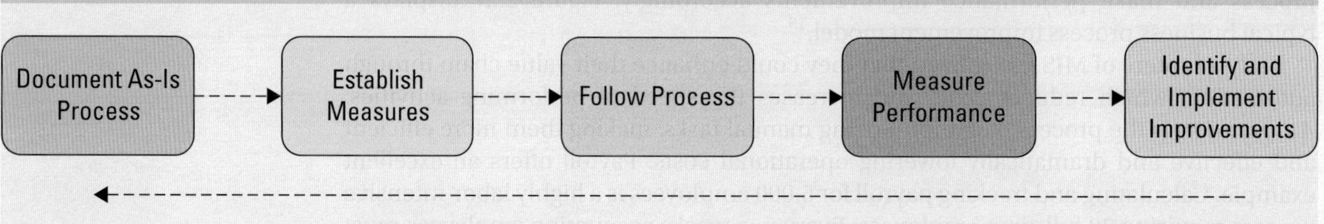

FIGURE 2.28
Steps in Business Process Improvement

competitive bar and the need to improve business processes dramatically. For example, Amazon.com reinvented the supply chain for selling books online. After gaining from automation, companies began to look for new ways to use MIS to improve operations, and managers recognized the benefits of pairing MIS with business processes by streamlining. We look at this improvement method next.

Improving Managerial Business Processes—Streamlining

Streamlining improves business process efficiencies by simplifying or eliminating unnecessary steps. ***Bottlenecks*** occur when resources reach full capacity and cannot handle any additional demands; they limit throughput and impede operations. A computer working at its maximum capacity will be unable to handle increased demand and will become a bottleneck in the process. Streamlining removes bottlenecks, an important step if the efficiency and capacity of a business process are being increased. It also eliminates redundancy. ***Redundancy*** occurs when a task or activity is unnecessarily repeated, for example, if both the sales department and the accounting department check customer credit.

APPLY YOUR KNOWLEDGE

BUSINESS DRIVEN MIS

Streamlining Your Email

The biggest problem with email is that it interferes with workflow. Many employees stop what they are working on and begin checking new email as soon as it arrives. If they do not have the time or capacity to answer it immediately, however, they leave it in the in-box, creating a bottleneck. This process continues all day, and eventually the in-box is overflowing with hundreds of emails, most of which require a response or action. Employees begin dreading email and feel stressed because their workflow process is off track, and they do not know which tasks need to be completed and when.

To streamline workflow, you can designate certain times for email processing (at the top of the hour, or for 30 minutes at three set times a day, for example). Turning off email notification also ensures you are not interrupted during your workflow. When you do begin to check your emails, review them one at a time from top to bottom, and deal with each one immediately. Either reply, put a note on your to-do list, forward the email, or delete it. Now you are working far more efficiently and effectively, and you are less stressed because your in-box is empty.[18]

Choose a process in your life that is inefficient or ineffective and causing you stress. Using the principles of streamlining, remove the bottlenecks and reduce redundancies. Be sure to diagram the As-Is process and your newly created To-Be process.

Automating a business process that contains bottlenecks or redundancies will magnify or amplify these problems if they are not corrected first. Here's an example based on a common source of tension in an organization. Increasing orders is a standard KPI for most marketing/sales departments. To meet this KPI, the sales department tends to say yes to any customer request, such as for rush or custom orders. Reducing ***cycle time,*** the time required to process an order, is a common KPI for operations management. Rush and custom orders tend to create bottlenecks, causing operations to fall below its benchmarked cycle time. Removing these bottlenecks, however, can create master streamlined business processes that deliver both standard and custom orders reliably and profitably. The goal of streamlining is not only to automate but also to improve by monitoring, controlling, and changing the business process.

FedEx streamlined every business process to provide a CSF of speedy and reliable delivery of packages. It created one central hub in Memphis, Tennessee, that processed all its orders. It purchased its own planes to be sure it could achieve the desired level of service. FedEx combined MIS and traditional distribution and logistics processes to create a competitive advantage. FedEx soon identified another market segment of customers who cared a little less about speed and were willing to trade off early-morning delivery for delivery any time *within* the next day at a significantly lower price. The firm had to reevaluate its strategy and realign its business processes to capture this market segment. Had Federal Express focused only on improving its traditional delivery process to handle increased volume faster and more reliably, it could have missed an entire customer segment.[19]

Improving Strategic Business Processes—Reengineering

The flat world (see Chapter 1) is bringing more companies and more customers into the marketplace, greatly increasing competition. Wine wholesalers in the United States must now compete globally, for instance, because customers can just as easily order a bottle of wine from a winery in France as from them. Companies need breakthrough performance and business process changes just to stay in the game. As the rate of change increases, companies looking for rapid change and dramatic improvement are turning to ***business process reengineering (BPR),*** the analysis and redesign of workflow within and between enterprises. Figure 2.29 highlights an analogy to process improvement by explaining the different means of traveling along the same route. A company could improve the way it travels by changing from foot to horse and then from horse to car. With a BPR mind-set, however, it would look beyond automating and streamlining to find a completely different approach. It would ignore the road and travel by air to get from point A to point B. Companies often follow the same indirect path for doing business, not realizing there might be a different, faster, and more direct way.

An organization can reengineer its cross-departmental business processes or an individual department's business processes to help meet its CSFs and KPIs. When selecting a business process to reengineer, wise managers focus on those core processes that are critical to performance, rather than marginal processes that have little impact. The effort to reengineer a business process as a strategic activity requires a different mind-set than that required in continuous business process improvement programs. Because companies have tended to overlook the powerful contribution that processes can make to strategy, they often undertake process improvement efforts using their current processes as the starting point. Managers focusing on reengineering can instead use several criteria to identify opportunities:

- Is the process broken?
- Is it feasible that reengineering of this process will succeed?
- Does it have a high impact on the agency's strategic direction?
- Does it significantly impact customer satisfaction?
- Is it antiquated?
- Does it fall far below best-in-class?
- Is it crucial for productivity improvement?
- Will savings from automation be clearly visible?
- Is the return on investment from implementation high and preferably immediate?

BPR relies on a different school of thought than business process improvement. *In the extreme,* BPR assumes the current process is irrelevant, does not work, or is broken and must be overhauled from scratch. Starting from such a clean slate enables business process designers to disassociate themselves from today's process and focus on a new process. It is as if they are projecting themselves into the future and asking: What should the process look like? What do customers want it to look like? What do other employees want it to look like? How do best-in-class companies do it? How can new technology facilitate the process?

Figure 2.30 displays the basic steps in a business process reengineering effort. It begins with defining the scope and objectives of the reengineering project and then takes the process designers through a learning process with customers, employees, competitors, and new technology. Given this knowledge base, the designers can create a plan

FIGURE 2.29
Different Ways to Travel the Same Route

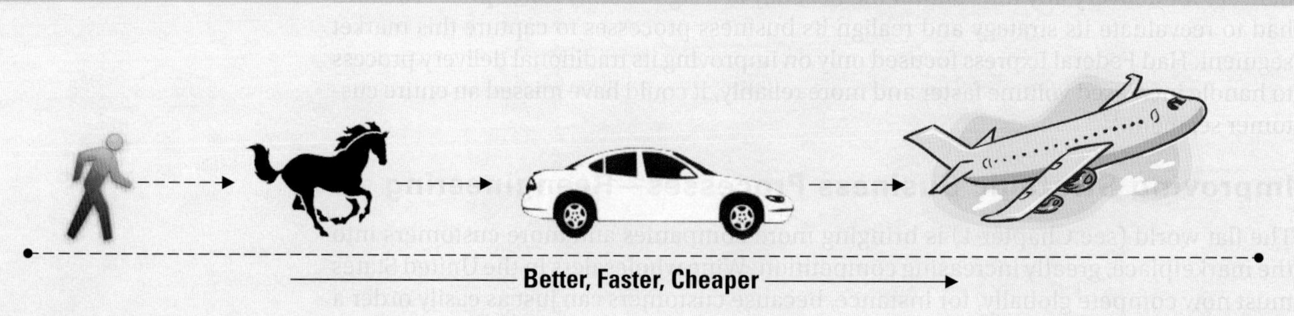

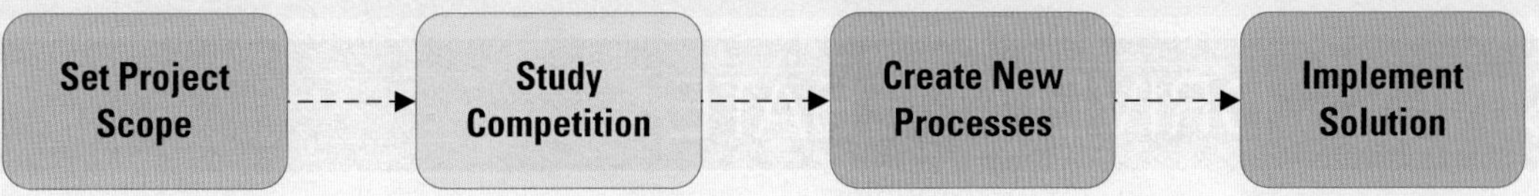

FIGURE 2.30

Business Process Reengineering Model

of action based on the gap between current processes, technologies, and structures and their vision of the processes of the future. It is then top management's job to implement the chosen solution.[20]

System thinking plays a big role in BPR. Automation and streamlining operate departmentally, whereas BPR occurs at the systems level or companywide level and the end-to-end view of a process.

Creating value for the customer is the leading reason for instituting BPR, and MIS often plays an important enabling role. Fundamentally new business processes enabled Progressive Insurance to slash its claims settlement time from 31 days to four hours, for instance. Typically, car insurance companies follow this standard claims resolution process: The customer gets into an accident, has the car towed, and finds a ride home. The customer then calls the insurance company to begin the claims process, which includes an evaluation of the damage, assignment of fault, and an estimate of the cost of repairs, and which usually takes about a month (see Figure 2.31). Progressive Insurance's innovation was to offer a mobile claims process. When a customer has a car accident, he or she calls in the claim on the spot. The Progressive claims adjuster comes to the accident site, surveying the scene and taking digital photographs. The adjuster then offers the customer on-site payment, towing services, and a ride home. A true BPR effort does more for a company than simply improve a process by performing it better, faster, and cheaper. Progressive Insurance's BPR effort redefined best practices for an entire industry.[21]

The Business Process Systems View Leveraging business processes has enormous implications for the business system as a whole. It requires recognition that any meaningful change within the organization affects the entire organization. Without a systems view, the identification of business process flaws and implementation of proposed solutions will often fix only symptoms. Many times what can make one process effective is what makes another process ineffective. Therefore, the redesign of any process within an integrated system requires appreciating the impact of the redesign on other processes. For example, operations management often wants to wait until a

FIGURE 2.31

Auto Insurance Claims Processes

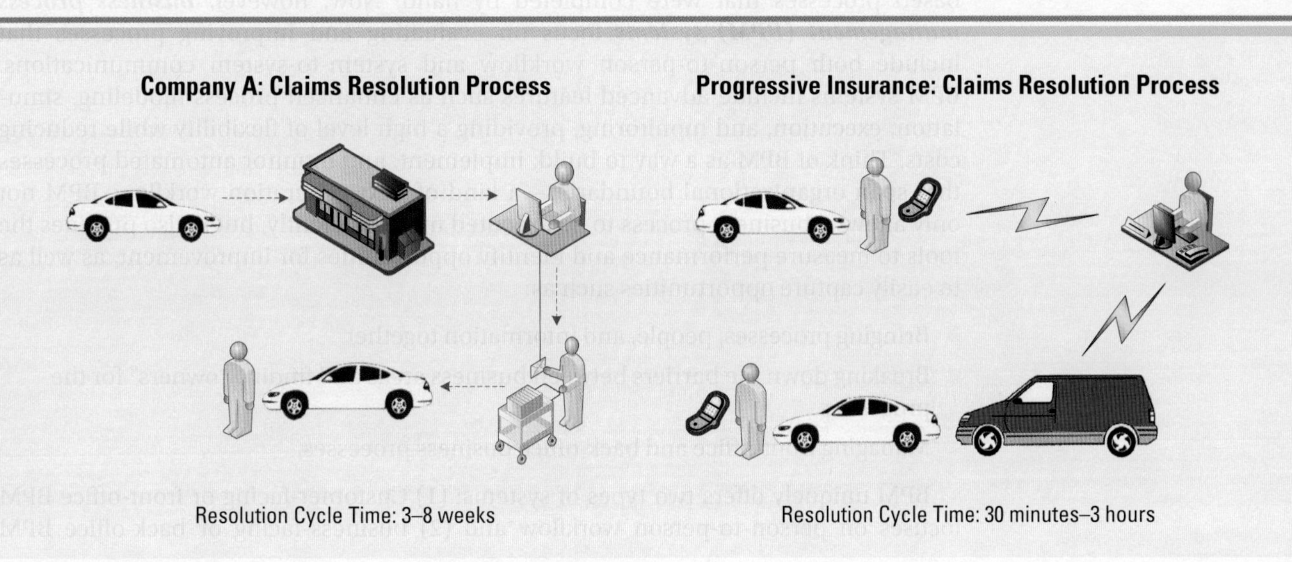

APPLY YOUR KNOWLEDGE

BUSINESS DRIVEN DEBATE

Education Processes

Trina Thompson, a New York City resident, is filing a lawsuit against Monroe College stating that she is unable to find employment after graduating with her bachelor's degree. Thompson is seeking tuition reimbursement of $70,000 and states that she has been unable to find gainful employment since graduating because the school's Office of Career Advancement failed to provide her with the leads and career advice it promised. Monroe College spokesman Gary Axelbank says Thompson's lawsuit is completely without merit and insists it helps its graduates find jobs.[22]

Do you agree that students should be allowed to hold their academic institutions liable for their inability to find a job after graduation? Design the current (As-Is) business process at your school from the time a student begins his or her program until graduation. How could your school reengineer the process to ensure it does not end up in litigation over an individual's expectation of automatically receiving a job after graduation?

truck is full before sending it out for deliveries because the department's KPI measures cost-per-mile-transported. Conversely, the customer satisfaction KPIs measure the ability to make the order-to-delivery cycle time as short as possible, requiring the truck to leave as soon as the product is available, whether it is full or not. Changing business processes to meet operations management KPIs will thus reduce customer satisfaction KPIs. Changing business processes to meet customer satisfaction KPIs will lower operations management KPIs. A systems view, on the other hand, will allow managers to understand the impact business processes have across the entire organization, so both can be improved.

LO 2.8: Describe business process management and its value to an organization.

THE FUTURE: BUSINESS PROCESS MANAGEMENT

Creating a company that can quickly adapt to market, industry, and economic changes to create a competitive advantage requires a new set of operating rules based on achieving speed, performance, and improved delivery. Until recently, business process improvement initiatives focused on improving workflow or document-based processes that were completed by hand. Now, however, ***business process management (BPM) systems*** focus on evaluating and improving processes that include both person-to-person workflow and system-to-system communications. BPM systems include advanced features such as enhanced process modeling, simulation, execution, and monitoring, providing a high level of flexibility while reducing costs. Think of BPM as a way to build, implement, and monitor automated processes that span organizational boundaries—a kind of next-generation workflow. BPM not only allows a business process to be executed more efficiently, but it also provides the tools to measure performance and identify opportunities for improvement, as well as to easily capture opportunities such as:

- Bringing processes, people, and information together.
- Breaking down the barriers between business areas and finding "owners" for the processes.
- Managing front-office and back-office business processes.

BPM uniquely offers two types of systems: (1) Customer-facing or front-office BPM focuses on person-to-person workflow and (2) business-facing or back-office BPM focuses on system-to-system workflow. With BPM the two systems function as one, allowing continual improvements to many business processes simultaneously and in real time. BPM's unified environment encourages people to observe, think, and provide feedback, harnessing the power of ideas and insight and promoting systems thinking throughout the organization. Providing the flexibility for quick BPM change drives efficiency and effectiveness, creating optimal business processes. This ability is the foundation for creating an operation that gives a company competitive advantage.

LEARNING OUTCOME REVIEW

Learning Outcome 2.1: Explain the importance of decision making for managers at each of the three primary organization levels along with the associated decision characteristics.

Decision-making skills are essential for all business professionals, at every company level, who make decisions that run the business. At the operational level, employees develop, control, and maintain core business activities required to run the day-to-day operations. Operational decisions are considered structured decisions, which arise in situations where established processes offer potential solutions. Structured decisions are made frequently and are almost repetitive in nature; they affect short-term business strategies.

At the managerial level, employees are continuously evaluating company operations to hone the firm's abilities to identify, adapt to, and leverage change. Managerial decisions cover short- and medium-range plans, schedules, and budgets along with policies, procedures, and business objectives for the firm. These types of decisions are considered semistructured decisions; they occur in situations in which a few established processes help to evaluate potential solutions, but not enough to lead to a definite recommended decision.

At the strategic level, managers develop overall business strategies, goals, and objectives as part of the company's strategic plan. They also monitor the strategic performance of the organization and its overall direction in the political, economic, and competitive business environment. Strategic decisions are highly unstructured decisions, occurring in situations in which no procedures or rules exist to guide decision makers toward the correct choice. They are infrequent, extremely important, and typically related to long-term business strategy.

Learning Outcome 2.2: Define critical success factors (CSFs) and key performance indicators (KPIs), and explain how managers use them to measure the success of MIS projects.

Metrics are measurements that evaluate results to determine whether a project is meeting its goals. Two core metrics are critical success factors and key performance indicators. CSFs are the crucial steps companies perform to achieve their goals and objectives and implement their strategies and include creating high-quality products, retaining competitive advantages, and reducing product costs. KPIs are the quantifiable metrics a company uses to evaluate progress toward critical success factors. KPIs are far more specific than CSFs; examples include turnover rates of employees, percentage of help-desk calls answered in the first minute, and number of products returned.

It is important to understand the relationship between critical success factors and key performance indicators. CSFs are elements crucial for a business strategy's success. KPIs measure the progress of CSFs with quantifiable measurements, and one CSF can have several KPIs. Of course, both categories will vary by company and industry. Imagine improved graduation rates as a CSF for a college.

Learning Outcome 2.3: Classify the different operational support systems, managerial support systems, and strategic support systems, and explain how managers can use these systems to make decisions and gain competitive advantages.

Being able to sort, calculate, analyze, and slice-and-dice information is critical to an organization's success. Without knowing what is occurring throughout the organization there is no way that managers and executives can make solid decisions to support the business. The different operational, managerial, and strategic support systems include:

- Operational: A transaction processing system (TPS) is the basic business system that serves the operational level (analysts) in an organization. The most common example of a TPS is an operational accounting system such as a payroll system or an order-entry system.
- Managerial: A decision support system (DSS) models information to support managers and business professionals during the decision-making process.
- Strategic: An executive information system (EIS) is a specialized DSS that supports senior-level executives within the organization.

Learning Outcome 2.4: Describe artificial intelligence, and identify its five main types.

Artificial intelligence (AI) simulates human thinking and behavior, such as the ability to reason and learn. The five most common categories of AI are:

1. Expert systems—computerized advisory programs that imitate the reasoning processes of experts in solving difficult problems.
2. Neural networks—attempts to emulate the way the human brain works.
3. Genetic algorithm—a system that mimics the evolutionary, survival-of-the-fittest process to generate increasingly better solutions to a problem.
4. Intelligent agents—a special-purpose knowledge-based information system that accomplishes specific tasks on behalf of its users.
5. Virtual reality—a computer-simulated environment that can be a simulation of the real world or an imaginary world.

Learning Outcome 2.5: Explain the value of business processes for a company, and differentiate between customer-facing and business-facing process.

A business process is a standardized set of activities that accomplish a specific task, such as processing a customer's order. Business processes transform a set of inputs into a set of outputs (goods or services) for another person or process by using people and tools. Without processes, organizations would not be able to complete activities. Customer-facing processes result in a product or service that is received by an organization's external customer. Business-facing processes are invisible to the external customer but essential to the effective management of the business.

Learning Outcome 2.6: Demonstrate the value of business process modeling, and compare As-Is and To-Be models.

Business process modeling (or mapping) is the activity of creating a detailed flowchart or process map of a work process showing its inputs, tasks, and activities, in a structured sequence. A business process model is a graphic description of a process, showing the sequence of process tasks, which is developed for a specific purpose and from a selected viewpoint.

Business process modeling usually begins with a functional process representation of what the process problem is, or an As-Is process model. As-Is process models represent the current state of the operation that has been mapped, without any specific improvements or changes to existing processes. The next step is to build a To-Be process model that displays how the process problem will be solved or implemented. To-Be process models show the results of applying change improvement opportunities to the current (As-Is) process model. This approach ensures that the process is fully and clearly understood before the details of a process solution are decided upon.

Learning Outcome 2.7: Differentiate among business process improvements, streamlining, and reengineering.

Business process improvement attempts to understand and measure the current process and make performance improvements accordingly. Streamlining improves business process efficiencies by simplifying or eliminating unnecessary steps. Bottlenecks occur when resources reach full capacity and cannot handle any additional demands; they limit throughput and impede operations. Streamlining removes bottlenecks, an important step if the efficiency and capacity of a business process are being increased. Business process reengineering (BPR) is the analysis and redesign of workflow within and between enterprises and occurs at the systems level or companywide level and the end-to-end view of a process.

Learning Outcome 2.8: Describe business process management and its value to an organization.

Business process management (BPM) systems focus on evaluating and improving processes that include both person-to-person workflow and system-to-system communications. BPM systems include advanced features such as enhanced process modeling, simulation, execution, and monitoring, providing a high level of flexibility while reducing costs.

OPENING CASE QUESTIONS

1. **Knowledge:** Define the three primary types of decision-making systems, and explain how Obama's campaign team used them to win votes.
2. **Comprehension:** Describe the difference between transactional and analytical information, and determine which types Spotlight Analysis used to identify its 10 tribes.
3. **Application:** Illustrate the business process model used to identify the 10 tribes.
4. **Analysis:** Explain business process reengineering and how Obama's team used it to develop political micro-targeting.
5. **Synthesis:** Formulate different metrics the Obama team used to measure the success of political micro-targeting.
6. **Evaluation:** Argue for or against the following statement: Political micro-targeting signals the dehumanization of politics.

KEY TERMS

Analytical information, 52
Artificial intelligence (AI), 57
As-Is process model, 64
Automation, 69
Benchmarking, 50
Benchmarks, 50
Bottlenecks, 70
Business-facing process, 62
Business process improvement, 69
Business process management (BPM) system, 74
Business process model, 63
Business process modeling (or mapping), 63
Business process reengineering (BPR), 72
Consolidation, 56
Critical success factors (CSFs), 47

REVIEW QUESTIONS

1. Why must business professionals understand how MIS supports decision making and problem solving?
2. What is the relationship between critical success factors and key performance indicators? How can a manager use them to understand business operations?
3. What are the three different levels found in a company? What types of decisions are made at each level?
4. Define transaction processing systems and describe the role they play in a business.
5. Define decision support systems and describe the role they play in a business.
6. Define expert systems and describe the role they play in a business.
7. What are the capabilities associated with digital dashboards?
8. What are the common DSS analysis techniques?
9. How does an electronic spreadsheet program, such as Excel, provide decision support capabilities?
10. What is the difference between the ability of a manager to retrieve information instantly on demand using an MIS and the capabilities provided by a DSS?
11. What is artificial intelligence? What are the five types of AI systems? What applications of AI offer the greatest business value?
12. What is a business process and what role does it play in an organization?
13. Why do managers need to understand business processes? Can you make a correlation between systems thinking and business processes?
14. Why would a manager need to review an As-Is and To-Be process model?
15. How can a manager use automation, streamlining, and business process reengineering to gain operational efficiency and effectiveness?
16. Explain the difference between customer-facing processes and business-facing processes. Which one is more important to an organization?
17. Explain how finding different ways to travel the same road relates to automation, streamlining, and business process reengineering.

CLOSING CASE ONE

Defense Advanced Research Projects Agency (DARPA) Grand Challenge

The goal of the DARPA Grand Challenge is to save lives by making one-third of ground military forces autonomous or driverless vehicles by 2015. Created in response to a congressional and U.S. Department of Defense (DoD) mandate, the DARPA Grand Challenge brings together individuals and organizations from industry, the research and development (R&D) community, government, the armed services, and academia and includes students, backyard inventors, and automotive enthusiasts.

The DARPA Grand Challenge 2004

The DARPA Grand Challenge 2004 field test of autonomous ground vehicles ran from Barstow, California, to Primm, Nevada, and offered a $1 million prize. From the qualifying round at the California Speedway, 15 finalists emerged to attempt the Grand Challenge. However, the prize went unclaimed when no vehicles were able to complete the difficult desert route.

The DARPA Grand Challenge 2005

The DARPA Grand Challenge 2005 was held in the Mojave Desert and offered a $2 million prize to the team that completed the 132-mile course in the shortest time under 10 hours. The race, over desert terrain, included narrow tunnels, sharp turns, and a winding mountain pass with a sheer drop-off on one side and a rock face on the other. Five teams completed the course, and "Stanley," the Stanford Racing Team's car, won the $2 million prize with a time of 6 hours, 53 minutes.

The DARPA Grand Challenge 2007

The third DARPA Grand Challenge was an urban challenge on the site of the now-closed George Air Force Base in Victorville, California. It offered a $2 million prize to the autonomous vehicle that could cover the 60-mile course in less than 6 hours. The vehicles had to obey stop lights, navigate around other vehicles, and even merge into heavy traffic. Tartan Racing, a collaborative effort by Carnegie Mellon University and General Motors Corporation, won the prize with "Boss," a Chevy Tahoe. The Stanford Racing Team's "Junior," a 2006 Volkswagen Passat, won second prize of $1 million. "Victor Tango," a 2005 Ford Escape hybrid from Virginia Tech, won third place along with a $500,000 prize.[23]

Questions

1. How is the DoD using AI to improve its operations and save lives?
2. Why would the DoD use an event like the DARPA Grand Challenge to further technological innovation?
3. Describe how autonomous vehicles could be used by organizations around the world to improve business efficiency and effectiveness.
4. The Ansari X is another technological innovation competition focusing on spacecraft. To win the $10 million Ansari X Prize, a private spacecraft had to be the first to carry the weight equivalent of three people to an altitude of 62.14 miles twice within two weeks. SpaceShipOne, a privately built spacecraft, won on October 4, 2004. Describe the potential business impacts of the Ansari X competition.

CLOSING CASE TWO

Second Life: Succeeding in Virtual Times

Second Life is a virtual world built and owned by its residents. It opened to the public in 2003, and today it is inhabited by millions of residents from around the world. The three main parts to Second Life are:

- **The World:** The world of Second Life is constantly changing and growing. It is filled with hundreds of games, from multiplayer role-playing games to puzzles and grid-wide contests. There are also dance clubs, shopping malls, space stations, vampire castles, and movie theaters. To find something to do at any time of the day or night, residents simply open the Search menu and click on Events for a listing of discussions, sports, entertainment, games, pageants, education, arts and culture, and charity/support groups.
- **The Creations:** Second Life is dedicated to creativity. Everything in Second Life is resident-created, from the strobe lights in the nightclubs to the cars (or spaceships) in driveways. Imagine tinkering with the steering and handling program of a motorcycle while a friend tweaks the shape of the fuel tank and gives it a wicked flame paint job, in-world and in real-time, before taking it for a spin down a newly created road to look for land to buy. Have you ever wondered what it would be like to have a pair of black leather wings? Build them and give it a go.
- **The Marketplace:** The Marketplace currently supports millions of U.S. dollars in monthly transactions. This commerce is transacted with the in-world unit of trade, the Linden dollar, which can be converted to U.S. dollars at several thriving online Linden dollar exchanges or at LindeX, the official exchange. Users can make real money in a virtual world because Second Life has a fully integrated economy designed to reward risk, innovation, and craftsmanship. Residents create their own virtual goods and services, retain the intellectual property rights of their creations, and sell them at various in-world venues. Businesses succeed on the ingenuity, artistic ability, entrepreneurial acumen, and good reputation of their owners.

Businesses on Second Life

Second Life is an exciting new venue for collaboration, business ventures, distance learning, new media studies, and marketing. Business possibilities there are endless; a few examples include:

- Holding a virtual meeting with sales managers located in Europe and Asia.
- Presenting new sales initiatives and discussing them with the team real-time.
- Allowing Second Life residents to interact with company products or services and test new designs and concepts before they are introduced to the real world.
- Selling products and services in Second Life by creating an event to promote the product: a concert, a class, a famous speaker, a party, a contest. Many companies are excited about the numerous ways they can use Second Life to support their business.[24] A few companies paving the way on Second Life include the following:

1-800-flowers.com	BBC Radio 1	Cisco
Adidas	Best Buy Co. Inc.	Coca-Cola
Amazon	BMW	Coldwell Banker
American Apparel	Calvin Klein	Comcast
American Cancer Society	Circuit City	Crayola

Dell
H&R Block
IBM
Intel
Kraft Food
Lacoste
Major League Baseball
Mazda
Mercedes-Benz
Microsoft
MTV
NASA
National Basketball Association
NBC
Nissan
NPR
Sony
Sprint
Student Travel Association
Starwood Hotels
Sundance Channel
Toyota
Universal Motown Records
Visa
Warner Bros. Music
Weather Channel
Wired magazine
Xerox
Yahoo
Yankee Stadium

Questions

1. How could financial companies use neural networks in Second Life to help their businesses?
2. How could a company such as Nike use decision support systems on Second Life to help its business?
3. How could an apparel company use Second Life to build a digital dashboard to monitor virtual operations?
4. How could a company use Second Life to revamp its customer service process?
5. How could a company use Second Life to revamp its order-entry process?
6. How could a company use Second Life to reinvent its relationships with customers, partners, and employees?

CRITICAL BUSINESS THINKING

1. Modeling a Business Process

Do you hate waiting in line at the grocery store? Do you find it frustrating when you go to the video rental store and cannot find the movie you wanted? Do you get annoyed when the pizza delivery person brings you the wrong order? This is your chance to reengineer the process that drives you crazy. Choose a problem you are currently experiencing and reengineer the process to make it more efficient. Be sure to provide an As-Is and To-Be process model.

2. Revamping Accounts

The accounting department at your company deals with the processing of critical documents that include invoices, purchase orders, statements, purchase requisitions, financial statements, sales orders, and price quotes. These documents must arrive at their intended destination in a secure and efficient manner.

Processing is currently done manually, which causes a negative ripple effect. Documents tend to be misplaced or delayed, becoming vulnerable to unauthorized changes or exposure of confidential information. In addition, the accounting department incurs costs such as for preprinted forms, inefficient distribution, and storage. Explain automation, streamlining, and business process reengineering and how they can be used to revamp the accounting department.

3. What Type of System Would You Use?

You have been assigned as senior director for a large manufacturing company. Your first assignment is to decide which type of MIS can best support your decision-making needs. For all of the following, determine which type of system you would use to help solve the business problem or make a business decision.

a. You need to analyze daily sales transactions for each region.
b. You need to analyze staffing requirements for each plant.
c. You need to determine which customers are at risk of defaulting on their bills.
d. You need to analyze your competition including prices, discounts, goods, and services.
e. You need to analyze critical success factors and key performance indicators for status on operations.
f. You need to produce a graphical display of patterns and complex relationships for large amounts of data.

4. **Unstructured Communications**

You have just received a job as a business analyst for a large sports marketing company. Your boss, Sandy Fiero, wants you to evaluate and improve the current corporate communication process. With the current process, employees receive a great deal of unstructured information in the form of emails, including corporate policies, corporate announcements, and human resource information. You quickly realize that using an email system for communication is causing a great deal of issues including inaccessible information for any new hires, lost productivity as employees search through hundreds of emails to find information, and miscommunication as global divisions of your organization send out regional human resource policies.

To begin analyzing the processes, create a list of issues you might encounter by using email as a primary communication tool for corporate information. What are the redundancies associated with an email communication process? What are the bottlenecks with an email communication process? Document the As-Is process for sending email communications to employees. Then, reengineer the process and document your suggestions for improving the process and the To-Be communication process.

5. **IGoogle Digital Dashboard**

Executives find information from a variety of sources coming across their computers every day. The digital dashboard containing this information might include their calendar, email, issues such as production delays or accounts past due, and even financial and industry information. Although it would be impossible to fit all of an organization's information into a single screen, it can summarize the data in ways tailored to meet the executive's needs.

IGoogle is a type of digital dashboard you can create for your own personal view of the world through Google. IGoogle allows users to create personalized home pages containing Google search along with a number of Google gadgets that provide access to activities and information from all over the Internet. If you want one location where you can view Gmail messages, peruse Google news, review weather forecasts, stock quotes, and movie showtimes, iGoogle is for you. Visit iGoogle and determine how you could customize your Google home page as a digital dashboard for your computer.

6. **Bot Shopping**

For those of us who love (or hate) shopping, a shopping bot can become your best friend. Regardless of whether you are shopping in a store or online you still have to research products, compare prices, select a seller, and find the safest way to pay. Shopping in the information age is easier than ever, especially with the help of a shopping bot. Shopping bots are price comparison websites that automatically search the inventory of different vendors to find the lowest possible price, saving you time and money. Shopping bots will rank the product you are looking for by price and link you directly to the vendor's website. Popular shopping bots include mysimon.com, Gomez.com, Bizrate.com, shopzilla.com, and Google's shopping bot at www.google.com/products.

Choose a product you are interested in purchasing and use three of the different shopping bots to compare prices. Did the different shopping bots return the same information and prices? Which shopping bot was the easiest to use? Will you continue using shopping bots? What are the advantages and disadvantages for a company using shopping bots to purchase office supplies or raw materials?

7. **Networking Neural**
   Neural networks are a category of AI that attempts to emulate the way the human brain works. A neural network could be a great asset for any college student. If a neural network could scan each brain for all of the students in your course, what types of information would it acquire? How could you use the student neural network to improve your grades? How could you use the student neural network to identify trends and new market segments? What would be the risks of using this neural network for academic improvement? What types of confidentiality and privacy issues would be encountered with this neural network?

8. **Driving Your Business**
   You have recently opened your own business—choose the business of your dreams and assume you have it up and running. What types of decision will you need to make to operate your business? How can you use MIS to support your decision-making efforts? What types of processes will you find throughout your business? How can you use MIS to revamp your business process for efficiency and effectiveness? Overall, how dependent will your business be on MIS? Do you think you could be just as successful running your business without MIS? Can you name a business that can operate efficiently and effectively without MIS?

ENTREPRENEURIAL CHALLENGE

BUILD YOUR OWN BUSINESS

1. You realize that you need a digital dashboard to help you operate your business. Create a list of all of the components you would want to track in your digital dashboard that would help you run your business. Be sure to justify how each component would help you gain insight into the operations of your business and flag potential issues that could ruin your business. (Be sure to identify your business and the name of your company as you defined it in Chapter 1.)
2. Explain three customer-facing processes and three business-facing process associated with your business. Be sure to detail why the process is customer facing or business facing.
3. Your friends have asked you to review the customer ordering process for their restaurant, The Broadway Café. To make the café as efficient and effective as possible, you want to redesign processes to remove bottlenecks, reduce redundancies, and streamline workflow. Review The Broadway Café's customer ordering process highlighted in the accompanying image and reengineer it for improvements in efficiency and effectiveness. If you are looking for a real challenge, create your As-Is and To-Be process diagrams using PowerPoint or Visio.

After revamping the ordering process for your friends, you decide to create a To-Be process model of the most important business processes required for your startup to find success. Create the To-Be process model for your most critical business process to ensure you know how to operate your startup in the most efficient and effective manner.

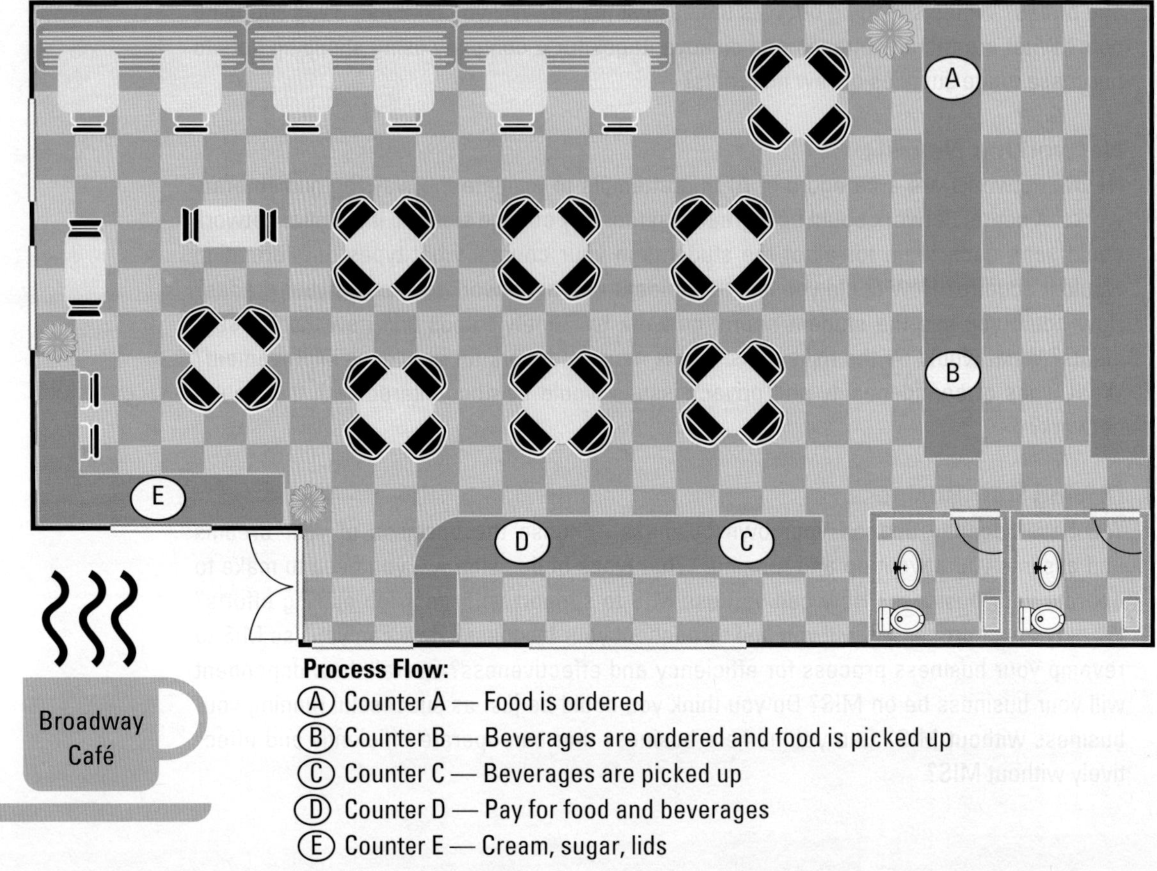
A
B
C
D
E
Broadway Café
Process Flow:
(A) Counter A — Food is ordered
(B) Counter B — Beverages are ordered and food is picked up
(C) Counter C — Beverages are picked up
(D) Counter D — Pay for food and beverages
(E) Counter E — Cream, sugar, lids

APPLY YOUR KNOWLEDGE BUSINESS PROJECTS

PROJECT I Making Business Decisions

You are the vice president of human resources for a large consulting company. You are compiling a list of questions that you want each job interviewee to answer. The first question on your list is, "How can MIS enhance your ability to make decisions at our organization?" Prepare a one-page report to answer this question.

PROJECT II DSS and EIS

Dr. Rosen runs a large dental conglomerate—Teeth Doctors—that employs more than 700 dentists in six states. Dr. Rosen is interested in purchasing a competitor called Dentix that has 150 dentists in three additional states. Before deciding whether to purchase Dentix, Dr. Rosen must consider several issues:

- The cost of purchasing Dentix.
- The location of the Dentix offices.
- The current number of customers per dentist, per office, and per state.
- The merger between the two companies.
- The professional reputation of Dentix.
- Other competitors.

Explain how Dr. Rosen and Teeth Doctors can benefit from the use of information systems to make an accurate business decision about whether to purchase Dentix.

PROJECT III Finding Information on Decision Support Systems

You are working on the sales team for a small catering company that maintains 75 employees and generates $1 million in revenues per year. The owner, Pam Hetz, wants to understand how she can use decision support systems to help expand her business. Hetz has an initial understanding of DSS and is interested in learning more about what types are available, how they can be used in a small business, and the costs associated. In a group, research the website www.dssresources.com and compile a presentation that discusses DSSs in detail. Be sure to answer all Hetz's questions on DSS in your presentation.

PROJECT IV Discovering Reengineering Opportunities

In an effort to increase efficiency, your college has hired you to analyze its current business processes for registering for classes. Analyze the current process and determine which steps are:

- Broken
- Redundant
- Antiquated

Be sure to define how you would reengineer the processes for efficiency.

PROJECT V Dashboard Design

Digital dashboards offer an effective and efficient way to view enterprisewide information at near real time. According to Nucleus Research, there is a direct correlation between use of digital dashboards and a company's return on investment (ROI); hence, all executives should be using or pushing the development of digital dashboards to monitor and analyze organizational operations.

Design a digital dashboard for a customer tracking and enterprise operations system. Be sure to address at least four of the following indicators by showing how you would measure it, such as red, yellow, green status; percentage complete status; and so on.

Customer Tracking System	Enterprise Operations
Customers	Accounting
Marketing	Finance
Order entry	Logistics
Collections	Production
Sales	Distribution
Customer service	Manufacturing
Billing	Human resources
Credit limits	Sales
Transportation	Total profit

AYK APPLICATION PROJECTS

If you are looking for Excel projects to incorporate into your class, try any of the following after reading this chapter.

Project Number	Project Name	Project Type	Plug-In Focus Area	Project Focus	Project Skill Set	Page Number
1	Financial Destiny	Excel	T2	Personal Budget	Introductory Formulas	AYK.4
2	Cash Flow	Excel	T2	Cash Flow	Introductory Formulas	AYK.4
3	Technology Budget	Excel	T1, T2	Hardware and Software	Introductory Formulas	AYK.4
4	Tracking Donations	Excel	T2	Employee Relationships	Introductory Formulas	AYK.4
5	Convert Currency	Excel	T2	Global Commerce	Introductory Formulas	AYK.5
6	Cost Comparison	Excel	T2	Total Cost of Ownership	Introductory Formulas	AYK.5
7	Time Management	Excel or Project	T2 or T12	Project Management	Introductory Gantt Charts	AYK.6
8	Maximize Profit	Excel	T2, T4	Strategic Analysis	Intermediate Formulas or Solver	AYK.6
9	Security Analysis	Excel	T3	Filtering Data	Intermediate Conditional Formatting, Autofilter, Subtotal	AYK.7
10	Gathering Data	Excel	T3	Data Analysis	Intermediate Conditional Formatting, PivotTable	AYK.8
11	Scanner System	Excel	T2	Strategic Analysis	Intermediate	AYK.8
12	Competitive Pricing	Excel	T2	Profit Maximization	Intermediate	AYK.9
13	Adequate Acquisitions	Excel	T2	Break-Even Analysis	Intermediate	AYK.9

Ebusiness: Electronic Business Value

CHAPTER 3

CHAPTER OUTLINE

SECTION 3.1
WEB 1.0: Ebusiness

- Disruptive Technologies and Web 1.0
- Advantages of Ebusiness
- Ebusiness Models
- Ebusiness Tools for Connecting and Communicating
- The Challenges of Ebusiness

SECTION 3.2
WEB 2.0: Business 2.0

- Web 2.0: Advantages of Business 2.0
- Networking Communities with Business 2.0
- Business 2.0 Tools for Collaborating
- The Challenges of Business 2.0
- Web 3.0: Defining the Next Generation of Online Business Opportunities

What's in IT for Me?

Internet and communication technologies have revolutionized the way business operates, improving upon traditional methods and even introducing new opportunities and ventures that were simply not possible before. More than just giving organizations another means of conducting transactions, online business provides the ability to develop and maintain customer relationships, supplier relationships, and even employee relationships between and within enterprises.

As future managers and organizational knowledge workers, you need to understand the benefits ebusiness can offer an organization and your career, the challenges that accompany Web technologies and their impact on organizational communication and collaboration. You need to be aware of the strategies organizations can use to deploy ebusiness and the methods of measuring ebusiness success. This chapter will give you this knowledge and help prepare you for success in tomorrow's electronic global marketplace.

opening case study

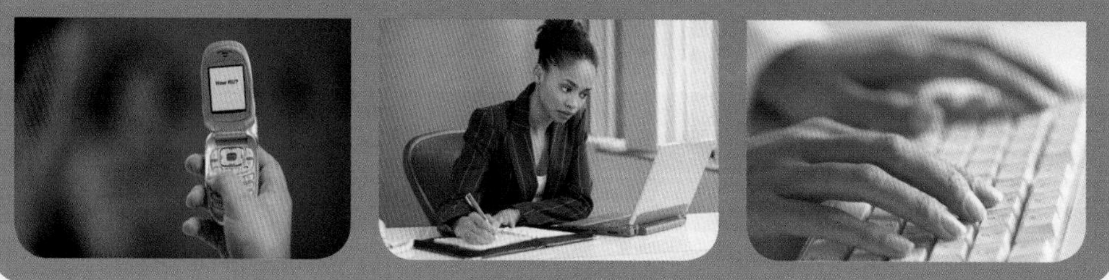

Social Media and Ashton Kutcher

Where celebrities go, fans follow. The truism applies as much in social media as in the real world, David Karp noticed after famous artists began using his blogging service Tumblr. As a result, encouraging celebrities to set up accounts on the site has become "absolutely part of our road map and our business plan," Karp says. In fact, he recently hired a full-time employee to help high-profile users design and manage their blogs.

It's no secret that well-recognized players in a host of fields—from acting to athletics, music to politics—are using social media sites to connect with fans and promote their brands. Celebrities used to seek out promotion "in *People* magazine or *Vogue,*" says Robert Passikoff, president of Brand Keys, a researcher that tracks the value of celebrity brands. "It's now become a necessity to have a Facebook page."

But the benefits go both ways. Sites benefit greatly from the online cavalcade of stars. Oprah Winfrey's recent debut on microblogging service Twitter sent visits to the site skyrocketing 43 percent over the previous week, according to analytics firm Hitwise. Facebook, Google's YouTube, Ning, and other Web 2.0 destinations have also seen swarms of activity around the profile pages of their famous members. And like Tumblr, social sites are going out of their way to keep the celebrities happy and coming back.

Obama on MySpace, Facebook, and Twitter

The Obama administration created profile pages on MySpace, Facebook, and Twitter. To accommodate 1600 Pennsylvania Avenue, News Corp.'s MySpace agreed to build ad-free pages and equipped the profile to get automatic updates from the White House's official blog. In some cases social networks give VIPs a heads-up on changes. Recently, Facebook worked with the handlers of select celebrity members, including CBS news anchor Katie Couric and French President Nicolas Sarkozy, to get feedback on the new design of the site before it was opened to the public. "We don't have a formalized support program for public figures, but we do offer some support," says Facebook spokeswoman Brandee Barker.

Some privileged members of Facebook have also been assigned "vanity URLs," or short, simple, personalized Web addresses such as www.facebook.com/KatieCouric. Elsewhere the perks of fame are offered up more casually. Twitter co-founder Biz Stone credits high-profile users like actor Ashton Kutcher and basketball professional Shaquille O'Neal for bringing attention to the site of 140-character messages but says the company doesn't reserve any "special resources" for them.

"Sometimes celebrities who love Twitter stop by and say hello," Stone says. "It's usually just a quiet tour and a lunchtime chat but it's really fun for us."

John Legend Taps Tumblr

In addition to their promotional value, social networking celebrities represent a potential revenue source for these young startups. Tumblr recently helped musician John Legend design a professional-looking blog that matches the look of his promotional site, created by Sony Music Entertainment. Tumblr's Karp says he took that project on at no charge—in part to bring in Legend's fans but also to explore whether it makes sense to offer similar services at a cost. "For people who want the reach on our network, who want to be able to take advantage of our platform, at some point this does turn into a premium service," he says.

Ning already collects monthly fees from some of its users, many of whom are celebrities. The site is free for anyone who wants to build their own social network but charges as much as $55 a month to users who prefer to keep their pages clear of ads or who want to collect revenue generated by ads on their pages. Although the service is not exclusive to stars, many of the most successful networks on Ning draw on the fame of their operators, including hip-hop artists 50 Cent and Q-Tip, rock band Good Charlotte, and Ultimate Fighting Championship titleholder BJ Penn. "The next generation of celebrities and social networks is in much richer and deeper collaborations [with fans] than what you see today on the more general social networks out there," says Ning CEO Gina Bianchini.

Many big names in business, including Dell CEO Michael Dell, use professional networking site LinkedIn more as a business tool than to amass legions of followers. Whatever their reasons for being on the site, LinkedIn uses the fact that executives from all of the 500 biggest companies are among its members to encourage other businesspeople to join the site, too.[1]

section 3.1 WEB 1.0: EBUSINESS

LEARNING OUTCOMES

3.1 Compare disruptive and sustaining technologies, and explain how the Internet and WWW caused business disruption.

3.2 Describe Web 1.0 along with ebusiness and its associated advantages.

3.3. Compare the four categories of ebusiness models.

3.4. Describe the six ebusiness tools for connecting and communicating.

3.5 Identify the four challenges associated with ebusiness.

LO 3.1: Compare disruptive and sustaining technologies, and explain how the Internet and WWW caused business disruption.

DISRUPTIVE TECHNOLOGIES AND WEB 1.0

Polaroid, founded in 1937, produced the first instant camera in the late 1940s. The Polaroid camera, whose pictures developed themselves, was one of the most exciting technological advances the photography industry had ever seen. The company eventually went public, becoming one of Wall Street's most prominent enterprises, with its stock trading above $60 per share in 1997. In 2002, the stock dropped to 8 cents and the company declared bankruptcy.[2]

How could a company such as Polaroid, which had innovative technology and a captive customer base, go bankrupt? Perhaps company executives failed to use Porter's Five Forces Model to analyze the threat of substitute products or services. If they had, would they have noticed the two threats—one-hour film processing and digital cameras—which eventually stole Polaroid's market share? Would they have understood that their customers, people who want instant access to their pictures, would be the first to try these alternatives? Could the company have found a way to compete with one-hour film processing and the digital camera to save Polaroid?

Many organizations face the same dilemma as Polaroid—what's best for the current business might not be what's best for it in the long term. Some observers of our business environment have an ominous vision of the future—digital Darwinism. ***Digital Darwinism*** implies that organizations that cannot adapt to the new demands placed on them for surviving in the information age are doomed to extinction.

Disruptive versus Sustaining Technology

A ***disruptive technology*** is a new way of doing things that initially does not meet the needs of existing customers. Disruptive technologies tend to open new markets and destroy old ones. A ***sustaining technology,*** on the other hand, produces an improved product customers are eager to buy, such as a faster car or larger hard drive. Sustaining technologies tend to provide us with better, faster, and cheaper products in established markets. Incumbent companies most often lead sustaining technology to market, but they virtually never lead in markets opened by disruptive technologies. Figure 3.1 positions companies expecting future growth from new investments (disruptive technology) and companies expecting future growth from existing investments (sustaining technology).[3]

Disruptive technologies typically enter the low end of the marketplace and eventually evolve to displace high-end competitors and their reigning technologies. Sony is a perfect example. Sony started as a tiny company that built portable, battery-powered transistor radios. The sound quality was poor, but customers were willing to overlook that for the convenience of portability. With the experience and revenue stream from the portables, Sony improved its technology to produce cheap, low-end transistor amplifiers that were suitable for home use and invested those revenues in improving the technology further, which produced still-better radios.[4]

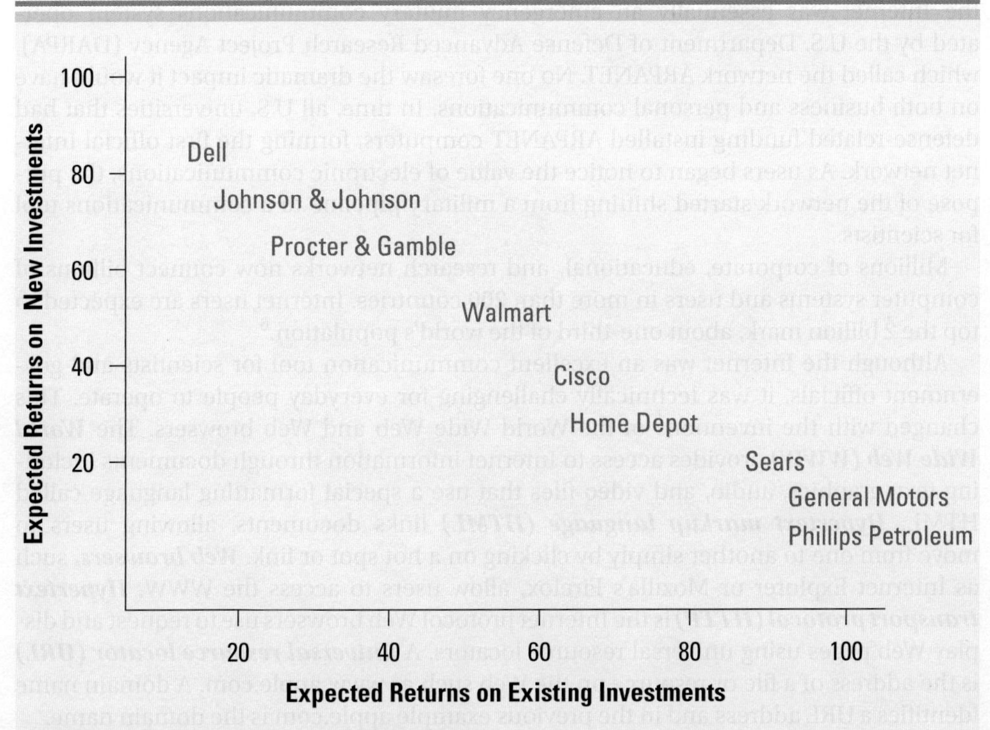

FIGURE 3.1

Disruptive and Sustaining Technologies

Source: Reprinted by permission of Harvard Business School Press. From *The Innovator's Dilemma*, by Clayton Christensen. Boston, MA. Copyright © by the Harvard Business School Publishing Corporation; all rights reserved.

The Innovator's Dilemma, a book by Clayton M. Christensen, discusses how established companies can take advantage of disruptive technologies without hindering existing relationships with customers, partners, and stakeholders. Xerox, IBM, Sears, and DEC all listened to existing customers, invested aggressively in technology, had their competitive antennae up, and still lost their market-dominant positions. They may have placed too much emphasis on satisfying customers' current needs, while neglecting new disruptive technology to meet customers' future needs and thus losing market share. Figure 3.2 highlights several companies that launched new businesses by capitalizing on disruptive technologies.[5]

The Internet and World Wide Web—The Ultimate Business Disruptors

The ***Internet*** is a massive network that connects computers all over the world and allows them to communicate with one another. Computers connected via the Internet can send and receive information including text, graphics, voice, video, and software. Originally

Company	Disruptive Technology
Apple	iPod, iPhone, iPad
Charles Schwab	Online brokerage
Hewlett-Packard	Microprocessor-based computers, ink-jet printers
IBM	Minicomputers; personal computers
Intel	Low-end microprocessors
Intuit	QuickBooks software; TurboTax software; Quicken software
Microsoft	Internet-based computing; operating system software; SQL and Access database software
Oracle	Database software
Quantum	3.5-inch disks
Sony	Transistor-based consumer electronics

FIGURE 3.2

Companies That Capitalized on Disruptive Technologies

Source: Reprinted by permission of Harvard Business School Press. From *The Innovator's Dilemma*, by Clayton Christensen. Boston, MA. Copyright © by the Harvard Business School Publishing Corporation; all rights reserved.

the Internet was essentially an emergency military communications system operated by the U.S. Department of Defense Advanced Research Project Agency (DARPA), which called the network ARPANET. No one foresaw the dramatic impact it would have on both business and personal communications. In time, all U.S. universities that had defense-related funding installed ARPANET computers, forming the first official Internet network. As users began to notice the value of electronic communications, the purpose of the network started shifting from a military pipeline to a communications tool for scientists.

Millions of corporate, educational, and research networks now connect billions of computer systems and users in more than 200 countries. Internet users are expected to top the 2 billion mark, about one-third of the world's population.[6]

Although the Internet was an excellent communication tool for scientists and government officials, it was technically challenging for everyday people to operate. This changed with the inventions of the World Wide Web and Web browsers. The ***World Wide Web (WWW)*** provides access to Internet information through documents including text, graphics, audio, and video files that use a special formatting language called HTML. ***Hypertext markup language (HTML)*** links documents, allowing users to move from one to another simply by clicking on a hot spot or link. ***Web browsers,*** such as Internet Explorer or Mozilla's Firefox, allow users to access the WWW. ***Hypertext transport protocol (HTTP)*** is the Internet protocol Web browsers use to request and display Web pages using universal resource locators. A ***universal resource locator (URL)*** is the address of a file or resource on the Web such as www.apple.com. A domain name identifies a URL address and in the previous example apple.com is the domain name.

Notice that the Internet and the World Wide Web are not synonymous. The WWW is just one part of the Internet, and its primary use is to correlate and disseminate information. The Internet includes the WWW and also other forms of communication systems such as email. Figure 3.3 lists the reasons for the massive growth of the WWW.[7]

Web 1.0: The Catalyst for Ebusiness

As people began learning about the WWW and the Internet, they understood that it enabled a company to communicate with anyone, anywhere, at anytime, creating a new way to participate in business. The competitive advantages for first movers would be enormous, thus spurring the beginning of the Web 1.0 Internet boom. ***Web 1.0*** is a term to refer to the World Wide Web during its first few years of operation between 1991 and 2003. ***Ecommerce*** is the buying and selling of goods and services over the Internet. Ecommerce refers only to online transactions. ***Ebusiness*** includes ecommerce along with all activities related to internal and external business operations such as servicing customer accounts, collaborating with partners, and exchanging real-time information. During Web 1.0, entrepreneurs began creating the first forms of ebusiness.

Ebusiness opened up a new marketplace for any company willing to move its business operations online. A ***paradigm shift*** occurs when a new radical form of business enters the market that reshapes the way companies and organizations behave. Ebusiness created a paradigm shift, transforming entire industries and changing enterprise-wide business processes that fundamentally rewrote traditional business rules. Deciding not to make the shift to ebusiness proved fatal for many companies (see Figure 3.4 for an overview of industries revamped by the disruption of ebusiness.)[8]

FIGURE 3.3
Reasons for Growth of the World Wide Web

The microcomputer revolution made it possible for an average person to own a computer.
Advancements in networking hardware, software, and media made it possible for business computers to be connected to larger networks at a minimal cost.
Browser software such as Microsoft's Internet Explorer and Netscape Navigator gave computer users an easy-to-use graphical interface to find, download, and display Web pages.
The speed, convenience, and low cost of email have made it an incredibly popular tool for business and personal communications.
Basic Web pages are easy to create and extremely flexible.

APPLY YOUR KNOWLEDGE

BUSINESS DRIVEN ETHICS AND SECURITY

Unethical Disruption

Did you know you can make a living naming things? Eli Altman has been naming things since he was six years old and has named more than 400 companies and brands while working for A Hundred Monkeys, a branding consulting company. Altman recently noticed an unfamiliar trend in the industry: nonsensical names such as Flickr, Socializr, Zoomr, Rowdii, Yuuguu, and Oooooc. Why are names like this becoming popular?

The reason is "domain squatting" or "cyber squatting," the practice of buying a domain to profit from a trademarked name. For example, if you wanted to start a business called Drink, chances are a domain squatter has already purchased drink.com and is just waiting for you to pay big bucks for the right to buy it. Domain squatting is illegal and outlawed under the 1999 Anticybersquatting Consumer Protection Act.[9]

Do you agree that domain squatting should be illegal? Why or why not? If you were starting a business and someone were squatting on your domain, what would you do?

FIGURE 3.4

Ebusiness Disruption of Traditional Industries

Industry	Business Changes Due to Technology
Auto	AutoTrader.com is the world's largest used-car marketplace, listing millions of cars from both private owners and dealers. AutoTrader.com actually helps to increase used-car dealer's business as it drives millions of qualified leads (potential used-car buyers) to participating automotive dealers and private sellers.
Publishing	With the Internet, anyone can publish online content. Traditionally, publishers screened many authors and manuscripts and selected those that had the best chances of succeeding. Lulu.com turned this model around by providing self-publishing along with print-on-demand capabilities.
Education and Training	Continuing medical education is costly, and just keeping up-to-date with advances often requires taking training courses and traveling to conferences. Now continuing education in many fields is moving online, and by 2016 over 50 percent of doctors will be building their skills through online learning. Companies such as Cisco save millions by moving training to the Internet.
Entertainment	The music industry was hit hard by ebusiness, and online music traders such as iTunes average billions of annual downloads. Unable to compete with online music, the majority of record stores closed. The next big entertainment industry to feel the effects of ebusiness will be the multibillion-dollar movie business. Video rental stores are closing their doors as they fail to compete with online streaming and home rental delivery companies such as Netflix.
Financial Services	Nearly every public efinance company makes money, with online mortgage service Lending Tree leading the pack. Processing online mortgage applications is over 50 percent cheaper for customers.
Retail	Forrester Research predicts ebusiness retail sales will grow at a 10 percent annual growth rate through 2014. It forecasts U.S. online retail sales will be nearly $250 billion, up from $155 billion in 2009. Online retail sales were recently up 11 percent, compared to 2.5 percent for all retail sales.
Travel	Travel site Expedia.com is now the biggest leisure-travel agency, with higher profit margins than even American Express. The majority of travel agencies closed as a direct result of ebusiness.

LO 3.2: **Describe Web 1.0 along with ebusiness and its associated advantages.**

ADVANTAGES OF EBUSINESS

Both individuals and organizations have embraced ebusiness to enhance productivity, maximize convenience, and improve communications. Companies today need to deploy a comprehensive ebusiness strategy, and business students need to understand its advantages, outlined in Figure 3.5. Let's look at each.

Expanding Global Reach

Easy access to real-time information is a primary benefit of ebusiness. ***Information richness*** refers to the depth and breadth of details contained in a piece of textual, graphic, audio, or video information. ***Information reach*** measures the number of people a firm can communicate with all over the world. Buyers need information richness to make informed purchases, and sellers need information reach to properly market and differentiate themselves from the competition.

Ebusinesses operate 24 hours a day, 7 days a week. This availability directly reduces transaction costs, since consumers no longer have to spend a lot of time researching purchases or traveling great distances to make them. The faster delivery cycle for online sales helps strengthen customer relationships, improving customer satisfaction and ultimately sales.

A firm's website can be the focal point of a cost-effective communications and marketing strategy. Promoting products online allows the company to precisely target its customers whether they are local or around the globe. A physical location is restricted by size and limited to those customers who can get there, while an online store has a global marketplace with customers and information seekers already waiting in line.

Opening New Markets

Ebusiness is perfect for increasing niche-product sales. ***Mass customization*** is the ability of an organization to tailor its products or services to the customers' specifications. For example, customers can order M&M's in special colors or with customized sayings such as "Marry Me." ***Personalization*** occurs when a company knows enough about a customer's likes and dislikes that it can fashion offers more likely to appeal to that person, say by tailoring its website to individuals or groups based on profile information, demographics, or prior transactions. Amazon uses personalization to create a unique portal for each of its customers.

Chris Anderson, editor-in-chief of *Wired* magazine, describes niche-market ebusiness strategies as capturing the ***long tail,*** referring to the tail of a typical sales curve. This strategy demonstrates how niche products can have viable and profitable business models when selling via ebusiness. In traditional sales models, a store is limited by shelf space when selecting products to sell. For this reason, store owners typically purchase products that will be wanted or needed by masses, and the store is stocked with broad products as there is not room on the shelf for niche products that only a few customers might purchase. Ebusinesses such as Amazon and eBay eliminated the shelf-space dilemma and were able to offer infinite products.

FIGURE 3.5
Ebusiness Advantages

Ebusiness Advantages
• Expanding global reach
• Opening new markets
• Reducing costs
• Improving operations
• Improving effectiveness

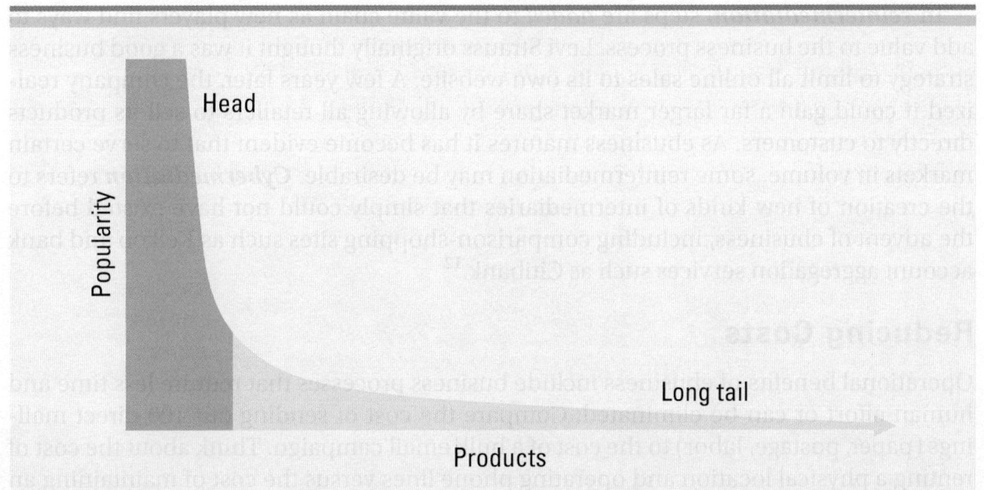

FIGURE 3.6
The Long Tail

Source: Reprinted with permission of Chris Anderson.

Netflix offers an excellent example of the long tail. Let's assume that an average Blockbuster store maintains 3,000 movies in its inventory, whereas Netflix, without physical shelf limitations, can maintain 100,000 movies in its inventory. Looking at sales data, the majority of Blockbuster's revenue comes from new releases that are rented daily, whereas older selections are rented only a few times a month and don't repay the cost of keeping them in stock. Thus Blockbuster's sales tail ends at title 3,000 (see Figure 3.6) However, Netflix, with no physical limitations, can extend its tail beyond 100,000 (and with streaming video perhaps 200,000). By extending its tail, Netflix increases sales, even if a title is rented only a few times.[10]

Intermediaries are agents, software, or businesses that provide a trading infrastructure to bring buyers and sellers together. The introduction of ebusiness brought about ***disintermediation,*** which occurs when a business sells directly to the customer online and cuts out the intermediary (see Figure 3.7). This business strategy lets the company shorten the order process and add value with reduced costs or a more responsive and efficient service. The disintermediation of the travel agent occurred as people began to book their own vacations online, often at a cheaper rate. At Lulu.com anyone can publish and sell print-on-demand books, online music, and custom calendars, making the publisher obsolete.[11]

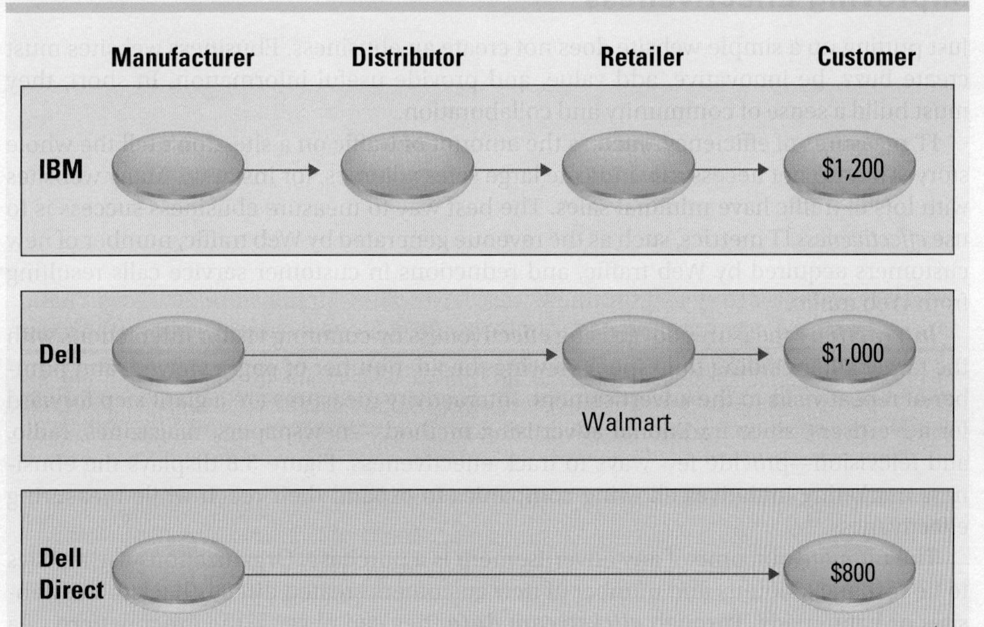

FIGURE 3.7
Business Value of Disintermediation

The more intermediaries that are cut from the distribution chain, the lower the product price. When Dell decided to sell its PCs through Walmart many were surprised, because Dell's direct-to-customer sales model was the competitive advantage that had kept Dell the market leader for years.

In ***reintermediation,*** steps are *added* to the value chain as new players find ways to add value to the business process. Levi Strauss originally thought it was a good business strategy to limit all online sales to its own website. A few years later, the company realized it could gain a far larger market share by allowing all retailers to sell its products directly to customers. As ebusiness matures it has become evident that to serve certain markets in volume, some reintermediation may be desirable. ***Cybermediation*** refers to the creation of new kinds of intermediaries that simply could not have existed before the advent of ebusiness, including comparison-shopping sites such as Kelkoo and bank account aggregation services such as Citibank.[12]

Reducing Costs

Operational benefits of ebusiness include business processes that require less time and human effort or can be eliminated. Compare the cost of sending out 100 direct mailings (paper, postage, labor) to the cost of a bulk email campaign. Think about the cost of renting a physical location and operating phone lines versus the cost of maintaining an online site. Switching to an ebusiness model can eliminate many traditional costs associated with communicating by substituting systems, such as Live Help, that let customers chat live with support or sales staff.

Online air travel reservations cost less than those booked over the telephone. Online ordering also offers the possibility of merging a sales order system with order fulfillment and delivery so customers can check the progress of their orders at all times. Ebusinesses can also inexpensively attract new customers with innovative marketing and retain present customers with improved service and support.[13]

One of the most exciting benefits of ebusiness is its low start-up costs. Today, anyone can start an ebusiness with just a website and a great product or service. Even a dog-walking operation can benefit from being an ebusiness.

Improving Operations

Ebusiness has had some of its biggest impacts on customer service. Communication is often faster, more available, and more effective, encouraging customers to learn more about the product. Customers can often help themselves, using the content richness only a website can provide, and they can both shop and pay online without having to leave the house. Companies can also use email, special messages, and private password access to special areas for top customers.

Improving Effectiveness

Just putting up a simple website does not create an ebusiness. Ebusiness websites must create buzz, be innovative, add value, and provide useful information. In short, they must build a sense of community and collaboration.

IT measures of efficiency, such as the amount of traffic on a site, don't tell the whole story. They do not necessarily indicate large sales volumes, for instance. Many websites with lots of traffic have minimal sales. The best way to measure ebusiness success is to use *effectiveness* IT metrics, such as the revenue generated by Web traffic, number of new customers acquired by Web traffic, and reductions in customer service calls resulting from Web traffic.

Interactivity measures advertising effectiveness by counting visitor interactions with the target ad, including time spent viewing the ad, number of pages viewed, and number of repeat visits to the advertisement. Interactivity measures are a giant step forward for advertisers, since traditional advertising methods—newspapers, magazines, radio, and television—provide few ways to track effectiveness. Figure 3.8 displays the ebusiness marketing initiatives allowing companies to expand their reach while measuring effectiveness.[14]

The ultimate outcome of any advertisement is a purchase. Organizations use metrics to tie revenue amounts and number of new customers created directly back to the websites or banner ads. Through ***clickstream data*** they can observe the exact pattern of a consumer's navigation through a site. Figure 3.9 displays different types of clickstream

Marketing via Ebusiness
An **associate (affiliate) program** allows a business to generate commissions or referral fees when a customer visiting its website clicks on a link to another merchant's website. For example, if a customer to a company website clicks on a banner ad to another vendor's website, the company will receive a referral fee or commission when the customer performs the desired action, typically making a purchase or completing a form.
A **banner ad** is a box running across a website that advertises the products and services of another business, usually another ebusiness. The banner generally contains a link to the advertiser's website. Advertisers can track how often customers click on a banner ad resulting in a click-through to their website. Often the cost of the banner ad depends on the number of customers who click on the banner ad. Web-based advertising services can track the number of times users click the banner, generating statistics that enable advertisers to judge whether the advertising fees are worth paying. Banner ads are like living, breathing classified ads. Tracking the number of banner ad clicks is an excellent way to understand the effectiveness of the ad on the website.
A **click-through** is a count of the number of people who visit one site and click on an advertisement that takes them to the site of the advertiser. Tracking effectiveness based on click-throughs guarantees exposure to target ads; however, it does not guarantee that the visitor liked the ad, spent any substantial time viewing the ad, or was satisfied with the information contained in the ad.
A **cookie** is a small file deposited on a hard drive by a website containing information about customers and their browsing activities. Cookies allow websites to record the comings and goings of customers, usually without their knowledge or consent.
A **pop-up ad** is a small Web page containing an advertisement that appears outside of the current website loaded in the browser. A pop-under ad is a form of a pop-up ad that users do not see until they close the current Web browser screen.
Viral marketing is a technique that induces websites or users to pass on a marketing message to other websites or users, creating exponential growth in the message's visibility and effect. One example of successful viral marketing is Hotmail, which promotes its service and its own advertisers' messages in every user's email notes. Viral marketing encourages users of a product or service supplied by an ebusiness to encourage friends to join. Viral marketing is a word-of-mouth type advertising program.

FIGURE 3.8

Marketing Received Tremendous Benefits from Ebusiness

metrics, and Figure 3.10 provides definitions of common metrics based on clickstream data. To interpret such data properly, managers try to benchmark against other companies. For instance, consumers seem to visit their preferred websites regularly, even checking back multiple times during a given session.[15]

EBUSINESS MODELS

LO 3.3: Compare the four categories of ebusiness models.

A ***business model*** is a plan that details how a company creates, delivers, and generates revenues. Some models are quite simple: A company produces a good or service and sells it to customers. If the company is successful, sales exceed costs and the company generates a profit. Other models are less straightforward, and sometimes it's not immediately clear who makes money and how much. Radio and network television are broadcast free to anyone with a receiver, for instance; advertisers pay the costs of programming.

The majority of online business activities consist of the exchange of products and services either between businesses or between businesses and consumers. An ***ebusiness model*** is a plan that details how a company creates, delivers, and generates revenues

Types of Clickstream Data Metrics
The number of page views (i.e., the number of times a particular page has been presented to a visitor).
The pattern of websites visited, including most frequent exit page and most frequent prior website.
Length of stay on the website.
Dates and times of visits.
Number of registrations filled out per 100 visitors.
Number of abandoned registrations.
Demographics of registered visitors.
Number of customers with shopping carts.
Number of abandoned shopping carts.

FIGURE 3.9

Clickstream Data Metrics

METRICS MEASURING WEBSITE SUCCESS	
Website Visit Metrics	
Stickiness (visit duration time)	The length of time a visitor spends on a website.
Raw visit depth (total Web pages exposure per session)	The total number of pages a visitor is exposed to during a single visit to a website.
Visit depth (total unique Web pages exposure per session)	The total number of unique pages a visitor is exposed to during a single visit to a website.
Website Visitor Metrics	
Unidentified visitor	A visitor is an individual who visits a website. An "unidentified visitor" means that no information about that visitor is available.
Unique visitor	A unique visitor is one who can be recognized and counted only once within a given period of time.
Identified visitor	An ID is available that allows a user to be tracked across multiple visits to a website.
Website Hit Metrics	
Hits	When visitors reach a website, their computer sends a request to the site's computer server to begin displaying pages. Each element of a requested page is recorded by the website's server log file as a "hit."

FIGURE 3.10
Website Metrics

on the Internet. Ebusiness models fall into one of the four categories: (1) business-to-business, (2) business-to-consumer, (3) consumer-to-business, and (4) consumer-to-consumer (see Figure 3.11).

Business-to-Business (B2B)

Business-to-business (B2B) applies to businesses buying from and selling to each other over the Internet. Examples include medical billing service, software sales and licensing, and virtual assistant businesses. B2B relationships represent 80 percent of all online business and are more complex with greater security needs than the other types.

Electronic marketplaces, or emarketplaces, are interactive business communities providing a central market where multiple buyers and sellers can engage in ebusiness activities. By tightening and automating the relationship between the two parties, they create structures for conducting commercial exchange, consolidating supply chains, and creating new sales channels.

Business-to-Consumer (B2C)

Business-to-consumer (B2C) applies to any business that sells its products or services directly to consumers online. Carfax offers car buyers detailed histories of used vehicles for a fee. An ***eshop,*** sometimes referred to as an ***estore*** or ***etailer,*** is an online version of

FIGURE 3.11
Ebusiness Models

Ebusiness Term	Definition
Business-to-business (B2B)	Applies to businesses buying from and selling to each other over the Internet.
Business-to-consumer (B2C)	Applies to any business that sells its products or services to consumers over the Internet.
Consumer-to-business (C2B)	Applies to any consumer that sells a product or service to a business over the Internet.
Consumer-to-consumer (C2C)	Applies to sites primarily offering goods and services to assist consumers interacting with each other over the Internet.

	Business	Consumer
Business	B2B	B2C
Consumer	C2B	C2C

Brick-and-Mortar Business
A business that operates in a physical store without an Internet presence.
Example: T.J. Maxx

Click-and-Mortar Business
A business that operates in a physical store and on the Internet.
Example: Barnes & Noble

Pure-Play (Virtual) Business
A business that operates on the Internet only without a physical store.
Example: Google

FIGURE 3.12

Forms of Business-to-Consumer Operations

a retail store where customers can shop at any hour. It can be an extension of an existing store such as The Gap or operate only online such as Amazon.com. There are three ways to operate as a B2C: brick-and-mortar, click-and-mortar, and pure play (see Figure 3.12).

Consumer-to-Business (C2B)

Consumer-to-business (C2B) applies to any consumer who sells a product or service to a business on the Internet. One example is customers of Priceline.com, who set their own prices for items such as airline tickets or hotel rooms and wait for a seller to decide whether to supply them. The demand for C2B ebusiness will increase over the next few years due to customers' desire for greater convenience and lower prices.

Consumer-to-Consumer (C2C)

Consumer-to-consumer (C2C) applies to customers offering goods and services to each other on the Internet. A good example of a C2C is an auction where buyers and sellers solicit consecutive bids from each other and prices are determined dynamically. EBay, the Internet's most successful C2C online auction website, links like-minded buyers and sellers for a small commission. Other types of online auctions include forward auctions where sellers market to many buyers and the highest bid wins, and reverse auctions where buyers select goods and services from the seller with the lowest bid.

Ebusiness Forms and Revenue-Generating Strategies

As more and more companies began jumping on the ebusiness bandwagon new forms of ebusiness began to emerge (see Figure 3.13). Many of the new forms of ebusiness went to market without clear strategies on how they were going to generate revenue. Google is an excellent example of an ebusiness that did not figure out a way to generate profits until many years after its launch.[16]

Google's primary line of business is its search engine; however, the company does not generate revenue from people using its site to search the Internet. It generates revenue from the marketers and advertisers that pay to place their ads on the site. About 200 million times each day, people from all over the world access Google to perform searches. AdWords, a part of the Google site, allows advertisers to bid on common search terms. The advertisers simply enter in the keywords they want to bid on and the maximum amounts they want to pay per click per day. Google then determines a price and a search ranking for those keywords based on how much other advertisers are willing to pay for

FIGURE 3.13

Ebusiness Forms

Form	Description	Examples
Content providers	Generate revenues by providing digital content such as news, music, photos, or videos.	Netflix.com, iTunes.com, CNN.com
Infomediaries	Provide specialized information on behalf of producers of goods and services and their potential customers	Edmunds.com, BizRate.com, Bloomberg.com, Zillow.com
Online marketplaces	Bring together buyers and sellers of products and services.	Amazon.com, eBay.com, Priceline.com
Portals	Operate central website for users to access specialized content and other services.	Google.com, Yahoo.com, MSN.com
Service providers	Provide services such as photo sharing, video sharing, online backup and storage.	Flickr.com Mapquest.com YouTube.com
Transaction brokers	Process online sales transactions.	Etrade.com, Charlesschwab.com, Fidelity.com

the same terms. Pricing for keywords can range from 5 cents to $10 a click. Paid search is the ultimate in targeted advertising because consumers type in exactly what they want. A general search term such as *tropical vacation* costs less than a more specific term such as *Hawaiian vacation.* Whoever bids the most for a term appears in a sponsored advertisement link either at the top or along the side of the search-results page.[17]

Ebusinesses must have a revenue model, or a model for making money. For instance, will it accept advertising, or sell subscriptions or licensing rights? Figure 3.14 lists the different benefits and challenges of various ebusiness revenue models.[18]

FIGURE 3.14

Ebusiness Revenue Models

Ebusiness Revenue Model	Benefits	Challenges
Advertising fees	■ Well-targeted advertisements can be perceived as value-added content by trading participants. ■ Easy to implement	■ Limited revenue potential ■ Overdone or poorly targeted advertisements can be disturbing elements on the website.
License fees	■ Creates incentives to do many transactions ■ Customization and back-end integration lead to lock-in of participants.	■ Up-front fee is a barrier to entry for participants. ■ Price differentiation is complicated.
Subscription fees	■ Creates incentives to do transactions ■ Price can be differentiated. ■ Possibility to build additional revenue from new user groups	■ Fixed fee is a barrier to entry for participants.
Transaction fees	■ Can be directly tied to savings (both process and price savings) ■ Important revenue source when high level of liquidity (transaction volume) is reached	■ If process savings are not completely visible, use of the system is discouraged (incentive to move transactions offline). ■ Transaction fees likely to decrease with time
Value-added services fees	■ Service offering can be differentiated. ■ Price can be differentiated. ■ Possibility to build additional revenue from established and new user groups (third parties)	■ Cumbersome process for customers to continually evaluate new services

APPLY YOUR KNOWLEDGE

BUSINESS DRIVEN START-UP

Go for It!

Rich Aberman and Bill Clerico found themselves in the difficult position of deciding whether to graduate from college and pursue their dreams of building their own company or heading off to graduate school and entry-level jobs. Aberman choose to head off to law school while Clerico choose an entry-level job as an investment banker. After several months they both decided that it was now or never if they truly wanted to build their dream business as they were both becoming more and more comfortable with their new lifestyles. Obviously, it would become harder and harder to leave their comfortable positions for the uncertainty of being an entrepreneur.

Aberman left law school and Clerico quit his job and the pair cofounded WePay, an online funds management company. WePay allows individuals and groups all over the world to establish an account and collect money in a variety of ways—from paper checks to credit cards—and then use a debit card to spend the money in the account. WePay collects transaction fees ranging from 50 cents to 3 percent of credit card payments. Luckily, their decision paid off and a little over a year after founding the company, Aberman and Clerico had raised nearly $2 million from high-profile Internet investors. WePay boasts several thousand customers ranging from sports teams to fraternities to groups of roommates managing rent and utilities.[19]

Have you thought of starting your own business? What are the advantages and challenges associated with building your own business early in your career? Research the Internet and find three examples of highly successful college start-ups. What do you think were the primary reasons the start-ups found success? What are the advantages of starting your own business while you are still in college? What are a few of the challenges you might face if you choose to start your own business today?

EBUSINESS TOOLS FOR CONNECTING AND COMMUNICATING

LO 3.4: **Describe the six ebusiness tools for connecting and communicating.**

As firms began to move online, more MIS tools were created to support ebusiness processes and requirements. The tools supporting and driving ebusiness are highlighted in Figure 3.15 and covered below in detail.

Email

Email, short for electronic mail, is the exchange of digital messages over the Internet. No longer do business professionals have to wait for the mail to receive important documents as email single-handedly increased the speed of business by allowing the transfer of documents with the same speed as the telephone. Its chief business advantage is the ability to inform and communicate with many people simultaneously, immediately, and with ease. There are no time or place constraints, and users can check, send, and view emails whenever they require.

An ***Internet service provider (ISP)*** is a company that provides access to the Internet for a monthly fee. Major ISPs in the United States include AOL, AT&T, Comcast, Earthlink, and Netzero, as well as thousands of local ISPs including regional telephone companies.

Instant Messaging

Real-time communication occurs when a system updates information at the same rate it receives it. Email was a great advancement over traditional communication methods

FIGURE 3.15
Ebusiness Tools

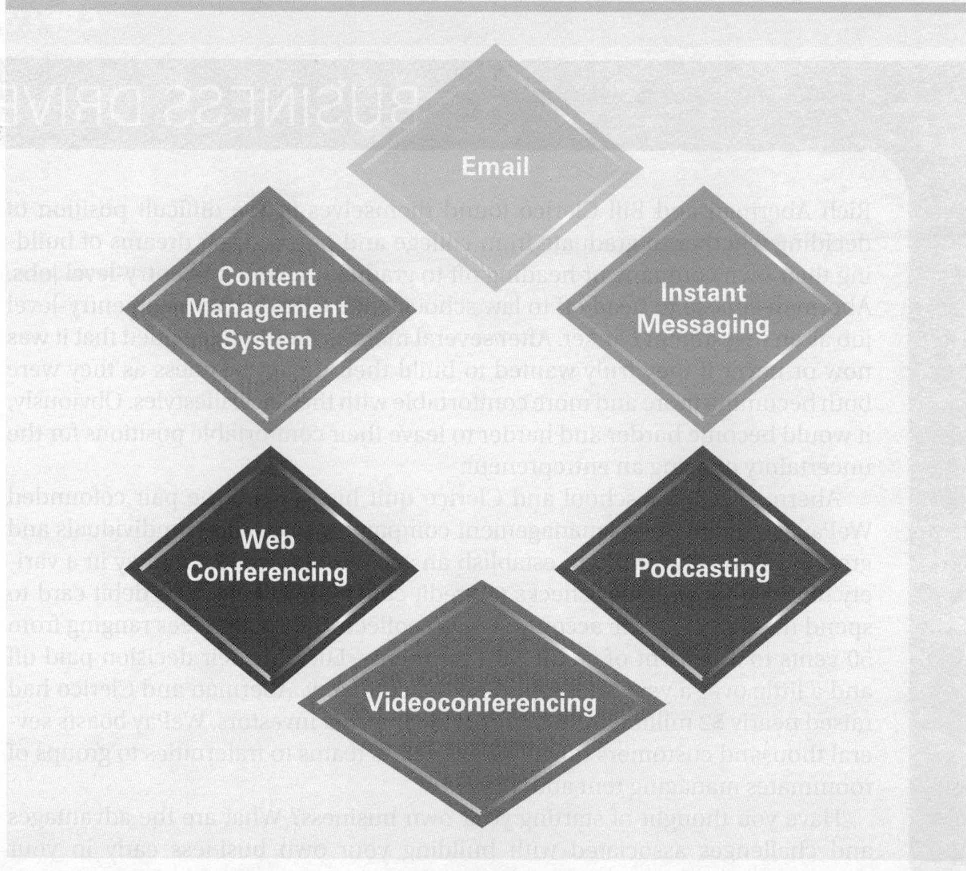

such as the U.S. mail, but it did not operate in real time. ***Instant messaging (IMing)*** is a service that enables instant or real-time communication between people. Businesses immediately saw what they could do:

- Answer simple questions quickly and easily.
- Resolve questions or problems immediately.
- Transmit messages as fast as naturally flowing conversation.
- Easily hold simultaneous IM sessions with multiple people.
- Eliminate long-distance phone charges.
- Quickly identifying which employees are at their computers.

Podcasting

Podcasting converts an audio broadcast to a digital music player. Podcasts can increase marketing reach and build customer loyalty. Companies use podcasts as marketing communication channels discussing everything from corporate strategies to detailed product overviews. The senior executive team can share weekly or monthly podcasts featuring important issues or expert briefings on new technical or marketing developments.

Videoconferencing

A videoconference allows people at two or more locations to interact via two-way video and audio transmissions simultaneously as well as share documents, data, computer displays, and whiteboards. Point-to-point videoconferences connect two people, and multipoint conferences connect more than two people at multiple locations.

Videoconferences can increase productivity because users participate without leaving their offices. It can improve communication and relationships, because participants see each other's facial expressions and body language, both important aspects of communication that are lost with a basic telephone call or email. It also reduces travel expenses, a big win for firms facing economic challenges. Of course, nothing can replace meeting someone face-to-face and shaking hands, but videoconferencing offers a viable and cost-effective alternative.

Web Conferencing

Web conferencing, or a ***webinar,*** blends videoconferencing with document sharing and allows the user to deliver a presentation over the Web to a group of geographically dispersed participants. Regardless of the type of hardware or software the attendees are running, every participant can see what is on anyone else's screen. Schools use Web conferencing tools such as Illuminate Live to deliver lectures to students, and businesses use tools such as WebEx to demonstrate products. Web conferencing is not quite like being there, but professionals can accomplish more sitting at their desks than in an airport waiting to make travel connections.

Content Management Systems

In the fourth century BC Aristotle catalogued the natural world according to a systematic organization, and the ancient library at Alexandria was reportedly organized by subject, connecting like information with like. Today ***content management systems (CMS)*** help companies manage the creation, storage, editing, and publication of their website content. CMSs are user-friendly; most include Web-based publishing, search, navigation, and indexing to organize information; and they let users with little or no technical expertise make website changes.

A search is typically carried out by entering a keyword or phrase (query) into a text field and clicking a button or a hyperlink. Navigation facilitates movement from one Web page to another. Content management systems play a crucial role in getting site visitors to view more than just the home page. If navigation choices are unclear, visitors may hit the "Back" button on their first (and final) visit to a website. One rule of thumb to remember is that each time a user has to click to find search information, there is a 50 percent chance the user will leave the website instead. A key principle of good website design, therefore, is to keep the number of clicks to a minimum.

Taxonomy is the scientific classification of organisms into groups based on similarities of structure or origin. Taxonomies are also used for indexing the content on the website into categories and subcategories of topics. For example, car is a subtype of vehicle. Every car is a vehicle, but not every vehicle is a car; some vehicles are vans, buses, and trucks. Taxonomy terms are arranged so that narrower/more specific/"child" terms fall under broader/more generic/"parent" terms. ***Information architecture*** is the set of ideas about how all information in a given context should be organized. Many companies hire information architects to create their website taxonomies. A well-planned taxonomy ensures search and navigation are easy and user-friendly. If the taxonomy is confusing, the site will soon fail.

THE CHALLENGES OF EBUSINESS

LO 3.5: Identify the four challenges associated with ebusiness.

Although the benefits of ebusiness are enticing, developing, deploying, and managing ebusiness systems is not always easy. Figure 3.16 lists the challenges facing ebusiness.[20]

Identifying Limited Market Segments

The main challenge of ebusiness is the lack of growth in some sectors due to product or service limitations. The online food sector has not grown in sales, in part because food products are perishable and consumers prefer to buy them at the supermarket as needed. Other sectors with limited ebusiness appeal include fragile or consumable goods and highly sensitive or confidential businesses such as government agencies.

FIGURE 3.16

Challenges Facing Ebusiness

Managing Consumer Trust

Trust in the ebusiness exchange deserves special attention. The physical separation of buyer and seller, the physical separation of buyer and merchandise, and customer perceptions about the risk of doing business online provide unique challenges. Internet marketers must develop a trustworthy relationship to make that initial sale and generate customer loyalty. A few ways to build trust when working online include being accessible and available to communicate in person with your customers; using customers' testimonials that link to your client website or to provide their contact information; accepting legitimate forms of payment such as credit cards.

Ensuring Consumer Protection

An organization that wants to dominate with superior customer service as a competitive advantage must not only serve but also protect its customers, guarding them against unsolicited goods and communication, illegal or harmful goods, insufficient information about goods and suppliers, invasion of privacy and misuse of personal information, and online fraud. System security, however, must not make ebusiness websites inflexible or difficult to use.

Adhering to Taxation Rules

Many believe that U.S. tax policy should provide a level playing field for traditional retail businesses, mail-order companies, and online merchants. Yet the Internet marketplace remains mostly free of traditional forms of sales tax, partly because ecommerce law is vaguely defined and differs from state to state. For now, companies that operate online must obey a patchwork of rules about which customers are subject to sales tax on their purchases and which are not.

section 3.2 WEB 2.0: BUSINESS 2.0

LEARNING OUTCOMES

3.6 Explain Web 2.0, and identify its four characteristics.

3.7 Explain how Business 2.0 is helping communities network and collaborate.

3.8 Describe the three Business 2.0 tools for collaborating.

3.9 Explain the three challenges associated with Business 2.0.

3.10 Describe Web 3.0 and the next generation of online business.

BUSINESS DRIVEN GLOBALIZATION

Collaborating for Nonprofits—Kiva

Kiva's mission is to connect people through lending for the sake of alleviating poverty. Kiva is a micro-lending online nonprofit organization that enables individuals to lend directly to entrepreneurs throughout the world. If you want to participate in Kiva you simply browse the website (www.kiva.org) and choose an entrepreneur that interests you, make a loan, then track your entrepreneur for the next 6 to 12 months while he or she builds the business and makes the funds to repay the loan. When the loan is up you can relend the money to someone else who is in need.[21]

Kiva is an excellent example of blending ethics and information technology. How is Kiva operating differently than traditional nonprofits? What are the risks associated with investing in Kiva? When you invest in Kiva you run three primary risks: entrepreneur risk, local field partner risk, and country risk. Analyze each of these risks for potential unethical issues that might arise when donating to Kiva.

WEB 2.0: ADVANTAGES OF BUSINESS 2.0

LO 3.6: Explain Web 2.0, and identify its four characteristics.

In the mid-1990s the stock market reached an all-time high as companies took advantage of ebusiness and Web 1.0, and many believed the Internet was the wave of the future. When new online businesses began failing to meet earning expectations, however, the bubble burst. Some then believed the ebusiness boom was over, but they could not have been more wrong.

Web 2.0 (or ***Business 2.0***) is the next generation of Internet use—a more mature, distinctive communications platform characterized by new qualities such as collaboration, sharing, and free. Business 2.0 encourages user participation and the formation of communities that contribute to the content. In Business 2.0, technical skills are no longer required to use and publish information to the World Wide Web, eliminating entry barriers for online business.

Traditional companies tended to view technology as a tool required to perform a process or activity, and employees picked up information by walking through the office or hanging out around the water cooler. Business 2.0 technologies provide a virtual environment that, for many new employees, is just as vibrant and important as the physical environment. Figure 3.17 highlights the common characteristics of Business 2.0.[22]

Content Sharing Through Open Sourcing

An ***open system*** consists of nonproprietary hardware and software based on publicly known standards that allows third parties to create add-on products to plug into or interoperate with the system. Thousands of hardware devices and software applications created and sold by third-party vendors interoperate with computers, such as iPods, drawing software, and mice.

Source code contains instructions written by a programmer specifying the actions to be performed by computer software. ***Open source*** refers to any software whose source code is made available free (not on a fee or licensing basis as in ebusiness) for any third party to review and modify. Business 2.0 is capitalizing on open source software. Mozilla, for example, offers its Firefox Web browser and Thunderbird email software free. Mozilla believes the Internet is a public resource that must remain open and accessible to all; it continuously develops free products by bringing together thousands of dedicated volunteers from around the world. Mozilla's Firefox now holds over 20 percent of the browser

FIGURE 3.17
Characteristics of Business 2.0

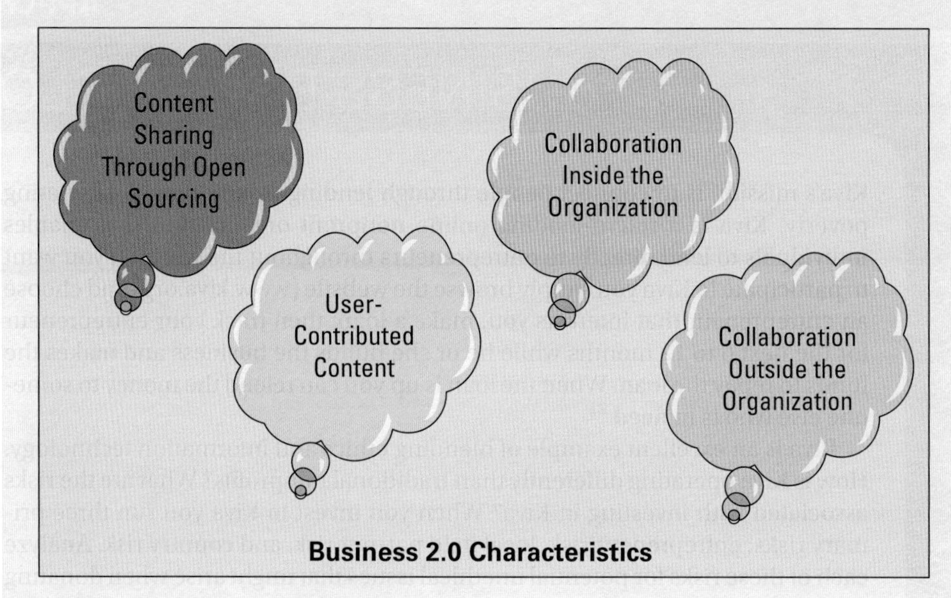

market and is quickly becoming a threat to Microsoft's Internet Explorer. How do open source software companies generate revenues? Many people are still awaiting an answer to this very important question.[23]

User-Contributed Content

Ebusiness was characterized by a few companies or users posting content for the masses. Business 2.0 is characterized by the masses posting content for the masses. ***User-contributed content*** (or ***user-generated content***) is created and updated by many users for many users. Websites such as Flickr, Wikipedia, and YouTube, for example, move control of online media from the hands of leaders to the hands of users. Netflix and Amazon both use user-generated content to drive their recommendation tools, and websites such as Yelp use customer reviews to express opinions on products and services. Companies are embracing user-generated content to help with everything from marketing to product development and quality assurance.

One of the most popular forms of user-generated content is a ***reputation system,*** where buyers post feedback on sellers. EBay buyers voluntarily comment on the quality of service, their satisfaction with the item traded, and promptness of shipping. Sellers comment about prompt payment from buyers or respond to comments left by the buyer. Companies ranging from Amazon to restaurants are using reputation systems to improve quality and enhance customer satisfaction.

Collaboration Inside the Organization

A ***collaboration system*** is a set of tools that supports the work of teams or groups by facilitating the sharing and flow of information. Business 2.0's collaborative mind-set generates more information faster from a wider audience. ***Collective intelligence*** is collaborating and tapping into the core knowledge of all employees, partners, and customers. Knowledge can be a real competitive advantage for an organization. The most common form of collective intelligence found inside the organization is ***knowledge management (KM),*** which involves capturing, classifying, evaluating, retrieving, and sharing information assets in a way that provides context for effective decisions and actions. The primary objective of knowledge management is to be sure that a company's knowledge of facts, sources of information, and solutions are readily available to all employees whenever it is needed. A ***knowledge management system (KMS)*** supports the capturing, organization, and dissemination of knowledge (i.e., know-how) throughout an organization. KMS can distribute an organization's knowledge base by interconnecting people and digitally gathering their expertise.

A great example of a knowledge worker is a golf caddie. Golf caddies give advice such as, "The rain makes the third hole play 10 yards shorter." If a golf caddie is good and gives accurate advice it can lead to big tips. Collaborating with other golf caddies can provide bigger tips for all. How can knowledge management make this happen? Caddies could be rewarded for sharing course knowledge by receiving prizes for sharing knowledge. The course manager could compile all of the tips and publish a course notebook for distribution to all caddies. The goal of a knowledge management system is that everyone wins. Here the caddies make bigger tips and golfers improve their play by benefiting from the collaborative experiences of the caddies, and the course owners win as business increases.

KM has assumed greater urgency in American business over the past few years as millions of baby boomers prepare to retire. When they punch out for the last time, the knowledge they gleaned about their jobs, companies, and industries during their long careers will walk out with them—unless companies take measures to retain their insights.

Explicit and Tacit Knowledge Not all information is valuable. Individuals must determine what information qualifies as intellectual and knowledge-based assets. In general, intellectual and knowledge-based assets fall into one of two categories: explicit or tacit. As a rule, ***explicit knowledge*** consists of anything that can be documented, archived, and codified, often with the help of IT. Examples of explicit knowledge are assets such as patents, trademarks, business plans, marketing research, and customer lists. ***Tacit knowledge*** is the knowledge contained in people's heads. The challenge inherent in tacit knowledge is figuring out how to recognize, generate, share, and manage knowledge that resides in people's heads. While information technology in the form of email, instant messaging, and related technologies can help facilitate the dissemination of tacit knowledge, identifying it in the first place can be a major obstacle.

Collaboration Outside the Organization

The most common form of collective intelligence found outside the organization is ***crowdsourcing,*** which refers to the wisdom of the crowd. The idea that collective intelligence is greater than the sum of its individual parts has been around for a long time (see Figure 3.18). With Business 2.0 the ability to efficiently tap into its power is emerging. For many years organizations believed that good ideas came from the top. CEOs

FIGURE 3.18

Crowdsourcing: The Crowd Is Smarter Than the Individual

APPLY YOUR KNOWLEDGE

BUSINESS DRIVEN INNOVATION

Is It Web 1.0 or Web 2.0?

Deciding whether a given site is Web 1.0 or Web 2.0 is not as straightforward as it appears. Websites do not have version numbers and many are dynamic enough to be in "permanent beta testing." Facebook and MySpace are good Web 2.0 examples, primarily due to their social networking functions and their reliance on user-generated content. Some sites are easy to identify as Web 1.0 in their approach: Craigslist, for example, emulates an email list server and has no public user profiles or dynamic pages. Many other sites are hard to categorize. Amazon.com launched in the mid-1990s and has gradually added features over time. The principal content (product descriptions) is not user-created, but much of the site's value is added by user reviews and ratings. Profiles of users do exist, but social features such as friend links, although present, are not widely adopted.[24]

Review the following websites and categorize them as Web 1.0, Web 2.0, or both. Be sure to justify your answer with the characteristics that classify the website as 1.0, 2.0, or both. Why would certain types of businesses choose to remain Web 1.0 and not offer collaboration or open source capabilities?

- www.ebay.com; www.amazon.com; www.facebook.com; www.foursquare.com; www.paypal.com; www.vatican.va; www.twitter.com; www.irs.gov; www.google.com; www.youtube.com.
- For the following be sure to use your personal websites as references. www.Your college's website.com; www.Your Visa Card.com; www.Your Bank.com

collaborated only with the heads of sales and marketing, the quality assurance expert, or the road warrior salesman. The organization chart governed who should work with whom and how far up the chain of command a suggestion or idea would travel. With Buisness 2.0 this belief is being challenged, as firms capitalize on crowdsourcing by opening up a task or problem to a wider group to find better or cheaper results from outside the box.

With Business 2.0, people can be continuously connected, a driving force behind collaboration. Traditional ebusiness communications were limited to face-to-face conversations and one-way technologies that used ***asynchronous communications,*** or communication such as email in which the message and the response do not occur at the same time. Business 2.0 brought ***synchronous communication,*** or communications that occur at the same time such as IM or chat. Ask a group of college students when they last spoke to their parents. For most the answer is less than hour ago, as opposed to the traditional response of a few days ago. In business too, continuous connections are now expected in today's collaborative world.

LO 3.7: Explain how Business 2.0 is helping communities network and collaborate.

NETWORKING COMMUNITIES WITH BUSINESS 2.0

Social media refers to websites that rely on user participation and user-contributed content, such as Facebook, YouTube, and Digg. A ***social network*** is an application that connects people by matching profile information. Providing individuals with the ability to network is by far one of the greatest advantages of Business 2.0. ***Social networking*** is the practice of expanding your business and/or social contacts by constructing a personal network (see Figure 3.19). Social networking sites provide two basic functions. The first is the ability to create and maintain a profile that serves as an online identity within the environment. The second is the ability to create connections between other people

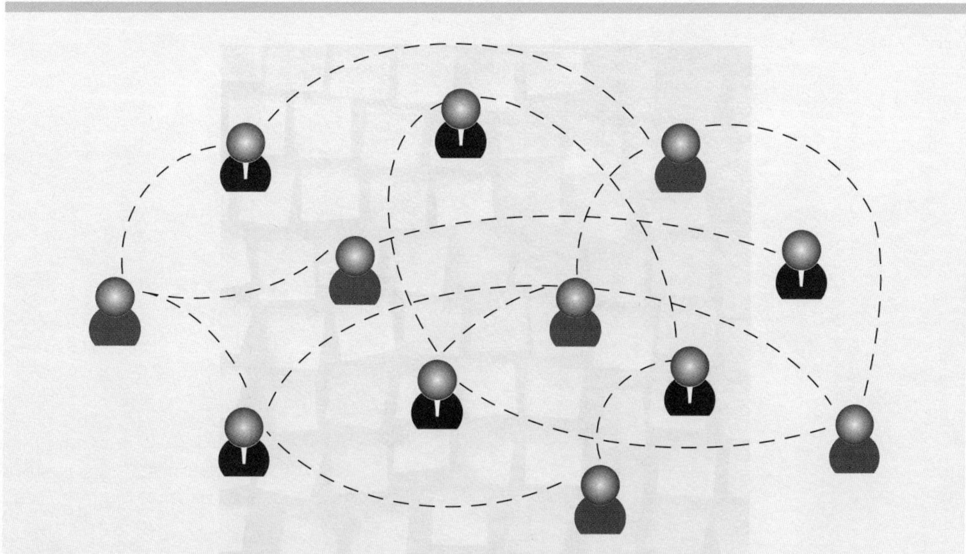

FIGURE 3.19

Social Network Example[25]

within the network. ***Social networking analysis (SNA)*** maps group contacts (personal and professional) identifying who knows each other and who works together. In a company it can provide a vision of how employees work together. It can also identify key experts with specific knowledge such as how to solve a complicated programming problem or launch a new product.

Business 2.0 simplifies access to information and improves the ability to share it. Instead of spending $1,000 and two days at a conference to meet professional peers, business people can now use social networks such as LinkedIn to meet new contacts for recruiting, prospecting, and identifying experts on a topic. With executive members from all the *Fortune* 500 companies, LinkedIn has become one of the more useful recruiting tools on the Web.

Social networking sites can be especially useful to employers trying to find job candidates with unique or highly specialized skill sets that may be harder to locate in larger communities. Many employers also search social networking sites to find "dirt" and character references for potential employees. Keep in mind that what you post on the Internet stays on the Internet.[26]

Social Tagging

Tags are specific keywords or phrases incorporated into website content for means of classification or taxonomy. An item can have one or more tags associated with it, to allow for multiple browseable paths through the items, and tags can be changed with minimal effort (see Figure 3.20). ***Social tagging*** describes the collaborative activity of marking shared online content with keywords or tags as a way to organize it for future navigation, filtering, or search. The entire user community is invited to tag, and thus essentially defines, the content. Flickr allows users to upload images and tag them with appropriate keywords. After enough people have done so, the resulting tag collection will identify images correctly and without bias.

Folksonomy is similar to taxonomy except that crowdsourcing determines the tags or keyword-based classification system. Using the collective power of a community to identify and classify content significantly lowers content categorization costs, because there is no complicated nomenclature to learn. Users simply create and apply tags as they wish. For example, while cell phone manufacturers often refer to their products as mobile devices, the folksonomy could include mobile phone, wireless phone, smart phone, iPhone, BlackBerry, and so on. All these keywords, if searched, should take a user to the same site. Folksonomies reveal what people truly call things (see Figure 3.21). They have been a point of discussion on the Web because the whole point of having a website is for your customers to find it. The majority of websites are found through search terms that match the content.[27]

FIGURE 3.20
Social Tagging Occurs When Many Individuals Categorize Content

FIGURE 3.21
Folksonomy Example: The User-Generated Names for Cellular Phones

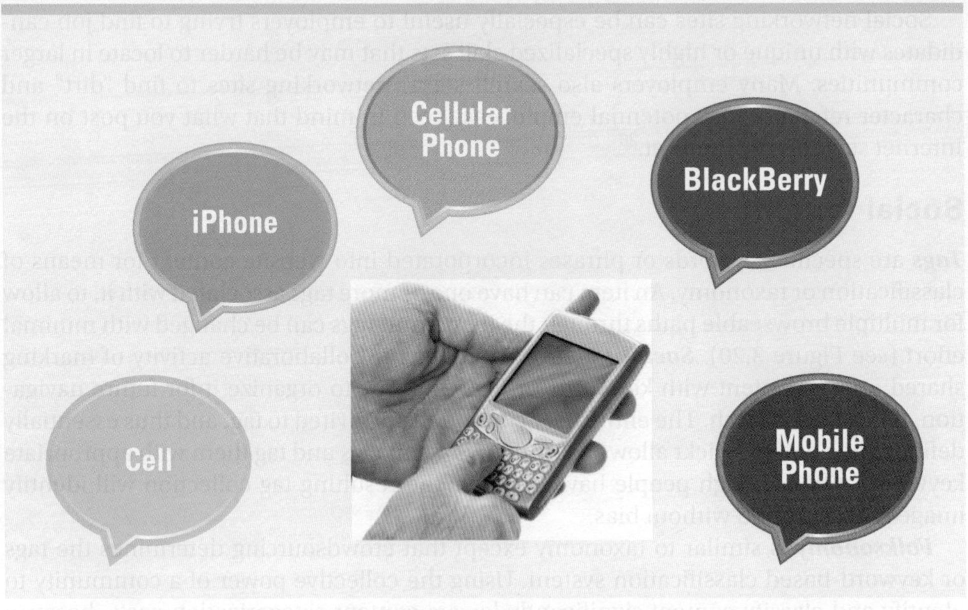

A ***website bookmark*** is a locally stored URL or the address of a file or Internet page saved as a shortcut. ***Social bookmarking*** allows users to share, organize, search, and manage bookmarks. Del.icio.us, a website dedicated to social bookmarking, provides users with a place to store, categorize, annotate, and share favorites. StumbleUpon is another popular social bookmarking website that allows users to locate interesting websites based on their favorite subjects. The more you use the service, the more the system "learns" about your interests and the better it can show you websites that interest

APPLY YOUR KNOWLEDGE

BUSINESS DRIVEN DEBATE

Anti-Social Networking

Before the Internet, angry customers could write letters or make phone calls, but their individual power to find satisfaction or bring about change was relative weak. Now, disgruntled consumers can create a website or upload a video bashing a product or service, and their efforts can be instantly seen by millions of people. Though many companies monitor the Internet and try to respond to such postings quickly, power has clearly shifted to the consumer. Create an argument for or against the following statement: "Social networking has given power to the consumer that benefits society and creates socially responsible corporations."

you. StumbleUpon represents a new social networking model in which content finds the users instead of the other way around. StumbleUpon is all about the users and the content they enjoy.[28]

BUSINESS 2.0 TOOLS FOR COLLABORATING

LO 3.8: Describe the three Business 2.0 tools for collaborating.

Social networking and collaborating are leading businesses in new directions, and Figure 3.22 provides an overview of the tools that harness the "power of the people," allowing users to share ideas, discuss business problems, and collaborate on solutions.

Blogs

A ***blog,*** or ***Web log,*** is an online journal that allows users to post their own comments, graphics, and video. Unlike traditional HTML Web pages, blog websites let writers communicate—and reader's respond—on a regular basis through a simple yet customizable interface that does not require any programming.

From a business perspective, blogs are no different from marketing channels such as video, print, audio, or presentations. They all deliver results of varying kinds. Consider Sun Microsystem's Jonathan Schwartz and GM's Bob Lutz, who use their blogs for marketing, sharing ideas, gathering feedback, press response, and image shaping. Starbucks has developed a blog called My Starbucks Idea, allowing customers to share ideas, tell Starbucks what they think of other people's ideas, and join discussions. Blogs are an ideal mechanism for many businesses since they can focus on topic areas more easily than traditional media, with no limits on page size, word count, or publication deadline.[29]

Microblogs ***Microblogging*** is the practice of sending brief posts (140 to 200 characters) to a personal blog, either publicly or to a private group of subscribers who can read

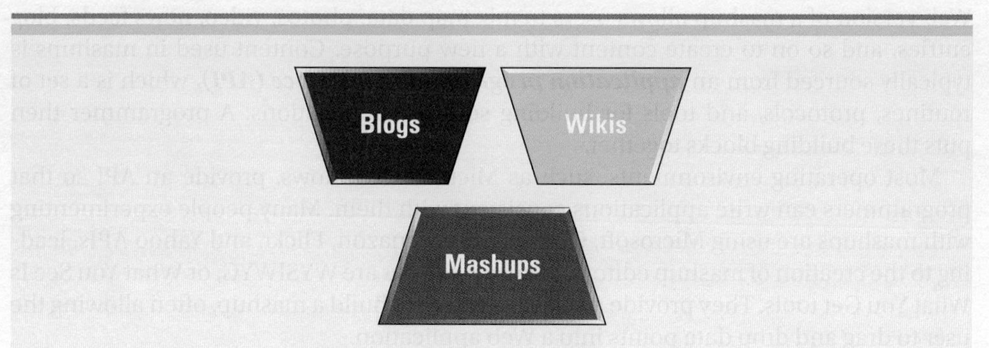

FIGURE 3.22
Business 2.0 Communication and Collaboration Tools

the posts as IMs or as text messages. The main advantage of microblogging is that posts can be submitted by a variety of means, such as instant messaging, email, or the Web. By far the most popular microblogging tool is Twitter, which allows users to send microblog entries called tweets to anyone who has registered to "follow" them. Senders can restrict delivery to people they want to follow them or, by default, allow open access. Microblogging is covered in detail in Chapter 7.[30]

Real Simple Syndication (RSS) ***Real Simple Syndication (RSS)*** is a Web format used to publish frequently updated works, such as blogs, news headlines, audio, and video, in a standardized format. An RSS document or feed includes full or summarized text, plus other information such as publication date and authorship. News websites, blogs, and podcasts use RSS, constantly feeding news to consumers instead of having them search for it. In addition to facilitating syndication, RSS allows a website's frequent readers to track updates on the site.

Wikis

A ***wiki*** (the word is Hawaiian for quick) is a type of collaborative Web page that allows users to add, remove, and change content, which can be easily organized and reorganized as required. While blogs have largely drawn on the creative and personal goals of individual authors, wikis are based on open collaboration with any and everybody. Wikipedia, the open encyclopedia that launched in 2001, has become one of the 10 most popular Web destinations, reaching an estimated 217 million unique visitors a month.[31]

A wiki user can generally alter the original content of any article, while the blog user can only add information in the form of comments. Large wikis, such as Wikipedia, protect the quality and accuracy of their information by assigning users roles such as reader, editor, administrator, patroller, policy maker, subject matter expert, content maintainer, software developer, and system operator. Access to some important or sensitive Wikipedia material is limited to users in these authorized roles.[32]

The ***network effect*** describes how products in a network increase in value to users as the number of users increases. The more users and content managers on a wiki, the greater the network affect because more users attract more contributors, whose work attracts more users, and so on. For example, Wikipedia becomes more valuable to users as the number of its contributors increases.

Wikis internal to firms can be vital tools for collecting and disseminating knowledge throughout an organization, across geographic distances, and between functional business areas. For example, what U.S. employees call a "sale" may be called "an order booked" in the United Kingdom, an "order scheduled" in Germany, and an "order produced" in France. The corporate wiki can answer any questions about a business process or definition. Companies are also using wikis for documentation, reporting, project management, online dictionaries, and discussion groups. Of course, the more employees who use the corporate wiki, the greater the network effect and valued added for the company.

Mashups

A ***mashup*** is a website or Web application that uses content from more than one source to create a completely new product or service. The term is typically used in the context of music; putting Jay-Z lyrics over a Radiohead song makes something old new. The Web version of a mashup allows users to mix map data, photos, video, news feeds, blog entries, and so on to create content with a new purpose. Content used in mashups is typically sourced from an ***application programming interface (API),*** which is a set of routines, protocols, and tools for building software applications. A programmer then puts these building blocks together.

Most operating environments, such as Microsoft Windows, provide an API so that programmers can write applications consistent with them. Many people experimenting with mashups are using Microsoft, Google, eBay, Amazon, Flickr, and Yahoo APIs, leading to the creation of mashup editors. ***Mashup editors*** are WYSIWYG, or What You See Is What You Get tools. They provide a visual interface to build a mashup, often allowing the user to drag and drop data points into a Web application.

APPLY YOUR KNOWLEDGE

BUSINESS DRIVEN MIS

Steve Jobs Resurrected from the Afterlife

It's a common, if not a little morbid, practice for news organizations to prepare obituaries well in advance of celebrities' actual death. So *Bloomberg* had a 17-page obituary for Apple's Steve Jobs ready to run on his death; unfortunately, the obit was accidently published in 2008 on *Bloomberg*'s financial website. The error occurred despite the markers on the story saying "Hold for Release" and "Do Not Use."

In addition to publishing the obituary, *Bloomberg* also accidentally published the list of people its reporters should contact when Steve Jobs does die. That list includes Microsoft founder Bill Gates, former Vice President Al Gore (a member of Apple's board of directors), and Google CEO Eric Schmidt. *Bloomberg* caught the mistake and pulled the obituary within minutes, but in today's instant information culture, the damage was already done. Now Jobs' obituary is all over the Web, and if he so desires, he has the unique opportunity to read his own obituary.[33]

While Jobs was very much alive, a few stockholders may have gone into cardiac arrest after reading the obituary. What kind of financial impact could a story like this have on Apple? With so many different forms of collaboration, how does a company monitor and track each one to ensure the content is error-free? Once erroneous content is posted to the Internet or written in a text message, what can a company do to rectify the situation? What types of safeguards can a company implement to ensure false information is not posted to a wiki or blog?

Whoever thought technology could help sell bananas? Dole Organic now places three-digit farm codes on each banana and creates a mashup using Google Earth and its banana database. Socially and environmentally conscious buyers can plug the numbers into Dole's website and look at a bio of the farm where the bananas were raised. The site tells the story of the farm and its surrounding community, lists its organic certifications, posts some photos, and offers a link to satellite images of the farm in Google Earth. Customers can personally monitor the production and treatment of their fruit from the tree to the grocer. The process assures customers that their bananas have been raised to proper organic standards on an environmentally friendly, holistically minded plantation.[34]

THE CHALLENGES OF BUSINESS 2.0

LO 3.9: **Explain the three challenges associated with Business 2.0.**

As much as Business 2.0 has positively changed the global landscape of business, a few challenges remain in open source software, user-contributed content systems, and collaboration systems, all highlighted in Figure 3.23. We'll briefly describe each one.

Technology Dependence

Many people today expect to be continuously connected, and their dependence on technology glues them to their Web connections for everything from Web conferencing for a university class or work project to making plans with friends for dinner. If a connection is down, how will they function? How long can people go without checking email, text messaging, or listening to free music on Pandora or watching on-demand television? As society becomes more technology-dependent, outages hold the potential to cause ever-greater havoc for people, businesses, and educational institutions.

FIGURE 3.23

Challenges of Business 2.0

Information Vandalism

Open source and sharing are both major advantages of Business 2.0, and ironically they are major challenges as well. Allowing anyone to edit anything opens the door for individuals to purposely damage, destroy, or vandalize website content. One of the most famous examples of wiki vandalism occurred when a false biography entry read that John Seigenthaler Sr. was assistant to Attorney General Robert F. Kennedy in the early 1960s and was thought to have been directly involved in the assassinations of both Kennedy and his brother, President John F. Kennedy. Seigenthaler did work as an assistant to Robert Kennedy, but he was never involved in the assassinations. Wiki vandalism is a hot issue and for this reason wiki software can now store all versions of a Web page, tracking updates and changes and ensuring the site can be restored to its original form if the site is vandalized. It can also color-code the background ensuring the user understands which areas have been validated and which areas have not. The real trick to wiki software is to determine which statements are true and which are false, a huge issue when considering how easy and frequently wiki software is updated and changed.[35]

Violations of Copyright and Plagiarism

Online collaboration makes plagiarism as easy as clicking a mouse. Unfortunately a great deal of copyrighted material tends to find its ways to blogs and wikis where many times blame cannot be traced to a single person. Clearly stated copyright and plagiarism policies are a must for all corporate blogs and wikis. These topics are discussed in detail in Chapter 4.

LO 3.10: Describe Web 3.0 and the next generation of online business.

WEB 3.0: DEFINING THE NEXT GENERATION OF ONLINE BUSINESS OPPORTUNITIES

While Web 1.0 refers to static text-based information websites and Web 2.0 is about user-contributed content, Web 3.0 is based on "intelligent" Web applications using natural language processing, machine-based learning and reasoning, and intelligent applications. Web 3.0 is the next step in the evolution of the Internet and Web applications. Business leaders who explore its opportunities will be the first to market with competitive advantages.

Web 3.0 offers a way for people to describe information such that computers can start to understand the relationships among concepts and topics. To demonstrate the power of Web 3.0, let's look at a few sample relationships, such as Adam Sandler is a comedian, Lady Gaga is a singer, and Hannah is friends with Sophie. These are all examples of descriptions that can be added to Web pages allowing computers to learn about relationships while displaying the information to humans. With this kind of information in place, there will be a far richer interaction between people and machines with Web 3.0.

Applying this type of advanced relationship knowledge to a company can create new opportunities. After all, businesses run on information. Where Web 2.0 brings people closer together with information using machines, Web 3.0 brings *machines* closer together using *information.* These new relationships unite people, machines, and information so a business can be smarter, quicker, more agile, and more successful.

APPLY YOUR KNOWLEDGE

BUSINESS DRIVEN DISCUSSION

Connectivity Breakdown

When you are considering connectivity services for your business, you need to take continuous access and connectivity seriously. What if one of your employees is about to close a huge multimillion-dollar deal and loses the Internet connection, jeopardizing the deal? What if a disgruntled employee decides to post your business's collective intelligence on an open-source blog or wiki? What if your patient scheduling software crashes and you have no idea which patients are scheduled to which operating rooms with which doctors? These are far worse scenarios than a teenage boy not gaining access to his email or Facebook page. What management and technical challenges do you foresee as people and businesses become increasingly dependent on connectivity? What can managers do to meet these challenges and prevent problems?

One goal of Web 3.0 is to tailor online searches and requests specifically to users' preferences and needs. For example, instead of making multiple searches, the user might type a complex sentence or two in a Web 3.0 browser, such as "I want to see a funny movie and then eat at a good Mexican restaurant. What are my options?" The Web 3.0 browser will analyze the request, search the Web for all possible answers, organize the results, and present them to the user.

Tim Berners-Lee, one of the founders of the Internet, has described the ***semantic Web*** as a component of Web 3.0 that describes things in a way that computers can understand. The semantic Web is not about links between Web pages; rather it describes the relationships between *things* (such as A is a part of B and Y is a member of Z) and the properties of things (size, weight, age, price). If information about music, cars, concert tickets, and so on is stored in a way that describes the information and associated resource files, semantic Web applications can collect information from many different sources, combine it, and present it to users in a meaningful way. Although Web 3.0 is still a bit speculative, some topics and features are certain to be included in it, such as:[36]

- Integration of legacy devices: the ability to use current devices such as iPhones, laptops, and so on, as credit cards, tickets, and reservations tools.
- Intelligent applications: the use of agents, machine learning, and semantic Web concepts to complete intelligent tasks for users.
- Open ID: the provision of an online identity that can be easily carried to a variety of devices (cell phones, PCs) allowing for easy authentication across different websites.
- Open technologies: the design of websites and other software so they can be easily integrated and work together.
- A worldwide database: the ability for databases to be distributed and accessed from anywhere.

Egovernment: The Government Moves Online

Recent business models that have arisen to enable organizations to take advantage of the Internet and create value are within egovernment. ***Egovernment*** involves the use of strategies and technologies to transform government(s) by improving the delivery of services and enhancing the quality of interaction between the citizen-consumer within all branches of government.

One example of an egovernment portal, FirstGov.gov, the official U.S. gateway to all government information, is the catalyst for a growing electronic government. Its powerful search engine and ever-growing collection of topical and customer-focused links

FIGURE 3.24
Extended Ebusiness Models

	Business	Consumer	Government
Business	B2B conisint.com	B2C dell.com	B2G lockheedmartin.com
Consumer	C2B priceline.com	C2C ebay.com	C2G egov.com
Government	G2B export.gov	G2C medicare.gov	G2G disasterhelp.gov

connect users to millions of Web pages, from the federal government, to local and tribal governments, to foreign nations around the world. Figure 3.24 highlights specific egovernment models.

Mbusiness: Supporting Anywhere Business

Internet-enabled mobile devices are quickly outnumbering personal computers. ***Mobile business*** (or ***mbusiness, mcommerce***) is the ability to purchase goods and services through a wireless Internet-enabled device. The emerging technology behind mbusiness is a mobile device equipped with a Web-ready micro-browser that can perform the following services:

- Mobile entertainment—downloads for music, videos, games, voting, ring tones, as well as text-based messaging services.
- Mobile sales/marketing—advertising, campaigns, discounts, promotions, and coupons.
- Mobile banking—manage accounts, pay bills, receive alerts, and transfer funds.
- Mobile ticketing—purchase tickets for entertainment, transportation, and parking including the ability to automatically feed parking meters.
- Mobile payments—pay for goods and services including in-store purchases, home delivery, vending machines, taxis, gas, and so on.

Organizations face changes more extensive and far reaching in their implications than anything since the modern industrial revolution occurred in the early 1900s. Technology is a primary force driving these changes. Organizations that want to survive must recognize the immense power of technology, carry out required organizational changes in the face of it, and learn to operate in an entirely different way.

LEARNING OUTCOME REVIEW

Learning Outcome 3.1: Compare disruptive and sustaining technologies, and explain how the Internet and WWW caused business disruption.

Disruptive technologies offer a new way of doing things that initially does not meet the needs of existing customers. Disruptive technologies redefine the competitive playing fields of their respective markets, open new markets and destroy old ones, and cut into the low end of the marketplace and eventually evolve to displace high-end competitors and their reigning technologies.

Sustaining technologies produce improved products customers are eager to buy, such as a faster car or larger hard drive. Sustaining technologies tend to provide us with better, faster, and cheaper products in established markets and virtually never lead in markets opened by new and disruptive technologies.

The Internet and WWW caused business disruption by allowing people to communicate and collaborate in ways that were not possible before the information age. The Internet and WWW completely disrupted the way businesses operate, employees communicate, and products are developed and sold.

Learning Outcome 3.2: Describe Web 1.0 along with ebusiness and its associated advantages.

Web 1.0 is a term to refer to the World Wide Web during its first few years of operation between 1991 and 2003. Ebusiness includes ecommerce along with all activities related to internal and external business operations such as servicing customer accounts, collaborating with partners, and exchanging real-time information. During Web 1.0, entrepreneurs began creating the first forms of ebusiness. Ebusiness advantages include expanding global reach, opening new markets, reducing costs, and improving operations and effectiveness.

Learning Outcome 3.3: Compare the four categories of ebusiness models.

- Business-to-business (B2B) applies to businesses buying from and selling to each other over the Internet.
- Business-to-consumer (B2C) applies to any business that sells its products or services to consumers over the Internet.
- Consumer-to-business (C2B) applies to any consumer that sells a product or service to a business over the Internet.
- Consumer-to-consumer (C2C) applies to sites primarily offering goods and services to assist consumers interacting with each other over the Internet.

The primary difference between B2B and B2C are the customers; B2B customers are other businesses while B2C markets to consumers. Overall, B2B relations are more complex and have higher security needs; plus B2B is the dominant ebusiness force, representing 80 percent of all online business.

Learning Outcome 3.4: Describe the six ebusiness tools for connecting and communicating.

As firms began to move online, more MIS tools were created to support ebusiness processes and requirements. The ebusiness tools used to connect and communicate include email, instant messaging, podcasting, content management systems, videoconferencing, and Web conferencing.

Learning Outcome 3.5: Identify the four challenges associated with ebusiness.

Although the benefits of ebusiness are enticing, developing, deploying, and managing ebusiness systems is not always easy. The challenges associated with ebusiness include identifying limited market segments, managing consumer trust, ensuring consumer protection, and adhering to taxation rules.

Learning Outcome 3.6: Explain Web 2.0, and identify its four characteristics.

Web 2.0, or Business 2.0, is the next generation of Internet use—a more mature, distinctive communications platform characterized by new qualities such as collaboration, sharing, and free. Web 2.0 encourages user participation and the formation of communities that contribute to the content. In Web 2.0, technical skills are no longer required to use and publish information to the World Wide Web, eliminating entry barriers for online business. The four characteristics of Web 2.0 include:

- Content sharing through open sourcing.
- User-contributed content.
- Collaboration inside the organization.
- Collaboration outside the organization.

Learning Outcome 3.7: Explain how Business 2.0 is helping communities network and collaborate.

A social network is an application that connects people by matching profile information. Providing individuals with the ability to network is by far one of the greatest advantages of Business 2.0. Social networking is the practice of expanding your business and/or social contacts by constructing a personal network. Business 2.0 simplifies the way individuals communicate, network, find employment, and search for information.

Learning Outcome 3.8: Describe the three Business 2.0 tools for collaborating.

The three tools that harness the "power of the people" for Business 2.0 include blogs, wikis, and mashups. A blog, or Web log, is an online journal that allows users to post their own comments, graphics, and video. Blog websites let writers communicate—and reader's respond—on a regular basis through a simple yet customizable interface that does not require any programming. A wiki is a type of collaborative Web page that allows users to add, remove, and change content, which can be easily organized and reorganized as required. While blogs have largely drawn on the creative and personal goals of individual authors, wikis are based on open collaboration with any and everybody. A mashup is a website or Web application that uses content from more than one source to create a completely new product or service. A mashup allows users to mix map data, photos, video, news feeds, blog entries, and so on to create content with a new purpose.

Learning Outcome 3.9: Explain the three challenges associated with Business 2.0.

As much as Business 2.0 has positively changed the global landscape of business, a few challenges remain in open source software, user-contributed content systems, and collaboration systems. These challenges include individuals forming unrealistic dependencies on technology, vandalism of information on blogs and wikis, and the violation of copyrights and plagiarism.

Learning Outcome 3.10: Describe Web 3.0 and the next generation of online business.

Web 3.0 is based on "intelligent" Web applications using natural language processing, machine-based learning and reasoning, and intelligent applications. Web 3.0 is the next step in the evolution of the Internet and Web applications. Business leaders who explore its opportunities will be the first to market with competitive advantages.

Web 3.0 offers a way for people to describe information such that computers can start to understand the relationships among concepts and topics.

OPENING CASE QUESTIONS

1. **Knowledge:** Do you consider Facebook, MySpace, and LinkedIn forms of disruptive or sustaining technology?
2. **Comprehension:** Create a list of the online businesses discussed in the case and determine if they are examples of Web 1.0 (ebusiness) or Web 2.0 (Business 2.0).

3. **Application:** Describe the ebusiness model and revenue model for Linked In, MySpace, or Facebook.
4. **Analysis:** What is open source software and can a business use it for a social networking platforms?
5. **Synthesis:** Create a plan for how a start-up company could take advantage of Web 3.0 and generate the idea for the next great website.
6. **Evaluation:** Evaluate the challenges facing social networking websites and identify ways companies can prepare to face these issues.

KEY TERMS

Application programming interface (API), 112
Asynchronous communication, 108
Blog, or Web log, 111
Business model, 97
Business-to-business (B2B), 98
Business-to-consumer (B2C), 98
Clickstream data, 96
Collaboration system, 106
Collective intelligence, 106
Consumer-to-business (C2B), 99
Consumer-to-consumer (C2C), 99
Content management system (CMS), 103
Crowdsourcing, 107
Cybermediation, 96
Digital Darwinism, 90
Disintermediation, 95
Disruptive technology, 90
Ebusiness, 92
Ebusiness model, 97
Ecommerce, 92
Egovernment, 115
Eshop (estore or etailer), 98
Explicit knowledge, 107
Folksonomy, 109
Hypertext markup language (HTML), 92
Hypertext transport protocol (HTTP), 92
Information architecture, 103
Information reach, 94
Information richness, 94
Instant messaging (sometimes called IM or IMing), 102
Interactivity, 96
Intermediaries, 95
Internet, 91
Internet service provider (ISP), 101
Knowledge management (KM), 106
Knowledge management system (KMS), 106
Long tail, 94
Mashup, 112
Mashup editor, 112
Mass customization, 94
Microblogging, 111
Mobile business (mcommerce, mbusiness), 116
Network effect, 112
Open source, 105
Open system, 105
Paradigm shift, 92
Personalization, 94
Podcasting, 102
Real Simple Syndication (RSS), 112
Real-time communication, 101
Reintermediation, 96
Reputation system, 106
Semantic Web, 115
Social bookmarking, 110
Social media, 108
Social network, 108
Social networking, 108
Social networking analysis (SNA), 109
Social tagging, 109
Source code, 105
Sustaining technology, 90
Synchronous communication, 108
Tacit knowledge, 107
Tags, 109
Taxonomy, 103
Universal resource locator (URL), 92
User-contributed content (also referred to as user-generated content), 106
Web 1.0, 92
Web 2.0 (or Business 2.0), 105
Web browser, 92
Web conferencing (webinar), 103
Website bookmark, 110
Wiki, 112
World Wide Web (WWW), 92

REVIEW QUESTIONS

1. What is the different between sustaining and disruptive technology?
2. Do you consider the Internet and WWW forms of sustaining or disruptive technology?
3. How has the Internet and WWW created a global platform for business?
4. What is the difference between ebusiness and ecommerce?

5. What are the benefits and challenges associated with ebusiness?
6. What are the benefits and challenges associated with Business 2.0?
7. Explain business models and their role in a company. How did ebusiness change traditional business models?
8. How can a company use mass customization and personalization to decrease buyer power?
9. How does ebusiness differ from Business 2.0?
10. What are the differences among collective intelligence, knowledge management, and crowdsourcing?
11. Why is knowledge management critical to a business?
12. What are the benefits and challenges associated with wikis?
13. How do disintermediation, reintermediation, and cybermediation differ?
14. What is the semantic Web?
15. How does mbusiness different from ebusiness?

CLOSING CASE ONE

BBC Taps Web 3.0 for New Music Site

The BBC's recently launched semantic Web music project could indicate the future direction of the corporation's online presence. The public beta of the BBC Music website has been recently relaunched incorporating semantic Web technology in its artist pages resource. The BBC artist pages, a repository of information on singers and bands played on several BBC radio stations, has been running as a closed beta project since June 2008, but with the launch of the new BBC Music website, its semantic Web technology has now been exposed to the wider public.

For the BBC, the site represents a new way of thinking about online content—where the priority is publishing data rather than simply publishing Web pages. Such thinking is likely to filter through to other parts of the BBC, with discussions taking place between editorial departments on how to aggregate and meaningfully link data. Matthew Shorter, interactive editor for music at the BBC, told silicon.com: "We're kind of on a journey of moving from what's effectively a magazine/print publication-based metaphor around Web publishing . . . to a world where we recognize that that's not the way that people use the Web. We're working towards a scenario where we really don't want to see any dead ends between bits of the BBC online offering."

The semantic technology is not the only improvement on the BBC Music site. The way in which the BBC's online music resource is constructed now makes it easier to search for content due to the way it's been tagged and linked to other content, according to Shorter. From an SEO point of view, once we start generating a lot of meaningful links among our pages, then we're going to improve the find-ability of our content via Web search which is a part of our strategy of doing this.

The BBC is also making its music-related application programming interfaces (APIs) available for third-party developers so they can reuse the content—in a similar way as YouTube and Flickr. The open platform could see individuals use the artist play-count data as shown on the BBC Music homepage and display it in a different way, for example. By having an open system, the BBC hopes that people will create unique content that will benefit from incoming links.[37]

Questions

1. Do you consider the BBC's use of semantic technology a disruptive or sustaining technology?
2. Do you consider the BBC's new music site a form of Web 1.0 or Web 2.0?

3. What benefits will the BBC receive from using an open system?
4. Why would collaboration, collective intelligence, and crowdsourcing be important to the BBC's radio station?
5. Brainstorm a few of the security issues a company should prepare for when using Halo.

CLOSING CASE TWO

Amazon.com—Not Your Average Bookstore

Jeffrey Bezos, CEO and founder of Amazon.com, is running what some people refer to as the "world's biggest bookstore." The story of Bezos' virtual bookstore teaches many lessons about online business. Out of nowhere, this digital bookstore turned an industry upside down. What happened here was more than just creating a website. Bezos conceived and implemented an intelligent, global digital business. Its business is its technology; its technology is its business. Shocking traditional value chains in the bookselling industry, Amazon opened thousands of virtual bookstores in its first few months of operation.

Bezos graduated from Princeton and was the youngest vice president at Banker's Trust in New York. He had to decide if he would stay and receive his 1994 Wall Street bonus or leave and start a business on the Internet. "I tried to imagine being 80 years old, looking back on my life. I knew that I would hardly regret having missed the 1994 Wall Street bonus. But having missed being part of the Internet boom—that would have really hurt," stated Bezos. One evening he compiled a list of 20 products he believed would sell on the Internet. Books, being small-ticket items that are easy and inexpensive to ship, were on the top of the list. It was also apparent that no bookstore could conceivably stock more than a fraction of the 5 million books published annually. Bezos, who had never sold a book in his life, developed a strategic plan for selling books on the Internet. Amazon launched three years later. In the fall of 1994, Amazon filled its first book order—personally packaged by Bezos and his wife.

Amazon's Ebusiness Strategy

Amazon is a pure-play business and does not operate any physical stores. All of its sales occur through its website. It is consistently pushing the technological envelope in its search to provide a satisfying, personalized experience for its customers. What started as a human-edited list of product suggestions morphed into a sophisticated computer-generated recommendation engine. The company captures the comments and recommendations of buyers for site visitors to read—similar to the friendly salesperson in a store offering advice on which books to buy. The website tracks customer traffic, the number of visitors who access the site, how long they stay, what pages they click on, and so forth. The company uses the information to evaluate buying and selling patterns and the success of promotions. Amazon has quickly become a model success story for ebusinesses around the globe.

Amazon retains customers with website features such as personalized recommendations, online customer reviews, and "1-click ordering"—the creation of a true one-stop shopping establishment where customers can find anything they want to buy online. Through the Amazon.com Auctions, zShops (independent third-party sellers), and more recently the Amazon.com Marketplace (where customers can sell used items), the company is able to offer its customers almost everything.

Shaping Amazon's Future

Amazon released a free Web service that enables its business partners (whom Amazon calls "associates") to interact with its website. More specifically, this service allows its partners to access catalog data, to create and populate an Amazon.com shopping cart, and even to initiate the checkout process. In 16 months, the company has inspired 30,000 associates to invent new ways to extend Amazon's visibility on the Internet. With over 30 million customers, Amazon has become a household brand. Amazon is always looking for new ways to take advantage of ebusiness. Here are a few of its creations:

- **Amazon S3:** Amazon launched an online storage service called Amazon Simple Storage Service (Amazon S3). Any type of data, from 1 byte to 5 gigabytes in size, can be stored on the service and the customer is charged monthly fees for data stored and transferred.
- **Amazon MP3:** The online music store sells downloadable MP3s. Amazon MP3 is selling music from the top four record labels—EMI, Universal, Warner Music, and Sony BMG—as well as many independents.
- **Vine:** Amazon launched Amazon Vine, which rewards top product reviewers by providing them with free access to products from vendors participating in the program.
- **Kindle:** Amazon launched Amazon Kindle, an ebook reader that downloads content over "Whispernet," a free wireless service on the Sprint Nextel network. Initial offerings include approximately 90,000 books, newspapers, magazines, and blogs. The screen uses E Ink technology to reduce battery consumption.

Mobile Amazon

Amazon.com has collaborated with Nokia to pioneer a new territory. With the launch of its Amazon.com Any-where service, it has become one of the first major online retailers to recognize and do something about the potential of Internet-enabled wireless devices. As content delivery over wireless devices becomes faster, more secure, and scalable, mcommerce will surpass landline ebusiness (traditional telephony) as the method of choice for digital commerce transactions. According to the research firm Strategy Analytics, the global mcommerce market was expected to be worth more than $200 billion by 2005, with some 350 million customers generating almost 14 billion transactions annually. Additionally, information activities such as email, news, and stock quotes will progress to personalized transactions, "one-click" travel reservations, online auctions, and videoconferencing.[38]

Questions

1. How has Amazon used technology to revamp the bookselling industry?
2. Is Amazon using disruptive or sustaining technology to run its business?
3. How is Amazon using personalization to keep customers loyal?
4. What is Amazon's ebusiness model?
5. How can Amazon use mbusiness to increase sales?
6. What are the Web 1.0 characteristics of Amazon.com?
7. What are the Web 2.0 characteristics of Amazon.com?
8. How can Amazon.com use Web 3.0 to create the future bookstore?

CRITICAL BUSINESS THINKING

1. **Anything but Online**

   Your best friend, Susan Stewart, has started a highly successful custom T-shirt business from your dorm room. Susan is art major, and each week she creates a limited edition T-shirt focusing on the lyrics from up-and-coming indie bands. Being an MIS major, you see the advantages Susan could reap by porting her business to the Internet. Susan, being an art major, does not like technology and does not believe she needs it to grow her business. Do you agree or disagree that Susan needs to compete online? How can creating an ebusiness benefit Susan? What are the challenges Susan will face as she moves her business to the Internet? How could Susan use Web 2.0 to build loyalty among her followers?

2. **The Future of Wikipedia**
Wikipedia is a multilingual, Web-based, free-content encyclopedia project written collaboratively by volunteers around the world. Since its creation in 2001, it has grown rapidly into one of the largest reference websites. Some people believe Wikipedia will eventually fail under an assault by marketers and self-promoting users. Eric Goldman, a professor at the Santa Clara University School of Law, argues that Wikipedia will see increasingly vigorous efforts to subvert its editorial process, including the use of automated marketing tools to alter Wikipedia entries to generate online traffic. The site's editors will burn out trying to maintain it, he projects, or Wikipedia will change its open-access architecture and its mission. Do you agree or disagree with Professor Goldman's argument? What can Wikipedia do to combat the challenges of information vandalism and copyright/plagiarism issues?[39]

3. **Is Facebook Becoming the Whole World's Social Network?**
Facebook's growth, which we already know is massive, is truly a global phenomenon. Nations with the fastest membership growth rate are in South America and Asia. Is Facebook becoming the global phone book? If you review InsideFacebook.com, you'll find a detailed analysis of the numerical growth rate of members per nation and the penetration Facebook is achieving among each nation's population. Particularly interesting was the monthly growth rate for Indonesia, the Philippines, Mexico, Argentina, and Malaysia—each of which showed about a 10 percent jump in Facebook membership in a single month. In a group answer the following:[40]

   - What potential business opportunities could be created by a worldwide social media network or phone book?
   - Facebook, which contains personal data on each member, is becoming the world's phone book. What are the implications of a world phone book for social change?
   - What do you think would be the benefits and challenges of global social networking?
   - How would tags and crowdsourcing be impacted by a global social network?

4. **The Toughest College Test You'll Ever Take**
If your professor asked you today to kick your social networking habits, do you think you could do it? Can you go without Facebook, cell phones, or the Internet for a week? For a day? Recently, a University of Minnesota professor challenged her public relations class to go five days without media or gadgets that didn't exist before 1984. Out of the 43 students in the class, just a handful made it even three days without new technology. Among those who didn't, one student said, "My mother thought I died." How long could you go without any social media? What types of issues might you encounter without constant connections to your friends? How has social media impacted society? How has social media impacted businesses?[41]

5. **Competing with the Big Boys**
Provenzo's Rentals is a small privately owned business that rents sports equipment in Denver, Colorado. The company specializes in winter rentals including ski, snowboard, and snowmobile equipment. Provenzo's has been in business for 20 years and, for the first time, it is experiencing a decline in rentals. Greg Provenzo, the company's owner, is puzzled by the recent decreases. The snowfall for the past two years has been

outstanding, and the ski resorts have opened earlier and closed later than most previous years. Reports say tourism in the Colorado area is up, and the invention of loyalty programs has significantly increased the number of local skiers. Overall, business should be booming. The only reason for the decrease in sales might be the fact that big retailers such as Walmart and Gart's Sports are now renting winter sports equipment. Provenzo would like your team's help in determining how he can use ebusiness and Business 2.0 to help his company increase sales, decrease costs, and compete with these big retailers.

6. **Book'em**

You are the CIO of Book'em, a company that creates and sells custom book bags. Book'em currently holds 28 percent of market share with over 3,000 employees operating in six countries. You have just finished reading *The Long Tail* by Chris Andersen and *The Innovator's Dilemma* by Clayton Christensen, and you are interested in determining how you can grow your business while reducing costs. Summarize each book and explain how Book'em could implement the strategies explained in each book to create competitive advantages and increase sales.

7. **Five Ways Google Docs Speeds Up Collaboration**

Google Docs wants you to skip Microsoft Office and collaborate with your group in your browser for free, especially when you're not in the same physical space. Visit Google Docs and answer the following questions.

- What are five ways the new Google Docs can help your team accomplish work more efficiently, even when you're not in the same room together.
- Is Google Docs open source software? What revenue model is Google Docs following?
- Why would putting Google Docs and Microsoft Office on your résumé help differentiate your skills?
- What other applications does Google create that you are interested in learning to help collaborate and communicate with peers and co-workers?

8. **Secure Collaboration**

As the methods and modes of communication continue to evolve, challenges will mount for businesses trying to secure their data and for law enforcement agencies looking to monitor communications as part of their investigations. That was the theme of the keynote that Sun Microsystems chief security officer and renowned cryptographer Whitfield Diffie delivered at the AT&T Cyber Security Conference.

Diffie believes that with millions of people joining Second Life and companies building facilities there, it may be that virtual communities will become the preferred communication method for humans as virtual communities become a growing source of collective intelligence that can be easily watched and monitored.[42]

Who would be interested in monitoring and spying on the collective intelligence of virtual communities? What is your answer to the following question: As we create new and better ways to collaborate, what happens to information security?

9. **City Council Member Fired for Playing Farmville Game at Work**

More than 80 million Facebook users are obsessed with Farmville, and one of the more devoted players is Bulgaria's Plovidv City Council member Dimitar Kerin. During council meetings, Kerin would take advantage of the city hall's laptops and wireless connection to tend to his farm. This caught the attention of the council chair, who many times scolded Kerin for his virtual farming, warning him that the game was not allowed during meetings. Kerin kept on, arguing that he had to catch up with other council members, who achieved higher levels on the game. Kerin pointed out logically that many other members used city hall for their Farmville pleasures, and he cited the fact that one councilman had reached level 46, whereas Kerin was stuck at level 40. Shockingly, council members voted Kerin off the board in a split 20–19 decision, suggesting that perhaps half the council members in Bulgaria's second-largest city are committed to the Facebook application. Do you agree with the firing of Dimitar Kerin? Do you agree that it is inappropriate to use social networking applications at work? If Dimitar Kerin was fired for playing Farmville, should all other council members who use social networking applications at work be fired? Have you ever been reprimanded for playing a game while at school or at work? What could you do differently to ensure this situation does not happen to you?[43]

10. ***48 Hour Magazine***

    That sound you hear, of thousands of writers, designers, and photographers banging their heads against the wall to the beat of a ticking clock? That's the sound of *48 Hour Magazine*, an innovative publication that aims to go from inspiration to execution in 48 hours and begins . . . now. *48 Hour* is available to the eager public as a real, printed magazine and as a website too. What are the limitations of "old media"? How are the editors of the *48 Hour Magazine* using Web 2.0 to overcome these limitations? What are the advantages and disadvantages of *48 Hour Magazine's* model? What type of revenue model would you recommend *48 Hour Magazine* implement? If you had $50,000 would you invest in the *48 Hour Magazine?* Why or why not?[44]

ENTREPRENEURIAL CHALLENGE

BUILD YOUR OWN BUSINESS

1. To build a sense of community, you have provided a mechanism on your business website where customers can communicate and post feedback. You review the communication daily to help understand customer issues and concerns. You log in and find the following anonymous posting: "I do not recommend visiting this business on Thursdays at 2:00 p.m. because the Children's Story Hour is taking place. I hate children, especially in a business. I'm not sure why this business encourages people to bring their children. In fact, I recommend that children should be banned from this business altogether." How would you respond to the above post? Is the customer's viewpoint ethical? How do you encourage an open line of communication with your customers and still maintain an open forum on your website?
2. Your business needs to take advantage of ebusiness and Business 2.0 strategies if it wants to remain competitive. Detail how your business could use Web 1.0 and Web 2.0 to increase sales and decrease costs. Be sure to focus on the different areas of business such as marketing, finance, accounting, sales, customer service, and human resources. You would like to build a collaboration tool for all of your customers and events. Answer the questions below as they pertain to your business.

    - What type of collaboration tool would you build?
    - How could you use the tool to facilitate planning, product development, product testing, feedback, and so on.
    - What additional benefits could a customer collaboration tool provide that could help you run your business?

3. The Yankee Group reports that 66 percent of companies determine website success solely by measuring the amount of traffic. Unfortunately, large amounts of website traffic do not necessarily indicate large sales. Many websites with lots of traffic have minimal sales. The best way to measure a website's success is to measure such things as the revenue generated by Web traffic, the number of new customers acquired by Web traffic, any reductions in customer service calls resulting from Web traffic. As you deploy your Business 2.0 strategy, you want to build a website that creates stickiness and a sense of community for your customers. Explain why measuring Web traffic is not a good indicator of Web sales or website success. How would you implement Business 2.0 characteristics to create a sense of community for your customers? How could a wiki help grow your business? Could you use blogs to create a marketing buzz? What else can you do to ensure your website finds financial success?[45]

APPLY YOUR KNOWLEDGE BUSINESS PROJECTS

PROJECT I Analyzing Websites

Stars Inc. is a large clothing corporation that specializes in reselling clothes worn by celebrities. The company's four websites generate 75 percent of its sales. The remaining 25 percent of sales occur directly through the company's warehouse. You have recently been hired as the director of sales. The only information you can find about the success of the four websites follows:

Website	Classic	Contemporary	New Age	Traditional
Traffic analysis	5,000 hits/day	200 hits/day	10,000 hits/day	1,000 hits/day
Stickiness (average)	20 minutes	1 hour	20 minutes	50 minutes
Number of abandoned shopping carts	400/day	0/day	5,000/day	200/day
Number of unique visitors	2,000/day	100/day	8,000/day	200/day
Number of identified visitors	3,000/day	100/day	2,000/day	800/day
Average revenue per sale	$1,000	$ 1,000	$50	$1,300

Project Focus

You decide that maintaining four separate websites is expensive and adds little business value. You want to propose consolidating to one site. Create a report detailing the business value gained by consolidating to a single website, along with your recommendation for consolidation. Be sure to include your website profitability analysis. Assume that at a minimum 10 percent of hits result in a sale, at an average 30 percent of hits result in a sale, and at a maximum 60 percent of hits result in a sale.

PROJECT II Wiki Your Way

Wikis are Web-based tools that make it easy for users to add, remove, and change online content. Employees at companies such as Intel, Motorola, IBM, and Sony use them for a host of tasks, from setting internal meeting agendas to posting documents related to new products.

Project Focus

Many companies rely on wikis to engage customers in ongoing discussions about products. Wikis for Motorola and T-Mobile handsets serve as continually updated user guides. TV networks, including ABC and CBS, created fan wikis that let viewers interact with each other as they unraveled mysteries from such shows as *Lost* and *CSI: Crime Scene Investigation.* You would like to implement wikis at your new company, The Consulting Edge, a small computer consulting company catering to mid- and large-sized businesses. Answer the following questions:

- How can a wiki help you attract customers and grow your business?
- How can a wiki help your partners and employees?
- What ethical and security concerns would you have with the wiki?
- What could you do to minimize these concerns?

PROJECT III Blogging for Dollars

You have purchased a financial investment company, The Financial Level, that caters to individuals and families. You would like to develop a few blogs for your customers, employees, and partners. The goals for your customer blog are to gather honest feedback, provide a place for customers to interact, and help find new opportunities for your businesses. The goals for the employee blog are to gather knowledge, collect employment feedback, and offer a place where employees can post anonymous feedback for issues and concerns so you can better manage your staff.

Project Focus

a. Research the Internet and find several customer blogs and employee blogs.

b. Determine the top three blogs for customers and for employees, and critique the blogs for content, ease of use, and overall value.

c. Design a prototype customer blog and a prototype employee blog for The Financial Level using Word, PowerPoint, or a tool of your choice.

PROJECT IV 14th Annual Webby Awards Nominees

Who needs the Academy Awards when you can witness the Webby Awards? The Webby Awards are the leading international awards honoring excellence in interactive design, creativity, usability, and functionality on the Internet. With nearly 70 categories, website entries make up the majority of Webby winners, nominees, and honorees. Some are beautiful to look at and interact with. Others are a testament to usability and functionality. And a handful excel across the board. To be selected among the best is an incredible achievement worthy of praise and perhaps a little bragging.[46]

Project Focus

Visit the latest edition of the Webby Awards at www.webbyawards.com and answer the following questions:

- Which nominations were the most surprising?
- Which nominations were you unfamiliar with but will now use?
- Were there any examples of Web 1.0 winners?
- Were there any examples of Web 3.0 winners?
- List the top five websites you think deserve to win a Webby.

PROJECT V Creating a Podcast

Podcasting is a form of audio broadcasting on the Internet. The reason it became linked with the iPod in name was because people download podcasts (audio shows) to listen to on their iPods. However, you don't have to listen to podcasts only on iPods; you can use your computer with some music software such as Windows built-in Media Player or Winamp, or other portable music players (iPod competitors) such as Creative Zen or iRiver. As long as you have some way to play music on your computer, you will be able to listen to podcasts.

Project Focus

a. Download Audacity from audacity.sourceforge.net. It is open source, is cross-platform, is free, and lets you mix multiple audio files. Windows, Mac OS 9 or X, and Linux/Unix versions are available. You will also have to download the LAME MP3 encoder, which allows Audacity to export MP3 files. You will see the download link for that on the same page as the Audacity download. Once you download the LAME MP3 encoder, place it in the Audacity program folder (C:Program\Files\Audacity\Plug-Ins\). Then, open a .WAV file in Audacity, and select the menu option "File" then choose "Export As MP3." When you do, you will see this message: At this Point, browse to where you placed the "lame_enc.dll" file (such as C:Program\Files\Audacity\Plug-Ins). Click on the "lame_enc.dll" file. Once finished, you can now effectively use the Export As MP3 menu option to create MP3 files.

b. Open Audacity and check the preferences. Make sure your playback and recording device are set. If you are going to record a stereo signal, set the number of channels to record to 2 (Stereo) on the Audio I/O preferences. When picking a device to record from, make sure you have set up all the connections properly, such as plugging a microphone into the Mic Input, and any other device into the Line In of your sound card.

c. Click on the red "Record" button to begin recording. You can also click on the blue "Pause" button to pause the recording. Press it again to continue. Click on the yellow "Stop" button to cease recording. The cursor will return to its previous position, before the recording was started.

d. MP3 is the standard format for podcasts. When saving, use the minimum bit rate that provides good results. Here are some suggested settings:

- 48–56k Mono—sermons, audio books, talk radio.
- 64k Stereo—music, music and talk combinations.
- 128k Stereo—good-quality music.

e. Create a two-to-three-minute podcast that you can share with your class about a successful Business 2.0 entrepreneurial company. A few examples include Digg.com, karmaloop.com, Foursquare.com, Flickr.com. Figure out what will be said (or not said) during the show. There are almost no limits to what content can be included in podcasts. Podcasting allows you to create shows, dramatizations, vignettes, commentaries, documentaries, and any other content imaginable. However, you need to script out your content before you start to record.

PROJECT VI Photo Story 3—Creating a Video Résumé

Microsoft Photo Story 3 for Windows helps create exciting video stories from pictures. For example, you could create a video story that features narrated photographs from a family vacation or a video story that includes pictures and sounds of an athletic race or game. In a few simple steps, you can import and edit your pictures, add titles, record narration, add background music, and save your story using the optimal quality settings (profile) for the way your story will be played.

Project Focus

Download Photo Story 3 from www.microsoft.com/windowsxp/using/digitalphotography/photostory/default.mspx. Review the requirements section to make sure your computer is able to run this application. Click the "Continue" button in the Validation Required section to begin the short validation process. Once validated, you will be sent to a page with specific instructions for obtaining the download.

When you run Photo Story 3, with the view to making a new project, the first option is to select "Begin a new story." After clicking this option, your first task is to "import" pictures. You can import pictures from your computer, a network folder, or a website. For each story, you can import up to 300 pictures, which can be files with .bmp, .dib, .eps, .gif, .jhif, .jpe, .jpeg, .jpg, .pcd, .pcx, .png, .psd, .rle, .tga, and .tif file name extensions.

Your pictures appear in the filmstrip at the bottom of the page. If you import more pictures, Microsoft Photo Story 3 adds them at the end of the filmstrip.

By clicking on a series of buttons or options, you can remove black borders, add titles to your picture, add narration and custom motion, and add background music to your story.

Develop a 30-second professional commercial. This is a short description of who you are, what job you are looking for, and the skills that make you suited for the job. Building a quality 30-second commercial can be tougher than it sounds. The goal is to be able to contact a stranger and let him or her know who you are, what your skills are, and why you are approaching the person. Create a list of words describing your skills and interests. Begin broadly and then narrow your list to skills related to your current job search.

PROJECT VII Sticky Wiki

Wiki (Hawaiian for "quick") is software that allows users to freely create and edit Web page content using any Web browser. The most common wiki is Wikipedia. Wikis offer a powerful yet flexible collaborative communication tool for developing websites. The best part of a wiki is that it grows and evolves by the collaborative community adding content—the owner of the wiki does not have to add all of the content as is typical in a standard Web page.

Many sites offer free wiki software such as Socialtext, a group-editable website. As one of the first wiki companies, Socialtext wikis are designed for anyone that wants to accelerate team communications, better enable knowledge sharing, foster collaboration, and build online communities. Socialtext also offers WikiWidgets, which make it easy for nontechnical business users to create rich, dynamic wiki content. Today, more than 3,000 organizations use Socialtext, including Symantec, Nokia, IKEA, Conde Nast, Ziff-Davis, Kodak, University of Southern California, Boston College, and numerous others.

Project Focus

Create your own wiki. Wikis can address a variety of needs from student involvement, fraternities and sororities, group activities, sport team updates, local band highlights, and so on. Choose a free wiki software vendor from the list below and create a wiki for something you are involved in or excited about and want to share with others. This could include a student organization, fraternity or sorority, academic organization, favorite author, book, movie, band, musician, or sports team.

- www.socialtext.com—easy-to-use, business-grade wikis proven by *Fortune* 500 companies.
- www.wetpaint.com—a free easy-to-use wiki building site.
- www.CentralDesktop.com—Easy-to-use, a wiki for non-techies.
- www.xwiki.com—Open source and free hosting with professional services.

If you have different wiki software you prefer, feel free to use it to create your wiki.

AYK APPLICATION PROJECTS

If you are looking for Excel projects to incorporate into your class, try any of the following after reading this chapter.

Project Number	Project Name	Project Type	Plug-In Focus Area	Project Focus	Project Skill Set	Page Number
1	Financial Destiny	Excel	T2	Personal Budget	Introductory Formulas	AYK.4
2	Cash Flow	Excel	T2	Cash Flow	Introductory Formulas	AYK.4
3	Technology Budget	Excel	T1, T2	Hardware and Software	Introductory Formulas	AYK.4
4	Tracking Donations	Excel	T2	Employee Relationships	Introductory Formulas	AYK.4
5	Convert Currency	Excel	T2	Global Commerce	Introductory Formulas	AYK.5
6	Cost Comparison	Excel	T2	Total Cost of Ownership	Introductory Formulas	AYK.5
7	Time Management	Excel or Project	T2 or T12	Project Management	Introductory Gantt Charts	AYK.6
8	Maximize Profit	Excel	T2, T4	Strategic Analysis	Intermediate Formulas or Solver	AYK.6
9	Security Analysis	Excel	T3	Filtering Data	Intermediate Conditional Formatting, Autofilter, Subtotal	AYK.7
10	Gathering Data	Excel	T3	Data Analysis	Intermediate Conditional Formatting, PivotTable	AYK.8
11	Scanner System	Excel	T2	Strategic Analysis	Intermediate	AYK.8
12	Competitive Pricing	Excel	T2	Profit Maximization	Intermediate	AYK.9
13	Adequate Acquisitions	Excel	T2	Break-Even Analysis	Intermediate	AYK.9
24	Electronic Resumes	HTML	T9, T10, T11	Electronic Personal Marketing	Introductory Structural Tags	AYK.16
25	Gathering Feedback	Dreamweaver	T9, T10, T11	Data Collection	Intermediate Organization of Information	AYK.16

Ethics and Information Security: MIS Business Concerns

4

CHAPTER

CHAPTER OUTLINE

SECTION 4.1
Ethics

- Information Ethics
- Developing Information Management Policies
- Ethics in the Workplace

SECTION 4.2
Information Security

- Protecting Intellectual Assets
- The First Line of Defense—People
- The Second Line of Defense—Technology

What's in IT for me?

This chapter concerns itself with protecting information from potential misuse. Organizations must ensure they collect, capture, store, and use information in an ethical manner. This means any type of information they collect and utilize, including about customers, partners, and employees. Companies must ensure that personal information collected about someone remains private. This is not just a nice thing to do. The law requires it. Perhaps more important, information must be kept physically secure to prevent access and possible dissemination and use by unauthorized sources.

You, the business student, must understand ethics and security because they are the top concerns voiced by customers today. The way they are handled directly influences a customer's likelihood of embracing electronic technologies and conducting business over the Web–and thus the company's bottom line. You can find evidence in recent news reports about how the stock price of organizations falls dramatically when information privacy and security breaches are made known. Further, organizations face potential litigation if they fail to meet their ethical, privacy, and security obligations in the handling of information.

opening case study

E-Espionage

BusinessWeek magazine recently probed the rising attacks on America's most sensitive computer networks, uncovering startling security gaps. The email message addressed to a Booz Allen Hamilton executive from the Pentagon was mundane—a shopping list of weaponry India wanted to buy. But the missive was a brilliant fake. Lurking beneath the description of aircraft, engines, and radar equipment was an insidious piece of computer code, known as Poison Ivy, designed to suck sensitive data out of the $4 billion consulting firm's computer network.

The Pentagon had not sent the email. Its origin is unknown, but the message traveled through Korea on its way to Booz Allen. Its authors knew enough about the "sender" and "recipient" to craft a message unlikely to arouse suspicion. Had the Booz Allen executive clicked on the attachment, his every keystroke would have been reported back to a mysterious master at the Internet address cybersyndrome.3322.org, which is registered through an obscure company headquartered on the banks of China's Yangtze River.

The email aimed at Booz Allen paints a vivid picture of the alarming new capabilities of America's cyberenemies. The email message was sent to John F. "Jack" Mulhern, vice president for international military assistance programs at Booz Allen. In the high-tech world of weapons sales, Mulhern's specialty, the email looked authentic enough. "Integrate U.S., Russian, and Indian weapons and avionics," the email noted, describing the Indian government's expectations for its fighter jets. "Source code given to India for indigenous computer upgrade capability." Such lingo could easily be understood by Mulhern. The 62-year-old former U.S. Naval officer and 33-year veteran of Booz Allen's military consulting business is an expert in helping to sell U.S. weapons to foreign governments.

The email was more convincing because of its apparent sender: Stephen J. Moree, a civilian who works for a group that reports to the office of Air Force Secretary Michael W. Wynne. Among its duties, Moree's unit evaluates the security of selling U.S. military aircraft to other countries. There would be little reason to suspect anything seriously amiss in Moree passing along the highly technical document with "India MRCA Request for Proposal" in the subject line. The Indian government had just released the request a week earlier, on August 28, and the language in the email closely tracked the request. Making the message appear more credible still, it referred to upcoming Air Force communiqués and a "Team Meeting" to discuss the deal.

But the correspondence from Moree to Jack Mulhern was a fake. An analysis of the email's path and attachment, conducted for *BusinessWeek* by three cybersecurity specialists, shows it was sent by an unknown attacker, bounced through an Internet address in South Korea, relayed through a Yahoo! server in New York, and finally made its way to Mulhern's Booz Allen in-box. The analysis also shows the code—known as malware, for malicious software—tracks keystrokes on the computers of people who open it. A separate program disables security measures such as password protection on Microsoft Access database files, a program often used by large organizations such as the U.S. defense industry to manage big batches of data.

Global Threats

The U.S. government and its sprawl of defense contractors have been the victims of an unprecedented rash of similar attacks, say current and former U.S. government officials. "It's espionage on a massive scale," said Paul B. Kurtz, a former high-ranking national security official. Government agencies reported 12,986 cybersecurity incidents to the U.S. Homeland Security Department in one fiscal year, triple the number from two years earlier. Incursions on the military's networks were up 55 percent, said Lieutenant General Charles E. Croom, head of the Pentagon's Joint Task Force for Global Network Operations. Private targets such as Booz Allen are just as vulnerable and pose just as much potential security risk. "They have our information on their networks. They're building our weapon systems. You wouldn't want that in enemy hands," Croom said. Cyber attackers "are not denying, disrupting, or destroying operations—yet. But that doesn't mean they don't have the capability."

Poison Ivy

Commercial computer security firms have dubbed the malicious code hidden inside the email attachment Poison Ivy, and it has a devious—and worrisome—capability known as a RAT, a remote administration tool. RAT gives the attacker control over the host PC, capturing screen shots and perusing files. It lurks in the background of Microsoft Internet Explorer browsers while users surf the Web. Then it phones home to its "master" at an Internet address currently registered under the name cybersyndrome.3322.org.

The digital trail to cybersyndrome.3322.org, followed by analysts at *BusinessWeek*'s request, leads to one of China's largest free domain-name-registration and email services. Called 3322.org, it is registered to a company called Bentium in the city of Changzhou, an industrial hub outside Shanghai. A range of security experts say that 3322.org provides names for computers and servers that act as the command and control centers for more than 10,000 pieces of malicious code launched at government and corporate networks in recent years. Many of those PCs are in China; the rest could be anywhere.

The founder of 3322.org, a 37-year-old technology entrepreneur named Peng Yong, says his company merely allows users to register domain names. "As for what our users do, we cannot completely control it," Peng said. The bottom line: If Poison

Ivy infected Jack Mulhern's computer at Booz Allen, any secrets inside could be seen in China. And if it spread to other computers, as malware often does, the infection opens windows on potentially sensitive information there, too.

Many security experts worry the Internet has become too unwieldy to be tamed. New threats appear every day, each seemingly more sophisticated than the previous one. The Defense Department, whose Advanced Research Projects Agency (DARPA) developed the Internet in the 1960s, is beginning to think it created a monster. "You don't need an Army, a Navy, an Air Force to beat the U.S.," said General William T. Lord, commander of the Air Force Cyber Command, a unit formed to upgrade Air Force computer defenses. "You can be a peer force for the price of the PC on my desk."[1]

section 4.1 ETHICS

LEARNING OUTCOMES

4.1 Explain the ethical issues in the use of information technology.

4.2 Identify the six epolicies organizations should implement to protect themselves.

INFORMATION ETHICS

LO 4.1: Explain the ethical issues in the use of information technology.

Ethics and security are two fundamental building blocks for all organizations. In recent years, enormous business scandals along with 9/11 have shed new light on the meaning of ethics and security. When the behavior of a few individuals can destroy billion-dollar organizations, the value of ethics and security should be evident.

Copyright is the legal protection afforded an expression of an idea, such as a song, book, or video game. ***Intellectual property*** is intangible creative work that is embodied in physical form and includes copyrights, trademarks, and patents. As it becomes easier for people to copy everything from words and data to music and video, the ethical issues surrounding copyright infringement and the violation of intellectual property rights are consuming the ebusiness world. Technology poses new challenges for our ***ethics***—the principles and standards that guide our behavior toward other people.

The protection of customers' privacy is one of the largest, and murkiest, ethical issues facing organizations today. ***Privacy*** is the right to be left alone when you want to be, to have control over your personal possessions, and not to be observed without your consent. Privacy is related to ***confidentiality,*** which is the assurance that messages and information remain available only to those authorized to view them. Each time employees make a decision about a privacy issue, the outcome could sink the company.

Trust among companies, customers, partners, and suppliers is the support structure of ebusiness. Privacy is one of its main ingredients. Consumers' concerns that their privacy will be violated because of their interactions on the Web continue to be one of the primary barriers to the growth of ebusiness.

Information ethics govern the ethical and moral issues arising from the development and use of information technologies, as well as the creation, collection, duplication, distribution, and processing of information itself (with or without the aid of computer technologies). Ethical dilemmas in this area usually arise not as simple, clear-cut situations but as clashes among competing goals, responsibilities, and loyalties. Inevitably, there will be more than one socially acceptable or "correct" decision. The two primary areas concerning software include pirated software and counterfeit software. ***Pirated software*** is the unauthorized use, duplication, distribution, or sale of copyrighted software. ***Counterfeit software*** is software that is manufactured to look like the real thing and sold as such. Figure 4.1 contains examples of ethically questionable or unacceptable uses of information technology.[2]

Unfortunately, few hard and fast rules exist for always determining what is ethical. Many people can either justify or condemn the actions in Figure 4.1, for example. Knowing the law is important but that knowledge will not always help, because what is legal

FIGURE 4.1

Ethically Questionable or Unacceptable Information Technology Use

Individuals copy, use, and distribute software.
Employees search organizational databases for sensitive corporate and personal information.
Organizations collect, buy, and use information without checking the validity or accuracy of the information.
Individuals create and spread viruses that cause trouble for those using and maintaining IT systems.
Individuals hack into computer systems to steal proprietary information.
Employees destroy or steal proprietary organization information such as schematics, sketches, customer lists, and reports.

APPLY YOUR KNOWLEDGE

BUSINESS DRIVEN DISCUSSION

Information - Does It Have Ethics?

A high school principal decided it was a good idea to hold a confidential conversation about teachers, salaries, and student test scores on his cellular phone in a local Starbucks. Not realizing that one of the student's parents was sitting next to him, the principal accidentally divulged sensitive information about his employees and students. The irate parent soon notified the school board about the principal's inappropriate behavior and a committee was formed to decide how to handle the situation.[3]

With the new wave of collaboration tools, electronic business, and the Internet, employees are finding themselves working outside the office and beyond traditional office hours. Advantages associated with remote workers include increased productivity, decreased expenses, and boosts in morale as employees are given greater flexibility to choose their work location and hours. Unfortunately, there are also disadvantages associated with remote workers such as new forms of ethical challenges and information security risks.

In a group, discuss the following statement: Information Does Not Have Any Ethics. If you were elected to the committee to investigate the principal's inappropriate Starbucks phone conversation, what types of questions would you want answered? What type of punishment, if any, would you enforce on the principal? What types of policies would you implement across the school district to ensure this scenario is never repeated? Be sure to highlight how remote workers impact business along with any potential ethical challenges and information security issues.

might not always be ethical, and what might be ethical is not always legal. For example, Joe Reidenberg received an offer for AT&T cell phone service. AT&T used Equifax, a credit reporting agency, to identify potential customers such as Joe Reidenberg. Overall, this seemed like a good business opportunity between Equifax and AT&T wireless. Unfortunately, the Fair Credit Reporting Act (FCRA) forbids repurposing credit information except when the information is used for "a firm offer of credit or insurance." In other words, the only product that can be sold based on credit information is credit. A representative for Equifax stated, "As long as AT&T Wireless (or any company for that matter) is offering the cell phone service on a credit basis, such as allowing the use of the service before the consumer has to pay, it is in compliance with the FCRA." However, the question remains—is it ethical?[4]

This is a good example of the ethical dilemmas, many still being defined, that organizations face. Figure 4.2 shows the four quadrants of ethical and legal behavior. The goal for organizations is to make decisions within quadrant I that are *both* legal and ethical.

BUSINESS DRIVEN ETHICS AND SECURITY

Is IT Really Worth the Risk?

Ethics. It's just one tiny word, but it has monumental impact on every area of business. From the magazines, blogs, and newspapers you read to the courses you take, you will encounter ethics as it is a hot topic in today's electronic world. Technology has provided so many incredible opportunities, but it has also provided those same opportunities to unethical people. Discuss the ethical issues surrounding each of the following situations (yes, these are true stories):

- A student raises her hand in class and states, "I can legally copy any DVD I get from Netflix because Netflix purchased the DVD and the copyright only applies to the company who purchased the product."
- A student stands up the first day of class before the professor arrives and announces that his fraternity scans textbooks and he has the textbook for this course on his thumb drive, which he will gladly sell for $20. Several students pay on the spot and upload the scanned textbook to their PCs. One student takes down the student information and contacts the publisher about the incident.
- A senior marketing manager is asked to monitor his employee's email because there is a rumor that the employee is looking for another job.
- A vice president of sales asks her employee to burn all of the customer data onto an external hard drive because she made a deal to provide customer information to a strategic partner.
- A senior manager is asked to monitor his employee's email to discover if she is sexually harassing another employee.
- An employee is looking at the shared network drive and discovers his boss's entire hard drive, including his email backup, has been copied to the network and is visible to all.
- An employee is accidently copied on an email listing the targets for the next round of layoffs.

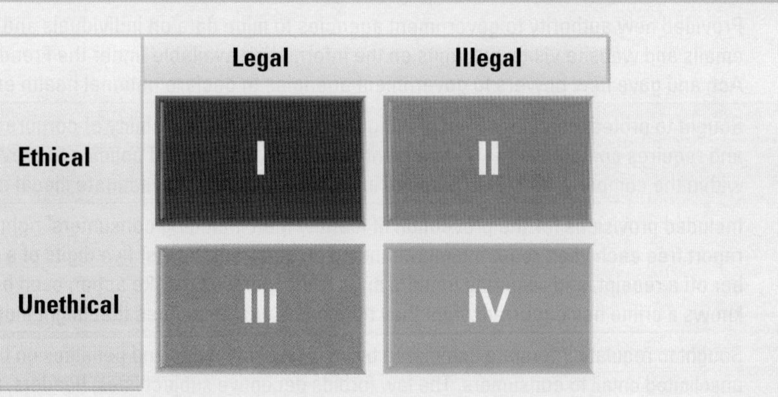

FIGURE 4.2

Acting Ethically and Acting Legally Are Not Always the Same

Information Does Not Have Ethics, People Do

Information itself has no ethics. It does not care how it is used. It will not stop itself from spamming customers, sharing itself if it is sensitive or personal, or revealing details to third parties. Information cannot delete or preserve itself. Therefore, it falls to those who own the information to develop ethical guidelines about how to manage it. ***Information management*** examines the organizational resource of information and regulates its definitions, uses, value, and distribution ensuring it has the types of data/information required to function and grow effectively. ***Information governance*** is a method or system of government for information management or control. ***Information***

FIGURE 4.3
Established Information-Related Laws

Established Information-Related Laws	
Privacy Act—1974	Restricts what information the federal government can collect; allows people to access and correct information on themselves; requires procedures to protect the security of personal information; and forbids the disclosure of name-linked information without permission.
Family Education Rights and Privacy Act—1974	Regulates access to personal education records by government agencies and other third parties and ensures the right of students to see their own records.
Cable Communications Act—1984	Requires written or electronic consent from viewers before cable TV providers can release viewing choices or other personally identifiable information.
Electronic Communications Privacy Act—1986	Allows the reading of communications by a firm and says that employees have no right to privacy when using their companies' computers.
Computer Fraud and Abuse Act—1986	Prohibits unauthorized access to computers used for financial institutions, the U.S. government, or interstate and international trade.
The Bork Bill (officially known as the Video Privacy Protection Act, 1988)	Prohibits the use of video rental information on customers for any purpose other than that of marketing goods and services directly to the customer.
Communications Assistance for Law Enforcement Act—1994	Requires that telecommunications equipment be designed so that authorized government agents are able to intercept all wired and wireless communications being sent or received by any subscriber. The act also requires that subscriber call-identifying information be transmitted to a government when and if required.
Freedom of Information Act—1967, 1975, 1994, and 1998	Allows any person to examine government records unless it would cause an invasion of privacy. It was amended in 1974 to apply to the FBI, and again in 1994 to allow citizens to monitor government activities and information gathering, and once again in 1998 to access government information on the Internet.
Health Insurance Portability and Accountability Act (HIPAA)—1996	Requires that the health care industry formulate and implement regulations to keep patient information confidential.
Identity Theft and Assumption Deterrence Act—1998	Strengthened the criminal laws governing identity theft making it a federal crime to use or transfer identification belonging to another. It also established a central federal service for victims.
USA Patriot Act—2001 and 2003	Allows law enforcement to get access to almost any information, including library records, video rentals, bookstore purchases, and business records when investigating any act of terrorist or clandestine intelligence activities. In 2003, Patriot II broadened the original law.
Homeland Security Act—2002	Provided new authority to government agencies to mine data on individuals and groups including emails and website visits; put limits on the information available under the Freedom of Information Act; and gave new powers to government agencies to declare national health emergencies.
Sarbanes-Oxley Act—2002	Sought to protect investors by improving the accuracy and reliability of corporate disclosures and requires companies to (1) implement extensive and detailed policies to prevent illegal activity within the company, and (2) to respond in a timely manner to investigate illegal activity.
Fair and Accurate Credit Transactions Act—2003	Included provisions for the prevention of identity theft including consumers' right to get a credit report free each year, requiring merchants to leave all but the last five digits of a credit card number off a receipt, and requiring lenders and credit agencies to take action even before a victim knows a crime has occurred when they notice any circumstances that might indicate identity theft.
CAN-Spam Act—2003	Sought to regulate interstate commerce by imposing limitations and penalties on businesses sending unsolicited email to consumers. The law forbids deceptive subject lines, headers, return addresses, etc., as well as the harvesting of email addresses from websites. It requires businesses that send spam to maintain a do-not-spam list and to include a postal mailing address in the message.

compliance is the act of conforming, acquiescing, or yielding information. A few years ago the ideas of information management, governance, and compliance were relatively obscure. Today, these concepts are a must for virtually every company, both domestic and global, primarily due to the role digital information plays in corporate legal proceedings or litigation. Frequently, digital information serves as key evidence in legal proceedings and it is far easier to search, organize, and filter than paper documents. Digital information is also extremely difficult to destroy especially if it is on a corporate network or sent via email. In fact, the only reliable way to truly obliterate digital information is to destroy the hard drives where the file was stored. ***Ediscovery*** (or ***electronic discovery***) refers to the ability of a company to identify, search, gather, seize, or export digital information in responding to a litigation, audit, investigation, or information inquiry. As the importance of ediscovery grows, so does information governance and information compliance. Figure 4.3 provides an overview of some of the important laws individuals and firms must follow in managing and protecting information.[5]

DEVELOPING INFORMATION MANAGEMENT POLICIES

LO 4.2: Identify the six epolicies organizations should implement to protect themselves.

Treating sensitive corporate information as a valuable resource is good management. Building a corporate culture based on ethical principles that employees can understand and implement is responsible management. Organizations should develop written policies establishing employee guidelines, employee procedures, and organizational rules for information. These policies set employee expectations about the organization's practices and standards and protect the organization from misuse of computer systems and IT resources. If an organization's employees use computers at work, the organization should, at a minimum, implement epolicies. ***Epolicies*** are policies and procedures that address information management along with the ethical use of computers and the Internet in the business environment. Figure 4.4 displays the epolicies a firm should implement to set employee expectations.

Ethical Computer Use Policy

In a case that illustrates the perils of online betting, a leading Internet poker site reported that a hacker exploited a security flaw to gain an insurmountable edge in high-stakes, no-limit Texas hold-'em tournaments—the ability to see his opponents' hole cards. The cheater, whose illegitimate winnings were estimated at between $400,000 and $700,000 by one victim, was an employee of AbsolutePoker.com and hacked the system to show that it could be done. Regardless of what business a company operates—even one that many view as unethical—the company must protect itself from unethical employee behavior.[6]

One essential step in creating an ethical corporate culture is establishing an ethical computer use policy. An ***ethical computer use policy*** contains general principles to guide computer user behavior. For example, it might explicitly state that users should refrain from playing computer games during working hours. This policy ensures the users know how to behave at work and the organization has a published standard to deal

FIGURE 4.4

Overview of Epolicies

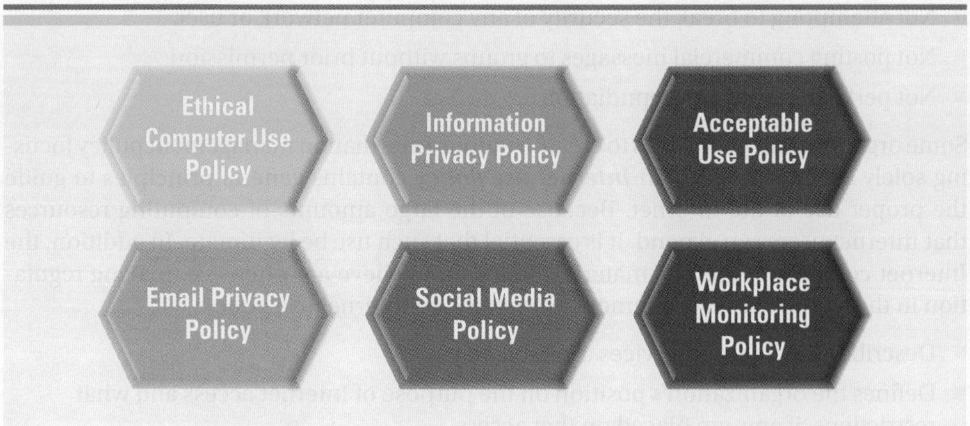

with infractions. For example, after appropriate warnings, the company may terminate an employee who spends significant amounts of time playing computer games at work.

Organizations can legitimately vary in how they expect employees to use computers, but in any approach to controlling such use, the overriding principle should be informed consent. The users should be *informed* of the rules and, by agreeing to use the system on that basis, *consent* to abide by them.

Managers should make a conscientious effort to ensure all users are aware of the policy through formal training and other means. If an organization were to have only one epolicy, it should be an ethical computer use policy because that is the starting point and the umbrella for any other policies the organization might establish.

Information Privacy Policy

An organization that wants to protect its information should develop an ***information privacy policy,*** which contains general principles regarding information privacy. Visa created Inovant to handle all its information systems including its coveted customer information, which details how people are spending their money, in which stores, on which days, and even at what time of day. Just imagine what a sales and marketing department could do if it gained access to this information. For this reason, Inovant bans the use of Visa's customer information for anything outside its intended purpose—billing. Innovant's privacy specialists developed a strict credit card information privacy policy, which it follows.

Now Inovant is being asked if it can guarantee that unethical use of credit card information will never occur. In a large majority of cases, the unethical use of information happens not through the malicious scheming of a rogue marketer, but rather unintentionally. For instance, information is collected and stored for some purpose, such as record keeping or billing. Then, a sales or marketing professional figures out another way to use it internally, share it with partners, or sell it to a trusted third party. The information is "unintentionally" used for new purposes. The classic example of this type of unintentional information reuse is the Social Security number, which started simply as a way to identify government retirement benefits and then was used as a sort of universal personal ID, found on everything from drivers' licenses to savings accounts.

Acceptable Use Policy

An ***acceptable use policy (AUP)*** requires a user to agree to follow it to be provided access to corporate email, information systems, and the Internet. ***Nonrepudiation*** is a contractual stipulation to ensure that ebusiness participants do not deny (repudiate) their online actions. A nonrepudiation clause is typically contained in an acceptable use policy. Many businesses and educational facilities require employees or students to sign an acceptable use policy before gaining network access. When signing up with an email provider, each customer is typically presented with an AUP, which states the user agrees to adhere to certain stipulations. Users agree to the following in a typical acceptable use policy:

- Not using the service as part of violating any law.
- Not attempting to break the security of any computer network or user.
- Not posting commercial messages to groups without prior permission.
- Not performing any nonrepudiation.

Some organizations go so far as to create a unique information management policy focusing solely on Internet use. An ***Internet use policy*** contains general principles to guide the proper use of the Internet. Because of the large amounts of computing resources that Internet users can expend, it is essential that such use be legitimate. In addition, the Internet contains numerous materials that some believe are offensive, making regulation in the workplace a requirement. Generally, an Internet use policy:

- Describes the Internet services available to users.
- Defines the organization's position on the purpose of Internet access and what restrictions, if any, are placed on that access.

APPLY YOUR KNOWLEDGE

BUSINESS DRIVEN GLOBALIZATION

Censoring Google

The Google debate over operations in China is an excellent example of types of global ethical and security issues U.S. companies face as they expand operations around the world. Google's systems were targeted by highly sophisticated hacker attacks aimed at obtaining proprietary information including personal data belonging to Chinese human rights activists who use Google's Gmail service. Google, which originally agreed to filter search results based on Chinese government censorship rules, decided to unfilter search results after what it called an infiltration of its technology and the email accounts of Chinese human-rights activists. China called Google's plan to defy government censorship rules unfriendly and irresponsible and demanded Google shut down all operations in China.

Why would China want to filer search results? Do you agree or disagree with China's censorship rules? Do you think Google was acting ethically when it agreed to implement China's censorship rules? Why do companies operating abroad need to be aware of the different ethical perspective found in other cultures?[7]

- Describes user responsibility for citing sources, properly handling offensive material, and protecting the organization's good name.
- States the ramifications if the policy is violated.

Email Privacy Policy

An ***email privacy policy*** details the extent to which email messages may be read by others. Email is so pervasive in organizations that it requires its own specific policy. Most working professionals use email as their preferred means of corporate communications. While email and instant messaging are common business communication tools, there are risks associated with using them. For instance, a sent email is stored on at least three or four computers (see Figure 4.5). Simply deleting an email from one computer does not delete it from the others. Companies can mitigate many of the risks of using electronic messaging systems by implementing and adhering to an email privacy policy.

One major problem with email is the user's expectations of privacy. To a large extent, this expectation is based on the false assumption that email privacy protection exists somehow analogous to that of U.S. first-class mail. Generally, the organization that owns the email system can operate the system as openly or as privately as it wishes. Surveys indicate that the majority of large firms regularly read and analyze employees' email looking for confidential data leaks such as unannounced financial results or the sharing of trade secrets that result in the violation of an email privacy policy and eventual termination of the employee. That means that if the organization wants to read everyone's email, it can do so. Basically, using work email for anything other than work is not a good idea. A typical email privacy policy:

- Defines legitimate email users and explains what happens to accounts after a person leaves the organization.
- Explains backup procedure so users will know that at some point, even if a message is deleted from their computer, it is still stored by the company.
- Describes the legitimate grounds for reading email and the process required before such action is performed.
- Discourages sending junk email or spam to anyone who does not want to receive it.

FIGURE 4.5
Email Is Stored on Multiple Computers

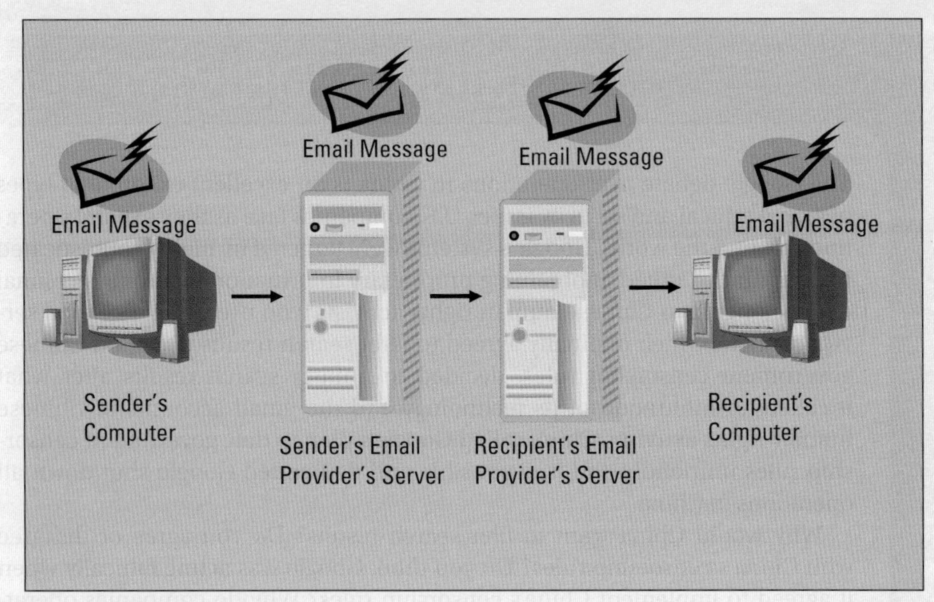

- Prohibits attempting to mail bomb a site. A ***mail bomb*** sends a massive amount of email to a specific person or system that can cause that user's server to stop functioning.
- Informs users that the organization has no control over email once it has been transmitted outside the organization.

Spam is unsolicited email. It plagues employees at all levels within an organization, from receptionist to CEO, and clogs email systems and siphons MIS resources away from legitimate business projects. An ***anti-spam policy*** simply states that email users will not send unsolicited emails (or spam). It is difficult to write anti-spam policies, laws, or software because there is no such thing as a universal litmus test for spam. One person's spam is another person's newsletter. End users have to decide what spam is, because it can vary widely not just from one company to the next, but from one person to the next.

Social Media Policy

Did you see the YouTube video showing two Domino's Pizza employees violating health codes while preparing food by passing gas on sandwiches? Millions of people did and the company took notice when disgusted customers began posting negative comments all over Twitter. Not having a Twitter account, corporate executives at Domino's did not know about the damaging tweets until it was too late. The use of social media can contribute many benefits to an organization, and implemented correctly it can become a huge opportunity for employees to build brands. But there are also tremendous risks as a few employees representing an entire company can cause tremendous brand damage. Defining a set of guidelines implemented in a social media policy can help mitigate that risk. Companies can protect themselves by implementing a ***social media policy*** outlining the corporate guidelines or principles governing employee online communications. Having a single social media policy might not be enough to ensure the company's online reputation is protected. Additional, more specific, social media policies a company might choose to implement include:[8]

- Employee online communication policy detailing brand communication.
- Employee blog and personal blog policies.
- Employee social network and personal social network policies.

APPLY YOUR KNOWLEDGE

BUSINESS DRIVEN MIS

Sources Are Not Friends

The Canadian Broadcasting Company (CBC) has issued a social networking policy directing journalists to avoid adding sources or contacts as friends on social networking sites such as Facebook or LinkedIn. Basic rules state that reporters never allow one source to view what another source says and reporters want to ensure private conversations with sources remain private. Adding sources as "friends" can compromise a journalist's work by allowing friends to view other friends in the network. It may also not be in a journalist's best interest to become a "friend" in a source's network. The CBC also discourages posting any political preferences in personal profiles, commenting on bulletin boards or people's "Facebook wall."

This might seem like common sense, but for employees who do not spend countless hours on the Internet, using social networking sites can be confusing and overwhelming. Why is it critical for any new hire to research and review all policies, especially social media policies? Research three companies you would like to work for upon graduation, and detail the types of social media policies that the company currently has or should implement.[9]

- Employee Twitter, corporate Twitter, and personal Twitter policies.
- Employee LinkedIn policy.
- Employee Facebook usage and brand usage policy.
- Corporate YouTube policy.

Organizations must protect their online reputations and continuously monitor blogs, message boards, social networking sites, and media sharing sites. However, monitoring the hundreds of different social media sites can quickly become overwhelming. To combat these issues, a number of companies specialize in online social media monitoring; for example, Trackur.com creates digital dashboards allowing executives to view at a glance the date published, source, title, and summary of every item tracked. The dashboard not only highlights what's being said, but also the influence of the particular person, blog, or social media site.

Workplace Monitoring Policy

Increasingly, employee monitoring is not a choice; it is a risk-management obligation. Michael Soden, CEO of the Bank of Ireland, issued a mandate stating that company employees could not surf illicit websites with company equipment. Next, he hired Hewlett-Packard to run the MIS department and illicit websites were discovered on Soden's own computer, forcing Soden to resign. Monitoring employees is one of the biggest challenges CIOs face when developing information management policies.[10]

New technologies make it possible for employers to monitor many aspects of their employees' jobs, especially on telephones, computer terminals, through electronic and voice mail, and when employees are using the Internet. Such monitoring is virtually unregulated. Therefore, unless company policy specifically states otherwise (and even this is not assured), your employer may listen, watch, and read most of your workplace communications. ***Information technology monitoring*** tracks people's activities by such measures as number of keystrokes, error rate, and number of transactions processed (see Figure 4.6 for an overview). The best path for an organization planning to engage in employee monitoring is open communication including an ***employee monitoring policy*** stating explicitly how, when, and where the company monitors its employees.

FIGURE 4.6
Internet Monitoring Technologies

Common Internet Monitoring Technologies	
Key logger, or key trapper, software	A program that records every keystroke and mouse click.
Hardware key logger	A hardware device that captures keystrokes on their journey from the keyboard to the motherboard.
Cookie	A small file deposited on a hard drive by a website containing information about customers and their web activities. Cookies allow websites to record the comings and goings of customers, usually without their knowledge or consent.
Adware	Software that generates ads that install themselves on a computer when a person downloads some other program from the Internet.
Spyware (sneakware or stealthware)	Software that comes hidden in free downloadable software and tracks online movements, mines the information stored on a computer, or uses a computer's CPU and storage for some task the user knows nothing about.
Web log	Consists of one line of information for every visitor to a website and is usually stored on a web server.
Clickstream	Records information about a customer during a Web surfing session such as what websites were visited, how long the visit was, what ads were viewed, and what was purchased.

Several common stipulations an organization can follow when creating an employee monitoring policy include:

- Be as specific as possible stating when and what (email, IM, Internet, network activity, etc.) will be monitored.
- Expressly communicate that the company reserves the right to monitor all employees.
- State the consequences of violating the policy.
- Always enforce the policy the same for everyone.

Many employees use their company's high-speed Internet access to shop, browse, and surf the Web. Most managers do not want their employees conducting personal business during working hours, and they implement a Big Brother approach to employee monitoring. Many management gurus advocate that organizations whose corporate cultures are based on trust are more successful than those whose corporate cultures are based on mistrust. Before an organization implements monitoring technology, it should ask itself, "What does this say about how we feel about our employees?" If the organization really does not trust its employees, then perhaps it should find new ones. If an organization does trust its employees, then it might want to treat them accordingly. An organization that follows its employees' every keystroke might be unwittingly undermining the relationships with its employees, and it might find the effects of employee monitoring are often worse than lost productivity from employee Web surfing.

section 4.2 INFORMATION SECURITY

LEARNING OUTCOMES

4.3 Describe the relationships and differences between hackers and viruses.

4.4 Describe the relationship between information security policies and an information security plan.

4.5 Provide an example of each of the three primary information security areas: (1) authentication and authorization, (2) prevention and resistance, and (3) detection and response.

BUSINESS DRIVEN DEBATE

Fired for Smoking on the Weekend

New technologies make it possible for employers to monitor many aspects of their employees' jobs, especially on telephones, computer terminals, through electronic and voice mail, and when employees are using the Internet. Such monitoring is virtually unregulated. Therefore, unless company policy specifically states otherwise (and even this is not assured), your employer may listen, watch, and read most of your workplace communications.

Employers are taking monitoring activity a step further and monitoring employees, and employees' spouses, at home and on weekends. Yes, you read that correctly. Numerous employees have been fired for smoking cigarettes on the weekend in the privacy of their own home. As health care costs escalate, employers are increasingly seeking to regulate employee behavior—at home as well as in the workplace. Weyco, an insurance benefits administrator in Michigan, initiated a program requiring mandatory breath tests to detect for nicotine, and any employee testing positive would be sent home without pay for one month. If the employee failed the nicotine test a second time, that person would be fired—no matter how long the employee had been with the company. Weyco's smoking prohibition does not stop with employees but extends to spouses also who must pass monthly nicotine tests. A positive test means the employee must pay a monthly fee of $80 until the spouse takes a smoking-cessation program and tests nicotine-free.[11]

Do you agree that companies have the right to hold employees accountable for actions they perform on weekends in the privacy of their own homes? If you were the CEO of Weyco, what would be your argument supporting its smoking prohibition policies? Do you think Weyco's monitoring practices are ethical? Do you think Weyco's monitoring practices are legal?

PROTECTING INTELLECTUAL ASSETS

LO 4.3: Describe the relationships and differences between hackers and viruses.

To accurately reflect the crucial interdependence between MIS and business processes, we should update the old business axiom "Time is money" to say "Uptime is money." ***Downtime*** refers to a period of time when a system is unavailable. Unplanned downtime can strike at any time for any number of reasons, from tornadoes to sink overflows to network failures to power outages (see Figure 4.7). Although natural disasters may appear to be the most devastating causes of MIS outages, they are hardly the most frequent or most expensive. Figure 4.8 demonstrates that the costs of downtime are not only associated with lost revenues, but also with financial performance, damage to reputations, and even travel or legal expenses. A few questions managers should ask when determining the cost of downtime are:[12]

- How many transactions can the company afford to lose without significantly harming business?
- Does the company depend upon one or more mission-critical applications to conduct business?
- How much revenue will the company lose for every hour a critical application is unavailable?
- What is the productivity cost associated with each hour of downtime?
- How will collaborative business processes with partners, suppliers, and customers be affected by an unexpected IT outage?
- What is the total cost of lost productivity and lost revenue during unplanned downtime?

FIGURE 4.7
Sources of Unplanned Downtime

Sources of Unplanned Downtime		
Bomb threat	Frozen pipe	Snowstorm
Burst pipe	Hacker	Sprinkler malfunction
Chemical spill	Hail	Static electricity
Construction	Hurricane	Strike
Corrupted data	Ice storm	Terrorism
Earthquake	Insects	Theft
Electrical short	Lightning	Tornado
Epidemic	Network failure	Train derailment
Equipment failure	Plane crash	Smoke damage
Evacuation	Power outage	Vandalism
Explosion	Power surge	Vehicle crash
Fire	Rodents	Virus
Flood	Sabotage	Water damage (various)
Fraud	Shredded data	Wind

FIGURE 4.8
The Cost of Downtime

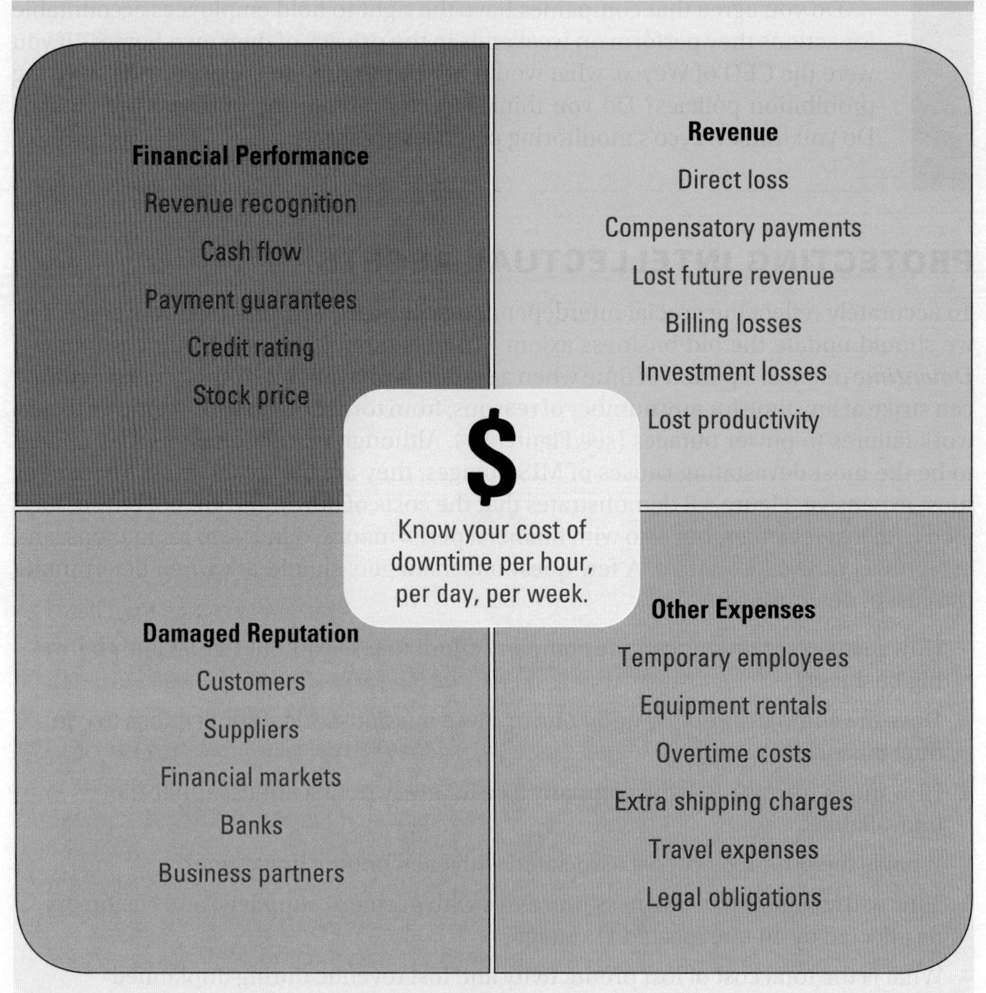

The reliability and resilience of IT systems have never been more essential for success as businesses cope with the forces of globalization, 24/7 operations, government and trade regulations, global recession, and overextended IT budgets and resources. Any unexpected downtime in today's business environment has the potential to cause both short- and long-term costs with far-reaching consequences.

Information security is a broad term encompassing the protection of information from accidental or intentional misuse by persons inside or outside an organization. Information security is the primary tool an organization can use to combat the threats associated with downtime. Understanding how to secure information systems is critical to keeping downtime to a minimum and uptime to a maximum. Hackers and viruses are two of the hottest issues currently facing information security.

Security Threats Caused by Hackers and Viruses

Hackers are experts in technology who use their knowledge to break into computers and computer networks, either for profit or just motivated by the challenge. Smoking is not just bad for a person's health; it seems it is also bad for company security as hackers regularly use smoking entrances to gain building access. Once inside they pose as employees from the MIS department and either ask for permission to use an employee's computer to access the corporate network, or find a conference room where they simply plug-in their own laptop. Figure 4.9 lists the various types of hackers organizations need to be aware of, and Figure 4.10 shows how a virus is spread.

FIGURE 4.9

Types of Hackers

Common Types of Hackers
■ ***Black-hat hackers*** break into other people's computer systems and may just look around or may steal and destroy information.
■ ***Crackers*** have criminal intent when hacking.
■ ***Cyberterrorists*** seek to cause harm to people or to destroy critical systems or information and use the Internet as a weapon of mass destruction.
■ ***Hactivists*** have philosophical and political reasons for breaking into systems and will often deface the website as a protest.
■ ***Script kiddies*** or ***script bunnies*** find hacking code on the Internet and click-and-point their way into systems to cause damage or spread viruses.
■ ***White-hat hackers*** work at the request of the system owners to find system vulnerabilities and plug the holes.

FIGURE 4.10

How Computer Viruses Spread

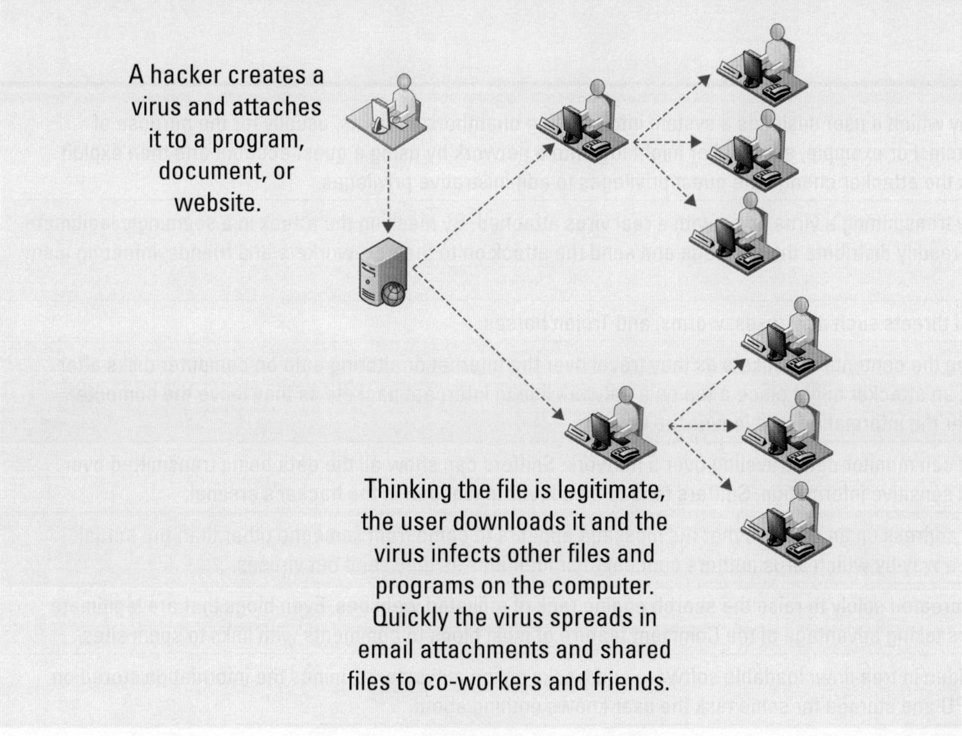

A hacker creates a virus and attaches it to a program, document, or website.

Thinking the file is legitimate, the user downloads it and the virus infects other files and programs on the computer. Quickly the virus spreads in email attachments and shared files to co-workers and friends.

One of the most common forms of computer vulnerabilities is a virus. A ***virus*** is software written with malicious intent to cause annoyance or damage. Some hackers create and leave viruses causing massive computer damage. Figure 4.11 provides an overview of the most common types of viruses. Two additional computer vulnerabilities include adware and spyware. ***Adware*** is software that, while purporting to serve some useful function and often fulfilling that function, also allows Internet advertisers to display advertisements without the consent of the computer user. ***Spyware*** is a special class of adware that collects data about the user and transmits it over the Internet without the user's knowledge or permission. Spyware programs collect specific data about the user, ranging from general demographics such as name, address, and browsing habits to credit card numbers, Social Security numbers, and user names and passwords. Not all adware programs are spyware and used correctly it can generate revenue for a company allowing users to receive free products. Spyware is a clear threat to privacy. Figure 4.12 displays a few additional weapons hackers use for launching attacks.[13]

Organizational information is intellectual capital. Just as organizations protect their tangible assets—keeping their money in an insured bank or providing a safe working environment for employees—they must also protect their intellectual capital, everything

FIGURE 4.11

Common Forms of Viruses

Backdoor programs open a way into the network for future attacks.
Denial-of-service attack (DoS) floods a website with so many requests for service that it slows down or crashes the site.
Distributed denial-of-service attack (DDoS) attacks from multiple computers that flood a website with so many requests for service that it slows down or crashes. A common type is the Ping of Death, in which thousands of computers try to access a website at the same time, overloading it and shutting it down.
Polymorphic viruses and worms change their form as they propagate.
Trojan-horse virus hides inside other software, usually as an attachment or a downloadable file.
Worm spreads itself, not only from file to file, but also from computer to computer. The primary difference between a virus and a worm is that a virus must attach to something, such as an executable file, to spread. Worms do not need to attach to anything to spread and can tunnel themselves into computers.

FIGURE 4.12

Hacker Weapons

Elevation of privilege is a process by which a user misleads a system into granting unauthorized rights, usually for the purpose of compromising or destroying the system. For example, an attacker might log onto a network by using a guest account and then exploit a weakness in the software that lets the attacker change the guest privileges to administrative privileges.
Hoaxes attack computer systems by transmitting a virus hoax, with a real virus attached. By masking the attack in a seemingly legitimate message, unsuspecting users more readily distribute the message and send the attack on to their co-workers and friends, infecting many users along the way.
Malicious code includes a variety of threats such as viruses, worms, and Trojan horses.
Packet tampering consists of altering the contents of packets as they travel over the Internet or altering data on computer disks after penetrating a network. For example, an attacker might place a tap on a network line to intercept packets as they leave the computer. The attacker could eavesdrop or alter the information as it leaves the network.
A **sniffer** is a program or device that can monitor data traveling over a network. Sniffers can show all the data being transmitted over a network, including passwords and sensitive information. Sniffers tend to be a favorite weapon in the hacker's arsenal.
Spoofing is the forging of the return address on an email so that the message appears to come from someone other than the actual sender. This is not a virus but rather a way by which virus authors conceal their identities as they send out viruses.
Splogs (spam blogs) are fake blogs created solely to raise the search engine rank of affiliated websites. Even blogs that are legitimate are plagued by spam, with spammers taking advantage of the Comment feature of most blogs to comments with links to spam sites.
Spyware is software that comes hidden in free downloadable software and tracks online movements, mines the information stored on a computer, or uses a computer's CPU and storage for some task the user knows nothing about.

from patents to transactional and analytical information. With security breaches and viruses on the rise and computer hackers everywhere, an organization must put in place strong security measures to survive.

THE FIRST LINE OF DEFENSE—PEOPLE

LO 4.4: Describe the relationship between information security policies and an information security plan.

Organizations today are able to mine valuable information such as the identity of the top 20 percent of their customers, who usually produce 80 percent of revenues. Most organizations view this type of information as intellectual capital and implement security measures to prevent it from walking out the door or falling into the wrong hands. At the same time, they must enable employees, customers, and partners to access needed information electronically. Organizations address security risks through two lines of defense; the first is people, the second technology.

Surprisingly, the biggest problem is people as the majority of information security breaches result from people misusing organizational information. ***Insiders*** are legitimate users who purposely or accidentally misuse their access to the environment and cause some kind of business-affecting incident. For example, many individuals freely give up their passwords or write them on sticky notes next to their computers, leaving the door wide open for hackers. Through ***social engineering,*** hackers use their social skills to trick people into revealing access credentials or other valuable information. ***Dumpster diving,*** or looking through people's trash, is another way hackers obtain information.

Information security policies identify the rules required to maintain information security, such as requiring users to log off before leaving for lunch or meetings, never sharing passwords with anyone, and changing passwords every 30 days. An ***information security plan*** details how an organization will implement the information security policies. The best way a company can safeguard itself from people is by implementing and communicating its information security plan. This becomes even more important with Web 2.0 and as the use of mobile devices, remote workforce, and contractors are growing. A few details managers should consider surrounding people and information security policies include defining the best practices for[14]

- Applications allowed to be placed on the corporate network, especially various file sharing applications (Kazaz), IM software, and entertainment or freeware created by unknown sources (iPhone applications).
- Corporate computer equipment used for personal reason on personal networks.
- Password creation and maintenance including minimum password length, characters to be included while choosing passwords, and frequency for password changes.
- Personal computer equipment allowed to connect to the corporate network.
- Virus protection including how often the system should be scanned and how frequently the software should be updated. This could also include if downloading attachments is allowed and practices for safe downloading from trusted and untrustworthy sources.

THE SECOND LINE OF DEFENSE—TECHNOLOGY

LO 4.5: Provide an example of each of the three primary information security areas: (1) authentication and authorization, (2) prevention and resistance, and (3) detection and response.

Once an organization has protected its intellectual capital by arming its people with a detailed information security plan, it can begin to focus on deploying technology to help combat attackers. Figure 4.13 displays the three areas where technology can aid in the defense against attacks.

People: Authentication and Authorization

Identity theft is the forging of someone's identity for the purpose of fraud. The fraud is often financial, because thieves apply for and use credit cards or loans in the victim's name. Two means of stealing an identity are phishing and pharming. ***Phishing*** is a technique to gain personal information for the purpose of identity theft, usually by means of fraudulent emails that look as though they came from legitimate businesses. The messages appear to be genuine, with official-looking formats and logos, and typically

FIGURE 4.13

Three Areas of Information Security

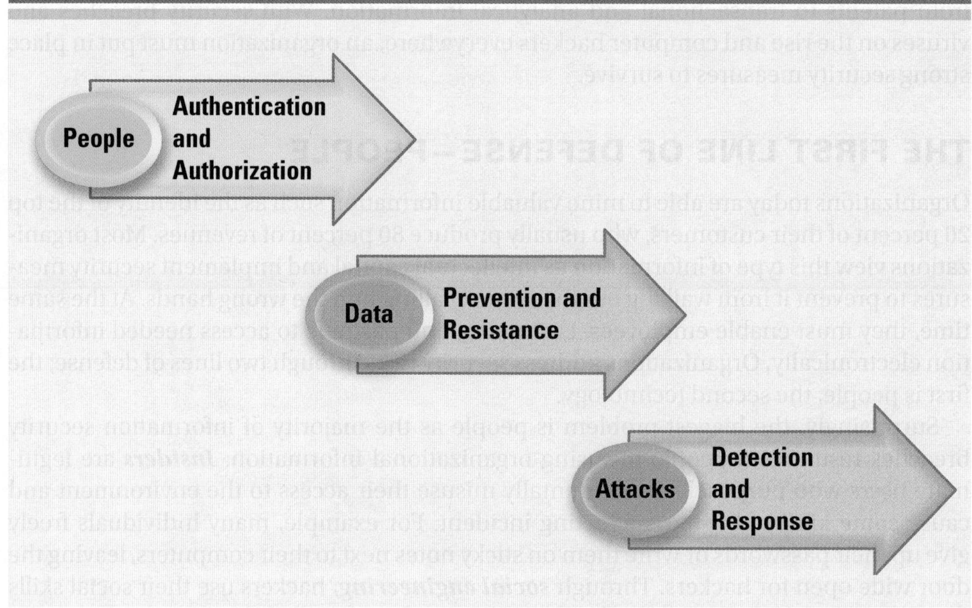

ask for verification of important information such as passwords and account numbers, ostensibly for accounting or auditing purposes. Since the emails look authentic, up to one in five recipients responds with the information and subsequently becomes a victim of identity theft and other fraud. Figure 4.14 displays a phishing scam attempting to gain information for Bank of America; you should never click on emails asking you to verify your identity as companies will never contact you directly asking for your user name or password.[15]

Pharming reroutes requests for legitimate websites to false websites. For example, if you were to type in the URL to your bank, pharming could redirect to a fake site that collects your information. Authentication and authorization technologies can prevent identity theft, phishing, and pharming scams. ***Authentication*** is a method for confirming users' identities. Once a system determines the authentication of a user, it can then determine the access privileges (or authorization) for that user. ***Authorization*** is the process of providing a user with permission including access levels and abilities such as file access, hours of access, and amount of allocated storage space. Authentication and authorization techniques fall into three categories; the most secure procedures combine all three:

1. Something the user knows, such as a user ID and password.
2. Something the user has, such as a smart card or token.
3. Something that is part of the user, such as a fingerprint or voice signature.

Something the User Knows Such as a User ID and Password The first type of authentication, using something the user knows, is the most common way to identify individual users and typically consists of a unique user ID and password. However, this is actually one of the most *ineffective* ways for determining authentication because passwords are not secure. All it typically takes to crack one is enough time. More than 50 percent of help-desk calls are password related, which can cost an organization significant money, and a social engineer can coax a password from almost anybody.

Something the User Has Such as a Smart Card or Token The second type of authentication, using something the user has, offers a much more effective way to identify individuals than a user ID and password. Tokens and smart cards are two of the primary forms of this type of authentication. ***Tokens*** are small electronic devices that change user passwords automatically. The user enters his or her user ID and token-displayed password to gain access to the network. A ***smart card*** is a device about the size of a credit card, containing embedded technologies that can store information and

FIGURE 4.14
Bank of America Phishing Scam

From: Bank of America Online [ealert@replies.em.bankofamerica.com]
Sent: Friday, May 21, 2010 5:40 PM
Subject: Customer Alert: Your Account was been Attended

Bank of America **Higher Standards**

The sooner you sign in to Online Banking, the simpler your life will get.

Important Notification

Dear **Valued Customer**,

As part of Bank of America Online commitment to provide you with exceptional service, Bank of America Online is taking additional steps to ensure that your account data is secure.

Therefore, we are sending you this e-mail as a security precaution to confirm to you the Inability to accurately verify your account information due to an internal error within server

You are required to confirm your account information to forestall a re-occurence of any future attention with your online banking.

However, failure to update your account information might result in your account being suspended.. Click below to get started.

Get Started

Thank you,
Bank of America Online Banking.

* Please do not respond to this email as your reply will not be received.

Bank of America Email, 8th Floor, 101 South Tryon St., Charlotte, NC 28255-0001

small amounts of software to perform some limited processing. Smart cards can act as identification instruments, a form of digital cash, or a data storage device with the ability to store an entire medical record.

Something That Is Part of the User Such as a Fingerprint or Voice Signature The third kind of authentication, something that is part of the user, is by far the best and most effective way to manage authentication. ***Biometrics*** (narrowly defined) is the identification of a user based on a physical characteristic, such as a fingerprint, iris, face, voice, or handwriting. Unfortunately, biometric authentication can be costly and intrusive.

Data: Prevention and Resistance

Prevention and resistance technologies stop intruders from accessing and reading data by means of content filtering, encryption, and firewalls. ***Content filtering*** occurs when organizations use software that filters content, such as emails, to prevent the accidental or malicious transmission of unauthorized information. Organizations can use content filtering technologies to filter email and prevent emails containing sensitive information from transmitting, whether the transmission was malicious or accidental. It can also filter emails and prevent any suspicious files from transmitting such as potential virus-infected files. Email content filtering can also filter for spam, a form of unsolicited email.

APPLY YOUR KNOWLEDGE

BUSINESS DRIVEN INNOVATION

Doodling Passwords

As our online world continues to explode, people are finding the number of user names and passwords they need to remember growing exponentially. For this reason many users will assign the same password for every log-on, choose easy to remember names and dates, or simply write down their passwords on sticky notes and attach them to their computers. Great for the person who needs to remember 72 different passwords, but not so great for system security.

Of course the obvious answer is to deploy biometrics across the board, but once you start reviewing the costs associated with biometrics you quickly realize that this is not feasible. What is coming to the rescue to help with the password nightmare we have created? The doodle. Background Draw-a-Secret (BDAS) is a new program created by scientists at Newcastle University in England. BDAS begins by recording the number of strokes it takes a user to draw a doodle and when the user wants to gain access to the system he simply redraws the doodle on a touchpad and it is matched against the stored prototype. If the doodle matches, the user is granted access. Doodles are even described as being far more anonymous, therefore offering great security, than biometrics.

You are probably thinking that you'll end up right back in the same position having to remember all 72 of your password doodles. The good news is that with doodle passwords you don't have to remember a thing. The doodle password can be displayed to users, and they simply have to redraw it since the system analyzes how the user draws or the user's unique hand strokes, not the actual doodle (similar to handwriting recognition technologies).[16]

If you were going to deploy doodle passwords to your organization, what issues and concerns do you think might occur? Do you agree that doodles are easier to remember than text passwords? Do you agree that doodles offer the most effective way to manage authentication and authorization, even greater than biometrics? What types of unethical issues do you think you might encounter with doodle passwords?

Encryption scrambles information into an alternative form that requires a key or password to decrypt. If there were a security breach and the stolen information were encrypted, the thief would be unable to read it. Encryption can switch the order of characters, replace characters with other characters, insert or remove characters, or use a mathematical formula to convert the information into a code. Companies that transmit sensitive customer information over the Internet, such as credit card numbers, frequently use encryption.

Some encryption technologies use multiple keys. ***Public key encryption (PKE)*** uses two keys: a public key that everyone can have and a private key for only the recipient (see Figure 4.15). The organization provides the public key to all customers, whether end consumers or other businesses, who use that key to encrypt their information and send it via the Internet. When it arrives at its destination, the organization uses the private key to unscramble it.

Public keys are becoming popular to use for authentication techniques consisting of digital objects in which a trusted third party confirms correlation between the user and the public key. A ***certificate authority*** is a trusted third party, such as VeriSign, that validates user identities by means of digital certificates. A ***digital certificate*** is a data file that identifies individuals or organizations online and is comparable to a digital signature.

A ***firewall*** is hardware and/or software that guard a private network by analyzing incoming and outgoing information for the correct markings. If they are missing, the

FIGURE 4.15

Public Key Encryption (PKE)

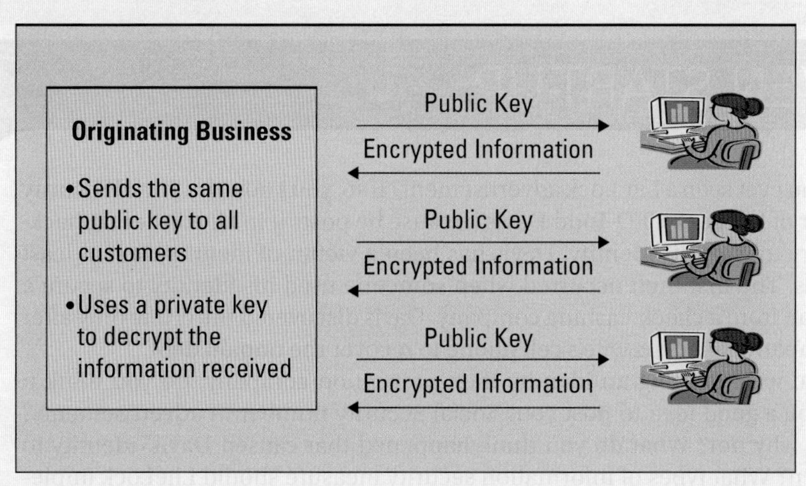

firewall prevents the information from entering the network. Firewalls can even detect computers communicating with the Internet without approval. As Figure 4.16 illustrates, organizations typically place a firewall between a server and the Internet. Think of a firewall as a gatekeeper that protects computer networks from intrusion by providing a filter and safe transfer points for access to and from the Internet and other networks. It screens all network traffic for proper passwords or other security codes and allows only authorized transmissions in and out of the network.

Firewalls do not guarantee complete protection, and users should enlist additional security technologies such as antivirus software and antispyware software. ***Antivirus software*** scans and searches hard drives to prevent, detect, and remove known viruses, adware, and spyware. Antivirus software must be frequently updated to protect against newly created viruses.

Attack: Detection and Response

The presence of an intruder can be detected by watching for suspicious network events such as bad passwords, the removal of highly classified data files, or unauthorized user attempts. ***Intrusion detection software (IDS)*** features full-time monitoring tools that search for patterns in network traffic to identify intruders. IDS protects against suspicious

FIGURE 4.16

Sample Firewall Architecture Connecting Systems Located in Chicago, New York, and Boston

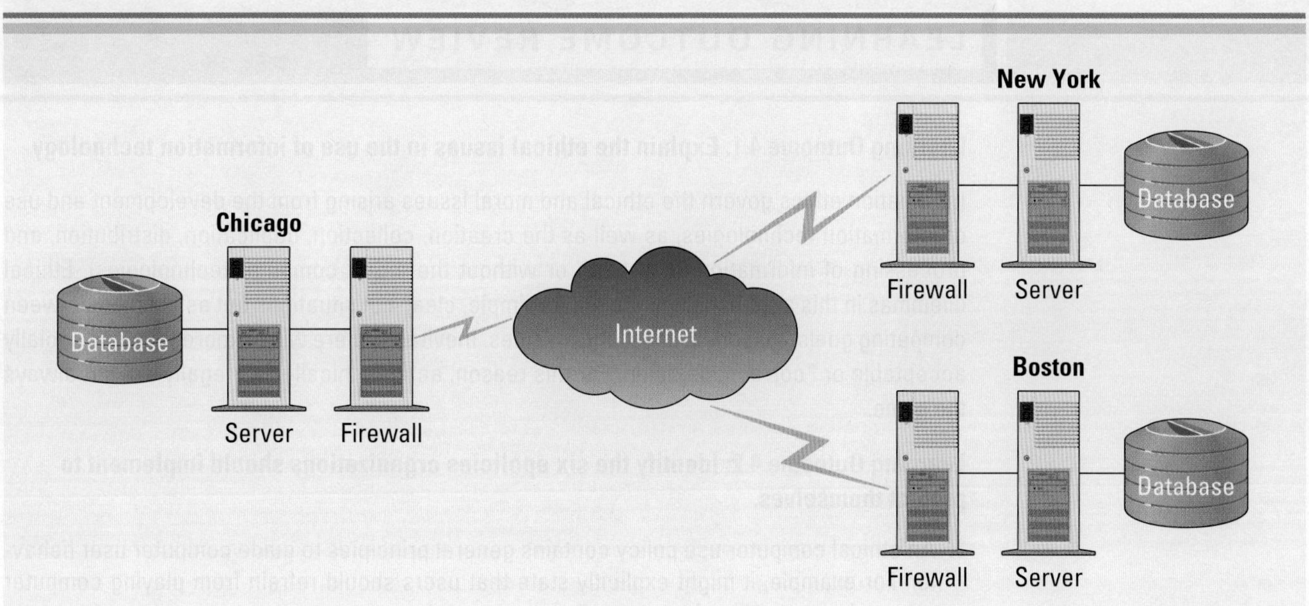

APPLY YOUR KNOWLEDGE

BUSINESS DRIVEN START-UP

LifeLock: Keeping Your Identity Safe

Have you ever seen a LifeLock advertisement? If so, you know the Social Security number of LifeLock CEO Todd Davis because he posts it in all ads daring hackers to try to steal his identity. Davis has been a victim of identity theft at least 13 times. The first theft occurred when someone used his identity to secure a $500 loan from a check-cashing company. Davis discovered the crime only after the company called his wife's cell phone to recover the unpaid debt.[17]

If you were starting an identity theft prevention company, do you think it would be a good idea to post your Social Security number in advertisements? Why or why not? What do you think happened that caused Davis' identity to be stolen? What types of information security measure should LifeLock implement to ensure Davis' Social Security number is not stolen again? If you were LifeLock's CEO, what type of marketing campaign would you launch next?

network traffic and attempts to access files and data. If a suspicious event or unauthorized traffic is identified, the IDS will generate an alarm and can even be customized to shut down a particularly sensitive part of a network. After identifying an attack, an MIS department can implement response tactics to mitigate the damage. Response tactics outline procedures such as how long a system under attack will remain plugged in and connected to the corporate network, when to shut down a compromised system, and how quickly a backup system will be up and running.

Guaranteeing the safety of organization information is achieved by implementing the two lines of defense: people and technology. To protect information through people, firms should develop information security policies and plans that provide employees with specific precautions they should take in creating, working with, and transmitting the organization's information assets. Technology-based lines of defense fall into three categories: authentication and authorization; prevention and resistance; and detection and response.

LEARNING OUTCOME REVIEW

Learning Outcome 4.1: Explain the ethical issues in the use of information technology.

Information ethics govern the ethical and moral issues arising from the development and use of information technologies, as well as the creation, collection, duplication, distribution, and processing of information itself (with or without the aid of computer technologies). Ethical dilemmas in this area usually arise not as simple, clear-cut situations but as clashes between competing goals, responsibilities, and loyalties. Inevitably, there will be more than one socially acceptable or "correct" decision. For this reason, acting ethically and legally are not always the same.

Learning Outcome 4.2: Identify the six epolicies organizations should implement to protect themselves.

1. An ethical computer use policy contains general principles to guide computer user behavior. For example, it might explicitly state that users should refrain from playing computer games during working hours.

2. An information privacy policy contains general principles regarding information privacy.
3. An acceptable use policy (AUP) is a policy that a user must agree to follow in order to be provided access to corporate email, information systems, and to the Internet.
4. An email privacy policy details the extent to which email messages may be read by others.
5. A social media policy outlines the corporate guidelines or principles governing employee online communications.
6. An employee monitoring policy states explicitly how, when, and where the company monitors its employees.

Learning Outcome 4.3: Describe the relationships and differences between hackers and viruses.

Hackers are experts in technology who use their knowledge to break into computers and computer networks, either for profit or just motivated by the challenge. A virus is software written with malicious intent to cause annoyance or damage. Some hackers create and leave viruses causing massive computer damage.

Learning Outcome 4.4: Describe the relationship between information security policies and an information security plan.

Information security policies identify the rules required to maintain information security, such as requiring users to log off before leaving for lunch or meetings, never sharing passwords with anyone, and changing passwords every 30 days. An information security plan details how an organization will implement the information security policies. The best way a company can safeguard itself from people is by implementing and communicating its information security plan.

Learning Outcome 4.5: Provide an example of each of the three primary information security areas: (1) authentication and authorization, (2) prevention and resistance, and (3) detection and response.

Authentication and authorization: Authentication is a method for confirming users' identities. Once a system determines the authentication of a user, it can then determine the access privileges (or authorization) for that user. Authorization is the process of providing a user with permission including access levels and abilities such as file access, hours of access, and amount of allocated storage space.

Prevention and resistance: Content filtering occurs when organizations use software that filters content, such as emails, to prevent the accidental or malicious transmission of unauthorized information. Encryption scrambles information into an alternative form that requires a key or password to decrypt. In a security breach, a thief is unable to read encrypted information. A firewall is hardware and/or software that guard a private network by analyzing incoming and outgoing information for the correct markings.

Detection and response: Intrusion detection software (IDS) features full-time monitoring tools that search for patterns in network traffic to identify intruders.

OPENING CASE QUESTIONS

1. **Knowledge:** Define information ethics and information security and explain why each are critical to any government operation.
2. **Comprehension:** Identify two epolicies the government should implement to help combat cyberterrorism.

3. **Application:** Demonstrate how the government can use authentication and authorization technologies to prevent information theft.
4. **Analysis:** Analyze how the government can use prevention and resistance technologies to safeguard its employees from hackers and viruses.
5. **Synthesis:** Propose a plan for how the government can implement information security plans to ensure its critical information is safe and protects.
6. **Evaluate:** Evaluate the information security issues facing the government and identify its three biggest concerns.

KEY TERMS

REVIEW QUESTIONS

1. What are ethics and why are they important to a company?
2. What is the relationship between information management, governance, and compliance?
3. Why are epolicies important to a company?
4. What is the correlation between privacy and confidentiality?
5. What is the relationship between adware and spyware?
6. What are the positive and negative effects associated with monitoring employees?
7. What is the relationship between hackers and viruses?
8. Why is security a business issue, not just a technology issue?
9. What are the growing issues related to employee communication methods and what can a company do to protect itself?
10. How can a company participating in ebusiness keep its information secure?
11. What technologies can a company use to safeguard information?

12. Why is ediscovery important to a company?
13. What are the reasons a company experiences downtime?
14. What are the costs associated with downtime?

CLOSING CASE ONE

Banks Banking on Security

Bank of America, Commerce Bancorp, PNC Financial Services Group, and Wachovia were victims of a crime where a person tried to steal customer data and sell it to law firms and debt-collection agencies. The thief was selling 670,000 account numbers and balances to the undercover New Jersey police. Increasing network security is a key factor for banks as this is a deciding factor when customers compare financial institutions.

Bank of America

Bank of America is moving toward a stronger authentication process using SiteKey. A service designed to spoil scams in which customers think they are entering data on the bank's website but are actually on a thief's website that is stealing customer data. Worms tell the computers to reroute the URL for the bank into a different site that looks exactly like the banks cite. With SiteKey, a customer can select an image and associate a brief written passage. Whenever the customer signs onto the website, they will see their selected image along with the passage ensuring they are on the bank's website. If the customer is using a different computer the website will ask additional identification questions.

Wells Fargo & Company

"Out-of-wallet" questions contain information not found on identification cards in a wallet such as a driver's license or ATM card. Wells Fargo is implementing a security strategy that operates based on "out-of-wallet" questions for passwords.

E-Trade Financial Corporation

E-Trade Financial Corporation provides customers who have account balances exceeding $50,000 a free Digital Security ID for network authentication. The device displays a new six-digit code every 60 seconds, which the customer must use to log on. Accounts under $50,000 can purchase the Digital Security ID device for $25.

Barclays Bank

Barclays Bank delays money transfers between several hours and one day allowing the company the ability to detect suspicious activity, such as a large number of transfers from multiple accounts into a single account. The online-transfer delay keeps transfers safe from mules, or people who open bank accounts based on an email solicitation. Thieves withdraw cash or open credit cards from the mule accounts.[18]

Questions

1. What reason would a bank have for not wanting to adopt an online-transfer delay policy?
2. What are the two primary lines of security defense and why are they important to financial institutions?
3. Explain the differences between the types of security offered by the banks in the case. Which bank would you open an account with and why?

4. What additional types of security, not mentioned in the case, would you recommend a bank implement?
5. Identify three epolicies a bank should implement to help it improve information security.
6. Describe monitoring policies along with the best way for a bank to implement monitoring technologies.

CLOSING CASE TWO

Hacker Hunters

Hacker hunters are the new breed of crime fighter. They employ the same methodology used to fight organized crime in the 1980s—informants and the cyberworld equivalent of wiretaps. Daniel Larking, a 20-year veteran who runs the FBI's Internet Crime Complaint Center, taps online service providers to help track down criminal hackers. Leads supplied by the FBI and eBay helped Romanian police round up 11 members of a gang that set up fake eBay accounts and auctioned off cell phones, laptops, and cameras they never intended to deliver.

The FBI unleashed Operation Firewall, targeting the ShadowCrew, a gang whose members were schooled in identity theft, bank account pillage, and selling illegal goods on the Internet. ShadowCrew's 4,000 gang members lived in a dozen countries and across the United States. For months, agents had been watching their every move through a clandestine gateway into their website, shadowcrew.com. One member turned informant and called a group meeting, ensuring the members would be at home on their computers during a certain time, when the Secret Service issued orders to move in on the gang. The move was synchronized around the globe to prevent gang members from warning each other via instant messages. Twenty-eight gang members in eight states and six countries were arrested, most still at their computers. Authorities seized dozens of computers and found 1.7 million credit card numbers and more than 18 million email accounts.

ShadowCrew's Operations

The alleged ringleaders of ShadowCrew included Andres Mantovani, 23, a part-time community college student in Arizona, and David Appleyard, 45, a former New Jersey mortgage broker. Mantovani and Appleyard allegedly were administrators in charge of running the website and recruiting members. The site created a marketplace for more than 4,000 gang members who bought and sold hot information and merchandise. The website was open for business 24 hours a day, but since most of the members held jobs, the busiest time was from 10 p.m. to 2 a.m. on Sundays. Hundreds of gang members would meet online to trade credit card information, passports, and even equipment to make fake identity documents. Platinum credit cards cost more than gold ones, and discounts were offered for package deals. One member known as "Scarface" sold 115,695 stolen credit card numbers in a single trade. Overall, the gang made more than $4 million in credit card purchases over two years. ShadowCrew was equivalent to an eBay for the underworld. The site even posted crime tips on how to use stolen credit cards and fake IDs at big retailers.

The gang stole credit card numbers and other valuable information through clever tricks. One of the favorites was sending millions of phishing emails—messages that appeared to be from legitimate companies such as Yahoo!—designed to steal passwords and credit card numbers. The gang also hacked into corporate databases to steal account data. According to sources familiar with the investigation, the gang cracked the networks of 12 unidentified companies that were not even aware their systems had been breached.

Police Operations

Brian Nagel, an assistant director at the Secret Service, coordinated the effort to track the ShadowCrew. Allies included Britain's national high-tech crimes unit, the Royal Canadian Mounted Police, and the Bulgarian Interior Ministry. Authorities turned one of the high-ranking members of the gang into a snitch and had the man help the Secret Service set up a new electronic doorway for ShadowCrew members to enter their website. The snitch spread the word that the new gateway was a more secure way to the website. It was the first-ever tap of a private computer network. "We became shadowcrew.com," Nagel said. Mantovani and Appleyard were slated for trial. Authorities anticipated making additional arrests.[19]

Questions

1. What types of technology could big retailers use to prevent identity thieves from purchasing merchandise?
2. What can organizations do to protect themselves from hackers looking to steal account data?
3. Authorities frequently tap online service providers to track down hackers. Do you think it is ethical for authorities to tap an online service provider and read people's email? Why or why not?
4. Do you think it was ethical for authorities to use one of the high-ranking officials to trap other gang members? Why or why not?
5. In a team, research the Internet and find the best ways to protect yourself from identity theft.

CRITICAL BUSINESS THINKING

1. Cheerleader Charged $27,750 for File Sharing 37 Songs

A federal appeals court is ordering a university student to pay the Recording Industry Association of America $27,750—$750 a track—for file sharing 37 songs when she was a high school cheerleader. Have you ever illegally copied or downloaded a song or movie? If you have and you were forced to pay $750 per track, how much would you owe? What is the difference between file sharing and Internet radio streaming? Do you agree or disagree with the federal appeals decision? Why or why not? Why is claiming a lack of copyright knowledge not a good defense against illegally sharing movies or music? If you do not have a good understanding of information laws, what can you do to ensure you are never placed in a federal lawsuit for violating information laws?[20]

2. Police Records Found in Old Copy Machine

Copy machines made after 2002 all contain a hard drive that stores a copy of every document the machine has ever scanned, printed, copied, or faxed. If the hard drive is not erased or scrubbed when the copy machine is resold, all of that digital information is still maintained inside the machine. The Buffalo, New York, Police Sex Crimes Division recently sold several copy machines without scrubbing the hard drives. The hard drives yielded detailed domestic violence complaints and a list of wanted sex offenders. A machine from the Buffalo Police Narcotics Unit contained targets in a major drug raid, and a copier once used by a New York construction company stored 95 pages of pay stubs with names, addresses, and Social Security numbers.[21]

Who do you think should be held responsible for the information issues caused at the Buffalo police department? What types of ethical issues and information security issues are being violated? What types of epolicies could a company implement to ensure these situations do not occur? What forms of information security could a company implement to ensure these situations do not occur? How does this case support the primary reason why ediscovery is so important to litigation?

3. **Firewall Decisions**

You are the CEO of Inverness Investments, a medium-size venture capital firm that specializes in investing in high-tech companies. The company receives more than 30,000 email messages per year. On average, there are two viruses and three successful hackings against the company each year, which result in losses to the company of about $250,000. Currently, the company has antivirus software installed but does not have any firewalls.

Your CIO is suggesting implementing 10 firewalls for a total cost of $80,000. The estimated life of each firewall is about three years. The chances of hackers breaking into the system with the firewalls installed are about 3 percent. Annual maintenance costs on the firewalls are estimated around $15,000. Create an argument for or against supporting your CIO's recommendation to purchase the firewalls. Are there any considerations in addition to finances?

4. **Preventing Identity Theft**

The FBI states that identity theft is one of the fastest-growing crimes. If you are a victim of identity theft, your financial reputation can be ruined, making it impossible for you to cash a check or receive a bank loan. Learning how to avoid identity theft can be a valuable activity. Research the following websites and draft a document stating the best ways to prevent identity theft.

- The Federal Trade Commission Consumer Information on ID theft at www.consumer.gov/idtheft.
- The Office of the Comptroller of the Currency at www.occ.treas.gov/chcktfd.idassume.htm.
- The Office of the Inspector General at www.ssa.gov/oig/when.htm.
- U.S. Department of Justice at www.usdoj.gov/criminal/fraud/idtheft.html.

5. **Discussing the Three Areas of Information Security**

Great Granola Inc. is a small business operating out of northern California. The company specializes in selling homemade granola, and its primary sales vehicle is through its website. The company is growing exponentially and expects its revenues to triple this year to $12 million. The company also expects to hire 60 additional employees to support its growth. Joan Martin, the CEO, is aware that if her competitors discover the recipe for her granola, or who her primary customers are, it could easily ruin her business. Martin has hired you to draft a document discussing the different areas of information security, along with your recommendations for providing a secure ebusiness environment.

6. **Spying on Email**

Technology advances now allow individuals to monitor computers that they do not even have physical access to. New types of software can capture an individual's incoming and outgoing email and then immediately forward that email to another person. For example, if you are at work and your child is home from school and she receives an email from John at 3:00 p.m., at 3:01 p.m. you can receive a copy of that email sent to your email address. If she replies to John's email, within seconds you will again receive a copy of what she sent to John. Describe two scenarios (other than those described here) for the use of this type of software: one in which the use would be ethical and one in which it would be unethical.

7. Stealing Software

The software industry fights against pirated software on a daily basis. The major centers of software piracy are in places such as Russia and China where salaries and disposable income are comparatively low. People in developing and economically depressed countries will fall behind the industrialized world technologically if they cannot afford access to new generations of software. Considering this, is it reasonable to blame someone for using pirated software when it could cost him or her two months' salary to purchase a legal copy? Create an argument for or against the following statement: Individuals who are economically less fortunate should be allowed access to software free of charge in order to ensure that they are provided with an equal technological advantage.

ENTREPRENEURIAL CHALLENGE

BUILD YOUR OWN BUSINESS

1. Providing employees with computer access is one of the perks offered by your business. Employees enjoy checking their personal email and surfing the Internet on their breaks. So far, computer access has been a cherished employee benefit. When you came into work this morning you found the following anonymous letter from one of your employees on your desk. "I received a highly inappropriate joke from a fellow employee that I found extremely offensive. The employee who sent the joke was Debbie Fernandez and I believe she should be reprimanded for her inappropriate actions. Signed—a disturbed employee." What would you do? What could you have done to ensure situations such as these would be easily handled if they did arise? What could you do to ensure such situations do not happen in the future and if they do all employees are aware of the ramifications of inappropriate emails? (Be sure to identify your business and the name of your company.)
2. The local community has always been a big part of your grandfather's business and he knew almost everyone in the community. Your grandfather attended all types of community events and would spend hours talking with friends and neighbors soliciting feedback and ideas on his business. As you know, data are important to any business. In fact, data are an essential business asset. You have decided to start tracking detailed customer information for all business events from fund-raising to promotions. Since you took over the business you have been collecting more and more event data to help you run marketing campaigns across events and optimize the event schedules. One day, a sophisticated businessman walks into your business and asks to speak to the owner. He introduces himself as Lance Smith and says that he would like to talk to you in private. Smith is retiring and is closing his business that was located just down the street, and he wants to sell you his detailed customer information. Smith would like a large sum of money to sell you his confidential customer contact information and sales reports for the past 20 years. He says he has more than 10,000 customers in his unique database. What do you do?
3. Yesterday you had an interesting conversation with one of your loyal customers, Dan Martello. He asked you the following question: "If I find a digital camera on the street is it OK to look at the contents, or am I invading the owner's privacy?" You have a lengthy debate and decided that in some scenarios it is an invasion of privacy to be looking at someone else's photos and is similar to looking in their windows. In other scenarios, it is not an invasion of privacy if you do not know the person and it is the primary way to identify the owner to return the camera, similar to looking in a wallet. As you are cleaning your business, you find a 30 gigabyte thumb drive and you know that it probably belongs to one of your valuable customers and contains their sensitive information. What do you do? What security concerns are associated with the thumb drive? How could information security policies or an information security plan help your business with this type of situation?

APPLY YOUR KNOWLEDGE BUSINESS PROJECTS

PROJECT I Grading Security

Making The Grade is a nonprofit organization that helps students learn how to achieve better grades in school. The organization has 40 offices in 25 states and more than 2,000 employees. The company wants to build a website to offer its services online. Making The Grade's online services will provide parents seven key pieces of advice for communicating with their children to help them achieve academic success. The website will offer information on how to maintain open lines of communication, set goals, organize academics, regularly track progress, identify trouble spots, get to know their child's teacher, and celebrate their children's successes.

Project Focus

You and your team work for the director of information security. Your team's assignment is to develop a document discussing the importance of creating information security polices and an information security plan. Be sure to include the following:

- The importance of educating employees on information security.
- A few samples of employee information security policies specifically for Making The Grade.
- Other major areas the information security plan should address.
- Signs the company should look for to determine if the website is being hacked.
- The major types of attacks the company should expect to experience.

PROJECT II Eyes Everywhere

The movie *Minority Report* chronicled a futuristic world where people are uniquely identifiable by their eyes. A scan of each person's eyes gives or denies them access to rooms, computers, and anything else with restrictions. The movie portrayed a black market in new eyeballs to help people hide from the authorities. (Why did they not just change the database entry instead? That would have been much easier, but a lot less dramatic.)

The idea of using a biological signature is entirely plausible because biometrics is currently being used and is expected to gain wider acceptance in the near future because forging documents has become much easier with the advances in computer graphics programs and color printers. The next time you get a new passport, it may incorporate a chip that has your biometric information encoded on it. Office of Special Investigations agents with fake documents found that it was relatively easy to enter the United States from Canada, Mexico, and Jamaica, by land, sea, and air.

The task of policing the borders is daunting. Some 500 million foreigners enter the country every year and go through identity checkpoints. More than 13 million permanent-resident and border-crossing cards have been issued by the U.S. government. Also, citizens of 27 countries do not need visas to enter this country. They are expected to have passports that comply with U.S. specifications that will also be readable at the border.

In the post-9/11 atmosphere of tightened security, unrestricted border crossing is not acceptable. The Department of Homeland Security is charged with securing the nation's borders, and as part of this plan, new entry/exit procedures were instituted at the beginning of 2003. An integrated system, using biometrics, will be used to identify foreign visitors to the United States and reduce the likelihood of terrorists entering the country.

Early in 2003, after 6 million biometric border-crossing cards had been issued, a pilot test conducted at the Canadian border detected more than 250 imposters. The testing started with two biometric identifiers: photographs for facial recognition and fingerprint scans. As people enter and leave the country, their actual fingerprints and facial features are compared to the data on the biometric chip in the passport.

Project Focus

In a group, discuss the following:

a. How do you feel about having your fingerprints, facial features, and perhaps more of your biometric features encoded in documents such as your passport? Explain your answer.

b. Would you feel the same way about having biometric information on your driver's license as on your passport? Why or why not?

c. Is it reasonable to have different biometric identification requirements for visitors from different nations? Explain your answer. What would you recommend as criteria for deciding which countries fall into what categories?

d. The checkpoints U.S. citizens pass through upon returning to the country vary greatly in the depth of the checks and the time spent. The simplest involves simply walking past the border guards who may or may not ask you your citizenship. The other end of the spectrum requires that you put up with long waits in airports where you have to line up with hundreds of other passengers while each person is questioned and must produce a passport to be scanned. Would you welcome biometric information on passports if it would speed the process, or do you think that the disadvantages of the reduction in privacy, caused by biometric information, outweigh the advantages of better security and faster border processing? Explain your answer.

PROJECT III Setting Boundaries

Even the most ethical people sometimes face difficult choices. Acting ethically means behaving in a principled fashion and treating other people with respect and dignity. It is simple to say, but not so simple to do since some situations are complex or ambiguous. The important role of ethics in our lives has long been recognized. As far back as 44 B.C., Cicero said that ethics are indispensable to anyone who wants to have a good career. Having said that, Cicero, along with some of the greatest minds over the centuries, struggled with what the rules of ethics should be.

Our ethics are rooted in our history, culture, and religion, and our sense of ethics may shift over time. The electronic age brings with it a new dimension in the ethics debate—the amount of personal information that we can collect and store, and the speed with which we can access and process that information.

Project Focus

In a group, discuss how you would react to the following situations:

a. A senior marketing manager informs you that one of her employees is looking for another job and she wants you to give her access to look through her email.

b. A vice president of sales informs you that he has made a deal to provide customer information to a strategic partner, and he wants you to copy all of the customer information to a thumb drive.

c. You are asked to monitor your employee's email to discover whether he is sexually harassing another employee.

d. You are asked to install a video surveillance system in your office to find out whether employees are taking office supplies home with them.

e. You are looking on the shared network drive and discover that your boss's entire hard drive has been copied to the network for everyone to view. What do you do?

f. You have been accidentally copied on an email from the CEO, which details who will be the targets of the next round of layoffs. What do you do?

PROJECT IV Contemplating Sharing

Bram Cohen created BitTorrent which allows users to upload and download large amounts of data. Cohen demonstrated his program at the world hacker conference, as a free, open source project aimed at computer users who need a cheap way to swap software online. Soon many TV and movie fanatics began using the program to download copyrighted materials. As a result of the hacker conference, more than 20 million people downloaded the BitTorrent program and began sharing movies and television shows across the Internet.

Project Focus

There is much debate surrounding the ethics of peer-to-peer networking. Do you believe BitTorrent is ethical or unethical? Justify your answer.

AYK APPLICATION PROJECTS

If you are looking for Excel projects to incorporate into your class, try any of the following after reading this chapter.

Project Number	Project Name	Project Type	Plug-In Focus Area	Project Focus	Project Skill Set	Page Number
1	Financial Destiny	Excel	T2	Personal Budget	Introductory Formulas	AYK.4
2	Cash Flow	Excel	T2	Cash Flow	Introductory Formulas	AYK.4
3	Technology Budget	Excel	T1, T2	Hardware and Software	Introductory Formulas	AYK.4
4	Tracking Donations	Excel	T2	Employee Relationships	Introductory Formulas	AYK.4
5	Convert Currency	Excel	T2	Global Commerce	Introductory Formulas	AYK.5
6	Cost Comparison	Excel	T2	Total Cost of Ownership	Introductory Formulas	AYK.5
7	Time Management	Excel or Project	T2 or T12	Project Management	Introductory Gantt Charts	AYK.6
8	Maximize Profit	Excel	T2, T4	Strategic Analysis	Intermediate Formulas or Solver	AYK.6
9	Security Analysis	Excel	T3	Filtering Data	Intermediate Conditional Formatting, Autofilter, Subtotal	AYK.7
10	Gathering Data	Excel	T3	Data Analysis	Intermediate Conditional Formatting, PivotTable	AYK.8
11	Scanner System	Excel	T2	Strategic Analysis	Intermediate	AYK.8
12	Competitive Pricing	Excel	T2	Profit Maximization	Intermediate	AYK.9
13	Adequate Acquisitions	Excel	T2	Break-Even Analysis	Intermediate	AYK.9
24	Electronic Resumes	HTML	T9, T10, T11	Electronic Personal Marketing	Introductory Structural Tags	AYK.16
25	Gathering Feedback	Dreamweaver	T9, T10, T11	Data Collection	Intermediate Organization of Information	AYK.16

Technical Foundations of MIS

module 2

Module 2 concentrates on the technical foundations of MIS. The power of MIS comes from its ability to carry, house, and support information. And information is power to an organization. This module highlights this point and raises awareness of the significance of information to organizational success. Understanding how the MIS infrastructure supports business operations, how business professionals access and analyze information to make business decisions, and how wireless and mobile technologies can make information continuously and instantaneously available are important for strategically managing any company, large or small. Thus, these are the primary learning outcomes of Module 2.

The module begins by reviewing the role of MIS in supporting business growth, operations, and performance. We quickly turn to the need for MIS to be sustainable given today's focus on being "green," and then dive into databases, data warehousing, networking, and wireless technologies—all fundamental components of MIS infrastructures. A theme throughout the module is the need to leverage and yet safeguard the use of information as key to the survival of any company. Information must be protected from misuse and harm, especially with the continued use, development, and exploitation of the Internet and the Web.

MODULE ONE: Business Driven MIS

MODULE TWO: Technical Foundations of MIS

MODULE THREE: Enterprise MIS

Module 2: TECHNICAL FOUNDATIONS OF MIS

5 CHAPTER

Infrastructures: Sustainable Technologies

CHAPTER OUTLINE

SECTION 5.1
MIS Infrastructures

- The Business Benefits of a Solid MIS Infrastructure
- Supporting Operations: Information MIS Infrastructure
- Supporting Change: Agile MIS Infrastructure

SECTION 5.2
Building Sustainable MIS Infrastructures

- MIS and the Environment
- Supporting the Environment: Sustainable MIS Infrastructure

What's in IT for me?

Why do you, as a business student, need to understand the underlying technology of any company? Most people think "that technical stuff" is something they will never personally encounter and for that reason do not need to know anything about MIS infrastructures. Well, those people will be challenged in the business world. When your database fails and you lose all of your sales history, you will personally feel the impact when you are unable to receive your bonus. When your computer crashes and you lose all of your confidential information, not to mention your emails, calendars, and messages, then you will understand why everyone needs to learn about MIS infrastructures. You never want to leave the critical task of backing up your data to your MIS department. You want to personally ensure that your information is not only backed up, but also safeguarded and recoverable. For these reasons, business professionals in the 21st century need to acquire a base-level appreciation of what MIS can and cannot do for their company. Understanding how MIS supports growth, operations, profitability, and most recently sustainability, is crucial whether one is new to the workforce or a seasoned *Fortune* 500 employee. One of the primary goals of this chapter is to create a more level playing field between you as a business professional and the MIS specialists with whom you will work. After reading it you should have many of the skills you need to assist in analyzing current and even some future MIS infrastructures; in recommending needed changes in processes; and in evaluating alternatives that support a company's growth, operations, and profits.

PANDORA®
internet radio

opening case study

Pandora's Music Box

Napster was one of the first service providers for sharing online music. Many other companies have attempted to legally jump into the online music business, and most found little success. However, Pandora, the Internet radio site, is becoming the exception. Pandora provides users with the ability to choose specific artists or categories of music and then creates individualized playlists. Based on user feedback to Pandora's suggestions of similar tracks, the site "learns" what selections each listener prefers for his or her playlist and uses that information to generate a unique customized listening experience for each.

At the heart of Pandora's business is the Music Genome Project (MGP), a computerized jukebox of more than 700,000 works by 80,000 artists, with new ones added every day. Each selection within the MGP is categorized by hundreds of characteristics, including artist and genre and covering the qualities of melody, harmony, rhythm, form, composition, and lyrics. For example, if someone is looking for a song with a certain tempo or wants to know what the lyrics are about, Pandora can supply that information. The company has 50 employees whose sole job is to listen to and analyze music along with assigning more than 400 characteristics to each track.

Computing Merges with Connectivity

Pandora is a perfect example of cloud computing as a result of three major trends:

1. The marriage of computing and connectivity can now occur without having to be tethered to a single location. It's among the biggest disruptive forces of modern times; one that will redefine business models for decades to come.
2. The mobile Internet is now pervasive.
3. The availability of low-cost, always-on computers—smart phones—that allow sophisticated software to conduct complex tasks on the go.

Pandora is strategically planning to reach a broad, global market by embedding itself in all sorts of Internet-enabled electronic devices that can access its services directly through the cloud. Pandora's music offerings are now being embedded in everything from thin LED televisions to Blu-ray players to digital frames. Customers are listening to Pandora through their Blu-ray players, iPods, iPhones, and BlackBerrys, and soon cars will come with Pandora preinstalled.

The Pandora team envisions Pandora playing everywhere, allowing users to create as many as 100 stations, allowing for a nearly infinite list of musical opportunities. Since its founding in 2000, Pandora has registered more than 50 million listeners and adds thousands more every day.

A basic membership, which includes an occasional advertisement or two, is free. Members are allowed 40 hours a month to listen to their personal stations. If users want more than 40 hours, they can purchase unlimited playing time for 99 cents per month. Users can upgrade even further to a Pandora One account for $36 a year that includes unlimited playing time, no advertisements, and a higher-quality sound.

What drives Pandora's business? Other than its valued customer base, it is the company's solid MIS infrastructure that supports its growth, operations, and profits. So far, Pandora's investment in MIS infrastructure has delivered wonderful results as well as future opportunities. The company can now develop new applications that support its core functions more rapidly than ever. And since Pandora is located in the cloud, the company has created an MIS infrastructure that is accessible, available, flexible, scalable, reliable, and usable and that performs to meet the needs of its growing customer community.[1]

section 5.1 MIS INFRASTRUCTURES

LEARNING OUTCOMES

5.1 Explain MIS infrastructure and its three primary types.

5.2 Identify the three primary areas associated with an information MIS infrastructure.

5.3 Describe the characteristics of an agile MIS infrastructure.

THE BUSINESS BENEFITS OF A SOLID MIS INFRASTRUCTURE

LO 5.1: Explain MIS infrastructure and its three primary types.

Management information systems have played a significant role in business strategies, affected business decisions and processes, and even changed the way companies operate. What is the foundation supporting all of these systems that enable business growth, operations, and profits? What supports the volume and complexity of today's user and application requirements? What protects systems from failures and crashes? It is the ***MIS infrastructure,*** which includes the plans for how a firm will build, deploy, use, and share its data, processes, and MIS assets. A solid MIS infrastructure can increase reduce costs, improve productivity, optimize business operations, generate growth, and increase profitability.

Briefly defined, ***hardware*** consists of the physical devices associated with a computer system, and ***software*** is the set of instructions the hardware executes to carry out specific tasks. In today's business environment, most hardware and software is run via a network. A ***network*** is a communications system created by linking two or more devices and establishing a standard methodology in which they can communicate. As more companies need to share more information, the network takes on greater importance in the infrastructure. Most companies use a specific form of network infrastructure called a client and server network. A ***client*** is a computer designed to request information from a server. A ***server*** is a computer dedicated to providing information in response to requests. A good way to understand this is when someone uses a Web browser (this would be the client) to access a website (this would be a server that would respond with the Web page being requested by the client). Anyone not familiar with the basics of hardware, software, or networks should review Appendix A, "Hardware and Software," and Appendix B, "Networks and Telecommunications," for more information.

In the physical world, a detailed blueprint would show how public utilities, such as water, electricity, and gas support the foundation of a building. MIS infrastructure is similar as it shows in detail how the hardware, software, and network connectivity support the firm's processes. Every company, regardless of size, relies on some form of MIS infrastructure, whether it is a few personal computers networked together sharing an Excel file or a large multinational company with thousands of employees interconnected around the world.

An MIS infrastructure is dynamic; it continually changes as the business needs change. Each time a new form of Internet-enabled device, such as an iPhone or BlackBerry, is created and made available to the public, a firm's MIS infrastructure must be revised to support the device. This moves beyond just innovations in hardware to include new types of software and network connectivity. An ***enterprise architect*** is a person grounded in technology, fluent in business, and able to provide the important bridge between MIS and the business. Firms employ enterprise architects to help manage change and dynamically update MIS infrastructure. Figure 5.1 displays the three primary areas where enterprise architects focus when maintaining a firm's MIS infrastructure.

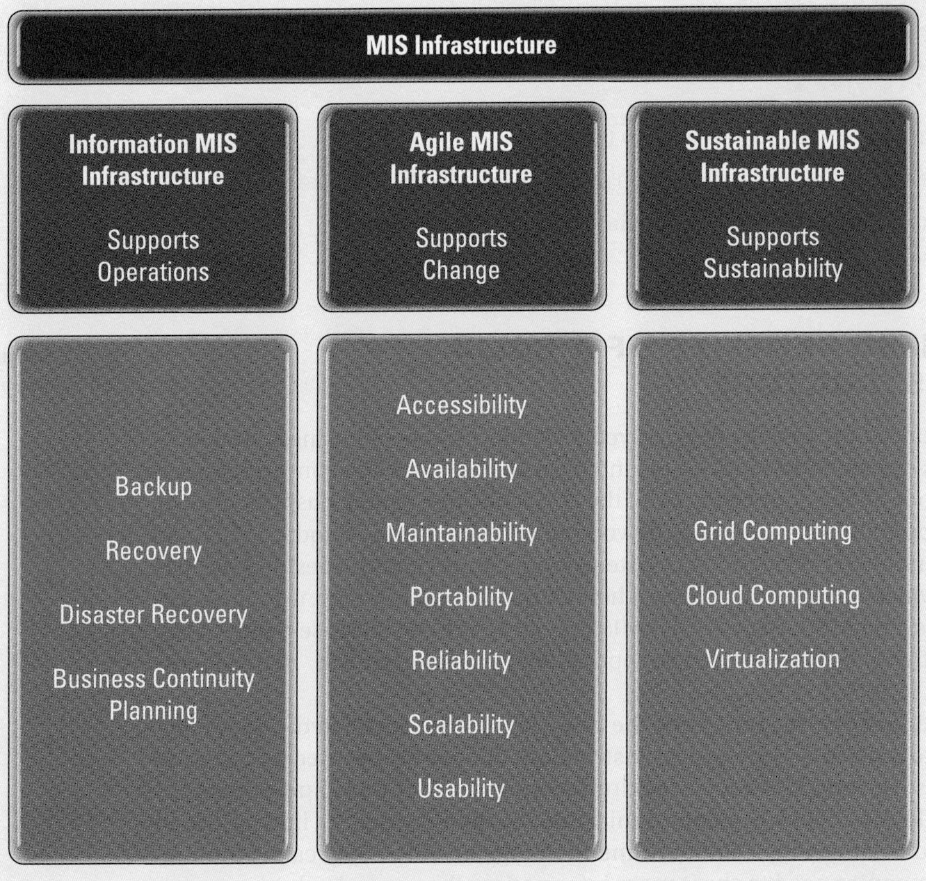

FIGURE 5.1
MIS Infrastructures

- **Supporting operations:** ***Information MIS infrastructure*** identifies where and how important information, such as customer records, is maintained and secured.
- **Supporting change:** ***Agile MIS Infrastructure*** includes the hardware, software, and telecommunications equipment that, when combined, provides the underlying foundation to support the organization's goals.
- **Supporting the environment:** ***Sustainable MIS infrastructure*** identifies ways that a company can grow in terms of computing resources while simultaneously becoming less dependent on hardware and energy consumption.

LO 5.2: Identify the three primary areas associated with an information MIS infrastructure.

SUPPORTING OPERATIONS: INFORMATION MIS INFRASTRUCTURE

Imagine taking a quick trip to the printer on the other side of the room, and when you turn around you find that your laptop has been stolen. How painful would you find this experience? What types of information would you lose? How much time would it take you to recover all of that information? A few things you might lose include music, movies, emails, assignments, saved passwords, not to mention that all-important 40-page paper that took you more than a month to complete. If this sounds painful then you want to pay particular attention to this section and learn how to eliminate this pain.

An information MIS infrastructure identifies where and how important information is maintained and secured. An information infrastructure supports day-to-day business operations and plans for emergencies such as power outages, floods, earthquakes, malicious attacks via the Internet, theft, and security breaches to name just a few. Managers must take every precaution to make sure their systems are operational and protected around the clock every day of the year. Losing a laptop or experiencing bad weather in one part of the country simply cannot take down systems required to operate core business processes. In the past, someone stealing company information would have to carry out boxes upon boxes of paper. Today, as data storage technologies grow in capabilities while shrinking in size, a person can simply walk out the front door of the building with the company's data files stored on a thumb drive or external hard drive. Today's managers must act responsibly to protect one of their most valued assets, information. To support continuous business operations, an information infrastructure provides three primary elements:

- Backup and recovery plan.
- Disaster recovery plan.
- Business continuity plan (see Figure 5.2).

Backup and Recovery Plan

Each year businesses lose time and money because of system crashes and failures. One way to minimize the damage of a system crash is to have a backup and recovery strategy in place. A ***backup*** is an exact copy of a system's information. ***Recovery*** is the ability to get a system up and running in the event of a system crash or failure that includes restoring the information backup. Many different types of backup and recovery media are available, including maintaining an identical replica or redundant of the storage server, external hard drives, thumb drives, and even DVDs. The primary differences between them are speed and cost.

Fault tolerance is the ability for a system to respond to unexpected failures or system crashes as the backup system immediately and automatically takes over with no loss of service. For example, fault tolerance enables a business to support continuous business operations if there is a power failure or flood. Fault tolerance is an expensive form of backup, and only mission-critical applications and operations use it. ***Failover,*** a specific type of fault tolerance, occurs when a redundant storage server offers an exact replica of the real-time data, and if the primary server crashes, the users are automatically directed to the secondary server or backup server. This is a high-speed and high-cost method of backup and recovery. ***Failback*** occurs when the primary machine recovers and resumes operations, taking over from the secondary server.

FIGURE 5.2

Areas of Support Provided by Information Infrastructure

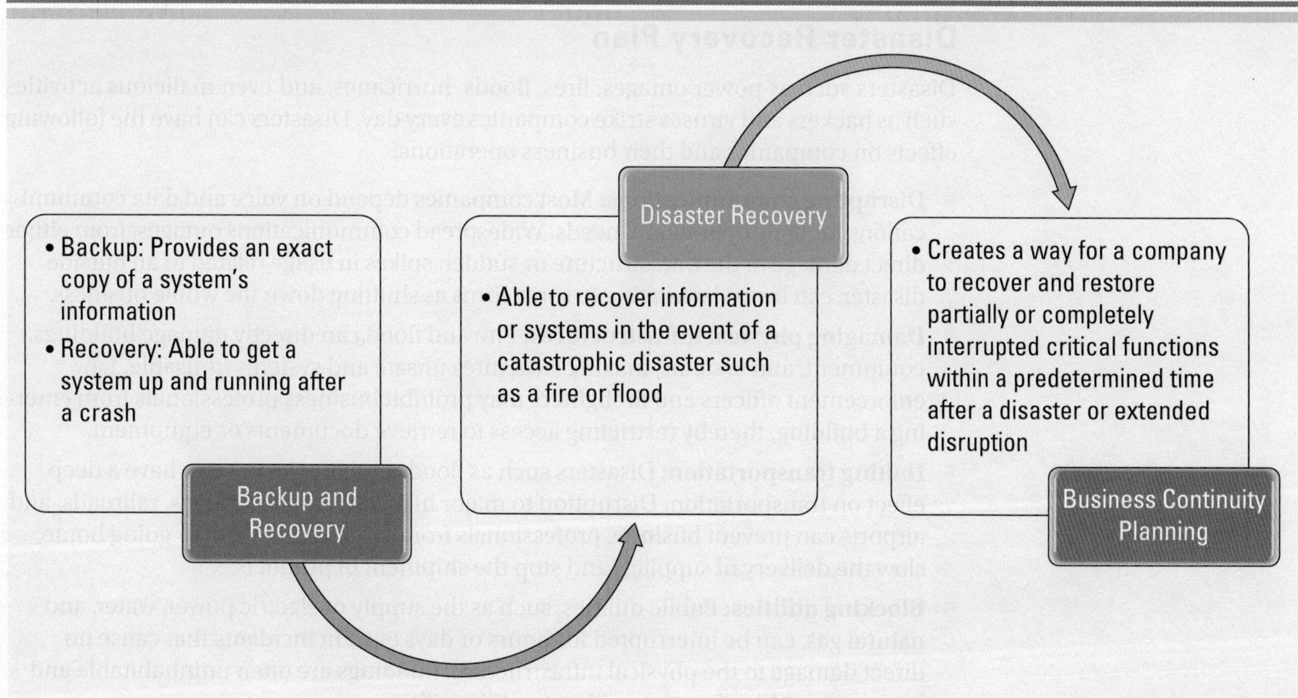

• Backup: Provides an exact copy of a system's information
• Recovery: Able to get a system up and running after a crash
Backup and Recovery
Disaster Recovery
• Able to recover information or systems in the event of a catastrophic disaster such as a fire or flood
• Creates a way for a company to recover and restore partially or completely interrupted critical functions within a predetermined time after a disaster or extended disruption
Business Continuity Planning

APPLY YOUR KNOWLEDGE

BUSINESS DRIVEN START-UP

I Don't Have a Temperature, but I'm Positive I Have a Virus

Think how horrible it would be to finish your term paper at 4 A.M. and find out that your computer has a virus and you just lost your entire document. Or perhaps you submit your final paper, which is worth 50 percent of your grade, and then head off to Colorado for winter break. You return to find that you failed the course, and you frantically check email to find out what happened. A message from your professor informs you that your document was corrupt and couldn't be opened and that you had 24 hours to resend the file, which you missed because you were skiing down the slopes.

Have you ever experienced having a file corrupted? If so, what could you have done to recover from this situation? Do you think your instructor ever receives corrupted files? How did the file become corrupted? Do you think your instructor would be suspicious if you submitted a corrupted file? How could an instructor prove that your file was purchased from this site?

Using DVDs or thumb drives to store your data offers a low-speed and low-cost backup method. It is a good business practice to back up data at least once a week using a low-cost method. This will alleviate the pain of having your laptop stolen or your system crash as you will still have access to your data, and it will only be a few days old.

Deciding how often to back up information and what media to use is a critical decision. Companies should choose a backup and recovery strategy in line with their goals and operational needs. If the company deals with large volumes of critical information, it will require daily, perhaps hourly, backups to storage servers. If it relies on small amounts of noncritical information, then it might require only weekly backups to external hard drives or thumb drives. A company that backs up on a weekly basis is taking the risk that, if a system crash occurs, it could lose a week's worth of work. If this risk is acceptable, a weekly backup strategy will work. If it is unacceptable, the company needs more frequent backup.

Disaster Recovery Plan

Disasters such as power outages, fires, floods, hurricanes, and even malicious activities such as hackers and viruses strike companies every day. Disasters can have the following effects on companies and their business operations.

- **Disrupting communications:** Most companies depend on voice and data communications for daily operational needs. Widespread communications outages, from either direct damage to the infrastructure or sudden spikes in usage related to an outside disaster, can be as devastating to some firms as shutting down the whole business.
- **Damaging physical infrastructures:** Fire and flood can directly damage buildings, equipment, and systems, making structures unsafe and systems unusable. Law enforcement officers and firefighters may prohibit business professionals from entering a building, thereby restricting access to retrieve documents or equipment.
- **Halting transportation:** Disasters such as floods and hurricanes can have a deep effect on transportation. Disruption to major highways, roads, bridges, railroads, and airports can prevent business professionals from reporting to work or going home, slow the delivery of supplies, and stop the shipment of products.
- **Blocking utilities:** Public utilities, such as the supply of electric power, water, and natural gas, can be interrupted for hours or days even in incidents that cause no direct damage to the physical infrastructure. Buildings are often uninhabitable and systems unable to function without public utilities.

These effects can devastate companies by causing them to cease operations for hours, days, or longer and risk losing customers whom they cannot then supply. Therefore, to combat these disasters a company can create a ***disaster recovery plan,*** which is a detailed process for recovering information or a system in the event of a catastrophic disaster. This plan includes such factors as which files and systems need to have backups and their corresponding frequency and methods along with the strategic location of the storage in a separate physical site that is geographically dispersed. A company might strategically maintain operations in New York and San Francisco, ensuring that a natural disaster would not impact both locations. A disaster recovery plan also foresees the possibility that not only the computer equipment but also the building where employees work may be destroyed. A ***hot site*** is a separate and fully equipped facility where the company can move immediately after a disaster and resume business. A ***cold site*** is a separate facility that does not have any computer equipment but is a place where employees can move after a disaster. A ***warm site*** is a separate facility with computer equipment that requires installation and configuration. Figure 5.3 outlines these resources that support disaster recovery.

A disaster recovery plan usually has a disaster recovery cost curve to support it. A ***disaster recovery cost curve*** charts (1) the cost to the company of the unavailability of information and technology and (2) the cost to the company of recovering from a disaster over time. Figure 5.4 displays a disaster recovery cost curve and shows that the best recovery plan in terms of cost and time is where the two lines intersect. Creating such a curve is no small task. Managers must consider the cost of losing information and technology within each department or functional area, and across the whole company. During the first few hours of a disaster, those costs may be low, but they rise over time. With those costs in hand, a company must then determine the costs of recovery.

FIGURE 5.3
Sites to Support Disaster Recovery

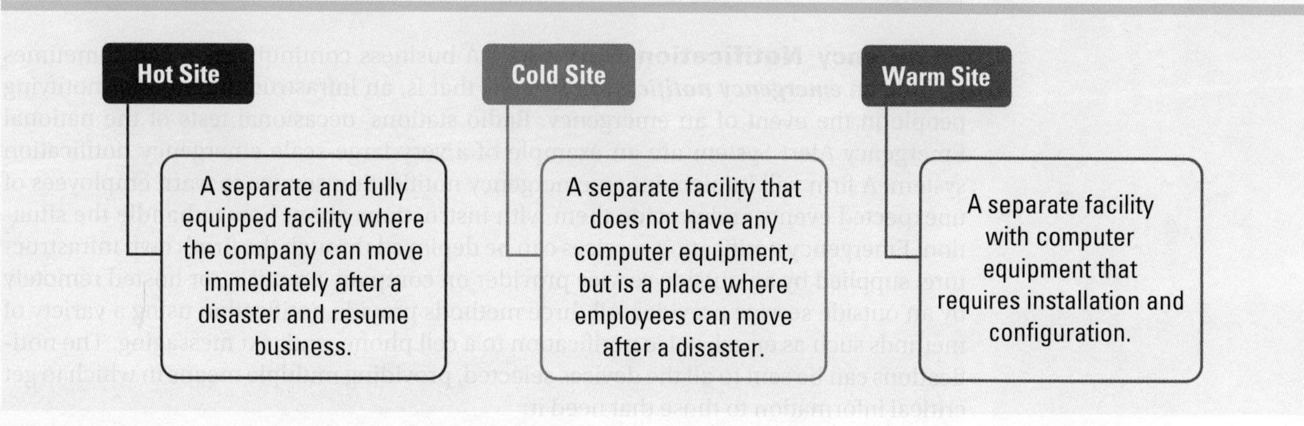

FIGURE 5.4
Disaster Recovery Cost Curve

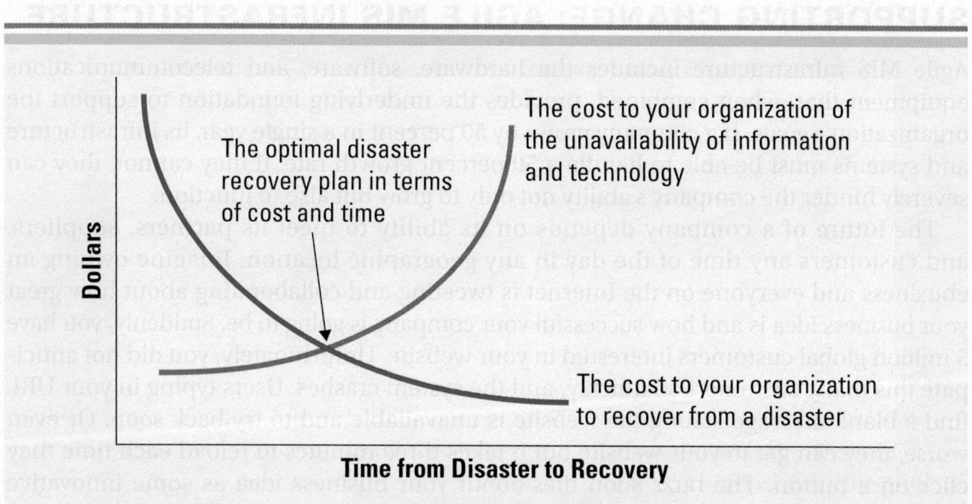

Business Continuity Plan

Natural disasters and terrorist attacks are on the minds of business professionals who take safeguarding their information assets seriously. Disaster recovery plans traditionally contained information on systems and data, ignoring cross-functional and intraorganizational issues for business processes and supply chain management. For this reason many are turning to a more comprehensive and all-encompassing plan known as ***business continuity planning (BCP),*** which details how a company recovers and restores critical business operations and systems after a disaster or extended disruption. This plan includes such factors such as identifying critical systems, business processes, departments, and the maximum amount of time the business can continue to operate without functioning systems. The plan will even detail the order in which functional areas should be restored, ensuring the most critical are focused on first.

On April 18, 1906, San Francisco was rocked by an earthquake that destroyed large sections of the city and claimed the lives of more than 3,000 inhabitants. More than a century later, a rebuilt and more durable San Francisco serves as a central location for major MIS corporations as well as a major world financial center. Managers of these corporations are well aware of the potential disasters that exist along the San Andreas Fault and actively update their business continuity plans anticipating such issues as earthquakes and floods. The Union Bank of California is located in the heart of downtown San Francisco and maintains a highly detailed and well-developed business continuity plan. The company employs hundreds of business professionals scattered around the world that coordinate plans for addressing the potential loss of a facility, business professionals, or critical systems so that the company can continue to operate if a disaster happens. Its disaster recovery plan includes hot sites where staff can walk in and start working exactly as if they were in their normal location. It would be a matter of minutes, not hours, for the Union Bank of California to be up and running again in the event of a disaster.[2]

Emergency Notification Services A business continuity plan can sometimes include an ***emergency notification service,*** that is, an infrastructure built for notifying people in the event of an emergency. Radio stations' occasional tests of the national Emergency Alert System are an example of a very large-scale emergency notification system. A firm will implement an emergency notification service to warn employees of unexpected events and provide them with instructions about how to handle the situation. Emergency notification services can be deployed through the firm's own infrastructure, supplied by an outside service provider on company premises, or hosted remotely by an outside service provider. All three methods provide notification using a variety of methods such as email, voice notification to a cell phone, and text messaging. The notifications can be sent to all the devices selected, providing multiple means in which to get critical information to those that need it.

LO 5.3: Describe the characteristics of an agile MIS infrastructure.

SUPPORTING CHANGE: AGILE MIS INFRASTRUCTURE

Agile MIS infrastructure includes the hardware, software, and telecommunications equipment that, when combined, provides the underlying foundation to support the organization's goals. If a company grows by 50 percent in a single year, its infrastructure and systems must be able to handle a 50 percent growth rate. If they cannot, they can severely hinder the company's ability not only to grow but also to function.

The future of a company depends on its ability to meet its partners, suppliers, and customers any time of the day in any geographic location. Imagine owning an ebusiness and everyone on the Internet is tweeting and collaborating about how great your business idea is and how successful your company is going to be. Suddenly, you have 5 million global customers interested in your website. Unfortunately, you did not anticipate this many customers so quickly, and the system crashes. Users typing in your URL find a blank message stating the website is unavailable and to try back soon. Or even worse, they can get to your website but it takes three minutes to reload each time they click on a button. The buzz soon dies about your business idea as some innovative Web-savvy fast follower quickly copies your idea and creates a website that can handle

APPLY YOUR KNOWLEDGE

BUSINESS DRIVEN MIS

Disaster Recovery

Backup and recovery are essential for any computer system. How painful would it be if someone stole your laptop right now? How much critical information would you lose? How many hours would it take you to re-create your data? Perhaps that will motivate you to implement a backup procedure. How many of you have a disaster recovery plan? Disaster recovery is needed when your best friend dumps a grande latte on your computer or you accidently wash your thumb drive.

Disaster recovery plans are crucial for any business, and you should ensure that your company has everything it needs to continue operations if there is ever a disaster, such as 9/11. You need to decide which disasters are worth worrying about and which ones are probably never going to occur. For example, if you live in Colorado, chances are good you don't have to worry about hurricanes, but avalanches are another story.

How often does a company need to back up its data? Where should the backup be stored? What types of disasters should companies in your state prepare for in case of an emergency? Why is it important to test the backup? What could happen to a company if it failed to create a disaster recovery plan?

the massive number of customers. The characteristics of agile MIS infrastructures can help ensure your systems can meet and perform under any unexpected or unplanned changes. Figure 5.5 lists the seven abilities of an agile infrastructure.

Accessibility

Accessibility refers to the varying levels that define what a user can access, view, or perform when operating a system. Imagine the people at your college accessing the main student information system. Each person that accesses the system will have different needs and requirements; for example, a payroll employee will need to access vacation information and salary information, or a student will need to access course information and billing information. Each system user is provided with an access level that details which parts of the system the user can and cannot access and what the user can do when in the system. For example, you would not want your students to be able to view payroll information or professor's personal information; also, some users can only view information and are not allowed to create or delete information. Top-level MIS employees require ***administrator access,*** or unrestricted access to the entire system. Administrator access can perform functions such as resetting passwords, deleting accounts, and shutting down entire systems.

Availability

In a 24/7/365 ebusiness environment, business professionals need to use their systems whenever they want from wherever they want. ***Availability*** refers to the time frames when the system is operational. A system is called ***unavailable*** when it is not operating and cannot be used. ***High availability*** occurs when a system is continuously operational at all times. Availability is typically measured relative to "100 percent operational" or "never failing." A widely held but difficult-to-achieve standard of availability for a system is known as "five 9s" (99.999 percent) availability. Some companies have systems available around the clock to support ebusiness operations, global customers, and online suppliers.

Sometimes systems must be taken down for maintenance, upgrades, and fixes, which are completed during downtime. One challenge with availability is determining when to

FIGURE 5.5
Agile MIS Infrastructure Characteristics

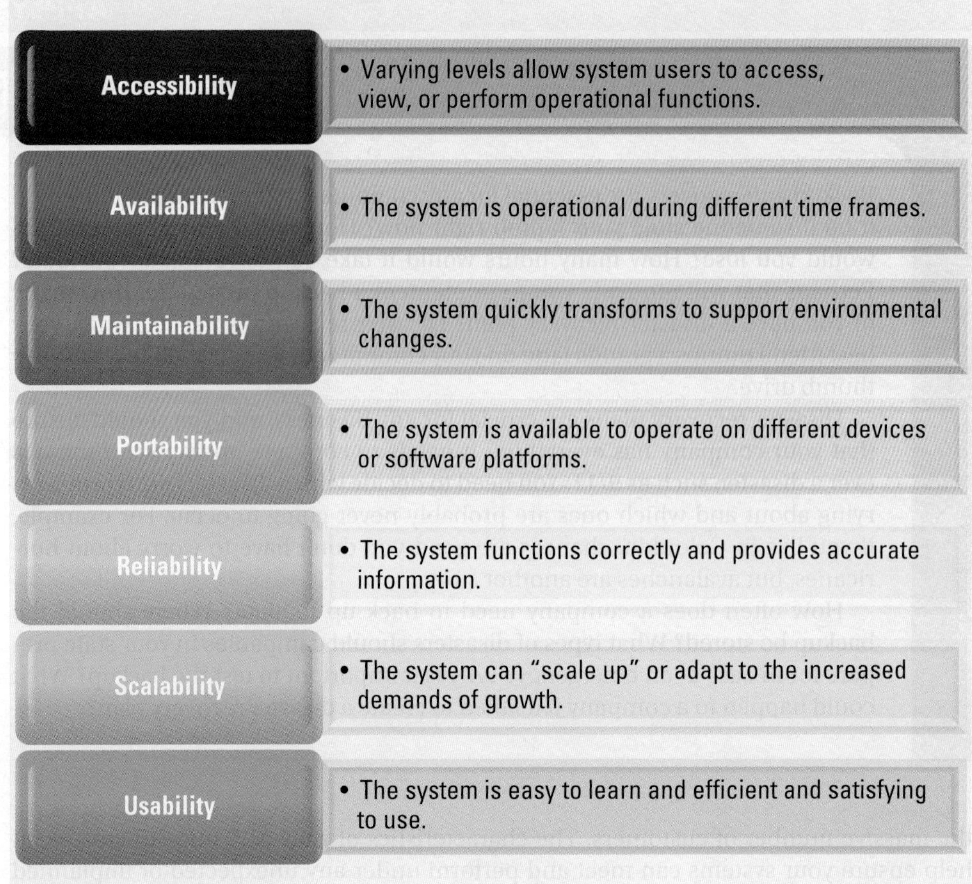

schedule system downtime if the system is expected to operate continuously. Performing maintenance during the evening might seem like a great idea, but evening in one city is morning somewhere else in the world, and business professionals scattered around the globe may not be able to perform specific job functions if the systems they need are unavailable. This is where companies deploy failover systems so they can take the primary system down for maintenance and activate the secondary system to ensure continuous operations.

Accessibility
• Varying levels allow system users to access, view, or perform operational functions.
Availability
• The system is operational during different time frames.
Maintainability
• The system quickly transforms to support environmental changes.
Portability
• The system is available to operate on different devices or software platforms.
Reliability
• The system functions correctly and provides accurate information.
Scalability
• The system can "scale up" or adapt to the increased demands of growth.
Usability
• The system is easy to learn and efficient and satisfying to use.

Maintainability

Companies must watch today's needs, as well as tomorrow's, when designing and building systems that support agile infrastructures. Systems must be flexible enough to meet all types of company changes, environmental changes, and business changes. ***Maintainability*** (or ***flexibility***) refers to how quickly a system can transform to support environmental changes. For example, when starting a small business you might not consider that you will have global customers, a common mistake. When building your systems, you might not design them to handle multiple currencies and different languages, which might make sense if the company is not currently performing international business. Unfortunately, when the first international order arrives, which happens easily with ebusiness, the system will be unable to handle the request because it does not have the flexibility to be easily reconfigured for a new language or currency. When the company does start growing and operating overseas, the system will need to be redeveloped, which is not an easy or cheap task, to handle multiple currencies and different languages.

Building and deploying flexible systems allow easy updates, changes, and reconfigurations for unexpected business or environmental changes. Just think what might have happened if Facebook had to overhaul its entire system to handle multiple languages.

Another social networking business could easily have stepped in and become the provider of choice. That certainly would not be efficient or effective for business operations.

Portability

Portability refers to the ability of an application to operate on different devices or software platforms, such as different operating systems. Apple's iTunes is readily available to users of Mac computers and also users of PC computers, smart phones, iPods, iPhones, iPads, and so on. It is also a portable application. Because Apple insists on compatibility across its products, both software and hardware, Apple can easily add to its product, device, and service offerings without sacrificing portability. Many software developers are creating programs that are portable to all three devices—the iPhone, iPod, and iPad—which increases their target market and they hope their revenue.

Reliability

Reliability (or ***accuracy***) ensures a system is functioning correctly and providing accurate information. Inaccuracy can occur for many reasons, from the incorrect entry of information to the corruption of information during transmissions. Many argue that the information contained in Wikipedia is unreliable. Because the Wikipedia entries can be edited by any user, there are examples of rogue users inaccurately updating information. Many users skip over Google search findings that correlate to Wikipedia for this reason. Housing unreliable information on a website can put a company at risk of losing customers, placing inaccurate supplier orders, or even making unreliable business decisions.

Scalability

Estimating company growth is a challenging task, in part because growth can occur in a number of different forms—the firm can acquire new customers, new product lines, or new markets. ***Scalability*** describes how well a system can scale up, or adapt to the increased demands of growth. If a company grows faster than anticipated, it might experience a variety of problems, from running out of storage space to taking more time to complete transactions. Anticipating expected, and unexpected, growth is key to building scalable systems that can support that development.

Performance measures how quickly a system performs a process or transaction. Performance is a key component of scalability as systems that can't scale suffer from performance issues. Just imagine your college's content management system suddenly taking five minutes to return a page after a button is pushed. Now imagine if this occurs during your midterm exam and you miss the two-hour deadline because the system is so slow. Performance issues experienced by firms can have disastrous business impacts causing loss of customers, loss of suppliers, and even loss of help-desk employees. Most users will wait only a few seconds for a website to return a request before growing frustrated and either calling the support desk or giving up and moving on to another website.

Capacity planning determines future environmental infrastructure requirements to ensure high-quality system performance. If a company purchases connectivity software that is outdated or too slow to meet demand, its employees will waste a great deal of time waiting for systems to respond to user requests. It is cheaper for a company to design and implement agile infrastructure that envisions growth requirements than to update all the equipment after the system is already operational. If a company with 100 workers merges with another company and suddenly there are 400 people using the system, performance time could suffer. Planning for increases in capacity can ensure systems perform as expected. Waiting for a system to respond to requests is not productive.

Web 2.0 is a big driver for capacity planning to ensure agile infrastructures can meet the business's operational needs. Delivering videos over the Internet requires enough bandwidth to satisfy millions of users during peak periods such as Friday and Saturday evenings. Video transmissions over the Internet cannot tolerate packet loss (blocks of data loss), and allowing one additional user to access the system could degrade the video quality for every user.

APPLY YOUR KNOWLEDGE

BUSINESS DRIVEN MIS

Ranking the Ab-"ilities"

Do you know how Google makes so much money? Unlike traditional businesses, Google does not make money from the users of its service. Google makes money by charging the companies that want to appear in the sponsored section of a search result. After performing a Google search, you will notice three sections on the resulting page. Along the top and side are the sponsored search results, and the middle lists the organic search results. Google's innovative marketing program, called AdWords, allows companies to bid on common search terms, and the highest bidder is posted first in the sponsored search results. Every time a user clicks on a sponsored link, the company that owns the link has to pay Google. This is also called pay-per-click and can cost anywhere from a few cents to a few dollars for each click. A general search term such as "tropical vacation" costs less than a more specific search term like "Hawaiian vacation." Whichever company bids the most for the search term appears at the top of the sponsored section. Clicking on the links in the organic search results does not incur any charges for the company that owns the link.

Rank the agile infrastructure ab-"ilities" for Google from most important to least important in terms of supporting Google's MIS infrastructure and business operations. Be sure to provide the justification behind your ranking.

Usability

Usability is the degree to which a system is easy to learn and efficient and satisfying to use. Providing hints, tips, shortcuts, and instructions for any system, regardless of its ease of use, is recommended. Apple understood the importance of usability when it designed the first iPod. One of the iPod's initial attractions was the usability of the click wheel. One simple and efficient button operates the iPod, making it usable for all ages. And to ensure ease of use, Apple also made the corresponding iTunes software intuitive and easy to use.

section 5.2 BUILDING SUSTAINABLE MIS INFRASTRUCTURES

LEARNING OUTCOMES

5.4 Identify the environmental impacts associated with MIS.

5.5 Explain the three components of a sustainable MIS infrastructure along with their business benefits.

LO 5.4: Identify the environmental impacts associated with MIS.

MIS AND THE ENVIRONMENT

The general trend in MIS is toward smaller, faster, and cheaper devices. Gordon Moore, co-founder of Intel, the world's largest producer of computer chips or microprocessors, observed in 1965 that continued advances in technological innovation made it possible to reduce the size of a computer chip (the brains of a computer, or even a cell phone now) while doubling its capacity every two years. His prediction that this trend would continue has come to be known as ***Moore's Law,*** which refers to the computer chip

APPLY YOUR KNOWLEDGE

BUSINESS DRIVEN DEBATE

Laptop? Notebook? Netbook? Tablet?

Thanks to Moore's Law, computing devices are getting smaller, cheaper, and faster every year, allowing innovative companies to create new devices that are smaller and more powerful than current devices. Just look at desktop, laptop, notebook, and tablet computers. These are all different devices allowing users to connect and compute around the globe. Moore's Law has been accurate about computing power roughly doubling every 18 months. Do you agree or disagree that Moore's Law will continue to apply for the next 20 years? Why or why not?

performance per dollar doubles every 18 months. Although Moore originally assumed a two-year period, many sources today refer to the 18-month figure.

Moore's Law is great for many companies as they can acquire large amounts of MIS equipment for cheaper and cheaper costs. As ebusinesses continue to grow, companies equip their employees with multiple forms of electronic devices ranging from laptops to cell phones to iPads. This is great for supporting a connected corporation, significant unintended side effects include our dependence upon fossil fuels and increased need for safe disposal of outdated computing equipment. Concern about these side effects has led many companies to turn to an ecological practice known as sustainable MIS. ***Sustainable,*** or ***green, MIS*** describes the production, management, use, and disposal of technology in a way that minimizes damage to the environment. Sustainable MIS is a critical part of ***corporate social responsibility,*** that is, companies' acknowledged responsibility to society. Building sustainable MIS infrastructures is a core initiative and critical success factor for socially responsible corporations. Figure 5.6 displays the three primary side effects of businesses' expanded use of technology.

Increased Electronic Waste

Moore's Law has made technological devices smaller, cheaper, and faster, allowing more people from all income levels to purchase computing equipment. This increased demand is causing numerous environmental issues. ***Ewaste*** refers to discarded, obsolete, or broken electronic devices. Ewaste includes CDs, DVDs, thumb drives, printer cartridges, cell phones, iPods, external hard drives, TVs, VCRs, DVD players, microwaves, and so on. Some say one human year is equivalent to seven years of technological advancements. A personal computer has a life expectancy of only three to five years and a cell phone is less than two years.

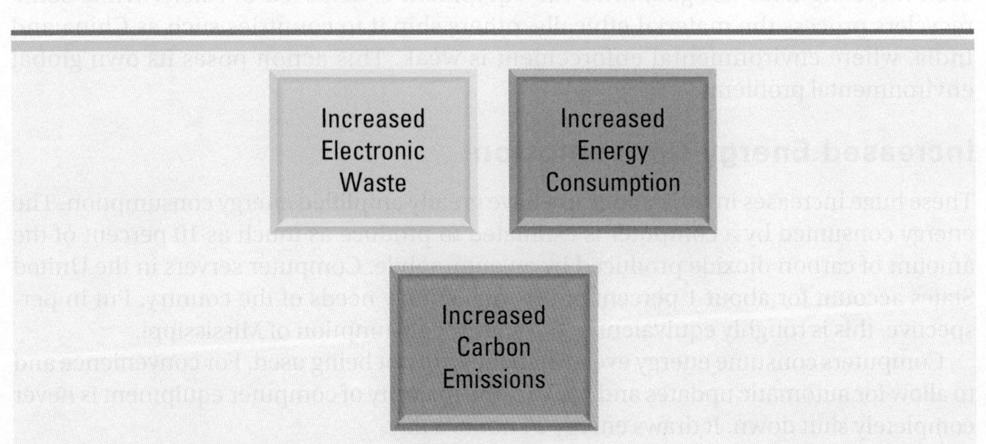

FIGURE 5.6
Three Pressures Driving Sustainable MIS Infrastructures

APPLY YOUR KNOWLEDGE

BUSINESS DRIVEN ETHICS AND SECURITY

Ewaste and the Environment

By some estimates, there may be as many as 1 billion surplus or obsolete computers and monitors in the world. Consider California, where 6,000 computers become surplus every day. If not disposed of properly, this enormous ewaste stream, which can contain more than 1,000 different toxic substances, is harmful to human beings and the environment. Beryllium is found in computer motherboards, chromium in floppy disks, lead in batteries and computer monitors, and mercury in alkaline batteries. One of the most toxic chemicals known is cadmium, found in many old laptops and computer chips.

In poorer countries, where the United States and Europe export some of their ewaste, the full impact of the environmental damage is quickly being realized. These areas have little use for obsolete electronic equipment so local recyclers resell some parts and burn the rest in illegal dumps, often near residential areas, releasing toxic and carcinogenic substances into the air, land, and water.[3]

Have you ever participated in ewaste? What can you do to ensure you are safely disposing of electronic equipment including batteries? What can governments do to encourage companies to safely dispose of ewaste? What can be done to protect poorer countries from receiving ewaste? Create a list of the ways you can safely dispose of cell phones, computers, printers, ink cartridges, MP3 players, and batteries. What could you do to inform citizens of the issues associated with ewaste and educate them on safe disposal practices?

Sustainable MIS disposal refers to the safe disposal of MIS assets at the end of their life cycle. It ensures that ewaste does not end up in landfills causing environmental issues. A single computer contains more than 700 chemicals; some are toxic, such as mercury, lead, and cadmium. If a computer ends up in a landfill, the toxic substances it contains can leach into our land, water, and air. Recycling costs from $15 to $50 for a monitor or computer. Many companies, including public schools and universities, simply can't afford the recycling costs.[4]

Ewaste also occurs when unused equipment stored in attics, basements, and storage facilities never reaches a recycling center. Retrieving the silver, gold, and other valuable metals from these devices is more efficient and less environmentally harmful than removing it from its natural environment.

Currently, less than 20 percent of ewaste in the United States is recycled; however, even recycling does not guarantee the equipment is disposed of safely. While some recyclers process the material ethically, others ship it to countries such as China and India, where environmental enforcement is weak. This action poses its own global environmental problems.

Increased Energy Consumption

These huge increases in technology use have greatly amplified energy consumption. The energy consumed by a computer is estimated to produce as much as 10 percent of the amount of carbon dioxide produced by an automobile. Computer servers in the United States account for about 1 percent of the total energy needs of the country. Put in perspective, this is roughly equivalent to the energy consumption of Mississippi.

Computers consume energy even when they are not being used. For convenience and to allow for automatic updates and backup, the majority of computer equipment is never completely shut down. It draws energy 24 hours a day.

APPLY YOUR KNOWLEDGE

BUSINESS DRIVEN DISCUSSION

Facebook's Energy Use

Cheap electricity is great for keeping business costs down, but it often means relying on coal for power. Facebook recently commissioned a new computing facility in Oregon and is using power from PacifiCorp, a utility that gets the majority of its energy from coal-fired power stations, which are major contributors of greenhouse gas emissions. As more and more people subscribe to Facebook, its energy needs are increasing almost exponentially.

Do you agree that Facebook made a wise business decision in selecting a utility provider that uses coal-fired power stations? What alternative sources of energy could Facebook have used to power its computing facility? Do you think Facebook's core customers care about the environment? What types of business challenges might Facebook encounter if it continues using coal-fired power stations?

Increased Carbon Emissions

The major human-generated greenhouse gases, such as carbon emissions from energy use, are very likely responsible for thc increases in climatic temperature over the past half a century. Additional temperature increases are projected over the next hundred years, with serious consequences for Earth's environment, if greenhouse gas emissions are not reduced.

In the United States, coal provides more than 50 percent of electrical power. When left on continuously, a single desktop computer and monitor can consume at least 100 watts of power per hour. To generate that much energy 24 hours a day for a year would require approximately 714 pounds of coal. When that coal is burned, it releases on average 5 pounds of sulfur dioxide, 5 pounds of nitrogen oxides, and 1,852 pounds (that is almost a ton) of carbon dioxide.[5]

SUPPORTING THE ENVIRONMENT: SUSTAINABLE MIS INFRASTRUCTURE

LO 5.5: **Explain the three components of a sustainable MIS infrastructure along with their business benefits.**

Combating ewaste, energy consumption, and carbon emissions requires a firm to focus on creating sustainable MIS infrastructures. A sustainable MIS infrastructure identifies ways that a company can grow in terms of computing resources while simultaneously becoming less dependent on hardware and energy consumption. The components of a sustainable MIS infrastructure include:

- Grid computing
- Cloud computing
- Virtualized computing

Grid Computing

When a light is turned on, the power grid delivers exactly what is needed, instantly. Computers and networks can now work that way using grid computing. ***Grid computing*** is a collection of computers, often geographically dispersed, that are coordinated to solve a common problem. With grid computing a problem is broken into pieces and distributed to many machines, allowing faster processing than could occur with a single system. Computers typically use less than 25 percent of their processing power, leaving more than 75 percent available for other tasks. Innovatively, grid computing takes advantage

FIGURE 5.7
Grid Computing

of this unused processing power by linking thousands of individual computers around the world to create a "virtual supercomputer" that can process intensive tasks. Grid computing makes better use of MIS resources, allowing greater scalability as systems can easily grow to handle peaks and valleys in demand, become more cost efficient, and solve problems that would be impossible to tackle with a single computer (see Figure 5.7).[6]

The uses of grid computing are numerous, including the creative environment of animated movies. DreamWorks Animation used grid computing to complete many of its hit films including *Antz, Shrek, Madagascar,* and *How to Train Your Dragon.* The third *Shrek* film required more than 20 million computer hours to make (compared to 5 million for the first *Shrek* and 10 million for the second). At peak production times, DreamWorks dedicated more than 4,000 computers to its *Shrek* grid, allowing it to complete scenes in days and hours instead of months. With the increased grid computing power, the DreamWork's animators were able to add more realistic movement to water, fire, and magic scenes (see Figure 5.8). With grid computing a company can work faster or more efficiently, providing a potential competitive advantage and additional cost savings.[7]

Solving the Energy Issue with Smart Grids A ***smart grid*** delivers electricity using two-way digital technology. It is meant to solve the problem of the world's outdated electrical grid, making it more efficient and reliable by adding the ability to remotely monitor, analyze, and control the transmission of power. The current U.S. power grid is said to have outlived its life expectancy by as much as 30 years. Smart grids provide users with real-time usage monitoring, allowing them to choose off-peak times for noncritical or less urgent applications or processes. Residents of Boulder, Colorado, can monitor their use of electricity and control appliances remotely due to the city's large-scale smart grid system. Xcel Energy has installed 21,000 smart grid meters since the $100 million program started several years ago. Energy use by early adopters is down as much as 45 percent.[8]

Cloud Computing

Marketing materials continually promote new technologies that promise to radically change the way businesses operate; unfortunately, these devices rarely live up to the hype. However, it might actually be true for one new development making this promise. Cloud computing could change not only the way businesses operate, but also the

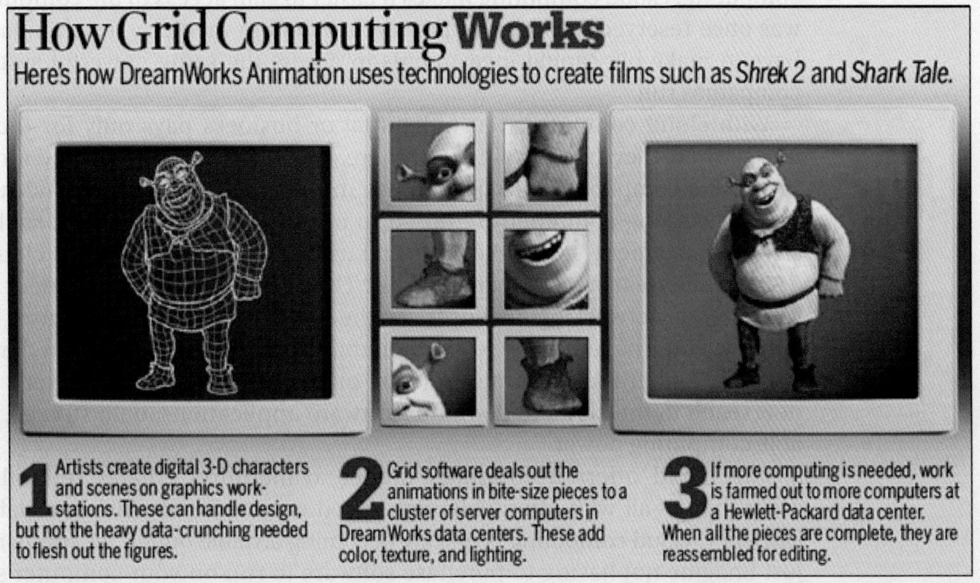

How Grid Computing Works
Here's how DreamWorks Animation uses technologies to create films such as Shrek 2 and Shark Tale.
1 Artists create digital 3-D characters and scenes on graphics workstations. These can handle design, but not the heavy data-crunching needed to flesh out the figures.
2 Grid software deals out the animations in bite-size pieces to a cluster of server computers in DreamWorks data centers. These add color, texture, and lighting.
3 If more computing is needed, work is farmed out to more computers at a Hewlett-Packard data center. When all the pieces are complete, they are reassembled for editing.

FIGURE 5.8

Making *Shrek 2* with Grid Computing

Source: Reprinted with special permission from Bloomberg Business Week, http://www.businessweek.com/magazine/content/04_42/b3904109_mz063.htm.

way people interact with technology. ***Cloud computing*** refers to the use of resources and applications hosted remotely on the Internet. The term comes (at least in part) from the image of a cloud to represent the Internet or some large networked environment. As shown in Figure 5.9, users connect to the cloud from their personal computers or portable devices using a client, such as a Web browser. To these individual users, the cloud appears as their personal application, device, or document. It is like storing all of your software and documents "in the cloud" and all you need is a device to access the cloud. No more hard drives, software, or processing power—that is all located in the cloud, transparent to the users.[9]

Cloud computing services are changing the way everyone can access, deliver, and use information. For example, social networking sites such as Facebook or MySpace

FIGURE 5.9

Cloud Computing

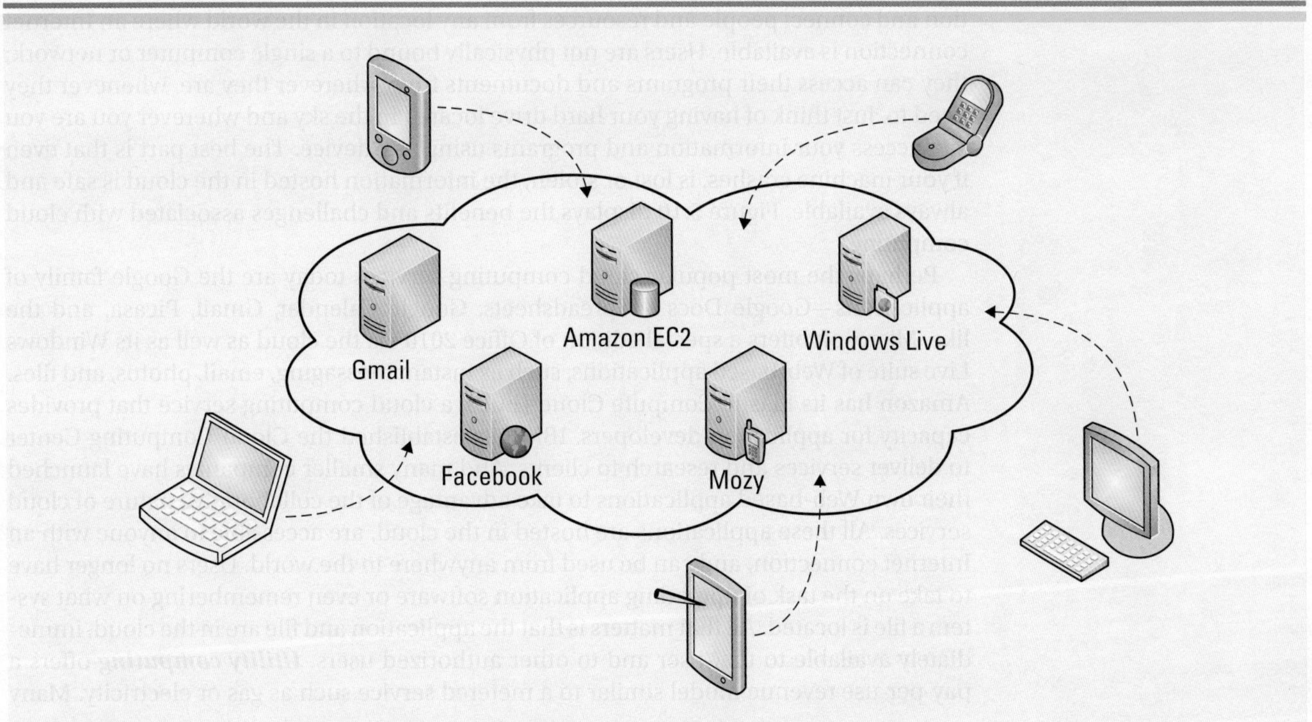

along with collaboration tools like videoconferencing and document storage use cloud computing. Cloud computing makes it easier to gain access to the computing power that was once reserved for large corporations. Small to medium-size companies no longer have to make big capital investments to access the same powerful systems that large companies run.

With cloud computing, an individual or business pays only for the services they need, when they need them and where, much as we use and pay for electricity. In the past, a company would have to pay millions of dollars for the hardware, software, and networking equipment required to implement a large system such as payroll or sales management. A cloud computing user can simply access the cloud and request a single license to a payroll application. The user does not have to incur any hardware, software, or networking expenses. As the business grows and the user requires more employees to have access to the system, the business simply purchases additional licenses. Rather than running software on a local computer or server, companies can now reach to the cloud to combine software applications, data storage, and considerable computing power.

The cloud offers a company higher availability, greater reliability, improved accessibility—all with affordable high-speed access. For flexibility, scalability, and cost efficiency, cloud computing is quickly becoming a viable option for companies of all sizes. Just imagine not having to purchase software to run on your computer such as Microsoft Office or Outlook. With the cloud, you could simply purchase a single license at a far discounted rate and not worry about the hassle of installing and upgrading the software on your computer. No more worries that you don't have enough memory to run a new program as the hardware is provided in the cloud, along with the software. You simply pay to access the program. You can think of this the same way you do with your telephone service. You simply pay to access a vendor's service, and you do not have to pay for the equipment required to carry the call around the globe. You also don't have to worry about scalability as the system automatically handles peak loads, which can be spread out among the systems in the cloud. Because additional cloud resources are always available, companies no longer have to purchase systems for infrequent computing tasks that need intense processing power, such as preparing tax returns during tax season or increased sales transactions during certain holiday seasons. If a company needs more processing power, it is always there in the cloud, and available on a cost-efficient basis.

Cloud computing also offers new ways to store, access, process, and analyze information and connect people and resources from any location in the world where an Internet connection is available. Users are not physically bound to a single computer or network; they can access their programs and documents from wherever they are, whenever they need to. Just think of having your hard drive located in the sky and wherever you are you can access your information and programs using any device. The best part is that even if your machine crashes, is lost or stolen, the information hosted in the cloud is safe and always available. Figure 5.10 displays the benefits and challenges associated with cloud computing.

Perhaps the most popular cloud computing services today are the Google family of applications—Google Docs & Spreadsheets, Google Calendar, Gmail, Picasa, and the like. Microsoft offers a special edition of Office 2010 via the cloud as well as its Windows Live suite of Web-based applications, such as instant messaging, email, photos, and files. Amazon has its Elastic Compute Cloud (EC2), a cloud computing service that provides capacity for application developers. IBM has established the Cloud Computing Center to deliver services and research to clients. And many smaller companies have launched their own Web-based applications to take advantage of the collaborative nature of cloud services. All these applications are hosted in the cloud, are accessible to anyone with an Internet connection, and can be used from anywhere in the world. Users no longer have to take on the task of upgrading application software or even remembering on what system a file is located. All that matters is that the application and file are in the cloud, immediately available to that user and to other authorized users. ***Utility computing*** offers a pay-per-use revenue model similar to a metered service such as gas or electricity. Many

CLOUD COMPUTING BENEFITS
Decreased maintenance issues: With less hardware, such as servers, maintenance costs are lowered for companies of all sizes. In addition, maintaining software, such as upgrades and patches, is eliminated.
Decreased labor costs: Less hardware and software maintenance means that companies need fewer MIS business professionals.
Increased computing power: Users benefit from the power of the entire cloud. They are no longer limited to what a single computer can do but can now have access to the power of (potentially) thousands of computers and servers.
Increased performance: Fewer applications on a client computer means the computer memory is freed up, which will allow users to get better performance. New PCs will not require the same burly capabilities as their predecessors.
Increased information security: All the information stored in the cloud stays in the cloud. A computer crashing in the cloud does not affect the storage of information because information in the cloud is automatically duplicated, so nothing is ever lost. In a world where few individual computer users back up their information on a regular basis, cloud computing can keep that asset safe.
Increased software updates: When an application is delivered via cloud computing, updates happen automatically and are available the next time someone accesses it. This provides all users of a cloud computing application with the latest version, including any fixes with a prior version. In most cases, users do not have to pay for or download an upgrade.
Increased storage capacity: Cloud computing offers increased, if not virtually limitless storage capacity.
CLOUD COMPUTING CHALLENGES
Limited features: Initially this is a small disadvantage, but it is bound to change. Many of the cloud computing applications today do not have the same full-featured functions as their personal computer counterparts. Google Presentations, for instance, lacks many of Microsoft PowerPoint's advanced features.
Internet connection required: Because cloud computing users need the Internet to connect to both their applications and their information, if the Internet is not available, they cannot access anything, even their own documents. Where Internet connections are few or unreliable, cloud computing is probably not feasible.
Security can be questionable: Information is stored in the cloud, but there are security issues with this, such as unauthorized users gaining access to confidential data. For some users, contractual or legal issues may prevent information from being stored remotely, especially if the cloud computing service is in another country operating under different laws and regulations.

FIGURE 5.10

Cloud Computing Benefits and Challenges

cloud computing service providers use utility computing cloud infrastructures, which are detailed in Figure 5.11. Other examples of cloud computing, some of which are free, are:[10]

- **Microsoft HealthVault**—online medical records storage.
- **Microsoft Hotmail**—Web-based email services.
- **Mozy**—online computer backup services.
- **Prezi**—online presentation services.
- **YouSendIt**—file transfer services.
- **Zoho Office**—word processor, spreadsheet, online presentation tool services.

Infrastructure as a Service ***Infrastructure as a Service (IaaS)*** is a service that delivers hardware networking capabilities, including the use of servers, networking, and storage over the cloud using a pay-per-use revenue model. With IaaS the customer rents the hardware and provides its own custom applications or programs. IaaS customers save money by not having to spend a large amount of capital purchasing expensive servers, which is a great business advantage considering some servers cost more than $100,000. The service is typically paid for on a usage basis, much like a basic utility service such as electricity or gas. IaaS offers a cost-effective solution for companies that need their computing resources to grown and shrink as business demand changes. This is known as ***dynamic scaling,*** which means the MIS infrastructure can be automatically scaled up or down based on needed requirements.

Currently the most popular IaaS operation is Amazon's Elastic Compute Cloud, generally known as Amazon EC2, or simply EC2. EC2 provides a Web interface through which customers can load and run their own applications on Amazon's computers. Customers control their own operating environment, so they can create, run, and stop services as needed, which is why Amazon describes EC2 as *elastic.*

FIGURE 5.11

Three Cloud Computing Service Delivery Models

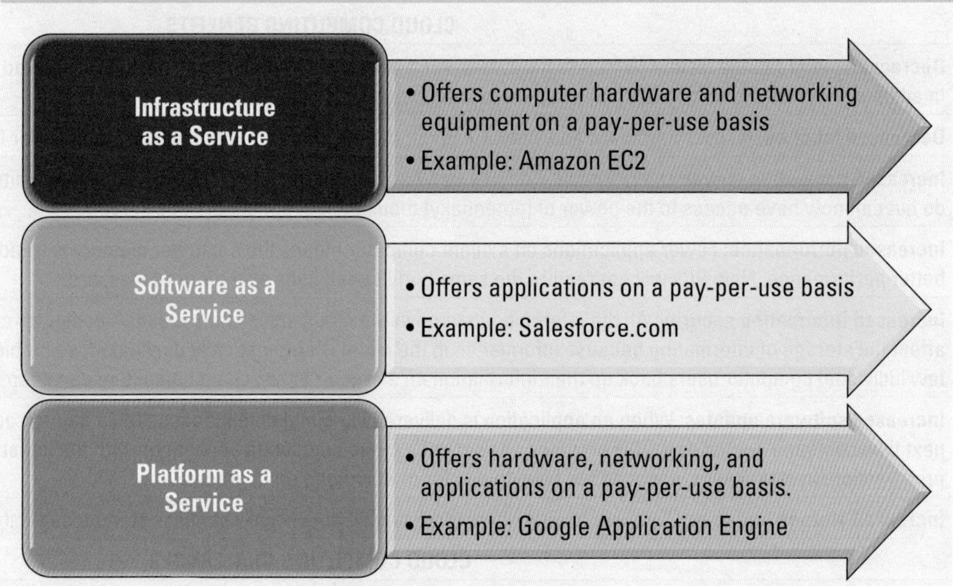

IaaS is a perfect fit for companies with research-intensive projects that need to process large amounts of information at irregular intervals, such as those in the scientific or medical field. Cloud computing services offer these companies considerable cost savings where they can perform testing and analysis at levels that are not possible without access to additional and very costly computing infrastructure.

Software as a Service Software as a Service was one of the first implementations of cloud computing ***Software as a Service (SaaS)*** delivers applications over the cloud using a pay-per-use revenue model. Before its introduction, companies often spent huge amounts of money implementing and customizing specialized applications to satisfy their business requirements. Many of these applications were difficult to implement, expensive to maintain, and challenging to use. Usability was one of the biggest drivers for creating interest in and success for cloud computing service providers.

SaaS offers a number of advantages; the most obvious is tremendous cost savings. The software is priced on a per-use basis with no up-front costs, so companies get the immediate benefit of reducing capital expenditures. They also get the added benefits of scalability and flexibility to test new software on a rental basis.

Salesforce.com is one of the most popular SaaS providers. Salesforce.com built and delivered a sales automation application, suitable for the typical salesperson, that automates functions such as tracking sales leads and prospects and forecasting. Tapping the power of SaaS can provide access to a large-scale, secure infrastructure, along with any needed support, which is especially valuable for a start-up or small company with few financial resources.

Platform as a Service ***Platform as a Service (PaaS)*** supports the deployment of entire systems including hardware, networking, and applications using a pay-per-use revenue model. PaaS is a perfect solution for a business as it passes on to the service provider the headache and challenges of buying, managing, and maintaining Web development software. With PaaS the development, deployment, management, and maintenance is based entirely in the cloud and performed by the PaaS provider, allowing the company to focus resources on its core initiatives. Every aspect of development, including the software needed to create it and the hardware to run it, lives in the cloud. PaaS helps companies minimize operational costs and increase productivity by providing all the following without up-front investment:

- Access to information anywhere and anytime.
- Centralized information management.

- Easy collaboration with partners, suppliers, and customers.
- Increased speed to market with significantly less costs.
- Increased security.

One of the most popular PaaS services is Google's App Engine, which builds and deploys Web applications for a company. Google's App Engine is easy to build, easy to maintain, and easy to scale as a company's Web-based application needs grow. Google's App Engine is free and offers a standard storage limit and enough processing power and network usage to support a Web application serving about 5 million page views a month. When a customer scales beyond these initial limits, it can pay a fee to increase capacity and performance. This can turn into some huge costs savings for a small business that does not have enough initial capital to buy expensive hardware and software for its Web applications. Just think, a two-person company can access the same computing resources as Google. That makes good business sense.[11]

Virtualized Computing

Most computers and even servers typically run only one operating system, such as Windows or Mac OS, and only one application. When a company invests in a large system such as inventory management, it dedicates a single server to house the system. This ensures the system has enough capacity to run during peak times and to scale to meet demand. Also, many systems have specific hardware requirements along with detailed software requirements, making it difficult to find two systems with the same requirements that could share the same machine. Through the use of virtualization, computers can run multiple operating systems along with multiple software applications—all at the same time. ***Virtualization*** creates multiple "virtual" machines on a single computing device. A good analogy is a computer printer. In the past you had to purchase a fax machine, copy machine, answering machine, and computer printer separately. This was expensive, required enough energy to run four separate machines, not to mention created additional amounts of ewaste. Today, you can buy a virtualized computer printer that functions as a fax machine, answering machine, and copy machine all on one physical machine, thereby reducing costs, power requirements, and ewaste. Virtualization is essentially a form of consolidation that can benefit sustainable MIS infrastructures in a variety of ways, for example:

- By increasing availability of applications that can give a higher level of performance depending on the hardware used.
- By increasing energy efficiency by requiring less hardware to run multiple systems or applications.
- By increasing hardware usability by running multiple operating systems on a single computer.

Originally, computers were designed to run a single application on a single operating system. This left most computers vastly underutilized (as mentioned earlier, 75 percent of most computing power is available for other tasks). Virtualization allows multiple virtual computers to exist on a single machine, which allows it to share its resources, such as memory and hard disk space, to run different applications and even different operating systems. Mac computers have the ability to run both the Apple operating system and the Windows PC operating system, with the use of virtualization software (see Figure 5.12). Unfortunately, virtualization, at least at the moment, is not available for a PC to run Mac software.

Virtualization is also one of the easiest and quickest ways to achieve a sustainable MIS infrastructure because it reduces power consumption and requires less equipment that needs to be manufactured, maintained, and later disposed of safely. Managers no longer have to assign servers, storage, or network capacity permanently to single applications. Instead, they can assign the hardware resources when and where they are needed, achieving the availability, flexibility, and scalability a company needs to thrive and grow. Also, by virtually separating the operating system and applications from the hardware, if there is a disaster or hardware failure, it is easy to port the virtual machine to a new

APPLY YOUR KNOWLEDGE

BUSINESS DRIVEN INNOVATION

Virtualization for Your Cell Phone

Virtualization is a challenging concept to understand. The formal definition is that it creates multiple "virtual" machines on a single computing device. OK, let's try that again in English. Imagine you have three cell phones, one for the company you work for, one for a company you are starting on the side, and one for personal calls. For the most part the phones are idle and they seldom ever ring at the same time. Since the phones are idle the majority of the time, you notice that it is a waste of time and resources to support idle time, especially when you are paying for cell service on each phone. You decide to use virtualization to help your situation.

Essentially, this would put three virtual cell phones on one device. The individual services and application for each phone would be independently stored on the one device. From the device's perspective, it sees three separate virtual phones. This saves time and money in expenses and maintenance. You could even use virtualization to turn your cell phone into a scanner. Visit ScanR.com and for just $5 a month you can use the camera on your phone to scan documents. Take a photo of any document, business card, or whiteboard and upload it to ScanR's website and in minutes it is returned to you in a digital file. Could be helpful if your friend has to miss class and you want to copy your lecture notes.[12]

Virtualization is a hot topic these days as more and more businesses are focusing on social responsibility and attempting to find ways to reduce their carbon footprints. Create an analogy similar to the cell phone that demonstrates virtualization. What are the potential environmental impacts associated with virtualization? What are the business advantages of virtualization? What are the business risks associated with virtualization?

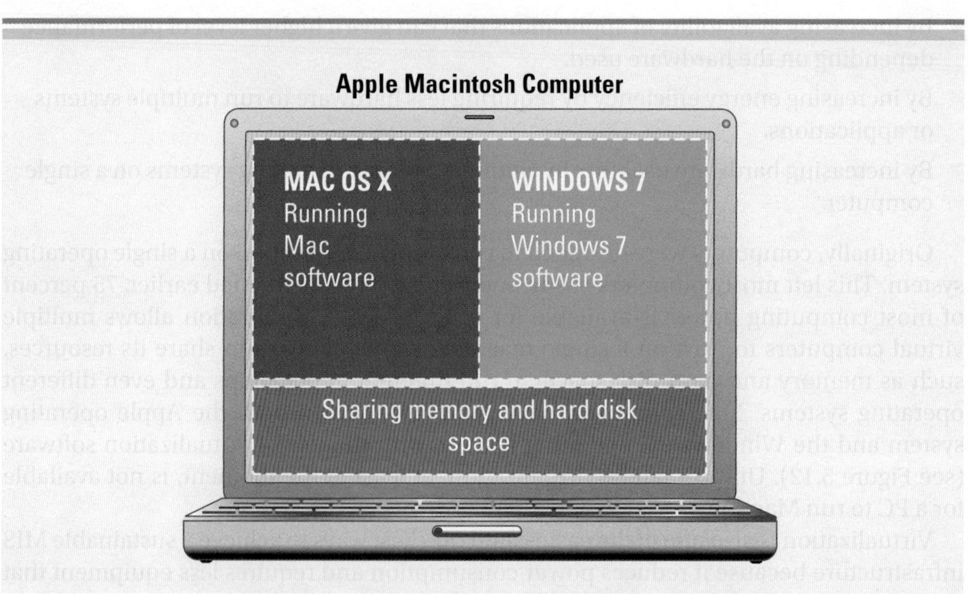

FIGURE 5.12

Virtualization Allows an Apple Macintosh Computer to Run OS X and Windows 7

physical machine allowing a company to recovery quickly from disasters. One of the primary uses of virtualization is for performing backup, recovery, and disaster recovery. Using virtual servers or a virtualization service provider, such as Google, Microsoft, or Amazon, to host disaster recovery is more sustainable than a single company incurring

APPLY YOUR KNOWLEDGE

BUSINESS DRIVEN GLOBALIZATION

Data Centers on the High Seas

Google is considering constructing a floating data center three to seven miles offshore that could be both powered and cooled by the ocean. It would consist of containers stacked with servers, data storage systems, and networking equipment on barges or other platforms and could be located close to users wherever it is not feasible, cost-effective, or efficient to build on land. Bringing the data closer to the user allows the data to arrive quicker. And since the ocean is a rent-free space, data centers can be as large as 100,000 square feet without real estate fees. The ocean can provide two critical factors that support a sustainable MIS infrastructure—water for cooling and power.[13]

What are the advantages and disadvantages of housing data centers in the ocean? Do you foresee any issues for these data centers with natural disasters? What types of security issues would Google encounter with a floating data center? Do you agree that it is good business sense to house a data center on a barge in the ocean? Why or why not?

the expense of having redundant physical systems. Also, these providers' data centers are built to withstand natural disasters and are typically located far away from big cities.

Virtual Data Centers A ***data center*** is a facility used to house management information systems and associated components, such as telecommunications and storage systems. Data centers, sometimes referred to as server farms, consume power and require cooling and floor space while working to support business growth without disrupting normal business operations and the quality of service. The amount of data a data center stores has grown exponentially over the years as our reliance on information increases. Backups, graphics, documents, presentations, photos, audio and video files all contribute to the ever-expanding information footprint that requires storage. One of the most effective ways to limit the power consumption and cooling requirements of a data center is to consolidate parts of the physical infrastructure, particularly by reducing the number of physical servers through virtualization. For this reason, virtualization is having a profound impact on data centers as the sheer number of servers a company requires to operate decreases, thereby boosting growth and performance while reducing environmental impact, as shown in Figure 5.13. Google, Microsoft, Amazon, and Yahoo! have all created data centers along the Columbia River in the northwestern United States. In this area, each company can benefit from affordable land, high-speed Internet access, plentiful water for cooling, and even more important, inexpensive electricity. These factors are critical to today's large-scale data centers, whose sheer size and power needs far

FIGURE 5.13
Ways for Data Centers to Become Sustainable

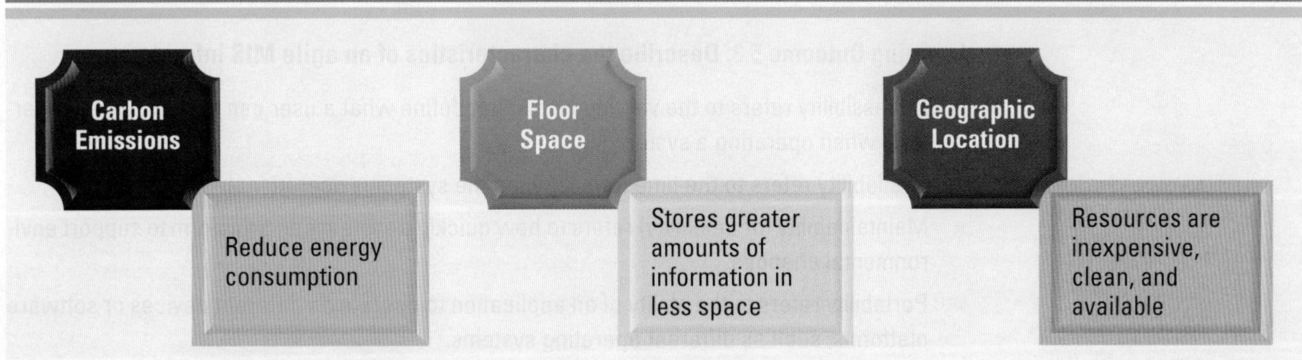
Carbon Emissions
Reduce energy consumption
Floor Space
Stores greater amounts of information in less space
Geographic Location
Resources are inexpensive, clean, and available

surpass those of the previous generation. Microsoft's data center in Quincy, Washington, is larger than 10 football fields and is powered entirely by hydroelectricity, power generated from flowing water rather than from the burning of coal or other fossil fuel.[14]

If we take a holistic and integrated approach to overall company growth, the benefits of integrating information MIS infrastructures, environmental MIS infrastructures, and sustainable MIS infrastructures become obvious. For example, a company could easily create a backup of its software and important information in one or more geographically dispersed locations using cloud computing. This would be far cheaper than building its own hot and cold sites in different areas of the country. In the case of a security breach, failover can be deployed as a virtual machine in one location of the cloud can be shut down as another virtual machine in a different location on the cloud comes online.

LEARNING OUTCOME REVIEW

Learning Outcome 5.1: Explain MIS infrastructure and its three primary types.

The three primary areas where enterprise architects focus when maintaining a firm's MIS infrastructure are:

- Supporting operations: Information MIS infrastructure identifies where and how important information, such as customer records, is maintained and secured.
- Supporting change: Agile MIS infrastructure includes the hardware, software, and telecommunications equipment that, when combined, provides the underlying foundation to support the organization's goals.
- Supporting the environment: Sustainable MIS infrastructure identifies ways that a company can grow in terms of computing resources while simultaneously becoming less dependent on hardware and energy consumption.

Learning Outcome 5.2: Identify the three primary areas associated with an information MIS infrastructure.

The three primary areas an information infrastructure provides to support continuous business operations are:

- Backup and recovery: A backup is an exact copy of a system's information. Recovery is the ability to get a system up and running in the event of a system crash or failure that includes restoring the information backup.
- Disaster recovery plan: This plan provides a detailed process for recovering information or a system in the event of a catastrophic disaster.
- Business continuity plan: This details how a company recovers and restores critical business operations and systems after a disaster or extended disruption.

Learning Outcome 5.3: Describe the characteristics of an agile MIS infrastructure.

- Accessibility refers to the varying levels that define what a user can access, view, or perform when operating a system.
- Availability refers to the time frames when the system is operational.
- Maintainability (or flexibility) refers to how quickly a system can transform to support environmental changes.
- Portability refers to the ability of an application to operate on different devices or software platforms, such as different operating systems.

- Reliability (or accuracy) ensures a system is functioning correctly and providing accurate information.
- Scalability describes how well a system can "scale up" or adapt to the increased demands of growth.
- Usability is the degree to which a system is easy to learn and efficient and satisfying to use.

Learning Outcome 5.4: Identify the environmental impacts associated with MIS.

Increased energy consumption, increased electronic waste, and increased carbon emissions are all associated with MIS. Ewaste refers to discarded, obsolete, or broken electronic devices. Sustainable MIS disposal refers to the safe disposal of MIS assets at the end of their life cycle.

Learning Outcome 5.5: Explain the three components of a sustainable MIS infrastructure along with their business benefits.

The components of a sustainable MIS infrastructure include:

- Grid computing: A collection of computers, often geographically dispersed, that are coordinated to solve a common problem.
- Cloud computing: The use of resources and applications hosted remotely on the Internet. The term comes (at least in part) from the image of a cloud to represent the Internet or some large networked environment.
- Virtualized computing: The creation of multiple "virtual" machines on a single computing device.

OPENING CASE QUESTIONS

1. **Knowledge:** List the ways that an agile MIS infrastructure supports Pandora's business.
2. **Comprehension:** Describe the reasons Pandora would create a disaster recovery plan and a business continuity plan.
3. **Application:** Apply the concepts of cloud computing to Pandora's business model.
4. **Analysis:** Analyze how Pandora is using sustainable MIS infrastructures.
5. **Synthesis:** Develop a way that Pandora could benefit from grid computing.
6. **Evaluate:** Assess the use of virtualization to support Pandora's business growth while helping the environment.

KEY TERMS

Fault tolerance, 171
Grid computing, 181
Hardware, 169
High availability, 175
Hot site, 173
Information MIS infrastructure, 170
Infrastructure as a Service (IaaS), 185
Maintainability (or flexibility), 176
MIS infrastructure, 169
Moore's Law, 178
Network, 169
Performance, 177
Platform as a Service (PaaS), 186
Portability, 177
Recovery, 171
Reliability (or accuracy), 177
Scalability, 177
Server, 169
Smart grid, 182
Software, 169
Software as a Service (SaaS), 186
Sustainable MIS disposal, 180
Sustainable MIS infrastructure, 170
Sustainable, or green, MIS, 179
Unavailable, 175
Usability, 178
Utility computing, 184
Virtualization, 187
Warm site, 173

REVIEW QUESTIONS

1. How often should a business back up its data?
2. Why is it important to ensure backups are working and can be restored?
3. What is the difference between a disaster recovery plan and a business continuity plan?
4. What are the three forms of MIS infrastructures and what do they support?
5. List the characteristics of an agile MIS infrastructure and explain why they are all critical for supporting change.
6. Explain what capacity planning is and how it can help a business prepare for growth.
7. Explain the difference between fault tolerance and failover.
8. Compare the differences among a hot, cold, and warm site.
9. What is Moore's Law and how does it affect companies?
10. List the business benefits of using grid computing.
11. Identify the benefits and challenges of cloud computing
12. What is a data center and why would a business develop one.
13. List and describe the three most popular cloud computing delivery models.
14. Why would a company want to use virtualization?
15. Explain why a business today would want to follow sustainable MIS practices.
16. Explain why ebusiness is contributing to the three pressures driving sustainable MIS infrastructures.

CLOSING CASE ONE

UPS Invests $1 Billion to Go Green

United Parcel Service (UPS) will make about $1 billion in technology investments to improve the efficiency of its operations, with the goal of cutting billions more from its costs over the long term. One of its main goals is to improve the speed and efficiency of its delivery operations. To achieve that, UPS is equipping its vans with sensors that allow it to collect data about things such as fuel consumption, chosen routes, and how much time its engines spend idling. Reducing fuel consumption will help UPS not only to cut costs, but also to be more environmentally responsible. A big portion of the company's costs comes from transporting packages by air. In fact, UPS is the world's ninth-largest airline, so it is trying to conserve aircraft fuel as well by lowering flight speeds and better planning to avoid duplication of routes. But a lot of fuel is also burned by its trucks, and the sensors being implemented there could save the company millions of dollars.

UPS is installing about 200 sensors in its vehicles—in the brakes, engine box, and on the exterior—to collect data and pinpoint opportunities where drivers can adjust their driving to maximize fuel efficiency. The company wants to reduce idle time of its delivery trucks, as each hour spent idling burns about a gallon of fuel.

The company is also installing equipment to track the routes drivers take to deliver packages. Every morning the drivers are briefed on the data captured by the sensors and how they could drive differently to save fuel. UPS wants to optimize the number of times a vehicle has to start, stop, reverse, turn, or back up.

Green Data Center

The company is also investing in more efficient cooling technologies at its two data centers, which are in Mahwah, New Jersey, and Alpharetta, Georgia. During the winter, the company can shut off its chiller equipment and use outside air for cooling.

The Alpharetta data center has a 650,000-gallon water tank outside for cooling and a heat exchanger to faster dissipate the heat captured in the fluid. The water flows in a circular motion around the data center, cooling the equipment, and the heat exchanger helps lower the temperature of the hot exhaust water more quickly.

UPS is also investing in faster server processors, allowing it to consolidate existing servers through virtualization. That helps lower energy costs and also reduces the physical footprint of its servers. And the company has been consolidating smaller server rooms that were scattered around the world. These changes are saving UPS around $400,000 each year.[15]

Questions

1. Why do you think UPS is embracing sustainable technologies?
2. How is UPS developing a sustainable MIS infrastructure?
3. What business benefits will UPS gain from virtualization?
4. What role does each characteristics of an agile MIS infrastructure play in helping UPS to operate its business?
5. How could UPS benefit from cloud or grid computing?
6. What types of ethical issues might UPS encounter with the tracking technology it has placed in its trucks?
7. What types of security issues might UPS encounter with the tracking technology it has placed in its trucks?

CLOSING CASE TWO

Turning Ewaste into Gold

During the 2010 Winter Olympic Games in Vancouver, champions were not just taking home gold, silver, or bronze medals—they were also playing a role in reducing electronic waste. For the first time in Olympic history, each medal, more than 1,000 of them, was made with a tiny bit of the more than 140,000 tons of ewaste that otherwise would have been sent to landfills. The medals are the first containing metal salvaged from televisions, circuit boards, computer monitors, and electronic waste. The so-called urban ore was supplied by Teck Resources Ltd.,

Canada's largest base-metals producer, which provided gold, silver, and copper used to make the medals. Historically, Olympic medals have been made from mined mineral deposits; this is the first time that recycled materials have been added to them. First-place winners get gold-plated medals that are 92.5 percent silver. The second-place prizes are also 92.5 percent silver, while the third-place bronze medals are mostly copper.

All the medals have some ewaste materials from Teck's electronic recycling program located in Trail, British Columbia. Teck mixed gold, silver, and copper from the program with metals mined from the ground. The company said it couldn't provide the exact percentage of mined versus recycled material in the finished medals. Each gold medal contained a little more than 1.5 percent of ewaste materials, while each copper medal contained just over 1 percent, and the silver medals contained only small pieces. The ewaste came from old computer monitor's glass, various computer parts, and other surplus or discarded technologies.

Several different processing methods were used to extract the materials. First, the company shredded the equipment to separate out the various metals, glass, and other usable parts. To remove the metals that could not be recovered by the shredding process, the parts were fed into a furnace operating at a temperature greater than 2,000 degrees (Fahrenheit). The materials were then combined with other metals to create the medals. Each medal was hand-cropped, ensuring no two are alike, another first in Olympic history. The medals, designed by Canadian artist Corrine Hunt, were also the first nonflat medals made for the Games, with a wavy form to represent the ocean and mountain snowdrifts, both characteristic of Vancouver's environment. In addition to representing the athletes' outstanding achievements, the 2010 Olympic medals gave new life to the precious metals recoverable from ewaste.[16]

Questions

1. Why would the Olympics benefit from creating a strong environmental MIS infrastructure?
2. How can the Olympics help support ethical ewaste initiatives?
3. Why would a sporting event like the Olympics be concerned with reducing its carbon footprint?
4. What could the Olympics do to help shed light on global environmental MIS issues?
5. How could Moore's Law enable future Olympic medals to be made from more ewaste?

CRITICAL BUSINESS THINKING

1. Universities Are Switching to Gmail

Schools around the world are moving to cloud computing applications such as Google Docs & Spreadsheets and Google Calendar. Yale had planned to move from its own email system to Google Mail, but at the last minute decided to cancel the project. The reason was because school administrators and faculty members did not believe the move could support their business requirements. Do you agree or disagree that Google Gmail would be unable to replace a university's private email system? What are the advantages and disadvantages of a private email system? What are the advantages and disadvantages of using a cloud application such as Google Gmail? What choice would you make if you were the primary decision maker for choosing your school's email system?[17]

2. Desktop Virtualization

Every day users are becoming more comfortable with accessing and storing information in the cloud. This creates increased demand on MIS personnel to help manage, control, and provide access to that information—not just on company-issued computers, but on any number of devices, including personal ones. More and more employees want to be able to utilize their own computing devices—cell phones, netbooks, laptops– instead of company-issued ones. For instance, many students graduating from college have been exposed to Macs and may even own one, yet they are finding PCs as the standard computer of choice for most companies. Do you think it is a good business practice to allow your employees to use their personal devices for work-related business? What are the challenges of allowing users to port business applications to their personal devices? What are the challenges of allowing users to connect to corporate systems with personal devices?

3. **ITunes in the Cloud**
   Apple is considering a cloud version of its iTunes software that could possibly provide a host of new services for its users as they would no longer be required to save iTunes to their computers as it would reside in the cloud. With cloud computing, the software for iTunes would reside in centralized servers in data centers, rather than on a specific user computer. What would be the benefits to customers if they could host iTunes in the clouds and access it using a variety of devices? What would be your fears if you were to use iTunes in the cloud?

4. **Sustainable Departments**
   Energy prices and global warming are discussed daily in the news as the environmental impact of ewaste is just beginning to be recognized. Sustainability and corporate social responsibility need to be taken seriously by all managers as everyone should take an active role in helping to preserve the environment. List the different departments in a business and the types of environmental issues they typically encounter. Which department do you think creates the most ewaste? Which department uses the greatest amount of electricity or has the largest carbon footprint? What can each department do to help combat its environmental issues? Why do all managers, and for that matter all employees, need to be aware of environmental issues and ways they can create sustainable MIS infrastructures?

5. **Making the Smart Grid Smart**
   ISO, a regional electricity company in New England, has launched an $18 million project in part because of an $8 million three-year federal grant. The project is designed to speed up the installation of 30 smart-grid devices covering every state in New England. The smart-grid devices will provide control room operators at ISO with enhanced tools to monitor and measure performance of the region's electrical grid, allowing the company to improve its ability to detect and address problems on the system. System status information coming into ISO will increase from once every four seconds to 30 times per second. Would you invest in ISO if you had the chance? Why or why not? If you were awarded an $8 million three-year federal grant, what type of sustainable infrastructure would you create?[18]

6. **Planning for Disaster Recovery**
   You are the new senior analyst in the MIS department at Beltz, a large snack food manufacturing company. The company is located on the beautiful shoreline in Charleston, North Carolina. The company's location is one of its best and worst features. The weather and surroundings are beautiful, but the threat of hurricanes and other natural disasters is high. What types of information should be contained in Beltz's disaster recovery plan that will minimize any risks involved with a natural disaster?

7. **Comparing Backup and Recovery Systems**
   Research the Internet to find three different vendors of backup and recovery systems. Compare and contrast the three systems and determine which one you would recommend if you were installing a backup and recovery system for a medium-sized business, with 3,500 employees, that maintains information on the stock market. Compile your findings in a presentation that you can give to your class that details the three systems' strengths and weaknesses, along with your recommendation.

8. **Cool Schools**

Very large computers and data centers incur huge energy costs keeping electronic components cooled. Where is your school's data center located? How big is it? What security measures does the facility enforce? Can you get a tour of it? If it is on campus, how is the facility cooled? How is the power supplied? Heating and cooling computer systems are certainly a big issue. Think of ways you could reuse the heat from a data center, such as sending it to a college dorm. Could alternative resources, such as a nearby river or a lake, provide added cooling? What unanticipated environmental issues could this create?

9. **Box.net in the Cloud**

Box.net was started by two college students, Aaron Levie and Dylan Smith, who needed a secure place to collaborate on group projects. The two immediately understood the value of cloud computing, and they created Box.net to allow them to share ideas and collaborate on documents in a virtual work space located in the cloud. They knew the cloud would allow them to access their documents from anywhere and on any device and that there was no chance of their papers being stolen or accidently destroyed. Levie and Smith recognized the business opportunity of their site and jumped at turning Box.net into a real business. Explain how Box.net could help you if you were working on a project with four other students. What would be the challenges of using Box.net?[19]

ENTREPRENEURIAL CHALLENGE

BUILD YOUR OWN BUSINESS

1. On your way to work this morning, you stopped for gas. When you were inside paying, someone broke into your car and stole your computer bag. You did not notice until you arrived at your business and began looking for your bag. As you begin to realize all of the data you just lost—customer lists, profit and loss analysis, tax returns, email, sales information, payroll files, and so on—you begin to wonder when you last backed up your hard drive. Now that you have been stung by a painful data loss experience, you realize the importance of having a backup strategy. Create a detailed backup strategy and disaster recovery plan for your business. Be sure to include details such as the types of backup you will perform, frequency of backups, and location of backups. (Be sure to identify your business and the name of your company.)
2. Rank the characteristics of an agile MIS infrastructure in order of importance to your business and be sure to provide detailed information on each characteristic and your justification for its ranking.
3. Cloud computing is a business driven MIS infrastructure that supports growth, operations, and profits. It helps today's businesses innovate by using resources and applications hosted remotely as a shared service on the Internet. You have decided to research the different types of cloud computing services. Create a report listing the types of services your business should implement and the advantages and disadvantages of each.

APPLY YOUR KNOWLEDGE BUSINESS PROJECTS

PROJECT I Ranking MIS characteristics

In a group, review the list of MIS infrastructure characteristics that support growth and rank them in order of their impact on a company's success, using 1 to indicate the biggest impact and 7 the least.

MIS Infrastructure Characteristics	Business Impact
Accessibility	
Availability	
Maintainability	
Portability	
Reliability	
Scalability	
Usability	

PROJECT II Designing a Company Infrastructure

Components of an MIS infrastructure include everything from documentation to business concepts to software and hardware. Deciding which components to implement and how to implement them can be a challenge. New MIS components are released daily, and business needs continually change. An MIS infrastructure that meets your company's needs today may not meet those needs tomorrow. Building an MIS infrastructure that is accessible, available, flexible, reliable, scalable, usable, and performs well is key to your company's growth, operations, and profitability.

Project Focus

You are the manager for a large clothing company called Xedous. You are responsible for developing the initial MIS infrastructure. Create a list of questions you will need answered to develop it. Here are examples of a few of the questions you might ask:

- What are the company's growth expectations?
- Will systems be able to handle additional users?
- How long will information be stored in the systems?
- How much customer history must be stored?
- What are the company's business hours?
- What are the company's backup requirements?

PROJECT III Recycle Your Cell Phone

For all those excited to get the new iPhone with its numerous applications and cool games, what are you going to do with your old cell phone? You can help the environment and recycle your phone, PDA, charger, and batteries. Recycling cell phones helps to save energy and keep reusable materials out of landfills. Cell phones are made of plastic, copper, and precious metals, which require energy to extract and manufacture. If you decide to recycle your cell phone be sure to terminate the service, delete any contacts or stored information, and take out the SIM card.

Project Focus

If your old cell phone is still working, you might also want to consider donating it to charity. Many programs will accept working cell phones that they donate to people in need, such as survivors of domestic violence, because old cell phones can still dial 911 even after the service is disconnected. To find local agencies where you can donate your cell phone, visit ncadv.org. Cell phones are only a small percentage of the total computer equipment organizations replace each year. What happens to all of those old laptops, notebooks, servers, and monitors? What is the environmental impact of throwing a computer system into a landfill? What can companies do to recycle their computer equipment? What can the government do to help motivate companies and individuals to recycle?

PROJECT IV Back on Your Feet

You are working for GetSmart, a document creation company for legal professionals. Due to the highly sensitive nature of their work, employees must store all information on the network drive and are not allowed to back up the data to a CD, flash drive, or any other type of external storage, including home computers. The company has been following this policy for the past three years without any problems. You return to work Monday morning after a long weekend to find that the building was struck by lightning, destroying several servers. Unfortunately, the backup network also failed, so all the data from your department has been lost.

Because of this loss, the MIS manager and four colleagues who developed the company backup policy were fired.

Project Focus

You have been placed on a committee with several of your peers to revamp the backup and recovery policies and create a new disaster recovery plan. You must create policies and procedures that will preserve the sensitive nature of the documents, while ensuring the company is safe from disasters. Be sure to address a worst-case scenario where the entire building is lost.

PROJECT V Growing, Growing, Gone

You are the founder of Black Pearl, a small comic book start-up. The good news is Black Pearl is tremendously successful, with 34 employees in a functional and creative office in downtown Chicago. The comics you produce are of extremely high quality. The artwork is unmatched, and fans find the storylines compelling. Black Pearl comics are quickly becoming classics with extremely loyal customers. You produce all the comics and sell them in your store and via the Internet to individuals all over the United States.

Project Focus

You had a vision when you started Black Pearl. You knew the potential of your business model to revamp the comic industry. You purchased high-end computers and customizable software to support your operations. Now, you are faced with a new dilemma. You have a large international following and you have decided to pursue international opportunities. You would like to open stores in Japan, France, and Brazil over the next year. To determine whether this is possible you need to evaluate if your MIS infrastructure is agile enough to support international requirements. Brainstorm all of the business nuances that will be different when working with international companies and customers. Create a list of questions your MIS department will need to answer to determine if your system is agile enough to support international business.

PROJECT VI Excuses, Excuses, Excuses

Here are a few examples of the strangest and most unusual excuses employees use when missing work.

- I have a sunburn.
- I'm not sure why but I woke up in Canada.
- I was caught selling an alligator.
- I was locked in the trunk of an abandoned car.
- I have a note from my mom that I could not go to work yesterday.
- I'm just not into it today.
- I was riding my motorcycle and I accidentally hit a nun.
- Some person threw poison ivy at me and now I have a rash on my face.

- I need to stay home as I am convinced I can catch my spouse having an affair.
- I was chasing a seagull and fell down and had to go to the hospital.
- I have a migraine from eating too many jalapeño peppers.

This chapter focuses on MIS infrastructures, the main building blocks that function together to control the entire organization's systems. If your systems cannot operate, then your organization cannot work, similar to how your health controls your ability to work. Attempting to do business with an organization when its systems have crashed, Internet access is down, or wireless network is malfunctioning is very frustrating. When these types of issues occur, companies do not want to broadcast that they are experiencing technical difficulties because of hackers, unpaid utility bill, or squirrels broke into the data center and ate through all of the wires (yes, that has really happened).

Project Focus

How many times have you called a company and the customer service representative has stated that the system is down or that the system is really slow today? How many times have you missed submitting an assignment because your Internet service was down? Why is it important for an organization to have its systems available 24 hours a day, 7 days a week, and 365 days a year? Why would a company hide the real reason that its systems are malfunctioning? What could happen if customers were informed that the systems were down due to hackers? How can an organization safeguard its systems?

PROJECT VII Ewaste Not, Want Not

On Earth Day every year many people, including corporate citizens, devote themselves to recycling and reducing, along with identifying items they can repurpose. Companies, such as Dell and Microsoft, two producers of materials that eventually become ewaste, have joined forces with an electronics recycling program run by Goodwill Industries International. Goodwill reports that the program has diverted about 96 million pounds in electronics from landfills.[20]

Assisting in a similar effort are office supply stores Office Depot and Staples that offer their own sorting and recycling services for used electronics. Apple has even jumped on this bandwagon, allowing customers to turn their old products in to retail locations when they buy something new.

Project Focus

There are so many opportunities to reduce ewaste. Make a list of how the popular technology manufacturers are already trying to reduce ewaste. Would starting a company that helped people locate used computers or other technologies for reuse be a worthwhile venture? Why or why not? Create a list of new alternatives any company could adopt to reuse, recycle, and reduce ewaste.

PROJECT VIII One Laptop Per Child

The One Laptop Per Child (OLPC) project intends to create a $100 laptop for distribution to the world's poorest children. The machine, called the OLPC or XO laptop, has a rubberized keyboard and an ultra-bright screen readable in daylight; when flipped, it converts to an electronic book reader. To keep the cost as low as possible (at $175 it is currently a bit more than the target), the computer has a host of free software and other tools to support learning opportunities. A special type of networking allows machines within a hundred feet or so to communicate with each other and relays a single Internet connection for them to use (where the Internet is available). The XO is targeted at communities where power generation is unreliable or nonexistent; it gets its power via a hand crank, pull cord, or foot pedal.[21]

Project Focus

Do you agree that the One Laptop Per Child project will help educate children around the world? How does the XO computer provide learning opportunities for children in economically poor regions of the world? What issues could these children encounter if they have an XO laptop? How will cloud computing play an important role in the XO laptop, especially in terms of keeping costs low and data safe? What do you think the typical environment will be like where the XO laptop will be used? What issues will users of the XO laptop encounter that are not common in the United States? What can the creators of the XO laptop do to ensure its functionality even in the most extreme environments?

AYK APPLICATION PROJECTS

If you are looking for Excel projects to incorporate into your class, try any of the following after reading this chapter.

Project Number	Project Name	Project Type	Plug-In	Focus Area	Project Level	Skill Set	Page Number
8	Book Boxes	Excel	T2, T4	Strategic Analysis	Intermediate	Formulas or Solver	AYK.6
9	Security Analysis	Excel	T3	Filtering Data	Intermediate	Conditional Formatting, Autofilter, Subtotal	AYK.7
10	Gathering Data	Excel	T3	Data Analysis	Intermediate	Conditional Formatting	AYK.8
11	Splashem	Excel	T2	Strategic Analysis	Intermediate	Formulas	AYK.8
12	Bill's Boots	Excel	T2	Profit Maximization	Intermediate	Formulas	AYK.9
13	Adequate Acquisitions	Excel	T2	Break Even Analysis	Intermediate	Formulas	AYK.9
15	Assessing the Value of Information	Excel	T3	Data Analysis	Intermediate	PivotTable	AYK.10
16	Growth, Trends, and Forecasts	Excel	T2, T3	Data Forecasting	Advanced	Average, Trend, Growth	AYK.11
18	Formatting Grades	Excel	T3	Data Analysis	Advanced	If, LookUp	AYK.12
22	Gizmo Turnover	Excel	T3	Data Mining	Advanced	PivotTable	AYK.15
24	Mountain Cycle	Excel	T4	Business Analysis	Advanced	Goal Seek	AYK.16
25	Lutz Motors	Excel	T4	Sales Analysis	Advanced	Scenario Manager	AYK.16

Data: Business Intelligence

6

CHAPTER

CHAPTER OUTLINE

SECTION 6.1
Data, Information, and Databases

- The Business Benefits of High-Quality Information
- Storing Information Using a Relational Database Management System
- Using a Relational Database for Business Advantages
- Driving Websites with Data

SECTION 6.2
Business Intelligence

- The Business Benefits of Data Warehousing
- Performing Business Analysis with Data Marts
- Uncovering Trends and Patterns with Data Mining
- Supporting Decisions with Business Intelligence

What's in IT for me?

This chapter introduces the concepts of information and data and their relative importance to business professionals and firms. It distinguishes between data stored in transactional databases and powerful business intelligence gleaned from data warehouses. Students who understand how to access, manipulate, summarize, sort, and analyze data to support decision making find success. Information has power, and understanding that power will help you compete in the global marketplace. This chapter will provide you with an overview of database fundamentals and the characteristics associated with high-quality information. It will also explain how the various bits of data stored across multiple, operational databases can be transformed in a centralized repository of summarized information in a data warehouse, which can be used for discovering business intelligence.

You, as a business student, need to understand the differences between transactional data and summarized information and the different types of questions you could use a transactional database to answer versus a data warehouse. You need to be aware of the complexity of storing data in databases and the level of effort required to transform operational data into meaningful, summarized information. You need to realize the power of information and the competitive advantage a data warehouse brings an organization in terms of facilitating business intelligence. Armed with the power of information, business students will make smart, informed, and data-supported managerial decisions.

opening case study

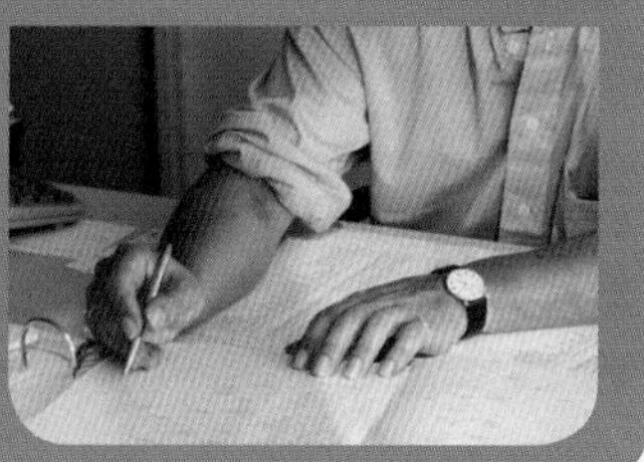

Business Intelligence Software's Time Is Now

With restaurants stretching from Seattle to the Osan Air Base in South Korea, the Chili's Grill & Bar chain gets many visitors. For parent company Brinker International, that makes many Triple Dippers to keep track of. In addition, as the owner of such chains as On The Border Mexican Grill & Cantina, Brinker has to gather information on sales, inventory, and other operations for 1,700 restaurants in 27 countries that receive more than 1 million customers a day. An even bigger challenge, though, is sifting through all that data, organizing it, and then using it to make the business run more profitably.

Making smart use of that information is all the more urgent as customers dine in more often and spend less even when they eat out. Amid falling revenue, Brinker already has resorted to cutting jobs and shutting restaurants. "At Brinker, we are not waiting for external actions to strengthen our company," states Brinker's CEO Doug Brooks. "We have taken considerable steps to remain competitive and position our brands for accelerated profitability once the economy eventually does improve."

One of those steps is analyzing the reams of data the company collects at its restaurants. Using what is known as business intelligence software, Brinker gets a better handle on consumer spending patterns to make a host of decisions, from altering staff levels to moving around menu items. Interest in business intelligence software is on the rise, analysts say, as economic woes force companies to pursue profit by delving deeper into the information already at their fingertips. "There's a tremendous pressure on cost containment, on developing accurate forecasts of sales and expenses, and on trying to align the expense stream with projected revenue stream," says John Van Decker, research vice president at research firm Gartner.

Top Priority for CIOs

Business intelligence (BI) software can bring together data from disparate parts of the company. Once that happens, companies can do analysis, run reports, and make predictions based on past performance. Some BI software lets companies weave in external information, such as the price of gas or the unemployment rate in certain regions, to understand how market swings or economic trends are affecting customer behavior and the company.

Brinker used BI to help with a challenge faced by many restaurants: determining how many staff should work each shift—a task that can be especially daunting during a recession. The company tapped a restaurant performance management system built with Information Builders' WebFOCUS business intelligence software.

Among other things, this software can calculate, based on sales, the optimal staffing level during a particular shift at a specific restaurant.

BI software tops the list of technology spending priorities for companies in 2009, according to a Gartner survey of more than 1,500 CIOs worldwide. That priority remains, even though IT budgets are expected to be essentially flat in 2009. Market researcher Forrester Research expects the BI market to generate more than $12 billion in revenue in 2014, compared with $8.5 billion in 2008.

Expectations for increasing demand helped fuel a wave of consolidation in the BI market. Software vendors including SAP, IBM, Oracle, and Microsoft all made big BI acquisitions in recent years.

Capitalizing on Quality Data

About two-thirds of large U.S. companies believe they need to improve their analytical capabilities and only half believe they are spending enough on business analytics, according to an Accenture survey of 250 executives. In it, about 57 percent of companies said they do not have a beneficial, consistently updated, companywide analytical capability, and 72 percent are working to increase their company's use of business analytics. Today, only 60 percent of major decisions are based on analytics, according to the survey, while 40 percent are based on intuition.

Business intelligence software can also help companies mine customer data that they already track to potentially sell new products or services. For example, Ingram Micro, a wholesale technology distributor, discovered it was missing out on opportunities to renew maintenance contracts. Ingram Micro sells hardware and software to smaller resellers, which sell it to businesses and consumers. "Our visibility into that piece of product evaporated as soon as it left the warehouse," says Justin Crotty, vice president for services at Ingram Micro North America. So, three years ago, the company started using online software from MaintenanceNet that analyzes data the company already captures to identify 80 to 90 percent of renewal opportunities, up from 30 percent previously. That has resulted in increased services revenues, even while hardware sales have slowed throughout the industry.

Strategic Modeling for the Future

The economic slowdown has also affected the number of bookings in the cruise industry. To cope, Carnival Cruise Lines is trying to lure back former travelers. "We're focusing on getting them to come back, refreshing in their minds what a fantastic time they had on their last cruise," says Shannon Balliet-Antorcha, director of database marketing and customer data integration for the Carnival Cruise Lines brand.

Trouble is, Carnival doesn't have an unlimited marketing budget to create material for all of its former travelers, so it concentrates on those likely to go on a cruise during a recession. Using software from SAS, Carnival can look at internal customer information and also third-party information about household income and composition. By analyzing that information, Carnival can quickly and easily create marketing campaigns for the right audience.

"Large companies are like large ships that are difficult to turn," says John Colbert, vice president for research and analysis at BPM Partners, a management consulting firm. Lots of companies use business intelligence to understand what has happened in the past, but it's really important, he says, to do strategic modeling to understand how to move forward, whether it means solidifying relationships with your most profitable clients or figuring out which employees are the least productive and will need to go in the next wave of layoffs.

Brinker hopes better information will give way to better management of labor costs going forward. "It's starting to help," says Kenny Sullivan, senior director of operational and analytical systems at Brinker. "We're starting to be more efficient."[1]

section 6.1 DATA, INFORMATION, AND DATABASES

LEARNING OUTCOMES

6.1 Explain the four primary traits that determine the value of information.

6.2 Describe a database, a database management system, and the relational database model.

6.3 Identify the business advantages of a relational database.

6.4 Explain the business benefits of a data-driven website.

THE BUSINESS BENEFITS OF HIGH-QUALITY INFORMATION

LO 6.1: Explain the four primary traits that determine the value of information.

Information is powerful. Information can tell an organization how its current operations are performing and help it estimate and strategize about how future operations might perform. The ability to understand, digest, analyze, and filter information is key to growth and success to any professional in any industry. Remember that new perspectives and opportunities can open up when you have the right data that you can turn into information and ultimately business intelligence.

Information is everywhere in an organization. Managers in sales, marketing, human resources, and management need information to run their departments and make daily decisions. When addressing a significant business issue, employees must be able to obtain and analyze all the relevant information so they can make the best decision possible. Information comes at different levels, formats, and granularities. ***Information granularity*** refers to the extent of detail within the information (fine and detailed or coarse and abstract). Employees must be able to correlate the different levels, formats, and granularities of information when making decisions. For example, a company might be collecting information from various suppliers to make needed decisions, only to find that the information is in different levels, formats, and granularities. One supplier might send detailed information in a spreadsheet, while another supplier might send summary information in a Word document, and still another might send a collection of information from emails. Employees will need to compare these different types of information for what they commonly reveal to make strategic decisions. Figure 6.1 displays the various levels, formats, and granularities of organizational information.

Successfully collecting, compiling, sorting, and finally analyzing information from multiple levels, in varied formats, and exhibiting different granularities can provide tremendous insight into how an organization is performing. Exciting and unexpected results can include potential new markets, new ways of reaching customers, and even new methods of doing business. After understanding the different levels, formats, and granularities of information, managers next want to look at the four primary traits that help determine the value of information:

- Information type: transactional and analytical.
- Information timeliness.
- Information quality.
- Information governance.

Information Type: Transactional and Analytical

As discussed previously in the text, the two primary types of information are transactional and analytical. Transactional information encompasses all of the information contained within a single business process or unit of work, and its primary purpose is to support daily operational tasks. Organizations need to capture and store transactional information to perform operational tasks and repetitive decisions such as analyzing daily

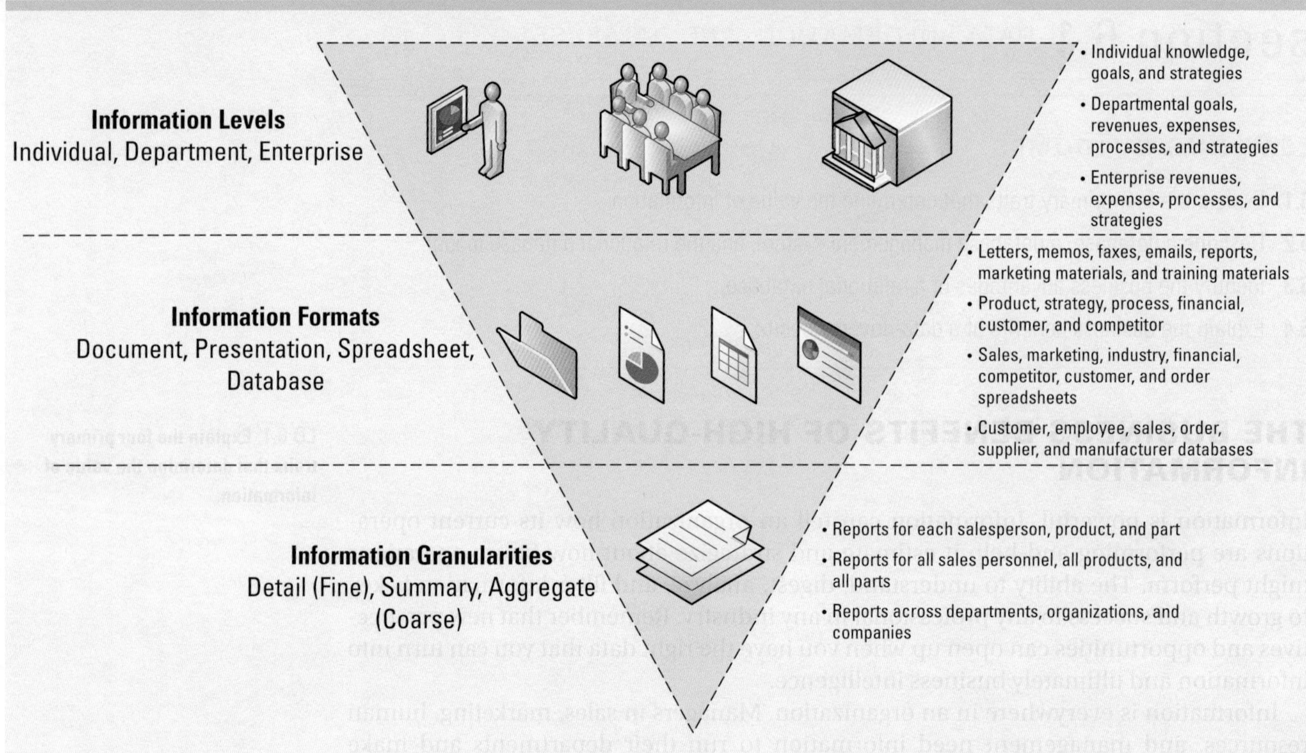

FIGURE 6.1

Levels, Formats, and Granularities of Organizational Information

sales reports and production schedules to determine how much inventory to carry. Consider Walmart, which handles more than 1 million customer transactions every hour, and Facebook, which keeps track of 400 million active users (along with their photos, friends, and Web links). In addition, every time a cash register rings up a sale, a deposit or withdrawal is made from an ATM, or a receipt is given at the gas pump, capturing and storing of the transactional information are required.

Analytical information encompasses all organizational information, and its primary purpose is to support the performing of managerial analysis tasks. Analytical information is useful when making important decisions such as whether the organization should build a new manufacturing plant or hire additional sales personnel. Analytical information makes it possible to do many things that previously were difficult to accomplish, such as spot business trends, prevent diseases, and fight crime. For example, credit card companies crunch through billions of transactional purchase records to identify fraudulent activity. Indicators such as charges in a foreign country or consecutive purchases of gasoline send a red flag highlighting potential fraudulent activity.

Walmart was able to use its massive amount of analytical information to identify many unusual trends, such as a correlation between storms and Pop-Tarts. Yes, Walmart discovered an increase in the demand for Pop-Tarts during the storm season. Armed with the valuable information the retail chain was able to stock up on Pop-Tarts that were ready for purchase when customers arrived. Figure 6.2 displays different types of transactional and analytical information.

Information Timeliness

Timeliness is an aspect of information that depends on the situation. In some firms or industries, information that is a few days or weeks old can be relevant, while in others information that is a few minutes old can be almost worthless. Some organizations, such as 911 response centers, stock traders, and banks, require up-to-the-second information. Other organizations, such as insurance and construction companies, require only daily or even weekly information.

Real-time information means immediate, up-to-date information. ***Real-time systems*** provide real-time information in response to requests. Many organizations

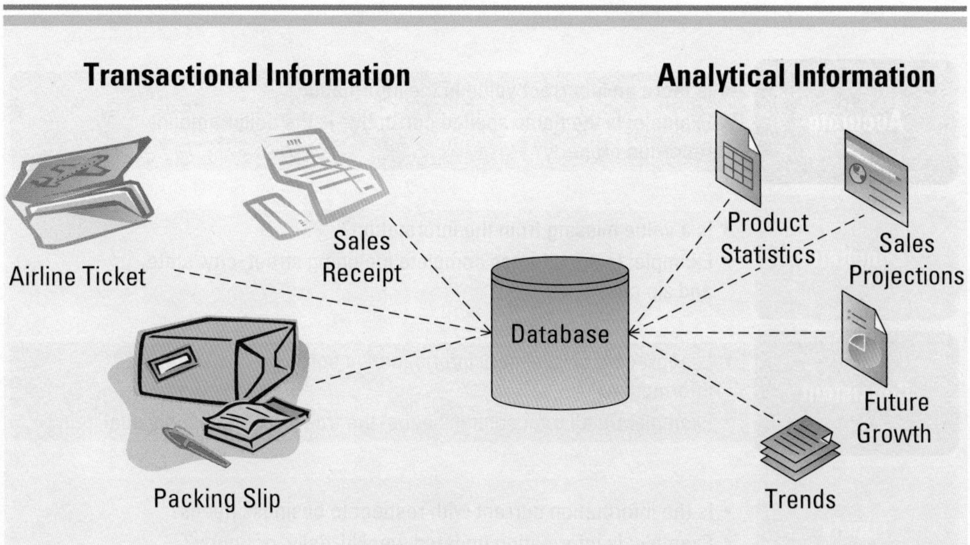

FIGURE 6.2

Transactional versus Analytical Information

use real-time systems to uncover key corporate transactional information. The growing demand for real-time information stems from organizations' need to make faster and more effective decisions, keep smaller inventories, operate more efficiently, and track performance more carefully. Information also needs to be timely in the sense that it meets employees' needs, but no more. If employees can absorb information only on an hourly or daily basis, there is no need to gather real-time information in smaller increments.

Most people request real-time information without understanding one of the biggest pitfalls associated with real-time information—continual change. Imagine the following scenario: Three managers meet at the end of the day to discuss a business problem. Each manager has gathered information at different times during the day to create a picture of the situation. Each manager's picture may be different because of the time differences. Their views on the business problem may not match because the information they are basing their analysis on is continually changing. This approach may not speed up decision making, and it may actually slow it down. Business decision makers must evaluate the timeliness for the information for every decision. Organizations do not want to find themselves using real-time information to make a bad decision faster.

Information Quality

Business decisions are only as good as the quality of the information used to make them. ***Data inconsistency*** occurs when the same data element has different values. Take for example the amount of work that needs to occur to update a customer who had changed her last name due to marriage. Changing this information in only a few organizational systems will lead to data inconsistencies causing customer 123456 to be associated with two last names. ***Data integrity issues*** occur when a system produces incorrect, inconsistent, or duplicate data. Data integrity issues can cause managers to consider the system reports invalid and will make decisions based on other sources.

To ensure your systems do not suffer from data integrity issues, review Figure 6.3 for the five characteristics common to high-quality information: accuracy, completeness, consistency, timeliness, and uniqueness. Figure 6.4 provides an example of several problems associated with using low-quality information including:

1. *Completeness.* The customer's first name is missing.
2. Another issue with *completeness.* The street address contains only a number and not a street name.
3. *Consistency.* There may be a duplication of information since there is a slight difference between the two customers in the spelling of the last name. Similar street addresses and phone numbers make this likely.

FIGURE 6.3

Five Common Characteristics of High-Quality Information

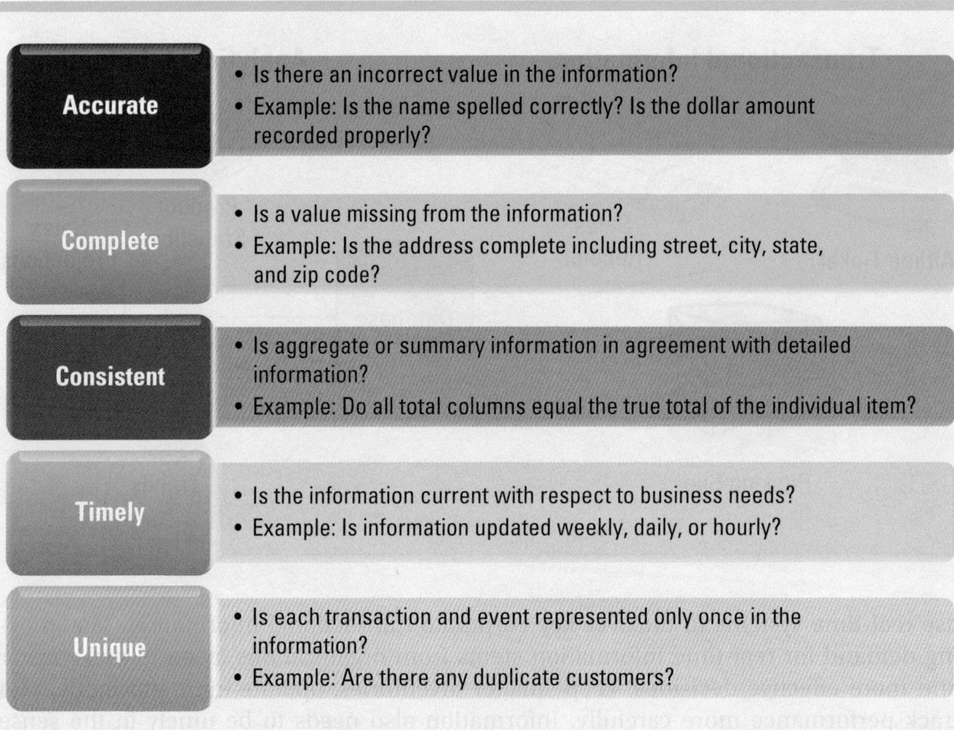

Accurate
• Is there an incorrect value in the information?
• Example: Is the name spelled correctly? Is the dollar amount recorded properly?
Complete
• Is a value missing from the information?
• Example: Is the address complete including street, city, state, and zip code?
Consistent
• Is aggregate or summary information in agreement with detailed information?
• Example: Do all total columns equal the true total of the individual item?
Timely
• Is the information current with respect to business needs?
• Example: Is information updated weekly, daily, or hourly?
Unique
• Is each transaction and event represented only once in the information?
• Example: Are there any duplicate customers?

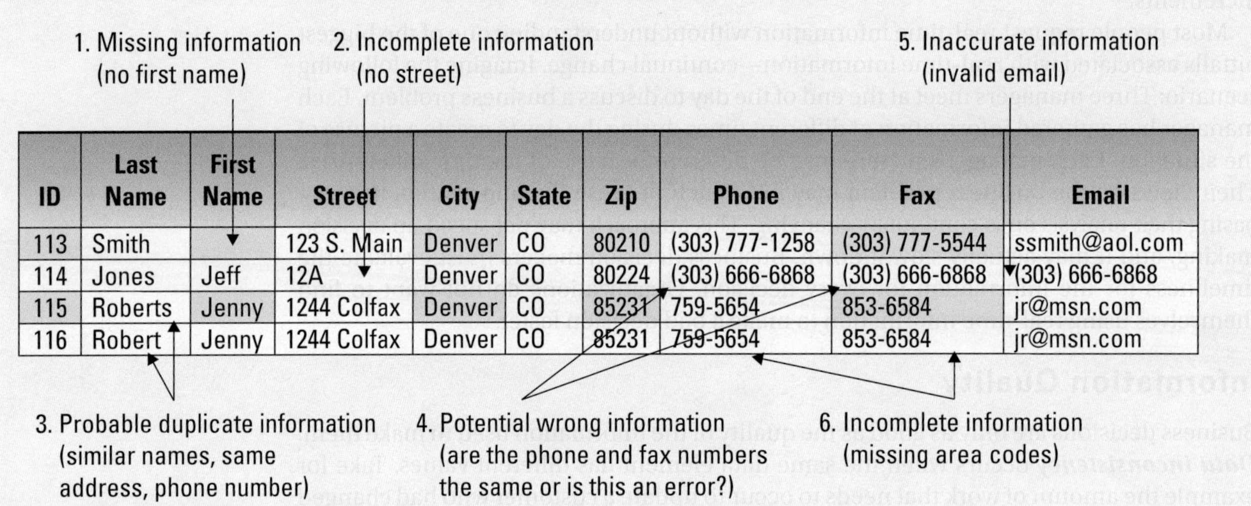

ID	Last Name	First Name	Street	City	State	Zip	Phone	Fax	Email
113	Smith		123 S. Main	Denver	CO	80210	(303) 777-1258	(303) 777-5544	ssmith@aol.com
114	Jones	Jeff	12A	Denver	CO	80224	(303) 666-6868	(303) 666-6868	(303) 666-6868
115	Roberts	Jenny	1244 Colfax	Denver	CO	85231	759-5654	853-6584	jr@msn.com
116	Robert	Jenny	1244 Colfax	Denver	CO	85231	759-5654	853-6584	jr@msn.com

FIGURE 6.4

Example of Low-Quality Information

4. *Accuracy.* This may be inaccurate information because the customer's phone and fax numbers are the same. Some customers might have the same number for phone and fax, but the fact that the customer also has this number in the email address field is suspicious.
5. Another issue with *accuracy.* There is inaccurate information because a phone number is located in the email address field.
6. Another issue with *completeness.* The information is incomplete because there is not a valid area code for the phone and fax numbers.

Nestlé uses 550,000 suppliers to sell more than 100,000 products in 200 countries. However, due to poor information, the company was unable to evaluate its business effectively. After some analysis, it found that it had 9 million records of vendors, customers, and materials, half of which were duplicated, obsolete, inaccurate, or incomplete. The analysis discovered that some records abbreviated vendor names while other

APPLY YOUR KNOWLEDGE

BUSINESS DRIVEN MIS

Determining Information Quality Issues

Real People magazine is geared toward working individuals and provides articles and advice on everything from car maintenance to family planning. The magazine is currently experiencing problems with its distribution list. More than 30 percent of the magazines mailed are returned because of incorrect address information, and each month it receives numerous calls from angry customers complaining that they have not yet received their magazines. Below is a sample of *Real People*'s customer information. Create a report detailing all the issues with the information, potential causes of the information issues, and solutions the company can follow to correct the situation.

ID	First Name	Middle Initial	Last Name	Street	City	State	Zip Code
433	M	J	Jones	13 Denver	Denver	CO	87654
434	Margaret	J	Jones	13 First Ave.	Denver	CO	87654
434	Brian	F	Hoover	Lake Ave.	Columbus	OH	87654
435	Nick	H	Schweitzer	65 Apple Lane	San Francisco	OH	65664
436	Richard	A		567 55th St.	New York	CA	98763
437	Alana	B	Smith	121 Tenny Dr.	Buffalo	NY	142234
438	Trevor	D	Darrian	90 Fresrdestil	Dallas	TX	74532

records spelled out the vendor names. This created multiple accounts for the same customer, making it impossible to determine the true value of Nestlé's customers. Without being able to identify customer profitability, a company runs the risk of alienating its best customers.[2]

Knowing how low-quality information issues typically occur can help a company correct them. Addressing these errors will significantly improve the quality of company information and the value to be extracted from it. The four primary reasons for low-quality information are:

1. Online customers intentionally enter inaccurate information to protect their privacy.
2. Different systems have different information entry standards and formats.
3. Data-entry personnel enter abbreviated information to save time or erroneous information by accident.
4. Third-party and external information contains inconsistencies, inaccuracies, and errors.

Understanding the Costs of Using Low-Quality Information Using the wrong information can lead managers to make erroneous decisions. Erroneous decisions in turn can cost time, money, reputations, and even jobs. Some of the serious business consequences that occur due to using low-quality information to make decisions are:

- Inability to accurately track customers.
- Difficulty identifying the organization's most valuable customers.
- Inability to identify selling opportunities.
- Lost revenue opportunities from marketing to nonexistent customers.

- The cost of sending nondeliverable mail.
- Difficulty tracking revenue because of inaccurate invoices.
- Inability to build strong relationships with customers.

Understanding the Benefits of Using High-Quality Information High-quality information can significantly improve the chances of making a good decision and directly increase an organization's bottom line. One company discovered that even with its large number of golf courses, Phoenix, Arizona, is not a good place to sell golf clubs. An analysis revealed that typical golfers in Phoenix are tourists and conventioneers who usually bring their clubs with them. The analysis further revealed that two of the best places to sell golf clubs in the United States are Rochester, New York, and Detroit, Michigan. Equipped with this valuable information, the company was able to strategically place its stores and launch its marketing campaigns.

High-quality information does not automatically guarantee that every decision made is going to be a good one, because people ultimately make decisions and no one is perfect. However, such information ensures that the basis of the decisions is accurate. The success of the organization depends on appreciating and leveraging the true value of timely and high-quality information.

Information Governance

Information is a vital resource and users need to be educated on what they can and cannot do with it. To ensure a firm manages its information correctly, it will need special policies and procedures establishing rules on how the information is organized, updated, maintained, and accessed. Every firm, large and small, should create an information policy concerning data governance. ***Data governance*** refers to the overall management of the availability, usability, integrity, and security of company data. A company that supports a data governance program has a defined a policy that specifies who is accountable for various portions or aspects of the data, including its accuracy, accessibility, consistency, timeliness, and completeness. The policy should clearly define the processes concerning how to store, archive, back up, and secure the data. In addition, the company should create a set of procedures identifying accessibility levels for employees. Then, the firm should deploy controls and procedures that enforce government regulations and compliance with mandates such as Sarbanes-Oxley.

LO 6.2: Describe a database, a database management system, and the relational database model.

STORING INFORMATION IN A RELATIONAL DATABASE MANAGEMENT SYSTEM

The core component of any system, regardless of size, is a database and a database management system. Broadly defined, a ***database*** maintains information about various types of objects (inventory), events (transactions), people (employees), and places (warehouses). A ***database management system (DBMS)*** creates, reads, updates, and deletes data in a database while controlling access and security. Managers send requests to the DBMS, and the DBMS performs the actual manipulation of the data in the database. Companies store their information in databases, and managers access these systems to answer operational questions such as how many customers purchased Product A in December or what were the average sales by region. There are two primary tools available for retrieving information from a DBMS. First is a ***query-by-example (QBE) tool*** that helps users graphically design the answer to a question against a database. Second is a ***structured query language (SQL)*** that asks users to write lines of code to answer questions against a database. Managers typically interact with QBE tools, and MIS professionals have the skills required to code SQL. Figure 6.5 displays the relationship between a database, a DBMS, and a user. Some of the more popular examples of DBMS include MySQL, Microsoft Access, SQL Server, FileMaker, Oracle, and FoxPro.

A ***data element*** (or ***data field***) is the smallest or basic unit of information. Data elements can include a customer's name, address, email, discount rate, preferred shipping method, product name, quantity ordered, and so on. ***Data models*** are logical data structures that detail the relationships among data elements using graphics or pictures.

APPLY YOUR KNOWLEDGE

BUSINESS DRIVEN DEBATE

Securing Credit Card Data

Without a data governance policy, a company might be leaving its data vulnerable to hackers and theft. Consider TJX Co., the parent company of T.J. Maxx, which had 45 million credit and debit card numbers stolen from its data systems. The credit card industry provides security rules that mandate vendors encrypt credit card data and limit storage of credit card numbers from point-of-sale terminals. T.J. Maxx did not have a data governance policy adhering to these stipulations and was actively storing the customer information and credit card numbers for years.[3]

Who do you think is to blame for the T.J. Maxx credit card data theft—the company for not implementing the proper data governance policies or the hackers?

Metadata provides details about data. For example, metadata for an image could include its size, resolution, and date created. Metadata about a text document could contain document length, data created, author's name, and summary. Each data element is given a description, such as Customer Name; metadata is provided for the type of data (text, numeric, alphanumeric, date, image, binary value) and descriptions of potential predefined values such as a certain area code; and finally the relationship is defined. A ***data dictionary*** compiles all of the metadata about the data elements in the data model. Looking at a data model along with reviewing the data dictionary provides tremendous insight into the database's functions, purpose, and business rules.

DBMS use three primary data models for organizing information—hierarchical, network, and the relational database, the most prevalent. A ***relational database model*** stores information in the form of logically related two-dimensional tables. A ***relational database management system*** allows users to create, read, update, and delete data in a relational database. Although the hierarchical and network models are important, this text focuses only on the relational database model.

Storing Data Elements in Entities and Attributes

For flexibility in supporting business operations, managers need to query or search for the answers to business questions such as which artist sold the most albums during a certain month. The relationships in the relational database model help managers extract this information. Figure 6.6 illustrates the primary concepts of the relational database model—entities, attributes, keys, and relationships. An ***entity*** (also referred to as a table)

FIGURE 6.5
Relationship of Database, DBMS, and User

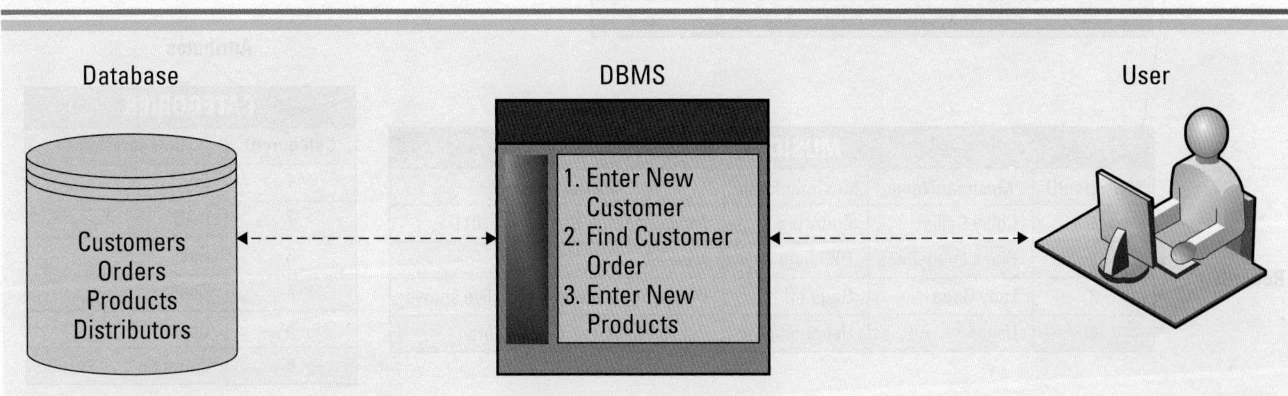

stores information about a person, place, thing, transaction, or event. The entities, or tables, of interest in Figure 6.6 are *TRACKS, RECORDINGS, MUSICIANS,* and *CATEGORIES.* Notice that each entity is stored in a different two-dimensional table (with rows and columns).

Attributes (also called columns or fields) are the data elements associated with an entity. In Figure 6.6 the attributes for the entity *TRACKS* are *TrackNumber, TrackTitle, TrackLength,* and *RecordingID.* Attributes for the entity *MUSICIANS* are *MusicianID, MusicianName, MusicianPhoto,* and *MusicianNotes.* A ***record*** is a collection of related data elements (in the *MUSICIANS* table these include "3, Lady Gaga, gag.tiff, Do not bring young kids to live shows"). Each record in an entity occupies one row in its respective table.

Creating Relationships Through Keys

To manage and organize various entities within the relational database model, you use primary keys and foreign keys to create logical relationships. A ***primary key*** is a field (or group of fields) that uniquely identifies a given record in a table. In the table *RECORDINGS,* the primary key is the field *RecordingID* that uniquely identifies each record in the table. Primary keys are a critical piece of a relational database because they provide a way of distinguishing each record in a table; for instance, imagine you need to find information on a customer named Steve Smith. Simply searching the customer name would not be an ideal way to find the information because there might be 20 customers with the name Steve Smith. This is the reason the relational database model uses primary keys to uniquely identify each record. Using Steve Smith's unique ID allows a manager to search the database to identify all information associated with this customer.

A ***foreign key*** is a primary key of one table that appears as an attribute in another table and acts to provide a logical relationship between the two tables. For instance, Black Eyed Peas in Figure 6.6 is one of the musicians appearing in the *MUSICIANS* table. Its primary key, *MusicianID,* is "2." Notice that *MusicianID* also appears as an attribute in the *RECORDINGS* table. By matching these attributes, you create a relationship

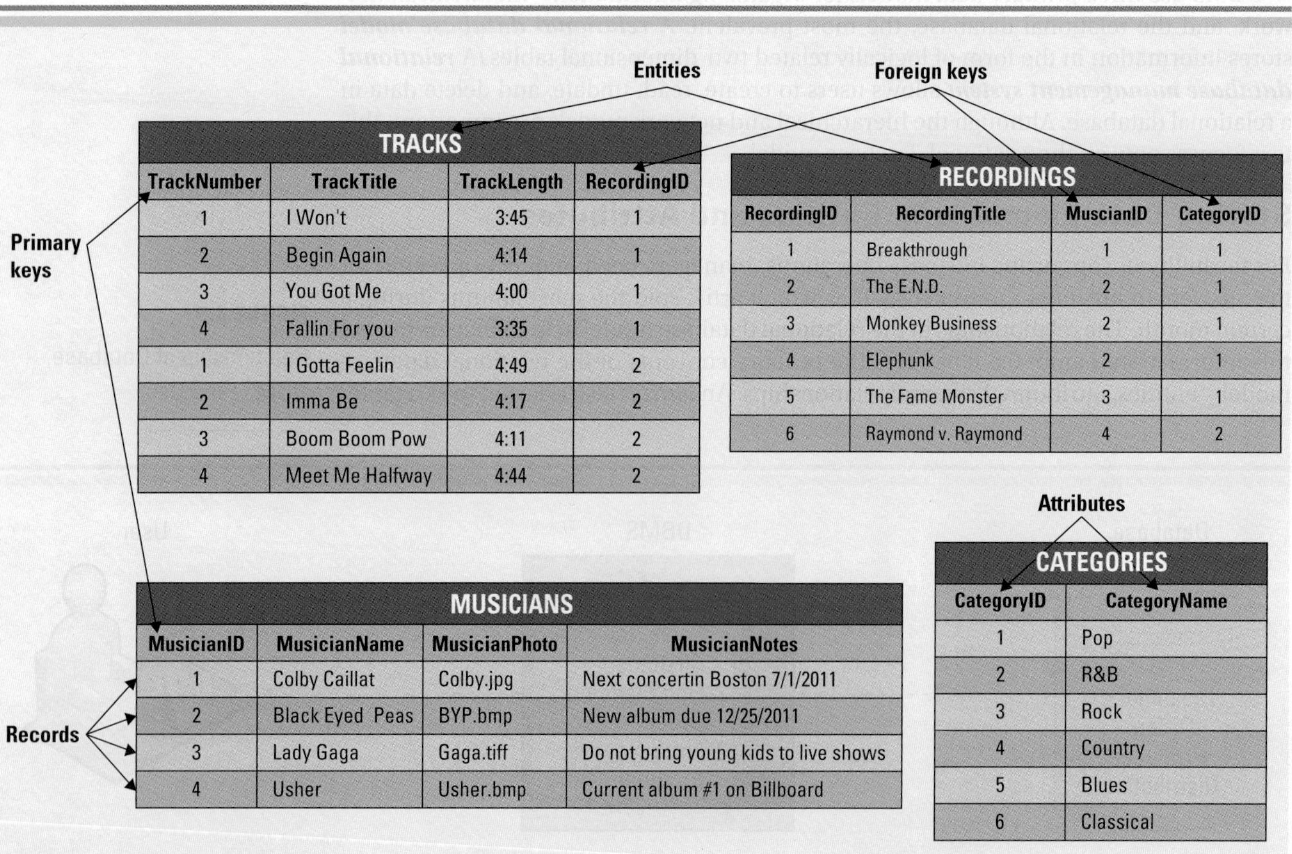

TRACKS

TrackNumber	TrackTitle	TrackLength	RecordingID
1	I Won't	3:45	1
2	Begin Again	4:14	1
3	You Got Me	4:00	1
4	Fallin For you	3:35	1
1	I Gotta Feelin	4:49	2
2	Imma Be	4:17	2
3	Boom Boom Pow	4:11	2
4	Meet Me Halfway	4:44	2

RECORDINGS

RecordingID	RecordingTitle	MusicianID	CategoryID
1	Breakthrough	1	1
2	The E.N.D.	2	1
3	Monkey Business	2	1
4	Elephunk	2	1
5	The Fame Monster	3	1
6	Raymond v. Raymond	4	2

MUSICIANS

MusicianID	MusicianName	MusicianPhoto	MusicianNotes
1	Colby Caillat	Colby.jpg	Next concertin Boston 7/1/2011
2	Black Eyed Peas	BYP.bmp	New album due 12/25/2011
3	Lady Gaga	Gaga.tiff	Do not bring young kids to live shows
4	Usher	Usher.bmp	Current album #1 on Billboard

CATEGORIES

CategoryID	CategoryName
1	Pop
2	R&B
3	Rock
4	Country
5	Blues
6	Classical

FIGURE 6.6

Primary Concepts of the Relational Database Model

APPLY YOUR KNOWLEDGE

BUSINESS DRIVEN START-UP

The Rylaxer

Living in a cramped dorm room is a common college occurrence. This was the experience of Ryan Dickerson, a Syracuse University student, who found himself wedged into a tiny dorm room with only enough room to fit a bed, desk, and chair. Spotting an entrepreneurial opportunity, Dickerson innovatively created a hybrid bed and couch, calling his new product the Rylaxer. During the day the Rylaxer functioned as a couch and during the night it transformed into a bed, solving his limited space issue. The Rylaxer is made of environmentally friendly foam and is available in two sizes and a variety of colors. Of course, you can pay extra for a custom cover with your school's name, Greek letters, or favorite sports team's logo.[4]

Why would a spreadsheet be ineffective for running Dickerson's business? Why would he want to create a database to support his business needs? If you were building the Rylaxer database, what are a few of the entities and associated attributes you might create? Why would you want to create primary and foreign keys? How will you use these keys to turn data into information?

between the *MUSICIANS* and *RECORDINGS* tables that states the Black Eyed Peas *(MusicianID 2)* have several recordings including The E.N.D., Monkey Business, and Elepunk. In essence, *MusicianID* in the *RECORDINGS* table creates a logical relationship (who was the musician that made the recording) to the *MUSICIANS* table. Creating the logical relationship between the tables allows managers to search the data and turn it into useful information.

USING A RELATIONAL DATABASE FOR BUSINESS ADVANTAGES

LO 6.3: Identify the business advantages of a relational database.

Many business managers are familiar with Excel and other spreadsheet programs they can use to store business data. Although spreadsheets are excellent for supporting some data analysis, they offer limited functionality in terms of security, accessibility, and flexibility and can rarely scale to support business growth. From a business perspective, relational databases offer many advantages over using a text document or a spreadsheet, including:

- Increased flexibility.
- Increased scalability and performance.
- Reduced information redundancy.
- Increased information integrity (quality).
- Increased information security.

Increased Flexibility

Databases tend to mirror business structures, and a database needs to handle changes quickly and easily, just as any business needs to be able to do. Equally important, databases need to provide flexibility in allowing each user to access the information in whatever way best suits his or her needs. The distinction between logical and physical views is important in understanding flexible database user views. The ***physical view*** of information deals with the physical storage of information on a storage device. The ***logical view*** of information focuses on how individual users logically access information to meet their own particular business needs.

In the database illustration from Figure 6.6, for example, one user could perform a query to determine which recordings had a track length of four minutes or more. At the same time, another user could perform an analysis to determine the distribution of recordings as they relate to the different categories. For example, are there more R&B recordings than rock, or are they evenly distributed? This example demonstrates that while a database has only one physical view, it can easily support multiple logical views that provides for flexibility.

Consider another example—a mail-order business. One user might want a report presented in alphabetical format, in which case last name should appear before first name. Another user, working with a catalog mailing system, would want customer names appearing as first name and then last name. Both are easily achievable, but different logical views of the same physical information.

Increased Scalability and Performance

In its first year of operation, the official website of the American Family Immigration History Center, www.ellisisland.org, generated more than 2.5 billion hits. The site offers immigration information about people who entered America through the Port of New York and Ellis Island between 1892 and 1924. The database contains more than 25 million passenger names that are correlated to 3.5 million images of ships' manifests.[5]

The database had to be scalable to handle the massive volumes of information and the large numbers of users expected for the launch of the website. In addition, the database needed to perform quickly under heavy use. Some organizations must be able to support hundreds or thousands of users including employees, partners, customers, and suppliers, who all want to access and share the same information. Databases today scale to exceptional levels, allowing all types of users and programs to perform information-processing and information-searching tasks.

Reduced Data Redundancy

Data redundancy is the duplication of data, or the storage of the same data in multiple places. Redundant data can cause storage issues along with data integrity issues, making it difficult to determine which values are the most current or most accurate. Employees become confused and frustrated when faced with incorrect information causing disruptions to business processes and procedures. One primary goal of a database is to eliminate information redundancy by recording each piece of information in only one place in the database. This saves disk space, makes performing information updates easier, and improves information quality.

Increased Information Integrity (Quality)

Information integrity is a measure of the quality of information. ***Integrity constraints*** are rules that help ensure the quality of information. The database design needs to consider integrity constraints. The database and the DBMS ensures that users can never violate these constraints. There are two types of integrity constraints: (1) relational and (2) business critical.

Relational integrity constraints are rules that enforce basic and fundamental information-based constraints. For example, a relational integrity constraint would not allow someone to create an order for a nonexistent customer, provide a markup percentage that was negative, or order zero pounds of raw materials from a supplier. ***Business-critical integrity constraints*** enforce business rules vital to an organization's success and often require more insight and knowledge than relational integrity constraints. Consider a supplier of fresh produce to large grocery chains such as Kroger. The supplier might implement a business-critical integrity constraint stating that no product returns are accepted after 15 days past delivery. That would make sense because of the chance of spoilage of the produce. Business-critical integrity constraints tend to mirror the very rules by which an organization achieves success.

The specification and enforcement of integrity constraints produce higher-quality information that will provide better support for business decisions. Organizations that establish specific procedures for developing integrity constraints typically see an increase in accuracy that then increases the use of organizational information by business professionals.

Increased Information Security

Managers must protect information, like any asset, from unauthorized users or misuse. As systems become increasingly complex and highly available over the Internet on many different devices, security becomes an even bigger issue. Databases offer many security features including passwords to provide authentication, access levels to determine who can access the data, and access controls to determine what type of access they have to the information.

For example, customer service representatives might need read-only access to customer order information so they can answer customer order inquiries; they might not have or need the authority to change or delete order information. Managers might require access to employee files, but they should have access only to their own employees' files, not the employee files for the entire company. Various security features of databases can ensure that individuals have only certain types of access to certain types of information.

Security risks are increasing as more and more databases and DBMS systems are moving to data centers run in the cloud. The biggest risks when using cloud computing are ensuring the security and privacy of the information in the database. Implementing data governance policies and procedures that outline the data management requirements can ensure safe and secure cloud computing.

DRIVING WEBSITES WITH DATA

LO 6.4: Explain the business benefits of a data-driven website.

Websites change for site visitors depending on the type of information they request. Consider, for example, an automobile dealer. The dealer would create a database containing data elements for each car it has available for sale including make, model, color, year, miles per gallon, a photograph, and so on. Website visitors might click on Porsche and then enter their specific requests such as price range or year made. Once the user hits "go" the website automatically provides a custom view of the requested information. The dealer must create, update, and delete automobile information as the inventory changes.

A ***data-driven website*** is an interactive website kept constantly updated and relevant to the needs of its customers using a database. Data-driven capabilities are especially useful when a firm needs to offer large amounts of information, products, or services. Visitors can become quickly annoyed if they find themselves buried under an avalanche of information when searching a website. A data-driven website can help limit the amount of information displayed to customers based on unique search requirements. Companies even use data-driven websites to make information in their internal databases available to customers and business partners.

There are a number of advantages to using the Web to access company databases. First, Web browsers are much easier to use than directly accessing the database using a custom-query tool. Second, the Web interface requires few or no changes to the database model. Finally, it costs less to add a Web interface in front of a DBMS than to redesign and rebuild the system to support changes. Additional data-driven website advantages include:

- **Easy to manage content:** Website owners can make changes without relying on MIS professionals; users can update data-driven website with little or no training.
- **Easy to store large amounts of data:** Data-driven websites can keep large volumes of information organized. Website owners can use templates to implement changes for layouts, navigation, or website structure. This improves website reliability, scalability, and performance.
- **Easy to eliminate human errors:** Data-driven websites trap data-entry errors, eliminating inconsistencies while ensuring all information is entered correctly.

APPLY YOUR KNOWLEDGE

BUSINESS DRIVEN ETHICS AND SECURITY

Facebook Fiasco

Peter Warden is not your typical Facebook user. He is a young entrepreneur from Boulder, Colorado, who used the online social networking site's data to illustrate people's interests and common names across the United States. Warden collected data from more than 200 million Facebook profiles, and then he created a visualization map showing connections between locations that share friends.

Warden gathered the data from public profiles using "crawling" software similar to what search engines use to find content. Analyzing these data could provide useful information, such as displaying links between people with similar income, employment, and social connections. When Facebook learned what Warden was doing, the company threatened to sue him unless he deleted the data immediately. Warden did not have the funds required to fight the lawsuit and was forced to comply with Facebook's request and deleted the data.[6]

Do you agree or disagree that Warden's use of the information was unethical? Do you agree with Facebook's decision to have Warden delete all the data he collected? What other social networking sites could Warden use to collect public information? How much of your personal information do you think is available to the public for data collection efforts such as Warden's?

Zappos credits its success as an online shoe retailer to its vast inventory of nearly 3 million products available through its dynamic data-driven website. The company built its data-driven website catering to a specific niche market: consumers who were tired of finding that their most-desired items were always out of stock at traditional retailers. Zappos' highly flexible, scalable, and secure database helped it rank as the most-available Internet retailer. Figure 6.7 displays Zappos data-driven website illustrating a user querying the database and receiving information that satisfies the user's request.[7]

FIGURE 6.7

Zappos.com—A Data-Driven Website

Source: © 2011 Zappos.com, Inc. and its affiliates. Reprinted with permission.

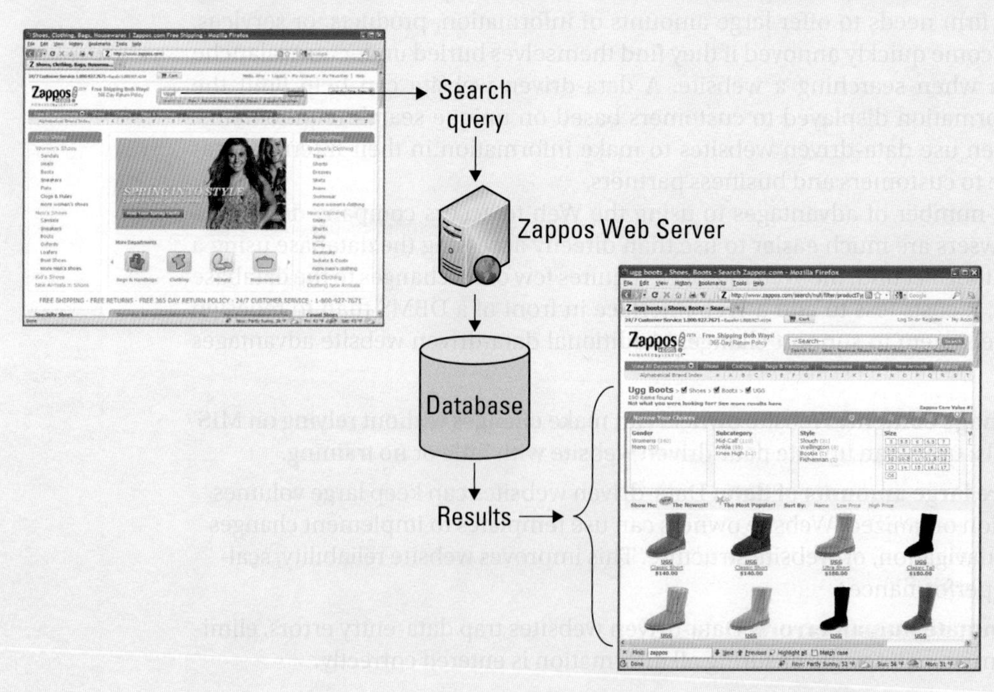

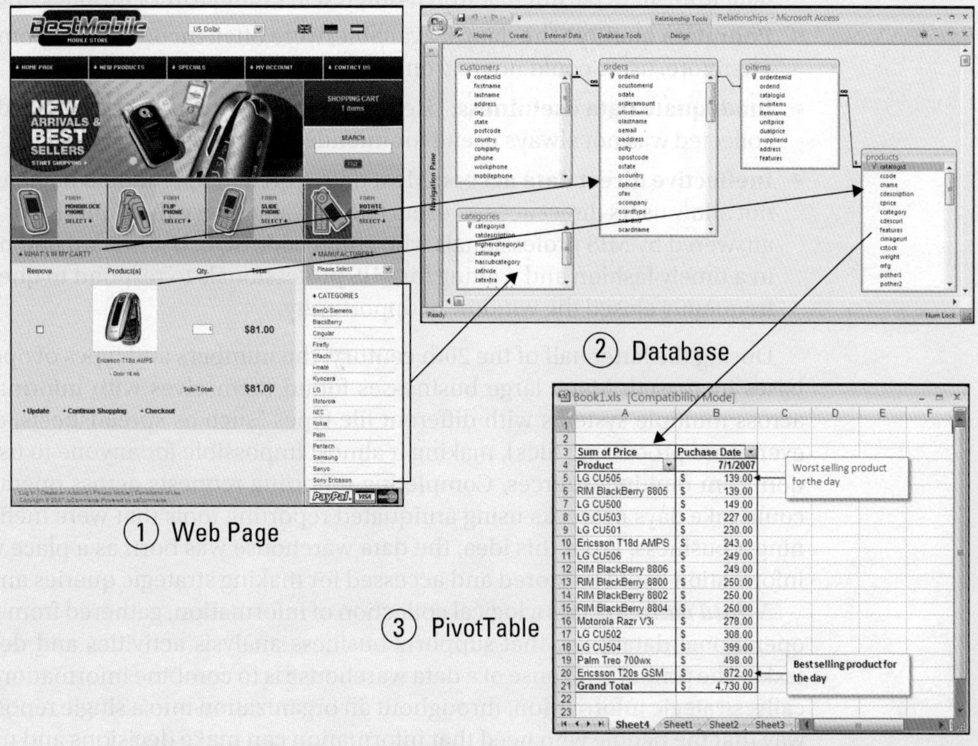

FIGURE 6.8
BI in a Data-Driven Website

Companies can gain valuable business knowledge by viewing the data accessed and analyzed from their website. Figure 6.8 displays how running queries or using analytical tools, such as a PivotTable, on the database that is attached to the website can offer insight into the business, such as items browsed, frequent requests, items bought together, and so on.

section 6.2 BUSINESS INTELLIGENCE

LEARNING OUTCOMES

6.5 Define a data warehouse, and provide a few reasons it can make a manager more effective.

6.6 Explain ETL and the role of a data mart in business.

6.7 Define data mining, and explain the three common forms for mining structured and unstructured data.

6.8 Identify the advantages of using business intelligence to support managerial decision making.

THE BUSINESS BENEFITS OF DATA WAREHOUSING

LO 6.5: Define a data warehouse, and provide a few reasons why it can make a manager more effective.

In the 1990s as organizations began to need more timely information about their business, they found that traditional management information systems were too cumbersome to provide relevant information efficiently and efficiently. Most of the systems were in the form of operational databases that were designed for specific business functions, such as accounting, order entry, customer service, and sales, and were not appropriate for business analysis for the following reasons:

- **Inconsistent data definitions:** Every department had its own method for recording data so when trying to share information, data did not match and users did not get the data they really needed.

- **Lack of data standards:** Managers need to perform cross-functional analysis using data from all departments, which differed in granularities, formats, and levels.
- **Poor data quality:** The data, if available, were often incorrect or incomplete. Therefore, users could not rely on the data to make decisions.
- **Inadequate data usefulness:** Users could not get the data they needed; what was collected was not always useful for intended purposes.
- **Ineffective direct data access:** Most data stored in operational databases did not allow users direct access; users had to wait to have their queries or questions answered by MIS professionals who could code SQL. Users want and need answers in a timely fashion and waiting for MIS professionals to respond to queries frequently closed the window of opportunity.

During the latter half of the 20th century, the numbers and types of operational databases increased. Many large businesses found themselves with information scattered across multiple systems with different file types (such as spreadsheets, databases, and even word processing files), making it almost impossible for anyone to use the information from multiple sources. Completing reporting requests across operational systems could take days or weeks using antiquated reporting tools that were ineffective for running a business. From this idea, the data warehouse was born as a place where relevant information could be stored and accessed for making strategic queries and reports.

A ***data warehouse*** is a logical collection of information, gathered from many different operational databases, that supports business analysis activities and decision-making tasks. The primary purpose of a data warehouse is to combine information, more specifically, strategic information, throughout an organization into a single repository in such a way that the people who need that information can make decisions and undertake business analysis. A key idea within data warehousing is to collect information from multiple systems in a common location that uses a universal querying tool. This allows operational databases to run where they are most efficient for the business, while providing a common location using a familiar format for the strategic or enterprisewide reporting information.

Data warehouses go even a step further by standardizing information. Gender, for instance can be referred to in many ways (Male, Female, M/F, 1/0), but it should be standardized on a data warehouse with one common way of referring to each data element that stores gender (M/F). Standardizing of data elements allows for greater accuracy, completeness, and consistency as well as increases the quality of the information in making strategic business decisions. The data warehouse then is simply a tool that enables business users, typically managers, to be more effective in many ways, including:

- Developing customer profiles.
- Identifying new-product opportunities.
- Improving business operations.
- Identifying financial issues.
- Analyzing trends.
- Understanding competitors.
- Understanding product performance.

LO 6.6: Explain ETL and the role of a data mart in business.

PERFORMING BUSINESS ANALYSIS WITH DATA MARTS

Businesses collect a tremendous amount of transactional information as part of their routine operations. Marketing, sales, and other departments would like to analyze these data to understand their operations better. While databases store the details of all transactions (for instance, the sale of a product) and events (hiring a new employee), data warehouses store that same information but in an aggregated form more suited to supporting decision-making tasks. Aggregation, in this instance, can include totals, counts, averages, and the like.

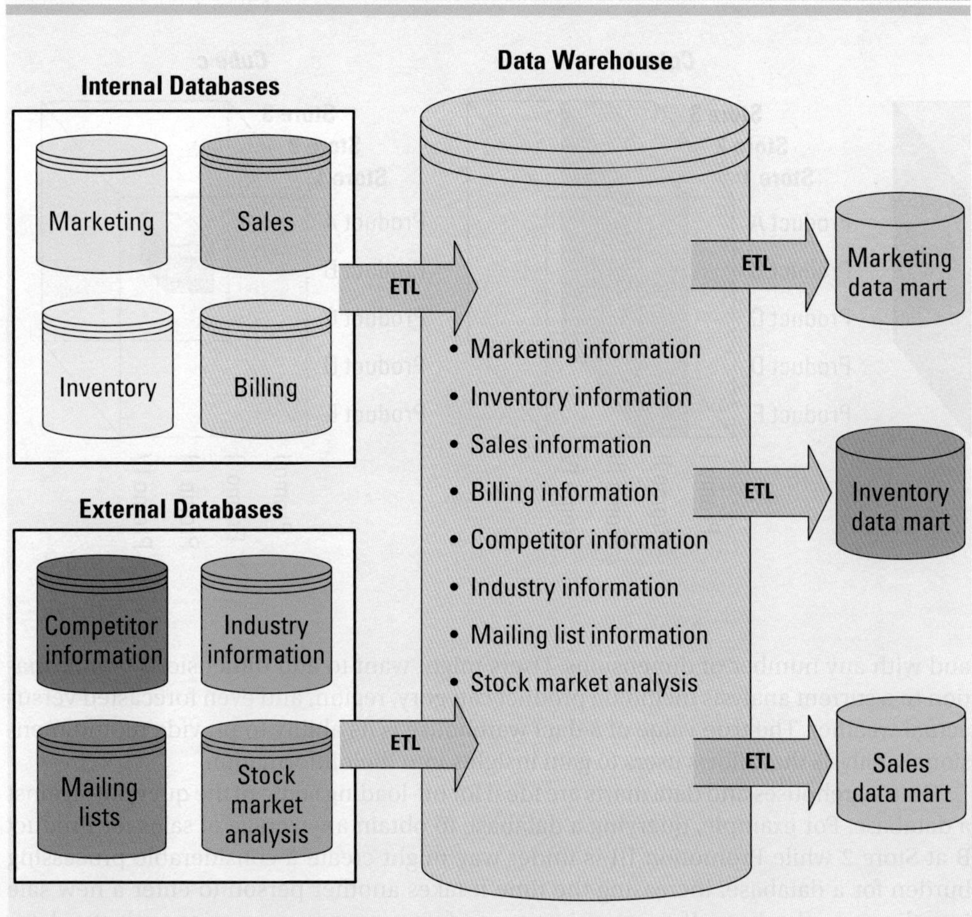

FIGURE 6.9

Data Warehouse Model

The data warehouse modeled in Figure 6.9 compiles information from internal databases (or transactional and operational databases) and external databases through extraction, transformation, and loading. ***Extraction, transformation, and loading (ETL)*** is a process that extracts information from internal and external databases, transforms it using a common set of enterprise definitions, and loads it into a data warehouse. The data warehouse then sends portions (or subsets) of the information to data marts. A ***data mart*** contains a subset of data warehouse information. To distinguish between data warehouses and data marts, think of data warehouses as having a more organizational focus and data marts as having a functional focus. Figure 6.9 provides an illustration of a data warehouse and its relationship to internal and external databases, ETL, and data marts.

Multidimensional Analysis

A relational database contains information in a series of two-dimensional tables. In a data warehouse and data mart, information contains layers of columns and rows. For this reason, most data warehouses and data marts are multidimensional databases. A dimension is a particular attribute of information. Each layer in a data warehouse or data mart represents information according to an additional dimension. A ***cube*** is the common term for the representation of multidimensional information. Figure 6.10 displays a cube (cube a) that represents store information (the layers), product information (the rows), and promotion information (the columns).

After creating a cube of information, users can begin to slice-and-dice the cube to drill down into the information. The second cube (cube b) in Figure 6.10 displays a slice representing promotion II information for all products at all stores. The third cube (cube c) in Figure 6.10 displays only information for promotion III, product B, at store 2. By using multidimensional analysis, users can analyze information in a number of ways

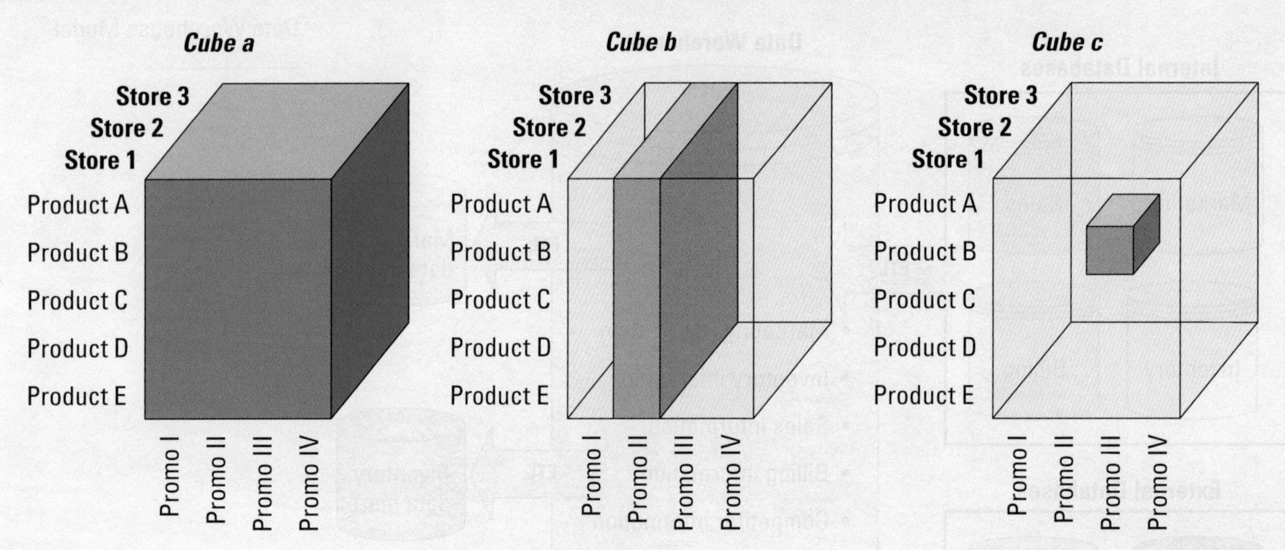

FIGURE 6.10

A Cube of Information for Performing a Multidimensional Analysis on Three Stores for Five Products and Four Promotions

and with any number of dimensions. Users might want to add dimensions of information to a current analysis including product category, region, and even forecasted versus actual weather. The true value of a data warehouse is its ability to provide multidimensional analysis that allows users to gain insights into their information.

Data warehouses and data marts are ideal for off-loading some of the querying against a database. For example, querying a database to obtain an average of sales for Product B at Store 2 while Promotion III is under way might create a considerable processing burden for a database, increasing the time it takes another person to enter a new sale into the same database. If an organization performs numerous queries against a database (or multiple databases), aggregating that information into a data warehouse will be beneficial.

Information Cleansing or Scrubbing

Maintaining quality information in a data warehouse or data mart is extremely important. To increase the quality of organizational information and thus the effectiveness of decision making, businesses must formulate a strategy to keep information clean. ***Information cleansing*** or ***scrubbing*** is a process that weeds out and fixes or discards inconsistent, incorrect, or incomplete information.

Specialized software tools exist that use sophisticated procedures to analyze, standardize, correct, match, and consolidate data warehouse information. This step is vitally important because data warehouses often contain information from several different databases, some of which can be external to the organization. In a data warehouse, information cleansing occurs first during the ETL process and again once the information is in the data warehouse. Companies can choose information cleansing software from several different vendors including Oracle, SAS, Ascential Software, and Group 1 Software. Ideally, scrubbed information is accurate and consistent.

Looking at customer information highlights why information cleansing is necessary. Customer information exists in several operational systems. In each system, all the details could change—from the customer ID to contact information—depending on the business process the user is performing (see Figure 6.11).

Figure 6.12 displays a customer name entered differently in multiple operational systems. Information cleansing allows an organization to fix these types of inconsistencies in the data warehouse. Figure 6.13 displays the typical events that occur during information cleansing.

Achieving perfect information is almost impossible. The more complete and accurate a company wants its information to be, the more it costs (see Figure 6.14). Companies may also trade accuracy for completeness. Accurate information is correct, while

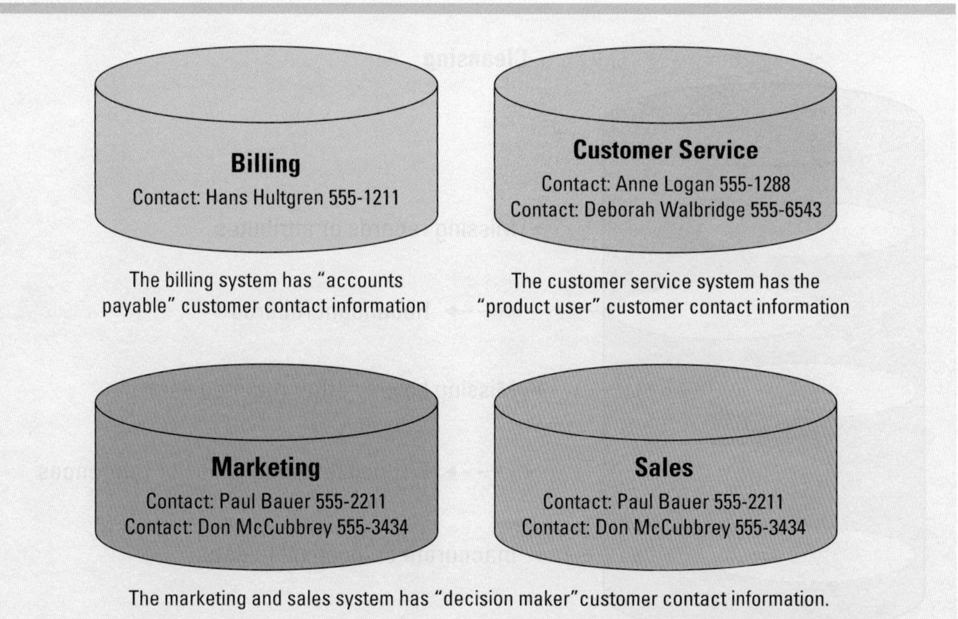

FIGURE 6.11

Contact Information in Operational Systems

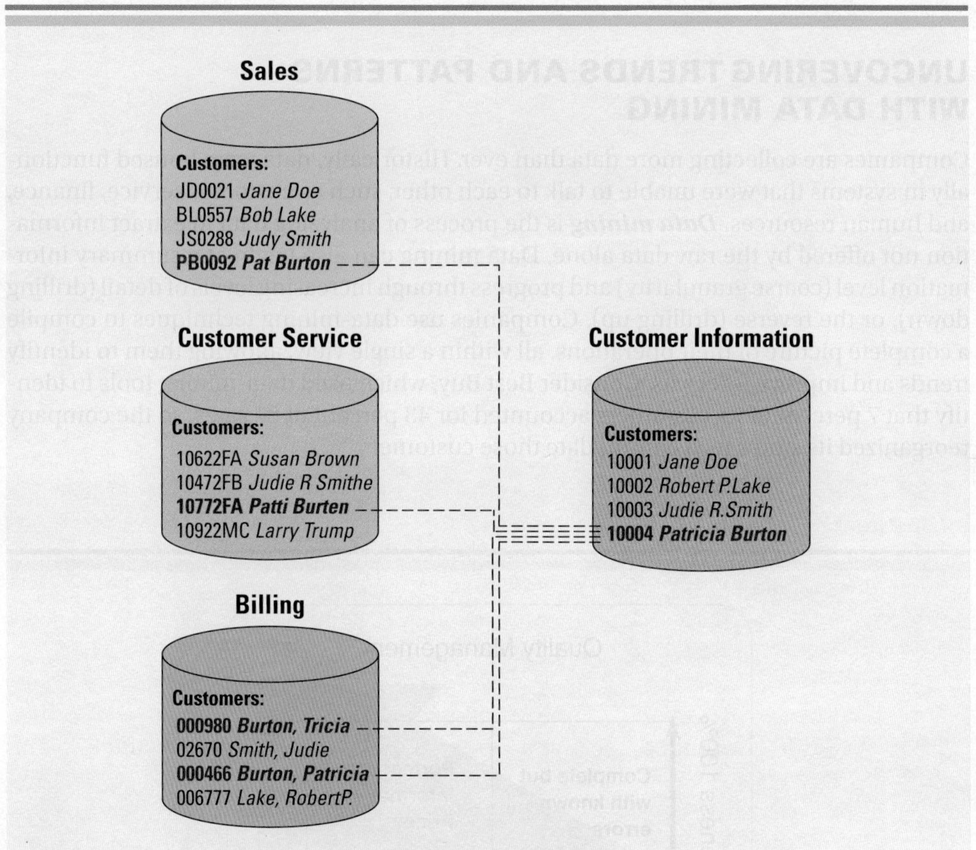

FIGURE 6.12

Standardizing a Customer Name in Operational Systems

complete information has no blanks. A birth date of 2/31/10 is an example of complete but inaccurate information (February 31 does not exist). An address containing Denver, Colorado, without a zip code is an example of accurate information that is incomplete. Many firms complete ***data quality audits*** to determine the accuracy and completeness of its data. Most organizations determine a percentage of accuracy and completeness high enough to make good decisions at a reasonable cost, such as 85 percent accurate and 65 percent complete.

FIGURE 6.13

Information Cleansing Activities

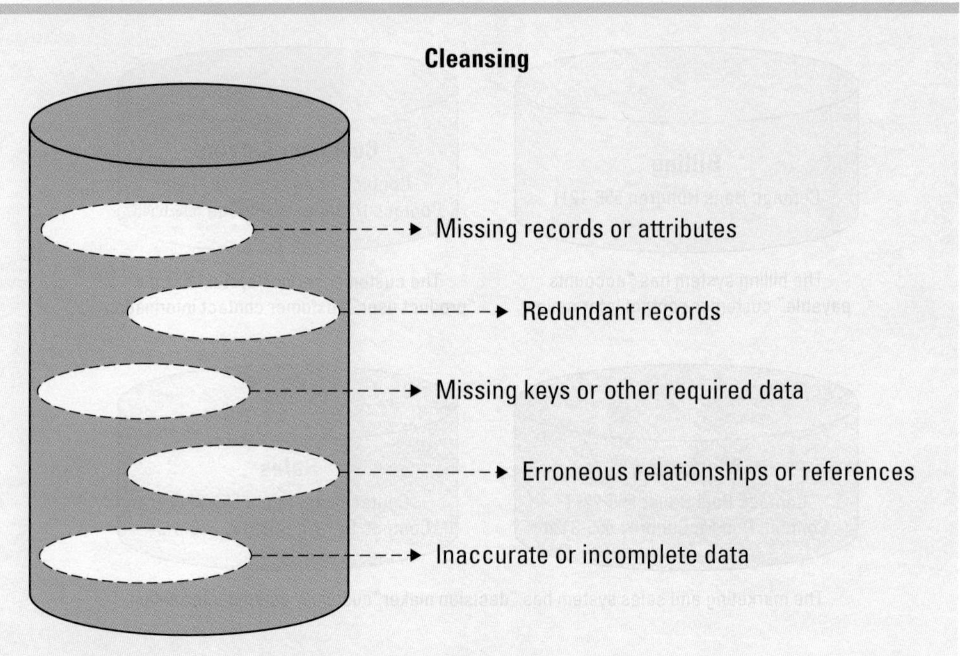

LO 6.7: Define data mining, and explain the three common forms for mining structured and unstructured data.

UNCOVERING TRENDS AND PATTERNS WITH DATA MINING

Companies are collecting more data than ever. Historically, data were housed functionally in systems that were unable to talk to each other, such as customer service, finance, and human resources. ***Data mining*** is the process of analyzing data to extract information not offered by the raw data alone. Data mining can also begin at a summary information level (coarse granularity) and progress through increasing levels of detail (drilling down), or the reverse (drilling up). Companies use data-mining techniques to compile a complete picture of their operations, all within a single view, allowing them to identify trends and improve forecasts. Consider Best Buy, which used data-mining tools to identify that 7 percent of its customers accounted for 43 percent of its sales, so the company reorganized its stores to accommodate those customers.[8]

FIGURE 6.14

The Cost of Accurate and Complete Information

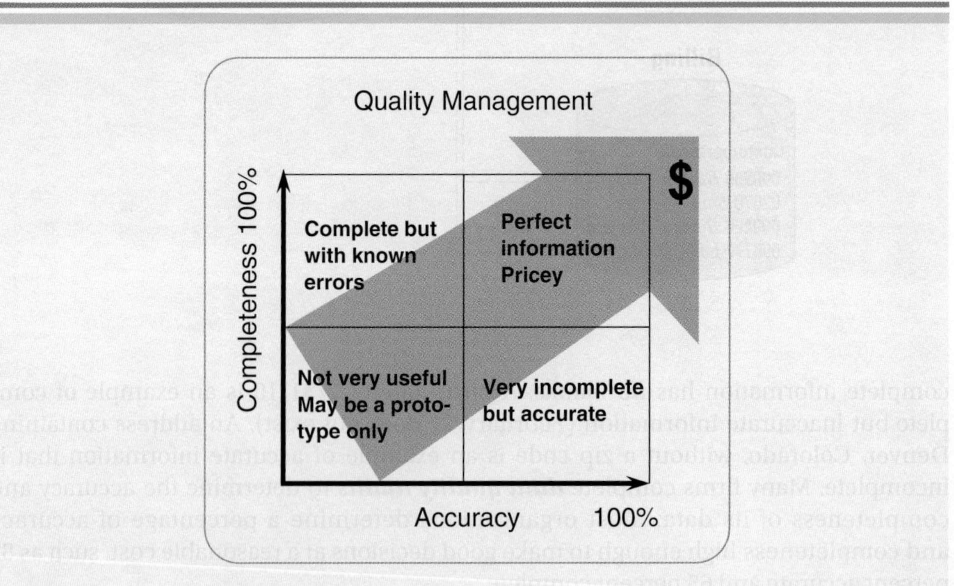

BUSINESS DRIVEN GLOBALIZATION

Integrity Information Inc.

Congratulations! You have just been hired as a consultant for Integrity Information Inc., a start-up business intelligence consulting company. Your first job is to help work with the sales department in securing a new client, The Warehouse. The Warehouse has been operating in the United States for more than a decade, and its primary business is to sell wholesale low-cost products. The Warehouse is interested in hiring Integrity Information Inc. to clean up the data that are stored in its U.S. database. To determine how good your work is, the client would like your analysis of the following spreadsheet. The Warehouse is also interested in expanding globally and wants to purchase several independent wholesale stores located in Australia, Thailand, China, Japan, and the United Kingdom. Before the company moves forward with the venture, it wants to understand what types of data issues it might encounter as it begins to transfer data from each global entity to the data warehouse. Please create a list detailing the potential issues The Warehouse can anticipate encountering as it consolidates the global databases into a single data warehouse.[9]

CUST ID	First Name	Last Name	Address	City	State	Zip	Phone	Last Order Date
233620	Christopher	Lee	12421 W Olympic Blvd	Los Angeles	CA	75080-1100	(972)680-7848	4/18/2010
233621	Bruce	Brandwen	268 W 44th St	New York	PA	10036-3906	(212)471-6077	5/3/2010
233622	Glr	Johnson	4100 E Dry Creek Rd	Littleton	CO	80122-3729	(303)712-5461	5/6/2010
233623	Dave	Owens	466 Commerce Rd	Staunton	VA	24401-4432	(540)851-0362	3/19/2010
233624	John	Coulbourn	124 Action St	Maynard	MA	1754	(978)987-0100	4/24/2010
233629	Dan	Gagliardo	2875 Union Rd	Cheektowaga	NY	14227-1461	(716)558-8191	5/4/2010
23362	Damanceee	Allen	1633 Broadway	New York	NY	10019-6708	(212)708-1576	
233630	Michael	Peretz	235 E 45th St	New York	NY	10017-3305	(212)210-1340	4/30/2010
233631	Jody	Veeder	440 Science Dr	Madison	WI	53711-1064	(608)238-9690 X227	3/27/2010
233632	Michael	Kehrer	3015 SSE Loop 323	Tyler	TX	75701	(903)579-3229	4/28/2010
233633	Erin	Yoon	3500 Carillon Pt	Kirkland	WA	98033-7354	(425)897-7221	3/25/2010
233634	Madeline	Shefferly	4100 E Dry Creek Rd	Littleton	CO	80122-3729	(303)486-3949	3/33/2010
233635	Steven	Conduit	1332 Enterprise Dr	West Chester	PA	19380-5970	(610)692-5900	4/27/2010
233636	Joseph	Kovach	1332 Enterprise Dr	West Chester	PA	19380-5970	(610)692-5900	4/28/2010
233637	Richard	Jordan	1700 N	Philadelphia	PA	19131-4728	(215)581-6770	3/19/2010
233638	Scott	Mikolajczyk	1655 Crofton Blvd	Crofton	MD	21114-1387	(410)729-8155	4/28/2010
233639	Susan	Shragg	1875 Century Park E	Los Angeles	CA	90067-2501	(310)785-0511	4/29/2010
233640	Rob	Ponto	29777 Telegraph Rd	Southfield	MI	48034-1303	(810)204-4724	5/5/2010
233642	Lauren	Butler	1211 Avenue Of The Americas	New York	NY	10036-8701	(212)852-7494	4/22/2010
233643	Christopher	Lee	12421 W Olympic Blvd	Los Angeles	CA	90064-1022	(310)689-2577	3/25/2010
233644	Michelle	Decker	6922 Hollywood Blvd	Hollywood	CA	90028-6117	(323)817-4655	5/8/2010
233647	Natalia	Galeano	1211 Avenue Of The Americas	New York	NY	10036-8701	(646)728-6911	4/23/2010
233648	Bobbie	Orchard	4201 Congress St	Charlotte	NC	28209-4617	(704)557-2444	5/11/2010
233650	Ben	Konfino	1111 Stewart Ave	Bethpage	NY	11714-3533	(516)803-1406	3/19/2010
233651	Lenee	Santana	1050 Techwood Dr NW	Atlanta	GA	30318-KKRR	(404)885-2000	3/22/2010
233652	Lauren	Monks	7700 Wisconsin Ave	Bethesda	MD	20814-3578	(301)771-4772	3/19/2005
233653	Mark	Woolley	10950 Washington Blvd	Culver City	CA	90232-4026	(310)202-2900	4/20/2010

To perform data mining, users need data-mining tools. ***Data-mining tools*** use a variety of techniques to find patterns and relationships in large volumes of information that predict future behavior and guide decision making. Data mining uncovers trends and patterns, which analysts use to build models that, when exposed to new information sets, perform a variety of information analysis functions. Data-mining tools for data warehouses help users uncover business intelligence in their data. Some of the key areas where businesses are using data mining include:

- Analyzing customer buying patterns to predict future marketing and promotion campaigns.
- Building budgets and other financial information.
- Detecting fraud by identifying deceptive spending patterns.
- Finding the best customers who spend the most money.
- Keeping customers from leaving or migrating to competitors.
- Promoting and hiring employees to ensure success for both the company and the individual.

Data mining enables these companies to determine relationships among such internal factors as price, product positioning, or staff skills, and external factors such as economic indicators, competition, and customer demographics. In addition, it enables companies to determine the impact on sales, customer satisfaction, and corporate profits and to drill down into summary information to view detail transactional data. With data mining, a retailer could use point-of-sale records of customer purchases to send targeted promotions based on an individual's purchase history. By mining demographic data from comment or warranty cards, the retailer could develop products and promotions to appeal to specific customer segments.

Netflix uses data mining to analyze each customer's film-viewing habits to provide recommendations for other customers with Cinematch, its movie recommendation system. Using Cinematch, Netflix can present customers with a number of additional movies they might want to watch based on the customer's current preferences. Netflix's innovative use of data mining provides its competitive advantage in the movie rental industry.[10]

Data mining uses specialized technologies and functionalities such as query tools, reporting tools, multidimensional analysis tools, statistical tools, and intelligent agents. Data mining approaches decision making with a few different activities in mind including:

- Classification—assigns records to one of a predefined set of classes.
- Estimation—determines values for an unknown continuous variable behavior or estimated future value.
- Affinity grouping—determines which things go together.
- Clustering—segments a heterogeneous population of records into a number of more homogeneous subgroups.

Data mining occurs on ***structured data*** that are already in a database or a spreadsheet. ***Unstructured data*** do not exist in a fixed location and can include text documents, PDFs, voice messages, emails, and so on. ***Text mining*** analyzes unstructured data to find trends and patterns in words and sentences. Text mining a firm's customer support email might identify which customer service representative is best able to handle the question, allowing the system to forward it to the right person. ***Web mining*** analyzes unstructured data associated with websites to identify consumer behavior and website navigation. Three common forms for mining structured and unstructured data are:

- Cluster analysis
- Association detection
- Statistical analysis.

APPLY YOUR KNOWLEDGE

BUSINESS DRIVEN DISCUSSION

Google Dashboard

Often criticized for accruing large amounts of data about people, Google is now giving users an easy way to find out what information it stores about them. The company provides a service called Google Dashboard that summarizes the data that it collects in users' accounts on their products such as Gmail, Picasa Reader, and YouTube. Using the Dashboard, users can then adjust their privacy settings for the various Google applications, even allowing users to review and delete recent Google searches.[11]

Google Dashboard is giving users what they want—control over their own data. How is Google using data mining to collect information on users? What privacy issues does Google create by the massive amounts of personal data it stores? Will the Dashboard prevent Google from tracking users across the Web if it wants to?

Cluster Analysis

Cluster analysis is a technique used to divide information sets into mutually exclusive groups such that the members of each group are as close together as possible to one another and the different groups are as far apart as possible. Cluster analysis segments customer information to help organizations identify customers with similar behavioral traits, such as clusters of best customers or onetime customers. Cluster analysis also has the ability to uncover naturally occurring patterns in information (see Figure 6.15).

A great example of using cluster analysis in business is to create target-marketing strategies based on zip codes. Evaluating customer segments by zip code allows a business to assign a level of importance to each segment. Zip codes offer valuable insight

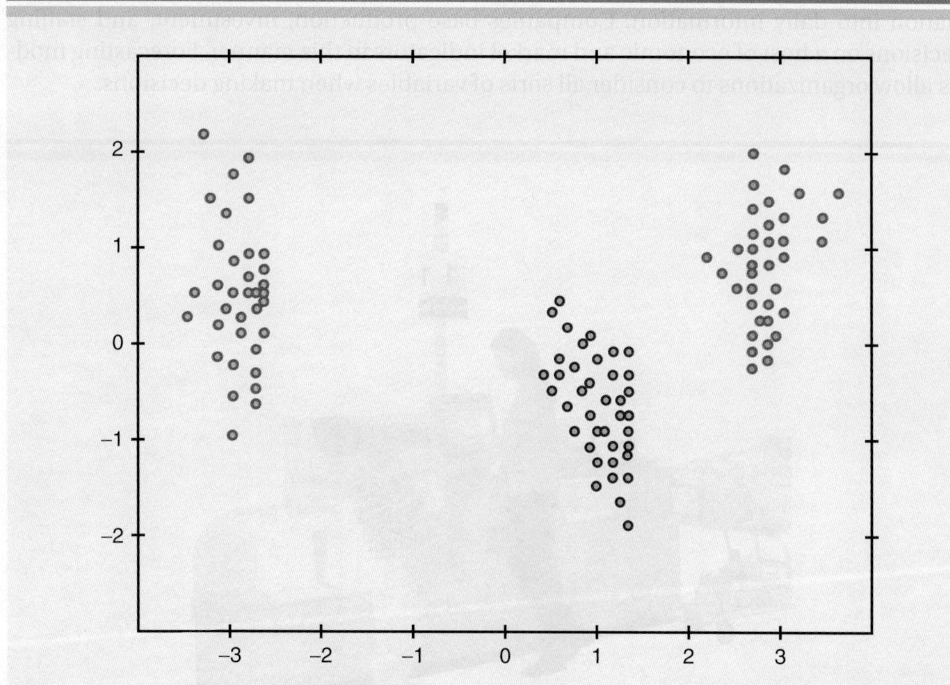

FIGURE 6.15
Example of Cluster Analysis

into such things as income levels, demographics, lifestyles, and spending habits. With target marketing, a business can decrease its costs while increasing the success rate of the marketing campaign.

Association Detection

Association detection reveals the relationship between variables along with the nature and frequency of the relationships. Many people refer to association detection algorithms as association rule generators because they create rules to determine the likelihood of events occurring together at a particular time or following each other in a logical progression. Percentages usually reflect the patterns of these events; for example, "55 percent of the time, events A and B occurred together," or "80 percent of the time that items A and B occurred together, they were followed by item C within three days."

One of the most common forms of association detection analysis is market basket analysis. ***Market basket analysis*** analyzes such items as websites and checkout scanner information to detect customers' buying behavior and predict future behavior by identifying affinities among customers' choices of products and services (see Figure 6.16). Market basket analysis is frequently used to develop marketing campaigns for cross-selling products and services (especially in banking, insurance, and finance) and for inventory control, shelf-product placement, and other retail and marketing applications.

Statistical Analysis

Statistical analysis performs such functions as information correlations, distributions, calculations, and variance analysis. Data-mining tools offer knowledge workers a wide range of powerful statistical capabilities so they can quickly build a variety of statistical models, examine the models' assumptions and validity, and compare and contrast the various models to determine the best one for a particular business issue.

Forecasting is a common form of statistical analysis. ***Time-series information*** is time-stamped information collected at a particular frequency. Formally defined, ***forecasts*** are predictions based on time-series information. Examples of time-series information include Web visits per hour, sales per month, and calls per day. Forecasting data-mining tools allow users to manipulate the time series for forecasting activities.

When discovering trends and seasonal variations in transactional information, use a time-series forecast to change the transactional information by units of time, such as transforming weekly information into monthly or seasonal information or hourly information into daily information. Companies base production, investment, and staffing decisions on a host of economic and market indicators in this manner. Forecasting models allow organizations to consider all sorts of variables when making decisions.

FIGURE 6.16
Market Basket Analysis

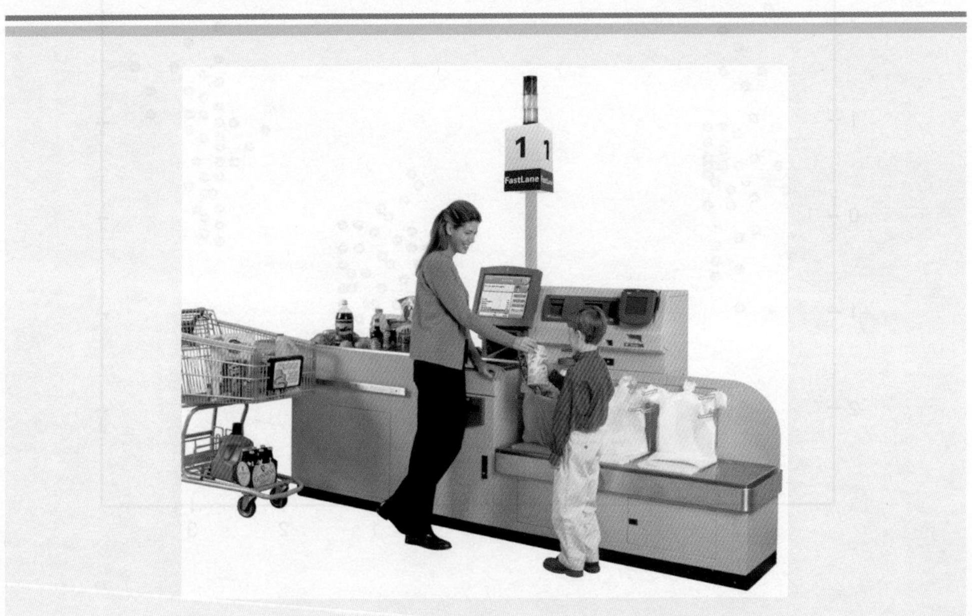

SUPPORTING DECISIONS WITH BUSINESS INTELLIGENCE

LO 6.8: Identify the advantages of using business intelligence to support managerial decision making.

Many organizations today find it next to impossible to understand their own strengths and weaknesses, let alone their biggest competitors, because the enormous volume of organizational data is inaccessible to all but the MIS department. Organization data include far more than simple structured data elements in a database; the set of data also includes unstructured data such as voice mail, customer phone calls, text messages, video clips, along with numerous new forms of data, such as tweets from Twitter.

The Problem: Data Rich, Information Poor

An ideal business scenario would be as follows: As a business manager on his way to meet with a client reviews historical customer data, he realizes that the client's ordering volume has substantially decreased. As he drills down into the data, he notices the client had a support issue with a particular product. He quickly calls the support team to find out all of the information and learns that a replacement for the defective part can be shipped in 24 hours. In addition, he learns that the client has visited the website and requested information on a new product line. Armed with all this information, the business manager is prepared for a productive meeting with his client. He now understands the client's needs and issues, and he can address new sales opportunities with confidence.

For many companies the above example is simply a pipe dream. Attempting to gather all of the client information would actually take hours or even days to compile. With so much data available, it is surprisingly hard for managers to get information, such as inventory levels, past order history, or shipping details. Managers send their information requests to the MIS department where a dedicated person compiles the various reports. In some situations, responses can take days, by which time the information may be outdated and opportunities lost. Many organizations find themselves in the position of being data rich and information poor. Even in today's electronic world, managers struggle with the challenge of turning their business data into business intelligence.

The Solution: Business Intelligence

Employee decisions are numerous and they include providing service information, offering new products, and supporting frustrated customers. Employees can base their decisions on data, experience, or knowledge and preferably a combination of all three. Business intelligence can provide managers with the ability to make better decisions. A few examples of how different industries use business intelligence include:

- **Airlines:** Analyze popular vacation locations with current flight listings.
- **Banking:** Understand customer credit card usage and nonpayment rates.
- **Health care:** Compare the demographics of patients with critical illnesses.
- **Insurance:** Predict claim amounts and medical coverage costs.
- **Law enforcement:** Track crime patterns, locations, and criminal behavior.
- **Marketing:** Analyze customer demographics.
- **Retail:** Predict sales, inventory levels, and distribution.
- **Technology:** Predict hardware failures.

Figure 6.17 displays how organizations using BI can find the cause to many issues and problems simply by asking "Why?" The process starts by analyzing a report such as sales amounts by quarter. Managers will drill down into the report looking for why sales are up or why sales are down. Once they understand why a certain location or product is experiencing an increase in sales, they can share the information in an effort to raise enterprisewide sales. Once they understand the cause for a decrease in sales, they can take effective action to resolve the issue. Here are a few examples of how managers can use BI to answer tough business questions:

- **Where has the business been?** Historical perspective offers important variables for determining trends and patterns.

APPLY YOUR KNOWLEDGE

BUSINESS DRIVEN INNOVATION

News Dots

Gone are the days of staring at boring spreadsheets and trying to understand how the data correlate. With innovative data visualization tools, managers can arrange different ways to view the data, providing new forms of pattern recognition not offered by simply looking at numbers. *Slate,* a news publication, developed a new data visualization tool called News Dots that offers readers a different way of viewing the daily news through trends and patterns. The News Dots tool scans about 500 stories a day from major publications and then tags the content with important keywords such as people, places, companies, and topics. Surprisingly, the majority of daily news overlaps as the people, places, and stories are frequently connected. Using News Dots you can visualize how the news fits together, almost similar to a giant social network. News Dots uses circles (or dots) to represent the tagged content and arranges them according to size. The more frequently a certain topic is tagged, the larger the dot and its relationship to other dots. The tool is interactive and users simply click on a dot to view which stories mention that topic and which other topics it connects to in the network such as a correlation among the U.S. government, Federal Reserve, Senate, bank, and Barack Obama.[12]

How can data visualization help identify trends? What types of business intelligence could you identify if your college used a data visualization tool to analyze student information? What types of business intelligence could you identify if you used a data visualization tool to analyze the industry where you plan to compete?

- **Where is the business now?** Looking at the current business situation allows managers to take effective action to solve issues before they grow out of control.
- **Where is the business going?** Setting strategic direction is critical for planning and creating solid business strategies.

Ask a simple question—such as Who is my best customer or What is my worst-selling product—and you might get as many answers as you have employees. Databases, data warehouses, and data marts can provide a single source of "trusted" data that can answer questions about customers, products, suppliers, production, finances, fraud, and even employees. They can also alert managers to inconsistencies or help determine the cause and effects of enterprisewide business decisions. All business aspects can benefit from the added insights provided by business intelligence and you, as a business student, will benefit from understanding how MIS can help you make intelligent decisions.

FIGURE 6.17

How BI Can Answer Tough Customer Questions

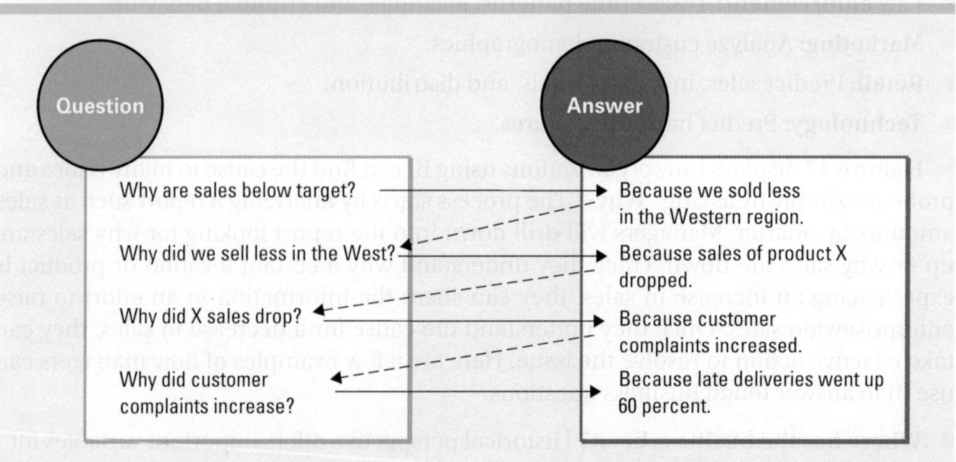

LEARNING OUTCOME REVIEW

Learning Outcome 6.1: Explain the four primary traits that determine the value of information.

Information is data converted into a meaningful and useful context. Information can tell an organization how its current operations are performing and help it estimate and strategize about how future operations might perform. It is important to understand the different levels, formats, and granularities of information along with the four primary traits that help determine the value of information, which include (1) information type: transactional and analytical; (2) information timeliness; (3) information quality; (4) information governance.

Learning Outcome 6.2: Describe a database, a database management system, and the relational database model.

A database maintains information about various types of objects (inventory), events (transactions), people (employees), and places (warehouses). A database management system (DBMS) creates, reads, updates, and deletes data in a database while controlling access and security. A DBMS provides methodologies for creating, updating, storing, and retrieving data in a database. In addition, a DBMS provides facilities for controlling data access and security, allowing data sharing, and enforcing data integrity. The relational database model allows users to create, read, update, and delete data in a relational database.

Learning Outcome 6.3: Identify the business advantages of a relational database.

Many business managers are familiar with Excel and other spreadsheet programs they can use to store business data. Although spreadsheets are excellent for supporting some data analysis, they offer limited functionality in terms of security, accessibility, and flexibility and can rarely scale to support business growth. From a business perspective, relational databases offer many advantages over using a text document or a spreadsheet, including increased flexibility, increased scalability and performance, reduced information redundancy, increased information integrity (quality), and increased information security.

Learning Outcome 6.4: Explain the business benefits of a data-driven website.

A data-driven website is an interactive website kept constantly updated and relevant to the needs of its customers using a database. Data-driven capabilities are especially useful when the website offers a great deal of information, products, or services because visitors are frequently annoyed if they are buried under an avalanche of information when searching a website. Many companies use the Web to make some of the information in their internal databases available to customers and business partners.

Learning Outcome 6.5: Define a data warehouse, and provide a few reasons it can make a manager more effective.

A data warehouse is a logical collection of information, gathered from many different operational databases, that supports business analysis and decision making. The primary value of a data warehouse is to combine information, more specifically, strategic information, throughout an organization into a single repository in such a way that the people who need that information can make decisions and undertake business analysis.

Learning Outcome 6.6: Explain ETL and the role of a data mart in business.

Extraction, transformation, and loading (ETL) is a process that extracts information from internal and external databases, transforms it using a common set of enterprise definitions, and loads it into a data warehouse. The data warehouse then sends portions (or subsets) of the information to data marts. A data mart contains a subset of data warehouse information. To distinguish between data warehouses and data marts, think of data warehouses as having a more organizational focus and data marts as having a functional focus.

Learning Outcome 6.7: Define data mining, and explain the three common forms for mining structured and unstructured data.

Data mining is the process of analyzing data to extract information not offered by the raw data alone. Data mining can also begin at a summary information level (coarse granularity) and progress through increasing levels of detail (drilling down), or the reverse (drilling up). Data mining occurs on structured data that are already in a database or a spreadsheet. Unstructured data do not exist in a fixed location and can include text documents, PDFs, voice messages, emails, and so on. Three common forms for mining structured and unstructured data are cluster analysis, association detection, and statistical analysis.

Learning Outcome 6.8: Identify the advantages of using business intelligence to support managerial decision making.

Many organizations today find it next to impossible to understand their own strengths and weaknesses, let alone their biggest competitors, due to enormous volumes of organizational data being inaccessible to all but the MIS department. Organization data include far more than simple structured data elements in a database; the set of data also includes unstructured data such as voice mail, customer phone calls, text messages, video clips, along with numerous new forms of data, such as tweets from Twitter. Managers today find themselves in the position of being data rich and information poor, and they need to implement business intelligence systems to solve this challenge.

OPENING CASE QUESTIONS

1. **Knowledge:** List the reasons a business would need consistently updated, enterprisewide analytical capabilities.
2. **Comprehension:** Describe how Brinker's is using business intelligence to reduce costs.
3. **Application:** Explain how the marketing department at Brinker's could use a data mart to help with the release of a new product.
4. **Analysis:** Categorize the five common characteristics of high-quality information and rank them in order of importance to Carnival Cruise.
5. **Synthesis:** Develop a list of some possible entities and attributes located in a Chili's restaurant database.
6. **Evaluate:** Assess how Brinker is using BI to identify trends and change associated business processes.

KEY TERMS

Association detection, 226
Attribute 212
Business-critical integrity constraint, 214
Cluster analysis, 225
Cube, 219
Data dictionary, 211
Data element (or data field), 210
Data governance, 210
Data inconsistency, 207
Data integrity issues, 207
Data mart, 219
Data mining, 222
Data model, 210
Data quality audit, 221

Data redundancy, 214
Data warehouse, 218
Database, 210
Database management system (DBMS), 210
Data-driven website, 215
Data-mining tool, 224
Entity, 211
Extraction, transformation, and loading (ETL), 219
Forecasts, 226
Foreign key, 212
Information cleansing or scrubbing, 220
Information granularity, 205
Information integrity, 214
Integrity constraint, 214
Logical view, 213
Market basket analysis, 226
Metadata, 211
Physical view, 213
Primary key, 212
Query-by-example (QBE) tool, 210
Real-time information, 206
Real-time system, 206
Record, 212
Relational database management system, 211
Relational database model, 211
Relational integrity constraint, 214
Statistical analysis, 226
Structured data, 221
Structured query language (SQL), 210
Text mining, 224
Time-series information, 226
Unstructured data, 224
Web mining, 224

REVIEW QUESTIONS

1. How does a database turn data elements into information?
2. Why does a business need to be concerned with the quality of its data?
3. How can data governance help protect a business from hackers?
4. Why would a company care about the timeliness of its data?
5. What are the five characteristics common to high-quality information?
6. What is data governance and its importance to a company?
7. What are the four primary traits that help determine the value of information?
8. What is the difference between an entity and an attribute?
9. What are the advantages of a relational database?
10. What are the advantages of a data-driven website?
11. What is a data warehouse and why would a business want to implement one?
12. Why would you need to use multidimensional analysis?
13. What is the purpose of information cleansing (or scrubbing)?
14. Why would a department want a data mart instead of just accessing the entire data warehouse?
15. Why would a business be data rich, but information poor?

CLOSING CASE ONE

Data Visualization: Stories for the Information Age

At the intersection of art and algorithm, data visualization schematically abstracts information to bring about a deeper understanding of the data, wrapping it in an element of awe. While the practice of visually representing information is arguably the foundation of all design, a newfound fascination with data visualization has been emerging. After *The New York Times* and *The Guardian* recently opened their online archives to the public, artists rushed to dissect nearly two centuries worth of information, elevating this art form to new prominence.

For artists and designers, data visualization is a new frontier of self-expression, powered by the proliferation of information and the evolution of available tools. For enterprise, it is a platform for displaying products and services in the context of the cultural interaction that surrounds them, reflecting consumers' increasing demand for corporate transparency.

"Looking at something ordinary in a new way makes it extraordinary," says Aaron Koblin, one of the more recent pioneers of the discipline. As technology lead of Google's Creative Labs in San Francisco, he spearheaded the search giant's Chrome Experiments series designed to show off the speed and reliability of the Chrome browser.

Forget Pie Charts and Bar Graphs

Data visualization has nothing to do with pie charts and bar graphs. And it's only marginally related to "infographics," information design that tends to be about objectivity and clarification. Such representations simply offer another iteration of the data—restating it visually and making it easier to digest. Data visualization, on the other hand, is an interpretation, a different way to look at and think about data that often exposes complex patterns or correlations.

Data visualization is a way to make sense of the ever-increasing stream of information with which we're bombarded and provides a creative antidote to the analysis paralysis that can result from the burden of processing such a large volume of information. "It's not about clarifying data," says Koblin. "It's about contextualizing it."

Today algorithmically inspired artists are reimagining the art-science continuum through work that frames the left-brain analysis of data in a right-brain creative story. Some use data visualization as a bridge between alienating information and its emotional impact—see Chris Jordan's portraits of global mass culture. Others take a more technological angle and focus on cultural utility—the Zoetrope project offers a temporal and historical visualization of the ephemeral Web. Still others are pure artistic indulgence—like Koblin's own Flight Patterns project, a visualization of air traffic over North America.

How Business Can Benefit

There are real implications for business here. Most cell phone providers, for instance, offer a statement of a user's monthly activity. Most often it's an overwhelming table of various numerical measures of how much you talked, when, with whom, and how much it cost. A visual representation of this data might help certain patterns emerge, revealing calling habits and perhaps helping users save money.

Companies can also use data visualization to gain new insight into consumer behavior. By observing and understanding what people do with the data—what they find useful and what they dismiss as worthless—executives can make the valuable distinction between what consumers say versus what they do. Even now, this can be a tricky call to make from behind the two-way mirror of a traditional qualitative research setting.

It's essential to understand the importance of creative vision along with the technical mastery of software. Data visualization isn't about using all the data available, but about deciding which patterns and elements to focus on, building a narrative, and telling the story of the raw data in a different, compelling way.

Ultimately, data visualization is more than complex software or the prettying up of spreadsheets. It's not innovation for the sake of innovation. It's about the most ancient of social rituals: storytelling. It's about telling the story locked in the data differently, more engagingly, in a way that draws us in, makes our eyes open a little wider and our jaw drop ever so slightly. And as we process it, it can sometimes change our perspective altogether.[13]

Questions

1. Identify the effects poor information might have on a data visualization project.
2. How does data visualization use database technologies?
3. How could a business use data visualization to identify new trends?

4. What is the correlation between data mining and data visualization?
5. Is data visualization a form of business intelligence? Why or why not?
6. What security issues are associated with data visualization?
7. What might happen to a data visualization project if it failed to cleanse or scrub its data?

CLOSING CASE TWO

Zillow

Zillow.com is an online Web-based real estate site helping homeowners, buyers, sellers, renters, real estate agents, mortgage professionals, property owners, and property managers find and share information about real estate and mortgages. Zillow allows users to access, anonymously and free of charge, the kinds of tools and information previously reserved for real estate professionals. Zillow's databases cover more than 90 million homes, which represents 95 percent of the homes in the United States. Adding to the sheer size of its databases, Zillow recalculates home valuations for each property every day, so they can provide historical graphs on home valuations over time. In some areas, Zillow is able to display 10 years of valuation history, a value-added benefit for many of its customers. This collection of data represents an operational data warehouse for anyone visiting the website.

As soon as Zillow launched its website, it immediately generated a massive amount of traffic. As the company expanded its services, the founders knew the key to its success would be the site's ability to quickly process and manage massive amounts of data, in real time. The company identified a need for accessible, scalable, reliable, secure databases that would enable it to continue to increase the capacity of its infrastructure indefinitely without sacrificing performance. Zillow's traffic continues to grow despite the weakening real estate market; the company is experiencing annual traffic growth of 30 percent and about a third of all U.S. mortgage professionals visit the site in a given month.

Data Mining and Business Intelligence

Zestimate values on Zillow use data-mining features for spotting trends across property valuations. Data mining also allows the company to see how accurate Zestimate values are over time. Zillow has also built the industry's first search by monthly payment, allowing users to find homes that are for sale and rent based on a monthly payment they can afford. Along with the monthly payment search, users can also enter search criteria such as the number of bedrooms or bathrooms.

Zillow also launched a new service aimed at changing the way Americans shop for mortgages. Borrowers can use Zillow's new Mortgage Marketplace to get custom loan quotes from lenders without having to give their names, addresses, phone numbers, or Social Security numbers, or field unwanted telephone calls from brokers competing for their business. Borrowers reveal their identities only after contacting the lender of their choice. The company is entering a field of established mortgage sites such as LendingTree .com and Experian Group's Lowermybills.com, which charge mortgage companies for borrower information. Zillow, which has an advertising model, says it does not plan to charge for leads.

For mortgage companies, the anonymous leads come free; they can make a bid based on information provided by the borrower, such as salary, assets, credit score, and the type of loan. Lenders can browse borrower requests and see competing quotes from other brokers before making a bid.[14]

Questions

1. List the reasons Zillow would need to use a database to run its business.
2. Describe how Zillow uses business intelligence to create a unique product for its customers.
3. How could the marketing department at Zillow use a data mart to help with the release of a new product launch?
4. Categorize the five common characteristics of high-quality information and rank them in order of importance to Zillow.
5. Develop a list of some possible entities and attributes of Zillow's mortgage database.
6. Assess how Zillow uses a data-driven website to run its business.

CRITICAL BUSINESS THINKING

1. Information—Business Intelligence or a Diversion from the Truth?

President Obama used part of his commencement address at Virginia's Hampton University last year to criticize the flood of incomplete information or downright incorrect information that flows in the 24-hour news cycle. The president said, "You're coming of age in a 24/7 media environment that bombards us with all kinds of content and exposes us to all kinds of arguments, some of which don't always rank all that high on the truth meter. With iPods and iPads and Xboxes and PlayStations—none of which I know how to work—information becomes a distraction, a diversion, a form of entertainment, rather than a tool of empowerment, rather than the means of emancipation."[15]

Do you agree or disagree with President Obama's statement? Who is responsible for verifying the accuracy of online information? What should happen to companies that post inaccurate information? What should happen to individuals who post inaccurate information? What should you remember when reading or citing sources for online information?

2. Illegal Database Access

Goldman Sachs has been hit with a $3 million lawsuit by a company that alleges the brokerage firm stole intellectual property from its database that had market intelligence facts. The U.S. District Court for the Southern District of New York filed the lawsuit in 2010 claiming Goldman Sachs employees used other people's access credentials to log into Ipreo's proprietary database, dubbed Bigdough. Offered on a subscription basis, Bigdough provides detailed information on more than 80,000 contacts within the financial industry. Ipreo complained to the court that Goldman Sachs employees illegally accessed Bigdough at least 264 times in 2008 and 2009.[16]

Do you agree or disagree with the lawsuit? Should Goldman Sachs be held responsible for rogue employees' behavior? What types of policies should Goldman Sachs implement to ensure this does not occur again?

3. Data Storage

Information is one of the most important assets of any business. Businesses must ensure information accuracy, completeness, consistency, timeliness, and uniqueness. In addition, business must have a reliable backup service. In part thanks to cloud computing, there are many data hosting services on the Internet. These sites offer storage of information that can be accessed from anywhere in the world.

These data hosting services include Hosting (www.hosting.com), Mozy (www.mozy.com), My Docs Online (www.mydocsonline.com), and Box (www.box.net). Visit a few of these sites along with a several others you find through research. Which sites are free? Are there limits to how much you can store? If so, what is the limit? What type of information can you store (video, text, photos, etc.)? Can you allow multiple users with different passwords to access your storage area? Are you contractually bound for a certain duration (annual, etc.)? Are different levels of services provided such as personal, enterprise, work group? Does it make good business sense to store business data on the Internet? What about personal data?

4. **Gathering Business Intelligence**
When considering new business opportunities, you need knowledge about the competition. One of the things many new business owners fail to do is to gather business intelligence on their competitors, such as how many there are and what differentiates each of them. You may find there are too many and that they would be tough competition for you. Or, you may find that there are few competitors and the ones who are out there offer very little value.

Generate a new business idea you could launch on the Internet. Research the Internet to find similar business in the area you have chosen. How many sites did you find that are offering the same products or services you are planning to offer? Did you come across any sites from another country that have a unique approach that you did not see on any of the sites in your own country? How would you use this information in pursuing your business idea?

5. **Free Data!**
The U.S. Bureau of Labor Statistics states that its role is as the "principal fact-finding agency for the federal government in the broad field of labor economics and statistics." And the data that the bureau provides via its website are available to anyone, free. This can represent a treasure trove of business intelligence and data mining for those who take advantage of this resource. Visit the website www.bls.gov. What type of information does the site provide? What information do you find most useful? What sort of information concerning employment and wages is available? How is this information categorized? How would this type of information be helpful to a business manager? What type of demographic information is available? How could this benefit a new start-up business?[17]

6. **Explaining Relational Databases**
You have been hired by Vision, a start-up clothing company. Your manager, Holly Henningson, is unfamiliar with databases and their associated business value. Henningson has asked you to create a report detailing the basics of databases. She would also like you to provide a detailed explanation of relational databases along with their associated business advantages.

7. **Entities and Attributes**
Martex Inc. is a manufacturer of athletic equipment, and its primary lines of business include running, tennis, golf, swimming, basketball, and aerobics equipment. Martex currently supplies four primary vendors including Sam's Sports, Total Effort, The Underline, and Maximum Workout. Martex wants to build a database to help it organize its products. In a group, identify the different types of entities, attributes, keys, and relationships Martex will want to consider when designing its relational database.

8. **Compiling Information**
You are currently working for the Public Transportation Department of Chatfield. The department controls all forms of public transportation, including buses, subways, and trains. Each department has about 300 employees and maintains its own accounting, inventory, purchasing, and human resource systems. Generating reports across departments is a difficult task and usually involves gathering and correlating the information from the many different databases. It typically takes about two weeks to generate the quarterly balance sheets and profit and loss statements. Your team has been asked to compile a report recommending what the Public Transportation Department of Chatfield can do to alleviate its information and system issues. Be sure that your report addresses the various reasons departmental reports are presently difficult to obtain as well as how you plan to solve this problem.[18]

9. Information Timeliness

Information timeliness is a major consideration for all organizations. Organizations need to decide the frequency of backups and the frequency of updates to a data warehouse. In a team, describe the timeliness requirements for backups and updates to a data warehouse for each of the following:

- Weather tracking systems.
- Car dealership inventories.
- Vehicle tire sales forecasts.
- Interest rates.
- Restaurant inventories.
- Grocery store inventories.

10. Improving Information Quality

HangUps Corporation designs and distributes closet organization structures. The company operates five systems—order entry, sales, inventory management, shipping, and billing. The company has severe information quality issues including missing, inaccurate, redundant, and incomplete information. The company wants to implement a data warehouse containing information from the five different systems to help maintain a single customer view, drive business decisions, and perform multidimensional analysis. Identify how the organization can improve its information quality when it begins designing and building its data warehouse.

ENTREPRENEURIAL CHALLENGE

BUILD YOUR OWN BUSINESS

Project Focus

1. Provide an example of your business data that fits each of the five common characteristics of high-quality information. Explain why each characteristic is important to your business data and what might happen if your business data were of low quality. (Be sure to identify your business and the name of your company.)
2. Identify the different entities and their associated attributes that would be found in your potential relational database model for your sales database.
3. Identify the benefits of having a data warehouse for your business. What types of data marts would you want to extract from you data warehouse to help you run your business and make strategic decisions.

APPLY YOUR KNOWLEDGE BUSINESS PROJECTS

PROJECT I Mining the Data Warehouse

Alana Smith is a senior buyer for a large wholesaler that sells different types of arts and crafts to greeting card stores such as Hallmark. Smith's latest marketing strategy is to send all of her customers a new line of handmade picture frames from Russia. All of her information supports her decision for the new line. Her analysis predicts that the frames should sell an average of 10 to 15 per store, per day. Smith is excited about the new line and is positive it will be a success.

One month later Smith learns the frames are selling 50 percent below expectations and averaging between five and eight frames sold daily in each store. She decides to access the company's data warehouse information to determine why sales are below expectations. Identify several different dimensions of information that Smith will want to analyze to help her decide what is causing the problems with the picture frame sales.

PROJECT II Different Dimensions

The focus of data warehousing is to extend the transformation of data into information. Data warehouses offer strategic level, external, integrated, and historical information so businesses can make projections, identify trends, and make key business decisions. The data warehouse collects and stores integrated sets of historical information from multiple operational systems and feeds them to one or more data marts. It may also provide end user access to support enterprisewide views of information.

Project Focus

You are currently working on a marketing team for a large corporation that sells jewelry around the world. Your boss has asked you to look at the following dimensions of data to determine which ones you want in your data mart for performing sales and market analysis (see Figure AYK.1). As a team, categorize the different dimensions ranking them from 1 to 5, with 1 indicating that the dimension offers the highest value and must be in your data mart and 5 indicating that the dimension offers the lowest value and does not need to be in your data mart.

FIGURE AYK.1

Data Warehouse Data

Dimension	Value (1–5)	Dimension	Value (1–5)
Product number		Season	
Store location		Promotion	
Customer net worth		Payment method	
Number of sales personnel		Commission policy	
Customer eating habits		Manufacturer	
Store hours		Traffic report	
Salesperson ID		Customer language	
Product style		Weather	
Order date		Customer gender	
Product quantity		Local tax information	
Ship date		Local cultural demographics	
Current interest rate		Stock market closing	
Product cost		Customer religious affiliation	
Customer's political affiliation		Reason for purchase	
Local market analysis		Employee dress code policy	
Order time		Customer age	
Customer spending habits		Employee vacation policy	
Product price		Employee benefits	
Exchange rates		Current tariff information	
Product gross margin			

PROJECT III Understanding Search

Pretend that you are a search engine. Choose a topic to query. It can be anything such as your favorite book, movie, band, or sports team. Search your topic on Google, pick three or four pages from the results, and print them out. On each printout, find the individual words from your query (such as "Boston Red Sox" or "The Godfather") and use a highlighter to mark each word with color. Do that for each of the documents that you print out. Now tape those documents on a wall, step back a few feet, and review your documents.

Project Focus

If you did not know what the rest of a page said and could judge only by the colored words, which document do you think would be most relevant? Is there anything that would make a document look more relevant? Is it better to have the words be in a large heading or to occur several times in a smaller font? Do you prefer it if the words are at the top or the bottom of the page? How often do the words need to appear? Come up with two or three things you would look for to see if a document matched a query well. This exercise mimics search engine processes and should help you understand why a search engine returns certain results over others.

PROJECT IV Predicting Netflix

Netflix Inc., the largest online movie rental service, provides more than 12 million subscribers access to more than 100,000 unique DVD titles along with a growing on-demand library in excess of 10,000 choices. Data and information are so important to Netflix that it created The Netflix Prize, an open competition for anyone who could improve the data used in prediction ratings for films (an increase of 10 percent), based on previous ratings. The winner would receive a $1 million prize.

Project Focus

The ability to search, analyze, and comprehend information is vital for any organization's success. It certainly was for Netflix, as it was happy to pay anyone $1 million to improve the quality of its information. In a group explain how Netflix might use databases, data warehouses, and data marts to predict customer movie recommendations. Here are a few characteristics you might want to analyze to get you started:

- Customer demographics.
- Movie genre, rating, year, producer, type.
- Actor information.
- Internet access.
- Location for mail pickup.

PROJECT V The Crunch Factory

The Crunch Factory is one of the fourth-largest gyms operating in Australia, and each gym operates its own system with its own database. Unfortunately, the company failed to develop any data-capturing standards and now faces the challenges associated with low-quality enterprisewide information. For example, one system has a field to capture email addresses while another system does not. Duplicate customer information among the different systems is another major issue, and the company continually finds itself sending conflicting or competing messages to customers from different gyms. A customer could also have multiple accounts within the company, one representing a membership, another representing additional classes, and yet another for a personal trainer. The Crunch Factory has no way to identify that the different customer accounts are actually for the same customer.

Project Focus

To remain competitive and be able to generate business intelligence The Crunch Factory has to resolve these challenges. The Crunch Factory has just hired you as its data quality expert. Your first task is to determine how the company can turn its low-quality information into high-quality business intelligence. Create a plan that The Crunch Factory can implement that details the following:

- Challenges associated with low-quality information.
- Benefits associated with high-quality information.
- Recommendations on how the company can clean up its data.

PROJECT VI Too Much of a Good Thing

The Castle, a premium retailer of clothes and accessories, created an enterprisewide data warehouse so all its employees could access information for decision making. The Castle soon discovered that it is possible to have too much of a good thing. The Castle employees found themselves inundated with data and unable to make any decisions, a common occurrence called analysis paralysis. When sales representatives queried the data warehouse to determine if a certain product in the size, color, and category was available, they would get hundreds of results showing everything from production orders to supplier contracts. It became easier for the sales representatives to look in the warehouse themselves than to check the system. Employees found the data warehouse was simply too big, too complicated, and contained too much irrelevant information.

Project Focus

The Castle is committed to making its data warehouse system a success and has come to you for help. Create a plan that details the value of the data warehouse to the business, how it can be easier for all employees to use, along with the potential business benefits the company can derive from its data warehouse.

PROJECT VII Twitter Buzz

Technology tools that can predict sales for the coming week, decide when to increase inventory, and determine when additional staff is required are extremely valuable. Twitter is not just for tweeting your whereabouts anymore. Twitter and other social-media sites have become great tools for gathering business intelligence on customers, including what they like, dislike, need, and want. Twitter is easy to use, and businesses can track every single time a customer makes a statement about a particular product or service. Good businesses turn this valuable information into intelligence spotting trends and patterns in customer opinion.

Project Focus

Do you agree that a business can use Twitter to gain business intelligence? How many companies do you think are aware of Twitter and exactly how they can use it to gain BI? How do you think Twitter uses a data warehouse? How do you think companies store Twitter information? How would a company use Twitter in a data mart? How would a company use cubes to analyze Twitter data?

AYK APPLICATION PROJECTS

If you are looking for Access projects to incorporate into your class, try any of the following after reading this chapter.

Project Number	Project Name	Project Type	Plug-In	Focus Area	Project Level	Skill Set	Page Number
28	Daily Invoice	Access	T5, T6, T7, T8	Business Analysis	Introductory	Entities, Relationships, and Databases	AYK.17
29	Billing Data	Access	T5, T6, T7, T8	Business Intelligence	Introductory	Entities, Relationships, and Databases	AYK.19
30	Inventory Data	Access	T5, T6, T7, T8	SCM	Intermediate	Entities, Relationships, and Databases	AYK.20
31	Call Center	Access	T5, T6, T7, T8	CRM	Intermediate	Entities, Relationships, and Databases	AYK.21
32	Sales Pipeline	Access	T5, T6, T7, T8	Business Intelligence	Advanced	Entities, Relationships, and Databases	AYK.23
33	Online Classified Ads	Access	T5, T6, T7, T8	Ecommerce	Advanced	Entities, Relationships, and Databases	AYK.23

Networks: Mobile Business

7

CHAPTER

CHAPTER OUTLINE

SECTION 7.1
Connectivity: The Business Value of a Networked World

- Overview of a Connected World
- Benefits of a Connected World
- Challenges of a Connected World

SECTION 7.2
Mobility: The Business Value of a Wireless World

- Wireless Network Categories
- Business Applications of Wireless Networks
- Benefits of Business Mobility
- Challenges of Business Mobility

What's in IT for me?

The pace of technological change never ceases to amaze as kindergarten classes are now learning PowerPoint and many elementary school children have their own cell phones. What used to take hours to download over a dial-up modem connection can now transfer in a matter of seconds through an invisible, wireless network connection from a computer thousands of miles away. We are living in an increasingly wireless present and hurtling ever faster toward a wireless future. The tipping point of ubiquitous, wireless, handheld, mobile computing is approaching quickly.

As a business student, understanding network infrastructures and wireless technologies allows you to take advantage of mobile workforces. Understanding the benefits and challenges of mobility is a critical skill for business executives, regardless if you are a novice or a seasoned *Fortune* 500 employee. By learning about the various concepts discussed in this chapter, you will develop a better understanding of how business can leverage networking technologies to analyze network types, improve wireless and mobile business processes, and evaluate alternative networking options.

opening case study

The Ironman

Florida-based World Triathlon Corporation (WTC), owner of the Ironman Triathlon World Championship, is in the business of fulfilling the dreams of endurance athletes in one of the world's most grueling events. The Ironman Triathlon World Championship brings more than 1,700 of the world's top athletes to rugged Kailua-Kona, Hawaii, for a world championship race every fall. Athletes attempt to swim 2.4 miles, cycle 112 miles, and run a full 26.2-mile marathon—all in a single day. The event features a remote course that threads around the side of an active volcano and offers breathtaking views but also rough terrain, intense heat, and shifting trade winds.

In the past, it was not easy for family and friends to know how a particular athlete was faring in the contest. "As a spectator, you'd see the start, and then the athletes would disappear, and that was pretty much it until the finish line," recalls Dave Scott, who ran his first triathlon in 1976. Now, however, Ironman is transforming the way audiences and athletes experience the race. By using WiMAX networks to enable remote cameras, the company also raised the bar for professional sports broadcasting and spotlighted a technology many say will help bring the next billion users into the Internet community.

Fans worldwide now can find any athlete's speed and location thanks to high-speed WiMAX broadband connections in various places along the 140-mile course. The company uses radio-frequency identification (RFID) ankle bracelets to track the athletes' progress and high-bandwidth communications to transmit professional-quality video and other data, making the information accessible on the Ironmanlive.com website.

Networking the course was a challenge due to the same factors that make it challenging for athletes. "We're on a very rough, rugged course on an island with an active volcano," explains Dan Gerson, Ironmanlive.com production manager. "It's hot, it's windy, and there's no infrastructure. If you can deploy WiMAX here, you can probably deploy it pretty much anywhere." Airspan Networks provided the WiMAX infrastructure, using its high-performance base stations and subscriber stations to create a high-performance network backbone capable of transmitting data rates required for top-quality video. The team set up its base station atop the hotel that served as the events' starting point and finish line, one of the lowest geographical points of the course.

The team was operating in a non-line-of-sight environment, and highly porous volcanic rock absorbed the wireless signals more than other types of rock would. Airspan set up relays on the ridge sides of the volcano, the side of the road, and the sides of buildings to keep signal fidelity. Cameras in locations without power used generators. This was a wireless deployment in every sense of the word, demonstrating the viability of WiMAX technology. Footage of the athletes could be incorporated into the live webcast, along with pre-event interviews, commentary, and film from cameras on motorcycles and helicopters. WTC produced the broadcast in a live production studio on-site that streamed the video data to the global servers that run the Ironmanlive.com website.

WTC also set up eight wireless hot spots, including five along the event course and at the finish line. An Internet café was stocked with laptops, providing convenient wireless access to event information and the Ironmanlive.com site. Two giant-screen displays showed the live program coverage from Ironmanlive.com. Staff used additional mobile devices to manage the race and monitor each athlete's progress. For example, if athletes needed medical care, the health care team used a PDA to scan their RFID tags and instantly access medical records and local contact information.

Ironman's transformative use of wireless computing makes sound business sense. It draws larger audiences and higher advertising revenues for WTC and NBC, which uses WTC's Ironman Triathlon programming in its own broadcast of the event a month or two later. Larger audiences and better experiences for athletes and their families ultimately lead to greater participation in the Ironman Triathlon and its more than two dozen qualifying races, and to increased popularity for the sport.[1]

section 7.1 CONNECTIVITY: THE BUSINESS VALUE OF A NETWORKED WORLD

LEARNING OUTCOMES

7.1 Explain the five different networking elements creating a connected world.

7.2 Identify the benefits of a connected world.

7.3 Identify the challenges of a connected world.

LO 7.1: Explain the five different networking elements creating a connected world.

OVERVIEW OF A CONNECTED WORLD

Computer networks are continuously operating all over the globe supporting our 24/7/365 always on and always connected lifestyles. You are probably using several different networks right now without even realizing it. You might be using a school's network to communicate with teachers, a phone network to communicate with friends, and a cable network to watch TV or listen to the radio. Networks enable telecommunications or the exchange of information (voice, text, data, audio, video). The telecommunication industry has morphed from a government-regulated monopoly to a deregulated market where many suppliers ferociously compete. Competing telecommunication companies offer local and global telephony services, satellite service, mobile radio, cable television, cellular phone services, and Internet access (all of which are detailed in this chapter). Businesses everywhere are increasingly using networks to communicate and collaborate with customers, partners, suppliers, and employees. As a manager, you will face many different communication alternatives, and the focus of this chapter is to provide you with an initial understanding of the different networking elements you will someday need to select (see Figure 7.1). A detailed technical overview of networking and telecommunications can be found in Appendix B.

Network Categories

The general idea of a network is to allow multiple devices to communicate at the highest achievable speeds and, very importantly, to reduce the cost of connecting. How a particular network achieves these goals depends in part on how it is physically constructed and connected. Networks are categorized based on geographic span: local area networks, wide area networks, and metropolitan area networks. Today's business networks include a combination of all three.

A ***local area network (LAN)*** connects a group of computers in close proximity, such as in an office building, school, or home. LANs allow sharing of files, printers, games, and other resources. A LAN also often connects to other LANs, and to wide area networks. A ***wide area network (WAN)*** spans a large geographic area such as a state, province, or country. Perhaps the best example is the Internet. WANs are essential for carrying out the day-to-day activities of many companies and government organizations, allowing

FIGURE 7.1
Networking Elements Creating a Connected World

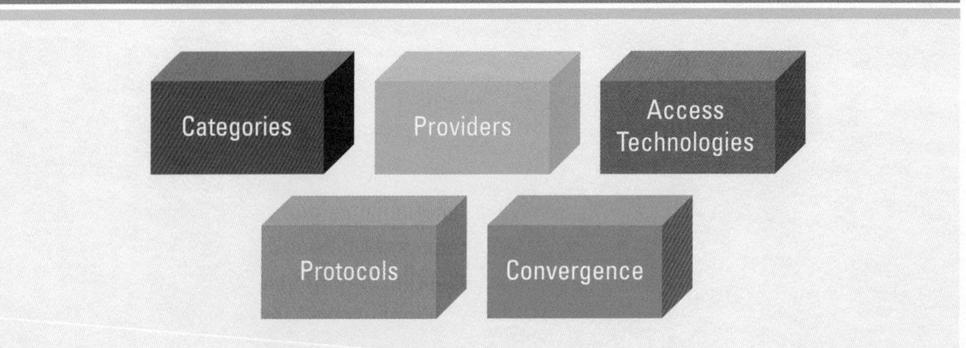

them to transmit and receive information among their employees, customers, suppliers, business partners, and other organizations across cities, regions, and countries and around the world.

WANs often connect multiple smaller networks, such as local area networks or metropolitan area networks. A ***metropolitan area network (MAN)*** is a large computer network usually spanning a city. Most colleges, universities, and large companies that span a campus use an infrastructure supported by a MAN. Figure 7.2 shows the relationships and a few differences between a LAN, WAN, and MAN. A cloud image often represents the Internet or some large network environment.

While LANs, WANs, and MANs all provide users with an accessible and reliable network infrastructure, they differ in many dimensions; two of the most important are cost and performance. It is easy to establish a network between two computers in the same room or building, but much more difficult if they are in different states or even countries. This means someone looking to build or support a WAN either pays more or gets less performance, or both.

Network Providers

The largest and most important network, the Internet has evolved into a global information superhighway. Think of it as a network made up of millions of smaller networks, each with the ability to operate independently of, or in harmony with, the others. Keeping the Internet operational is no simple task. No one owns or runs it, but it does have

FIGURE 7.2

Network Categories: LAN, WAN, and MAN

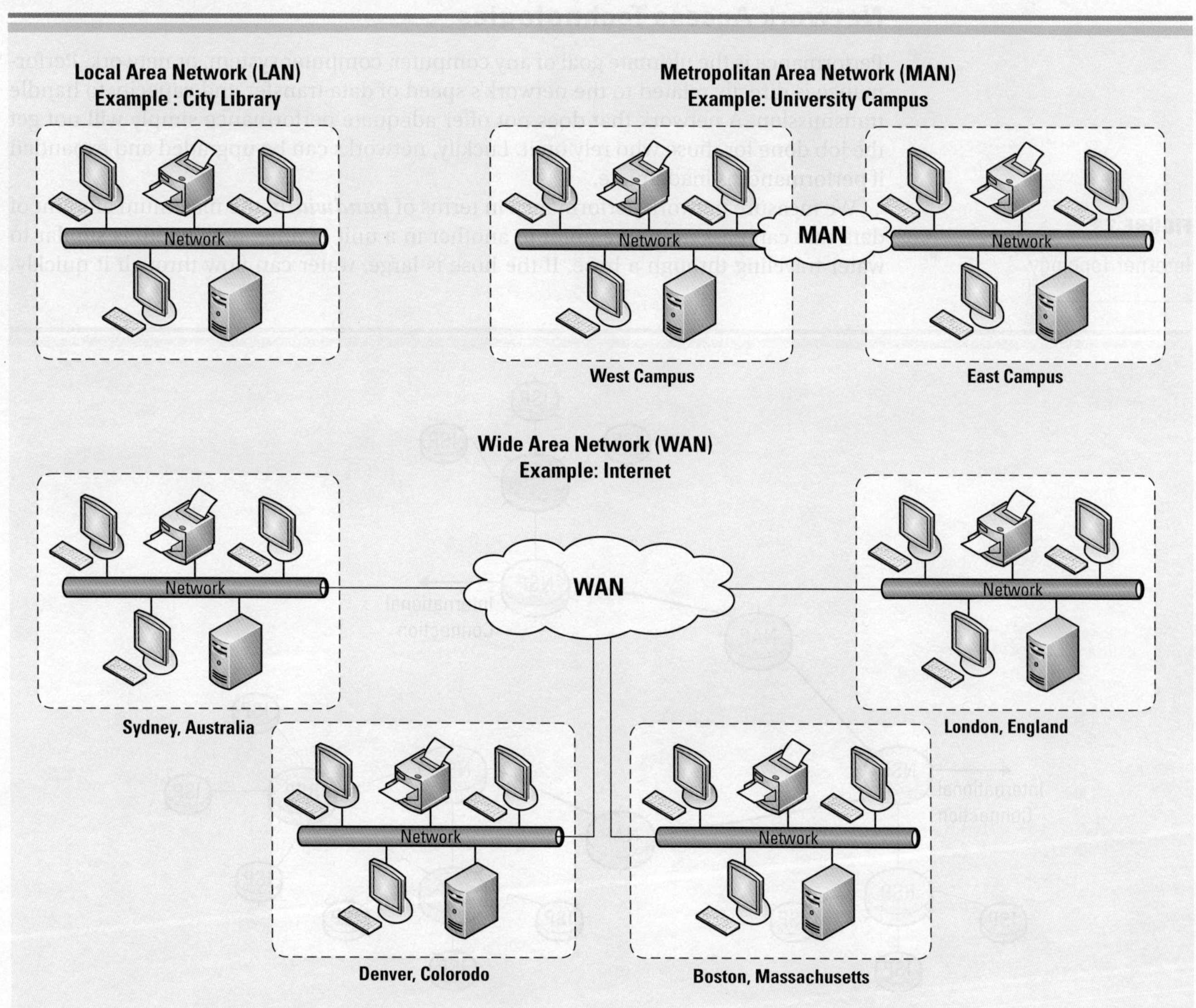

an organized network topology. The Internet is a hierarchical structure linking different levels of service providers, whose millions of devices, LANs, WANs, and MANs supply all the interconnections. At the top of the hierarchy are ***national service providers (NSPs),*** private companies that own and maintain the worldwide backbone that supports the Internet. These include Sprint, Verizon, MCI (previously UUNet/WorldCom), AT&T, NTT, Level3, Qwest, and Cable & Wireless Worldwide. ***Network access points (NAPs)*** are traffic exchange points in the routing hierarchy of the Internet that connects NSPs. They typically have regional or national coverage and connect to only a few NSPs. Thus, to reach a large portion of the global Internet, a NAP needs to route traffic through one of the NSPs to which it is connected.[2]

One step down in the hierarchy is the regional service provider. ***Regional service providers (RSPs)*** offer Internet service by connecting to NSPs, but they also can connect directly to each other. Another level down is the Internet service providers (ISPs), recall from Chapter 3 that an ISP provides access to the Internet for a monthly fee. ISPs vary services provided and available bandwidth rates. ISPs link to RSPs and, if they are geographically close, to other ISPs. Some also connect directly to NSPs, thereby sidestepping the hierarchy. Individuals and companies use local ISPs to connect to the Internet, and large companies tend to connect directly using an RSP. Major ISPs in the United States include AOL, AT&T, Comcast, Earthlink, and NetZero. The further up the hierarchy, the faster the connections and the greater the bandwidth. The backbone shown in Figure 7.3 is greatly simplified, but it illustrates the concept that basic global interconnections are provided by the NSPs, RSPs and ISPs.[3]

Network Access Technologies

Performance is the ultimate goal of any computer, computer system, or network. Performance is directly related to the network's speed of data transfer and capacity to handle transmission. A network that does not offer adequate performance simply will not get the job done for those who rely on it. Luckily, networks can be upgraded and expanded if performance is inadequate.

We measure network performance in terms of ***bandwidth,*** the maximum amount of data that can pass from one point to another in a unit of time. Bandwidth is similar to water traveling through a hose. If the hose is large, water can flow through it quickly.

FIGURE 7.3
Internet Topology

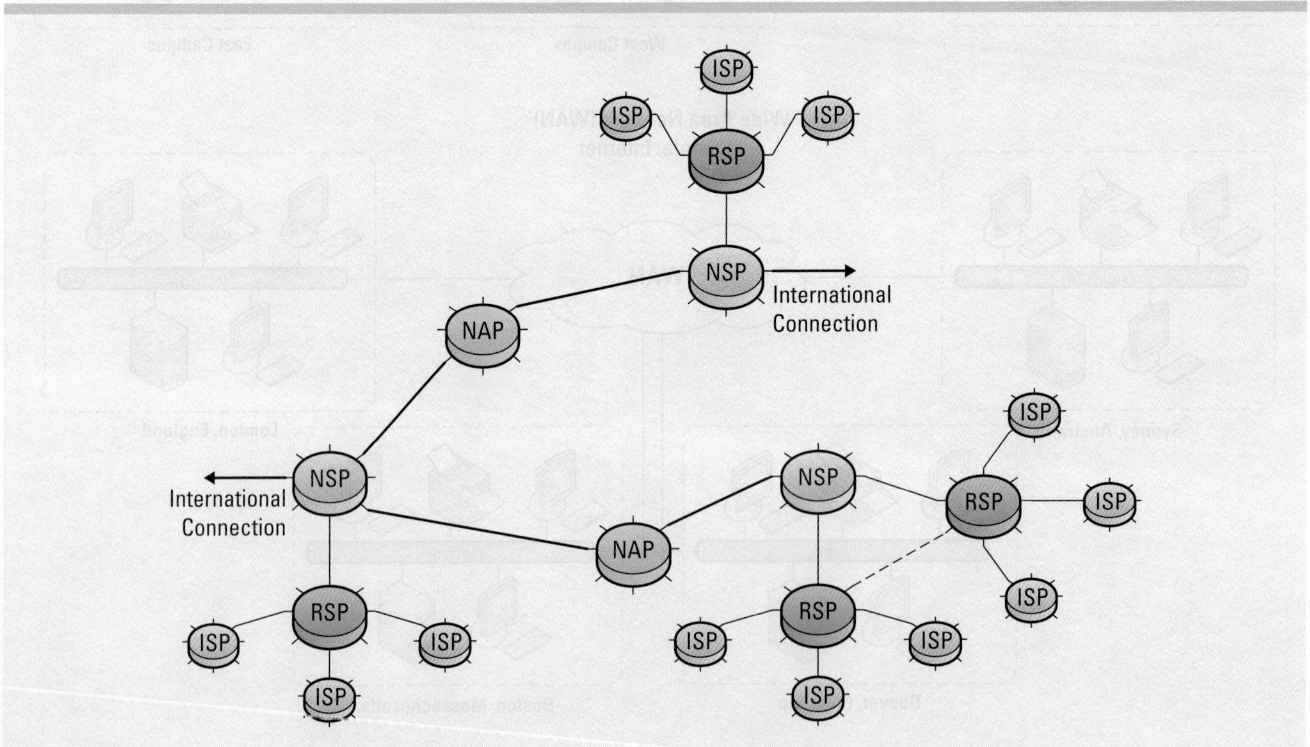

Bandwidth	Abbreviation	Bits per Second (bps)	Example
Kilobits	Kbps	1 Kbps = 1,000 bps	Traditional modem = 56 Kbps
Megabits	Mbps	1 Mbps = 1,000 Kbps	Traditional Ethernet = 10 Mbps Fast Ethernet = 100 Mbps
Gigabits	Gbps	1 Gbps = 1,000 Mbps	Gigabit Ethernet = 1,000 Mbps

FIGURE 7.4

Bandwidth Speeds

Data differs from a hose in that it must travel great distances, especially on a WAN, and not all areas of the network have the same bandwidth. A network essentially has many different hoses of unequal capacity connected together, which will restrict the flow of data when one is smaller than the others. Therefore, the speed of transmission of a network is determined by the speed of its smallest bandwidth.

A ***bit*** (short for binary digit) is the smallest element of data and has a value of either 0 or 1. Bandwidth is measured in terms of ***bit rate*** (or ***data rate***), the number of bits transferred or received per unit of time. Figure 7.4 represents bandwidth speeds in terms of bit rates.

A ***modem*** is a device that enables a computer to transmit and receive data. A connection with a traditional telephone line and a modem, which most residential users had in the 1990s, is called dial-up access. Today, many users in underdeveloped countries and in rural areas in developed countries still use dial-up. It has two drawbacks. First, it is slow, providing a maximum rate of 56 Kbps. (At 56 Kbps, it takes eight minutes to download a three-minute song and more than a day to download a two-hour movie.) Second, dial-up modem access ties up the telephone line so the user cannot receive and make phone calls while online. The good news is this is not as big an issue as it once was as many people have cell phones and no longer require using the telephone line for making phone calls.[4]

Once the most common connection method worldwide, dial-up is quickly being replaced by broadband. ***Broadband*** is a high-speed Internet connection that is always connected. High-speed in this case refers to any bandwidth greater than 2 Mbps. Not long ago, broadband speeds were available only at a premium price to support large companies' high-traffic networks. Today, inexpensive access is available for home use and small companies.

The two most prevalent types of broadband access are digital subscriber line and cable connection. ***Digital subscriber line (DSL)*** allows high-speed digital data transmission over standard telephone lines. Consumers typically obtain DSL Internet access from the same company that provides their wired local telephone access, such as AT&T or Qwest. Thus, a customer's telephone provider is also its ISP, and the telephone line carries both data and telephone signals using a DSL modem.

DSL has two major advantages over dial-up. First, it can transmit and receive data much faster—in the 1 to 2 Mbps range for downloading and 128 Kbps to 1 Mbps for uploading. (Most high-speed connections are designed to download faster than they upload, because most users download more—including viewing Web pages—than they upload.) The second major advantage is that because they have an "always on" connection to their ISP, users can simultaneously talk on the phone and access the Internet.[5]

While dial-up and DSL make use of local telephone infrastructure, ***Internet cable connections*** provide Internet access using a cable television company's infrastructure and a special cable modem. Unlike DSL, cable is a shared service, which means everyone in a certain radius, such as a neighborhood, shares the available bandwidth. Therefore, if several users are simultaneously downloading a video file, the actual transfer rate for each will be significantly lower than if only one person were doing so. On average, the available bandwidth using cable can range from 512 Kbps to 50 Mbps for downloading, and 786 Kbps for uploading.[6]

In rural areas where neither DSL nor cable is available, a satellite link can connect to the Internet at speeds of more than 1 Mbps. Satellite technologies are discussed in Section 7.2.

Access Technology	Description	Bandwidth	Comments
Dial-up	On-demand access using a modem and regular telephone line.	Up to 56 Kbps	Cheap but slow compared with other technologies.
DSL	Always-on connection. Special modem needed.	Download: 1 Mbps to 2 Mbps Upload: 128 Kbps to 1 Mbps	Makes use of the existing local telephone infrastructure.
Cable	Always-on connection. Special cable modem and cable line required.	Download: 512 Kbps to 50 Mbps Upload: 786 Kbps	It is a shared resource with other users in the area.
T1	Leased lines for high bandwidth.	1.544 Mbps	More expensive than dial-up, DSL, or cable.

FIGURE 7.5
Types of Internet Access

Another alternative to DSL or cable is dedicated communications lines leased from AT&T or another provider. The most common are ***T1 lines,*** a type of data connection able to transmit a digital signal at 1.544 Mpbs. Although this speed might not seem impressive, and T1 lines are more expensive than DSL or cable, they are more reliable than either. Each is composed of 24 channels, creating 24 separate connections through one line. If a company has three separate plants that experience a high volume of data traffic, it might make sense to lease lines to connect them all with a reliable high bandwidth.[7]

A company must match its needs with Internet access methods. If it always needs high bandwidth access to communicate with customers, partners, or suppliers, a T1 line may be the most cost effective method. Figure 7.5 provides an overview of the main methods for Internet access. The bandwidths there represent average speeds; actual speeds vary depending upon the service provider and other factors such as the type of cabling and speed of the computer.[8]

Network Protocols

A ***protocol*** is a standard that specifies the format of data as well as the rules to be followed during transmission. Computers using the same protocol can communicate easily, providing accessibility, scalability, and connectability between networks. Network access technologies use a standard Internet protocol called ***transmission control protocol/Internet protocol (TCP/IP),*** which provides the technical foundation for the public Internet as well as for large numbers of private networks. One of the primary reasons for developing TCP/IP was to allow diverse or differing networks to connect and communicate with each other, essentially allowing LANs, WANs, and MANs to grow with each new connection.

TCP (the TCP part of TCP/IP) verifies the correct delivery of data because data can become corrupt when traveling over a network. TCP ensures the size of the data packet is the same throughout its transmission and can even retransmit data until delivered correctly. IP (the IP part of TCP/IP) verifies the data are sent to the correct IP address, numbers represented by four strings of numbers ranging from 0 to 255 separated by periods. For example, the IP address of www.apple.com is 97.17.237.15.

Here is another way to understand TCP/IP. Consider a letter that needs to go from the University of Denver to Apple's headquarters in Cupertino, California. TCP makes sure the envelope is delivered and does not get lost along the way. IP acts as the sending and receiving labels, telling the letter carrier where to deliver the envelope and who it was from. The Postal Service mainly uses street addresses and zip codes to get letters to their destinations, which is really what IP does with its addressing method. Figure 7.6 illustrates this example. However, unlike the Postal Service, which allows multiple people to share the same physical address, each device using an IP address to connect to the Internet must have a unique address or else it could not detect which individual device a request should be sent to.

One of the most valuable characteristics of TCP/IP is how scalable its protocols have proven to be as the Internet has grown from a small network with just a few machines to a huge internetwork with millions of devices. While some changes have been required periodically to support this growth, the core of TCP/IP is the same as it was more than 25 years ago.[9]

BUSINESS DRIVEN DISCUSSION

Net Neutrality: The Great Debate

Net Neutrality—the great debate has been raging for some time now, with the battle lines clearly drawn. *Net neutrality* is about ensuring that everyone has equal access to the Internet. It is the founding principle that all consumers should be able to use the Internet and be free to access its resources without any form of discrimination. However, regulation on net neutrality is currently in flux. The Federal Communications Commission (FCC) recently required Comcast to stop slowing down or blocking subscriber access to many peer-to-peer file-sharing sites such as BitTorrent. Users of many peer-to-peer networks often transfer large files, which can be legitimate in nature (such as downloading open source applications) or pirated (such as illegal copies of the latest Hollywood video). Shortly after the FCC ruling, a federal appeals court overturned that decision, unanimously ruling that the agency did not have the legal authority to tell Comcast what to do.

On one side of the debate are the ISPs, such as Comcast, that are building the Internet infrastructure and want to charge customers relative to their use, namely, the amount of bandwidth they consume. The ISPs argue more and more users accessing bandwidth-intense resources provided by the likes of YouTube and Hulu place huge demands on their networks. They want Internet access to move from a flat-rate pricing structure to a metered service. The content providers, such as Google, support the counterargument that if ISPs move toward metered schemes, this may limit the usage of many resources on the Internet such as iTunes and Netflix. A metered service may also stifle the innovative opportunities the "open" Internet provides.

Do you agree that the government should control the Internet? Should website owners be legally forced to receive or transmit information from competitors or other websites they find objectionable? Provide examples of when net neutrality might be good for a business and when net neutrality might be bad for a business. Overall, is net neutrality good or bad for business?[10]

If there is one flaw in TCP/IP, it is the complexity of IP addresses. This is why we use a ***domain name system (DNS)*** to convert IP addresses into *domains,* or identifying labels that use a variety of recognizable naming conventions. Therefore, instead of trying to remember 97.17.237.15, users can simply specify a domain name to access a computer or website, such as www.apple.com. Figure 7.7 lists the most common Internet domains.[11]

The list of domain names is expected to expand in the coming years to include entities such as .pro (for accountants, lawyers, and physicians), .aero (for the air-transport industry), and .museum (for museums). The creation of an .xxx domain was recently approved for pornographic content. Countries also have domain names such as .au (Australia), .fr (France), and .sp (Spain).

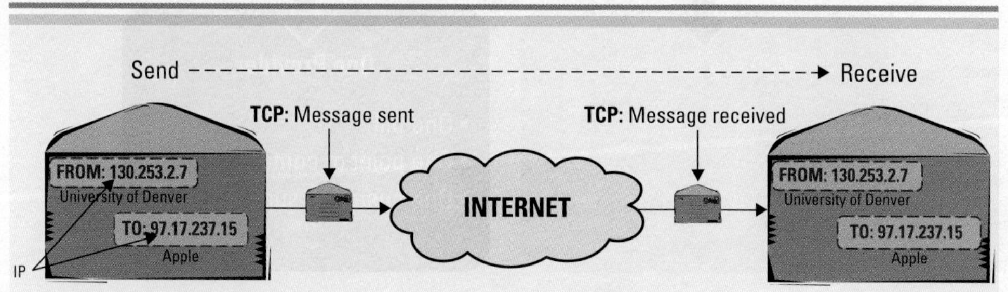

FIGURE 7.6
Example of TCP/IP

Domain Name	Use
.biz	Reserved for businesses
.com	Reserved for commercial organizations and businesses
.edu	Reserved for accredited postsecondary institutions
.gov	Reserved for U.S. government agencies
.info	Open to any person or entity, but intended for information providers
.mil	Reserved for U.S. military
.net	Open to any person or entity
.org	Reserved for nonprofit organizations

FIGURE 7.7

Internet Domains

Websites with heavy traffic often have several computers working together to share the load of requests. This offers load balancing and fault tolerance, so when requests are made to a popular site such as www.facebook.com, they will not overload a single computer and the site does not go down if one computer fails. A single computer can also have several host names—for instance, if a company is hosting several websites on a single server, much as an ISP works with hosting.

Domain names are essentially rented, with renewable rights, from a domain name registrar, such as godaddy.com. Some registrars only register domain names, while others provide hosting services for a fee. ICANN (Internet Corporation for Assigning Names and Numbers) is a nonprofit governance and standards organization that certifies all domain name registrars throughout the world. With the certification, each registrar is authorized to register domain names, such as .com, .edu, or .org.[12]

Network Convergence

In part due to the explosive use of the Internet and connectivity of TCP/IP, there is a convergence of network devices, applications, and services. Consumers, companies, educational institutions, and government agencies extensively engage in texting, Web surfing, videoconference applications, online gaming, and ebusiness. ***Network convergence*** is the efficient coexistence of telephone, video, and data communication within a single network, offering convenience and flexibility not possible with separate infrastructures. Almost any type of information can be converted into digital form and exchanged over a network. Network convergence then allows the weaving together of voice, data, and video. The benefits of network convergence allow for multiple services, multiple devices, but one network, one vendor, and one bill, as suggested by Figure 7.8.

FIGURE 7.8

The Benefits of Network Convergence

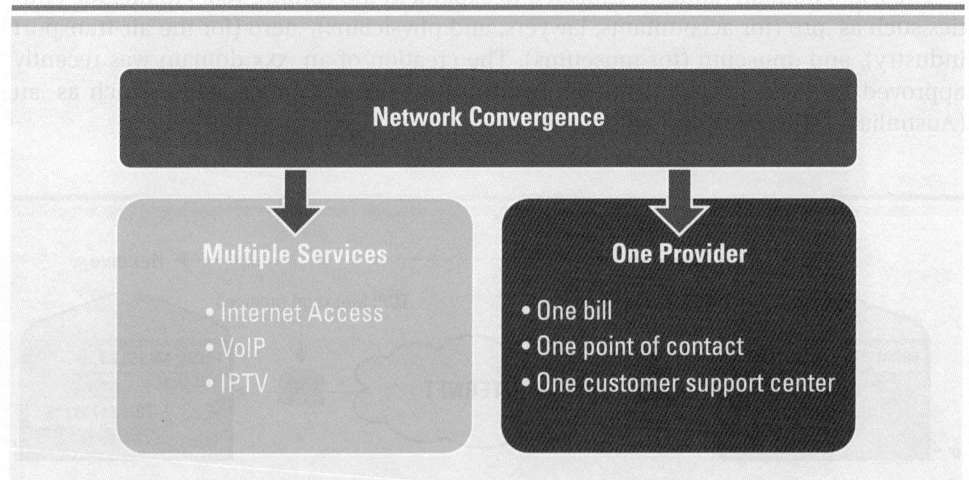

One of the challenges associated with network convergence is using the many different tools efficiently and productively. Knowing which communication channel—PC, text message, videoconference—to use with each business participant can be a challenge. ***Unified communications (UC)*** is the integration of communication channels into a single service. UC integrates communication channels allowing participants to communicate using the method that is most convenient for them. UC merges instant messaging, videoconferencing, email, voice mail, and VoIP. This can decrease the communication costs for a business while enhancing the way individuals communicate and collaborate.

One area experiencing huge growth in network convergence is the use of the Internet for voice transmission. ***Voice over IP (VoIP)*** uses IP technology to transmit telephone calls. For the first time in more than 100 years, VoIP is providing an opportunity to bring about significant change in the way people communicate using the telephone. VoIP service providers—specialists as well as traditional telephone and cable companies and some ISPs—allow users to call anyone with a telephone number, whether local, long distance, cellular, or international.

Two ways to use VoIP for telephone calls are through a Web interface that allows users to make calls from their computer and through a phone attached to a VoIP adapter that links directly to the Internet through a broadband modem. Figure 7.9 illustrates these two ways along with the use of VoIP-enabled phones, bypassing the need for an adapter.

VoIP services include fixed-price unlimited local and long-distance calling plans (at least within the United States and Canada), plus a range of interesting features, such as:

- The ability to have more than one phone number, including numbers with different area codes.
- Integrating email and voice mail so users can listen to their voice mail using their computer.
- The ability to receive personal or business calls via computer, no matter where the user is physically located.[13]

The biggest benefit of VoIP is its low cost. Because it relies on the Internet connection, however, service can be affected if the bandwidth is not appropriate or Internet access is not available.

Skype is a perfect example of IP applied to telephone use. Unlike typical VoIP systems that use a client and server infrastructure, Skype uses a peer-to-peer network. ***Peer-to-peer (P2P)*** is a computer network that relies on the computing power and bandwidth of the participants in the network rather than a centralized server. Skype's user directory is distributed among the users in its network, allowing scalability without a complex and expensive centralized infrastructure. Peer-to-peer networks became an overnight sensation years ago through a service called Napster that distributed digital music illegally. Skype has found a way to use this resource to provide value to its users.[14]

As the popularity of VoIP grows, governments are becoming more interested in regulating it as they do traditional telephone services. In the United States, the Federal Communications Commission requires compliance among VoIP service providers

FIGURE 7.9
VoIP Connectivity

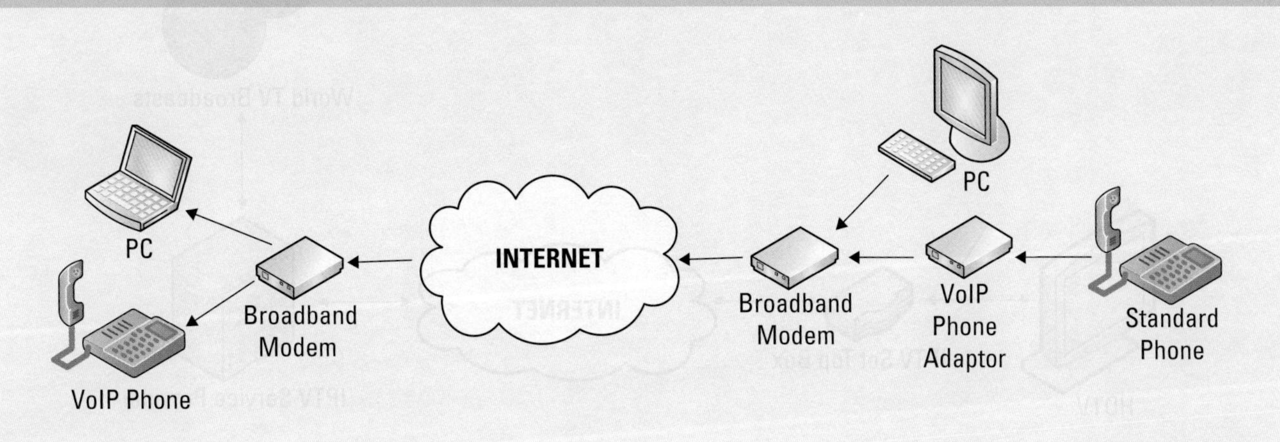

comparable to those for traditional telephone providers such as support for local number portability, services for the disabled, and law enforcement for surveillance, along with regulatory and other fees.

An exciting and new convergence is occurring in the area of television with ***Internet Protocol TV (IPTV),*** which distributes digital video content using IP across the Internet and private IP networks. Comcast provides an example of a private IP network that also acts as a cable TV provider. Traditional television sends all program signals simultaneously to the television, allowing the user to select the program by selecting a channel. With IPTV, the user selects a channel and the service provider sends only that single program to the television. Like cable TV, IPTV uses a box that acts like a modem to send and receive the content (see Figure 7.10). A few IPTV features include:

- **Support of multiple devices:** PCs and televisions can access IPTV services.
- **Interactivity with users:** Interactive applications and programs are supported by IPTV's two-way communication path.
- **Low bandwidth:** IPTV conserves bandwidth because the provider sends only a single channel.
- **Personalization:** Users can choose not only what they want to watch, but also when they want to watch it.[15]

LO 7.2: Identify the benefits of a connected world.

BENEFITS OF A CONNECTED WORLD

Before networks, transferring data between computers was time-consuming and labor-intensive. People had to physically copy data from machine to machine using a disk. Networks offer many advantages for a business including:

- Sharing resources
- Providing opportunities
- Reducing travel

Sharing Resources

Resource sharing makes all applications, equipment (such as a high-volume printer), and data available to anyone on the network, without regard to the physical location of the resource or the user. Sharing physical resources also supports a sustainable MIS infrastructure, allowing companies to be agile, efficient, and responsible at the same time. Cloud computing (see Chapter 5) and virtualization consolidate information as

FIGURE 7.10

IPTV Components

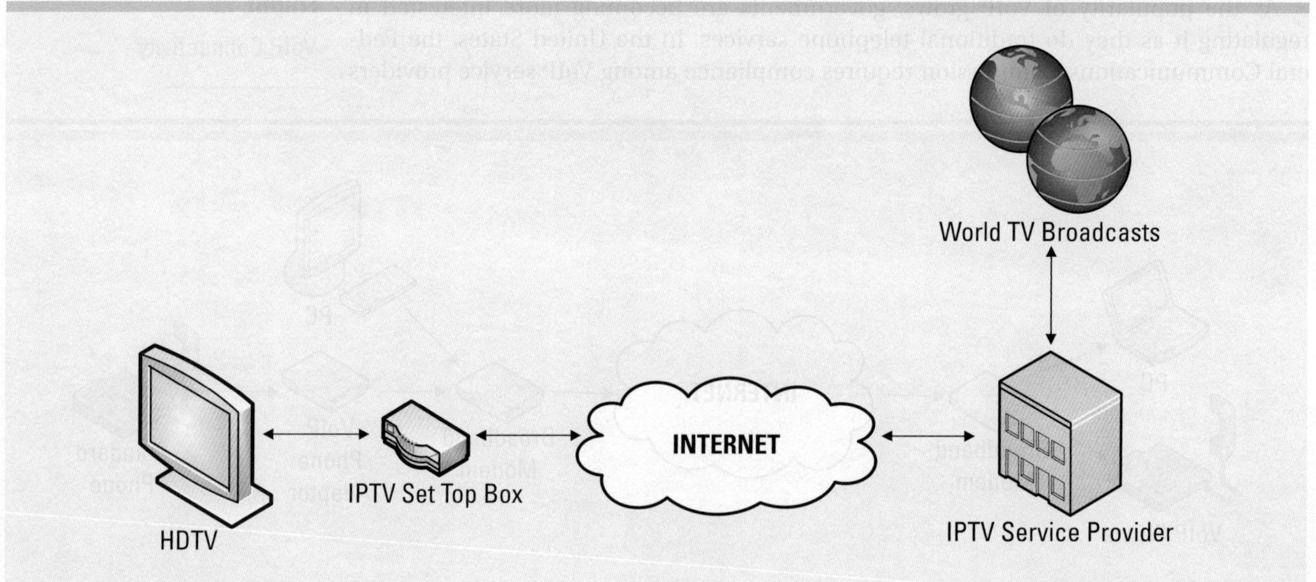

BUSINESS DRIVEN DEBATE

Google TV

As more Internet-related services move beyond delivering content just to the computer, Google wants to bring that content into the living room. In a joint venture, Google is teaming with Sony and Intel to introduce IPTV services either through new Internet accessible TVs or a new set-top box allowing consumers to search for content, browse the Web, view photo albums, and more. Google would provide the needed software, along with advertisement opportunities; Sony would manufacture the new TVs; and Intel would supply the processors that make it all happen. While consumers can already watch TV shows on their computers as well as on a TV, porting Internet content to a HDTV screen seems like the next logical step, which is the magic of IPTV.

However, this is a very crowded playing field with many firms competing for the living room space. Google is competing with the likes of VUDU, TiVo, Yahoo! Connected TV, Netflix, Roku, Rovi, DivX, Apple TV, Xbox 360, Boxee, CinemaNow, Popbox, and many others, with no clear winner, at least not at the moment.

Brainstorm the advantages and disadvantages of associated with IPTV. Do you think Google TV will be successful? Why or why not?[16]

well as systems that enhance the use of shared resources. By using shared resources, cloud computing and virtualization allow for collective computing power, storage, and software, in an on-demand basis.

Perhaps even more important than sharing physical resources is sharing data. Most companies, regardless of size, depend not just on their customer records, inventories, accounts receivable, financial statements, and tax information, but also on their ability to share these, especially with operations in remote locations. Networking with a LAN, WAN, or MAN allows employees to share data quickly and easily and to use applications such as databases and collaboration tools that rely on sharing. By sharing data, networks have made business processes more efficient. For example, as soon as an order is placed, anyone in the company who needs to view it—whether in marketing, purchasing, manufacturing, shipping, or billing—can do so.

Intranets and extranets let firms share their corporate information securely. An ***intranet*** is a restricted network that relies on Internet technologies to provide an Internet-like environment within the company for information sharing, communications, collaboration, Web publishing, and the support of business processes, as suggested in Figure 7.11. This network is protected by security measures such as passwords, encryption, and firewalls, and thus only authorized users can access it. Intranets provide a central location for all kinds of company-related information such as benefits, schedules, strategic directions, and employee directories.[17]

An ***extranet*** is an extension of an intranet that is available only to authorized outsiders, such as customers, partners, and suppliers. Having a common area where these parties can share information with employees about, for instance, order and invoice processing can be a major competitive advantage in product development, cost control, marketing, distribution, and supplier relations. Companies can establish direct private network links among themselves or create private, secure Internet access, in effect a "private tunnel" within the Internet, called a ***virtual private network (VPN).*** Figure 7.12 illustrates using a VPN to connect to a corporate server.

Extranets enable customers, suppliers, consultants, subcontractors, business prospects, and others to access selected intranet websites and other company network resources that allow the sharing of information. Consultants and contractors can facilitate the design of new products or services. Suppliers can ensure that the raw materials

FIGURE 7.11
Intranet Uses

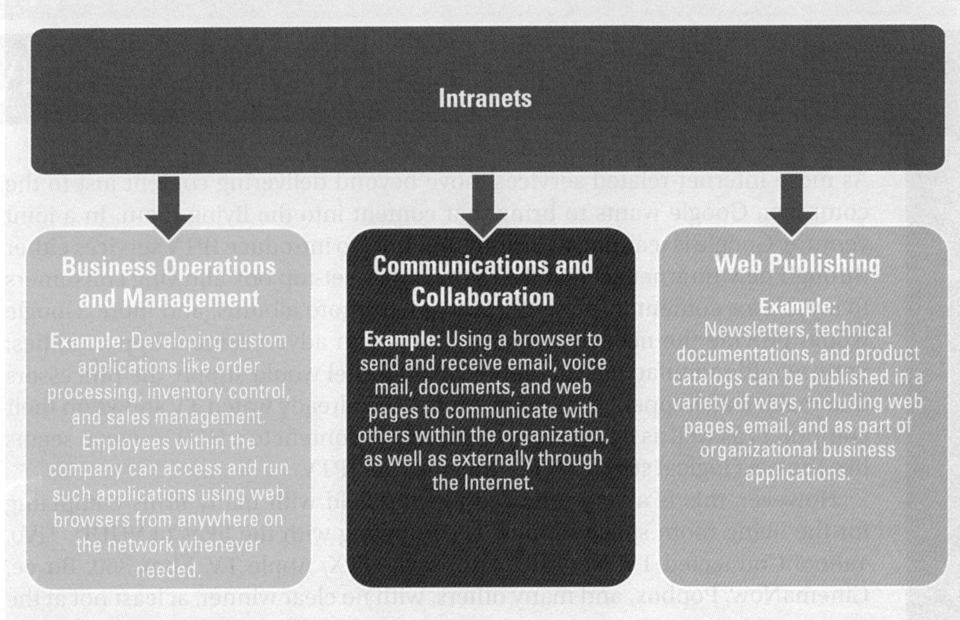

Intranets
Business Operations and Management
Example: Developing custom applications like order processing, inventory control, and sales management. Employees within the company can access and run such applications using web browsers from anywhere on the network whenever needed.
Communications and Collaboration
Example: Using a browser to send and receive email, voice mail, documents, and web pages to communicate with others within the organization, as well as externally through the Internet.
Web Publishing
Example: Newsletters, technical documentations, and product catalogs can be published in a variety of ways, including web pages, email, and as part of organizational business applications.

FIGURE 7.12
Using a VPN

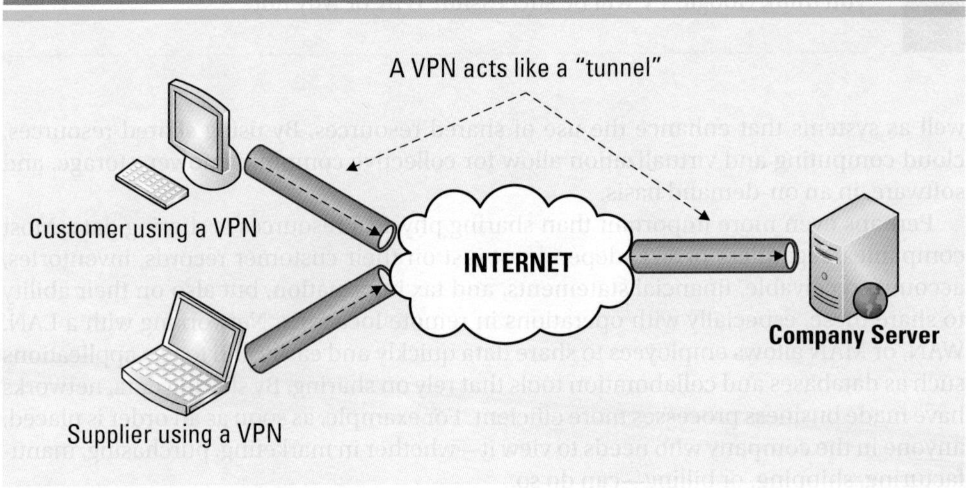

necessary for the company to function are in stock and can be delivered in a timely fashion. Customers can access ordering and payment functions and check order status. The extranet links the company to the outside world in a way that improves its operations.

Extranets provide business value in several ways. First, by relying on Web browsers they make customer and supplier access to company resources easy and fast. Second, they enable a company to customize interactive Web-enabled services for the intended audience, to build and strengthen strategic relationships with customers and suppliers. Finally, extranets can allow and improve collaboration with customers and other business partners.

Providing Opportunities

Ebusiness can enhance the opportunities of manufacturers that buy parts from a variety of suppliers. Using networks, they can order parts electronically when needed, reducing the need for large inventories and enhancing efficiency.

Networks allow companies to sell to consumers via the Internet too, offering books, clothing, airline tickets, and more. Most midsize and larger companies also have a marketing presence on the Web and provide extensive online information about their

APPLY YOUR KNOWLEDGE

BUSINESS DRIVEN STARTUP

ViVu Videoconferencing

ViVu is transforming the way people interact using videoconferencing. The company has several useful services, including VuRoom, which uses a Skype plug-in that allows remote users to collaborate with presentation and desktop sharing functionalities. The company uses a software-as-a-service (SaaS) model, allowing consumers to purchase a license to host an event of varying size. Teleconference members can participate from any platform (PC or Mac) using a Web browser without having to download any proprietary viewer or needing any special hardware. Attendees only need a regular broadband Internet connection to receive the service. VuRoom can be used for both small videoconferences and big corporate Web-based training sessions. The company's flagship service, VuCast, enables meeting organizers to create, publish, and manage large-scale, high-quality video events that can accommodate more than 10,000 participants.

What are the advantages of using videoconferencing? What are the disadvantages of using videoconferencing? Would you participate in a teleconference with 10,000 users? Why or why not? What types of events does ViVu best serve?[18]

products and services. The Internet has lowered entry barriers for start-ups and small companies, which can now immediately tap potential customers online without hiring an expensive marketing company.

Reducing Travel

Networks provide the means for videoconferencing. Using this technology, employees at distant locations can meet without spending time and money on travel, while seeing and hearing each other as if they were in the same location. Nor do all employees have to come to the office; some can telecommute using Internet connections for both data and voice and, thanks to intranets and extranets, maintain the same access to information as they do at work. Telecommuting has been greatly enhanced by VPNs, videoconferencing, and VoIP.

CHALLENGES OF A CONNECTED WORLD

LO 7.3: Identify the challenges of a connected world.

Networks have created a diverse, yet globally connected world. By eliminating time and distance, networks make it possible to communicate in ways not previously imaginable. Even though networks provide many business advantages, they also create increased challenges in (1) security and (2) social, ethical, and political issues.

Security

Networks are a tempting target for mischief and fraud. A company first has to ensure proper identification of users and authorization of network access. Outside suppliers might be allowed to access production plans via the company's extranet, for example, but they must not be able to see other information such as financial records. The company should also preserve the integrity of its data; only qualified users should be allowed to change and update data, and only well-specified data. Security problems intensify on the Internet where companies need to guard against fraud, invalid purchases, and misappropriation of credit card information.

Two methods for encrypting network traffic on the Web are secure sockets layer and secure hypertext transfer protocol. ***Secure sockets layer (SSL)*** is a standard security technology for establishing an encrypted link between a Web server and a browser, ensuring that all data passed between them remain private. Millions of websites use SSL to protect their online transactions with their customers.

To create an SSL connection, a Web server requires an ***SSL Certificate,*** an electronic document that confirms the identity of a website or server and verifies that a public key belongs to a trustworthy individual or company. (Public key is described in Chapter 4.) Typically, an SSL Certificate will contain a domain name, the company name and address, and the expiration date of the certificate and other details. Verisign is the leading Internet Certification Authority that issues SSL Certificates. When a browser connects to a secure site, it retrieves the site's SSL Certificate, makes sure it has not expired, and confirms a Certification Authority has issued it. If the certificate fails on any one of these validation measures, the browser will display a warning to the end user that the site is not secure. If a website is using SSL, a lock icon appears in the lower right-hand corner of the user's Web browser.

Secure hypertext transfer protocol (SHTTP or ***HTTPS)*** is a combination of HTTP and SSL to provide encryption and secure identification of an Internet server. HTTPS protects against interception of communications, transferring credit card information safely and securely with special encryption techniques. When a user enters a Web address using *https://* the browser will encrypt the message. However, the server receiving the message must be configured to receive HTTPS messages.

In summary, each company needs to create a network security policy that specifies aspects of data integrity availability and confidentiality or privacy as well as accountability and authorization. With a variety of security methods, such as SSL and SHTTP, a company can protect its most important asset, its data.

Social, Ethical, and Political Issues

Only a small fraction of the world's population has access to the Internet, and some people who have had access in the past have lost it due to changes in their circumstances such as unemployment or poverty. Providing network access to those who want or need it helps to level the playing field and removes the ***digital divide,*** a worldwide gap giving advantage to those with access to technology. Some organizations are trying to bridge the divide such as the Boston Digital Bridge Foundation, which concentrates on local schoolchildren and their parents, helping to make them knowledgeable about computers, programs, and the Internet. Other organizations provide inexpensive laptops and Internet access in low-income areas in developing countries.[19]

Another social issue with networking occurs with newsgroups or blogs where like-minded people can exchange messages. If the topics are technical in nature or sports related such as cycling, few issues arise. Problems can begin when social media feature topics people can be sensitive about, such as politics, religion, or sex, or when someone posts an offensive message to someone else. Different countries have different and even conflicting laws about Internet use, but because the Internet knows no physical boundaries, communication is hard to regulate, even if anyone could. Some people believe network operators should be responsible for the content they carry, just as newspapers and magazines are. Operators, however, feel that like the post office or phone companies, they cannot be expected to police what users say. If they censored messages, how would they avoid violating users' rights to free speech?

Many employers read and censor employee emails and limit employee access to distracting entertainment such as YouTube and social networks such as Facebook. Spending company time "playing" is not a good use of resources, they believe.

Social issues can even affect the government and its use of networks to snoop on citizens. The FBI has installed a system at many ISPs to scan all incoming and outgoing email for nuggets of interest. The system was originally called Carnivore but bad publicity caused it to be renamed DCS1000. While the name is much more generic, its goal is the same—locate information on illegal activities by spying on millions of people. A common conception associated with networking technologies is "Big Brother is watching!" People are wary of how much information is available on the Internet and how easily it can fall into the wrong hands.[20]

section 7.2 MOBILITY: THE BUSINESS VALUE OF A WIRELESS WORLD

LEARNING OUTCOMES

7.4 Explain the different wireless network categories.

7.5 Explain the different wireless network business applications.

7.6 Identify the benefits of business mobility.

7.7 Identify the challenges of business mobility.

WIRELESS NETWORK CATEGORIES

LO 7.4: Explain the different wireless network categories.

As far back as 1896, Italian inventor Guglielmo Marconi demonstrated a wireless telegraph, and in 1927, the first radiotelephone system began operating between the United States and Great Britain. Automobile-based mobile telephones were offered in 1947. In 1964, the first communications satellite, Telstar, was launched, and soon after, satellite-relayed telephone service and television broadcasts became available. Wireless networks have exploded since then, and newer technologies are now maturing that allow companies and home users alike to take advantage of both wired and wireless networks.[21]

Before delving into a discussion of wireless networks, we should distinguish between mobile and wireless, terms that are often use synonymously but actually have different meanings. *Mobile* means the technology can travel with the user, for instance, users can download software, email messages, and Web pages onto a laptop or other mobile device for portable reading or reference. Information collected while on the road can be synchronized with a PC or company server. *Wireless,* on the other hand, refers to any type of operation accomplished without the use of a hard-wired connection. There are many environments in which the network devices are wireless but not mobile, such as wireless home or office networks with stationary PCs and printers. Some forms of mobility do not require a wireless connection; for instance, a worker can use a wired laptop at home, shut down the laptop, drive to work, and attach the laptop to the company's wired network.

In many networked environments today, users are both wireless and mobile; for example, a mobile user commuting to work on a train can maintain a VoIP call and multiple TCP/IP connections at the same time. Figure 7.13 categorizes wireless networks by type.

Personal Area Networks

In addition to the three network types described in the previous section (LANs, WANs, and MANs), wireless networking includes ***personal area networks (PAN)*** that provide communication over a short distance that is intended for use with devices that are owned

FIGURE 7.13
Wireless Communication Network Categories

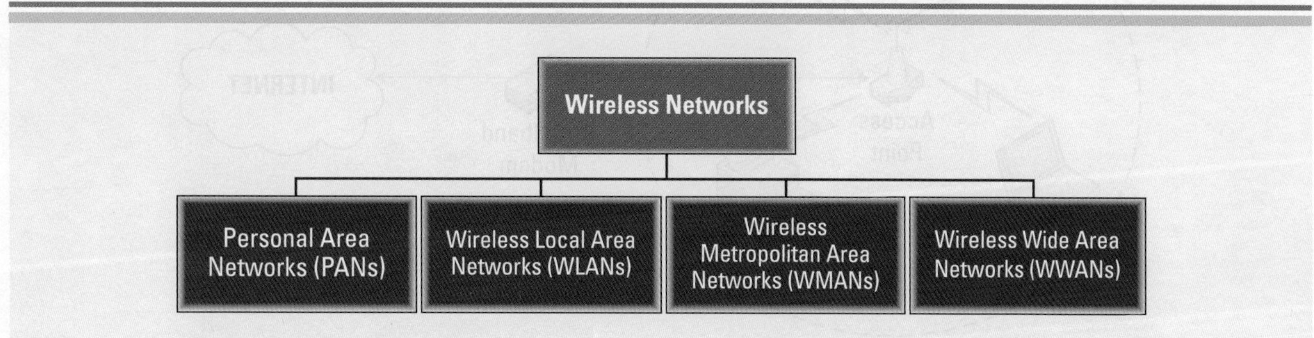

and operated by a single user. For example, a PAN can provide communication between a wireless headset and a cell phone or between a computer and a wireless mouse or keyboard. ***Bluetooth*** is a wireless PAN technology that transmits signals over short distances among cell phones, computers, and other devices. It eliminates the need for wires, docking stations or cradles, and all the special attachments that typically accompany personal computing devices. Bluetooth operates at speeds up to 1 Mbps within a range of 33 feet or less. Devices that are Bluetooth-enabled communicate directly with each other in pairs, like a handshake. Up to eight can be paired simultaneously. And Bluetooth is not just for technology devices. An array of Bluetooth-equipped appliances, such as a television set, a stove, and a thermostat, can be controlled from a cell phone—all from a remote location.[22]

Wireless LANs

Wireless LANs are everywhere in the workplace, home, educational institutions, cafés, and airports and are one of the most important access network technologies in the Internet today. A ***wireless LAN (WLAN)*** is a local area network that uses radio signals to transmit and receive data over distances of a few hundred feet. Most WLANs use an infrastructure in which a wireless device, often a laptop, communicates through an access point or base station by means of, for instance, wireless fidelity. ***Wireless fidelity (Wi-Fi)*** is a means by which portable devices can connect wirelessly to a local area network, using access points that send and receive data via radio waves. Wi-Fi has a maximum range of about 1,000 feet in open areas such as a city park and 250 to 400 feet in closed areas such as an office building. Areas around access points where users can connect to the Internet are often called *hotspots.* By positioning hotspots at strategic locations throughout a building, campus, or city, network administrators can keep Wi-Fi users continuously connected to a network or the Internet, no matter where they roam on the premises.[23]

In a Wi-Fi network, the user's laptop or other Wi-Fi-enabled device has a wireless adapter that translates data into a radio signal and transmits it to the wireless access point. The wireless access point, which consists of a transmitter with an antenna that is often built into the hardware, receives the signal and decodes it. The access point then sends the information to the Internet over a wired broadband connection, as illustrated in Figure 7.14. When receiving data, the wireless access point takes the information from the Internet, translates it into a radio signal, and sends it to the computer's wireless adapter. If too many people try to use the Wi-Fi network at one time, they can experience interference or dropped connections. Most laptop computers come with built-in wireless transmitters and software to enable computers to automatically discover the existence of a Wi-Fi network.[24]

FIGURE 7.14
Wi-Fi Network

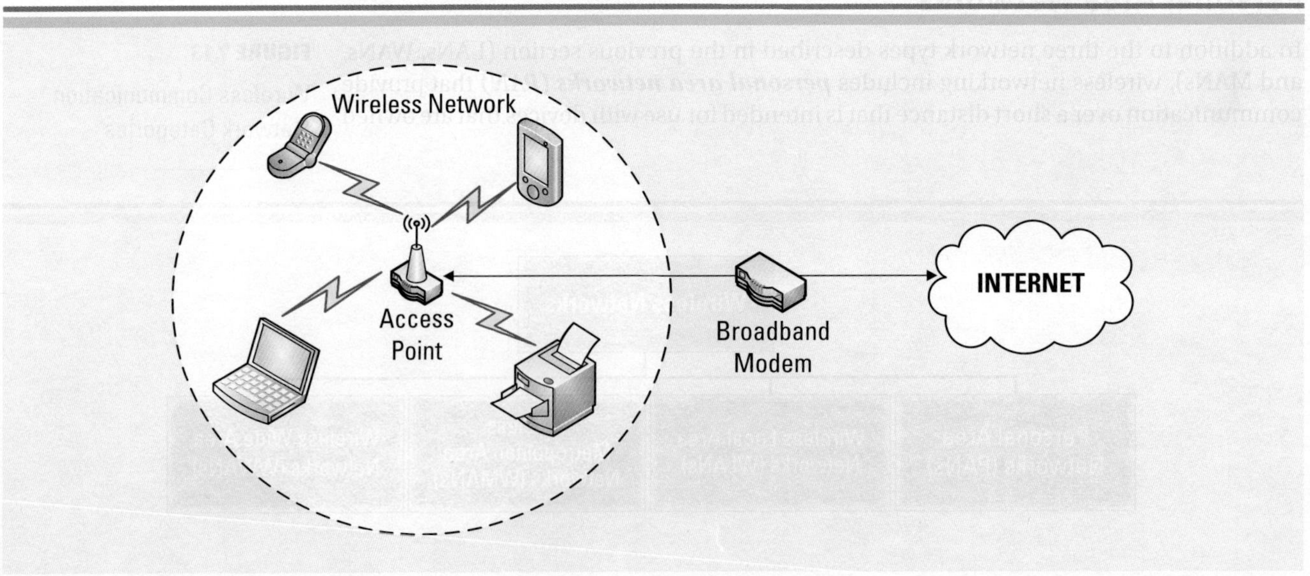

APPLY YOUR KNOWLEDGE

BUSINESS DRIVEN MIS

Cars Hacked

Who would have thought that a car could be hacked? But that is exactly what happened in Austin, Texas. About a hundred cars were broken into, not by the usual method of either picking the lock or smashing a window but instead via a Wi-Fi connection. A local dealership, where all the cars were purchased, had installed a Wi-Fi-enabled black box under the dashboard that could disable the car and set off the horn if the owner did not make payments. However, in this case, the owners were not in arrears, but the victims of a recently laid-off employee at the dealership who was seeking revenge by going into the Web-based system to disable the cars one by one. After someone at the dealership figured out the cars had been hacked, the password that allowed authorization to the black boxes was quickly changed.

Is the black box a good idea? Do you consider this an ethical business practice? If you had bought a car with a black box, would you have it removed? How many customers do you think will consider buying another car from that dealership?[25]

Wi-Fi operates at considerably higher frequencies than cell phones use, which allows greater bandwidth. The bandwidths associated with Wi-Fi are separated according to several wireless networking standards, known as ***802.11,*** for carrying out wireless local area network communication. Figure 7.15 outlines the bandwidths associated with a few of these standards.[26]

An increasing number of digital devices, including most laptops, netbooks, tablets such as the iPad, and even some printers are incorporating Wi-Fi technology into their design. Cell phones are incorporating Wi-Fi so they can automatically switch from the cell network to a faster Wi-Fi network where available for data communications. BlackBerrys and iPhones can connect to an access point for data communications such as email and Web browsing, but not for voice unless they use the services of Skype or another VoIP.

Wireless MANs

A ***wireless MAN (WMAN)*** is a metropolitan area network that uses radio signals to transmit and receive data. WMAN technologies have not been highly successful to date, mainly because they are not widely available, at least in the United States. One with the potential for success is ***Worldwide Interoperability for Microwave Access (WiMAX),*** a communications technology aimed at providing high-speed wireless data over metropolitan area networks. In many respects, WiMAX operates like Wi-Fi, only over greater distances and with higher bandwidths. A WiMAX tower serves as an access point and can connect to the Internet or another tower. A single tower can provide up to 3,000 square miles of coverage, so only a few are needed to cover an entire city. WiMAX can support data communications at a rate of 70 Mbps. In New York City, for example, one or two WiMAX access points around the city might meet the heavy demand more cheaply

FIGURE 7.15
Wi-Fi Standards and Bandwidths

Wi-Fi Standard	Bandwidth
802.11a	54 Mbps
802.11b	11 Mbps
802.11g	54 Mbps
802.11n	140 Mbps

than hundreds of Wi-Fi access points. WiMAX can also cover remote or rural areas where cabling is limited or nonexistent, and where it is too expensive or physically difficult to install wires for the relatively few users.[27]

WiMAX can provide both line-of-sight and non-line-of-sight service. A non-line-of-sight service uses a small antenna on a mobile device that connects to a WiMAX tower less than six miles away where transmissions are disrupted by physical obstructions. This form of service is similar to Wi-Fi but has much broader coverage area and higher bandwidths. A line-of-sight option offers a fixed antenna that points at the WiMAX tower from a rooftop or pole. This option is much faster than non-line-of-sight service, and the distance between the WiMAX tower and antenna can be as great as 30 miles. Figure 7.16 illustrates the WiMAX infrastructure.[28]

Some cellular companies are evaluating WiMAX as a means of increasing bandwidth for a variety of data-intensive applications such as those used by smart phones. Sprint Nextel and Clearwire are building a nationwide WiMAX network in the United States. WiMAX-capable gaming devices, laptops, cameras, and even cell phones are being manufactured by companies including Intel, Motorola, Nokia, and Samsung.[29]

Wireless WAN—Cellular Communication System

A ***wireless WAN (WWAN)*** is a wide area network that uses radio signals to transmit and receive data. WWAN technologies can be divided into two categories: cellular communication systems and satellite communication systems.

FIGURE 7.16

WiMAX Infrastructure

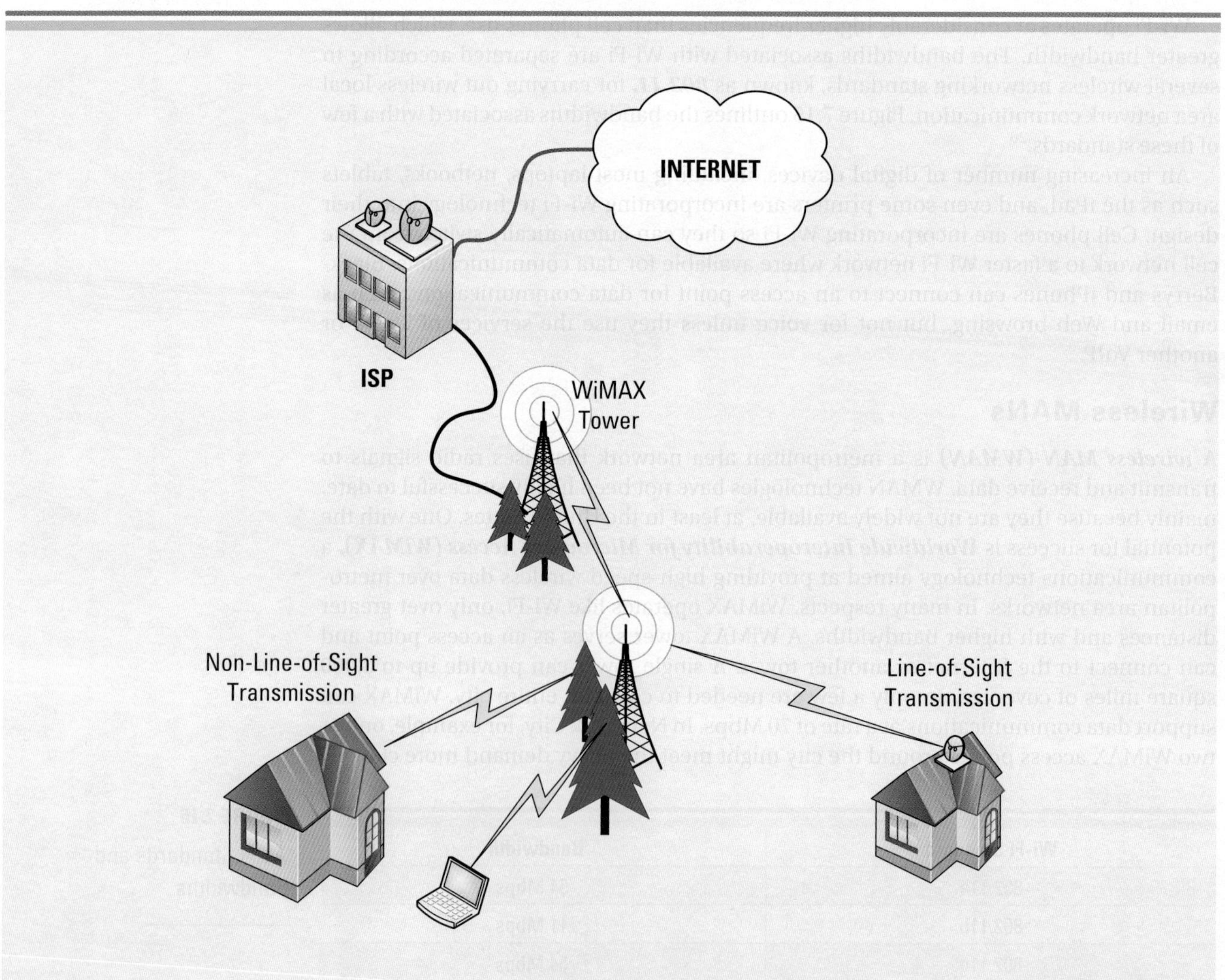

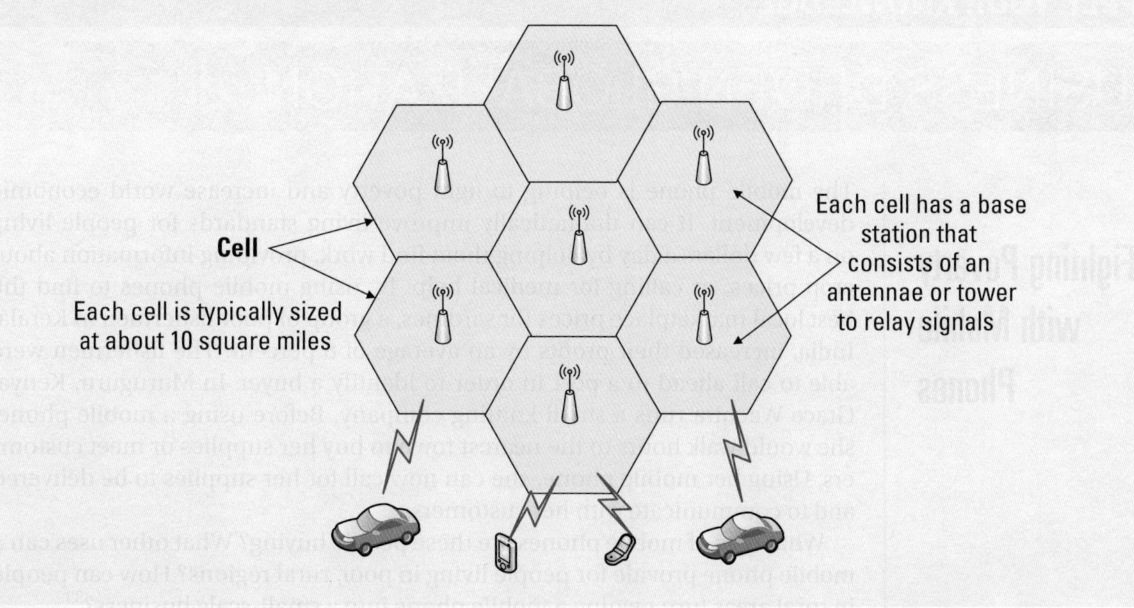
Cell
Each cell is typically sized at about 10 square miles
Each cell has a base station that consists of an antennae or tower to relay signals

FIGURE 7.17
Cell Phone Communication System Overview

Although mobile communications have been around for generations, including the walkie-talkies of the 1940s and mobile radiophones of the 1950s, it was not until 1983 that cellular telephony became available commercially. A cell phone is a device for voice and data, communicating wirelessly through a collection of stationary ground-based sites called base stations, each of which is linked to its nearest neighbor stations. Base station coverage areas are about 10 square miles and are called cells, as Figure 7.17 illustrates.[30]

The first cell phone was demonstrated in 1973 by Motorola (it weighed almost 2 pounds), but it took 10 years for the technology to become commercially available. The Motorola DynaTAC, marketed in 1983, weighed one pound and cost about $4,000. Cellular technology has come a long way since then.[31]

Cellular systems were originally designed to provide voice services to mobile customers and thus were designed to interconnect cells to the public telephone network. Increasingly, they provide data services and Internet connectivity. There are more cell phones than landline phones in many countries today, and it is no longer uncommon for cell phones to be the only phones people have.

Cell phones have morphed into ***smart phones*** that offer more advanced computing ability and connectivity than basic cell phones. They allow for Web browsing, emailing, listening to music, watching video, computing, keeping track of contacts, sending text messages, and taking and sending photos. The Apple iPhone and RIM BlackBerry are examples of smart phones.

Cell phones and smart phones, or mobile phones as they are collectively called, need a provider to offer services, much as computer users need an ISP to connect to the Internet. The most popular mobile phone providers in the United States are AT&T, Sprint, T-Mobile, and Verizon. They offer different cell phones, features, coverage areas, and services. One of the newer services is third-generation, or ***3G,*** services that bring wireless broadband to mobile phones. Figure 7.18 lists the cell phone generations. The 3G networks let users surf Web pages, enjoy streaming music, watch video-on-demand programming, download and play 3D games, and participate in social media and teleconferencing. ***Streaming*** is a method of sending audio and video files over the Internet in such a way that the user can view the file while it is being transferred. Streaming is not limited to cellular usage; all wireless and even wired networks can take advantage of this method. The most obvious advantage is speed, a direct benefit for mobile and wireless devices since they are still not as fast as their wired counterparts.[32]

APPLY YOUR KNOWLEDGE

BUSINESS DRIVEN GLOBALIZATION

Fighting Poverty with Mobile Phones

The mobile phone is helping to fight poverty and increase world economic development. It can dramatically improve living standards for people living on a few dollars a day by helping them find work, providing information about crop prices, or calling for medical help. By using mobile phones to find the best local marketplace prices for sardines, a group of poor fishermen in Kerala, India, increased their profits by an average of 8 percent. The fishermen were able to call ahead to a port in order to identify a buyer. In Muruguru, Kenya, Grace Wachira runs a small knitting company. Before using a mobile phone, she would walk hours to the nearest town to buy her supplies or meet customers. Using her mobile phone, she can now call for her supplies to be delivered and to communicate with her customers.

What type of mobile phones are these people buying? What other uses can a mobile phone provide for people living in poor, rural regions? How can people in rural areas turn owning a mobile phone into a small-scale business?[33]

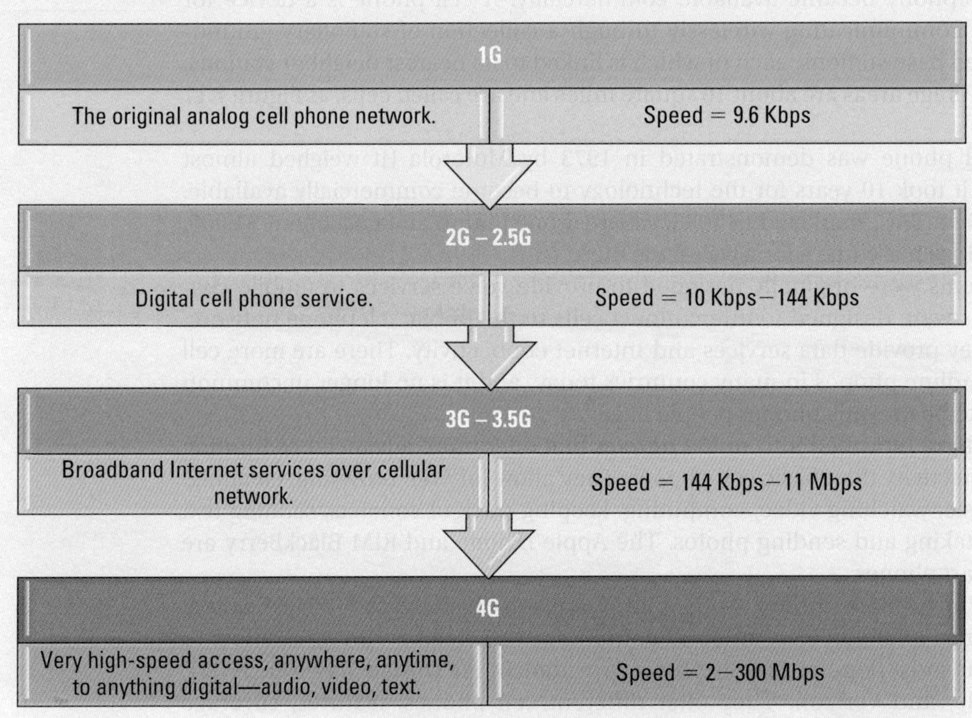

FIGURE 7.18
Cell Phone Generations

Wireless WAN—Satellite Communication System

The other wireless WAN technology is a satellite communication system. A ***satellite*** is a space station that orbits the Earth receiving and transmitting signals from Earth-based stations over a wide area. When satellite systems first came into consideration in the 1990s, the goal was to provide wireless voice and data coverage for the entire planet, without the need for mobile phones to roam between many different provider networks. But by the time satellite networks were ready for commercial use, they had already been overtaken by cellular systems.

The devices used for satellite communication range from handheld units to mobile base stations to fixed satellite dish receivers. The peak data transmission speeds range from 2.4 Kbps to 2 Mbps. For the everyday mobile professional, satellite communication may not provide a compelling benefit, but for people requiring voice and data access from remote locations or guaranteed coverage in nonremote locations, satellite technology is a viable solution.

Conventional communication satellites move in stationary orbits approximately 22,000 miles above Earth. A newer satellite medium, the low-orbit satellite, travels much closer to Earth and is able to pick up signals from weak transmitters. Low-orbit satellites also consume less power and cost less to launch than conventional satellites. With satellite networks, businesspeople almost anywhere in the world have access to full communication capabilities, including voice, videoconferencing, and Internet access. Figure 7.19 briefly illustrates the satellite communication system.[34]

BUSINESS APPLICATIONS OF WIRELESS NETWORKS

LO 7.5: Explain the different wireless network business applications.

Companies of all types and sizes have relied on wireless technology for years. Shipping and trucking companies developed some of the earliest wireless applications to help track vehicles and valuable cargo, optimize the logistics of their global operations, perfect their delivery capabilities, and reduce theft and damage. Government agencies such as the National Aeronautics and Space Administration and the Department of Defense have relied on satellite technologies for decades to track the movement of troops, weaponry, and military assets; to receive and broadcast data; and to communicate over great distances.

Wireless technologies have also aided the creation of new applications. Some build upon and improve existing capabilities. UPS, for example, is combining several types of wireless network technologies from Bluetooth to WWANs and deploying scanners and wearable data-collection terminals to automate and standardize package management and tracking across all its delivery centers. Areas experiencing tremendous growth using wireless technologies include:

- Radio-frequency identification (RFID).
- Global positioning system.
- Geographic information system.
- Location-based services.

Radio-Frequency Identification (RFID)

Radio-frequency identification (RFID) uses electronic tags and labels to identify objects wirelessly over short distances. It holds the promise of replacing existing identification technologies such as the bar code. RFID wirelessly exchanges information between a tagged object and a reader/writer. A RFID system is comprised of one or more tags, one

FIGURE 7.19

Satellite Communication System

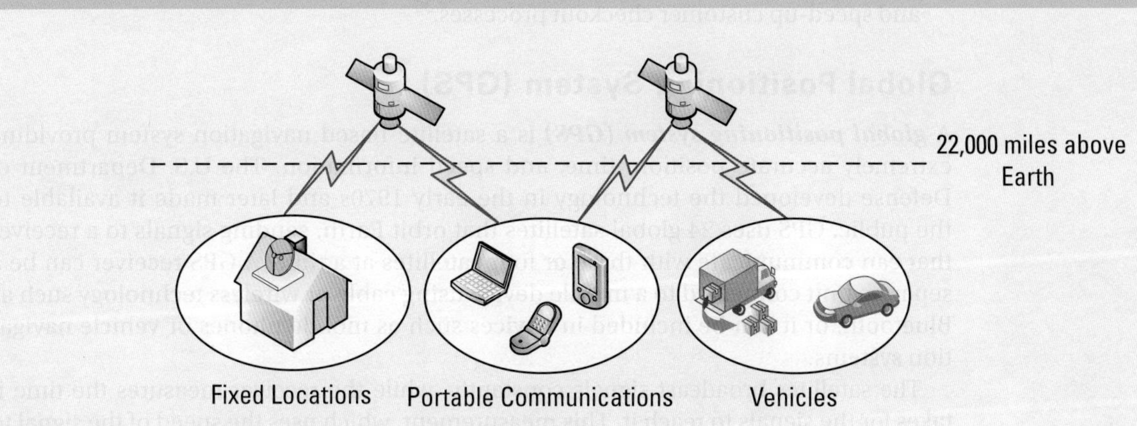

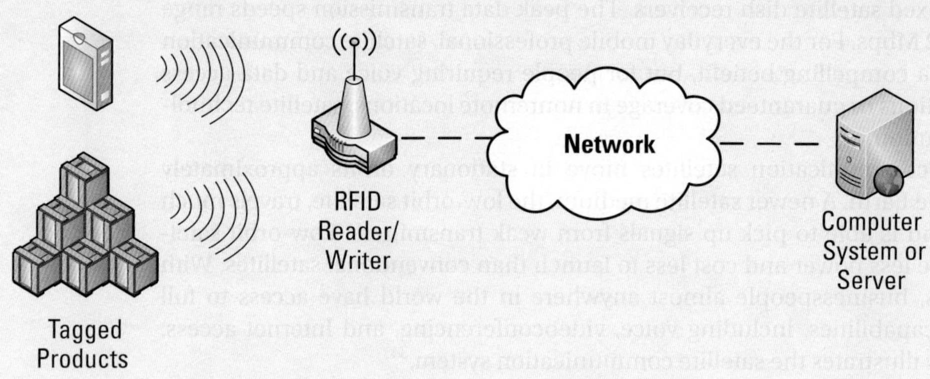

FIGURE 7.20
RFID Components

or more readers, two or more antennas (one on the tag and one on each reader), RFID application software, and a computer system or server, as Figure 7.20 illustrates. Tags, often smaller than a grain of rice, can be applied to books or clothing items as part of an adhesive bar-code label, or included in items such as ID cards or packing labels. Readers can be stand-alone devices, such as for self-checkout in a grocery store, integrated with a mobile device for portable use, or built-in as in printers. The reader sends a wireless request that is received by all tags in the area that have been programmed to listen to wireless signals. Tags receive the signal via their antennas and respond by transmitting their stored data. The tag can hold many types of data, including a product number, installation instructions, and history of activity (such as the date the item was shipped). The reader receives a signal from the tag using its antenna, interprets the information sent, and transfers the data to the associated computer system or server. Examples of the innovative uses of RFID include:

- RFID chips injected under the skin of animals using a syringe can help ranchers meet regulations, track wild animals for ecological studies, and return lost pets to their owners.
- Retail stores use RFID to track and monitor inventory. Hospitals and pharmaceutical companies meet government regulations and standards with RFID. Even local libraries are using RFID to control theft and speed up the checkout process.
- Car manufacturers install RFID antitheft systems. Toll roads use RFID to collect payments from passing cars, such as E-Pass and SunPass.
- Hospitals track patients', doctors', and nurses' locations to facilitate emergency situations and ensure safety. RFID also tracks equipment location to ensure quick response times during an emergency.
- American Express and MasterCard use RFID for automatic payments.
- Walmart and other large retailers use RFID to maintain inventory, stop shoplifting, and speed-up customer checkout processes.[35]

Global Positioning System (GPS)

A ***global positioning system (GPS)*** is a satellite-based navigation system providing extremely accurate position, time, and speed information. The U.S. Department of Defense developed the technology in the early 1970s and later made it available to the public. GPS uses 24 global satellites that orbit Earth, sending signals to a receiver that can communicate with three or four satellites at a time. A GPS receiver can be a separate unit connected to a mobile device using cable or wireless technology such as Bluetooth, or it can be included in devices such as mobile phones or vehicle navigation systems.

The satellites broadcast signals constantly, while the receiver measures the time it takes for the signals to reach it. This measurement, which uses the speed of the signal to determine the distance, is taken from three distinct satellites to provide precise location information. The time measurements depend on high-powered clocks on each satellite and must be precise, because an error of one-thousandth of a second can result in a location variation of more than 200 miles. GPS can produce very accurate results, typically within 5 to 50 feet of the actual location (military versions have higher accuracy). GPS also provides latitude, longitude, and elevation information.[36]

GPS applications are in every kind of company vehicle these days—from police cars to bulldozers, from dump trucks to mayoral limousines. Emergency response systems use GPS to track each of their vehicles and so dispatch those closest to the scene of an accident. If a vehicle is missing, its GPS locator can help locate it.

Geographic Information Systems (GIS)

GPS provides the foundation for geographic information systems. A ***geographic information system (GIS)*** consists of hardware, software, and data that provide location information for display on a multidimensional map. This information includes building locations, street layouts, and population densities. Companies that deal in transportation combine GISs with database and GPS technology. Airlines and shipping companies can plot routes with up-to-the-second information about the location of all their transport vehicles. Hospitals can locate their medical staff with GIS and sensors that pick up transmissions from ID badges. Automobiles have GPSs linked to GIS maps that display the car's location and driving directions on a dashboard screen. GM offers the OnStar system, which sends a continuous stream of information to the OnStar center about the car's exact location.

Some mobile phone providers combine GPS and GIS capabilities so they can locate users within a geographical area about the size of a tennis court to assist emergency services such as 911. Farmers can use GIS to map and analyze fields, telling them where to apply the proper amounts of seed, fertilizer, and herbicides.

A GIS can find the closest gas station or bank or determine the best way to get to a particular location. But it is also good at finding patterns, such as finding the most feasible location to hold a conference according to where the majority of a company's customers live and work. GIS can present this information in a visually effective way.

Some common GIS uses include:

- **Finding what is nearby.** Given a specific location, the GIS finds sources within a defined radius. These might be entertainment venues, medical facilities, restaurants, or gas stations. Users can also use GIS to locate vendors that sell a specific item they want and get the results as a map of the surrounding area or an address.
- **Routing information.** Once users have an idea where they want to go, GIS can provide directions to get there using either a map or step-by-step instructions. Routing information can be especially helpful when combined with search services.
- **Sending information alerts.** Users may want to be notified when information relevant to them becomes available near their location. A commuter might want to know that a section of the highway has traffic congestion, or a shopper might want to be notified when a favorite store is having a sale on a certain item.
- **Mapping densities.** GIS can map population and event densities based on a standard area unit, such as square miles, making it easy to see distributions and concentrations. Police can map crime incidents to determine where additional patrolling is required, and stores can map customer orders to identify ideal delivery routes.
- **Mapping quantities.** Users can map quantities to find out where the most or least of a feature may be. For example, someone interested in opening a specialty coffee shop can determine how many others are already in the area, and city planners can determine where to build more parks.[37]

A GIS can provide information and insight to both mobile users and people at fixed locations. Google Earth combines satellite imagery, geographic data, and Google's search capabilities to create a virtual globe that users can download to a computer or mobile device. Not only does this provide useful business benefits, but it also allows for many educational opportunities. Instead of just talking about the Grand Canyon, an instructor can use Google Earth to view that region.

Location-Based Services (LBS)

GPS and GIS both utilize ***location-based services (LBS),*** applications that use location information to provide a service. LBS is designed to give mobile users instant access to personalized local content and range from 911 applications to buddy finders ("Let me know when my friend is within 1,000 feet") to games (treasure hunts) to location-based advertising ("Visit the Starbucks on the corner and get $1.00 off a latte"). Many LBS applications complement GPS and GIS, such as:

- Emergency services
- Field service management
- Find-it services
- Mapping
- Navigation
- Tracking assets
- Traffic information
- Vehicle location
- Weather information
- Wireless advertising[38]

Just as Facebook and Twitter helped fuel the Web 2.0 revolution, applications such as Foursquare, Gowalla, and Loopt are bringing attention to LBS. Each application is a mobile phone service that helps social media users find their friends' location. Facebook and Twitter have added location-based services to complement their applications.

LO 7.6: Identify the benefits of business mobility.

BENEFITS OF BUSINESS MOBILITY

Mobile and wireless development has come a long way. Consider Dr Pepper/Seven-Up Inc., of Plano, Texas, which monitors the operation of its antenna-equipped vending machines via wireless technology. The company collects inventory, sales, and "machine-health" data and polls the machines daily; managers and salespeople can access the stored information via its intranet. Dr Pepper/Seven-Up Inc. understands the business value of the data, both for daily operations and for data-mining purposes. The information collected is helpful for deciding where to place new vending machines, such as in front of a Target store or a high-traffic supermarket. Figure 7.21 lists many of the advantages of wireless networks.[39]

Enhances Mobility

Enhancing mobility is one of the greatest advantages provided by wireless networks. It allows activities that were formerly tied to physical locations to be performed almost anywhere. Companies can bring employees, information, and computing resources to a job location instead of forcing the job to be located at the company's site. Consider how mobile phones alone have changed the way most companies operate. Executives and sales professionals can conduct business wherever they are, eliminating downtime during travel and speeding their response to customers. Mobility means more face-to-face contact with customers and business partners. Even people with internal jobs, such as custodians, floor salespeople, production supervisors, and emergency room doctors, keep moving throughout the day. Instead of returning periodically to their offices or other fixed location for information access or doing without, they can rely on wireless technology to bring that access to them, where and when they need it.

Mobility gives a company the power to place the right resources in the right place at the right time. It allows for the redistribution of operations to gain efficiencies or react to changing conditions. For example, a mobile checkout stand allows additional checkouts to be set up during holiday rushes and store sales events.

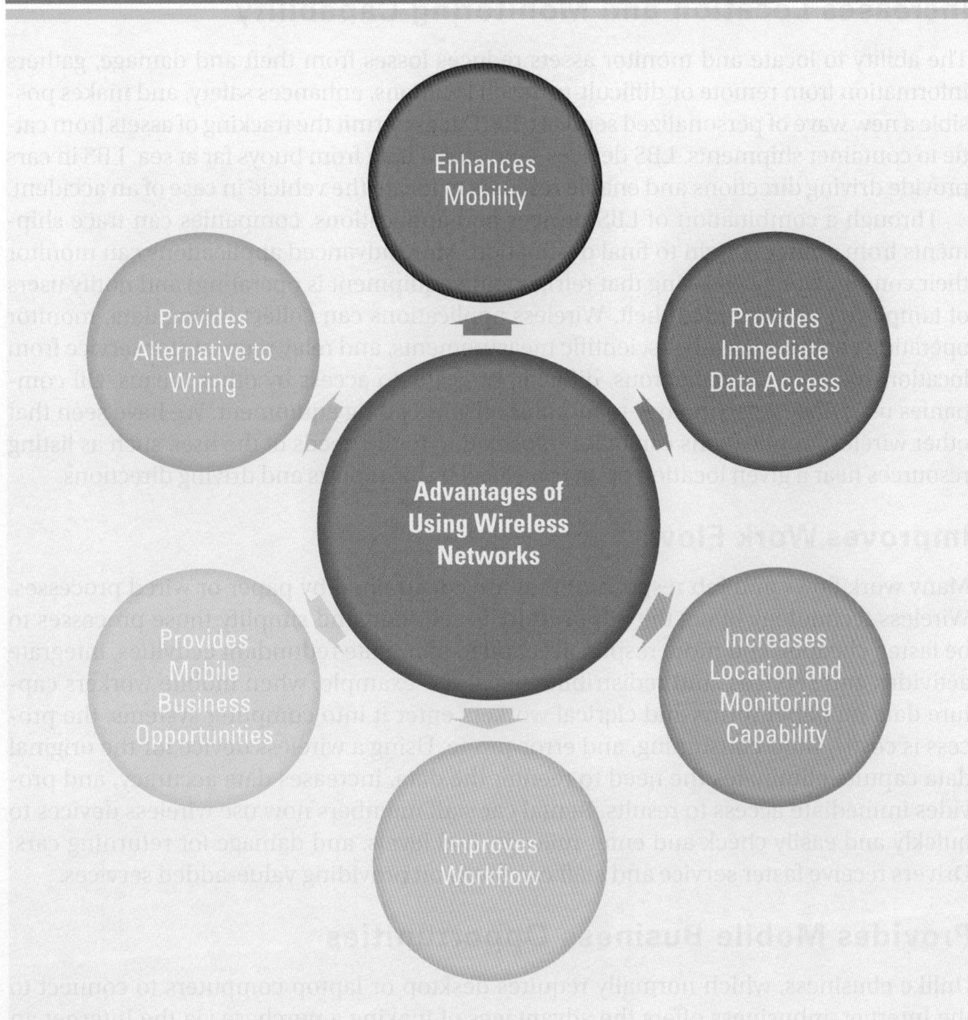

FIGURE 7.21
Advantages of Wireless Networks

Provides Immediate Data Access

Mobility allows activities to be performed where needed; however, providing immediate data access offers the value. Wireless networks can support a wide variety of immediate data access options, from collecting usage data using Wi-Fi or RFID technologies when driving past a water meter to having full Internet access on a laptop or other mobile device. A mobile worker can submit a status report or credit card scan or be notified about a new assignment. When up-to-the-second data are required, such as for stock transactions and credit card authorizations, wireless technology is the only mobile option. Employees can "pull" data by linking to the source and requesting the desired information, or "push" it by sending an alert to a user's device or automatically refreshing data.

Whether through voice, email, or text messaging, the quality and frequency of information exchange increases with wireless access. An emergency room doctor can be notified of lab test results immediately upon completion. A service worker and appropriate information can be rerouted to a higher-priority assignment. A salesperson can submit updates right after a sales call.

Instant access to customer profiles, account history, and current order status significantly improves the quality of interactions with customers, suppliers, and business partners. A salesperson can check inventories, generate quotes, take orders, and resolve problems all at the customer's site. Field workers can identify problems with online manuals and diagnostic tools. Decision making is always improved by access to accurate and current information.

Increases Location and Monitoring Capability

The ability to locate and monitor assets reduces losses from theft and damage, gathers information from remote or difficult-to-reach locations, enhances safety, and makes possible a new wave of personalized services. RFID tags permit the tracking of assets from cattle to container shipments. LBS devices send storm data from buoys far at sea. LBS in cars provide driving directions and enable rescuers to locate the vehicle in case of an accident.

Through a combination of LBS devices and applications, companies can trace shipments from point of origin to final destination. More advanced applications can monitor their condition (e.g., ensuring that refrigeration equipment is operating) and notify users of tampering or attempted theft. Wireless applications can collect billing data, monitor operating conditions, gather scientific measurements, and relay requests for service from locations that are too dangerous, difficult, or costly to access by other means. Oil companies use wireless technology to monitor offshore oil rig equipment. We have seen that other wireless applications can tailor information to the needs of the user, such as listing resources near a given location or offering local traffic reports and driving directions.

Improves Work Flow

Many work flows and job responsibilities are constrained by paper or wired processes. Wireless technology offers the opportunity to redesign and simplify those processes to be faster, cheaper, and more responsive, and to eliminate redundant activities, integrate activities and services, and redistribute tasks. For example, when mobile workers capture data on paper forms and clerical workers enter it into computer systems, the process is costly, time-consuming, and error-prone. Using a wireless device for the original data capture eliminates the need to reenter the data, increases data accuracy, and provides immediate access to results. Rental car staff members now use wireless devices to quickly and easily check and enter mileage, fuel levels, and damage for returning cars. Drivers receive faster service and staff can focus on providing value-added services.

Provides Mobile Business Opportunities

Unlike ebusiness, which normally requires desktop or laptop computers to connect to the Internet, mbusiness offers the advantages of making a purchase via the Internet an anywhere, anytime experience. It provides consumers with the ability to obtain information and order goods and services quickly and easily using a mobile device. The growing popularity of iPhones along with iPhone apps have helped fuel the growth of mbusiness.

A few mbusiness offerings include:

- **Digital purchases.** The most suitable purchase for a mobile user is for products that can be downloaded and used immediately such as music and (electronic) books.
- **Location-based services.** The ability for merchants to capture and react to a user's current location and requirements can be a powerful tool for selling products and services.
- **Mobile banking and payments.** Using a mobile device can provide access to personal bank accounts to view account history and execute transactions. In addition, a mobile device can be used for making payments, essentially acting as digital cash. For example, someone can order and pay for a Starbucks latte using a mobile device and app.
- **Mobile shopping.** Most forms of shopping may be impractical using mobile devices; however, some forms of purchases lend themselves to mbusiness. For example, having the ability to purchase movie tickets for a show playing the same evening can be quite valuable. Mobile devices can also be used for comparison shopping. Before making a purchase, a shopper in a retail store may want to first see what the current price of a product is from another vendor to ensure he is getting a good price.[40]

Provides Alternative to Wiring

Wireless networks provide an attractive alternative where physical constraints or convenience make wired solutions costly or impractical. Many office buildings already have a maze of wires in their ceilings, floors, and walls representing many generations of

APPLY YOUR KNOWLEDGE

BUSINESS DRIVEN INNOVATION

Crash Pad

Many National Football League teams use wireless devices for communicating between players and coaches, and now new devices can be used to communicate just how hard players are being hit in the head. The Chicago Bears, Dallas Cowboys, and Jacksonville Jaguars tucked Wi-Fi sensors into helmets that send data to the sidelines every time a player is hit or tackled. The sensors have been programmed to detect hard hits, triggering a warning to pull the player for further assessment.

The sensors look like marshmallows that are stuffed between the helmet's padding and the outside shell. Each sensor can measure the acceleration of a player's head during a hit, determine the direction, duration, location on the head, magnitude, and time of impact. Once a player's helmet is hit, the sensors immediately transmit the data to staff on the sideline using mobile devices to receive the information. If the data sent determine that the hit exceeds a certain threshold, a mobile device lights up, alerting staff that a player's condition needs to be assessed. The NFL's new injury-related rules state that if a player exhibits any signs of a concussion, he must leave the field for the day.

How else can wireless devices be used to prevent injury? Should all football teams, including professional, academic, and recreational, use wireless sensors in helmets? Why or why not? Should other sports such as hockey and cycling start using this technology? Why or why not?[41]

network technologies. Tracing existing wires or adding new lines becomes increasingly cumbersome and difficult. In other cases, building design or aesthetic considerations make wired networks unattractive. In manufacturing facilities or production lines with moving equipment or complex setups, wireless connections are simpler to implement and safer for workers. The higher per unit cost of a wireless solution may be more than offset by its advantages over physical lines.

WLANs allow MIS employees to relocate equipment at will, attractive for trade shows, temporary offices, and seasonal selling areas. In conference rooms, WLANs enable attendees to bring laptops or other Wi-Fi-enabled devices for Internet access.

Finally, wireless technology allows voice and data connections with ships at sea, passengers in airliners, and travelers in remote locations. In developing countries, it is a means to bypass the effort and expense of installing and maintaining telephone lines across inhospitable terrain.

CHALLENGES OF BUSINESS MOBILITY

LO 7.7: Identify the challenges of business mobility.

The mobile employee has become the norm rather than the exception, driven by lifestyle choices, productivity gains, and technology improvements. Although the advantages of using wireless networks are significant, added challenges exist such as protecting against theft, protecting wireless connections, preventing viruses on mobile devices, and addressing privacy concerns with RFID and LBS (see Figure 7.22).

Protecting Against Theft

Any mobile device is vulnerable to loss no matter how big or small it is. The company may face significant exposure from stolen IDs, passwords, encryption keys, and confidential information if the device falls into the wrong hands, especially if the theft is not discovered or reported immediately and the company does not have time to revoke access.

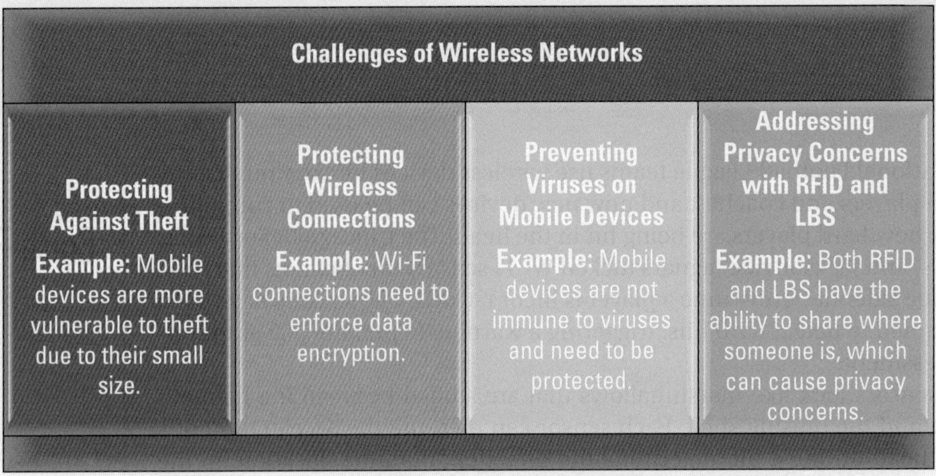

Challenges of Wireless Networks
Protecting Against Theft
Example: Mobile devices are more vulnerable to theft due to their small size.
Protecting Wireless Connections
Example: Wi-Fi connections need to enforce data encryption.
Preventing Viruses on Mobile Devices
Example: Mobile devices are not immune to viruses and need to be protected.
Addressing Privacy Concerns with RFID and LBS
Example: Both RFID and LBS have the ability to share where someone is, which can cause privacy concerns.

FIGURE 7.22
Challenges of Using Wireless Networks

Power-on passwords—passwords implemented at the hardware level that must be entered before gaining access to the computer—are the first line of defense against unauthorized use. Companies should activate these passwords before giving their workforce the devices. They should also prohibit storing passwords on devices and periodically monitor compliance with the policy. Companies need to consider encrypting and password-protecting data stored on the device, including any flash drives or other mobile storage devices. In addition, some device management tools can send messages to a device to lock it or destroy its contents, which can be an attractive security feature.

Protecting Wireless Connections

Network intrusions can occur if access codes or passwords are stored on a device that is lost or stolen. However, any time a wireless network connects to a wired one, the wireless network can serve as a conduit for a hacker to gain entry into an otherwise secure wired network. This risk is especially high if the wireless network is not sufficiently secured in its own right.

Before the emergence of the Internet, hackers generally had to be physically present within the corporate complex to gain access to a wired network. The thousands, if not millions, of access points enabled by the Internet now allow hackers to work from a distance. This threat has spawned a variety of different security techniques from firewalls to VPNs to SSL and HTTPS.

Several techniques can secure wireless networks from unauthorized access whether used separately or in combination. One method is authenticating Wi-Fi access points. Because Wi-Fi communications are broadcast, anyone within listening distance can intercept communications. Every time someone uses an unsecured website via a public Wi-Fi access point, his or her log-on name and password are sent over the open airwaves, with a high risk that someone might "eavesdrop" or capture log-on names, passwords, credit card numbers, and other vital information. WLANs that use Wi-Fi have a built-in security mechanism called ***Wi-Fi Protected Access (WPA),*** a wireless security protocol to protect Wi-Fi networks. It is an improvement on the original Wi-Fi security standard, Wired Equivalent Privacy (WEP), and provides more sophisticated data encryption and user authentication. Anyone who wants to use an access point must know the WPA encryption key to access the Wi-Fi connection.

Preventing Viruses on a Mobile Device

The potential for contracting viruses on mobile devices is becoming a reality. The need for virus protection at the device level is critical. Any device that can access the

BUSINESS DRIVEN ETHICS AND SECURITY

Geoblogging for Chimpanzees

Jane Goodall loved Tarzan and Dr. Dolittle when she was a young girl and dreamed of living in Africa among the wild chimpanzees. The Jane Goodall Institute continues Dr. Goodall's pioneering chimpanzee research that fundamentally changed the way many humans view these wild animals. Using Google Earth, you can now zoom right into the Gombe National Park in Tanzania to watch for yourself the amazing interaction among chimpanzees. New innovative blogs such as Google Earth's geoblog allows users to simply click on an entry, which causes the globe image to spin toward eastern Africa and then slowly zooms in on the park, allowing users to view satellite images of the animals. The Jane Goodall Institute was the first to create such a Google geoblog.

Now just imagine what you could do with Google Earth if you added GPS. What other types of research could be accomplished using GPS? How could other nonprofits use geoblogs and GPS to help their cause? How could a business user Google Earth and GPS to create a competitive advantage? Are there any ethical or security concerns with this type of geoblog?[42]

Internet or receive email is at risk of catching a virus and passing it on to other devices. Because of the memory limitations of most mobile devices, antivirus software has typically been hosted on a PC or laptop, with the mobile device physically connecting to a PC or laptop to perform virus scanning. The first known mobile phone virus, named Cabir, appeared several years ago and infected only a small number of Bluetooth-enabled phones that carried out no malicious action; the virus was created by a group of malware developers to prove it could be done. The developers sent Cabir to antivirus researchers, so they could begin to develop a solution to a problem that promises to get a lot worse. At present, mobile phone viruses do not do much damage, but if protective measures are not taken, they could be as devastating as their computer counterparts.[43]

The best way to protect against mobile phone viruses is the same way users protect themselves from computer viruses—never open anything that seems suspicious. Another method is to turn Bluetooth discoverable mode off. By setting the Bluetooth option to "hidden," other devices cannot detect it and send it the virus. In addition, install some type of security software on the mobile device. Many of the mobile phone manufacturers, such as Nokia and Samsung, have developed security software for their mobile phones that detect and remove a virus as well as protect it from getting certain viruses in the first place.

Addressing Privacy Concerns with RFID and LBS

As technology advances, the potential for privacy infringement does as well. RFID already has the capability to determine the distance of a tag from the reader location. It is not difficult to imagine that retailers could determine the location of individuals within the store and target specific advertisements to them based upon past purchases and shopping and behavior patterns. Many consumers would consider gathering such information intrusive enough, but the possibility that it could be sold to other retailers might lead consumers to refuse to give retailers any information.

Several steps are being taken to address these privacy concerns. For example, one proposal would require all RFID-tagged products to be clearly labeled. This would act as an alert mechanism to which items are being tracked. Another measure being considered is "Kill Codes," which would turn off all RFID tags when someone comes into contact with them. Another measure is "RSA Blocker Tags," which try to address privacy concerns while maintaining the integrity of the product. Only that store's authorized reader can track items with these tags; customers cannot be tracked outside the store in which they made a purchase.[44]

LBS can track and monitor objects much like RFID. Tracking vulnerable individuals and company assets is beneficial. But the dark side of LBS risks the invasion of privacy and security caused by indiscreet location tracking. For example, if a company is using LBS to know where each employee is on duty, it must not observe their positions when they are off duty. Advertising at random to users in a specific area may violate privacy if mobile users in the area do not want to receive these advertisements. Criminals might also take advantage of illegal location tracking. And because LBS are based on message exchange in a wireless network, there are always security risks because location information could be stolen, lost, or modified.

Security mechanisms must eliminate or minimize the potential for attacks against LBS entities and reduce exposure of the user's identity and location. One way to solve the location privacy problem is to provide strong privacy practices that counterbalance the invisible nature of location collection in the wireless world. LBS policies should specify that:

- Direct marketing purposes are permitted only with the business or service a user has a contract with.
- Electronic messages cannot hide the identity of the sender.
- Solicitation is allowed only if the user has given prior consent.
- The location service must tell the user about the type, duration, and purpose of the data they are collecting.
- The user must be given the opportunity to reject any direct marketing opportunities.[45]

For mobile service providers, an unwelcome push can lead to increased customer care cost. When a user has issues with her PC, she tries to fix it herself. However, when a user's mobile phone is not working, she usually contacts the service provider. As a result, subscribers receiving unsolicited messages through LBS would contact their mobile service providers with complaints.

With the power of a network, business professionals can share data and resources around the globe. With the power of a wireless network, business professionals can take advantage of mobility allowing them to work from anywhere, at any time, using many different devices.

Watching people work in airports, restaurants, stores, trains, planes, and automobiles is common, and soon even remote villages in Africa, South America, and Asia will have access to the Internet along with all the power that comes with wireless networking.

LEARNING OUTCOME REVIEW

Learning Outcome 7.1: Explain the five different networking elements creating a connected world.

- **Network categories:**
  Networks are categorized based on geographic span: local area networks, wide area networks, and metropolitan area networks.
- **Network providers:**
  At the top of the hierarchy are national service providers (NSPs), private companies that own and maintain the worldwide backbone that supports the Internet. Regional service providers (RSPs) offer Internet service by connecting to NSPs, but they also can connect

directly to each other. Another level down are the Internet service providers (ISPs); recall from Chapter 3 that an ISP provides access to the Internet for a monthly fee.

- **Network access technologies:**

  A modem is a device that enables a computer to transmit and receive data. Broadband is a high-speed Internet connection that is always connected. Digital subscriber line (DSL) allows high-speed digital data transmission over standard telephone lines. Internet cable connections provide Internet access using a cable television company's infrastructure and a special cable modem. A T1 line is a type of data connection able to transmit a digital signal at 1.544 Mpbs.

- **Network protocols:**

  A protocol is a standard that specifies the format of data as well as the rules to be followed during transmission. Network access technologies use a standard Internet protocol called transmission control protocol/Internet protocol (TCP/IP); it provides the technical foundation for the public Internet as well as for large numbers of private networks.

- **Network convergence:**

  Network convergence is the efficient coexistence of telephone, video, and data communication within a single network, offering convenience and flexibility not possible with separate infrastructures. Voice over IP (VoIP) uses IP technology to transmit telephone calls. Internet protocol TV (IPTV) distributes digital video content using IP across the Internet and private IP networks.

Learning Outcome 7.2: Identify the benefits of a connected world.

Before networks, transferring data between computers was time-consuming and labor-intensive. People had to physically copy data from machine to machine using a disk. Networks offer many advantages for a business including:

- Sharing resources
- Providing opportunities
- Reducing travel

Learning Outcome 7.3: Identify the challenges of a connected world.

Networks have created a diverse, yet globally connected world. By eliminating time and distance, networks make it possible to communicate in ways not previously imaginable. Even though networks provide many business advantages, they also create increased challenges in (1) security and (2) social, ethical, and political issues.

Learning Outcome 7.4: Explain the different wireless network categories.

There are four types of wireless networks—PAN, WLAN, WMAN, and WWAN. A PAN provides communication over a short distance that is intended for use with devices that are owned and operated by a single user. A WLAN is a local area network that uses radio signals to transmit and receive data over distances of a few hundred feet. A WMAN is a metropolitan area network that uses radio signals to transmit and receive data, and a WWAN is a wide area network that uses radio signals to transmit and receive data.

Learning Outcome 7.5: Explain the different wireless network business applications.

Mobile and wireless business applications and services are using satellite technologies. These technologies are GPS, GIS, and LBS. GPS is a satellite-based navigation system providing extremely accurate position, time, and speed information. GIS is location information that can be shown on a map. LBS are applications that use location information to provide a service used by both GPS and GIS.

Learning Outcome 7.6: Identify the benefits of business mobility.

A wireless network can enhance mobility, provide immediate data access, increase location and monitoring capabilities, provide mobile commerce opportunities, improve work flow, and provide an alternative to wiring.

Learning Outcome 7.7: Identify the challenges of business mobility.

There are several challenges of wireless networks including protecting against theft, protecting wireless connections, preventing viruses on mobile devices, and addressing privacy concerns with RFID and LBS.

Any mobile device is vulnerable to loss no matter how big or small it is. The company may face significant exposure from stolen IDs, passwords, encryption keys, and confidential information if the device falls into the wrong hands, especially if the theft is not discovered or reported immediately and the company does not have time to revoke access.

Network intrusions can occur if access codes or passwords are stored on a device that is lost or stolen. However, any time a wireless network connects to a wired one, the wireless network can serve as a conduit for a hacker to gain entry into an otherwise secure wired network.

The potential for contracting viruses on mobile devices is becoming a reality. The need for virus protection at the device level is critical. Any device that can access the Internet or receive email is at risk of catching a virus and passing it on to other devices.

As technology advances, the potential for privacy infringement does as well. RFID already has the capability to determine the distance of a tag from the reader location. LBS can track and monitor objects much like RFID. LBS risks the invasion of privacy and security caused by indiscreet location tracking.

OPENING CASE QUESTIONS

1. **Knowledge:** List the ways WTC is using networks to improve its competitive advantage in the professional sports broadcasting industry.
2. **Comprehension:** Describe the different types of networks WTC is using.
3. **Application:** Apply the concepts of TCP/IP to how the Ironman World Championships are broadcast from Ironmanlive.com.
4. **Analysis:** Analyze the various wireless technologies that WTC could use in promoting the Ironman World Championships.
5. **Synthesis:** Develop a use for LBS that the WTC could benefit from.
6. **Evaluate:** Assess the security dilemmas that WTC faces in using the various forms of wireless technology.

KEY TERMS

Internet Protocol TV (IPTV), 252
Intranet, 253
Local area network (LAN), 244
Location-based service (LBS), 266
Metropolitan area network (MAN), 245
Modem, 247
National service provider (NSP), 246
Network access point (NAP), 246
Network convergence, 250
Peer-to-peer (P2P), 251
Personal area network (PAN), 257
Protocol, 248
Radio-frequency identification (RFID), 263
Regional service provider (RSP), 246
Satellite, 262
Secure hypertext transfer protocol (SHTTP or HTTPS), 256
Secure sockets layer (SSL), 255
Smart phones, 261
SSL Certificate, 256
Streaming, 261
T1 line, 248
Transmission control protocol/Internet protocol (TCP/IP), 248
Unified communications (UC), 251
Virtual private network (VPN), 253
Voice over IP (VoIP), 251
Wide area network (WAN), 224
Wi-Fi protected access (WPA), 270
Wireless fidelity (Wi-Fi), 258
Wireless LAN (WLAN), 258
Wireless MAN (WMAN), 259
Wireless WAN (WWAN), 260
Worldwide Interoperability for Microwave Access (WiMAX), 259

REVIEW QUESTIONS

1. Why would a manager be concerned with bandwidth? How is bandwidth measured?
2. How have networks contributed to the digital divide?
3. What are the different levels of service providers that supply the interconnections to the Internet?
4. What are the different Internet access technologies you can use to connect to the Internet?
5. What is network convergence and why is it important to a business?
6. What is VoIP and how can it benefit a business?
7. What is the difference between an intranet and extranet?
8. How do SSL and SHTTP provide security for networks?
9. What is a personal area network?
10. How does Wi-Fi work?
11. What are GIS, GPS, and LBS? How are businesses using these applications to compete?
12. What is RFID and how could it help a large retailer track inventory?
13. What are the advantages of mobile business?
14. How does a domain name system work?
15. What is the difference between VoIP and IPTV?

CLOSING CASE ONE

Wireless Bikes

Bike-sharing programs have been a popular trend in many foreign countries for years but have just started in the United States, driven mainly by the desire to provide zero-emissions transportation for commuters and tourist in urban areas. A new Denver, Colorado, company, Denver B-cycle, offers one of the largest bike-sharing programs in the United States. The company has more than 500 bikes, all made by Trek, that are available through more than

50 bike stations, or B-stations as they are called, in the Denver metropolitan area. Each B-station is fully operated by using a variety of wireless technologies, such as RFID, GPS, and Wi-Fi, which have a number of locking docks that hold as few as 5 bikes or as many as 25. The number of bikes at each location is dependent upon the amount of use expected.

There are several methods in which a user can access a bike. One method is to use the B-station kiosk machine that allows users to unlock bikes with a credit card. This method is preferred for those who seek infrequent usage for short-term rentals. Here, the user receives a day pass that is good for a 24-hour rental. Another option is to purchase a 7-day, 30-day, or annual membership online or at the B-station kiosk for those planning to use bikes on a regular basis. Members receive an RFID-enabled card that allows them to retrieve any of the available bikes from the B-stations located around the city. Members can also download an iPhone app with the added convenience of using the device to unlock and locate bikes.

Once a user selects a bike by using the day pass, RFID-enabled membership card, or iPhone application, the transaction must be validated before the bike is unlocked. This is all done using RFID readers and Wi-Fi-enabled devices that validate the transaction with the company's main database. An RFID reader collects the ID number encoded to an RFID tag attached to the bike. The device then forwards the ID number using Wi-Fi to the company's central database, so that the system knows which particular bike to associate with which user. Once validated, the user is then alerted with a beep and a green light, indicating the selected bike is unlocked and available for use. When a user wants to return a bicycle, he or she only needs to find an empty dock at any B-station to roll the bike into the locking position. A beep and green light will signal that the bike has been securely locked, and the RFID reader records the tag ID from the bike and sends this information to the company database to complete the transaction.

In addition to having an RFID tag on each bike, embedded GPS units record the routes that a user travels. When a user returns the bike, the GPS information is uploaded to the company database, along with that bike's tag ID number. These data help Denver B-cycle understand the most common routes that its users take in addition to allowing the company to collaborate with Denver merchants to target product or service offerings to members, based on their daily routes. For example, a coffee shop might email a coupon to a user who rides by each day. The GPS units also help to protect the company in case a user does not return a bike, or a bike is stolen. B-cycle can use LBS to help find the "missing" bike.[46]

Questions

1. What advantages does a wireless network provide Denver B-cycle?
2. What challenges does a wireless network create for Denver B-cycle?
3. What information not described in the case can Denver B-cycle use with RFID and LBS data?
4. How could Denver B-cycle use other wired or wireless network technologies to gain a competitive advantage?

CLOSING CASE TWO

Google Latitude. . .Without an Attitude?

Google is at it again, creating applications that have the potential for disruption. Google Latitude is an upgrade to Google Maps, specifically developed for mobile users that allows people to track the location of friends or family using their mobile phone or PC. Latitude is integrated with a variety of other Google applications, such as Google Talk or Gmail, which allows someone to send a message to the person whom they are tracking.

Latitude can use Wi-Fi access points, cell towers, or GPS to find someone's location. And if all three are active and available, they each can be used collectively to validate location. The Latitude software is written for a location-based service that allows any mobile device with Wi-Fi, cellular, or GPS to determine its position with an accuracy of 30 to 60 feet.

Certainly, there are some real benefits to having this information, such as parents being able to easily track their children or companies knowing exactly where a delivery truck is located. Latitude is an opt-in service for those who are worried about privacy issues. Users can access a simple interface to allow only specific friends or family members to follow them. Once the opt-in agreement is activated, users can see their friends' or family members' profile pictures appear on a map using their mobile phone or PC. Latitude has many customized settings that can be changed on a person-by-person basis. For example, someone can choose to share his or her best available location or city-level location, or even hide their location.

Latitude even lets users lie about their location; for instance, if a user is in Rome, instead of having the approximate location detected and shared automatically, a manual location can be set for elsewhere—perhaps Washington, D.C.

Latitude is primarily developed for two broad classes of people: (1) a small circle of friends and family with whom users are willing to share their exact location and (2) a larger group with whom a user is happy to share city-level detail, convenient for finding out when somebody's in town, but not much more.[47]

Questions

1. What are the privacy and security issues with using Google Latitude?
2. If users can lie about the location, is this a very effective tool?
3. What are the advantages of using LBS?
4. If you wanted to use Google Latitude, what could you do to protect your privacy from someone you do not want to be able to locate you?

CRITICAL BUSINESS THINKING

1. Building Nationwide Broadband

The Federal Communications Commission is proposing a nationwide broadband plan, a sweeping initiative to provide—among other things—100 megabit-per-second Internet access to 100 million people by 2020. The FCC also proposes to deliver 1-gigabit-per-second access to places such as schools, libraries, and government buildings. "The national broadband plan is a 21st-century roadmap to spur economic growth and investment, create jobs, educate our children, protect our citizens, and engage in our democracy," said FCC Chairman Julius Genachowski.[48]

How will implementing nationwide broadband create technology jobs? Identify three new products or services you could create based on nationwide broadband. Will a nationwide broadband plan eliminate the digital divide in the United States?

2. Foursquare Cheating

Foursquare is one of the latest social networking sites that use location-based services. Users check-in to places they visit, such as a bar, restaurant, or library. The main goal in using Foursquare is to earn badges and "Mayor" titles for favorite establishments by checking in more than friends or other Foursquare users. However, users were found to be cheating, recording check-ins to places they had not been. In an effort to make it more difficult to cheat, the company introduced a new "cheater code," which uses a smart phone's GPS—where available—to validate the users' true location.[49]

Why is GPS important to Foursquare? How could individuals cheat on providing locations? Why would individuals cheat about their locations? What did Foursquare implement to halt cheating? Do you think Foursquare users will still find ways to cheat?

3. **Pandora Makes Users' Music Public**

Pandora, the online music company, lets users create personalized music stations that they can stream online, but it also makes those stations viewable to anyone on the Internet who knows someone's email address. For example, someone with the email address sergey@google.com likes a band called Rise Against. Using the email address of Steve Jobs implies he likes country music legend Willie Nelson and jazz trumpeter Chris Botti.[50]

Do you view your music selection as private or public information? How could someone use this information unethically? Do you see this as a threat for Pandora? Do you think customers will stop using the service? What can Pandora do to ensure customer privacy?

4. **Wireless Network Vulnerability**

Empty cans of Pringles could be helping malicious hackers spot wireless networks that are open to attack. Security companies have demonstrated that by using a simple Pringles can to create a homemade antenna, someone can easily identify wireless networks. Known as the "PringlesCantenna," these networks are rapidly becoming popular because they are cheap (under $10) and easy to set up.

Wireless network security is a big concern of network managers. As companies and home users have increasingly adopted wireless technology, security precautions need to be enforced. After all, the very nature of using wireless technology deliberately puts information out on the airwaves for anyone within range and equipped with an appropriate receiver (e.g., PringlesCantenna) can grab this information. This is why many wireless networks should apply authentication and encryption mechanisms to provide a trusted level of security.[51]

Create a report based on Internet research that discusses the tips, techniques, and best practices to protect against this type of amateur hacking. Include a summary on the types of detection and prevention technology available, specifically the use of firewalls and built-in wireless security mechanisms.

5. **Selecting an ISP**

You have been hired by Front Range Car Rental, a new company in Colorado, to research companies that can host its website. Because all ISPs are not created equal, you have been provided with some questions to help you identify their strengths, weaknesses, capabilities, and core competencies.

Does the ISP offer full life cycle services, including 24/7 accessibility, data storage, 24/7 customer support? What is the ISP's depth and breadth of technical expertise? What are its specialties? Does the ISP have actual customers online and if so, what results have they achieved? Can the ISP provide development expertise to customize the applications? How does the ISP handle updates? Adding product modules? Specifically, does the ISP's infrastructure deliver:

- High availability (uptime)?
- Assured data integrity?
- Scalability?
- Reliability?
- High performance?
- Security and access control?

Devolop a detailed report answering the questions presented here along with your ISP recommendation.

6. **Wireless Fitness**

   Sandifer's Fitness Club is located in central South Carolina. Rosie Sandifer has owned and operated the club for 20 years. The club has three outdoor pools, two indoor pools, 10 racquetball courts, 10 tennis courts, an indoor and outdoor track, along with a two-story exercise equipment and massage therapy building. Sandifer has hired you as a summer intern specializing in MIS. The extent of Sandifer's current technology includes a few PCs in the accounting department and two PCs with Internet access for the rest of the staff. Your first assignment is to create a report detailing networks and wireless technologies. The report should explain how the club could gain a business advantage by implementing a wireless network. If Sandifer likes your report, she will hire you as the full-time employee in charge of MIS. Be sure to include all of the different uses for wireless devices the club could implement to improve its operations.

7. **The End of the All-You-Can-Eat Wireless Data Plan**

   AT&T, along with other wireless service providers such as Verizon, are switching from an all-you-can-eat data plan to tiered pricing. The move comes as landline revenues are shrinking and mobile usage, especially on smart phones that require higher bandwidths, is greatly expanding. Subscribers who consume modest levels of data will pay slightly less every month than they do now, while heavy users will see extra fees.

   AT&T is said to be offering two new plans: one will cost $25 per month and offer 2 gigabytes of data per month, and a second plan will cost $15 per month for 200 megabytes of data. If users on the second plan go over, they will pay another $15 for 200 megabytes.[52]

   Does this make good business sense? Will these fees disappear when service providers start offering 4G or WiMAX services? How scalable do you think AT&T's network is?

8. **Could the Domain Name System Be Hacked?**

   Is it possible for someone to hack the DNS? If so, it would be a disaster! By hacking the DNS, someone could change a website's IP address, thereby redirecting someone to a fictitious or look-alike site that could collect passwords and even credit card information. This scenario really happened. A Brazilian ISP, NET Virtua, was hacked using a method called DNS *cache poisoning,* which takes advantage of a hole in DNS software that redirects users to websites they did not request. The NET Virtua users were trying to access Bradesco, a bank in Brazil, but were sent to a fraudulent website that tried to install malware and steal users' passwords. Luckily, the hack was detected before too much damage was done.[53]

   How can the DNS be protected from cache poisoning? Because every ISP maintains its own DNS, is this impossible?

9. **Shipment Routes**

   Mary Conzachi works in the logistics department for Loadstar, a large trucking company and barge operator in the Midwest. She has looked into a variety of systems to keep track of the location of trucks and barges so that the company can route shipments better and answer customer inquiries faster. Conzachi's major concern is with the trucks; the barges have commodities and take weeks to move something. She states that it is much harder to keep up with trucking. She needs to know the exact location of the truck at any given time. You have been hired to assist her in recommending a solution. What solution would you recommend? Why?

10. **Google Collected Public Wi-Fi Data. . .By Mistake**

    Google has admitted to mistakenly collecting data sent over unsecured Wi-Fi networks using its Street View cars. Google photographs homes from public streets, using a fleet of company cars. Google said it was trying to gather information about the location, strength, and configuration of Wi-Fi networks so it could improve the accuracy of location-based services such as Google Maps and driving directions. However, in the process, the cars were also collecting snippets of emails and other Internet activity from wireless networks in the homes, provided they had not been secured by passwords. Google blamed this on a programming error, temporarily halted the Street View data collection, and announced it would stop collecting all Wi-Fi data.[54] Do you believe this was a mistake by Google? If home users do not protect their wireless networks, what is to stop a neighbor from collecting the same information? Who is really at fault here?

ENTREPRENEURIAL CHALLENGE

BUILD YOUR OWN BUSINESS

Project Focus

1. In an effort to better connect with younger consumers, McDonald's restaurants in southern California are enticing customers through their mobile phones, offering mobile coupons for a free McFlurry. Under the promotion, customer's text the message "McFlurry" to a five-digit short code promotional phone line. An electronic coupon for the free dessert is then downloaded to their mobile phones; when consumers bring those phones to participating restaurants, they can redeem the coupon electronically. Mobile coupons (mcoupons) that are stored and carried in a mobile phone have higher redemption rates than paper or ecoupons because they are not forgotten, or left at home. Mcoupons can drastically reduce delivery and redemption cost, trigger impulse buys, and send offers to customers in real time that are location based. Your customers are mobile, and you want your business to take advantage of mobile technology, so you have decided to create an innovative system for mcoupons, allowing customers to capitalize on instant redemption coupons. As customers walk past your business (or within a 25-foot radius) a coupon will be pushed to their mobile device. As you prepare to deploy this new mobile marketing campaign, you need to create a detailed analysis of mcoupons, including all of the potential risks and benefits. In your analysis, be sure to discuss the types of coupons you would offer to your mobile customers along with all of the potential risks and benefits.
2. Radio-frequency identification technologies use active or passive tags in the form of chips or smart labels that can store unique identifiers and relay this information to readers. RFID tags represent the next big step forward from bar codes, and retailers are using RFID to control theft, increase efficiency, and improve demand planning. Businesses are using RFID for everything, including preventing toilets from overflowing, refilling customer's drinks, identifying human remains, and combating counterfeit drugs. Develop two new products using RFID that can help you reduce expenses, increase profits, and create a competitive advantage for your business.

APPLY YOUR KNOWLEDGE BUSINESS PROJECTS

PROJECT I GoGo Gadgets

Now that Wi-Fi and other types of high-speed wireless networks are becoming common, devices using that technology are multiplying rapidly. Wireless gadgets run the gamut from cell phones to kitchen appliances and digital cameras. Here are some of the hottest new wireless broadband gadgets.

- Samsung's $2,100 Zipel refrigerator features a touch screen with Wi-Fi to browse the Internet, stream media, take notes, and even pull up nutritional information for more than 500 different types of food. It will also show Google Calendar entries and weather reports, as well as news alerts and other articles.

- Toshiba's UX600 LED TV is a Wi-Fi-enabled HDTV that can stream content straight to its display without network cables.
- HTC EVO 4G mobile phone has the ultrafast WiMAX technology letting users surf the Web and download beyond broadband speeds with increased reliability. Users can enjoy VoD and IPTV, plus download music or electronic books all delivered on a 3.8-inch WVGA screen.
- Sony's Cybershot is a digital camera with Wi-Fi capabilities, allowing users to share their snapshots wirelessly using a built-in Web browser.[55]

Project Focus

New wireless technologies promise to make today's wireless fidelity networks seem like slow modem dial-up connections. New technologies will provide greater reach geographically of wireless networks along with new personal and business uses. Search the Internet and discover new wireless devices that entrepreneurs and established companies can use to improve their business.

- Explain how companies can use these devices to create competitive advantages, streamline production, and improve productivity.

PROJECT II WAP

Wireless Internet access is quickly gaining popularity among people seeking high-speed Internet connections when they are away from their home or office. The signal from a typical wireless access point (WAP) extends only about 300 feet in any direction, so the user must find a hotspot to be able to access the Internet while on the road. Sometimes hotspots are available for free or for a small fee. You work for a sales company, SalesTek, which has a sales force of 25 representatives and customers concentrated in Denver, Colorado; Salt Lake City, Utah; and Santa Fe, New Mexico. Your sales representatives are constantly on the road and they require 24/7 Internet access.

Project Focus

You have been asked to find hotspots for your colleagues to connect while they are on the road. It is critical that your sales force can access the Internet 24/7 to connect with customers, suppliers, and the corporate office. Create a document detailing how your mobile workforce will be able to stay connected to the Internet while traveling. Here are a few tips to get you started:

- Use websites such as www.wifinder.com and www.jiwire.com to determine which commercial hotspots would be the most appropriate for your sales force and the commercial network service that these hotspots use.
- Search the websites of two or three commercial networks that seem most appropriate to discover more about pricing and services. (Hint: T-Mobile is one example.)
- Use www.wifinder.com and www.wififreespot.com to determine how many free public hotspots are available in these cities. Are there enough for your company to rely on them or should you use a commercial Wi-Fi system. If so, which one?
- You might also research www.fon.com to see alternative methods of using home broadband connections.

PROJECT III Securing Your Home Wireless Network

Wireless networks are so ubiquitous and inexpensive that anyone can easily build one with less than $100 worth of equipment. However, wireless networks are exactly that—wireless—they do not stop at walls. Living in an apartment, dorm, or house means that your neighbors can access your network.

It is one thing to let neighbors borrow sugar or a cup of coffee, but problems occur when you allow them to borrow your wireless network. There are several good reasons for not sharing a home wireless network including:

- Slowing of Internet performance.
- Potential for others to view files on your computers and spread dangerous software such as viruses.
- Possibility for others to monitor the websites you visit, read your email and instant messages as they travel across the network, and copy your usernames and passwords.
- Availability for others to send spam or perform illegal activities with your Internet connection.

Project Focus

Securing a home wireless network makes it difficult for uninvited guests to connect through your wireless network. Create a document detailing how you can secure a home wireless network.

PROJECT IV Weather Bots

Warren Jackson designed a GPS-equipped robot when he was a graduate student at the University of Pennsylvania. The robot was created to bring weather balloons back down to Earth, allowing them to land in a predetermined location. The National Weather Service has collected most of its information using weather balloons that carry a device to measure items such as pressure, wind, and humidity. When the balloon reaches about 100,000 feet and pressure causes it to pop, the device falls and lands a substantial distance from its launch point. The weather service and researchers sometimes look for the $200 device, but of the 80,000 sent up annually, they write off many as lost.

Jackson's idea was so inventive that Penn's Weiss Tech House—a university organization that encourages students to innovate and bring their ideas to market—awarded Jackson and some fellow graduate engineering students first prize in its third annual PennVention Contest. Jackson won $5,000 and access to expert advice on prototyping, legal matters, and branding.[56]

Project Focus

GPS and GIS can be used in all sorts of devices, in many different industries, for multiple purposes. You want to compete, and win first prize, in the PennVention next year. Create a product, using a GPS or GIS, that is not currently in the market today that you will present at the next PennVention.

PROJECT V Free Wi-Fi in Africa

Covering Africa with free and low-cost Wi-Fi may not seem like a smart thing, but that is exactly what Paul English, the cofounder of travel search engine Kayak.com, plans to do. English has created a hybrid nonprofit/for-profit company, JoinAfrica, to explore the creation of two tiers of Wi-Fi access in Africa. The first tier will be free and offer basic email service (from Gmail, Yahoo!, etc.) and Web browsing (Wikipedia, BBC, etc.). The second tier will be fee-based and offer additional capabilities, including audio, video, and high-quality images.[57]

Although many countries in Africa struggle to have proper drinking water or even efficient electrical power, English and the JoinAfrica initiative believe having access to the Internet is just as important. JoinAfrica will work with for-profit telecommunication companies in Africa to first branch out with existing connections in villages, providing residents with the first-tier services, and residents can pay money to upgrade to the second tier. More bandwidth-intensive services such as streaming video and pornography will be throttled to ensure a basic level of service for all as the networks grow.

Project Focus

- List 10 ways wireless access might help remote villages in Africa.
- List 10 ways wireless access could hurt remote villages in Africa.
- What other infrastructure requirements will JoinAfrica need to implement to ensure the project's success?
- How will changes in technology over the next decade affect the JoinAfrica project?
- What types of security and ethical issues will JoinAfrica face?
- If you were given $1 million, would you invest it in JoinAfrica?

PROJECT VI Never Run with Your iPod

Jennifer Goebel was disqualified from her first-place spot in the Lakefront Marathon in Milwaukee after race officials spotted her using an iPod. A controversial 2007 rule banned portable music devices by all U.S. Track and Field participants because music could give a runner a competitive advantage and cause safety issues if the runner can't hear announcements. The officials for the Lakefront Marathon took action after viewing online photos of Goebel using her iPod; ironically, the photos were posted by Goeble herself on her own website.[58]

Project Focus

Do you agree with the USTAF's decision to disqualify Jennifer Goebel? How could an iPod give a runner a competitive advantage? With so many wireless devices entering the market, it is almost impossible to keep up with the surrounding laws. Do you think Goebel was aware of the headphone ban? In your state, what are the rules for using wireless devices while driving? Do you agree with these rules? How does a business keep up with the numerous, ever-changing rules surrounding wireless devices? What could happen to a company that fails to understand the laws surrounding wireless devices?

PROJECT VII Ding-a-Ling Took My $400!

A satellite television customer requested her service be disconnected due to poor reception. Soon after disconnecting the service, the customer noticed a direct bank withdrawal for a $430 early-termination fee from the satellite provider. To make matters worse, the unplanned charge caused hundreds of dollars in overdraft charges. To top it all off, a customer service representative apparently named Ding-A-Ling called the customer to see if she would consider reconnecting the service.[59]

Project Focus

Never give any company your checking account number or direct access to your bank account. If you want to establish a good relationship with a company, give it your credit card number. When a relationship with a supplier turns sour, the last thing you want is for that company to have direct access to your checking account.

Do you think what the satellite provider did was ethical? What could the customer do when disconnecting her service to avoid this type of issue? Can credit card companies enter your bank account and take out as much money as you owe at any time they want? Why is it important to never give a supplier direct access to your business checking account?

PROJECT VIII 911 McNuggets

Cellular technologies have changed the way we do business, and it is hard to imagine life without them. There are many wonderful advantages of using wireless technologies in business, but there are also some serious disadvantages, like the ability to make a bad decision faster.

A woman in Florida called 911 three times after a McDonald's employees told her they were out of Chicken McNuggets. The woman stated that this is an emergency and if she had known they didn't have any McNuggets, then she would not have given them any money. The woman said McDonald's offered her a McDouble, but that she didn't want one. The woman was cited on a misuse of 911 charge.[60]

Project Focus

It is so easy to pick up the phone, from anywhere, at any time, and make a bad call. How many times do you see people making calls on their cell phones from inappropriate locations? If this woman had to wait in line to use a pay phone, do you think it would have given her time to calm down and rethink her decision? With technology and the ability to communicate at our fingertips, do you agree that it is easier than ever to make a bad decision? What can you do to ensure you think before you communicate?

PROJECT IX Wireless Networks and Streetlights

Researchers at Harvard University and BBN Technologies are designing CitySense, a wireless network attached to streetlights that can report real-time data across the entire city of Cambridge, Massachusetts. The CitySense network mounts each node on a municipal streetlight, where it draws power from city electricity. Each node includes a Wi-Fi interface, weather sensors, along with download and uploading data capabilities.[61]

Project Focus

You are responsible for deploying a CitySense network around your city. What goals would you have for the system besides monitoring urban weather and pollution? What other benefits could a CitySense network provide? How could local businesses and citizens benefit from the network? What legal and ethical concerns should you understand before deploying the network? What can you do to protect your network and your city from these issues?

AYK APPLICATION PROJECTS

If you are looking for Excel projects to incorporate into your class, try any of the following after reading this chapter.

Project Number	Project Name	Project Type	Plug-In	Focus Area	Project Level	Skill Set	Page Number
9	Security Analysis	Excel	T3	Filtering Data	Intermediate	Conditional Formatting, Autofilter, Subtotal	AYK.7
10	Gathering Data	Excel	T3	Data Analysis	Intermediate	Conditional Formatting	AYK.8
11	Scanner System	Excel	T2	Strategic Analysis	Intermediate	Formulas	AYK.8
12	Competitive Pricing	Excel	T2	Profit Maximization	Intermediate	Formulas	AYK.9
13	Adequate Acquisitions	Excel	T2	Break Even Analysis	Intermediate	Formulas	AYK.9
15	Assessing the Value of Information	Excel	T3	Data Analysis	Intermediate	PivotTable	AYK.10
16	Growth, Trends, and Forecasts	Excel	T2, T3	Data Forecasting	Advanced	Average, Trend, Growth	AYK.11
18	Formatting Grades	Excel	T3	Data Analysis	Advanced	If, LookUp	AYK.12
22	Turnover Rates	Excel	T3	Data Mining	Advanced	PivotTable	AYK.15
23	Vital Information	Excel	T3	Data Mining	Advanced	PivotTable	AYK.15
24	Breaking Even	Excel	T4	Business Analysis	Advanced	Goal Seek	AYK.16
25	Profit Scenario	Excel	T4	Sales Analysis	Advanced	Scenario Manager	AYK.16

Enterprise MIS

module 3

Organizations use various types of information systems to help run their daily operations. These primarily transactional systems concentrate on the management and flow of low-level data items for basic business processes such as purchasing and order delivery. The data are often rolled up and summarized into higher-level decision support systems to help firms understand what is happening in their organizations and how best to respond. To achieve seamless and efficient handling of data and informed decision making, organizations must ensure that their enterprise systems are tightly integrated, providing an end-to-end view of operations.

This module introduces various types of enterprise information systems and their role in helping firms reach their strategic goals, including supply chain management, customer relationship management, and enterprise resource planning. Organizations that can correlate and summarize enterprisewide information are prepared to meet their strategic business goals and outperform their competitors.

This module then dives into how enterprise systems can be built to support global businesses, the challenges in that process, and how well things turn out if systems are built according to good design principles, sound management practices, and flexibility to support ever-changing business needs. Making this happen requires not only extensive planning, but also well-honed people skills.

Module 3: ENTERPRISE MIS

CHAPTER

Enterprise Applications: Business Communications

CHAPTER OUTLINE

SECTION 8.1 Enterprise Systems and Supply Chain Management	SECTION 8.2 Customer Relationship Management and Enterprise Resource Planning
■ Building a Connected Corporation through Integrations ■ Supply Chain Management ■ The Benefits of SCM ■ The Challenges of SCM ■ The Future of SCM	■ Customer Relationship Management ■ The Benefits of CRM ■ The Challenges of CRM ■ The Future of CRM ■ Enterprise Resource Planning ■ The Benefits of ERP ■ The Challenges of ERP ■ The Future of Enterprise Systems: Integrating SCM, CRM, and ERP

What's in IT for me?

This chapter introduces high-profile strategic initiatives an organization can undertake to help it gain competitive advantages and business efficiencies—supply chain management, customer relationship management, and enterprise resource planning. At the simplest level, organizations implement enterprise systems to gain efficiency in business processes, effectiveness in supply chains, and an overall understanding of customer needs and behaviors. Successful organizations recognize the competitive advantage of maintaining healthy relationships with employees, customers, suppliers, and partners. Doing so has a direct and positive effect on revenue and greatly adds to a company's profitability.

You, as a business student, must understand the critical relationship your business will have with its employees, customers, suppliers, and partners. You must also understand how to analyze your organizational data to ensure you are not just meeting but exceeding expectations. Enterprises are technologically empowered as never before to reach their goals of integrating, analyzing, and making intelligent business decisions.

opening case study

Zappos Is Passionate for Customers

Tony Hsieh's first entrepreneurial effort began at the age of 12 when he started his own custom button business. Realizing the importance of advertising, Hsieh began marketing his business to other kids through directories, and soon his profits soared to a few hundred dollars a month. Throughout his adolescence, Hsieh started several businesses, and by the time he was in college he was making money selling pizzas out of his Harvard dorm room. Another entrepreneurial student, Alfred Lin, bought pizzas from Hsieh and resold them by the slice, making a nice profit. Hsieh and Lin quickly became friends.

After Harvard, Hsieh founded LinkExchange in 1996, a company that helped small businesses exchange banner ads. A mere two years later Hsieh, sold LinkExchange to Microsoft for $265 million. Using the profits from the sale, Hsieh and Lin formed a venture capital company that invested in start-up businesses. One investment that caught their attention was Zappos, an online etailer of shoes. Both entrepreneurs viewed the $40 billion shoe market as an opportunity they could not miss, and in 2000 Hsieh took over as Zappos' CEO with Lin as his chief financial officer.

Today, Zappos is leading its market and offering an enormous selection of more than 90,000 styles of handbags, clothing, and accessories for more than 500 brands. One reason for Zappos' incredible success was Hsieh's decision to use the advertising and marketing budget for customer service, a tactic that would not have worked before the Internet. Zappos' passionate customer service strategy encourages customers to order as many sizes and styles of products as they want, ships them for free, and offers free return shipping. Zappos encourages customer communication, and its call center receives more than 5,000 calls a day with the longest call to date lasting more than four hours.

Zappos' extensive inventory is stored in a warehouse in Kentucky right next to a UPS shipping center. Only available stock is listed on the website, and orders as late as 11 p.m. are still guaranteed next-day delivery. To facilitate supplier and partner relationships, Zappos built an extranet that provides its vendors with all kinds of product information, such as items sold, times sold, price, customer, and so on. Armed with these kinds of details, suppliers can quickly change manufacturing schedules to meet demand.

Zappos Culture

Along with valuing its partners and suppliers, Zappos also places a great deal of value on its employee relationships. Zappos employees have fun, and walking through the offices you will see all kinds of things not normally seen in business environments—bottle-cap pyramids, cotton-candy machines, and bouncing balls. Building loyal employee relationships is a critical success factor at Zappos, and to facilitate this relationship the corporate headquarters are located in the same building as the call center (where most employees work) in Las Vegas. All employees receive 100 percent company-paid health insurance along with a daily free lunch.

Of course, the Zappos culture does not work for everyone, and the company pays to find the right employees through "The Offer," which extends to new employees the option of quitting and receiving payment for time worked plus an additional $1,000 bonus. Why the $1,000 bonus for quitting? Zappos management believes that is a small price to pay to find those employees who do not have the sense of commitment Zappos requires. Less than 10 percent of new hires take The Offer.

Zappos' unique culture stresses the following:

1. Delivering WOW through service.
2. Embracing and driving change.
3. Creating fun and a little weirdness.
4. Being adventurous, creative, and open-minded.
5. Pursuing growth and learning.
6. Building open and honest relationships with communication.
7. Building a positive team and family spirit.
8. Doing more with less.
9. Being passionate and determined.
10. Being humble.

Zappos' Sale to Amazon

Amazon.com purchased Zappos for $880 million in 2009. Zappos employees shared $40 million in cash and stock, and the Zappos management team remained in place. Having access to Amazon's world-class warehouses and supply chain is sure to catapult Zappos' revenues, though many wonder whether the Zappos culture will remain. It'll be interesting to watch![1]

section 8.1 SUPPLY CHAIN MANAGEMENT

LEARNING OUTCOMES

8.1. Explain integrations and the role they play in connecting a corporation.

8.2 Describe supply chain management and its role in supporting business operations.

8.3. Identify the benefits and challenges of SCM along with its future.

BUILDING A CONNECTED CORPORATION THROUGH INTEGRATIONS

LO 8.1: Explain integrations and the role they play in connecting a corporation.

Until the 1990s, each department in the United Kingdom's Ministry of Defense and Army headquarters had its own information system, and each system had its own database. Sharing information was difficult, requiring employees to manually input the same information into different systems multiple times. Often, management could not even compile the information it needed to answer questions, solve problems, and make decisions.

To combat this challenge the ministry integrated its systems, or built connections among its many databases. These connections or ***integrations*** allow separate systems to communicate directly with each other, eliminating the need for manual entry into multiple systems. Building integrations allows the sharing of information across databases along with dramatically increasing its quality. The army can now generate reports detailing its state of readiness and other essential intelligence, tasks that were nearly impossible before the integrations.

Two common methods are used for integrating databases. The first is to create forward and backward integrations that link processes (and their underlying databases) in the value chain. A ***forward integration*** takes information entered into a given system and sends it automatically to all downstream systems and processes. A ***backward integration*** takes information entered into a given system and sends it automatically to all upstream systems and processes. Figure 8.1 demonstrates how this method works across the systems or processes of sales, order entry, order fulfillment, and billing. In the order entry system, for example, an employee can update the customer's information. Via the integrations, that information is sent upstream to the sales system and downstream to the order fulfillment and billing systems. Ideally, an organization wants to build both forward and backward integrations, which provide the flexibility to create, update, and delete information in any of the systems. However, integrations are expensive and difficult to build and maintain, causing most organizations to invest in forward integrations only.

The second integration method builds a central repository for a particular type of information. Figure 8.2 provides an example of customer information integrated using

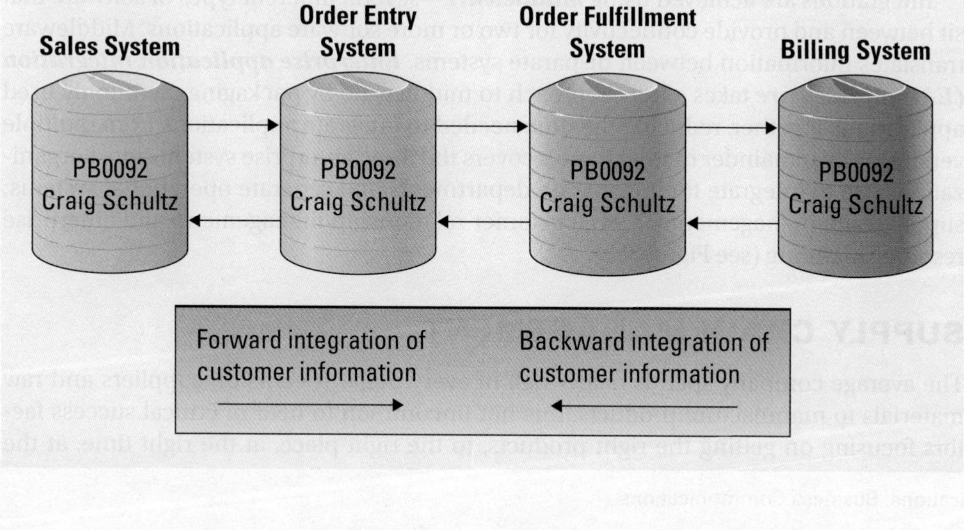

FIGURE 8.1

A Forward and Backward Customer Information Integration Example

FIGURE 8.2

Integrating Customer Information among Databases

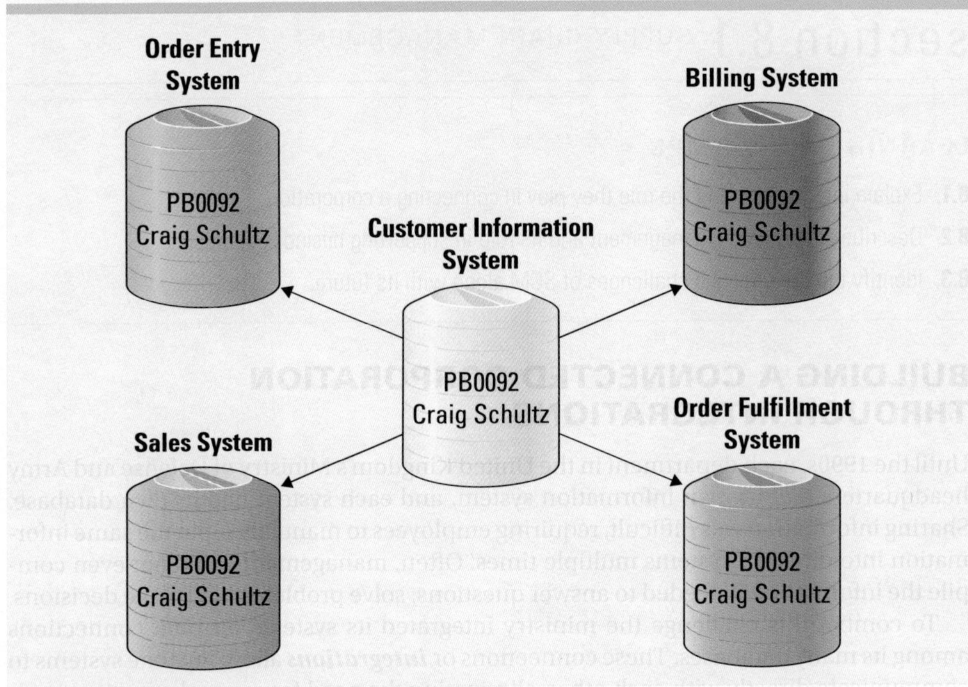

this method across four different systems in an organization. Users can create, update, and delete customer information only in the central customer database. As users perform these tasks, integrations automatically send the new and/or updated customer information to the other systems. The other systems limit users to read-only access of the customer information stored in them. Both integration methods do not entirely eliminate information redundancy, but they do ensure information consistency among multiple systems.

Integration Tools

Enterprise systems provide enterprisewide support and data access for a firm's operations and business processes. These systems can manage customer information across the enterprise, letting you view everything your customer has experienced from sales to support. Enterprise systems are often available as a generic, but highly customizable, group of programs for business functions such as accounting, manufacturing, and marketing. Generally, the development tools for customization are complex programming tools that require specialist capabilities.

Enterprise application integration (EAI) connects the plans, methods, and tools aimed at integrating separate enterprise systems. A ***legacy system*** is a current or existing system that will become the base for upgrading or integrating with a new system. EAI reviews how legacy systems fit into the new shape of the firm's business processes and devises ways to efficiently reuse what already exists while adding new systems and data.

Integrations are achieved using ***middleware***—several different types of software that sit between and provide connectivity for two or more software applications. Middleware translates information between disparate systems. ***Enterprise application integration (EAI) middleware*** takes a new approach to middleware by packaging commonly used applications together, reducing the time needed to integrate applications from multiple vendors. The remainder of this chapter covers the three enterprise systems most organizations use to integrate their disparate departments and separate operational systems: supply chain management (SCM), customer relationship management, and enterprise resource planning (see Figure 8.3).

LO 8.2: Describe supply chain management and its role in supporting business operations.

SUPPLY CHAIN MANAGEMENT

The average company spends nearly half of every dollar it earns on suppliers and raw materials to manufacture products. It is not uncommon to hear of critical success factors focusing on getting the right products, to the right place, at the right time, at the

Supply Chain Management

Customer Relationship Management

Enterprise Resource Planning

FIGURE 8.3

The Three Primary Enterprise Systems

right cost. For this reason, tools that can help a company source raw materials, manufacture products, and deliver finished goods to retailers and customers are in high demand. A ***supply chain*** consists of all parties involved, directly or indirectly, in obtaining raw materials or a product. Figure 8.4 highlights the five basic supply chain activities a company undertakes to manufacture and distribute products. To automate and enable

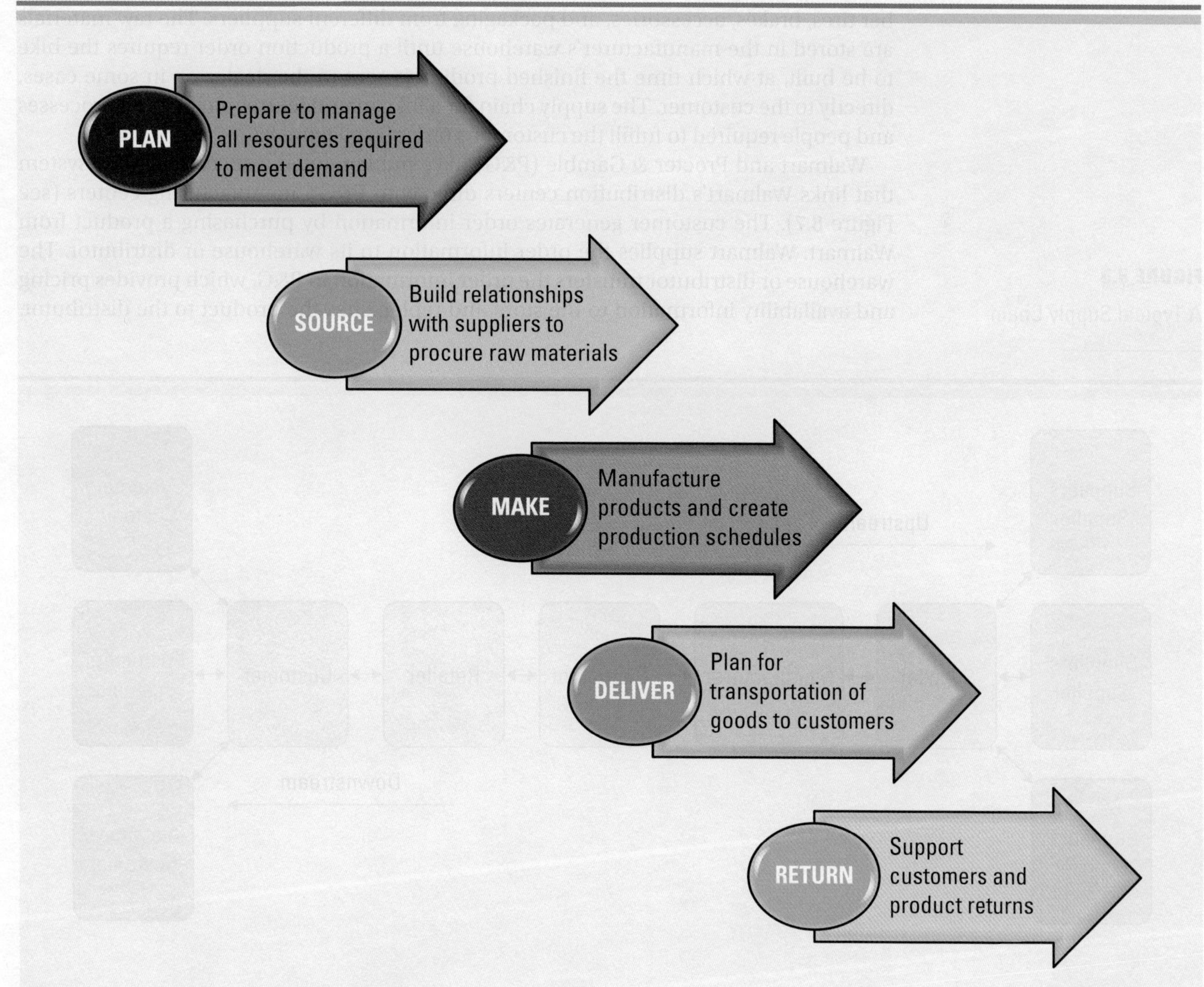
PLAN
Prepare to manage all resources required to meet demand
SOURCE
Build relationships with suppliers to procure raw materials
MAKE
Manufacture products and create production schedules
DELIVER
Plan for transportation of goods to customers
RETURN
Support customers and product returns

FIGURE 8.4

The Five Basic Supply Chain Activities

sophisticated decision making in these critical areas, companies are turning to systems that provide demand forecasting, inventory control, and information flows between suppliers and customers.

Supply chain management (SCM) is the management of information flows between and among activities in a supply chain to maximize total supply chain effectiveness and corporate profitability. In the past, manufacturing efforts focused primarily on quality improvement efforts within the company; today these efforts reach across the entire supply chain, including customers, customers' customers, suppliers, and suppliers' suppliers. Today's supply chain is an intricate network of business partners linked through communication channels and relationships. Supply chain management systems manage and enhance these relationships with the primary goal of creating a fast, efficient, and low-cost network of business relationships that take products from concept to market. SCM systems create the integrations or tight process and information linkages between all participants in the supply chain. Supply chain management performs three main business processes (see Figure 8.5):

1. Materials flow from suppliers and their upstream suppliers at all levels.
2. Materials are transformed into semifinished and finished products—the organization's own production processes.
3. Products are distributed to customers and their downstream customers at all levels.

Consider a customer purchasing a mountain bike from a dealer. Dozens of steps are required to complete this transaction from beginning to end. The customer places an order with the dealer. The dealer purchases the bike from the manufacturer. The manufacturer purchases the raw materials required to make the bike such as aluminum, rubber tires, brakes, accessories, and packaging from different suppliers. The raw materials are stored in the manufacturer's warehouse until a production order requires the bike to be built, at which time the finished product is sent to the dealer or, in some cases, directly to the customer. The supply chain for a bike manufacturer includes all processes and people required to fulfill the customer's order (see Figure 8.6).

Walmart and Procter & Gamble (P&G) have implemented a successful SCM system that links Walmart's distribution centers directly to P&G's manufacturing centers (see Figure 8.7). The customer generates order information by purchasing a product from Walmart. Walmart supplies the order information to its warehouse or distributor. The warehouse or distributor transfers the order information to P&G, which provides pricing and availability information to the store and replenishes the product to the distributor.

FIGURE 8.5

A Typical Supply Chain

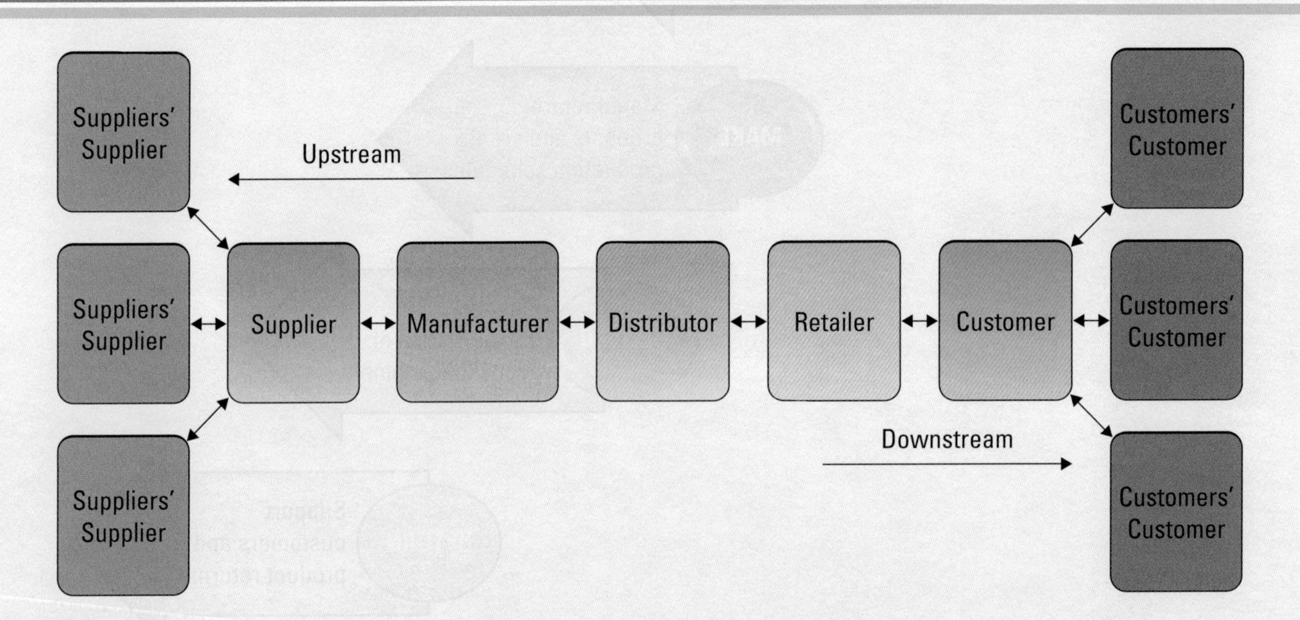

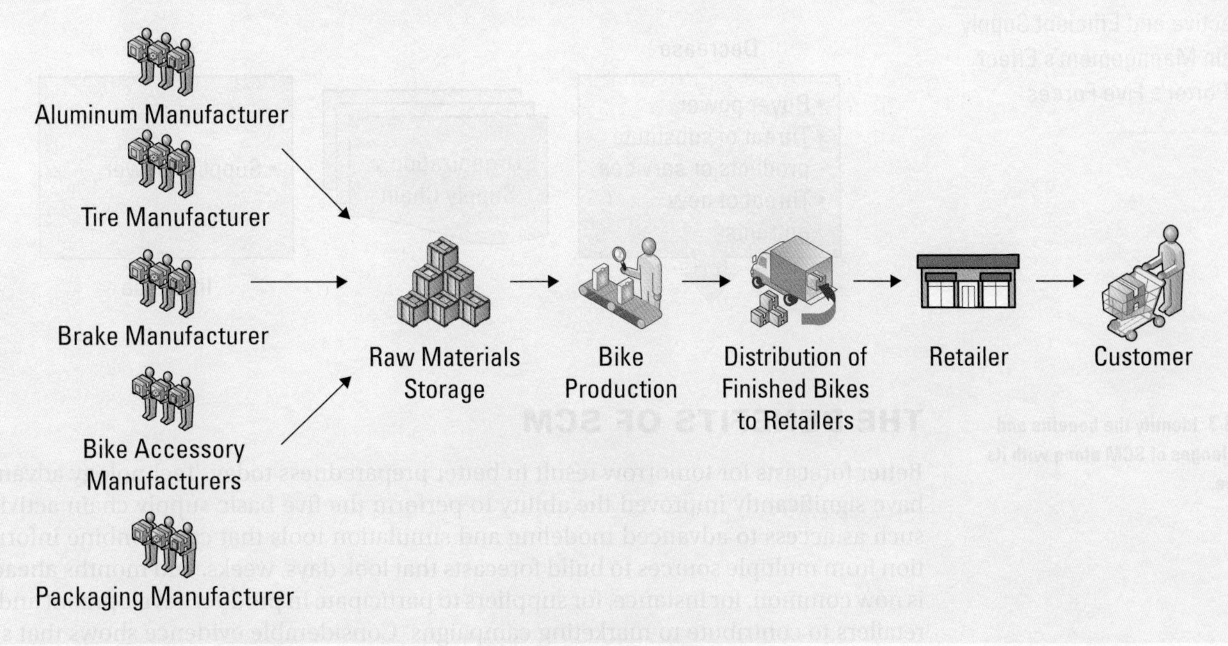

FIGURE 8.6

Supply Chain for a Bike Manufacturer

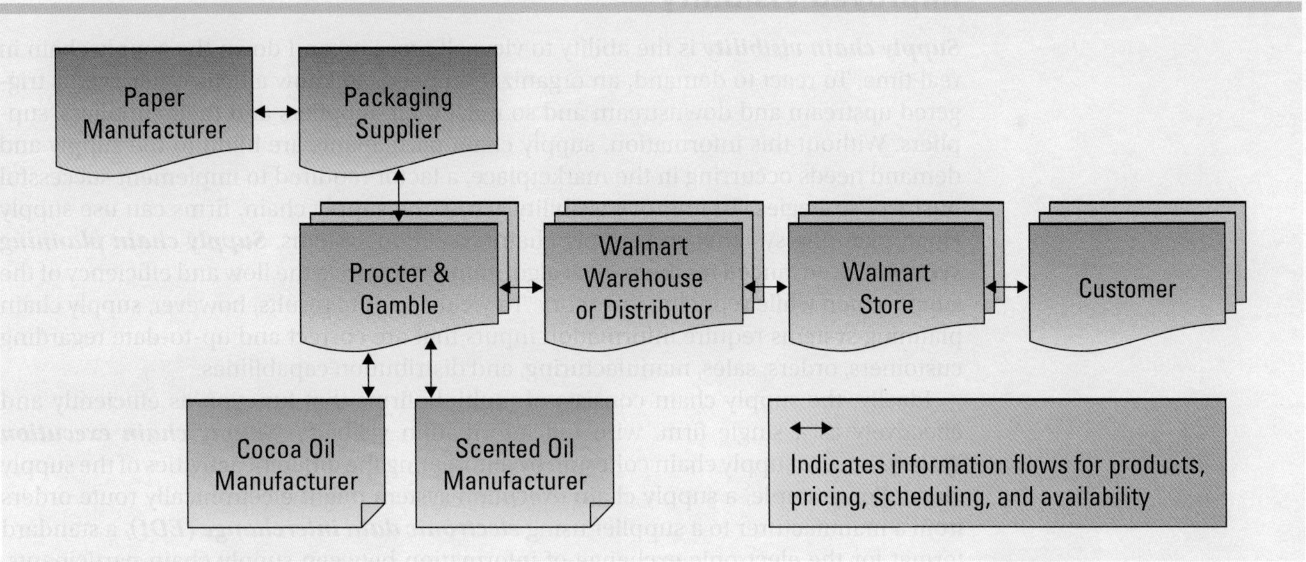

FIGURE 8.7

Supply Chain for a Product Purchased from Walmart

Payment is transferred electronically. Effective and efficient supply chain management systems can enable an organization to have these impacts on Porter's Five Forces Model[2]:

- Decrease the power of its buyers.
- Increase its supplier power.
- Increase buyers' switching costs to reduce the threat of substitute products or services.
- Create entry barriers to reduce the threat of new entrants.
- Increase efficiencies while seeking a competitive advantage through cost leadership (see Figure 8.8).

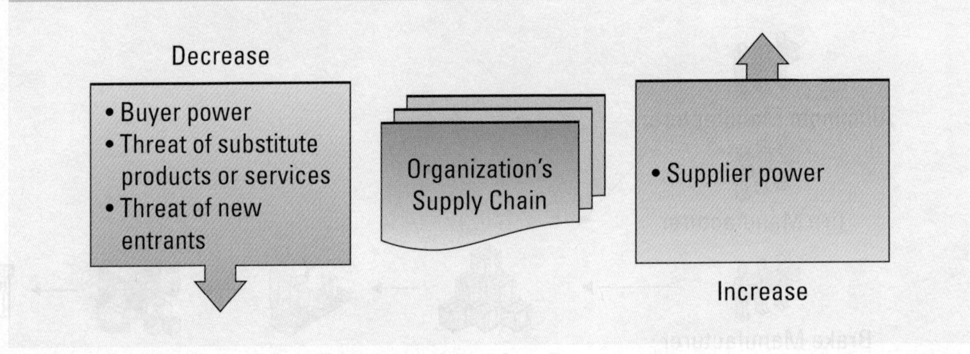

FIGURE 8.8

Effective and Efficient Supply Chain Management's Effect on Porter's Five Forces

LO 8.3: Identify the benefits and challenges of SCM along with its future.

THE BENEFITS OF SCM

Better forecasts for tomorrow result in better preparedness today. Technology advances have significantly improved the ability to perform the five basic supply chain activities such as access to advanced modeling and simulation tools that can combine information from multiple sources to build forecasts that look days, weeks, and months ahead. It is now common, for instance, for suppliers to participate in product development and for retailers to contribute to marketing campaigns. Considerable evidence shows that supply chain integration results in superior supply chain capabilities, which drives a firm's profitability. Although firms have dreamed of integrating their supply chains for a long time, it is only recently that advances in MIS have brought these dreams to life. Improved visibility across the supply chain and increased profitability for the firm are the primary business benefits received when implementing supply chain management systems.

Improved Visibility

Supply chain visibility is the ability to view all areas up and down the supply chain in real time. To react to demand, an organization needs to know all customer events triggered upstream and downstream and so must their suppliers and their suppliers' suppliers. Without this information, supply chain participants are blind to the supply and demand needs occurring in the marketplace, a factor required to implement successful business strategies. To improve visibility across the supply chain, firms can use supply chain planning systems and supply chain execution systems. ***Supply chain planning systems*** use advanced mathematical algorithms to improve the flow and efficiency of the supply chain while reducing inventory. To yield accurate results, however, supply chain planning systems require information inputs that are correct and up-to-date regarding customers, orders, sales, manufacturing, and distribution capabilities.

Ideally, the supply chain consists of multiple firms that function as efficiently and effectively as a single firm, with full information visibility. ***Supply chain execution systems*** ensure supply chain cohesion by automating the different activities of the supply chain. For example, a supply chain execution system might electronically route orders from a manufacturer to a supplier using ***electronic data interchange (EDI),*** a standard format for the electronic exchange of information between supply chain participants. Figure 8.9 details how supply chain planning and supply chain execution systems interact with the supply chain.

A good example of inventory issues that occur when a company does not have a clear vision of its entire supply chain is the bullwhip effect. The ***bullwhip effect*** occurs when distorted product-demand information ripples from one partner to the next throughout the supply chain. The misinformation regarding a slight rise in demand for a product could cause different members in the supply chain to stockpile inventory. These changes ripple throughout the supply chain, magnifying the issue and creating excess inventory and costs for all. For example, if a car dealership is having a hard time moving a particular brand of car, it might offer significant discounts to try to move the inventory. Without this critical information, the car manufacturer might see a rise in demand for this particular brand of car and increase production orders, not realizing that the dealerships are actually challenged with selling the inventory. Today, integrated supply chains provide

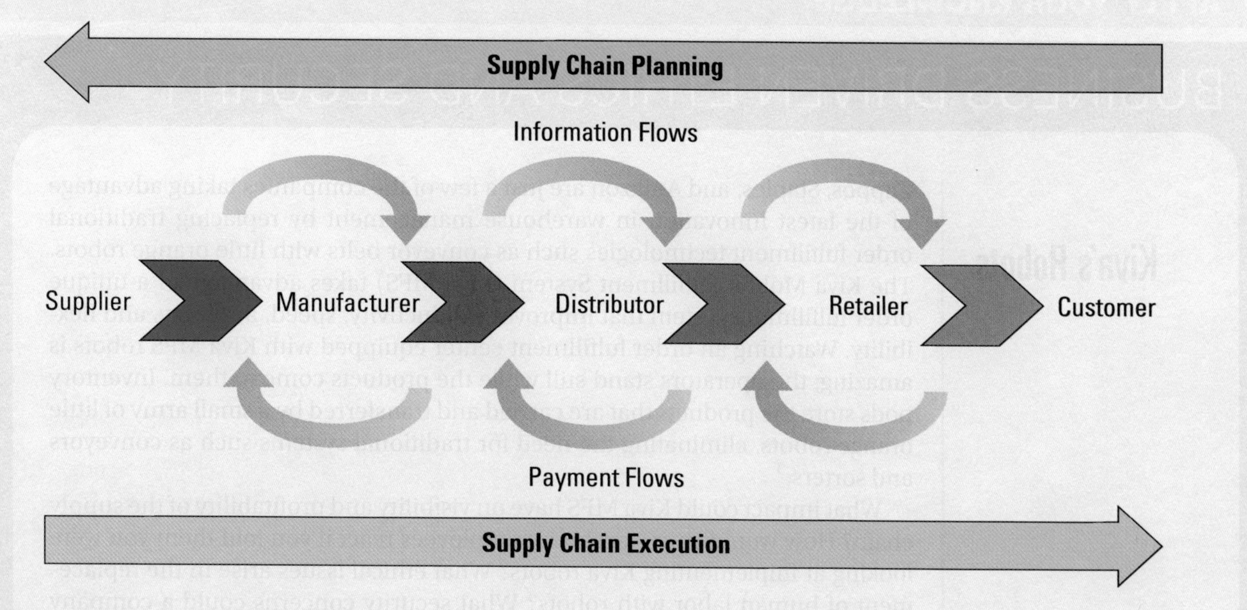

FIGURE 8.9

Supply Chain Planning's and Supply Chain Execution's Roles in the Supply Chain

managers with the visibility to see their suppliers' and customers' supply chains, ensuring that supply always meets demand.

Increased Profitability

Supply chain management systems can increase profitability across an organization. For example, a manufacturing plant manager might focus on keeping the inventory of Product A as low as possible, which will directly reduce the manufacturing costs and make the plant manager look great. However, the plant manager and the business might not realize that these savings are causing increased costs in other areas, such as having to pay more to procure raw materials for immediate production needs or increasing costs due to expedited shipping services. Only an end-to-end view or an integrated supply chain would uncover these issues, allowing a firm to adjust business strategies to increase profitability across the enterprise.

Customers are also more demanding than ever before. Because information is so readily available, they know exactly what they want, when they want it, and how they want it delivered. If your company can't meet their demand, the competition is simply a mouse-click away. Couple supply chain complexity with today's demanding customers and a firm's costs can easily escalate out of control. ***Demand planning systems*** generate demand forecasts using statistical tools and forecasting techniques, so companies can respond faster and more effectively to consumer demands through supply chain enhancements. Firms are implementing demand planning systems to understand customer demand and production capabilities so they can estimate supply chain costs that ultimately impact the firm's performance and business strategies. Innovative wireless technologies, such as radio-frequency identification (RFID), are also enabling companies to operate with improved speed and accuracy, ensuring that they can satisfy continuously changing customer demands.

A supply chain is only as strong as its weakest link. Companies use supply chain management metrics to measure the performance of supply chains to quickly identify weak links. A few of the common supply chain management metrics include:

- **Back order:** An unfilled customer order for a product that is out of stock.
- **Inventory cycle time:** The time it takes to manufacture a product and deliver it to the retailer.
- **Customer order cycle time:** The agreed upon time between the purchase of a product and the delivery of the product.
- **Inventory turnover:** The frequency of inventory replacement.

APPLY YOUR KNOWLEDGE

BUSINESS DRIVEN ETHICS AND SECURITY

Kiva's Robots

Zappos, Staples, and Amazon are just a few of the companies taking advantage of the latest innovation in warehouse management by replacing traditional order fulfillment technologies such as conveyor belts with little orange robots. The Kiva Mobile Fulfillment System (Kiva MFS) takes advantage of a unique order fulfillment system that improves productivity, speed, accuracy, and flexibility. Watching an order fulfillment center equipped with Kiva MFS robots is amazing; the operators stand still while the products come to them. Inventory pods store the products that are carried and transferred by a small army of little orange robots, eliminating the need for traditional systems such as conveyors and sorters.[3]

What impact could Kiva MFS have on visibility and profitability of the supply chain? How would your warehouse employees react if you told them you were looking at implementing Kiva robots? What ethical issues arise in the replacement of human labor with robots? What security concerns could a company face when implementing Kiva MFS robots?

THE CHALLENGES OF SCM

The primary challenges associated with supply chain management include costs and complexity. Supply chain management systems can cost millions of dollars for the software and millions of dollars more for help with the implementation. Just walk into any manufacturing plant, distribution center, or factory floor and you will witness the complexity and costs associated with supply chain management. Supply chains cross entire organizations touching multiple departments and spanning organizationwide business processes. Revamping just a single business process can be difficult for a company. Revamping all business processes that touch the supply chain is an incredibly difficult and complex task but is typically required for the SCM system to become effective. And, to top it all off, the supply chain reaches beyond the borders of the organization into partner, supplier, and customer domains, adding another layer of complexity for SCM. A lack of adequate collaboration among marketing, sales, and manufacturing within a company and suppliers, partners, and distributors outside of a company can easily sabotage SCM efforts sending the multimillion-dollar investment down the drain.

The move toward globalization is also increasing supply chain complexity. As supply chains span geographical locations, issues such as time zone differences, transportation fees, cultural and language barriers, and exchange rates all add additional layers to the already complex supply chain. Government relationships, taxes, and local laws also tend to differ across global regions, creating more confusion and issues in supplier relationships. The bottom line is that SCM systems are complex and costly and implementing them correctly can be challenging even for the most sophisticated organization.

THE FUTURE OF SCM

There is a great commercial that depicts the future of supply chain management. A man wearing a uniform is walking through a home and quietly replaces an empty cereal box with a full one just as the child opens the kitchen cabinet. He then produces a new bag of

APPLY YOUR KNOWLEDGE

BUSINESS DRIVEN DEBATE

Fixing the Post Office

Lines at the post office are frustrating, and they are also becoming unprofitable as the U.S. Postal Service faces billion-dollar losses for the first time in its history. What is causing this failure? It could be any number of things, but ebusiness competition is one of the primary challengers stealing the Postal Service's market share. Stamps.com allows you to customize and print your own stamps 24 hours a day. If you are getting married, you can place your engagement picture on the stamp for the invitations. If you are starting your own business, you can purchase stamps showing your business logo. And, Stamps.com goes beyond simply delivering a product by tracking customer spending and recommending optimal delivery methods along with postage discounts. Now that is something you can't get at the post office. Talk about a competitive advantage![4]

Why do you think the U.S. Postal Service is losing its market share and becoming unprofitable? What does the Postal Service's supply chain look like? Who are its partners, suppliers, distributors, and customers? What can the Postal Service do to revamp its supply chain so it can become profitable? Many people believe the Postal Service should not be supported by the government, and that if it can't operate efficiently it should fail. Do you agree? Why or why not?

dog food as soon as the hungry dog's bowl is empty and finally reaches into the shower to hand a new bottle of shampoo to the man in the shower who had just run out. The next wave in supply chain management will be home-based supply chain fulfillment. No more running to the store to replace your products as your store will come to you as soon as you need a new product.

Walgreens is differentiating itself from other national chains as the family's just-in-time supplier, developing custom websites for each household that allow families to order electronically and then pick up their goods at a self-service counter or drive-through window at their convenience. Walgreens even calls its customers to let them know their prescription medications are soon going to run out and offers to fulfill the new prescription.

As the supply chain management market matures, it is becoming even more sophisticated and incorporating additional functionality such as marketing, customer service, and even product development to its extended supply chain. Advanced communications tools, easy-to-use decision support systems, and building trust among participants when sharing information are all making the home-based supply chain possible. A few of the fastest-growing SCM components include:

- **Collaborative demand planning**—reduces inventory investments, while improving customer satisfaction.
- **Collaborative engineering**—reduces product development costs.
- **Selling chain management**—automates order processes from initial customer inquiry to final product delivery.
- **Supply chain event management (SCEM)**—increases real-time information sharing among supply chain partners focusing on reducing response time to unexpected events.

section 8.2 CUSTOMER RELATIONSHIP MANAGEMENT AND ENTERPRISE RESOURCE PLANNING

LEARNING OUTCOMES

8.4 Describe customer relationship management and its role in supporting business operations.

8.5. Identify the benefits and challenges of CRM along with its future.

8.6 Describe enterprise resource management and its role in supporting business operations.

8.7. Identify the benefits and challenges of ERP along with the future of the connected corporation.

LO 8.4: Describe customer relationship management and its role in supporting business operations.

CUSTOMER RELATIONSHIP MANAGEMENT

Today, most competitors are simply a mouse-click away, and this intense competition is forcing firms to switch from sales-focused business strategies to customer-focused business strategies. Customers are one of a firm's most valuable assets, and building strong loyal customer relationships is a key competitive advantage. Harley-Davidson offers an excellent example of a company that knows the value of customer loyalty, and it finds itself in the coveted position of demand outweighing its supply. No other motorcycle in the world has the look, feel, and sound of a Harley-Davidson. Demand for Harley-Davidson motorcycles outweighs supply and some models have up to a two-year waiting list. Knowing the value of its customers, Harley-Davidson started the Harley's Owners Group (HOG), which is the largest motorcycle club in the world with more than 600,000 members. HOG offers a wide array of events, rides, and benefits to its members and is a key competitive advantage as it helps to build a strong sense of community among Harley-Davidson owners. Harley-Davidson has built a customer following that is extremely loyal, a difficult task to accomplish in any industry.[5]

Customer relationship management (CRM) is a means of managing all aspects of a customer's relationship with an organization to increase customer loyalty and retention and an organization's profitability. CRM allows an organization to gain insights into customers' shopping and buying behaviors. Every time a customer communicates with a company, the firm has the chance to build a trusting relationship with that particular customer. Harley-Davidson realizes that it takes more than just building and selling motorcycles to fulfill the dreams of its loyal customers. For this reason, the company strives to deliver unforgettable experiences along with its top-quality products. When the company began selling products online it found itself facing a dilemma—its online strategy for selling accessories directly to consumers would bypass Harley-Davidson's dealers, who depend on the high-margin accessories for store revenues. The solution was to deploy Harley-Davidson.com, which prompts customers to select a participating Harley-Davidson dealership before placing any online orders. The selected dealership is then responsible for fulfilling the order. This strategy ensured that the dealers remained the focus point of each customer's buying experiences. To guarantee that every customer has a highly satisfying online buying experience, the company asks the dealers to agree to a number of standards including:

- Checking online orders twice daily.
- Shipping online orders within 24 hours.
- Responding to customer inquiries within 24 hours.[6]

Harley-Davidson still monitors online customer metrics such as time taken to process orders, number of returned orders, and number of incorrect orders, guaranteeing that the company delivers on its critical success factor of providing prompt, excellent customer service consistently to all its loyal customers.

A primary component of managing a customer relationship is knowing when and why the customer is communicating with the company. Imagine an irate customer that has just spent an hour on the phone with your call center complaining about a defective product. While the customer is on the phone, your sales representative decides to drop by the customer's office in an attempt to sell additional products. Obviously, this is not the ideal time to try to up-sell or cross-sell products to this particular customer. A customer relationship management system would inform the sales representative that the customer was on the phone with customer service and even provide details of the call. Then your sales representative could stop by and offer assistance in resolving the product issue, which might help restore the relationship with the customer and provide opportunities for future sales.

The complicated piece of this puzzle is that customers have many communication channels they can use to contact a company including call centers, websites, email, faxes, and telephones. To make matters even more complex, a single customer can communicate with a firm using all of the different communication channels multiple times. Keeping track of customer communications is important if the firm wants to continue to build and manage that relationship. A CRM system can track every form of customer communication providing this information to all employees (see Figure 8.10). The firm can then implement strategies for the best ways to communicate effectively with each and every customer. With a CRM system a firm can obtain an overview of the customer's products, preferences, account information, communications, and purchasing history, allowing it to send customized product offers, expedite shipping, ensure satisfaction, and other marketing and sales techniques that can greatly add to sales and profits.

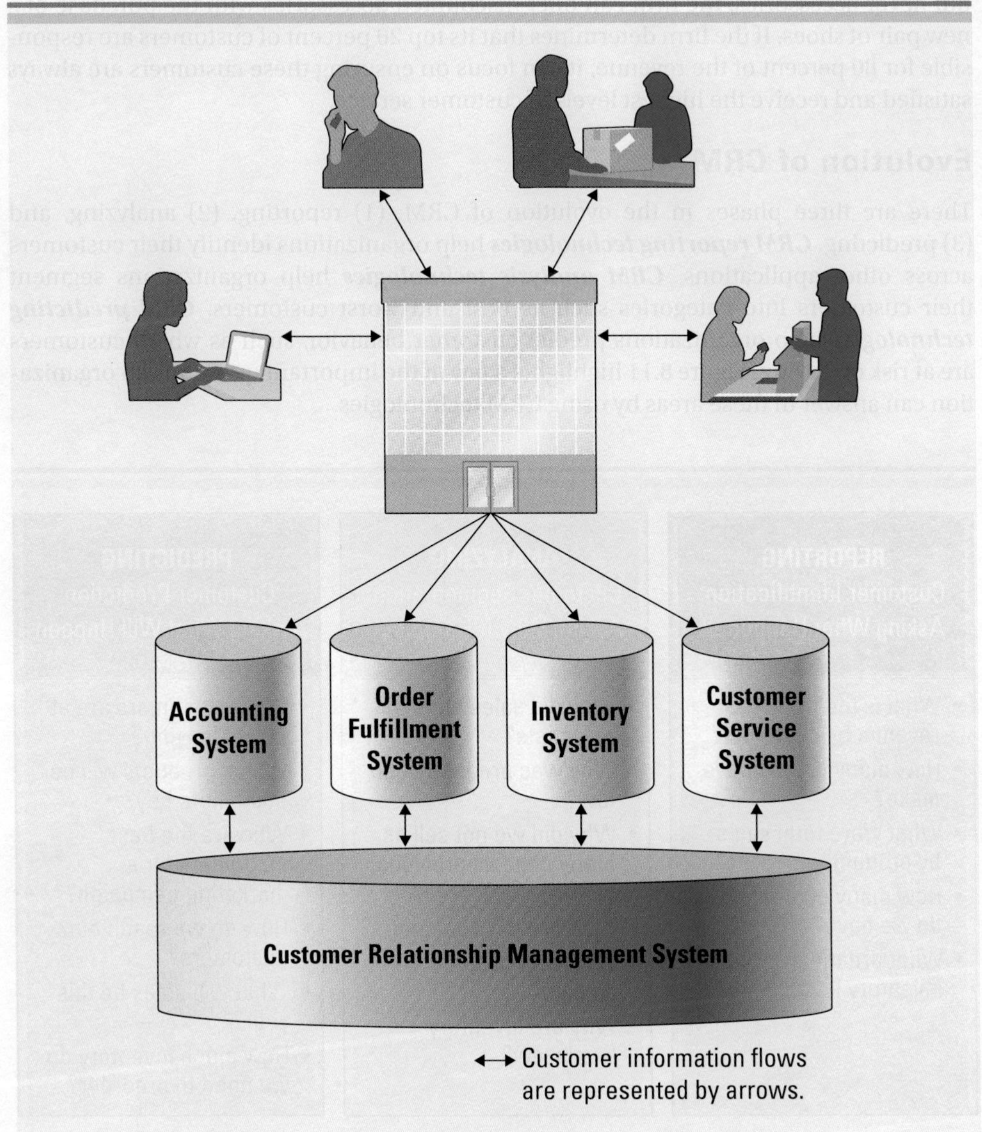

FIGURE 8.10
Customer Relationship Management Overview

LO 8.5: **Identify the benefits and challenges of CRM along with its future.**

THE BENEFITS OF CRM

Companies that understand individual customer needs are best positioned to achieve success. Of course, building successful customer relationships is not a new business practice; however, implementing CRM systems allows a company to operate more efficiently and effectively in the area of supporting customer needs. CRM moves far beyond technology by identifying customer needs and designing specific marketing campaigns tailored to each. This enables a firm to treat customers as individuals, gaining important insights into their buying preferences and shopping behaviors. Firms that treat their customers well reap the rewards and generally see higher profits and highly loyal customers. Identifying the most valuable customers allows a firm to ensure that these customers receive the highest levels of customer service and are offered the first opportunity to purchase new products. Firms can find their most valuable customers by using the RFM formula—recency, frequency, and monetary value. In other words, an organization must track:

- How *recently* a customer purchased items.
- How *frequently* a customer purchases items.
- The *monetary value* of each customer purchase.

After gathering this initial CRM information, the firm can analyze it to identify patterns and create marketing campaigns and sales promotions for different customer segments. For example, if a customer buys only at the height of the season, the firm should send a special offer during the off-season. If a certain customer segment purchases shoes but never accessories, the firm can offer discounted accessories with the purchase of a new pair of shoes. If the firm determines that its top 20 percent of customers are responsible for 80 percent of the revenue, it can focus on ensuring these customers are always satisfied and receive the highest levels of customer service.

Evolution of CRM

There are three phases in the evolution of CRM: (1) reporting, (2) analyzing, and (3) predicting. ***CRM reporting technologies*** help organizations identify their customers across other applications. ***CRM analysis technologies*** help organizations segment their customers into categories such as best and worst customers. ***CRM predicting technologies*** help organizations predict customer behavior, such as which customers are at risk of leaving. Figure 8.11 highlights a few of the important questions an organization can answer in these areas by using CRM technologies.

FIGURE 8.11

Evolution of CRM

REPORTING Customer Identification: Asking What Happened	ANALYZING Customer Segmentation: Asking Why It Happened	PREDICTING Customer Prediction: Asking What Will Happen
• What is the total revenue by customer? • How many units did we make? • What were total sales by product? • How many customers do we have? • What are the current inventory levels?	• Why did sales not meet forecasts? • Why was production so low? • Why did we not sell as many units as previous years? • Who are our customers? • Why was revenue so high? • Why are inventory levels low?	• What customers are at risk of leaving? • Which products will our customers buy? • Who are the best customers for a marketing campaign? • How do we reach our customers? • What will sales be this year? • How much inventory do we need to preorder?

APPLY YOUR KNOWLEDGE

BUSINESS DRIVEN GLOBALIZATION

Banking on Customer Relationships

Barclays Bank, a leader in the global financial markets, maintains business operations in more than 70 countries. Barclays chose to invest in CRM technologies to help it gain valuable insights into its personal and business customers, many of which carry credit cards. The purpose of the CRM system was to predict the financial behavior of individual customers and assess whether a customer is likely to pay back a loan in full within the agreed-upon time period and interest rate. Surprisingly, Barclays' CRM system quickly identified that about 50 percent of its customers were nonprofitable, and that 90 percent of its profits were generated by fewer than 30 percent of its customers.

This valuable information allowed Barclays to revamp its offerings and charge customers an interest rate based on risk assessment. Barclays also identifies groups of profitable customers, both on a corporate and personal level, which it can then target for new financial products.[7]

How can a business like Barclays use RFM (recency, frequency, and monetary value) to improve customer relations? Provide three examples of questions a bank would ask in each of the following categories: CRM reporting technologies, CRM analysis technologies, and CRM predicting technologies.

Operational and Analytical CRM

The two primary components of a CRM strategy are operational CRM and analytical CRM. ***Operational CRM*** supports traditional transactional processing for day-to-day front-office operations or systems that deal directly with the customers. ***Analytical CRM*** supports back-office operations and strategic analysis and includes all systems that do not deal directly with the customers. Figure 8.12 provides an overview of the two.

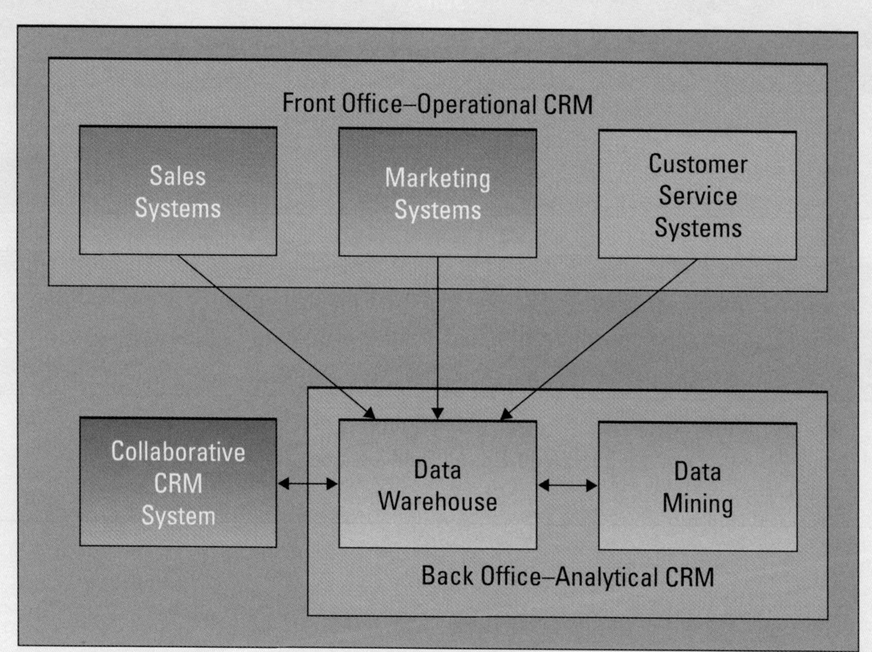

FIGURE 8.12
Operational CRM and Analytical CRM

Figure 8.13 shows the different technologies marketing, sales, and customer service departments can use to perform operational CRM.

Marketing and Operational CRM

Companies are no longer trying to sell one product to as many customers as possible; instead, they are trying to sell one customer as many products as possible. Marketing departments switch to this new way of doing business by using CRM technologies that allow them to gather and analyze customer information to tailor successful marketing campaigns. In fact, a marketing campaign's success is directly proportional to the organization's ability to gather and analyze the right customer information. The three primary operational CRM technologies a marketing department can implement to increase customer satisfaction are:

1. List generator.
2. Campaign management.
3. Cross-selling and up-selling.

List Generator ***List generators*** compile customer information from a variety of sources and segment it for different marketing campaigns. These sources include website visits, questionnaires, surveys, marketing mailers, and so on. After compiling the

FIGURE 8.13

Operational CRM Technologies

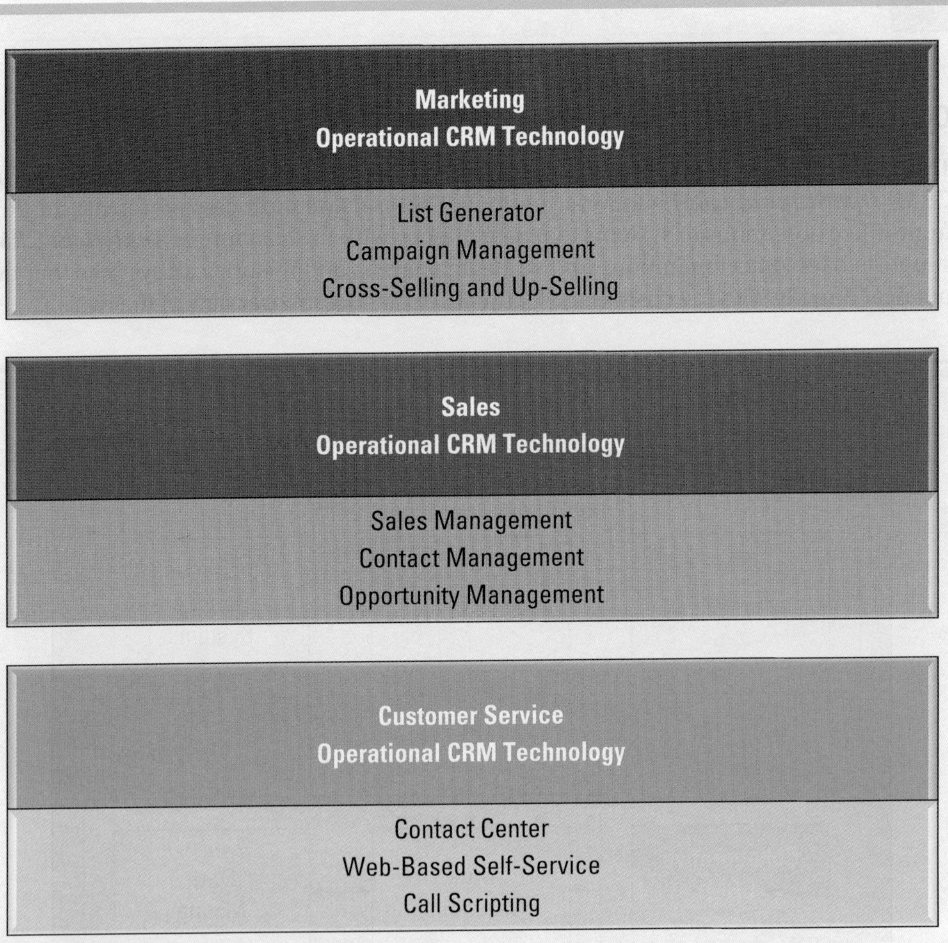

customer list, it can be filtered based on criteria such as household income, gender, education level, political facilitation, age, or other factors. List generators provide the marketing department with valuable information on the type of customer it must target to find success for a marketing campaign.

Campaign Management ***Campaign management systems*** guide users through marketing campaigns by performing such tasks as campaign definition, planning, scheduling, segmentation, and success analysis. These advanced systems can even calculate the profitability and track the results for each marketing campaign.

Cross-Selling and Up-Selling Two key sales strategies a marketing campaign can deploy are cross-selling and up-selling. ***Cross-selling*** is selling additional products or services to an existing customer. For example, if you were to purchase Tim Burton's movie *Alice in Wonderland* on Amazon, you would also be asked if you want to purchase the movie's soundtrack or the original book. Amazon is taking advantage of cross-selling by offering customers goods across its book, movie, and music product lines. ***Up-selling*** is increasing the value of the sale. McDonald's performs up-selling by asking customers whether they would like to super-size their meals for an extra cost. CRM systems offer marketing departments all kinds of information about customers and products, which can help identify up-selling and cross-selling opportunities to increase revenues.

Sales and Operational CRM

Sales departments were the first to begin developing CRM systems. They had two primary motivations to track customer sales information electronically. First, sales representatives were struggling with the overwhelming amount of customer account information they were required to maintain and track. Second, managers found themselves hindered because much of their vital customer and sales information remained in the heads of their sales representatives, even if the sales representative left the company. Finding a way to track customer information became a critical success factor for many sales departments.

Figure 8.14 depicts the typical sales process, which begins with an opportunity and ends with billing the customer for the sale. Leads and potential customers are the lifeblood of all sales organizations, whether they sell computers, clothing, consulting, or cars. How leads are handled can make the difference between revenue growth and decline.

FIGURE 8.14
A Typical Sales Process

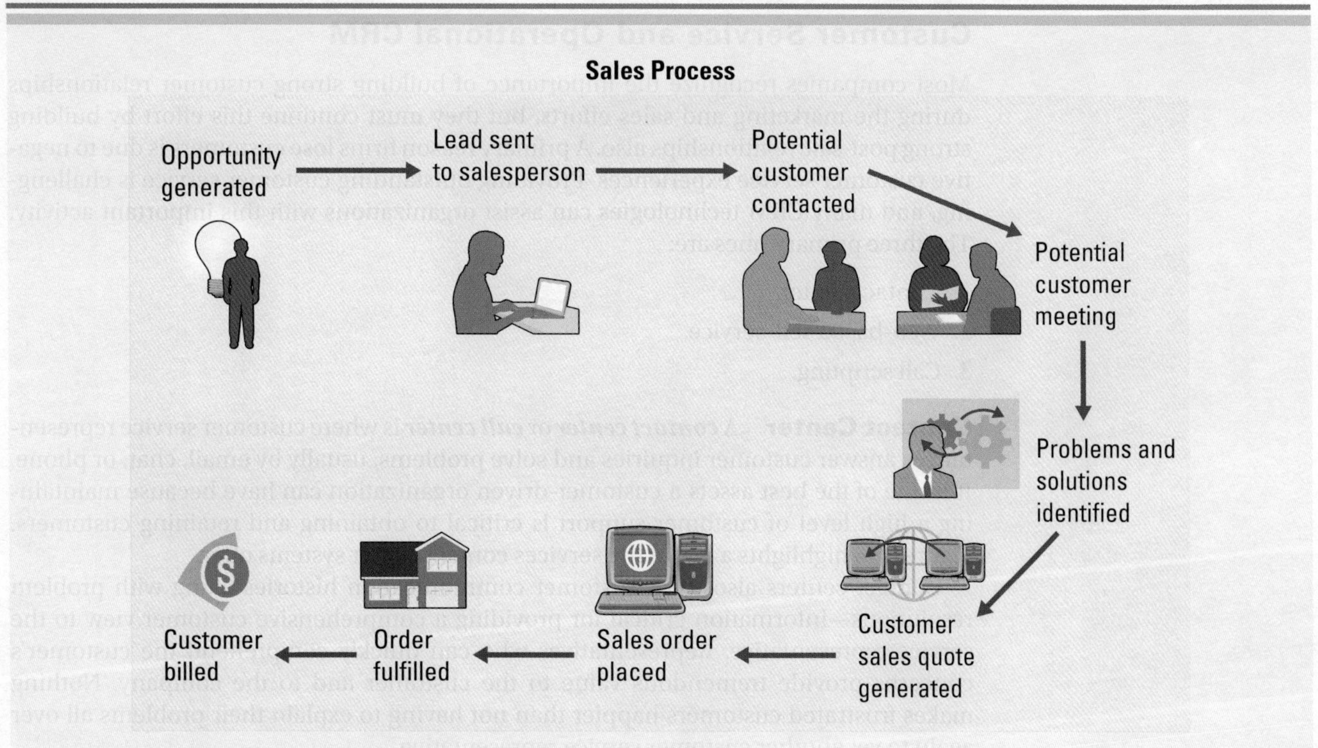

Sales force automation (SFA) automatically tracks all the steps in the sales process. SFA products focus on increasing customer satisfaction, building customer relationships, and improving product sales. The three primary operational CRM technologies a sales department can adopt are:

1. Sales management CRM systems.
2. Contact management CRM systems.
3. Opportunity management CRM systems.

Sales Management CRM Systems ***Sales management CRM systems*** automate each phase of the sales process, helping individual sales representatives coordinate and organize all their accounts. Features include calendars, reminders for important tasks, multimedia presentations, and document generation. These systems can even provide an analysis of the sales cycle and calculate how each individual sales representative is performing during the sales process.

Contact Management CRM Systems A ***contact management CRM system*** maintains customer contact information and identifies prospective customers for future sales, using tools such as organizational charts, detailed customer notes, and supplemental sales information. For example, a contact management system can take an incoming telephone number and automatically display the person's name along with a comprehensive history including all communications with the company. This allows the sales representative to personalize the phone conversation and ask such things as, "How is your new laptop working, Sue?" or "How was your family vacation to Colorado?" The customer feels valued since the sales associate knows her name and even remembers details of their last conversation.

Opportunity Management CRM Systems ***Opportunity management CRM systems*** target sales opportunities by finding new customers or companies for future sales. They determine potential customers and competitors and define selling efforts including budgets and schedules. Advanced systems can even calculate the probability of a sale, which can save sales representatives significant time and money when qualifying new customers. The primary difference between contact management and opportunity management is that contact management deals with existing customers and opportunity management with new or potential customers.

Customer Service and Operational CRM

Most companies recognize the importance of building strong customer relationships during the marketing and sales efforts, but they must continue this effort by building strong post-sale relationships also. A primary reason firms lose customers is due to negative customer service experiences. Providing outstanding customer service is challenging, and many CRM technologies can assist organizations with this important activity. The three primary ones are:

1. Contact center.
2. Web-based self-service.
3. Call scripting.

Contact Center A ***contact center*** or ***call center*** is where customer service representatives answer customer inquiries and solve problems, usually by email, chat, or phone. It is one of the best assets a customer-driven organization can have because maintaining a high level of customer support is critical to obtaining and retaining customers. Figure 8.15 highlights a few of the services contact center systems offer.

Contact centers also track customer communication histories along with problem resolutions—information critical for providing a comprehensive customer view to the service representative. Representatives who can quickly comprehend the customer's concerns provide tremendous value to the customer and to the company. Nothing makes frustrated customers happier than not having to explain their problems all over again to yet another customer service representative.

BUSINESS DRIVEN INNOVATION

Nice Emotions

New emotion-detection software called Perform, created by Nice Systems, helps firms improve customer service by identifying callers who are displeased or upset. Perform determines a baseline of emotion and can detect emotional issues during the first few seconds of a call; any variation from the baseline activates an alert. When an elderly person who was highly distressed over medical costs hung up during a phone call to the insurance company, Perform identified the customer's frustration and automatically emailed a supervisor. The supervisor was able to review a recording of the conversation and immediately called the customer back suggesting ways to lower the costs.[8]

How do you think emotion-detection software will affect customer relationships? What other departments or business processes could benefit from its use? Create a new product that uses emotion-detection software. What business problem would your product solve and who would be your primary customers?

FIGURE 8.15

Common Services Provided by Contact Centers

Automatic call distribution: Routes inbound calls to available agents.
Interactive voice response (IVR): Directs customers to use touch-tone phones or keywords to navigate or provide information.
Predictive dialing: Automatically dials outbound calls and forwards answered calls to an available agent.

Web-Based Self-Service ***Web-based self-service systems*** allow customers to use the Web to find answers to their questions or solutions to their problems. FedEx uses Web-based self-service systems to let customers electronically track packages without having to talk to a customer service representative. Another feature of Web-based self-service is ***click-to-talk*** functions, which allow customers to click on a button and talk with a representative via the Internet. Powerful customer-driven features such as these add value to any organization by providing customers with real-time information that helps resolve their concerns.

Call Scripting Companies that market and sell highly technical products have a difficult time finding competent customer service representatives. ***Call scripting systems*** gather product details and issue resolution information that can be automatically generated into a script for the representative to read to the customer. These systems even provide questions the representative can ask the customer to troubleshoot the problem and find a resolution. This feature not only helps reps answer difficult questions quickly but also presents a uniform response so customers don't receive different answers.

Analytical CRM

Analytical CRM provides information about customers and products that was once impossible to locate, such as which type of marketing and sales campaign to launch and which customers to target and when. Unlike operational CRM, which automates call centers and sales forces with the aim of enhancing customer service, analytical CRM works by using business intelligence to identify patterns in product sales and customer behaviors. Analytical CRM tools can slice-and-dice vast amounts of information to create custom views of customers, products, and market segments highlighting opportunities for cross-selling and up-selling. ***Website personalization*** occurs when a website has stored enough data about a person's likes and dislikes to fashion offers more likely to appeal to that person. Many marketers use CRM to personalize customer communications and decide which customers are worth pursuing. Here are a few examples of the information insights analytical CRM can help an organization gain.

- **Find new profitable customers:** Analytical CRM could highlight that the most profitable market segment consists of women between 35 and 45 years old who drive SUVs and live within 30 miles of the city limits. The firm could then find a way to locate these customers for mailings and other opportunities.
- **Exceed customer expectations:** Analytical CRM helps a firm move past the typical "Dear Mr. Smith" greeting by personalizing communications. For example, if the firm knows the customer's favorite brand and size of shoe it can notify the customer that a pair of size 12 Nike cross trainers are available for him to try on the next time he visits the store.
- **Discover the activities the firm performs the best:** Analytical CRM can determine what an organization does better than its competitors. If a restaurant caters more lunches to midsized companies than its competition does, it can purchase a specialized mailing targeting these customers for future mailings.
- **Eliminate competition:** Analytical CRM can determine sales trends allowing the company to provide customers with special deals outsmarting its competition. A sports store might identify its best customers for outdoor apparel and invite them to a private sale right before the competition runs its sale.
- **Care about customers:** Analytical CRM can determine what customers want and need, so a firm can contact them with an invitation to a private sale, reminder that a product needs a tune-up, or send them a personalized letter along with a discount coupon to help spark a renewed relationship.

Measuring CRM Success

Using CRM metrics to track and monitor performance is a best practice for many companies. Figure 8.16 displays a few common CRM metrics a manager can use to track the success of the system. Just remember that you only want to track between five and seven of the hundreds of CRM metrics available.

THE CHALLENGES OF CRM

A standard rule of business states that the customer is always right. Although most businesses use this as their motto, they do not actually mean it. Ebusiness firms must adhere to this rule as the power of the customer grows exponentially in the information age. Various websites and videos on YouTube reveal the power of the individual consumer (see Figure 8.17). A decade ago if you had a complaint against a company you could make a phone call or write a letter. Now you can contact hundreds or thousands of

FIGURE 8.16
CRM Metrics

Sales Metrics	Customer Service Metrics	Marketing Metrics
Number of prospective customers	Cases closed same day	Number of marketing campaigns
Number of new customers	Number of cases handled by agent	New customer retention rates
Number of retained customers	Number of service calls	Number of responses by marketing campaign
Number of open leads	Average number of service requests by type	Number of purchases by marketing campaign
Number of sales calls	Average time to resolution	Revenue generated by marketing campaign
Number of sales calls per lead	Average number of service calls per day	Cost per interaction by marketing campaign
Amount of new revenue	Percentage compliance with service-level agreement	Number of new customers acquired by marketing campaign
Amount of recurring revenue	Percentage of service renewals	Customer retention rate
Number of proposals given	Customer satisfaction level	Number of new leads by product

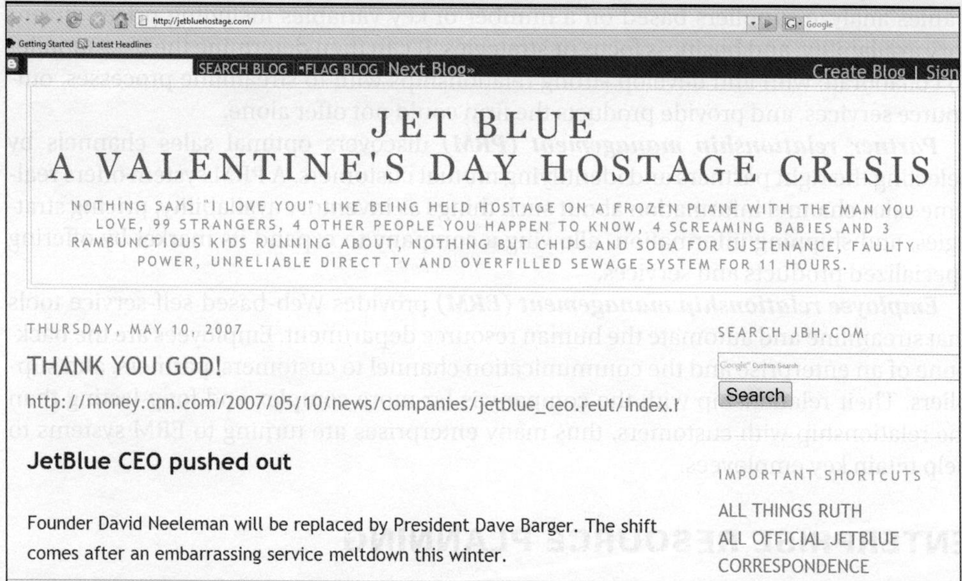

FIGURE 8.17

The Power of the Customer

APPLY YOUR KNOWLEDGE

BUSINESS DRIVEN START-UP

Straightjacket Customer Service

You might not want to put the fact that you won the Straightjacket Award on your résumé unless you worked for Rackspace, a Texas company that specializes in hosting websites. At Rackspace, the coveted Straightjacket Award is won by the employee who best delivers "fanatical customer support," one of the firm's critical success factors. The company motivates its customer service representatives by dividing them into teams, each responsible for its own profitability. The company then measures such things as customer turnover, up-selling, cross-selling, and referrals. The team with the highest scores wins the Straightjacket Award and each member receives a 20 percent bonus.[9]

Assume your professor has hired you as the employee relationship manager for your class. What type of award would you create to help increase class participation? What type of award would you create to help increase the overall average on exams? What type of award would you create to help increase student collaboration? Be sure to name your awards and describe their details. Also, what type of metrics would you create to measure your awards? How could a CRM system help you implement your awards?

people around the globe and voice your complaint or anger with a company or product. You—the customer—can now take your power directly to millions of people and companies have to listen.

THE FUTURE OF CRM

Organizations are discovering a wave of other key business areas where it is beneficial to build strong relationships beyond customers. These include supplier relationship management (SRM), partner relationship management (PRM), and employee relationship management (ERM).

Supplier relationship management (SRM) focuses on keeping suppliers satisfied by evaluating and categorizing suppliers for different projects. SRM applications help companies analyze suppliers based on a number of key variables including prices, inventory availability, and business focus or strategies. It can then determine the best supplier to collaborate with and develop strong relationships with to streamline processes, outsource services, and provide products the firm could not offer alone.

Partner relationship management (PRM) discovers optimal sales channels by selecting the right partners and identifying mutual customers. A PRM system offers real-time sales channel information about such things as inventory availability, pricing strategies, and shipping information, allowing a company to expand its market by offering specialized products and services.

Employee relationship management (ERM) provides Web-based self-service tools that streamline and automate the human resource department. Employees are the backbone of an enterprise and the communication channel to customers, partners, and suppliers. Their relationship with the company is far more complex and long-lasting than the relationship with customers, thus many enterprises are turning to ERM systems to help retain key employees.

LO 8.6: Describe enterprise resource management and its role in supporting business operations.

ENTERPRISE RESOURCE PLANNING

Today's managers require real-time views into their businesses so they can make decisions when they need to. ***Enterprise resource planning (ERP)*** integrates all departments and functions throughout an organization into a single IT system (or integrated set of IT systems) so employees can make decisions by viewing enterprisewide information about all business operations.

Many organizations fail to maintain consistency across business operations. If a single department, such as sales, decides to implement a new system without considering other departments, like marketing and accounting, inconsistencies can occur throughout the company, and operations can become discontinuous, like silos. Enterprise resource planning systems provide organizations with consistency. They allow for the effective planning and controlling of all the resources required to plan, source, make, and deliver goods and services. Figure 8.18 shows how an ERP system takes data from across the enterprise, consolidates and correlates it, and generates enterprisewide organizational reports.

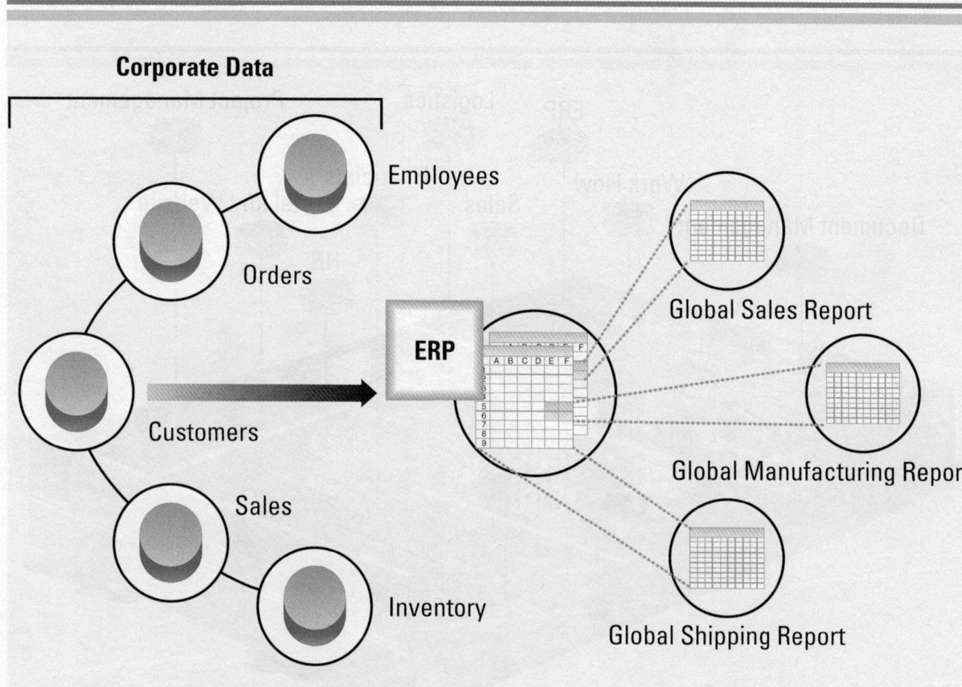

FIGURE 8.18
Enterprise Resource Planning System Overview

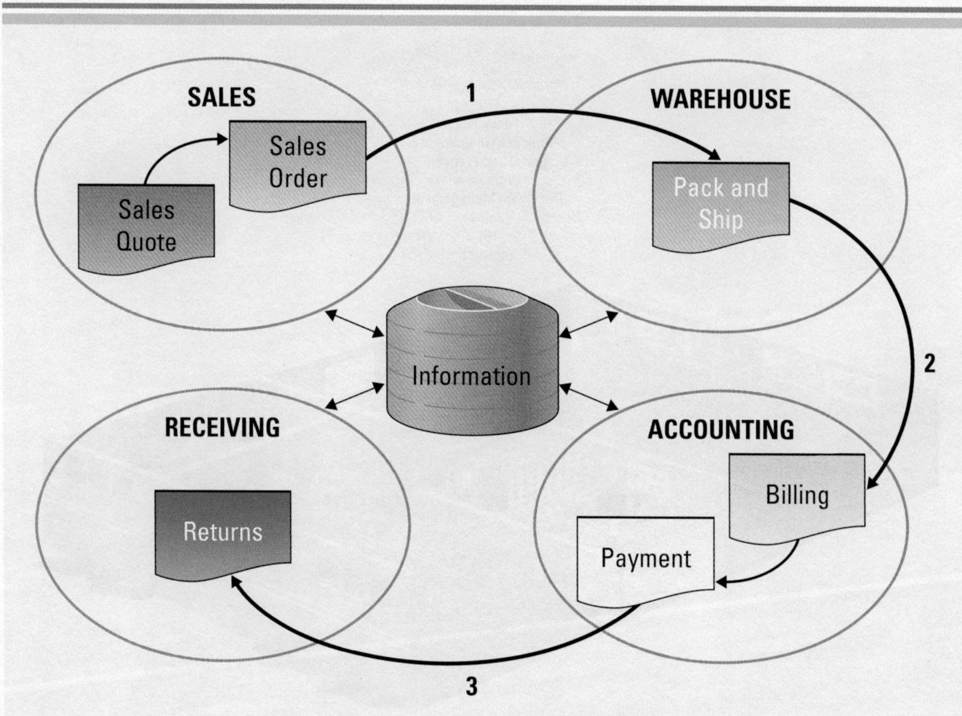

FIGURE 8.19
ERP Process Flow

The key word in enterprise resource planning is *enterprise*. At the core of an ERP system is a central database that gathers transactional data from operational systems across the company. Each time information is altered, it is automatically updated throughout the entire system. For example, sales representatives can access the ERP system to view all necessary information to process orders such as credit rating, order history, inventory levels, and delivery schedules. Once the order is complete, the ERP system automatically routes it to the next department in the order process, as illustrated in Figure 8.19. ERP systems facilitate the order process, ensuring customers receive their purchases faster and with fewer errors. ERP systems can support numerous business processes far beyond order processing, such as employee benefits and financial reporting. An ERP system can also support supplier and customer business processes infiltrating the entire value chain and helping the organization achieve greater operational efficiency (see Figure 8.20).

FIGURE 8.20

The Organization Before and After ERP

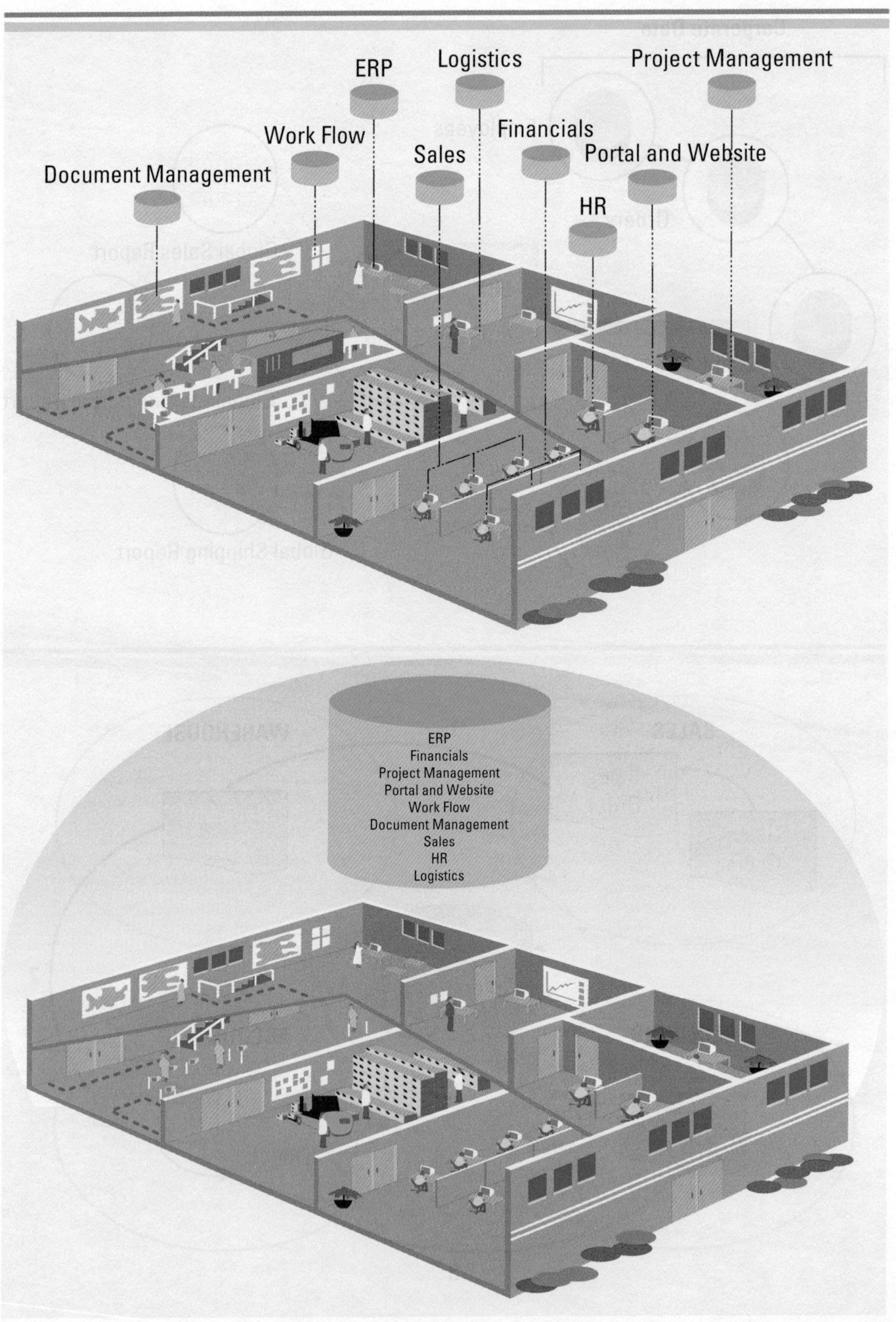

APPLY YOUR KNOWLEDGE

BUSINESS DRIVEN MIS

Classic Cars

Classic Cars Inc. operates high-end automotive dealerships that offer luxury cars along with luxury service. The company is proud of its extensive inventory, top-of-the-line mechanics, and especially its exceptional service, which includes operating a cappuccino bar at each dealership.

The company currently has 40 sales representatives at four locations. Each location maintains its own computer systems, and all sales representatives have their own contact management systems. This splintered approach to operations causes numerous problems in customer communication, pricing strategy, and inventory control, such as:

- A customer can get different quotes at different dealerships for the same car.
- Sales representatives frequently steal each other's customers and commissions.
- Sales representatives send their customers to other dealerships to see specific cars that turn out not to be on the lot.
- Marketing campaigns are typically generic and not designed to target specific customers.
- If a sales representative quits, all his or her customer information is lost.

You work for Customer One, a small consulting company that specializes in enterprisewide strategies. The owner of Classic Cars Inc. has hired you to help him formulate a strategy to put his company back on track. Develop a proposal detailing how an ERP system can alleviate the company's problems and create new sales opportunities.

THE BENEFITS OF ERP

LO 8.7: Identify the benefits and challenges of ERP along with the future of the connected corporation.

The first generation of ERP systems focused on improving the manufacturing process through automation, primarily addressing back-office business processes such as inventory ordering and product distribution. The second generation of ERP systems extended its reach into the front office and primarily addressed customer issues including marketing and sales. The third generation of ERP systems, known as ERP-II, allows a company to compete on a functional level by adopting an enterprisewide approach using the Internet to connect all participants in the value chain. Figure 8.21 shows how ERP has grown to accommodate the needs of the entire organization.

The current generation of ERP, ERP-II is composed of two primary components—core and extended. ***Core ERP components*** are the traditional components included in most ERP systems and primarily focus on internal operations. ***Extended ERP components*** are the extra components that meet organizational needs not covered by the core components and primarily focus on external operations. Figure 8.22 provides an example of an ERP system with its core and extended components.

Core ERP Components

The three most common core ERP components focusing on internal operations are:

1. Accounting and finance.
2. Production and materials management.
3. Human resources.

FIGURE 8.21
The Evolution of ERP

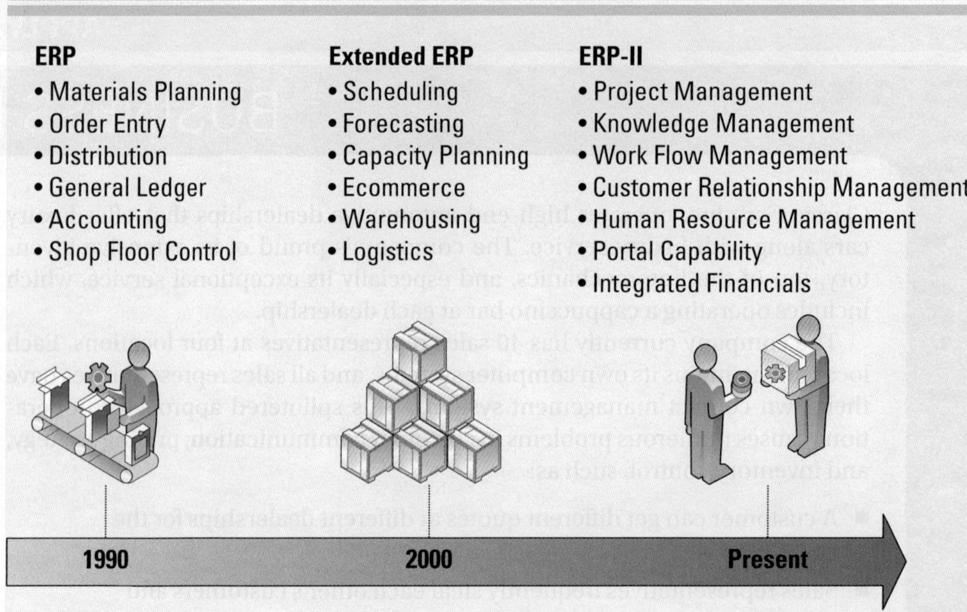

FIGURE 8.22
Core ERP Components and Extended ERP Components

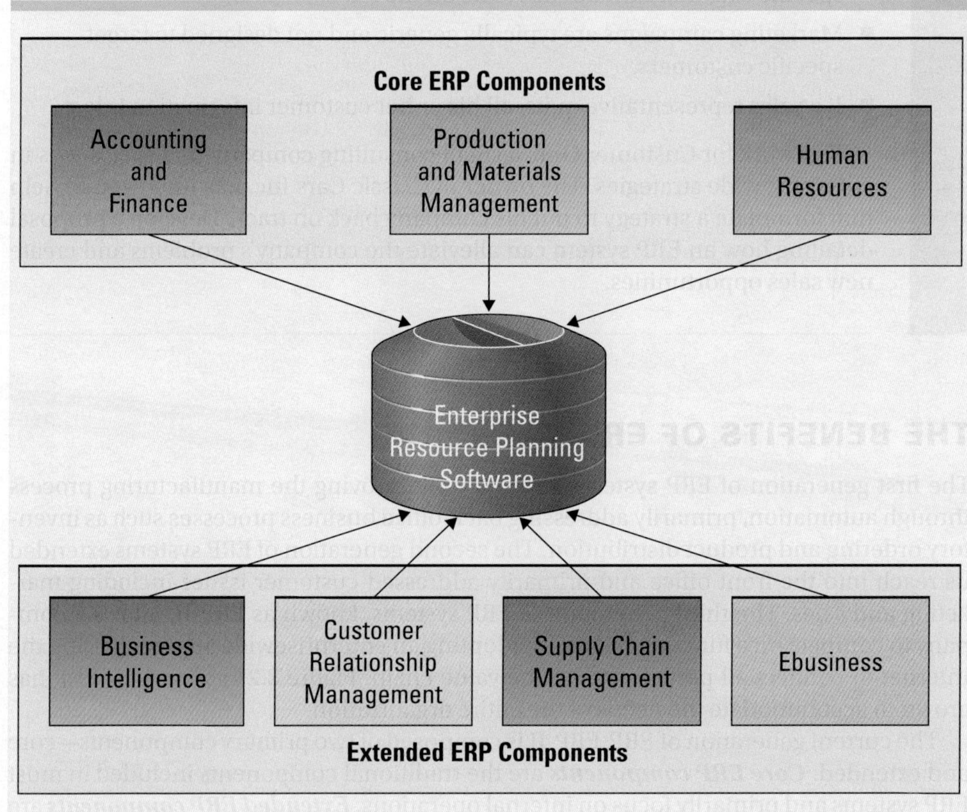

Accounting and Finance ERP Components ***Accounting and finance ERP components*** manage accounting data and financial processes within the enterprise with functions such as general ledger, accounts payable, accounts receivable, budgeting, and asset management. One of the most useful features of an ERP accounting/finance component is credit management. Most organizations manage their relationships with customers by setting credit limits, or limits on how much a customer can owe at any one time. ERP financial systems correlate customers' orders with their account balances to determine credit availability. They also perform all types of advanced profitability modeling techniques.

Production and Materials Management ERP Components ***Production and materials management ERP components*** handle production planning and execution tasks such as demand forecasting, production scheduling, job cost accounting, and quality control. Demand forecasting helps determine production schedules and materials purchasing. A company that makes its own product prepares a detailed production schedule, and a company that buys products for resale develops a materials requirement plan.

Human Resources ERP Components ***Human resources ERP components*** track employee information including payroll, benefits, compensation, and performance assessment and ensure compliance with all laws. They even allow the organization to perform detailed employee analysis, such as identifying who is likely to leave the company unless additional compensation or benefits are provided, and whether the most talented people are working in areas where they can have the greatest impact. Human resource components can also identify which employees are using which resources, such as online training and long-distance telephone services.

Extended ERP Components

Extended ERP components meet the organizational needs not covered by the core components and primarily focus on external operations. Many are Internet-enabled and require interaction with customers, suppliers, and business partners outside the organization. The four most common extended ERP components are:

1. Business intelligence.
2. Customer relationship management.
3. Supply chain management.
4. Ebusiness.

Business Intelligence ERP Components Many organizations have found that ERP tools can provide even greater value with the addition of powerful business intelligence systems. The business intelligence components of ERP systems typically collect information used throughout the organization (including data used in many other ERP components), organize it, and apply analytical tools to assist managers with decisions. Data warehouses are one of the most popular extensions to ERP systems.

Customer Relationship Management ERP Components ERP vendors now include additional functionality that provides services formerly found only in CRM systems. The CRM components in ERP systems include contact centers, sales force automation, and advanced marketing functions. The goal is to provide an integrated view of customer data, enabling a firm to effectively manage customer relationships by responding to customer needs and demands while identifying the most (and least) valuable customers so the firm can better allocate its marketing resources.

Supply Chain Management ERP Components ERP vendors are expanding their systems to include SCM functions that manage the information flows between and among supply chain stages, maximizing total supply chain effectiveness and profitability. SCM components allow a firm to monitor and control all stages in the supply chain from the acquisition of raw materials to the receipt of finished goods by customers.

Ebusiness ERP Components The newest extended ERP components are the ebusiness components that allow companies to establish an Internet presence and fulfill online orders. Two of the primary features of ebusiness components are elogistics and eprocurement. ***Elogistics*** manages the transportation and storage of goods. ***Eprocurement*** is the business-to-business (B2B) online purchase and sale of supplies and services. A common mistake many businesses make is jumping into online business without properly integrating the entire organization on the ERP system. One large toy manufacturer announced less than a week before Christmas that it would be unable to fulfill any of its online orders. The company had all the toys in the warehouse, but it could not organize the basic order processing function to get the toys delivered to consumers on time.

Measuring ERP Success

One of the best methods of measuring ERP success is the balanced scorecard, created by Dr. Robert Kaplan and Dr. David Norton, both from the Harvard Business School. The ***balanced scorecard*** is a management system, as well as a measurement system, that a firm uses to translate business strategies into executable tasks. It provides feedback for both internal and external business processes, allowing continuous improvement. Kaplan and Norton describe the balanced scorecard as follows: "The balanced scorecard retains traditional financial measures. But financial measures tell the story of past events, an adequate story for industrial age companies for which investments in long-term capabilities and customer relationships were not critical for success. These financial measures are inadequate, however, for guiding and evaluating the journey that information age companies must make to create future value through investment in customers, suppliers, employees, processes, technology, and innovation."[10] The balanced scorecard uses four perspectives to monitor an organization:

1. The learning and growth perspective.
2. The internal business process perspective.
3. The customer perspective.
4. The financial perspective (see Figure 8.23).

FIGURE 8.23

The Four Primary Perspectives of the Balanced Scorecard

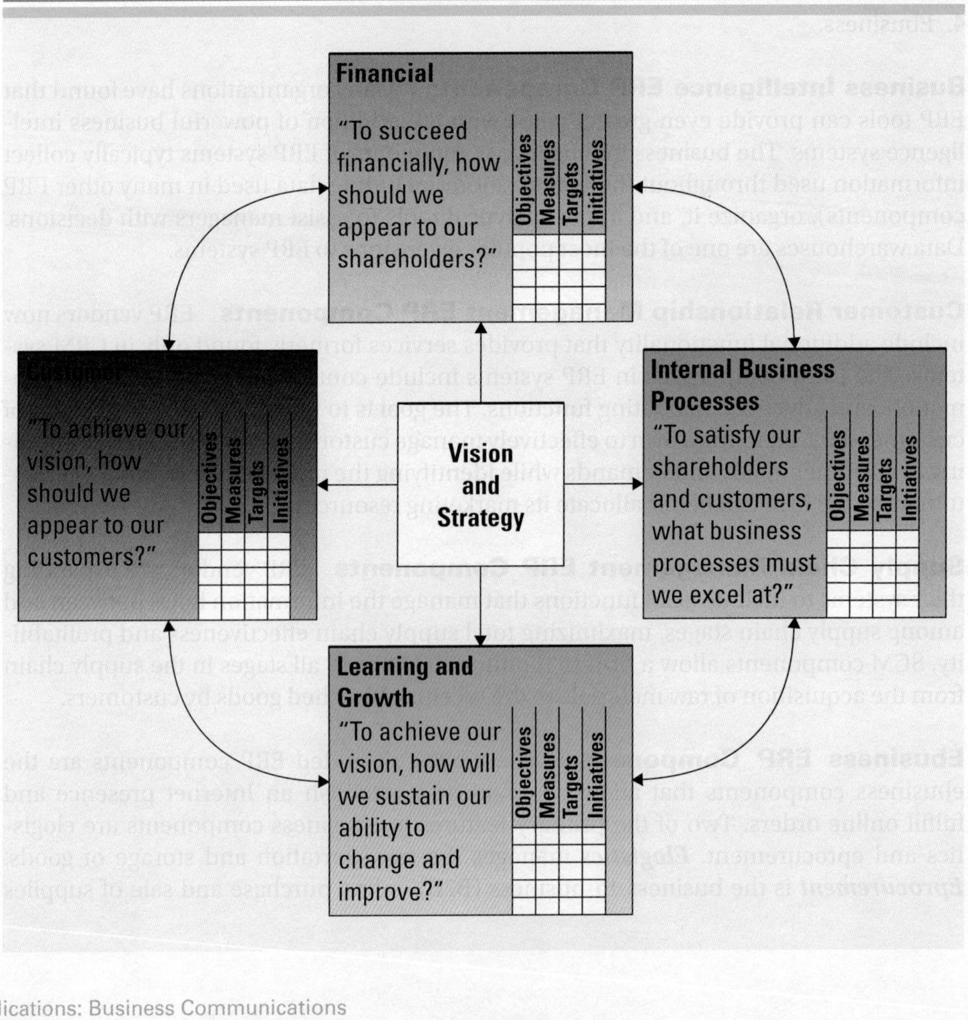

APPLY YOUR KNOWLEDGE

BUSINESS DRIVEN DISCUSSION

Bean Integration

At Flavors, a premium coffee shop, customers receive more than just a great cup of coffee—they also get exposure to music, art, literature, and town events. Flavors offers the following:

- Music center—information about all live music events occurring in the area and an open microphone two nights a week for local musicians.
- Art gallery—a space in the store filled with great pieces from local artists.
- Book clubs—a way for customers to meet to discuss current and classic literature.
- Coffee sampler—free tastings in which experts showcase coffees from around the world.
- Community calendar—weekly meetings to help customers find ways to become more involved in their community.
- Brewing courses—lessons in the finer details of the brewing, grinding, and blending equipment for sale in Flavor stores, from the traditional press to a digital espresso machine. Also includes a trouble-shooting guide developed by brewing specialists.

Flavors' sales are great and profits are soaring; however, operations need an overhaul. The following is a quick look at Flavors' current nonfood offerings.

- Flavors does not receive any information about how many customers attend live events in the music center. Musicians typically maintain a fan email list and CD sales records for the event; however, they don't always provide this information to the store.
- The art gallery is run by several local artists who pay Flavors a small commission on each sale. Flavors has no input on the art displayed in the store or information about who purchases it.
- Book club events are booked and run through the local bookstore, Pages Up, which runs a tab during the meetings and pays Flavor with a check at the end of each month. Flavors has no access to book club customer information or sales information.
- Coffee sampler events are run through Flavors' primary operations.
- Community event information is open to all members of the community. Each event is run by a separate organization, which provides monthly event feedback to Flavors in a variety of formats from Word to Access files.
- Brewing and machine resource courses are run by the equipment manufacturers, and all customer and sales information is provided to Flavors in a Word document at the end of each year.

Flavors' owners want to revamp the way the company operates so they can take advantage of enterprise systems, and they have hired you as an integration expert. They also want to gain a better understanding of how the different events they host affect the different areas of their business. For example, should they have more open-microphone nights and fewer book clubs? The other way around? Currently, they have no way to tell which events result in higher sales. Create an integration strategy so Flavors can take advantage of CRM, SCM, and ERP across the company.

THE CHALLENGES OF ERP

One of the biggest challenges of an ERP system is cost. ERP systems contain multiple complex components that are not only expensive to purchase, but also expensive to implement. Costs can include the software itself, plus consulting charges, hardware expenses, and training fees. A large firm can easily spend millions of dollars and many years completing an ERP implementation. The biggest issue facing an ERP implementation is that it fundamentally changes the way the entire organization operates, causing employees to learn and adjust to new business processes. Many ERP failures occur because the business managers and MIS professionals underestimate the complexity of the planning, development, and training required with an ERP implementation. As a manager, you must carefully assess your company's needs and choose the right ERP system and ensure proper support for all new processes, while avoiding too much change too fast.

THE FUTURE OF ENTERPRISE SYSTEMS: INTEGRATING SCM, CRM, AND ERP

Applications such as SCM, CRM, and ERP are the backbone of ebusiness, yet most organizations today have to piece together these systems. A firm might choose its CRM components from Siebel, SCM components from i2, and financial components and HR management components from Oracle. Figure 8.24 identifies the general audience and purpose for each of these applications, and Figure 8.25 shows where they are integrated and the underlying premise of an integrated organization. Integrating all of these enterprise systems allows an organization to function as a single unit meeting customer, partner, and supplier needs.

If one application performs poorly, the entire customer value delivery system is affected. For example, no matter how great a company is at CRM, if its SCM system does not work and the customer never receives the finished product, the company will lose that customer. The world-class enterprises of tomorrow must be built on world-class applications implemented today.

FIGURE 8.24

Primary Uses and Business Benefits of Strategic Initiatives

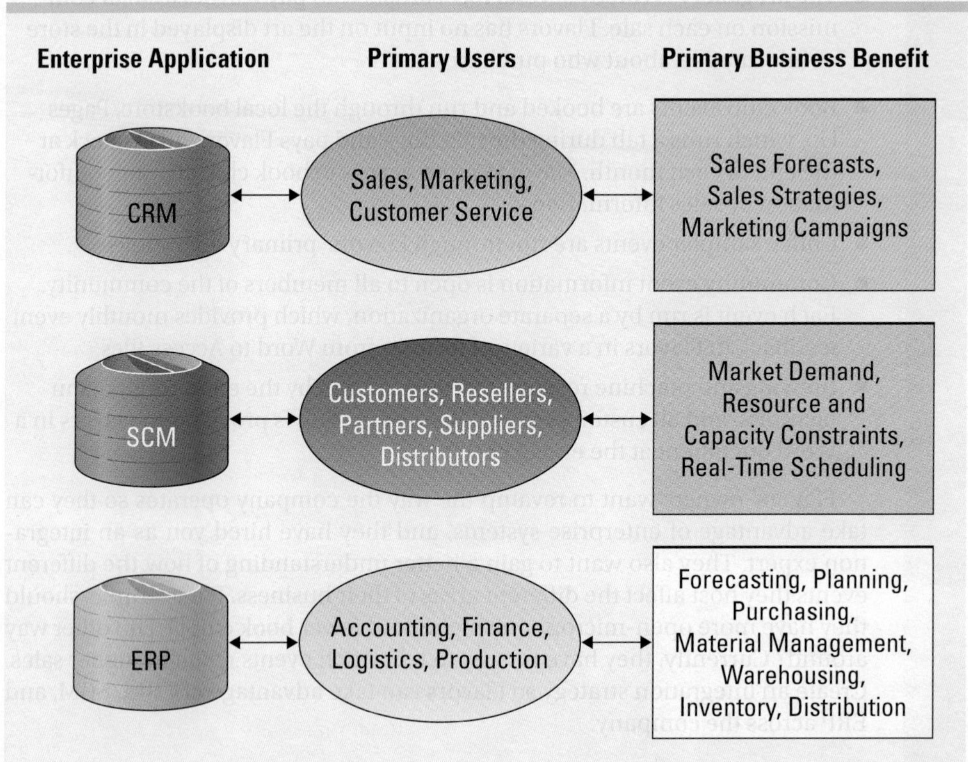

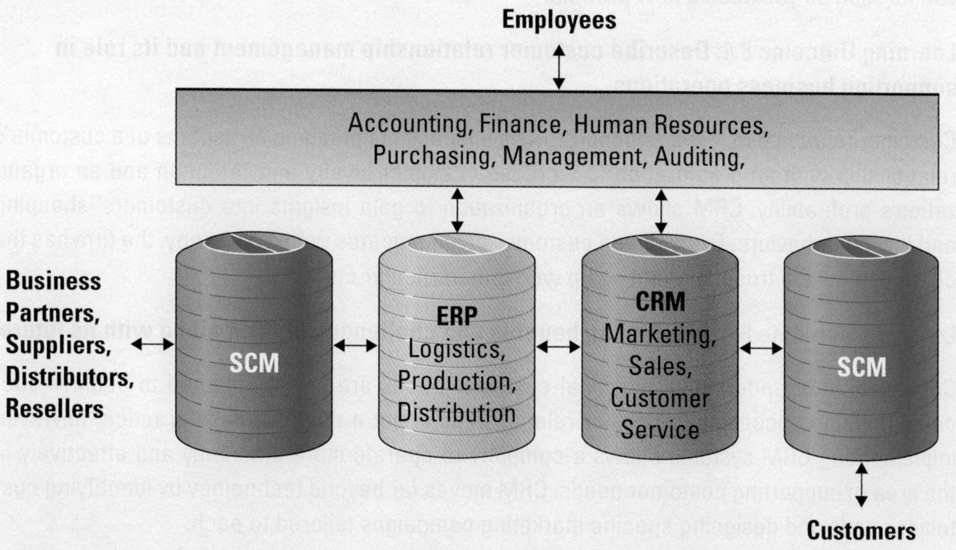

FIGURE 8.25
Integrations between SCM, CRM, and ERP

Employees

Accounting, Finance, Human Resources, Purchasing, Management, Auditing,

Business Partners, Suppliers, Distributors, Resellers ↔ SCM ↔ ERP Logistics, Production, Distribution ↔ CRM Marketing, Sales, Customer Service ↔ SCM

Customers

LEARNING OUTCOME REVIEW

Learning Outcome 8.1: Explain integrations and the role they play in connecting a corporation.

Integrations allow separate systems to communicate directly with each other, eliminating the need for manual entry into multiple systems. Building integrations allows the sharing of information across databases along with dramatically increasing its quality.

Learning Outcome 8.2: Describe supply chain management and its role in supporting business operations.

A supply chain consists of all parties involved, directly or indirectly, in obtaining raw materials or a product. To automate and enable sophisticated decision making in these critical areas, companies are turning to systems that provide demand forecasting, inventory control, and information flows between suppliers and customers. Supply chain management (SCM) is the management of information flows between and among activities in a supply chain to maximize total supply chain effectiveness and corporate profitability. In the past, manufacturing efforts focused primarily on quality improvement efforts within the company; today these efforts reach across the entire supply chain, including customers, customers' customers, suppliers, and suppliers' suppliers. Today's supply chain is an intricate network of business partners linked through communication channels and relationships.

Learning Outcome 8.3: Identify the benefits and challenges of SCM along with its future.

Improved visibility across the supply chain and increased profitability for the firm are the primary business benefits received when implementing supply chain management systems. Supply chain visibility is the ability to view all areas up and down the supply chain in real time. The primary challenges associated with supply chain management include costs and complexity. The next wave in supply chain management will be home-based supply chain fulfillment. No more running to the store to replace your products as your store will come to you as soon as you need a new product.

Learning Outcome 8.4: Describe customer relationship management and its role in supporting business operations.

Customer relationship management (CRM) is a means of managing all aspects of a customer's relationship with an organization to increase customer loyalty and retention and an organization's profitability. CRM allows an organization to gain insights into customers' shopping and buying behaviors. Every time a customer communicates with a company, the firm has the chance to build a trusting relationship with that particular customer.

Learning Outcome 8.5: Identify the benefits and challenges of CRM along with its future.

Companies that understand individual customer needs are best positioned to achieve success. Building successful customer relationships is not a new business practice; however, implementing CRM systems allows a company to operate more efficiently and effectively in the area of supporting customer needs. CRM moves far beyond technology by identifying customer needs and designing specific marketing campaigns tailored to each.

A decade ago if you had a complaint against a company you could make a phone call or write a letter. Now you can contact people around the globe and voice your complaint or anger with a company or product. Companies have to listen, making CRM the primary challenge facing organizations.

Organizations are discovering a wave of other key business areas where it is beneficial to build strong relationships beyond customers. These include supplier relationship management (SRM), partner relationship management (PRM), and employee relationship management (ERM).

Learning Outcome 8.6: Describe enterprise resource management and its role in supporting business operations.

Enterprise resource planning (ERP) integrates all departments and functions throughout an organization into a single IT system (or integrated set of IT systems) so employees can make decisions by viewing enterprisewide information about all business operations. Enterprise resource planning systems provide organizations with consistency. They allow for the effective planning and controlling of all the resources required to plan, source, make, and deliver goods and services.

Learning Outcome 8.7: Identify the benefits and challenges of ERP along with the future of the connected corporation.

The first generation of ERP systems focused on improving the manufacturing process through automation, primarily addressing back-office business processes such as inventory ordering and product distribution. The second generation of ERP systems extended its reach into the front office and primarily addressed customer issues including marketing and sales. The third generation of ERP systems, known as ERP-II, allows a company to compete on a functional level, adopting an enterprisewide approach using the Internet to connect all participants in the value chain

One of the biggest challenges of an ERP system is cost. ERP systems contain multiple complex components that are not only expensive to purchase, but also expensive to implement. Costs can include the software itself, plus consulting charges, hardware expenses, and training fees.

Applications such as SCM, CRM, and ERP are the backbone of ebusiness, yet most organizations today have to piece together these systems. A firm might choose its CRM components from Siebel, SCM components from i2, and financial components and HR management components from Oracle. Integrating all of these enterprise systems allows an organization to function as a single unit meeting customer, partner, and supplier needs.

OPENING CASE QUESTIONS

1. **Knowledge:** Define SCM and how it can benefit Zappos.
2. **Comprehension:** Explain CRM and why Zappos would benefit from the implementation of a CRM system.
3. **Application:** Demonstrate why Zappos would need to implement SCM, CRM, and ERP for a connected corporation.
4. **Analysis:** Analyze the merger between Zappos and Amazon and assess potential issues for Zappos customers.
5. **Synthesis:** Propose a plan for how Zappos can use Amazon's supply chain to increase sales and customer satisfaction.
6. **Evaluate:** Argue for or against the following statement: "In the electronic age customer relationships are more important than ever and Zappos provides the new benchmark that all corporations should follow."

KEY TERMS

Accounting and finance ERP component, 312
Analytical CRM, 301
Backward integration, 289
Balanced scorecard, 314
Bullwhip effect, 294
Call scripting system, 305
Campaign management system, 303
Click-to-talk, 305
Contact center or call center, 304
Contact management CRM system, 304
Core ERP component, 311
CRM analysis technologies, 300
CRM predicting technologies, 300
CRM reporting technologies, 300
Cross-selling, 303
Customer relationship management (CRM), 298
Demand planning system, 295
Electronic data interchange (EDI), 294
Elogistics, 313
Employee relationship management (ERM), 308
Enterprise application integration (EAI), 290
Enterprise application integration (EAI) middleware, 290
Enterprise resource planning (ERP), 308
Enterprise system, 290
Eprocurement, 313
Extended ERP component, 311
Forward integration, 289
Human resources ERP component, 313
Integration, 289
Legacy system, 290
List generator, 302
Middleware, 290
Operational CRM, 301
Opportunity management CRM system, 304
Partner relationship management (PRM), 308
Production and materials management ERP component, 313
Sales force automation (SFA), 304
Sales management CRM system, 304
Supplier relationship management (SRM), 308
Supply chain, 291
Supply chain execution system, 294
Supply chain management (SCM), 292
Supply chain planning system, 294
Supply chain visibility, 294
Up-selling, 303
Web-based self-service system, 305
Website personalization, 305

REVIEW QUESTIONS

1. How do integrations connect a corporation?
2. What is the difference between forward and backward integrations?
3. What are the five primary activities in a supply chain?

4. What is the bullwhip effect and how can it impact a supply chain and a firm's profitability?
5. What are supply chain planning systems, supply chain execution systems, and demand planning systems?
6. What are the challenges associated with SCM systems?
7. Why are customer relationships important to an organization? Do you agree that every business needs to focus on customers to survive in the information age?
8. What is the difference between operational and analytical CRM?
9. How can a sales department use CRM to improve operations?
10. How can a marketing department use CRM to improve operations?
11. What is the difference between customer relationship management, supplier relationship management, and employee relationship management?
12. What is an enterprise resource planning system?
13. What are the components in a core ERP system?
14. What are the components in an extended ERP system?
15. What does a company need to integrate to become connected?

CLOSING CASE ONE

Can Customer Loyalty Be a Bad Thing?

What happens when you find out that your business's most faithful customers aren't necessarily the most profitable ones? The economic crisis has jolted companies into the need to redouble efforts to foster customer loyalty. Numerous articles now tout the increased importance of giving customers premium service in troubled times to ensure customer retention. The underlying reasoning is simple—through their continued patronage, loyal customers help a company to weather the storm.

Without question, there is some truth to this logic. No firm can survive for long without loyal customers. The problem, however, is that success through loyalty isn't nearly so simple. Like most big ideas, there are conditions where it is unarguably correct, and less popular but equally true conditions where it is wrong.

Loyalty is a big idea. At its most basic level, it is a feeling of attachment that causes someone to be willing to continue a relationship. And while exclusive loyalty has been replaced in customers' hearts and minds with multiple loyalties for many if not most product categories, often greater than 50 percent of a company's customers would classify themselves as holding some level of loyalty to a particular company. Even if we narrow our classification of loyalty to customers who feel loyal and give the majority of their purchases in a category to the firm, typically we find this to represent one-third of a firm's customers.

The fly in the ointment is that typically only 20 perceny of a firm's customers are actually profitable. And many—often most—of a company's profitable customers are not loyal. This presents managers with a loyalty problem, although not one that they expect. If typically most loyal customers in a firm aren't profitable, how does a customer loyalty strategy ever generate a positive return on investment? Instead of asking whether you have enough loyal customers in your customer base, you need to ask yourself three more complex questions: (1) which loyal customers are good for the business, (2) how do we hang onto them, and (3) how do we get more customers like them.

In this slow economy, customers in both B2B and B2C settings are naturally much more sensitive to economic issues. Furthermore, companies in B2B relationships are often more reliant on their vendor partners to help them shoulder this burden. There is nothing inherently wrong with this, and managers need to recognize that their job is to meet customers' needs to deserve their loyalty.

But the simple solution to improving customer loyalty in a down market is to offer price deals. Firms that track their customer loyalty can be guaranteed that loyalty scores will increase with each substantial decrease in price.

But that's a bad loyalty strategy. This doesn't mean businesses shouldn't find ways to be more efficient so they can pass cost savings on to customers. But price-driven loyalty is always the lowest form of loyalty. It means the firm isn't offering differentiated value to its customers.

The place to begin any loyalty strategy is to determine which loyal customers are profitable and which are not. A closer examination of these two types of customers always reveals very different reasons for their loyalty. Unprofitable loyal customers tend to be loyal for one of two reasons: (1) they are driven by unprofitable pricing or exchange policies, or (2) they demand an excessive amount of service that they are not willing to pay fairly to receive.

Profitable loyal customers, on the other hand, are almost always driven by differentiating aspects of the product or service offering. The key to a successful loyalty strategy is to become clear as to what these differentiating aspects are, and to focus on tangibly improving these elements. It is also imperative to actively tell customers and prospective customers that these are the things the company stands for and that the firm is committed to being best at. By doing this, the best customers will have the necessary information to clearly articulate why an organization deserves their loyalty in good times and in bad.[11]

Questions

1. Why are customer relationships important to an organization? Do you agree that every business needs to focus on customers to survive in the information age?
2. How can a company find its most loyal customers?
3. Choose a business (maybe Starbucks, Disney, or Nissan). Answer each of the following questions based on your business choice.
   a. Which loyal customers are good for the business?
   b. How do we hang onto them?
   c. How do we get more customers like them?
4. Do you agree or disagree with the following statement: "The fly in the ointment is that typically only 20 percent of a firm's customers are actually profitable. And many—often most—of a company;s profitable customers are not loyal."

CLOSING CASE TWO

Got Milk? It's Good for You—Unless It's Contaminated!

Dong Lizhong bet that being a dairy farmer was his golden ticket out of a factory job in China. Unfortunately, a contamination crisis in 2008 shattered his dairy business when babies mysteriously started developing kidney stones from contaminated baby formula. A chemical called melamine, an additive used to make plastic, was discovered in the milk supply of one of China's third-largest dairy producers. Four infants died from the contamination and at least 53,000 fell ill. According to the official Xinhua news agency, officials knew about problems with the milk for months before informing the public.

China's four largest dairy organizations, accounting for nearly half the country's milk market, pulled their goods off shelves. More than 20 countries, including France, India, and South Korea, banned not only dairy products from China, but also candies, cookies, and chocolates. "This is a disastrous setback. I estimate that it will take one or two years to rebuild confidence in dairy products," says Luo Yunbo, dean of the College of Food Science & Nutritional Engineering at China Agricultural University.

The local milk-collection station in Dong Lizhong's village discontinued purchasing milk. Farmers continued to milk their cows, but they drank the milk themselves or poured the milk into their cabbage fields.

Cutting Corners

Chinese do not traditionally drink milk. However, as the country has grown more affluent over the past few decades, the domestic dairy industry has skyrocketed. China's two largest dairy companies have greatly benefited from this new trend: China Mengniu Dairy and Inner Mongolia Yili Industrial Group. Simultaneously, numerous entrepreneurs—from dairy farmers to milk-collection station owners to milk distributors—have jumped into the supply chain of dairy products to make their fortunes. Due to the fierce competition within China's dairy industry, a few companies decided to cut corners to reduce costs, regardless of the consequences.

As Mengniu and Yili expanded at breathtaking speed, they found themselves in the unique position where supply could not keep up with demand. According to KPMG, China consumes 25 million tons of milk yearly, putting its dairy market ahead of France and Germany. In their quest for more raw milk, Mengniu and Yili have expanded outside their base in the northern province of Inner Mongolia and set up production facilities in other parts of China. Most of the quality problems in milk were found in dairy farms in Hebei and Inner Mongolia provinces, where the competition for raw milk supplies has been the fiercest.

Most dairy farmers in Hebei province traditionally sold their milk to milk-collection stations established by local heavyweight Sanlu. In recent years, new privately owned milk-collection stations to buy raw milk for Mengniu and Yili started popping up next to existing stations. These new entrants captured raw milk supplies by offering dairy farmers slightly higher prices. "This competition broke the rules. As milk buyers fought over milk supplies, their standards for quality fell," says Roger Liu, vice chairman of American Dairy Inc., a Heilongjiang province-based powdered milk company.

Additives to Boost Protein

Many of the milking stations do not have the equipment to test milk for additives. At the Nanxincheng station, 16 households bring their dairy cows in the area to be milked in the red brick farmhouse. The farmers hook up the cows to a milking machine, which pumps the milk directly into a big vat. "They didn't test the milk here. They sent it to Sanlu for testing," says Du Yanjun, a government inspector who was posted to monitor the Nanxincheng station after the contamination crisis broke.

The milk is collected from the stations and shipped by middlemen to big dairy companies such as Sanlu, which would do their own testing and grading. It now appears that unscrupulous middlemen added melamine to the raw milk to increase protein levels in their milk samples, so their milk would be graded higher. However, ingesting melamine can also cause kidney stones or kidney failure, especially in infants.

Matthew Estes, president and CEO of BabyCare, had looked into switching from Australian and New Zealand sources of milk for the company's infant-formula business in China. BabyCare tested possible Chinese suppliers and realized it could not locate a suitable supplier in China. "We couldn't the find quality that met our standards. We chose to not sell in China rather than take the risk," he says.

Stiff Sentences

A Chinese court sentenced two of the middlemen to death and a dairy boss to life in prison for their roles in the milk contamination scandal. The swift trial and harsh sentences show

Beijing's resolve in tackling the country's stubborn food safety problems and an eagerness by the communist leadership to move past the embarrassing scandal.[12]

Questions

1. List 10 products that could possibly be affected by a problem in the U.S. milk supply chain. What would be the damages to an ice cream business that used contaminated milk in its manufacturing process? Who do you think should be held liable for such an issue?
2. Do you think a CRM system could have helped communicate issues in the milk production supply chain? How could a company use a CRM system to perform damage control after finding out about contaminated milk in the supply chain?
3. Do you agree with the Chinese court in sentencing of the middlemen to death and a dairy boss to life in prison for their roles in the milk contamination scandal? Do you think the United States should implement similar laws for unethical corporate behavior?
4. Many companies in the United States use Chinese suppliers in the sourcing of raw materials and manufacturing of products. Research the Internet and find three examples of recent issues for U.S. companies because of Chinese products. What will happen in the long run as companies use Chinese suppliers?

CRITICAL BUSINESS THINKING

1. Political Supply Chains

The U.S. government brokered a deal with the United Arab Emirates (UAE) allowing the UAE government-owned firm Dubai Ports World (DPW) to operate six major U.S. ports (New York, New Jersey, Baltimore, New Orleans, Miami, Philadelphia) after DPW purchased the current United Kingdom-based port operator, P&O, the fourth largest port company in the world.

Some citizens are worried that the federal government may be outsourcing U.S. port operations to a company prone to terrorist infiltration by allowing a firm from the United Arab Emirates to run port operations within the United States. The United Arab Emirates has had people involved in terrorism. Some of its financial institutions laundered the money for the 9/11 terrorists. You have been called in on an investigation to determine the potential effects on U.S. businesses' supply chains if these ports were shut down due to terrorist activities. Create an argument for or against outsourcing these ports to the UAE. Be sure to detail the effect on U.S. businesses' supply chains if these ports are subjected to terrorist acts.[12]

2. Analyzing Dell's Supply Chain Management System

Dell's supply chain strategy is legendary. If you want to build a successful SCM system, your best bet is to model your SCM system after Dell's. In a team, research Dell's supply chain management strategy on the Web and create a report discussing any new SCM updates and strategies the company is currently using that were not discussed in this text. Be sure to include a graphical presentation of Dell's current supply chain model.

3. Total Recall

The Firestone Tire Company issued a recall for all tires issued on a certain brand of Ford's sport-utility vehicles. The tire treads on some SUVs separated during use, which could cause a fatal accident as the defect caused vehicles to roll over. In the beginning Firestone denied it had a tire problem, stating that Ford had incorrectly matched its SUVs with the wrong brand of tires. It also suggested that the shock absorbers might have been rubbing against the tires, causing the defect. Firestone soon recalled the tires as the company received more and more pressure from government and consumer advocacy groups. Interestingly, all of the defective tires were manufactured at the same tire factory and the company soon shut down that facility. Information was soon found that Firestone had recalled the identical type of tire in South America and had already settled a lawsuit for an accident caused by the tread defect. Discuss each of the following factors in relation to this case: quality, inventory, ethics, supply chain visibility, profitability, customer loyalty.[13]

4. **Finding Shelf Space at Walmart**

Walmart's business strategy of being a low-cost provider by managing its supply chain down to the minutia has paid off greatly. Each week, approximately 100 million customers, or one-third of the U.S. population, visit Walmart's U.S. stores. Walmart is currently the world's largest retailer and the second-largest corporation behind ExxonMobil. It was founded by Sam Walton in 1962 and is the largest private employer in the United States and Mexico. Walmart is also the largest grocery retailer in the United States, with an estimated 20 percent of the retail grocery and consumables business, and the largest toy seller in the United States, with an estimated 45 percent of the retail toy business, having surpassed Toys "R" Us in the late 1990s.

Walmart's business model is based on selling a wide variety of general merchandise at "always low prices." The reason Walmart can offer such low prices is due to its innovative use of information technology tools to create its highly sophisticated supply chain. Walmart has famously invited its major suppliers to jointly develop powerful supply chain partnerships. These are designed to increase product flow efficiency and, consequently, Walmart's profitability.[14]

You are the owner of a high-end collectible toy company. You create everything from authentic sports figure replicas to famous musicians and movie characters including Babe Ruth, Hulk Hogan, Mick Jagger, Ozzy Osbourne, Alien, and the Terminator. It would be a huge win for your company if you could get your collectibles into Walmart. Compile a strategic plan highlighting the steps required to approach Walmart as your supply chain partner. Be sure to address the pros and cons of partnering with the chain, including the cost to revamp your current supply chain to meet Walmart's tough supply chain requirements.

5. **Customer Relationship Management Strategies**

On average, it costs an organization six times more to sell to a new customer than to sell to an existing customer. As the co-owner of a medium-sized sports equipment distributor, you have recently been notified that sales for the past three months have decreased by an average of 20 percent. The reasons for the decline in sales are numerous, including a poor economy and some negative publicity your company received regarding a defective product line. In a group, explain how implementing a CRM system can help you understand and combat the decline in sales. Be sure to justify why a CRM system is important to your business and its future growth.

Also, search the Internet for at least one recent and authoritative article that compares or ranks customer relationship management systems. Select two packages from the list and compare their functions and features as described in the article(s) you found as well as on each company's website. Find references in the literature where companies that are using each package have reported their experiences, both good and bad. Draw on any other comparisons you can find. Prepare a presentation for delivery in class on the strengths and weaknesses of each package, which one you favor, and why.

6. **Searching for Employee Loyalty**

You are the CEO of Razz, a start-up Web-based search company, which is planning to compete directly with Google. The company had an exceptional first year and is currently receiving over 500,000 hits a day from customers all over the world. You have hired 250 people in the past four months, doubling the size of your organization. With so many new employees starting so quickly you are concerned about how your company's culture will evolve and whether your employees are receiving enough attention. You are already familiar with customer relationship management and how CRM systems can help an organization create strong customer relationships. However, you are unfamiliar with employee relationship management and you are wondering what ERM systems might be able to offer your employees and your company. Research the Web, create a report detailing features and functions of ERM systems, and determine what value will be added to your organization if you decide to implement an ERM solution.

7. **Driving Up Profits with Loyalty (or Driving Down?)**
   The Butterfly Café is located in downtown San Francisco and offers specialty coffee, teas, and organic fruits and vegetables. The café holds a number of events to attract customers such as live music, poetry readings, book clubs, charity events, and local artist's night. A listing of all participants attending each event is tracked in the café's database. The café uses the information for marketing campaigns and offers customers who attend multiple events additional discounts. A marketing database company, InTheKnow.com, has offered to pay the Butterfly Café a substantial amount of money for access to its customer database, which it will then sell to other local businesses. The owner of the Butterfly Café, Penny Dirks, has come to you for advice. She is not sure if her customers would appreciate her selling their personal information and how it might affect her business. However, the amount of money InTheKnow.com is offering is enough to finance her much-needed new patio for the back of the café. InTheKnow.com has promised that the sale will be completely confidential. What should Dirks do?

8. **Supporting Customers**
   Creative.com is an ebusiness that sells craft materials and supplies over the Internet. You have just started as the vice president of customer service, and you have a team of 45 customer service representatives. Currently, the only form of customer service is the toll-free number and the company is receiving a tremendous number of calls regarding products, orders, and shipping information. The average wait time for a customer to speak to a customer service representative is 35 minutes. Orders are being cancelled and Creative.com is losing business due to its lack of customer service. Create a strategy to revamp the customer service center and get the company back on track.

9. **Implementing an ERP System**
   Blue Dog Inc. is a leading manufacturer in the high-end sunglasses industry, reaching record revenue levels of more than $250 million last year. Blue Dog is currently deciding on the possibility of implementing an ERP system to help decrease production costs and increase inventory control. Many of the executives are nervous about making such a large investment in an ERP system due to its low success rates. As a senior manager at Blue Dog Inc., you have been asked to compile a list of the potential benefits and risks associated with implementing an ERP system along with your recommendations for the steps the company can take to ensure a successful implementation. Be sure to also explain why ERP systems include CRM and SCM components, and the advantages the company can gain by implementing all of the components for a connected corporation.

ENTREPRENEURIAL CHALLENGE

BUILD YOUR OWN BUSINESS

1. Netflix reinvented the video rental business using supply chain technology. Netflix is the largest online DVD rental service, offering flat-rate rental by mail and over the Internet to customers. Customers can create their own personal list of movie favorites and the DVDs

are delivered by the US Post office from one of Netflix's warehouses. Customers can keep the DVDs for as long as they want and simply return it by mail to receive their next selection. Netflix's business is video rental, but it used technology to revamp its supply chain to completely disrupt the entire video rental industry. Define a way that you can revamp or reinvent your business using supply chain technologies.

2. Business is booming, and you have achieved your goal of driving operating costs down, which helps to drive revenues up. One of your best new products is from China, and it is accounting for a 20 percent increase in your profits. Yesterday, a dockworkers union strike began and shut down all of the West Coast shipping docks from San Francisco to Canada. Work will resume when the union agrees to new labor contracts, which could take months. You need to quickly assess the impact of the shutdown on your business. How will you keep business running if you cannot receive your shipments? What strategies do you recommend to help the business continue working while the supply chain is disrupted by the strike?

3. The Web contains numerous examples of customer power. Examples include www.ihatedell.net and www.donotbuydodge.ca. Customers are using YouTube, MySpace, blogs, and a number of other Web tools to slam or praise companies. Do you believe that the most influential person in your business is the customer? How could customers hurt or help your business? Will your employees agree that customers are the most important part of the business?

APPLY YOUR KNOWLEDGE BUSINESS PROJECTS

PROJECT I Shipping Problems

Entrepreneurship is in Alyssa Stuart's blood. Stuart has been starting businesses since she was 10 years old, and she finally has the perfect business of custom-made furniture. Customers who visit her shop can choose from a number of different fabrics and 50 different styles of couch and chair designs to create their custom-made furniture. Once the customer decides on a fabric pattern and furniture design, the information is sent to China where the furniture is built and shipped to the customer via the West Coast. Stuart is excited about her business; all of her hard work has finally paid off as she has more than 17,000 customers and 875 orders currently in the pipe.

Project Focus

Stuart's business is booming. Her high-quality products and outstanding customer service have created an excellent reputation for her business. But the business is at risk of losing everything and she has come to you for help solving her supply chain issues. The parcel delivery companies like Fed Ex and UPS are on strike and Alyssa is not sure how she is going to get her raw materials or finished products delivered. What strategies do you recommend for Alyssa's business to continue working to overcome the strike?

PROJECT II Great Stories

When customers have an unpleasant customer experience, the company no longer has to worry about them telling a few friends and family; the company now has to worry about them telling everyone. Internet service providers are giving frustrated consumers another means of fighting back. Free or low-cost computer space for Internet websites is empowering consumers to tell not only their friends, but also the world about the way they have been treated. A few examples of disgruntled customer stories from the Internet include:

- A bike-riding tourist requires stitches after being bitten on the leg by a dog. The tourism company is banned from renting bikes and in turn bars the tourist from taking any future tours.
- A customer leaving Best Buy refuses to voluntarily show the receipt to the guard at the door. The Best Buy employees try to seize the customer's cart and then decide to park a car behind the customer's vehicle.
- Enterprise Rent-A-Car operates a high-stress business, and frequently its customers find that the company did not honor reservations, did not have cars ready for reservations, rented cars with empty tanks of gas, and charged higher rates to corporate account holders.

Project Focus

The pervasive nature of the Internet is increasing customer power and changing business from product-focused to a customer-focused. Explain the difference between product-focused business and customer-focused business and why CRM is more important than ever before?

PROJECT III JetBlue on YouTube

JetBlue took an unusual and interesting CRM approach by using YouTube to apologize to its customers. JetBlue's founder and former CEO, David Neeleman, apologized to customers via YouTube after a very bad week for the airline: 1,100 flights were canceled due to snowstorms, causing thousands of passengers to be stranded at airports around the country. Neeleman's unrehearsed, unrefined, and sincere YouTube apology made customers understand the issues and accept the company's apology.

Project Focus

You are the founder and CEO of GoodDog, a large pet food manufacturing company. Recently, at least 16 pet deaths have been tied to tainted pet food, fortunately not manufactured by your company. A recall of potentially deadly pet food has dog and cat owners studying their animals for even the slightest hint of illness and swamping veterinarians nationwide with calls about symptoms. Create a strategy for using YouTube as a vehicle to communicate with your customers as they fear for their pets' lives. Be sure to highlight the pros and cons of using YouTube as a customer communication vehicle. Are there any other new technologies you could use as a customer communication vehicle that would be more effective than YouTube? With all the new advances in technology and the many ways to reach customers, do you think using YouTube is a smart approach? What else could you do to help gain back customers' trust?

PROJECT IV Gaining Business Intelligence from Strategic Initiatives

You are a new employee in the customer service department at Premier One, a large office supply distributor. The company, , has been in business for three years and focuses on providing top of the line office supplies at a low cost. The company currently has 90 employees and operates in seven states.

Project Focus

Sales over the past three years have tripled, and the manual systems currently in place are no longer sufficient to run the business. Your first task is to meet with your new team and create a presentation for the president and chief executive officer describing supply chain management, customer relationship management, and enterprise resource planning. The presentation should highlight the main benefits Premier One can receive from these enterprise systems along with any additional added business value that can be gained from the systems.

PROJECT V Second Life CRM

New virtual worlds such as Second Life are becoming the first point of contact between many firms and customers. To say the least, virtual relationships are far different from traditional relationships. Firms such as Adidas, Dell, Reuters, and Toyota are all embracing Second Life; however, beyond opening a virtual office in a virtual world, they are struggling with how to build virtual customer relationships.

PA Consulting quickly learned that building a virtual office to answer customer queries is not nearly good enough to find and attract loyal customers. The company realized that real people behind the avatars need to be housed in a real office similar to having a call center to answer questions for online shopping. When a potential customer wants to speak to a human, one must appear or else the customer will leave the website.

Project Focus

You are the executive director of CRM at StormPeak, an advanced technological company that develops robots. You are in charge of overseeing the first virtual site being built in Second Life. Create a CRM strategy for doing business in a virtual world. Here are a few questions to get you started:

- How will customer relationships be different in a virtual world?
- What is your strategy for managing customer relationships in this new virtual environment?
- How will supporting Second Life customers differ from supporting traditional customers?
- How will supporting Second Life customers differ from supporting website customers?
- What customer security issues might you encounter in Second Life?
- What customer ethical issues might you encounter in Second Life?

PROJECT VI Searching Telephone Calls

Imagine being able to search a database of customer phone calls to find specific requests or to be able to sort through digital customer complaints to detect the exact moment when the interaction between the customer service representative and the customer went wrong. A new tool called Find It allows the sorting of digital voice records as easily as using Google to sift through documents. Find It is opening limitless business opportunities as organizations begin to understand how they can use this technology to help employees search voice mails or recorded calls for keywords and phrases.

Project Focus

You have recently started your own marketing firm and you want to use the power of Find It to help your customers query all of their unique data records, including digital voice recordings. Now all you need is to prepare your marketing materials to send to potential customers. Create a marketing pitch that you will deliver to customers detailing the business opportunities they could uncover if they purchase Find It. Your marketing pitch can be a one-page document, a catchy tune, a video, or a PowerPoint presentation.

PROJECT VII Sharptooth Incorporated

Stephen Kern is the founder and CEO of Sharptooth, a small business that buys and sells comic strips to magazines and newspapers around the country. Some of Sharptooth's artists have made it big and are syndicated in hundreds of magazines and newspapers, while others are new to the industry. Kern started in the business as an artist and began contracting other artists when he realized he had a knack for promoting and marketing comic materials. His artistic background is great for spotting talented young artists, but not so great for running the business.

Project Focus

Kern recently began selling comics to new forms of media such as blogs, websites, and other online tools. He has hired you to build him a new system to track all online comic sales. You quickly notice that Kern has a separate system for each of his different lines of business including newspaper sources, magazine sources, billboard sources, and now online sources. You notice that each system works independently to perform its job of creating, updating, and maintaining sales information, but you are wondering how he operates his business as a whole. Create a list of issues Kern will encounter if he continues to run his business with four separate systems performing the same operations. What could happen to the business if he cannot correlate the details of each? Be sure to highlight at least 10 issues where separate systems could cause problems.

PROJECT VIII Eating In

Having been employed by the same company for more than 20 years, Mary Lou Smith was shocked when she was suddenly terminated along with about 900 of her co-workers. It took Smith a few weeks to recover from the shock, then she finally began focusing her efforts on searching for a new job. Smith was sure her loyal employment history and strong skill set would land her a new job in no time; however, after several months of searching she wasn't having any luck. With her emergency funds quickly being depleted, Smith knew she had to find a new job soon or else she'd need to start selling her assets or cashing in her retirement.

The one positive aspect of having so much free time was that she could focus on her true passion, cooking. She began making a little money by catering lunches and dinners for local businesses and neighbors. Smith overheard a neighbor remark that she was hosting a large party and didn't have enough time to prepare the meal. Almost jokingly, Smith asked her how much she'd be willing to pay for a catered event. Soon Smith was catering for numerous neighbors and small businesses and she knew she had to make a decision if she would go into business for herself or continue searching for other employment.

Project Focus

After a year in the catering business, Smith was earning a good living and building a stellar reputation. She began catering for all types of events, including weddings, and business was so good that she hired several employees to help grow her business. As Smith begins to plan her expansion, she has asked for you help in answering the following questions:

1. How important is customer loyalty for Smith's business? What can she do to ensure her customers remain loyal? How could one disgruntled customer hurt business? What can she do to combat this challenge?
2. Research the business Yelp.com. What service does Yelp.com perform? Would a small business see Yelp.com as an opportunity or a threat? What are the pros and cons a customer should be aware of when using yelp.com?
3. Smith's responsibilities include forecasting, inventory control, scheduling, and ensuring high-quality products. What types of forecasts would she require to run her business? What types of inventory would she want to track? What might happen if her inventory tracking tool was off by 50 percent? What types of schedules does Smith need to generate? What things might occur to disrupt schedules and cause her to reschedule? How can a supply chain management system help run the business?
4. Smith wants to create a business based on loyal customers and loyal employees. She offers her employees bonuses for new ideas, recipes, or business referrals. What risks

is Smith encountering by offering these bonuses? One employee idea that she has implemented is turning out to be a competitive advantage for her business; however, the employee has quit and is now working for a competitor. Should Smith still pay the employee the bonus? What should she do to ensure she is building strong employee relationships?

5. Smith overheard one of her customers talking about enterprise systems such as CRM, SCM, and ERP. However, she is sure they are available only to big companies that have lots of capital. Research the Internet and find examples of enterprise systems for small business. Do you think she should invest in these types of systems to run her business? Why or why not?

AYK APPLICATION PROJECTS

If you are looking for Excel projects to incorporate into your class, try any of the following after reading this chapter.

Project Number	Project Name	Project Type	Plug-In	Focus Area	Project Level	Skill Set	Page Number
9	Security Analysis	Excel	T3	Filtering Data	Intermediate	Conditional Formatting, Autofilter, Subtotal	AYK.7
10	Gathering Data	Excel	T3	Data Analysis	Intermediate	Conditional Formatting	AYK.8
11	Scanner System	Excel	T2	Strategic Analysis	Intermediate	Formulas	AYK.8
12	Competitive Pricing	Excel	T2	Profit Maximization	Intermediate	Formulas	AYK.9
13	Adequate Acquisitions	Excel	T2	Break Even Analysis	Intermediate	Formulas	AYK.9
15	Assessing the Value of Information	Excel	T3	Data Analysis	Intermediate	PivotTable	AYK.10
16	Growth, Trends, and Forecasts	Excel	T2, T3	Data Forecasting	Advanced	Average, Trend, Growth	AYK.11
18	Formatting Grades	Excel	T3	Data Analysis	Advanced	If, LookUp	AYK.12
22	Turnover Rates	Excel	T3	Data Mining	Advanced	PivotTable	AYK.15
23	Vital Information	Excel	T3	Data Mining	Advanced	PivotTable	AYK.15
24	Breaking Even	Excel	T4	Business Analysis	Advanced	Goal Seek	AYK.16
25	Profit Scenario	Excel	T4	Sales Analysis	Advanced	Scenario Manager	AYK.16

Systems Development and Project Management: Corporate Responsibility

CHAPTER OUTLINE

SECTION 9.1
Developing Enterprise Applications

- Developing Software
- The Systems Development Life Cycle (SDLC)
- Traditional Software Development Methodology: Waterfall
- Agile Software Development Methodologies
- Developing Successful Software

SECTION 9.2
Project Management

- Managing Software Development Projects
- Choosing Strategic Projects
- Understanding Project Planning
- Managing Projects
- Outsourcing Projects

What's in IT for me?

This chapter provides an overview of how organizations build information systems. As a business student, you need to understand this process because information systems are the underlying foundations of company operations. Your understanding of the principles of building information systems will make you a more valuable employee. You will be able to identify trouble spots early and make suggestions during the design process that will result in a better information systems project—one that satisfies both you and your business.

Building an information system is like constructing a house. You could sit back and let the developers do all the design work, construction, and testing and hope the finished product will satisfy your needs. However, participating in the process helps to guarantee that your needs are not only heard, but also met. It is good business practice to have direct user input steering the development of the finished product. Your knowledge of the systems development process will allow you to participate and ensure you are building flexible enterprise architectures that support not only current business needs, but also future ones.

opening case study

Getting Your Project on Track

June is the perfect time of year to reflect on the current state of all the key projects that were approved in January. At this stage, you and your management team should have enough data to know if each initiative will successfully meet its objectives. You may already know there are projects in your organization that are not positioned to succeed, yet they still receive funding and staff. When you assess the current state of your projects, do you see any of the following signs:

- Critical issues keep opening up, but they're not getting resolved.
- Project scope is constantly changing.
- The project is consistently behind its plan, despite efforts to get it back on schedule.
- Competing deliverables are distracting your attention.

If all of these signs appear, it may be time to cut your losses and cut the project—or at least radically restructure it. You know better than anyone that throwing good money after the bad will not save the project because it doesn't address the root cause of the project's woes. To determine a course of action, ask yourself the following questions about the project:

- What can be salvaged?
- What can be delivered with the time and budget that are left?
- Do you have the right leadership in place to complete the project successfully?
- Is the plan for the initiative sound and realistic?
- Am I and my management team doing everything we can to support the initiative?

If part of or the entire project can be salvaged and delivered on time and with the remaining budget, if the right leaders are present to steer the project, if the new plan is solid, and if management will continue to support the project, the following four steps will help you regain control and deliver the revised project successfully. These steps are basic blocking and tackling, but the detail behind the plan—and more importantly, the execution and focus the project team brings to the effort—will determine whether the project recovery effort will succeed.

Step One: Assess the Situation

Get as much information about the current state of the project as possible. Use that data to make informed decisions about what needs to happen next. Don't be afraid if, at this stage, there are more questions than answers; that is normal. The key is to ask the right question to obtain as accurate a picture of the project's status as possible. The following questions address key data points you need to collect:

- How critical is the delivery date?
- What functionality is exactly required by the delivery date?
- What has been completed and what is still outstanding?
- How willing will people be to change scope, dates, and budget?

The last question about change is critical because it touches on the people and political issues that are present in any project and any organization. Even when faced with sure failure, people find it hard to change unless there is a direct benefit to them and their team. For recovery to have a chance, expectations need to change, especially those of the key stakeholders.

When gathering data about the current state of the project, remember to ask the current team for their opinions on what went wrong. It can be easy to ignore their input since they're associated with the current failure. In fact, each individual can provide great insight into why the project arrived in its current state. Reach out to key team members and get their suggestions for correcting the situation.

Step Two: Prepare the Team for Recovery

Everyone involved in the project—from executive management to stakeholders to project team members—needs to accept that the current project is broken and needs to be fixed. They also need to accept that the existing project plan and approach to delivering the project is flawed and needs to be restructured. If they don't accept these facts, they will likely resist the steps needed for recovery.

Once everyone has accepted the need to change course, define realistic expectations for what can be delivered given the current state and time frame. Also establish metrics for success and control of the recovery. If you had metrics at the outset of the project, you may need to establish new ones, or you may simply need to hold yourself and others accountable to them.

Both management and the project manager in charge of the recovery need to develop a supportive environment for team members. Giving them realistic goals and providing them with the needed space, equipment, and training will position them for success.

Finally, take advantage of the new momentum associated with the recovery and involve all the key parties in the status of the project. This involvement will keep everyone focused and engaged. It will assure project team members and stakeholders that they're needed for more than just executing tasks.

Step Three: Develop a Game Plan for Recovery

Think of the recovery as a new project, separate from the old one. This new project requires its own scope of work to make the expectations around what is being delivered and the new criteria for judging success crystal clear. The new scope may require you to determine if you have the right resources on the project team or if you need to re-staff some team members.

Based on the new project scope, the project manager and project team should lay out a clear and realistic road map to achieve the objectives. The main difference in the plan this time is that it must not fail. It will also be under much greater scrutiny by management. Consequently, it will be critical to make sure the milestones are shorter in duration to demonstrate success and to allow for course correction if needed. The shorter milestones will provide valuable data points to determine the health of the project early.

Step Four: Execute the Game Plan

With the new plan in hand, it's time to get down to business. Remember that during execution, it is not just the project team members who are accountable. Everyone from management on down is on the hook. All facets of the project, from environment to support, need to be in sync at all times, and everyone needs to know they are accountable for the project recovery to succeed.

To make sure everyone is on the same page during the recovery, the project communication needs to be clear, informative, and frequent. Clearly define in your communication plan how information will be disseminated, how urgent items will be addressed, and how key decisions will be made.

Given the added level of scrutiny on the plan and the project, being able to provide the latest on the metrics to show the improved control over the project will be key. The data will also allow you to quickly make corrections when any sign of trouble surfaces.

Getting a flailing project back on track is not easy. It requires sustained effort, focus, commitment, and objectivity. During the project recovery there is no time for personal agendas. The ability to see and do what is best for the project is required from every team member.

It is also important to not lose sight of the pressure that everyone is under. Make sure there is a positive focus on people. The team needs to have the ability to bond, release a little steam, and be focused on the task at hand.

When the project has been successfully delivered, celebrate and recognize the effort of each and every team member. Finally, learn from this successful project recovery so that you and your organization can avoid having to recover a project again. Pay attention to the warning signs and act swiftly and decisively to make corrections early in the project's life cycle so that successful delivery is ensured the first time.[1]

section 9.1 DEVELOPING ENTERPRISE APPLICATIONS

LEARNING OUTCOMES

9.1 Explain the relationship between the systems development life cycle and software development along with the business benefits associated with successful software development.

9.2 Describe the seven phases of the systems development life cycle.

9.3 Summarize the different software development methodologies.

DEVELOPING SOFTWARE

LO 9.1: Explain the business benefits associated with successful software development.

The multimillion-dollar Nike SCM system failure is legendary as Nike CEO Philip Knight famously stated, "This is what we get for our $400 million?" Nike partnered with i2 to implement an SCM system that never came to fruition. i2 blamed the failed implementation on the fact that Nike failed to use the vendor's implementation methodology and templates. Nike blamed the failure on faulty software.[2]

It is difficult to get an organization to work if its systems do not work. In the information age, software success, or failure, can lead directly to business success, or failure. Companies rely on software to drive business operations and ensure work flows throughout the company. As more and more companies rely on software to operate, so do the business-related consequences of software successes and failures.

The potential advantages of successful software implementations provide firms with significant incentives to manage software development risks. However, an alarmingly high number of software development projects come in late or over budget, and successful projects tend to maintain fewer features and functions than originally specified. Understanding the basics of software development, or the systems development life cycle, will help organizations avoid potential software development pitfalls and ensure that software development efforts are successful.

THE SYSTEMS DEVELOPMENT LIFE CYCLE (SDLC)

LO 9.2: Describe the seven phases of the systems development life cycle.

The ***systems development life cycle (SDLC)*** is the overall process for developing information systems, from planning and analysis through implementation and maintenance. The SDLC is the foundation for all systems development methods, and hundreds of different activities are associated with each phase. These activities typically include determining budgets, gathering system requirements, and writing detailed user documentation.

The SDLC begins with a business need, proceeds to an assessment of the functions a system must have to satisfy the need, and ends when the benefits of the system no longer outweigh its maintenance costs. This is why it is referred to as a life cycle. The SDLC is comprised of seven distinct phases: planning, analysis, design, development, testing, implementation, and maintenance (see Figure 9.1).

1. **Planning:** The ***planning phase*** establishes a high-level plan of the intended project and determines project goals. Planning is the first and most critical phase of any systems development effort an organization undertakes, regardless of whether the effort is to develop a system that allows customers to order products online, determine the best logistical structure for warehouses around the world, or develop a strategic information alliance with another organization. Organizations must carefully plan the activities (and determine why they are necessary) to be successful.
2. **Analysis:** In the ***analysis phase*** the firm analyzes its end-user business requirements and refines project goals into defined functions and operations of the intended system. ***Business requirements*** are the specific business requests the system must meet to be successful, so the analysis phase is critical. The organization must spend as much time, energy, and resources as necessary to perform it accurately and in detail.

APPLY YOUR KNOWLEDGE

BUSINESS DRIVEN START-UP

Just Ask TED

You'll remember this day because it is the day you were introduced to Ted (www.ted.com). TED is a nonprofit devoted to "ideas worth spreading." The company hosts a yearly conference focusing on technology, entertainment, and design (TED). TED gathers the world's innovative minds who are challenged to give the talk of their lives in just 18 minutes. Each talk is posted to the Ted website and includes such famous speakers as:

- Chris Anderson, editor of *Wired* and author of *The Long Tail: Why the Future of Business Is Selling Less of More.*
- Tim Berners-Lee, inventor of the World Wide Web.
- Jeff Bezos, founder of Amazon.com.
- Richard Branson, founder of Virgin.
- Bill Clinton, former president of the United States.
- Peter Diamandis, chairman of the X Prize Foundation.
- Sergey Brin and Larry Page, co-founders of Google.
- Malcolm Gladwell, author of *Blink* and *The Tipping Point.*
- Bill Gates, founder of Microsoft.
- Seth Godin, a marketing guru.
- Steven Levitt, author of *Freakonomics.*[3]

As you brainstorm your future start-up hoping to become the next Bill Gates or Steve Jobs, how can you use TED to generate ideas? Review the TED website and choose three talks that could help lead to the next great business idea.

FIGURE 9.1
The Systems Development Life Cycle

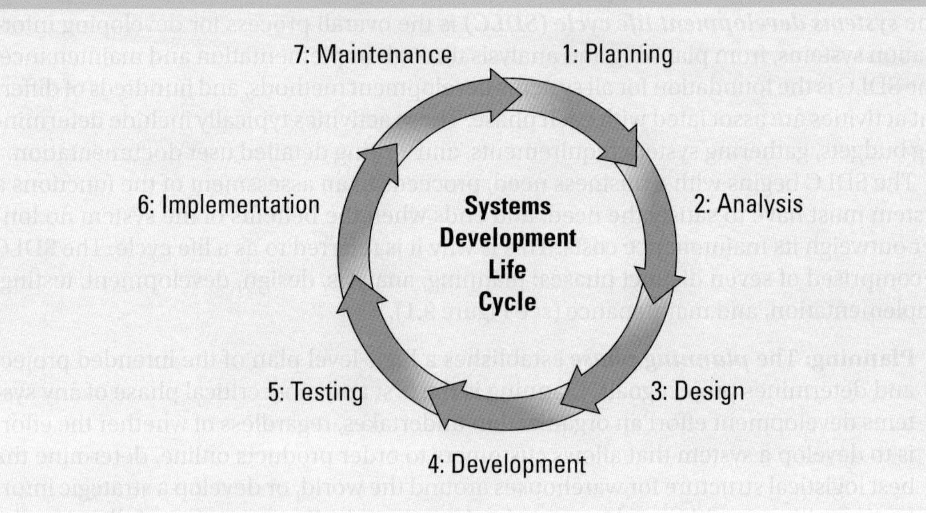

3. **Design:** The ***design phase*** establishes descriptions of the desired features and operations of the system including screen layouts, business rules, process diagrams, pseudo code, and other documentation.
4. **Development:** The ***development phase*** takes all the detailed design documents from the design phase and transforms them into the actual system. In this phase the project transitions from preliminary designs to actual physical implementation.

BUSINESS DRIVEN DEBATE

Flawed Development

Data must be secure! A computer programming course would teach you that security is a critical component that must be included in every system. Apparently, the employees that developed the new system for the state of Oklahoma were out sick during this important class. The new system mistakenly posted confidential data, including Social Security numbers, for thousands of Oklahoma residents on the state's website. The really unfortunate part of this systems blunder is that the error went unnoticed for more than three years. A programmer found the error when he realized that by changing his Web browser he could redirect his page to the entire database for the state of Oklahoma. To make matters even worse, due to development issues, a hacker could have easily changed all of the data in the database or added false data to elements such as the state's Sexual and Violent Offender Registry.[4]

Why is it important to secure data? What can happen if someone accesses your customer database? What could happen if someone changes the information in your customer database and adds fictitious data? What phases in the systems development life cycle should have found these errors? How could these errors go unnoticed for over three years? Who should be held responsible for the system issues?

5. **Testing:** The ***testing phase*** brings all the project pieces together into a special testing environment to eliminate errors and bugs, and verify that the system meets all the business requirements defined in the analysis phase.
6. **Implementation:** In the ***implementation phase*** the organization places the system into production so users can begin to perform actual business operations with it.
7. **Maintenance:** Maintaining the system is the final sequential phase of any systems development effort. In the ***maintenance phase*** the organization performs changes, corrections, additions, and upgrades to ensure the system continues to meet its business goals. This phase continues for the life of the system because the system must change as the business evolves and its needs change, which means conducting constant monitoring, supporting the new system with frequent minor changes (for example, new reports or information capturing), and reviewing the system to be sure it is moving the organization toward its strategic goals.

TRADITIONAL SOFTWARE DEVELOPMENT METHODOLOGY: THE WATERFALL

LO 9.3: Summarize the different software development methodologies.

Today, systems are so large and complex that teams of architects, analysts, developers, testers, and users must work together to create the millions of lines of custom-written code that drive enterprises. For this reason, developers have created a number of different systems development life cycle methodologies. A ***methodology*** is a set of policies, procedures, standards, processes, practices, tools, techniques, and tasks that people apply to technical and management challenges. Firms use a methodology to manage the deployment of technology with work plans, requirements documents, and test plans, for instance. A formal methodology can include coding standards, code libraries, development practices, and much more.

The oldest and the best known is the ***waterfall methodology,*** a sequence of phases in which the output of each phase becomes the input for the next (see Figure 9.2). In the SDLC, this means the steps are performed one at a time, in order, from planning through implementation and maintenance. The traditional waterfall method no longer

FIGURE 9.2

The Traditional Waterfall Methodology

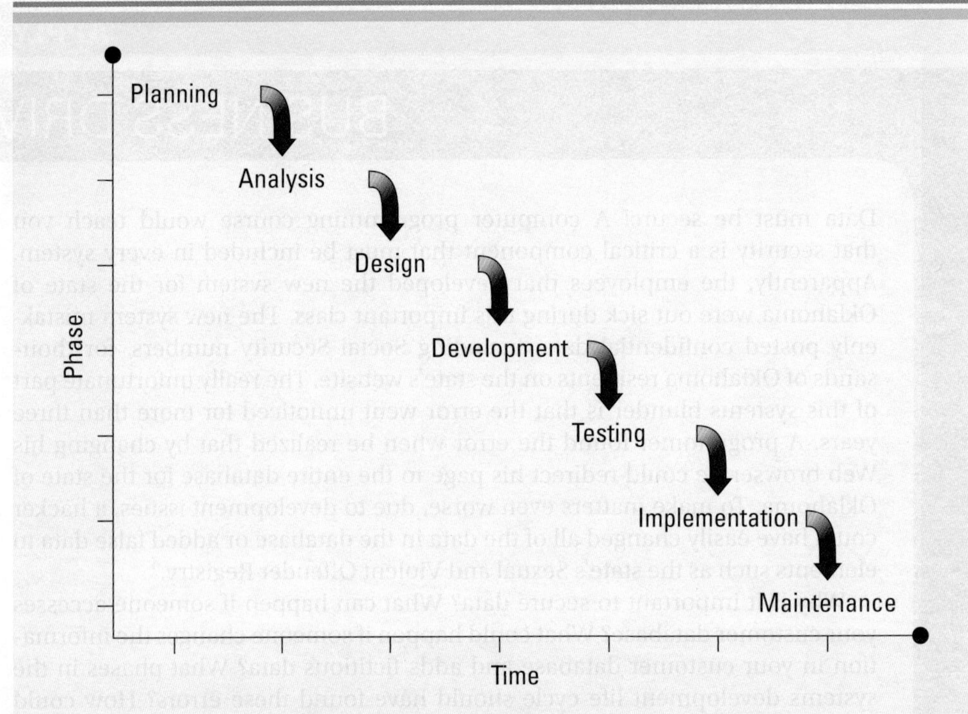

FIGURE 9.3

Disadvantages of the Waterfall Methodology

Issues Related to the Waterfall Methodology	
The business problem	Any flaws in accurately defining and articulating the business problem in terms of what the business users actually require flow onward to the next phase.
The plan	Managing costs, resources, and time constraints is difficult in the waterfall sequence. What happens to the schedule if a programmer quits? How will a schedule delay in a specific phase impact the total cost of the project? Unexpected contingencies may sabotage the plan.
The solution	The waterfall methodology is problematic in that it assumes users can specify all business requirements in advance. Defining the appropriate IT infrastructure that is flexible, scalable, and reliable is a challenge. The final IT infrastructure solution must meet not only current but also future needs in terms of time, cost, feasibility, and flexibility. Vision is inevitably limited at the head of the waterfall.

serves most of today's development efforts, however; it is inflexible and expensive, and it requires rigid adherence to the sequence of steps. Its success rate is only about 1 in 10. Figure 9.3 explains some issues related to the waterfall methodology.[5]

Today's business environment is fierce. The desire and need to outsmart and outplay competitors remains intense. Given this drive for success, leaders push internal development teams and external vendors to deliver agreed-upon systems faster and cheaper so they can realize benefits as early as possible. Even so, systems remain large and complex. The traditional waterfall methodology no longer serves as an adequate systems development methodology in most cases. Because this development environment is the norm and not the exception anymore, development teams use a new breed of alternative development methods to achieve their business objectives.

AGILE SOFTWARE DEVELOPMENT METHODOLOGIES

It is common knowledge that the smaller the project, the greater the success rate. The iterative development style is the ultimate in small projects. Basically, ***iterative development*** consists of a series of tiny projects. It has become the foundation of multiple agile methodologies. Figure 9.4 displays an iterative approach.

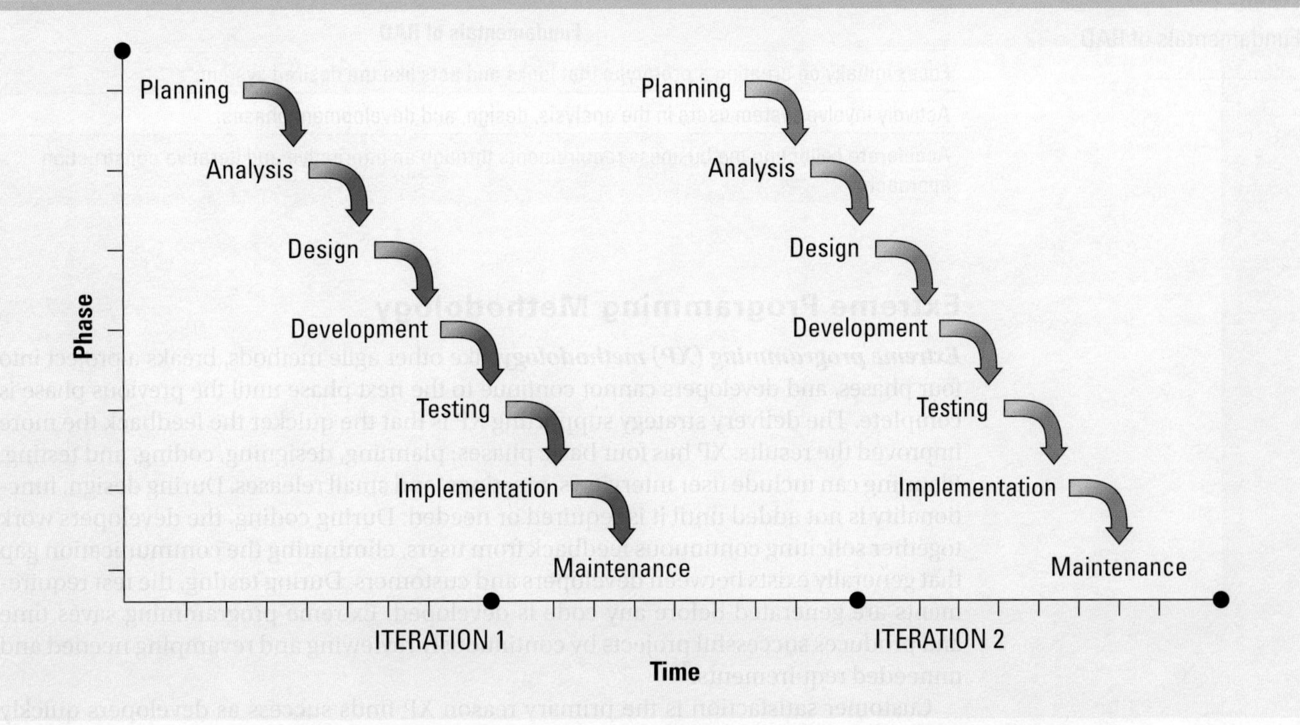

FIGURE 9.4

The Iterative Approach

An ***agile methodology*** aims for customer satisfaction through early and continuous delivery of useful software components developed by an iterative process using the bare minimum requirements. Agile methodology is what it sounds like: fast and efficient, with lower costs and fewer features. Using agile methods helps refine feasibility and supports the process for getting rapid feedback as functionality is introduced. Developers can adjust as they move along and better clarify unclear requirements.[6]

One key to delivering a successful product or system is to deliver value to users as soon as possible—give them something they want and like early to create buy-in, generate enthusiasm, and, ultimately, reduce scope. Using agile methodologies helps maintain accountability and helps to establish a barometer for the satisfaction of end users. It does no good to accomplish something on time and on budget if it does not satisfy the end user. The primary forms of agile methodologies include:

- Rapid prototyping or rapid application development methodology.
- Extreme programming methodology.
- Rational unified process (RUP) methodology.
- Scrum methodology.

It is important not to get hung up on the names of the methodologies—some are proprietary brand names, others are generally accepted names. It is more important to know how these alternative methodologies are used in today's business environment and the benefits they can deliver.

Rapid Application Development (RAD) Methodology

In response to the faster pace of business, rapid application development has become a popular route for accelerating systems development. ***Rapid application development (RAD) methodology*** (also called ***rapid prototyping***) emphasizes extensive user involvement in the rapid and evolutionary construction of working prototypes of a system, to accelerate the systems development process. Figure 9.5 displays the fundamentals of RAD.

A ***prototype*** is a smaller-scale representation or working model of the users' requirements or the proposed design for an information system. The prototype is an essential part of the analysis phase when using the RAD methodology.[7]

FIGURE 9.5
Fundamentals of RAD

Fundamentals of RAD
Focus initially on creating a prototype that looks and acts like the desired system.
Actively involve system users in the analysis, design, and development phases.
Accelerate collecting the business requirements through an interactive and iterative construction approach.

Extreme Programming Methodology

Extreme programming (XP) methodology, like other agile methods, breaks a project into four phases, and developers cannot continue to the next phase until the previous phase is complete. The delivery strategy supporting XP is that the quicker the feedback the more improved the results. XP has four basic phases: planning, designing, coding, and testing. Planning can include user interviews, meetings, and small releases. During design, functionality is not added until it is required or needed. During coding, the developers work together soliciting continuous feedback from users, eliminating the communication gap that generally exists between developers and customers. During testing, the test requirements are generated before any code is developed. Extreme programming saves time and produces successful projects by continuously reviewing and revamping needed and unneeded requirements.[8]

Customer satisfaction is the primary reason XP finds success as developers quickly respond to changing business requirements, even late in the life cycle. XP encourages managers, customers, and developers to work together as a team to ensure the delivery of high-quality systems. XP is similar to a puzzle; there are many small pieces and individually the pieces make no sense, but when they are pieced together they can create a new system.

Rational Unified Process (RUP) Methodology

The ***rational unified process (RUP) methodology,*** owned by IBM, provides a framework for breaking down the development of software into four "gates." Each gate consists of executable iterations of the software in development. A project stays in a gate waiting for the stakeholder's analysis, and then it either moves to the next gate or is cancelled. The gates include:[9]

- **Gate one: inception.** This phase ensures all stakeholders have a shared understanding of the proposed system and what it will do.
- **Gate two: elaboration.** This phase expands on the agreed-upon details of the system, including the ability to provide an architecture to support and build it.
- **Gate three: construction.** This phase includes building and developing the product.
- **Gate four: transition.** Primary questions answered in this phase address ownership of the system and training of key personnel.

Because RUP is an iterative methodology, the user can reject the product and force the developers to go back to gate one. RUP helps developers avoid reinventing the wheel and focuses on rapidly adding or removing reusable chunks of processes addressing common problems.

Scrum Methodology

Another agile methodology, ***scrum methodology,*** uses small teams to produce small pieces of software using a series of "sprints," or 30-day intervals, to achieve an appointed goal. In rugby, a scrum is a team pack and everyone in the pack works together to move the ball down the field. In scrum methodology, each day ends or begins with a stand-up meeting to monitor and control the development effort.

APPLY YOUR KNOWLEDGE

BUSINESS DRIVEN ETHICS AND SECURITY

Planning for the Unexpected

Unexpected situations happen all the time, and the more you plan for them the better prepared you'll be when developing software. Your employees will get into accidents, contract viruses and diseases, and other life issues. All of these scenarios lead to unplanned absenteeism, which can throw your project plan into a tailspin. What can happen to a project when a key employee suddenly quits or is forced to go on short-term disability? When reviewing all the different SDLC methodologies, which one offers the greatest flexibility for unplanned employee downtime? If you could choose when your employee was absent, which phase in the SDLC would be the safest for your project to still continue and achieve success? What can you do to ensure you are preparing for unplanned absenteeism on your project plan?

DEVELOPING SUCCESSFUL SOFTWARE

Developing projects within budget and on time is challenging. The primary reasons for project failure include:

- Unclear or missing business requirements.
- Skipping SDLC phases.
- Changing technology.
- The cost of finding errors.

Unclear or Missing Business Requirements

The most common reason systems fail is because the business requirements are either missing or incorrectly gathered during the analysis phase. The business requirements drive the entire system. If they are not accurate or complete, the system will not be successful.

Skipping Phases

The first thing individuals tend to do when a project falls behind schedule is to start skipping phases in the SDLC. For example, if a project is three weeks behind in the development phase, the project manager might decide to cut testing from six weeks to three weeks. Obviously, it is impossible to perform all the testing in half the time. Failing to test the system will lead to unfound errors, and chances are high that the system will fail. It is critical that an organization perform all phases in the SDLC during every project. Skipping any of the phases is sure to lead to system failure.

Changing Technology

Many real-world projects have hundreds of business requirements, take years to complete, and cost millions of dollars. As Moore's Law states, technology changes at an incredibly fast pace; therefore, it is possible to have to revise an entire project plan in the middle of a project as a result of a change in technology. Technology changes so fast that it is almost impossible to deliver an information system without feeling the pain of changing technology.

The Cost of Finding Errors in the SDLC

It is important to discuss the relationship between the SDLC and the cost for the organization to fix errors. An error found during the analysis and design phase is relatively

FIGURE 9.6
The Cost of Fixing Errors

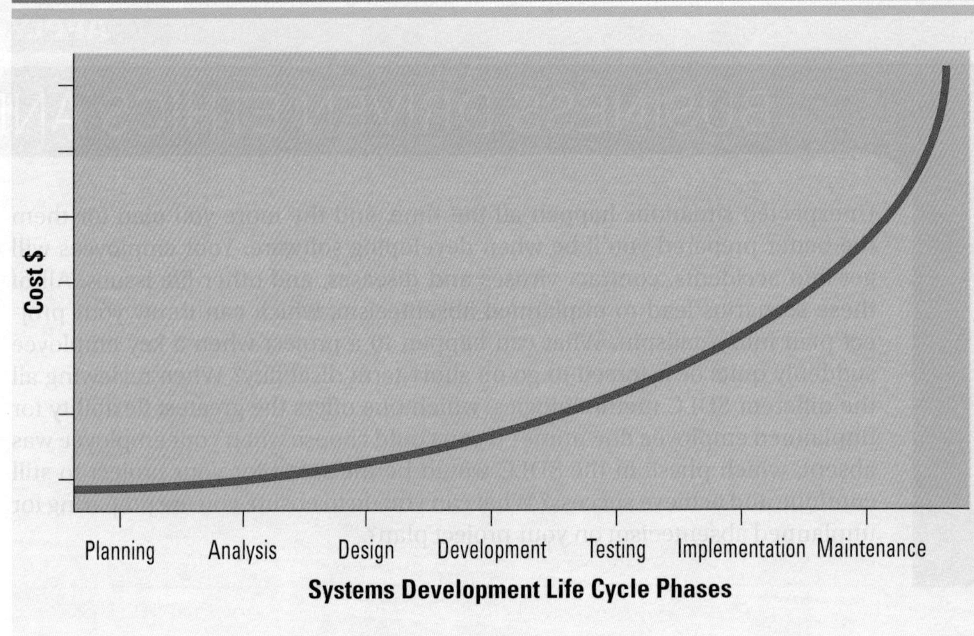

inexpensive to fix. All that is typically required is a change to a Word document. However, exactly the same error found during the testing or implementation phase is going to cost the organization an enormous amount to fix because it has to change the actual system. Figure 9.6 displays how the cost to fix an error grows exponentially the later the error is found in the SDLC.

section 9.2 PROJECT MANAGEMENT

LEARNING OUTCOMES

9.4 Explain project management, the triple constraint, and project stakeholder and executive sponsor's roles in choosing strategic projects.

9.5 Explain how project stakeholder's choose strategic projects.

9.6 Describe the two primary diagrams most frequently used in project planning.

9.7 Identify the three primary areas a project manager must focus on managing to ensure success.

9.8 Explain the three different types of outsourcing along with their benefits and challenges.

MANAGING SOFTWARE DEVELOPMENT PROJECTS

LO 9.4: Explain project management, the triple constraint, and the project stakeholder's and executive sponsor's roles in choosing strategic projects.

No one would think of building an office complex by turning loose 100 different construction teams to build 100 different rooms with no single blueprint or agreed-upon vision of the completed structure. Yet this is precisely the situation in which many large organizations find themselves when managing information technology projects. Organizations routinely overschedule their resources (human and otherwise), develop redundant projects, and damage profitability by investing in nonstrategic efforts that do not contribute to the organization's bottom line. Business leaders face a rapidly moving and unforgiving global marketplace that will force them to use every possible tool to sustain competitiveness; project management is one of those tools.

The ***Project Management Institute (PMI)*** develops procedures and concepts necessary to support the profession of project management (www.pmi.org). PMI defines a

project as a temporary activity a company undertakes to create a unique product, service, or result. ***Project management*** is the application of knowledge, skills, tools, and techniques to project activities to meet project requirements. A ***project manager*** is an individual who is an expert in project planning and management, defines and develops the project plan, and tracks the plan to ensure the project is completed on time and on budget. The project manager is the person responsible for executing the entire project. Project management terms all managers should know and understand include:

- ***Project deliverables*** are any measurable, tangible, verifiable outcome, result, or item that is produced to complete a project or part of a project. Examples of project deliverables include design documents, testing scripts, and requirements documents.[10]
- ***Project milestones*** represent key dates when a certain group of activities must be performed. For example, completing the planning phase might be a project milestone. If a project milestone is missed, then chances are the project is experiencing problems.[11]
- ***Project management office (PMO)*** is an internal department that oversees all organizational projects. This group must formalize and professionalize project management expertise and leadership. One of the primary initiatives of the PMO is to educate the organization on techniques and procedures necessary to run successful projects.[12]

The Triple Constraint

Figure 9.7 displays the relationships between the three primary and interdependent variables in any project—time, cost, and scope. All projects are limited in some way by these three constraints. The Project Management Institute calls the framework for evaluating these competing demands *the triple constraint.*

The relationship between these variables is such that if any one changes, at least one other is likely to be affected. For example, moving up a project's finish date could mean either increasing costs to hire more staff or decreasing the scope to eliminate features or functions. Increasing a project's scope to include additional customer requests could extend the project's time to completion or increase the project's cost—or both—to accommodate the changes. Project quality is affected by the project manager's ability to balance these competing demands. High-quality projects deliver the agreed upon product or service on time and on budget. Project management is the science of making intelligent trade-offs between time, cost, and scope. Benjamin Franklin's timeless advice—*by failing to prepare, you prepare to fail*—applies to many of today's software development projects.

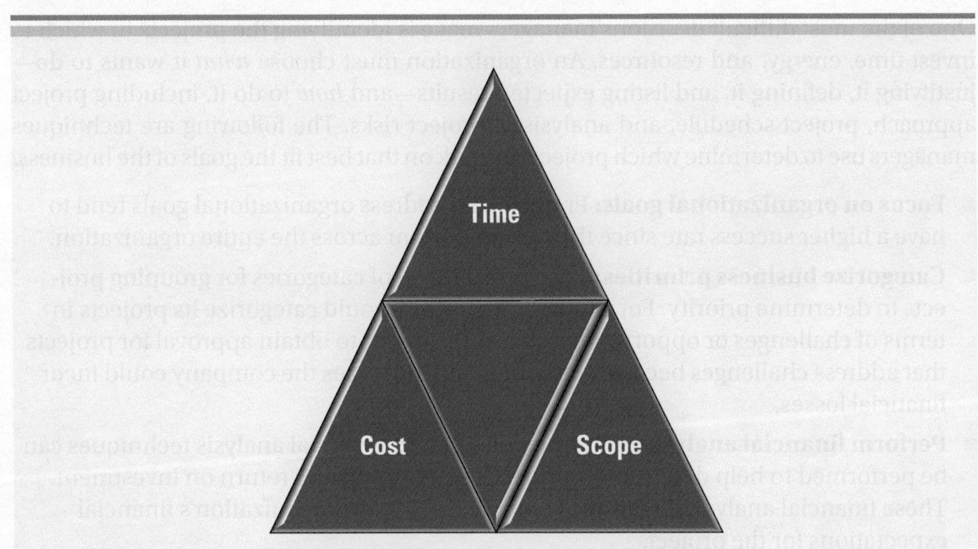

FIGURE 9.7
Project Management Interdependent Variables

Project Participants

Project stakeholders are individuals and organizations actively involved in the project or whose interests might be affected as a result of project execution or project completion. Stakeholders, such as the CFO, also can exert influence over the project's objectives and outcomes. It is important for all stakeholders to understand the business objective of the project—once again, it is about getting the big picture. Stakeholders measure projects based on such factors as customer satisfaction, increased revenue, or decreased cost.

The project management team must identify stakeholders, determine their requirements and expectations, and, to the extent possible, manage their influence in relationship to the requirements to ensure a successful project. While all stakeholders are important, one stands out as having the most impact on the success or failure of a project. That person is the executive sponsor. PMI defines the ***executive sponsor*** as the person or group who provides the financial resources for the project. Research has shown that the leadership strength of the executive sponsor has more to do with the success or failure of a project than any other critical success factor. In fact, the executive sponsor should be accountable to the project team for much more than the financial backing. The executive sponsor communicates up the chain on behalf of the project, supports the project manager by championing the project to others sharing the vision and benefit of the successfully completed project, and demonstrates the commitment and accountability necessary to survive a project! If a team has a hands-off sponsor who merely reviews invoices and inquires as to the status of a project, then that project surely is in trouble from the start.

Another part of the equation is influence. If the executive sponsor has influence, he or she can use that influence to gain and direct essential resources needed to accomplish the project. A highly connected executive sponsor could mean the difference between success and failure. The executive sponsor should be committed to use his or her influence to ensure the health of the project.

Most business managers are not project managers; however, all managers will be part of a project team. Therefore, future managers need to understand how a business manages its project and how the culture supports the effort. The art and science of project management must coordinate numerous activities, as shown in Figure 9.8. Project managers perform many of them, and the remainder of this section focuses on four:

1. Choosing strategic projects.
2. Understanding project planning.
3. Managing projects.
4. Outsourcing projects.

LO 9.5: Explain how project stakeholder's choose strategic projects.

CHOOSING STRATEGIC PROJECTS

One of the most difficult decisions managers make is identifying the projects in which to invest time, energy, and resources. An organization must choose *what* it wants to do—justifying it, defining it, and listing expected results—and *how* to do it, including project approach, project schedule, and analysis of project risks. The following are techniques managers use to determine which projects to work on that best fit the goals of the business.

- **Focus on organizational goals:** Projects that address organizational goals tend to have a higher success rate since they are important across the entire organization.
- **Categorize business priorities:** There are a range of categories for grouping projects to determine priority. For example, a business could categorize its projects in terms of challenges or opportunities. It is often easier to obtain approval for projects that address challenges because without fixing the issues the company could incur financial losses.
- **Perform financial analysis:** A number of different financial analysis techniques can be performed to help determine a project's priority, such as return on investment. These financial analysis techniques help determine the organization's financial expectations for the project.

APPLY YOUR KNOWLEDGE

BUSINESS DRIVEN MIS

Google Books Project

Google is scanning all or parts of the book collections of the University of Michigan, Harvard University, Stanford University, the New York Public Library, and Oxford University as part of its Google Print Library Project with the intent of making all of the copyrighted material free and searchable on Google. Of course many authors and publishers are furious with Google, claiming copyright infringement. According to Google, scanning books will help make out-of-print books accessible as customers can find, read, and print books directly from the website and will actually generate sales by giving customers the ability to buy books online.

Do you view Google's Print Library Project as a violation of copyright laws? Of all the projects Google can afford to tackle, why would the company choose one that directly violates copyright laws? If all books were available for free on Google, what would happen to the publishing industry? As you prioritize projects for your business, what types of competitive information will you want to view before choosing projects? What do you think the future of the book publishing industry will look like based on Google's radical new website? If you owned a publishing business, what could you do to combat Google's book project?[13]

FIGURE 9.8
Project Management Roles

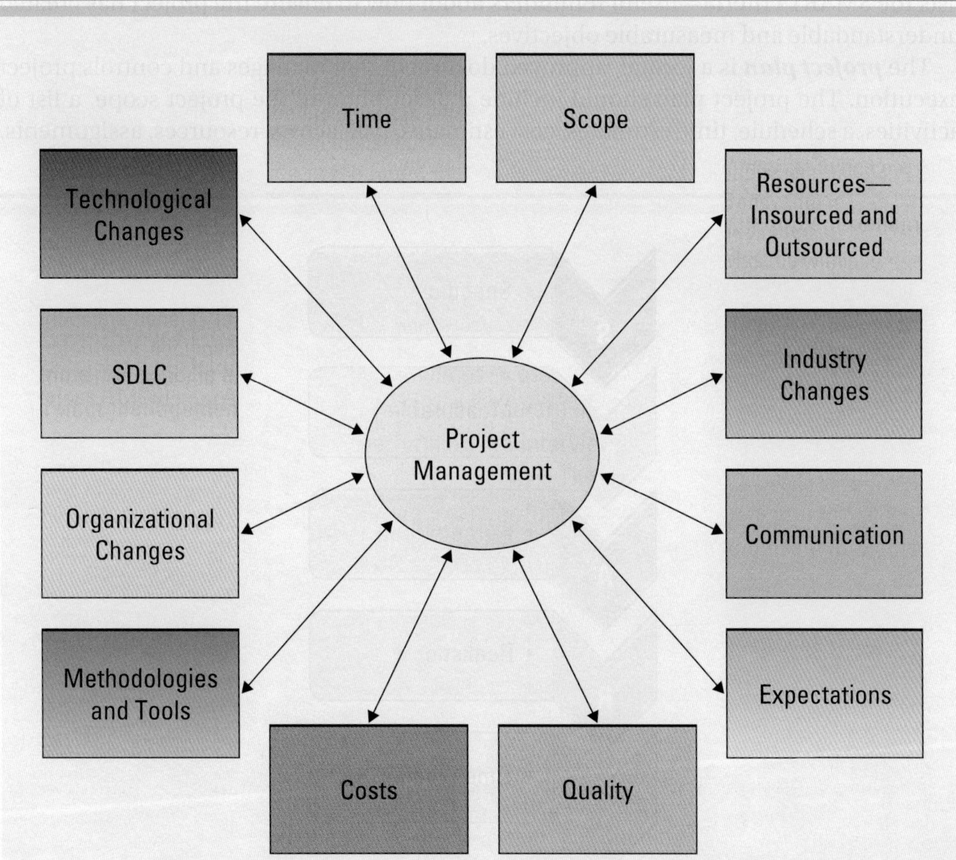

LO 9.6: Describe the two primary diagrams most frequently used in project planning.

UNDERSTANDING PROJECT PLANNING

Once an organization has selected strategic projects and identified its project manager, it is time to build the critical component—the project plan. Many project professionals believe a solid project begins with documentation that includes a project charter, a scope statement, and the project management plan. A ***project charter*** is a document issued by the project initiator or sponsor that formally authorizes the start of a project and provides the project manager with the authority to apply organizational resources to project activities. In short, this means someone has stepped up to pay for and support the project. A project charter typically includes several elements.

- The ***project scope statement*** links the project to the organization's overall business goals. It describes the business need (the problem the project will solve) and the justification, requirements, and current boundaries for the project. It defines the work that must be completed to deliver the product with the specified features and functions, and it includes constraints, assumptions, and requirements—all components necessary for developing accurate cost estimates.
- ***Project objectives*** are quantifiable criteria that must be met for the project to be considered a success.
- ***Project constraints*** are specific factors that can limit options. They include budget, delivery dates, available skilled resources, and organizational policies.
- ***Project assumptions*** are factors considered to be true, real, or certain without proof or demonstration. Examples include hours in a workweek or time of year the work will be performed.[14]

The project objectives are among the most important areas to define because they are essentially the major elements of the project. When an organization achieves the project objectives, it has accomplished the major goals of the project and the project scope is satisfied. Project objectives must include metrics so that the project's success can be measured. The metrics can include cost, schedule, and quality metrics. Figure 9.9 lists the SMART criteria—useful reminders about how to ensure the project has created understandable and measurable objectives.

The ***project plan*** is a formal, approved document that manages and controls project execution. The project plan should include a description of the project scope, a list of activities, a schedule, time estimates, cost estimates, risk factors, resources, assignments,

FIGURE 9.9

SMART Criteria for Successful Objective Creation

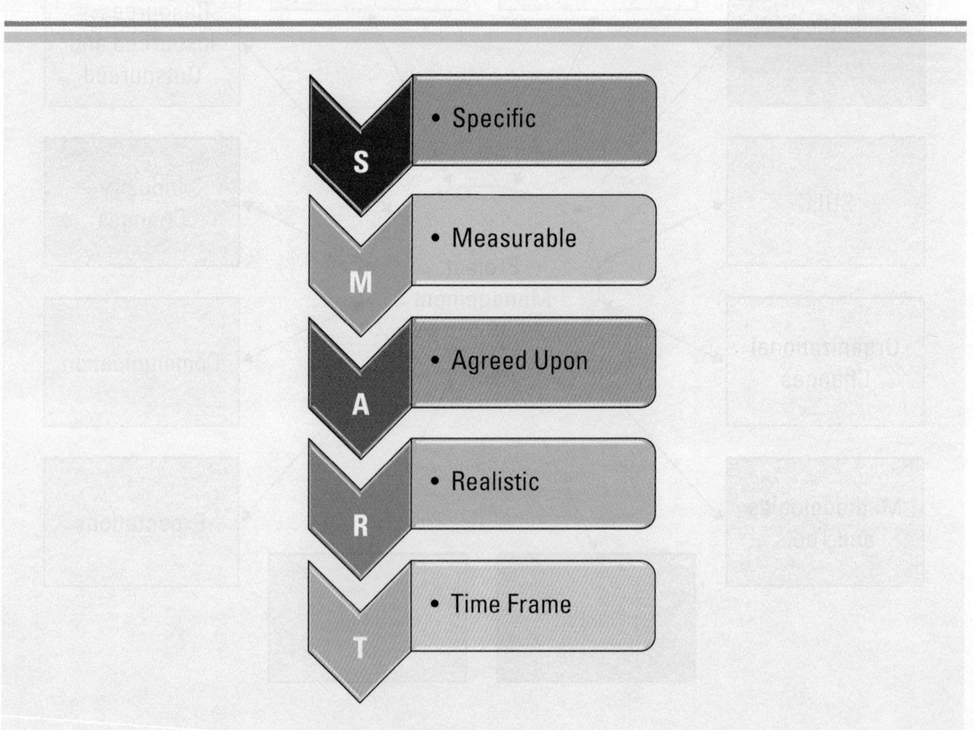

and responsibilities. In addition to these basic components, most project professionals also include contingency plans, review and communications strategies, and a ***kill switch***—a trigger that enables a project manager to close the project before completion.

A good project plan should include estimates for revenue and strategic necessities. It also should include measurement and reporting methods and details as to how top leadership will engage in the project. It also informs stakeholders of the benefits of the project and justifies the investment, commitment, and risk of the project as it relates to the overall mission of the organization.

Managers need to continuously monitor projects to measure their success. If a project is failing, the manager must cancel the project and save the company any further project costs. Canceling a project is not necessarily a failure as much as it is successful resource management as it frees resources that can be used on other projects that are more valuable to the firm.

The most important part of the plan is communication. The project manager must communicate the plan to every member of the project team and to any key stakeholders and executives. The project plan must also include any project assumptions and be detailed enough to guide the execution of the project. A key to achieving project success is earning consensus and buy-in from all key stakeholders. By including key stakeholders in project plan development, the project manager allows them to have ownership of the plan. This often translates to greater commitment, which in turn results in enhanced motivation and productivity. The two primary diagrams most frequently used in project planning are PERT and Gantt charts.

A ***PERT (Program Evaluation and Review Technique) chart*** is a graphical network model that depicts a project's tasks and the relationships between them. A ***dependency*** is a logical relationship that exists between the project tasks, or between a project task and a milestone. PERT charts define dependency between project tasks before those tasks are scheduled (see Figure 9.10). The boxes in Figure 9.10 represent project tasks, and the project manager can adjust the contents of the boxes to display various project attributes such as schedule and actual start and finish times. The arrows indicate that a task depends on the start or the completion of a different task. The ***critical path***

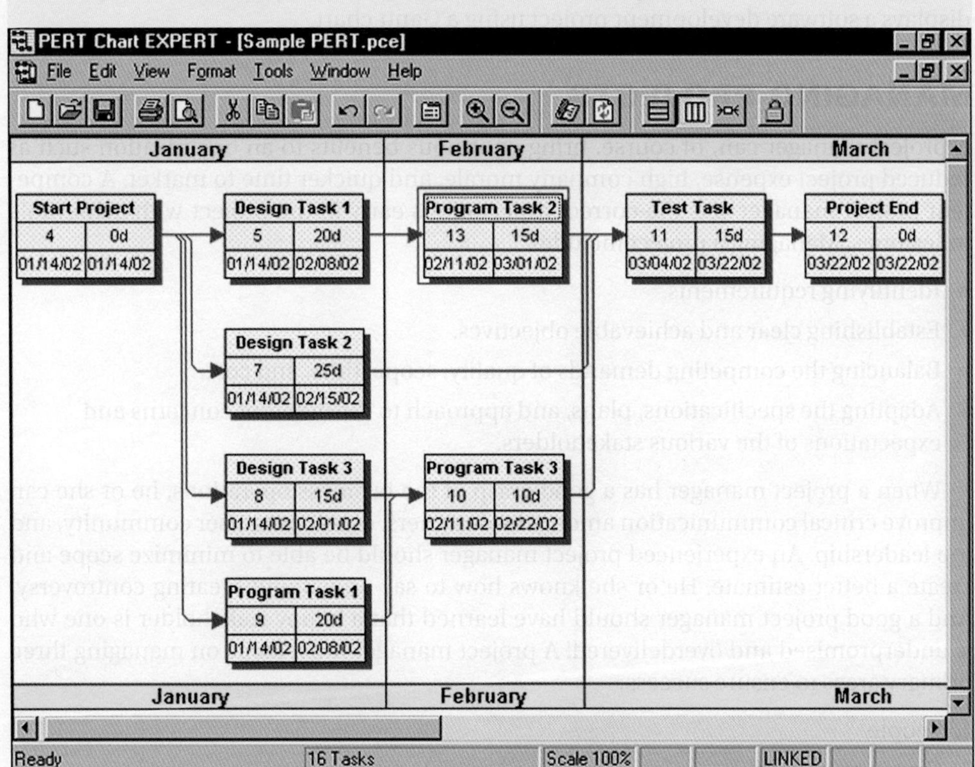

FIGURE 9.10

PERT Chart Expert, a PERT Chart Example

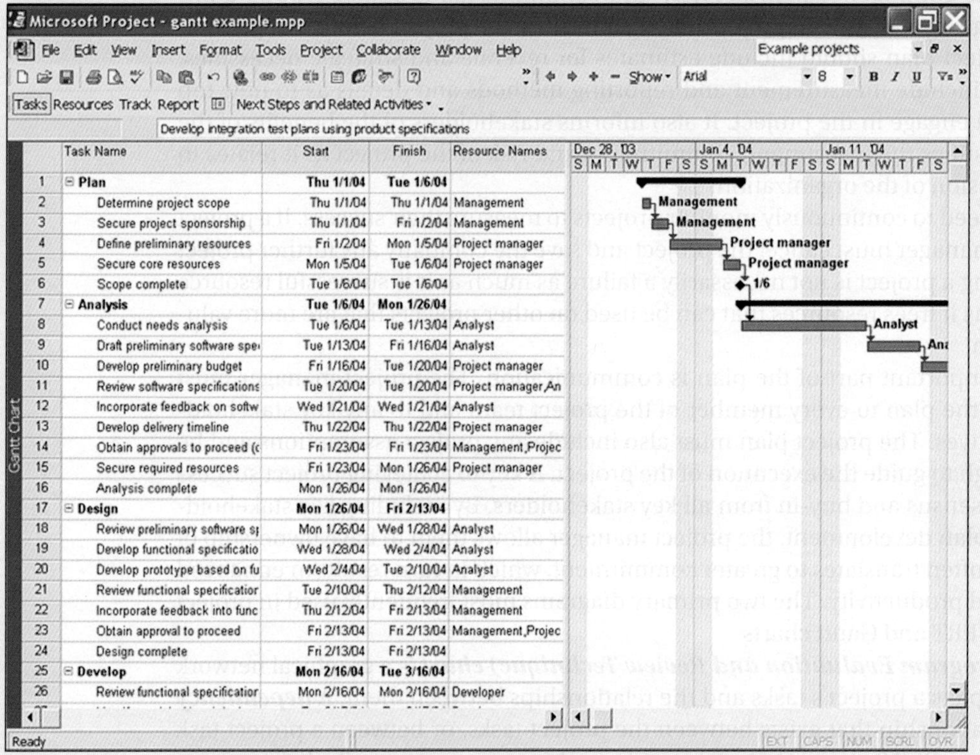

FIGURE 9.11

Microsoft Project, a Gantt Chart Example

estimates the shortest path through the project ensuring all critical tasks are completed from start to finish. The red line in Figure 9.10 displays the critical path for the project.

A ***Gantt chart*** is a simple bar chart that lists project tasks vertically against the project's time frame, listed horizontally. A Gantt chart works well for representing the project schedule. It also shows actual progress of tasks against the planned duration. Figure 9.11 displays a software development project using a Gantt chart.

MANAGING PROJECTS

LO 9.7: Identify the three primary areas a project manager must focus on to ensure success.

A project manager can, of course, bring enormous benefits to an organization such as reduced project expense, high company morale, and quicker time to market. A competent project manager sets the correct expectations early in the project with achievable milestones. Managing a project includes:

- Identifying requirements.
- Establishing clear and achievable objectives.
- Balancing the competing demands of quality, scope, time, and cost.
- Adapting the specifications, plans, and approach to the different concerns and expectations of the various stakeholders.

When a project manager has a good grasp of the business operations, he or she can improve critical communication among the designers, developers, user community, and top leadership. An experienced project manager should be able to minimize scope and create a better estimate. He or she knows how to say no without creating controversy. And a good project manager should have learned that a happy stakeholder is one who is underpromised and overdelivered! A project manager must focus on managing three primary areas to ensure success:

1. People
2. Communications
3. Change

Managing People

Managing people is among the most challenging efforts a project manager undertakes. Resolving conflicts within the team and balancing the needs of the project with the personal and professional needs of the team are two of the project manager's critical goals. Because project managers are often the client's main (and sometimes sole) contact person during the project, communication, negotiation, marketing, and salesmanship are just as important to the project manager as financial and analytical acumen. Many times, the people management side of project management makes the difference in pulling off a successful project.

Managing Communications

While many companies develop unique project management frameworks based on familiar project management standards, all agree that communication is the key to excellent project management. This is quite easy to state, but not so easy to accomplish! It is extremely helpful if a project manager plans what and how he or she will communicate as a formal part of the project management plan called a *communications plan.* A project manager distributes timely, accurate, and meaningful information regarding project objectives, including the schedule, cost, scope, quality, and status of each. The project manager also shares small wins as the project progresses, informs others of needed corrections, makes requests for additional resources, and keeps all stakeholders informed of the project schedule.

Another important aspect of a project management communications plan is to provide a method for continually obtaining and monitoring feedback from and for all stakeholders. This is not to say that a project manager needs to spend countless hours answering every email and responding to every question posed. Rather, the manager should develop a method for asking for specific feedback as part of the plan and responding to it in a timely, organized manner. Team members remain closest to the project and should be encouraged to share open and honest feedback. It is the project manager's role and responsibility to foster an environment of trust so that members feel safe to contribute their knowledge and ideas—even if it means relaying bad news or offering an opposing viewpoint.

Managing Change

Successful organizations and successful people learn to anticipate and react appropriately to change. Change comes in many forms from an environmental crisis to a labor shortage and can include:

- A misunderstanding or missing business requirement in the project scope.
- A new government regulation or law that requires changes to business processes.
- Mergers, acquisitions, or new business partnerships.
- An emerging technology.
- User change in business requirements for additional functionality.
- Resource constraints such as budget cuts or personal cutbacks.

Change management offers procedures and policies managers can use to help manage change during system development. A ***change management system*** includes a collection of procedures to document a change request and identifies the expected impact associated with the change. Most change management systems require that a change request form be initiated by one or more project stakeholders (systems owners, users, customers, developers). Ideally, these change requests are considered by a ***change control board (CCB)*** that is responsible for approving or rejecting all change requests. The CCB's composition typically includes a representative from each business area that has a stake in the project. The CCB's decision to accept or reject each change is based on an impact analysis of the change. For example, if one department wants to implement a change to the software that will increase both deployment time and cost, then the other business owners need to agree that the change is valid and that it warrants the extended time frame and increased budget.

APPLY YOUR KNOWLEDGE

BUSINESS DRIVEN INNOVATION

$7,500 Steak Dinner

The next time one of your employees submits an expense report, you might want to think twice as a number of websites offer phony documentation individuals can use to help cheat on their taxes, expense reports, or even spouses. Here are a few you should be aware of:

- **Customreceipts.com:** This website can print a fake ATM receipt. Why would people want a fake ATM receipt? To impress others with their massive balances of course!
- **Alibi Network:** This website can create you a customized excuse, such as an emergency phone call giving you a reason to leave that boring meeting, or a false invitation to a corporate or business event so an unfaithful partner can give physical proof of a false destination and location.
- **The Restaurant Maloney & Porcelli's:** This innovative, yet highly unethical, restaurant started a website that allows its customers to enter an amount for a meal and it generates fake receipts adding up to the cost of the meal.[15]

All these systems were created by software developers. If you were asked to participate in one of these website development efforts, what would you do? Who do you think should be held liable for unethical websites—the employee or the host of the website? Now that you know about the existence of these types of websites, how will you manage your employees? What would you do to an employee who was using one of these services? How can a project manager combat these types of issues without wasting enormous amounts of time and energy?

Change is an opportunity, not a threat. Realizing that change is the norm rather than the exception will help an organization stay ahead. Becoming a change leader and accepting the inevitability of change can help ensure that an organization can survive and even thrive in times of change.

LO 9.8: Explain the three different types of outsourcing along with their benefits and challenges.

OUTSOURCING PROJECTS

In the high-speed global business environment, an organization needs to increase profits, grow market share, and reduce costs. Two basic options are available to organizations wishing to develop and maintain their information systems—in-sourcing or outsourcing.

In-sourcing (in-house development) uses the professional expertise within an organization to develop and maintain its information technology systems. In-sourcing has been instrumental in creating a viable supply of IT professionals and in creating a better quality workforce combining both technical and business skills.

Outsourcing is an arrangement by which one organization provides a service or services for another organization that chooses not to perform them in-house. In some cases, the entire MIS department is outsourced, including planning and business analysis as well as the design, development, and maintenance of equipment and projects. Figure 9.12 displays the most common departments companies outsource. Outsourcing can range from a large contract under which an organization such as IBM manages all MIS services for another company, to hiring contractors and temporary staff on an individual basis. Common reasons companies outsource include:

- **Core competencies.** Many companies have recently begun to consider outsourcing as a way to acquire best-practices and the business process expertise of highly skilled technology resources for a low cost. Technology is advancing at such an accelerated rate that companies often lack the technical resources required to keep current.

- **Financial savings.** It is far cheaper to hire people in China and India than pay the required salaries for similar labor in the United States.
- **Rapid growth.** Firms must get their products to market quickly and still be able to react to market changes. By taking advantage of outsourcing, an organization can acquire the resources required to speed up operations or scale to new demand levels.
- **The Internet and globalization.** The pervasive nature of the Internet has made more people comfortable with outsourcing abroad as India, China, and the United States become virtual neighbors.

Outsourcing MIS enables organizations to keep up with market and technology advances—with less strain on human and financial resources and more assurance that the IT infrastructure will keep pace with evolving business priorities (see Figure 9.13). The three forms of outsourcing options available for a project are:

1. ***Onshore outsourcing***—engaging another company within the same country for services.
2. ***Nearshore outsourcing***—contracting an outsourcing arrangement with a company in a nearby country. Often this country will share a border with the native country.
3. ***Offshore outsourcing***—using organizations from developing countries to write code and develop systems. In offshore outsourcing the country is geographically far away.

Since the mid-1990s, major U.S. companies have been sending significant portions of their software development work offshore—primarily to vendors in India, but also to vendors in China, eastern Europe (including Russia), Ireland, Israel, and the Philippines. The big selling point for offshore outsourcing is inexpensive but good work. The overseas counterpart to an American programmer who earns as much as $63,000 per year is paid as little as $5,000 per year (see Figure 9.14). Developing countries in Asia and South Africa offer some outsourcing services but are challenged by language

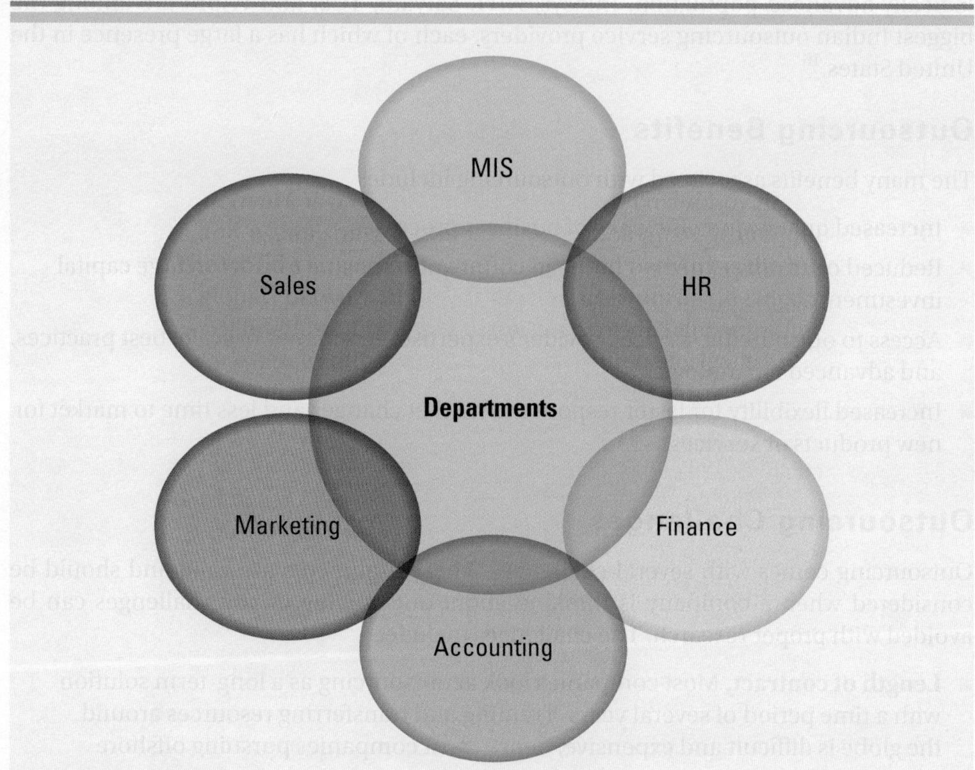

FIGURE 9.12

Departments Commonly Outsourced by Organizations

FIGURE 9.13
Outsourcing Models

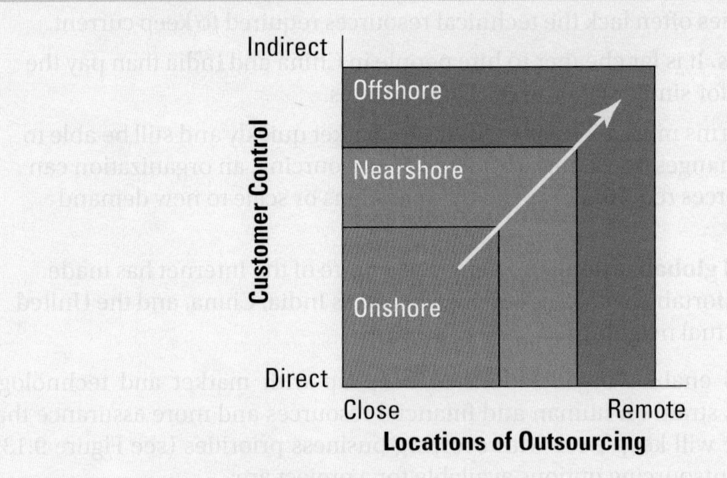

FIGURE 9.14
Typical Salary Ranges for Computer Programmers

Source: From Edward Yourdon, *Death March*, 2nd edition, © 2004. Reproduced by permission of Pearson Education, Inc., Upper Saddle River, New Jersey.

Country	Salary Range Per Year
China	$5,000–$9,000
India	6,000–10,000
Philippines	6,500–11,000
Russia	7,000–13,000
Ireland	21,000–28,000
Canada	25,000–50,000
United States	60,000–90,000

difference, inadequate telecommunication equipment, and regulatory obstacles. India is the largest offshore marketplace because it promotes English along with a technologically advanced population. Infosys, NIIT, Satyam, TCS, and Wipro are among the biggest Indian outsourcing service providers, each of which has a large presence in the United States.[16]

Outsourcing Benefits

The many benefits associated with outsourcing include:

- Increased quality and efficiency of business processes.
- Reduced operating expenses for head count and exposure to risk for large capital investments.
- Access to outsourcing service provider's expertise, economies of scale, best practices, and advanced technologies.
- Increased flexibility for faster response to market changes and less time to market for new products or services.

Outsourcing Challenges

Outsourcing comes with several challenges. These arguments are valid and should be considered when a company is thinking about outsourcing. Many challenges can be avoided with proper research. The challenges include:

- **Length of contract.** Most companies look at outsourcing as a long-term solution with a time period of several years. Training and transferring resources around the globe is difficult and expensive, hence most companies pursuing offshore

BUSINESS DRIVEN GLOBALIZATION

DUI in a Golf Cart

Swedish police stopped Bill Murray and charged him with drunk driving when he attempted to drive his golf cart around the city. A golf cart hits top speed at three miles per hour and although it might seem odd that you can be issued a DUI for driving one, many countries have laws against such practices. A few other culture blunders you want to avoid include:

- One American company learned that the name of the cooking oil they were marketing translated into "jackass oil" in Spanish.
- A deodorant marketing campaign displayed images of a strong courageous man washing his dog. The campaign failed in Islamic countries where dogs are considered unclean.
- A sports equipment company packaged golf balls in groups of four for sales throughout Japan. Sales plummeted because the word *four* pronounced in Japanese sounds the same as the word *death* and items packaged in fours are considered unlucky.[17]

Companies that are expanding globally are looking for opportunities, not problems. Yet local laws and procedures that come into play when setting up shop abroad—everything from hiring and firing to tax filings—can be a minefield. What types of culture, language, and legal issues should a company expect to encounter when dealing with outsourcing to another country? What can a company do to mitigate these risks?

outsourcing contract for multiple years of service. A few of the challenges facing the length of the contract include:

1. It can be difficult to break the contract.
2. Forecasting business needs for the next several years is challenging and the contract might not meet future business needs.
3. Re-creating an internal MIS department if the outsource provider fails is costly and challenging.

- **Threat to competitive advantage.** Many businesses view MIS as a competitive advantage and view outsourcing as a threat because the outsourcer could share the company's trade secrets.
- **Loss of confidentiality.** Information on pricing, products, sales, and customers can be a competitive asset and often critical for business success. Outsourcing could place confidential information in the wrong hands. Although confidentiality clauses contained in the contracts are supposed to protect the company, the potential risk and costs of a breach must be analyzed.

Every type of organization in business today relies on software to operate and solve complex problems or create exciting opportunities. Software built correctly can support nimble organizations and transform with them as they and their businesses transform. Software that effectively meets employee needs will help an organization become more productive and enhance decision making. Software that does not meet employee needs might have a damaging effect on productivity and can even cause a business to fail. Employee involvement in software development, along with the right implementation, is critical to the success of an organization.

BUSINESS DRIVEN DISCUSSION

Death March

Edward Yourdon's book *Death March* describes the complete software developer's guide to surviving "mission impossible" projects. MIS projects are challenging, and project managers are expected to achieve the impossible by pulling off a successful project even when pitted against impossible challenges. In *Death March,* infamous software developer Edward Yourdon presents his project classification displayed here. Yourdon measures projects based on the level of pain and chances for success.

- **Mission Impossible Project:** This project has a great chance of success and your hard work will pay off as you find happiness and joy in the work. For example, this is the type of project where you work all day and night for a year and become the project hero as you complete the mission impossible and reap a giant promotion as your reward.
- **Ugly Project:** This project has a high chance of success but is very painful and offers little happiness. For example, you work day and night to install a new accounting system and although successful, you hate accounting and dislike the company and its products.
- **Kamikaze Project:** This is a project that has little chance of success but you are so passionate about the content that you find great happiness working on the project. For example, you are asked to build a website to support a cancer foundation, a cause near to your heart, but the company is nonprofit and doesn't have any funds to help buy the software you need to get everything working. You patch the system together and implement many manual work-arounds just to keep the system functioning.
- **Suicide Project:** This project has no chance of success and offers you nothing but pain. This is the equivalent of your worst nightmare project. Word of caution, avoid suicide projects![18]

Analyze your school and work projects and find a project that would fit in each box. What could you have done differently on your suicide project to ensure its success? What can you do to avoid being placed on a suicide project? Given the choice, which type of project would you choose to work on and why?

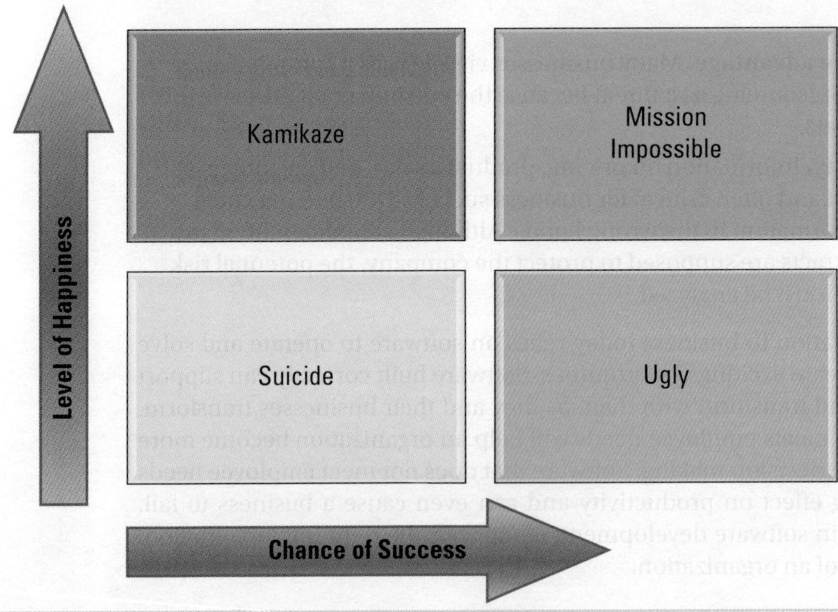

LEARNING OUTCOME REVIEW

Learning Outcome 9.1: Explain the business benefits associated with successful software development.

Software development uses the systems development life cycle to create software. The benefits associated with successful software development include increase in revenues, repair to brand reputation, limited liabilities, and increase in productivity

Learning Outcome 9.2: Describe the seven phases of the systems development life cycle.

The seven phases in the SDLC are:

- Planning—involves establishing a high-level plan of the intended project and determining project goals.
- Analysis—involves analyzing end-user business requirements and refining project goals into defined functions and operations of the intended system.
- Design—involves describing the desired features and operations of the system including screen layouts, business rules, process diagrams, pseudo code, and other documentation.
- Development—involves taking all of the detailed design documents from the design phase and transforming them into the actual system.
- Testing—involves bringing all the project pieces together into a special testing environment to test for errors, bugs, and interoperability and verify that the system meets all of the business requirements defined in the analysis phase.
- Implementation—involves placing the system into production so users can begin to perform actual business operations with the system.
- Maintenance—involves performing changes, corrections, additions, and upgrades to ensure the system continues to meet the business goals.

Learning Outcome 9.3: Summarize the different software development methodologies.

There are a number of different software development methodologies including:

- Agile methodology aims for customer satisfaction through early and continuous delivery of useful software components developed by an iterative process with a design point that uses the bare minimum requirements.
- Waterfall methodology follows an activity-based process in which each phase in the SDLC is performed sequentially from planning through implementation and maintenance.
- Rapid application development methodology (RAD) emphasizes extensive user involvement in the rapid and evolutionary construction of working prototypes of a system to accelerate the systems development process.
- Extreme programming (XP) methodology breaks a project into tiny phases, and developers cannot continue on to the next phase until the first phase is complete.
- Rational unified process (RUP) provides a framework for breaking down the development of software into four gates.
- Scrum uses small teams to produce small pieces of deliverable software using sprints, or 30-day intervals, to achieve an appointed goal.

Learning Outcome 9.4: Explain project management and the role the triple constraints play when managing a project.

A project is a temporary or short-term endeavor undertaken to create a unique product, service, or result, such as developing a custom ecommerce site or merging databases. Project management is the application of knowledge, skills, tools, and techniques to project activities to meet project requirements. A project manager is an individual who is an expert in project planning and management, defines and develops the project plan, and tracks the plan to ensure the project is completed on time and on budget.

The triple constraints are scope, resources, and time. These three components are interdependent, and if you change one the others must change. The three primary activities performed by a project manager include choosing strategic projects, setting the project scope, and managing resources and maintaining the project plan.

Learning Outcome 9.5: Describe the project stakeholder's and executive sponsor's roles in choosing strategic projects.

Project stakeholders are individuals and organizations actively involved in the project or whose interests might be affected as a result of project execution or project completion. While all stakeholders are important, one stands out as having the most impact on the success or failure of a project. That person is the executive sponsor or the person or group who provides the financial resources for the project. Techniques for choosing strategic projects include focusing on organizational goals, categorizing projects, or performing a financial analysis.

Learning Outcome 9.6: Describe the two primary diagrams most frequently used in project planning.

A PERT (Program Evaluation and Review Technique) chart is a graphical network model that depicts a project's tasks and the relationships between those tasks. A dependency is a logical relationship that exists between the project tasks, or between a project task and a milestone. A Gantt chart is a simple bar chart that depicts project tasks against a calendar. In a Gantt chart, tasks are listed vertically and the project's time frame is listed horizontally. A Gantt chart works well for representing the project schedule. It also shows actual progress of tasks against the planned duration.

Learning Outcome 9.7: Identify the three primary areas a project manager must focus on managing to ensure success.

The three primary areas a project manager must focus on managing to ensure success are managing people, communications, and change.

Learning Outcome 9.8: Explain the three different types of outsourcing along with their benefits and challenges.

- Onshore outsourcing—engaging another company within the same country for services.
- Nearshore outsourcing—contracting an outsourcing arrangement with a company in a nearby country.
- Offshore outsourcing—using organizations from developing countries to write code and develop systems.

The many benefits associated with outsourcing include increased quality and efficiency of a process, service, or function; reduction of operating expenses and exposure to risks involved with large capital investments; and access to outsourcing service provider's expertise, economies of scale, best practices, and advanced technologies. Outsourcing comes with several challenges including length of contracts, losing competitive advantages, and risking a breach of confidential information.

OPENING CASE QUESTIONS

1. **Knowledge:** List the signs for assessing if a current project is experiencing issues.
2. **Comprehension:** Identify the options a project manager can follow if a project is not meeting its success criteria.
3. **Application:** Illustrate the triple constraints role in a project.
4. **Analysis:** Analyze the four steps to recovering a project and determine which one is the most critical.
5. **Synthesis:** Propose how you would develop a game plan to recover a project.
6. **Evaluate:** Argue for or against the following statement: "Throwing good money after bad will not save a project."

KEY TERMS

Agile methodology, 339
Analysis phase, 335
Business requirement, 335
Change control board (CCB), 349
Change management, 349
Change management system, 349
Critical path, 347
Dependency, 347
Design phase, 336
Development phase, 336
Executive sponsor, 344
Extreme programming (XP) methodology, 340
Gantt chart, 348
Implementation phase, 337
In-sourcing (in-house development), 350
Iterative development, 338
Kill switch, 347
Maintenance phase, 337
Methodology, 337
Nearshore outsourcing, 351
Offshore outsourcing, 351
Onshore outsourcing, 351
Outsourcing, 350
PERT (Program Evaluation and Review Technique) chart, 347
Planning phase, 335
Project, 343
Project assumption, 346
Project charter, 346
Project constraint, 346
Project deliverable, 343
Project management, 343
Project Management Institute (PMI), 342
Project management office (PMO), 343
Project manager, 343
Project milestones, 343
Project objective, 346
Project plan, 346
Project scope statement, 346
Project stakeholder, 344
Prototype, 339
Rapid application development (RAD) methodology (also called rapid prototyping), 339
Rational unified process (RUP) methodology, 340
Scrum methodology, 340
Systems development life cycle (SDLC), 335
Testing phase, 337
Waterfall methodology, 337

REVIEW QUESTIONS

1. What role does project management play in the systems development effort?
2. What role does the project manager play in determining a project's success?
3. Why would a project require an executive sponsor?
4. Which phase in the systems development life cycle is the most important?
5. If you had to skip a phase during the development of a system, which phase would it be and why?
6. Which phase in the systems development life cycle contains the most risk? Be sure to explain your answer.

7. Which project management methodology would you choose to run your software development project?
8. If you started on a new software development project and the project plan was using the waterfall methodology, would you remain on the project? What could you do to better prepare your project for success?
9. What is change management and why is it important for a manager to plan for change?
10. Why should end users be involved in the systems development effort?
11. Why would a project manager use Gantt and PERT charts?
12. Why are gathering business requirements a challenge for most projects?
13. What are the different types of outsourcing available for a project?
14. What are the risks associated with outsourcing?
15. How can scope creep and feature creep kill a project?

CLOSING CASE ONE

Disaster at Denver International Airport

One good way to learn how to develop successful systems is to review past failures. One of the most infamous system failures is Denver International Airport's (DIA) baggage system. When the automated baggage system design for DIA was introduced, it was hailed as the savior of modern airport design. The design relied on a network of 300 computers to route bags and 4,000 cars to carry luggage across 21 miles of track. Laser scanners were to read bar-coded luggage tags, while advanced scanners tracked the movement of toboggan-like baggage carts.

When DIA finally opened its doors for reporters to witness its revolutionary baggage handling system, the scene was rather unpleasant. Bags were chewed up, lost, and misrouted in what has since become a legendary systems nightmare.

One of the biggest mistakes made in the baggage handling system fiasco was that not enough time was allowed to properly develop the system. In the beginning of the project, DIA assumed it was the responsibility of individual airlines to find their own way of moving the baggage from the plane to the baggage claim area. The automated baggage system was not involved in the initial planning of the DIA project. By the time the DIA developers decided to create an integrated baggage system, the time frame for designing and implementing such a complex and huge system was not possible.

Another common mistake that occurred during the project was that the airlines kept changing their business requirements. This caused numerous issues, including the implementation of power supplies that were not properly updated for the revised system design, which caused overloaded motors and mechanical failures. Besides the power supply design problem, the optical sensors did not read the bar codes correctly, causing issues with baggage routing.

Finally, BAE, the company that designed and implemented the automated baggage system for DIA, had never created a baggage system of this size before. BAE had created a similar system in an airport in Munich, Germany, where the scope was much smaller. Essentially, the baggage system had an inadequate IT infrastructure because it was designed for a much smaller system.

DIA simply could not open without a functional baggage system so the city had no choice but to delay the opening date for more than 16 months, costing taxpayers roughly $1 million per day, which totaled around $500 million.[19]

Questions

1. One problem with DIA's baggage system was inadequate testing. Why is testing important to a project's success? Why do so many projects decide to skip testing?
2. Evaluate the different systems development methodologies. Which one would have most significantly increased the chances of the project's success?
3. How could more time spent in the analysis and design phase have saved Colorado taxpayers hundreds of millions of dollars?
4. Why could BAE not take an existing IT infrastructure and simply increase its scale and expect it to work?

CLOSING CASE TWO

Reducing Ambiguity in Business Requirements

The main reason projects fail is bad business requirements. Business requirements are considered "bad" because of ambiguity or insufficient involvement of end users during analysis and design.

A requirement is unambiguous if it has the same interpretation for all parties. Different interpretations by different participants will usually result in unmet expectations. Here is an example of an ambiguous requirement and an example of an unambiguous requirement:

Ambiguous requirement: The financial report must show profits in local and U.S. currencies.

Unambiguous requirement: The financial report must show profits in local and U.S. currencies using the exchange rate printed in *The Wall Street Journal* for the last business day of the period being reported.

Ambiguity is impossible to prevent completely because it is introduced into requirements in natural ways. For example:

- Requirements can contain technical implications that are obvious to the IT developers but not to the customers.
- Requirements can contain business implications that are obvious to the customer but not to the IT developers.
- Requirements may contain everyday words whose meanings are "obvious" to everyone, yet different for everyone.
- Requirements are reflections of detailed explanations that may have included multiple events, multiple perspectives, verbal rephrasing, emotion, iterative refinement, selective emphasis, and body language—none of which are captured in the written statements.

Tips for Reviewing Business Requirements

When reviewing business requirements always look for the following words to help dramatically reduce ambiguity:

- *And* and *or* have well-defined meanings and ought to be completely unambiguous, yet they are often understood only informally and interpreted inconsistently. For example, consider the statement "The alarm must ring if button T is pressed and if button F is pressed." This statement may be intended to mean that to ring the alarm, both buttons must be pressed or it may be intended to mean that either one can be pressed. A statement like this should never appear in a requirement because the potential for misinterpretation is too great. A preferable approach is to be very explicit, for example, "The alarm must ring if both buttons T and F are pressed simultaneously. The alarm should not ring in any other circumstance."

- *Always* might really mean "most of the time," in which case it should be made more explicit. For example, the statement "We always run reports A and B together" could be challenged with "In other words, there is never any circumstance where you would run A without B and B without A?" If you build a system with an "always" requirement, then you are actually building the system to never run report A without report B. If a user suddenly wants report B without report A, you will need to make significant system changes.
- *Never* might mean rarely, in which case it should be made more explicit. For example, the statement "We never run reports A and B in the same month" could be challenged with, "So that means that if I see that A has been run, I can be absolutely certain that no one will want to run B." Again, if you build a system that supports a "never" requirement, then the system users can never perform that requirement. For example, the system would never allow a user to run reports A and B in the same month, no matter what the circumstances.
- Boundary conditions are statements about the line between true and false and do and do not. These statements may or may not be meant to include end points. For example, "We want to use method X when there are up to 10 pages, but method Y otherwise." If you were building this system, would you include page 10 in method X or in method Y? The answer to this question will vary causing an ambiguous business requirement.[20]

Questions

1. Why are ambiguous business requirements the leading cause of system development failures?
2. Why do the words *and* and *or* tend to lead to ambiguous requirements?
3. Research the Web and determine other reasons for "bad" business requirements.
4. What is wrong with the following business requirement: "The system must support employee birthdays because every employee always has a birthday every year."

CRITICAL BUSINESS THINKING

1. Selecting a Systems Development Methodology

Exus Incorporated is an international billing outsourcing company. Exus currently has revenues of $5 billion, more than 3,500 employees, and operations on every continent. You have recently been hired as the CIO. Your first task is to increase the software development project success rate, which is currently at 20 percent. To ensure that future software development projects are successful, you want to standardize the systems development methodology across the entire enterprise. Currently, each project determines which methodology it uses to develop software.

Create a report detailing three system development methodologies that were covered in this text. Compare each of these methodologies to the traditional waterfall approach. Finally, recommend which methodology you want to implement as your organizational standard. Be sure to highlight any potential roadblocks you might encounter when implementing the new standard methodology.

2. Understanding Project Failure

You are the director of project management for Stello, a global manufacturer of high-end writing instruments. The company sells to primarily high-end customers, and the average price for one of its fine writing instruments is about $350. You are currently implementing a new customer relationship management system, and you want to do everything you can to ensure a successful systems development effort. Create a document summarizing the primary reasons why this project could fail, along with your strategy to eliminate the possibility of system development failure on your project.

3. **Missing Phases in the Systems Development Life Cycle**
Hello Inc. is a large concierge service for executives operating in Chicago, San Francisco, and New York. The company performs all kinds of services from dog walking to airport transportation. Your manager, Dan Martello, wants to skip the testing phase during the company's financial ERP implementation. He feels that because the system came from a vendor, it should work correctly. Draft a memo explaining the importance of following the SDLC and the ramifications to the business if the financial system is not tested.

4. **Refusing to Sign Off**
You are the primary client on a large extranet development project. After carefully reviewing the requirements definition document, you are positive that there are missing, ambiguous, inaccurate, and unclear requirements. The project manager is pressuring you for your sign-off because he has already received sign-off from five of your co-workers. If you fail to sign off on the requirements, you are going to put the entire project at risk because the time frame is nonnegotiable. What would you do? Why?

5. **Saving Failing Systems**
Crik Candle Company manufactures low-end candles for restaurants. The company generates more than $40 million in annual revenues and has more than 300 employees. You are in the middle of a large multimillion-dollar supply chain management implementation. Your project manager has just come to you with the information that the project might fail for the following reasons:
   - Several business requirements were incorrect and the scope has to be doubled.
   - Three developers recently quit.
   - The deadline has been moved up a month.

   Develop a list of options that your company can follow to ensure the project remains on schedule and within budget.

6. **Explaining Project Management**
Prime Time Inc. is a large consulting company that specializes in outsourcing people with project management capabilities and skills. You are in the middle of an interview for a job with Prime Time. The manager performing the interview asks you to explain why managing a project plan is critical to a project's success. The manager also wants you to explain scope creep and feature creep and your tactics for managing them on a project. Finally, the manager wants you to elaborate on your strategies for delivering successful projects and reducing risks.

7. **Applying Project Management Techniques**
You have been hired by a medium-sized airline company, Sun Best. Sun Best currently flies more than 300 routes in the East. The company is experiencing tremendous issues coordinating its 3,500 pilots, 7,000 flight attendants, and 2,000 daily flights. Determine how Sun Best could use a Gantt chart to help it coordinate pilots, flight attendants, and daily flights. Using Excel, create a sample Gantt chart highlighting the different types of activities and resources Sun Best could track with the tool.

ENTREPRENEURIAL CHALLENGE

BUILD YOUR OWN BUSINESS

1. Your business is undertaking many new and exciting initiatives to boost growth, including employee blogs, customer wikis, and implementation of a new time and attendance system. Time and attendance software is critical to the business because it can ensure you have the right employees, at the right place, at the right time, which can increase sales. You never want to find yourself understaffed during busy times and overstaffed during slow times. Also, accurately accounting for employees' time is crucial to effectively analyzing labor expenses, which are the largest operating expense your business incurs. Conveniently, time and attendance solution providers, time clock manufacturers, and software development companies are developing high-quality affordable products. You have decided to replace the manual employee tracking system your grandfather implemented in the 1950s. You have a highly technical employee, Nick Zele, who has offered to build the system for you and ensures you it is a simple build. You could also purchase one of the many off-the-shelf applications and have an outsourcing firm customize the application for your business. What are the pros and cons of using an employee to build you a custom system? What are the pros and cons of purchasing an off-the-shelf time and attendance application and outsourcing custom development? How will your older employees feel about the new system and what can you do to ensure a smooth transition?
2. You have decided to implement a new payroll system for your business. Review the following business requirements and highlight any potential issues.
   - All employees must have a unique employee ID.
   - The system must track employee hours worked based on employee's last name.
   - Employees must be scheduled to work a minimum of eight hours per day.
   - Employee payroll is calculated by multiplying the employee's hours worked by $7.25.
   - Managers must be scheduled to work morning shifts.
   - Employees cannot be scheduled to work more than eight hours per day.
   - Servers cannot be scheduled to work morning, afternoon, or evening shifts.
   - The system must allow managers to change and delete employees from the system.
3. You are in the middle of a implementing a new system at your business. Your project team is failing for the following three reasons: (1) The project is using the traditional waterfall methodology; (2) the SDLC was not followed and the developers decided to skip the testing phase; (3) a project plan was developed during the analysis phase, but the old project manager never updated or followed the plan and never updated the business requirements. Detail your strategy for getting your project back on track.

APPLY YOUR KNOWLEDGE BUSINESS PROJECTS

PROJECT I Methods Behind Methodologies

Signatures Inc. specializes in producing personalized products such as coffee mugs and pens with company logos. The company generates more than $40 million in annual revenues and has more than 300 employees. The company is in the middle of a large multimillion-dollar SCM implementation, and it has just hired your project management outsourcing firm to take over the project management efforts.

Project Focus

On your first day, your team is told that the project is failing for the following reasons:

- The project is using the traditional waterfall methodology.
- The SDLC was not followed and the developers decided to skip the testing phase.
- A project plan was developed during the analysis phase, but the old project manager never updated or followed the plan.

Determine what your first steps would be to get this project back on track.

PROJECT II The Travel Store

The Travel Store is facing a dilemma as it tripled in size over the past three years and finds its online sales escalating beyond a billion dollars. The company is having a hard time continuing with operations as its business processes can't scale to meet the new demand. In the past six months, sales and profits have dropped and the stock price is plummeting.

Project Focus

The Travel Store is determined to take quick and decisive action to restore profitability and improve its credibility in the marketplace. One of its top priorities is to overhaul its inventory management system in an effort to create optimal levels of inventory to support sales demand. This would prevent higher-volume stores from running out of key sale items while also ensuring that lower-sales stores would not be burdened with excess inventory that could be moved only at closeout prices. The company would like to outsource this function but is worried about the challenges of transferring the responsibility of this important business function, as well as the issues surrounding confidentiality, and scope definition. List the competitive advantages outsourcing could give to The Travel Store, along with recommendations for addressing the company's outsourcing concerns.

PROJECT III GEM Athletic Center

First Information Corporation is a large consulting company that specializes in systems analysis and design. The company has more than 2,000 employees, and first-quarter revenues reached $15 million. The company prides itself on maintaining an 85 percent success rate for all project implementations. The primary reason attributed to the unusually high project success rate is the company's ability to define accurate, complete, and high-quality business requirements.

The GEM Athletic Center located in Cleveland, Ohio, is interested in implementing a new payroll system. The current payroll process is manual and takes three employees two days each month to complete. The GEM Athletic Center does not have an IT department and is outsourcing the entire procurement, customization, and installation of the new payroll system to First Information Corporation.

Project Focus

You have been working for First Information for a little over one month. Your team has just been assigned the GEM Athletic Center project, and your first task is to define the initial business requirements for the development of the new payroll system.

a. Review the testimony of three current GEM Athletic Center accounting employees who detail the current payroll process along with their wish list for the new system. Figure 9.15 presents the testimonies of Maggie Cleaver, Anne Logan, and Jim Poulos.

b. Review Closing Case Two, "Reducing Ambiguity in Business Requirements" and highlight several techniques you can use to develop solid business requirements.

c. After careful analysis, create a report detailing the business requirements for the new system. Be sure to list any assumptions, issues, or questions in your document.

FIGURE 9.15
Employee Testimonies

Jim Poulos, Director of Sales

Each week I have to review all of the new memberships sold in our club. Each of my seven sales representatives receives $50 from a new sale for the initiation fee. They also receive 10 percent of the type of membership sold. Membership types include:

- Adult, $450/month
- Youth, $300/month
- Family, $750/month
- Senior, $300/month

Each sales representative is also paid $4.50/hour and receives a 25 percent bonus for working overtime and holidays. If the sales representative sells over 200 percent of expected sales they receive an additional 25 percent bonus on their commissions. If the membership is sold during a promotion, the commission rate decreases. The payroll department uses time sheets to track my sales representatives' hourly pay. I have to sign all time sheets once they are completed by the payroll department. I check my sales representatives' schedule to validate the times on the employee time sheets. I then have to submit a separate listing of each employee and their corresponding commissions for initiation fees and memberships sold. I track all of my sales representatives' vacation and sick time. If they are over their vacation or sick time, I have them sign a form stating that if they quit they will pay back all negative vacation or sick time.

I would like a system that can automatically calculate commissions and be able to handle sales forecasting and "what if" analysis on my sales representatives' commission rates. I would like to be able to walk up to my sales representatives and tell them that if they sell four more family memberships and one adult they will receive their bonus. I would also like to be able to design promotions for our best customers. These types of things would really help boost sales at our club.

Maggie Cleaver, Payroll Manager

The first thing I do each week is collect the time sheets. I review each time sheet to ensure the employee punched in and out correctly. If the employee forgot to clock out, I contact that person's director to find the time that the employee should have clocked out. I then calculate all regular hours, overtime hours, and holiday hours and total these on the time sheet. I also track sick time and vacation time and total these on the time sheet. Once completed, I send the time sheet to the directors of each department for approval.

When I receive the signed time sheets back, I begin to calculate payments. First, I calculate regular pay, then overtime pay, and finally holiday pay. I then add in the sales representatives' commissions, which I receive from the director of sales. I then calculate payment amounts for aerobics instructors because they are paid by class, not by hour. I receive the aerobics class schedule from the fitness coordinator. I then total the entire pay and send a sheet with payment amounts to my co-worker Anne, who calculates taxes. I then calculate all sick time and vacation time and track this in a separate document. I then print labels that state each employee's name, department, and the pay period. I place the labels on a new time sheet, which is returned to the employee punch clock.

I would like a system that automatically tracks employee sick time and vacation time. I would also like a system that can automatically calculate regular pay, overtime pay, and holiday pay. I don't know if there is a system that can validate employee time sheets, but if there is that would be great.

Anne Logan, Tax Manager

I receive the payment amounts from Maggie. I then calculate all city, state, and federal taxes. I also deduct health benefits and retirement plan benefits. I then cut the check to the employee and the corresponding checks for the taxes to the government. I manually calculate W2s and all quarterly taxes. I'm also responsible for correcting personal information such as a change of address. I'm also responsible for cutting checks if an incorrect amount was issued. I also track amounts owed by employees that have gone over their sick time or vacation time. I also generate checks for all salaried employees.

The part of my job that takes the longest is correlating the total cash debit for all checks and the total amount calculated for all checks. It's amazing how many times these two figures do not match, which indicates that a check was written for the wrong amount.

I would like a system that determines taxes automatically, along with quarterly tax filing statements. I would also like a system that can perform audits.

PROJECT IV Confusing Coffee

Business requirements are the detailed set of business requests that any new system must meet to be successful. A sample business requirement might state, "The system must track all customer sales by product, region, and sales representative." This requirement states what the system must do from the business perspective, giving no details or information on how the system is going to meet this requirement.

Project Focus

You have been hired to build an employee payroll system for a new coffee shop. Review the following business requirements and highlight any potential issues.

- All employees must have a unique employee ID.
- The system must track employee hours worked based on employee's last name.
- Employees must be scheduled to work a minimum of eight hours per day.
- Employee payroll is calculated by multiplying the employee's hours worked by $7.25.
- Managers must be scheduled to work morning shifts.
- Employees cannot be scheduled to work more than eight hours per day.
- Servers cannot be scheduled to work morning, afternoon, or evening shifts.
- The system must allow managers to change and delete employees from the system.

PROJECT V Picking Projects

You are a project management contractor attempting to contract work at a large telecommunications company, Hex Incorporated. Your interview with Debbie Fernandez, the senior vice president of IT, went smoothly. The last thing she wants to see from you before she makes her final hiring decision is a prioritized list of the following projects. You are sure to land the job if Fernandez is satisfied with your prioritization.

Project Focus

Create a report prioritizing the following projects and be sure to include the business justifications for your prioritization.

- Upgrade accounting system.
- Develop employee vacation tracking system.
- Enhance employee intranet.
- Cleanse and scrub data warehouse information.
- Performance-test all hardware to ensure 20 percent growth scalability.
- Implement changes to employee benefits system.
- Develop backup and recovery strategy.
- Implement supply chain management system.
- Upgrade customer relationship management system.
- Build executive information system for CEO.

PROJECT VI Keeping Time

Time Keepers Inc. is a small firm that specializes in project management consulting. You are a senior project manager, and you have recently been assigned to the Tahiti Tanning Lotion account. The Tahiti Tanning Lotion company is currently experiencing a 10 percent success rate (90 percent failure rate) on all internal IT projects. Your first assignment is to analyze one of the current project plans being used to develop a new CRM system (see Figure 9.16).

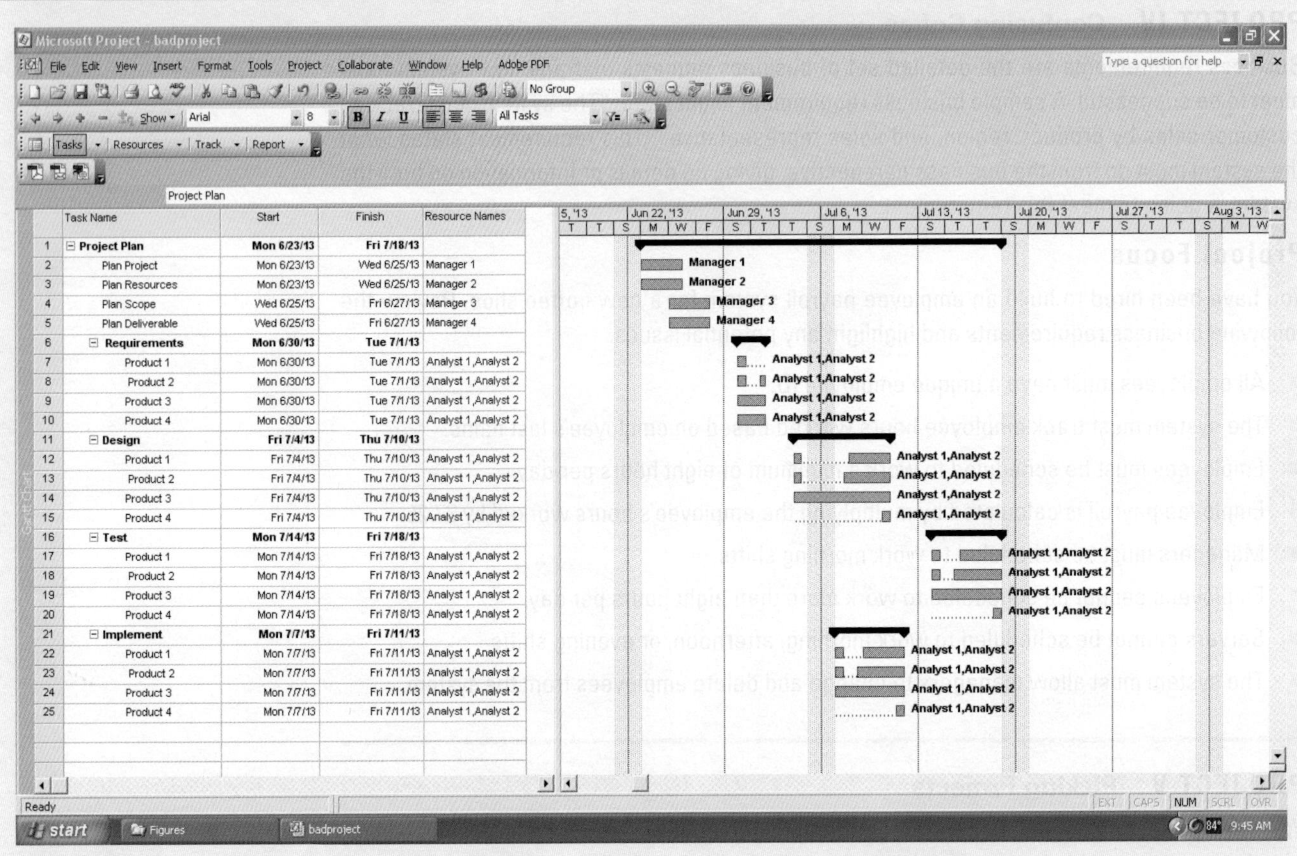

	Task Name	Start	Finish	Resource Names
1	**Project Plan**	**Mon 6/23/13**	**Fri 7/18/13**	
2	Plan Project	Mon 6/23/13	Wed 6/25/13	Manager 1
3	Plan Resources	Mon 6/23/13	Wed 6/25/13	Manager 2
4	Plan Scope	Wed 6/25/13	Fri 6/27/13	Manager 3
5	Plan Deliverable	Wed 6/25/13	Fri 6/27/13	Manager 4
6	**Requirements**	**Mon 6/30/13**	**Tue 7/1/13**	
7	Product 1	Mon 6/30/13	Tue 7/1/13	Analyst 1,Analyst 2
8	Product 2	Mon 6/30/13	Tue 7/1/13	Analyst 1,Analyst 2
9	Product 3	Mon 6/30/13	Tue 7/1/13	Analyst 1,Analyst 2
10	Product 4	Mon 6/30/13	Tue 7/1/13	Analyst 1,Analyst 2
11	**Design**	**Fri 7/4/13**	**Thu 7/10/13**	
12	Product 1	Fri 7/4/13	Thu 7/10/13	Analyst 1,Analyst 2
13	Product 2	Fri 7/4/13	Thu 7/10/13	Analyst 1,Analyst 2
14	Product 3	Fri 7/4/13	Thu 7/10/13	Analyst 1,Analyst 2
15	Product 4	Fri 7/4/13	Thu 7/10/13	Analyst 1,Analyst 2
16	**Test**	**Mon 7/14/13**	**Fri 7/18/13**	
17	Product 1	Mon 7/14/13	Fri 7/18/13	Analyst 1,Analyst 2
18	Product 2	Mon 7/14/13	Fri 7/18/13	Analyst 1,Analyst 2
19	Product 3	Mon 7/14/13	Fri 7/18/13	Analyst 1,Analyst 2
20	Product 4	Mon 7/14/13	Fri 7/18/13	Analyst 1,Analyst 2
21	**Implement**	**Mon 7/7/13**	**Fri 7/11/13**	
22	Product 1	Mon 7/7/13	Fri 7/11/13	Analyst 1,Analyst 2
23	Product 2	Mon 7/7/13	Fri 7/11/13	Analyst 1,Analyst 2
24	Product 3	Mon 7/7/13	Fri 7/11/13	Analyst 1,Analyst 2
25	Product 4	Mon 7/7/13	Fri 7/11/13	Analyst 1,Analyst 2

FIGURE 9.16

CRM Project Plan

Project Focus

Review the project plan and create a document listing the numerous errors in the plan. Be sure to also provide suggestions on how to fix the errors.

AYK APPLICATION PROJECTS

If you are looking for Excel projects to incorporate into your class, try any of the following after reading this chapter.

Project Number	Project Name	Project Type	Plug-In	Focus Area	Project Level	Skill Set	Page Number
9	Security Analysis	Excel	T3	Filtering Data	Intermediate	Conditional Formatting, Autofilter, Subtotal	AYK.7
10	Gathering Data	Excel	T3	Data Analysis	Intermediate	Conditional Formatting	AYK.8
11	Scanner System	Excel	T2	Strategic Analysis	Intermediate	Formulas	AYK.8
12	Competitive Pricing	Excel	T2	Profit Maximization	Intermediate	Formulas	AYK.9
13	Adequate Acquisitions	Excel	T2	Break Even Analysis	Intermediate	Formulas	AYK.9
15	Assessing the Value of Information	Excel	T3	Data Analysis	Intermediate	PivotTable	AYK.10
16	Growth, Trends, and Forecasts	Excel	T2, T3	Data Forecasting	Advanced	Average, Trend, Growth	AYK.11
18	Formatting Grades	Excel	T3	Data Analysis	Advanced	If, LookUp	AYK.12
22	Turnover Rates	Excel	T3	Data Mining	Advanced	PivotTable	AYK.12
23	Vital Information	Excel	T3	Data Mining	Advanced	PivotTable	AYK.15
24	Breaking Even	Excel	T4	Business Analysis	Advanced	Goal Seek	AYK.16
25	Profit Scenario	Excel	T4	Sales Analysis	Advanced	Scenario Manager	AYK.16

Hardware and Software Basics

Introduction

Managers need to determine what types of hardware and software will satisfy their current and future business needs, the right time to buy the equipment, and how to protect their investments. This does not imply that managers need to be experts in all areas of technology; however, building a basic understanding of hardware and software can help them make the right investment choices.

Information technology can be an important enabler of business success and innovation. Information technology can be composed of the Internet, a personal computer, a cell phone that can access the Web, a personal digital assistant, or presentation software. All of these technologies help to perform specific information processing tasks. There are two basic categories of information technology: hardware and software. ***Hardware*** consists of the physical devices associated with a computer system. ***Software*** is the set of instructions the hardware executes to carry out specific tasks. Software, such as Microsoft Excel, and various hardware devices, such as a keyboard and a monitor, interact to create a spreadsheet or a graph. This appendix covers the basics of computer hardware and software including terminology, characteristics, and the associated managerial responsibilities for building a solid enterprise architecture.

LEARNING OUTCOMES

A.1. Describe the six major categories of hardware, and provide an example of each.

A.2. Identify the different computer categories, and explain their potential business uses.

A.3. Explain the difference between primary and secondary storage.

A.4. List the common input, output, storage, and communication devices.

A.5. Describe the eight categories of computers by size.

A.6. Define the relationship between operating system software and utility software.

Hardware Basics

In many industries, exploiting computer hardware is key to gaining a competitive advantage. Frito-Lay gained a competitive advantage by using handheld devices to track the strategic placement and sale of items in convenience stores. Sales representatives could track sale price, competitor information, the number of items sold, and item location in the store all from their handheld device.[1]

A ***computer*** is an electronic device operating under the control of instructions stored in its own memory that can accept, manipulate, and store data. A computer system consists of six hardware components (see Figure A.1). Figure A.2 displays how these components work together to form a computer system.

CENTRAL PROCESSING UNIT

The dominant manufacturers of CPUs today include Intel (with its Celeron and Pentium lines for personal computers) and Advanced Micro Devices (AMD) (with its Athlon series).[2]

The ***central processing unit (CPU)*** (or ***microprocessor***) is the actual hardware that interprets and executes the program (software) instructions and coordinates how all the other hardware devices work together. The CPU is built on a small flake of silicon and

figure A.1
Hardware Components of a Computer System

Six Hardware Components	
Central processing unit (CPU)	The actual hardware that interprets and executes the program (software) instructions and coordinates how all the other hardware devices work together.
Primary storage	The computer's main memory, which consists of the random access memory (RAM), the cache memory, and the read-only memory (ROM) that is directly accessible to the central processing unit (CPU).
Secondary storage	Equipment designed to store large volumes of data for long-term storage (e.g., diskette, hard drive, memory card, CD).
Input devices	Equipment used to capture information and commands (e.g., keyboard, scanner).
Output devices	Equipment used to see, hear, or otherwise accept the results of information processing requests (e.g., monitor, printer).
Communication devices	Equipment used to send information and receive it from one location to another (e.g., modem).

figure A.2 How the Hardware Components Work Together

Input Device

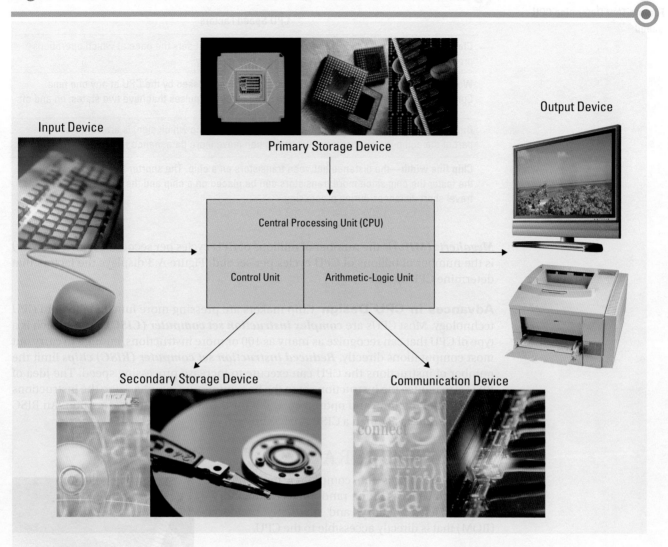

Primary Storage Device

Output Device

Central Processing Unit (CPU)

Control Unit

Arithmetic-Logic Unit

Secondary Storage Device

Communication Device

can contain the equivalent of several million transistors. CPUs are unquestionably one of the 20th century's greatest technological advances.

A CPU contains two primary parts: control unit and arithmetic/logic unit. The ***control unit*** interprets software instructions and literally tells the other hardware devices what to do, based on the software instructions. The ***arithmetic-logic unit (ALU)*** performs all arithmetic operations (for example, addition and subtraction) and all logic operations (such as sorting and comparing numbers). The control unit and ALU perform different functions. The control unit obtains instructions from the software. It then interprets the instructions, decides which tasks other devices perform, and finally tells each device to perform the task. The ALU responds to the control unit and does whatever it dictates, performing either arithmetic or logic operations.

The number of CPU cycles per second determines how fast a CPU carries out the software instructions; more cycles per second means faster processing, and faster CPUs cost more than their slower counterparts. CPU speed is usually quoted in megahertz and gigahertz.

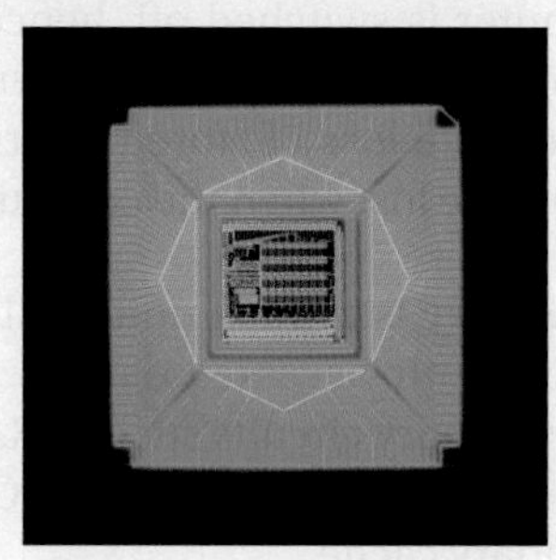

figure A.3

Factors That Determine CPU Speed

CPU Speed Factors
Clock speed—the speed of the internal clock of a CPU that sets the pace at which operations proceed within the computer's internal processing circuitry.
Word length—number of bits (0s and 1s) that can be processed by the CPU at any one time. Computers work in terms of bits and bytes using electrical pulses that have two states: on and off.
Bus width—the size of the internal electrical pathway along which signals are sent from one part of the computer to another. A wider bus can move more data, hence faster processing.
Chip line width—the distance between transistors on a chip. The shorter the chip line width the faster the chip since more transistors can be placed on a chip and the data and instructions travel short distances during processing.

Megahertz (MHz) is the number of millions of CPU cycles per second. ***Gigahertz (GHz)*** is the number of billions of CPU cycles per second. Figure A.3 displays the factors that determine CPU speed.

Advances in CPU Design Chip makers are pressing more functionality into CPU technology. Most CPUs are ***complex instruction set computer (CISC) chips,*** which is a type of CPU that can recognize as many as 100 or more instructions, enough to carry out most computations directly. ***Reduced instruction set computer (RISC) chips*** limit the number of instructions the CPU can execute to increase processing speed. The idea of RISC is to reduce the instruction set to the bare minimum, emphasizing the instructions used most of the time and optimizing them for the fastest possible execution. An RISC processor runs faster than a CISC processor.

PRIMARY STORAGE

Primary storage is the computer's main memory, which consists of the random access memory (RAM), cache memory, and read-only memory (ROM) that is directly accessible to the CPU.

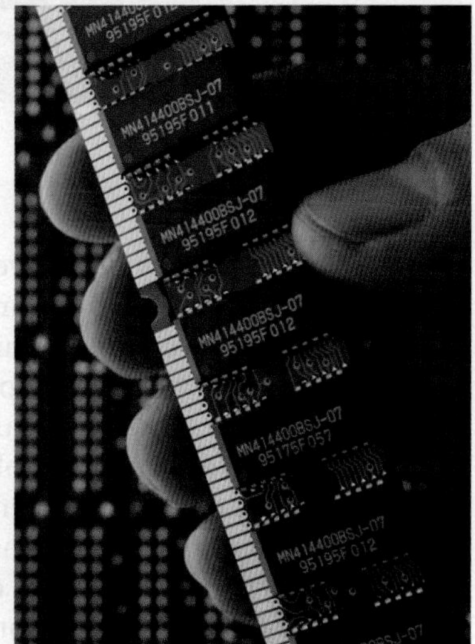

Random Access Memory ***Random access memory (RAM)*** is the computer's primary working memory, in which program instructions and data are stored so that they can be accessed directly by the CPU via the processor's high-speed external data bus.

RAM is often called read/write memory. In RAM, the CPU can write and read data. Most programs set aside a portion of RAM as a temporary workspace for data so that one can modify (rewrite) as needed until the data is ready for printing or storage on secondary storage media, such as a hard drive or memory key. RAM does not retain its contents when the power to the computer is switched off, hence individuals should save their work frequently. When the computer is turned off, everything in RAM is wiped clean. ***Volatility*** refers to RAM's complete loss of stored information if power is interrupted. RAM is volatile and its contents are lost when the computer's electric supply fails.

Cache Memory ***Cache memory*** is a small unit of ultra-fast memory that is used to store recently accessed or frequently accessed data so that the CPU does not have to retrieve this data from slower memory circuits such as RAM. Cache memory that is built directly into the CPU's circuits is called primary cache. Cache memory contained on an external circuit is called secondary cache.

Read-Only Memory (ROM) ***Read-only memory (ROM)*** is the portion of a computer's primary storage that does not lose its contents when one switches off the power. ROM contains essential system programs that neither the user nor the computer can erase. Since the computer's internal memory is blank during start-up, the computer cannot perform any functions unless given start-up instructions. These instructions are stored in ROM.

Flash memory is a special type of rewritable read-only memory (ROM) that is compact and portable. ***Memory cards*** contain high-capacity storage that holds data such as captured images, music, or text files. Memory cards are removable; when one is full the user can insert an additional card. Subsequently, the data can be downloaded from the card to a computer. The card can then be erased and used again. Memory cards are typically used in digital devices such as cameras, cellular phones, and personal digital assistants (PDA). ***Memory sticks*** provide nonvolatile memory for a range of portable devices including computers, digital cameras, MP3 players, and PDAs.

SECONDARY STORAGE

Storage is a hot area in the business arena as organizations struggle to make sense of exploding volumes of data. ***Secondary storage*** consists of equipment designed to store large volumes of data for long-term storage. Secondary storage devices are nonvolatile and do not lose their contents when the computer is turned off. Some storage devices, such as a hard disk, offer easy update capabilities and a large storage capacity. Others, such as CD-ROMs, offer limited update capabilities but possess large storage capacities.

Storage capacity is expressed in bytes, with megabytes being the most common. A ***megabyte (MB*** or ***M*** or ***Meg)*** is roughly 1 million bytes. Therefore, a computer with 256 MB of RAM translates into the RAM being able to hold roughly 256 million characters of data and software instructions. A ***gigabyte (GB)*** is roughly 1 billion bytes. A ***terabyte (TB)*** is roughly 1 trillion bytes (refer to Figure A.4).[3]

A typical double-spaced page of pure text is roughly 2,000 characters. Therefore, a 40 GB (40 gigabyte or 40 billion characters) hard drive can hold approximately 20 million pages of text.

Common storage devices include:

- Magnetic medium
- Optical medium

figure A.4
Binary Terms

Term	Size
Kilobyte (KB)	1,024 Bytes
Megabyte (MB)	1,024 KB 1,048,576 Bytes
Gigabyte (GB)	1,024 MB (10^9 bytes)
Terabyte (TB)	1,024 GB (10^{12} bytes) 1 TB = Printing of 1 TB would require 50,000 trees to be made into paper and printed
Petabyte (PB)	1,024 TB (10^{15} bytes) 200 PB = All production of digital magnetic tape in 1995
Exabyte (EB)	1,024 PB (10^{18} bytes) 2 EB = total volume of information generated worldwide annually 5 EB = all words ever spoken by human beings

Magnetic medium ***Magnetic medium*** is a secondary storage medium that uses magnetic techniques to store and retrieve data on disks or tapes coated with magnetically sensitive materials. Like iron filings on a sheet of waxed paper, these materials are reoriented when a magnetic field passes over them. During write operations, the read/write heads emit a magnetic field that orients the magnetic materials on the disk or tape to represent encoded data. During read operations, the read/write heads sense the encoded data on the medium.

One of the first forms of magnetic medium developed was magnetic tape. ***Magnetic tape*** is an older secondary storage medium that uses a strip of thin plastic coated with a magnetically sensitive recording medium. The most popular type of magnetic medium is a hard drive. A ***hard drive*** is a secondary storage medium that uses several rigid disks coated with a magnetically sensitive material and housed together with the recording heads in a hermetically sealed mechanism. Hard drive performance is measured in terms of access time, seek time, rotational speed, and data transfer rate.

Optical Medium Optical medium is a secondary storage medium for computers on which information is stored at extremely high density in the form of tiny pits. The presence or absence of pits is read by a tightly focused laser beam. Optical medium types include:

- **Compact disk-read-only memory (CD-ROM) drive**—an optical drive designed to read the data encoded on CD-ROMs and to transfer this data to a computer.
- **Compact disk-read-write (CD-RW) drive**—an optical drive that enables users to erase existing data and to write new data repeatedly to a CD-RW.
- **Digital video disk (DVD)**—a CD-ROM format capable of storing up to a maximum of 17 GB of data; enough for a full-length feature movie.
- **DVD-ROM drive**—a read-only drive designed to read the data encoded on a DVD and transfer the data to a computer.
- **Digital video disk-read/write (DVD-RW)**—a standard for DVD discs and player/recorder mechanisms that enables users to record in the DVD format.

CD-ROMs and DVDs offer an increasingly economical medium for storing data and programs. The overall trend in secondary storage is toward more direct-access methods, higher capacity with lower costs, and increased portability.

INPUT DEVICES

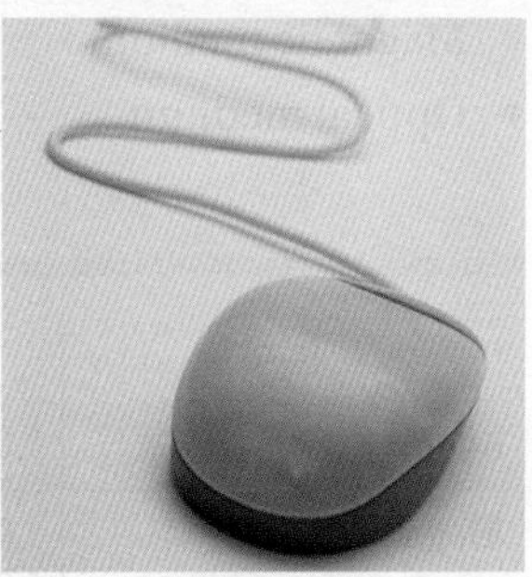

An ***input device*** is equipment used to capture information and commands. A keyboard is used to type in information, and a mouse is used to point and click on buttons and icons. Numerous input devices are available in many different environments, some of which have applications that are more suitable in a personal setting than a business setting. A keyboard, mouse, and scanner are the most common forms of input devices (see Figures A.5 and A.6).

New forms of input devices allow people to exercise and play video games at the same time. The Kilowatt Sport from Powergrid Fitness lets people combine strength training with their favorite video games. Players can choose any PlayStation or Xbox game that uses a joystick to run the elliptical trainer. After loading the game, participants stand on a platform while pushing and pulling a resistance rod in all directions to control what happens in the game. The varied movement targets muscle groups on the chest,

figure A.5
Manual Input Devices

Manual Input Devices
Joystick—widely used as an alternative to the keyboard for computer games and some professional applications, such as computer-aided design.
Keyboard—provides a set of alphabetic, numeric, punctuation, symbol, and control keys.
Microphone—captures sounds such as a voice for voice-recognition software.
Mouse—one or more control buttons housed in a palm-sized case and designed so that one can move it about on the table next to the keyboard.
Pointing stick—causes the pointer to move on the screen by applying directional pressure (popular on notebooks and PDAs).
Touch screen—allows the use of a finger to point at and touch a particular function to perform.
Touch pad—a form of a stationary mouse on which the movement of a finger causes the pointer on the screen to move.

figure A.6
Automated Input Devices

Automated Input Devices
Bar code scanner—captures information that exists in the form of vertical bars whose width and distance apart determine a number.
Digital camera—captures still images or video as a series of 1s and 0s.
Magnetic ink character reader—reads magnetic ink numbers printed on checks that identify the bank, checking account, and check number.
Optical-character recognition—converts text into digital format for computer input.
Optical-mark recognition (OMR)—detects the presence or absence of a mark in a predetermined place (popular for multiple-choice exams).
Point-of-sale (POS)—captures information at the point of a transaction, typically in a retail environment.
Radio frequency identification (RFID)—uses active or passive tags in the form of chips or smart labels that can store unique identifiers and relay this information to electronic readers.

arms, shoulders, abdomen, and back. The machine's display shows information such as pounds lifted and current resistance level, and players can use one-touch adjustment to vary the degree of difficulty.[4]

Another new input device is a stationary bicycle. A computer design team of graduate and undergraduate students at MIT built the Cyclescore, an integrated video game and bicycle. The MIT students tested current games on the market but found users would stop pedaling to concentrate on the game. To engage users, the team is designing games that interact with the experience of exercise itself, for example, monitoring heart rate and adjusting the difficulty of the game according to the user's bicycling capabilities. In one game, the player must pedal to make a hot-air balloon float over mountains, while collecting coins and shooting at random targets.[5]

OUTPUT DEVICES

An ***output device*** is equipment used to see, hear, or otherwise accept the results of information processing requests. Among output devices, printers and monitors are the most common; however, speakers and plotters (special printers that draw output on a page)

figure A.7

Output Devices

Output Devices
Cathode-ray tube (CRT)—a vacuum tube that uses an electron gun (cathode) to emit a beam of electrons that illuminates phosphors on a screen as the beam sweeps across the screen repeatedly. A monitor is often called a CRT.
Liquid crystal display (LCDs)—a low-powered display technology used in laptop computers where rod-shaped crystal molecules change their orientation when an electrical current flows through them.
Laser printer—a printer that forms images using an electrostatic process, the same way a photocopier works.
Ink-jet printer—a printer that makes images by forcing ink droplets through nozzles.
Plotter—a printer that uses computer-directed pens for creating high-quality images, blueprints, schematics, etc.

are widely used (see Figure A.7). In addition, output devices are responsible for converting computer-stored information into a form that can be understood.

A new output device based on sensor technology aims to translate American Sign Language (ASL) into speech, enabling the millions of people who use ASL to better communicate with those who do not know the rapid gesturing system. The AcceleGlove is a glove lined on the inside with sensors embedded in rings. The sensors, called accelerometers, measure acceleration and can categorize and translate finger and hand movements. Additional, interconnected attachments for the elbow and shoulder capture ASL signs that are made with full arm motion. When users wear the glove while signing ASL, algorithms in the glove's software translate the hand gestures into words. The translations can be relayed through speech synthesizers or read on a PDA-size computer screen. Inventor Jose L. Hernandez-Rebollar started with a single glove that could translate only the ASL alphabet. Now, the device employs two gloves that contain a 1,000-word vocabulary.[6]

Other new output devices are being developed every day. Needapresent.com, a British company, has developed a vibrating USB massage ball, which plugs into a computer's USB port to generate a warm massage for sore body parts during those long evenings spent coding software or writing papers. Needapresent.com also makes a coffee cup warmer that plugs into the USB port.[7]

COMMUNICATION DEVICES

A ***communication device*** is equipment used to send information and receive it from one location to another. A telephone modem connects a computer to a phone line in order to access another computer. The computer works in terms of digital signals, while a standard telephone line works with analog signals. Each digital signal represents a bit (either 0 or 1). The modem must convert the digital signals of a computer into analog signals so they can be sent across the telephone line. At the other end, another modem translates the analog signals into digital signals, which can then be used by the other computer. Figure A.8 displays the different types of modems.

Computer Categories

Supercomputers today can hit processing capabilities of well over 200 teraflops—the equivalent of everyone on Earth performing 35,000 calculations per second (see Figure A.9). For the past 20 years, federally funded supercomputing research has given

figure A.8
Comparing Modems

Carrier Technology	Description	Speed	Comments
Dial-up Access	On demand access using a modem and regular telephone line (POT).	2400 bps to 56 Kbps	■ Cheap but slow.
Cable	Special cable modem and cable line required.	512 Kbps to 20 Mbps	■ Must have existing cable access in area. ■ Bandwidth is shared.
DSL Digital Subscriber Line	This technology uses the unused digital portion of a regular copper telephone line to transmit and receive information. A special modem and adapter card are required.	128 Kbps to 8 Mbps	■ Doesn't interfere with normal telephone use. ■ Bandwidth is dedicated. ■ Must be within 5 km (3.1 miles) of telephone company switch.
Wireless (LMCS)	Access is gained by connection to a high-speed cellular-like local multipoint communications system (LMCS) network via wireless transmitter/receiver.	30 Mbps or more	■ Can be used for high-speed data, broadcast TV, and wireless telephone service.
Satellite	Newer versions have two-way satellite access, removing need for phone line.	6 Mbps or more	■ Bandwidth is not shared. ■ Some connections require an existing Internet service account. ■ Setup fees can range from $500–$1,000.

figure A.9
Supercomputer

birth to some of the computer industry's most significant technology breakthroughs including:

- Clustering, which allows companies to chain together thousands of PCs to build mass-market systems.
- Parallel processing, which provides the ability to run two or more tasks simultaneously and is viewed as the chip industry's future.
- Mosaic browser, which morphed into Netscape and made the Web a household name.

Federally funded supercomputers have also advanced some of the country's most dynamic industries, including advanced manufacturing, gene research in the life sciences, and real-time financial-market modeling.[8]

Computers come in different shapes, sizes, and colors. Some are small enough to carry around, while others are the size of a telephone booth. Size does not always correlate to power, speed, and price (see Figure A.10).

figure A.10
Computer Categories

Computer Category	Description	Size
Personal digital assistant (PDA)	A small handheld computer that performs simple tasks such as taking notes, scheduling appointments, and maintaining an address book and a calendar. The PDA screen is touch-sensitive, allowing a user to write directly on the screen, capturing what is written.	Fits in a person's hand
Laptop	A fully functional computer designed to be carried around and run on battery power. Laptops come equipped with all of the technology that a personal desktop computer has, yet weigh as little as two pounds.	Similar to a textbook
Tablet	A pen-based computer that provides the screen capabilities of a PDA with the functional capabilities of a laptop or desktop computer. Similar to PDAs, tablet PCs use a writing pen or stylus to write notes on the screen and touch the screen to perform functions such as clicking on a link while visiting a website.	Similar to a textbook
Desktop	Available with a horizontal system box (the box is where the CPU, RAM, and storage devices are held) with a monitor on top, or a vertical system box (called a tower) usually placed on the floor within a work area.	Fits on a desk

Workstation	Similar to a desktop but has more powerful mathematical and graphics processing capabilities and can perform more complicated tasks in less time. Typically used for software development, Web development, engineering, and ebusiness tools.	Fits on a desk
Minicomputer (midrange computer)	Designed to meet the computing needs of several people simultaneously in a small to medium-size business environment. A common type of minicomputer is a server and is used for managing internal company networks and websites.	Ranges from fitting on a desk to the size of a filing cabinet
Mainframe computer	Designed to meet the computing needs of hundreds of people in a large business environment. Mainframe computers are a step up in size, power, capability, and cost from minicomputers.	Similar to a refrigerator
Supercomputer	The fastest, most powerful, and most expensive type of computer. Organizations such as NASA that are heavily involved in research and number crunching employ supercomputers because of the speed with which they can process information. Other large, customer-oriented businesses such as General Motors and AT&T employ supercomputers just to handle customer information and transaction processing.	Similar to a car

figure A.10
(Continued)

MIT's Media Lab is developing a laptop that it will sell for $100 each to government agencies around the world for distribution to millions of underprivileged schoolchildren. Using a simplified sales model and reengineering the device helped MIT reach the $100 price point. Almost half the price of a current laptop comprises marketing, sales, distribution, and profit. Of the remaining costs, the display panel and backlight account for roughly half while the rest covers the operating system. The low-cost laptop will use a display system that costs less than $25, a 500 MHz processor from AMD, a wireless LAN connection, 1 GB of storage, and the Linux operating system. The machine will automatically connect with others. China and Brazil have already ordered 3 million and 1 million laptops, respectively. MIT's goal is to produce around 150 million laptops per year.[9]

Software Basics

Hardware is only as good as the software that runs it. Over the years, the cost of hardware has decreased while the complexity and cost of software have increased. Some large software applications, such as customer relationship management systems, contain millions of lines of code, take years to develop, and cost millions of dollars. The two main types of software are system software and application software.

SYSTEM SOFTWARE

System software controls how the various technology tools work together along with the application software. System software includes both operating system software and utility software.

Operating System Software Linus Torvalds, a Finnish programmer, may seem an unlikely choice to be one of the world's top managers. However, Linux, the software project he created while a university student, is now one of the most powerful influences on the computer world. Linux is an operating system built by volunteers and distributed for free and has become one of the primary competitors to Microsoft. Torvalds coordinates Linux development with a few dozen volunteer assistants and more than 1,000 programmers scattered around the globe. They contribute code for the kernel—or core piece—of Linux. He also sets the rules for dozens of technology companies that have lined up behind Linux, including IBM, Dell, Hewlett-Packard, and Intel.

figure A.11
Operating System Software

Operating System Software	
Linux	An open source operating system that provides a rich environment for high-end workstations and network servers. Open source refers to any program whose source code is made available for use or modification as users or other developers see fit.
Mac OS X	The operating system of Macintosh computers.
Microsoft Windows	Generic name for the various operating systems in the Microsoft Windows family, including Microsoft Windows CE, Microsoft Windows, Microsoft Windows ME, Microsoft Windows, Microsoft Windows XP, Microsoft Windows NT, and Microsoft Windows Server.
MS-DOS	The standard, single-user operating system of IBM and IBM-compatible computers, introduced in 1981. MS-DOS is a command-line operating system that requires the user to enter commands, arguments, and syntax.
UNIX	A 32-bit multitasking and multiuser operating system that originated at AT&T's Bell Laboratories and is now used on a wide variety of computers, from mainframes to PDAs.

While basic versions of Linux are available for free, Linux is having a considerable financial impact. According to market researcher IDC, the total market for Linux devices and software was expected to increase from $11 billion in 2004 to $35.7 billion by 2008.[10]

Operating system software controls the application software and manages how the hardware devices work together. When using Excel to create and print a graph, the operating system software controls the process, ensures that a printer is attached and has paper, and sends the graph to the printer along with instructions on how to print it.

Operating system software also supports a variety of useful features, one of which is multitasking. ***Multitasking*** allows more than one piece of software to be used at a time. Multitasking is used when creating a graph in Excel and simultaneously printing a word processing document. With multitasking, both pieces of application software are operating at the same time. There are different types of operating system software for personal environments and for organizational environments (see Figure A.11).

Utility Software ***Utility software*** provides additional functionality to the operating system. Utility software includes antivirus software, screen savers, and anti-spam software. Figure A.12 displays a few types of available utility software.

figure A.12
Utility Software

Types of Utility Software	
Crash-proof	Helps save information if a computer crashes.
Disk image for data recovery	Relieves the burden of reinstalling applications if a hard drive crashes or becomes irretrievably corrupted.
Disk optimization	Organizes information on a hard disk in the most efficient way.
Encrypt data	Protects confidential information from unauthorized eyes.
File and data recovery	Retrieves accidental deletion of photos or documents.
Text protect	In Microsoft Word, prevents users from typing over existing text after accidentally hitting the Insert key. Launch the Insert Toggle Key program, and the PC will beep whenever a user presses the Insert key.

Preventative security	Through programs such as Window Washer, erases file histories, browser cookies, cache contents, and other crumbs that applications and Windows leave on a hard drive.
Spyware	Removes any software that employs a user's Internet connection in the background without the user's knowledge or explicit permission.
Uninstaller	Can remove software that is no longer needed.

figure A.12
(Continued)

APPLICATION SOFTWARE

Application software is used for specific information processing needs, including payroll, customer relationship management, project management, training, and many others. Application software is used to solve specific problems or perform specific tasks. From an organizational perspective, payroll software, collaborative software such as videoconferencing (within groupware), and inventory management software are all examples of application software (see Figure A.13).

figure A.13
Application Software

Types of Application Software	
Browser	Enables the user to navigate the World Wide Web. The two leading browsers are Netscape Navigator and Microsoft Internet Explorer.
Communication	Turns a computer into a terminal for transmitting data to and receiving data from distant computers through the telephone system.
Data management	Provides the tools for data retrieval, modification, deletion, and insertion; for example, Access, MySQL, and Oracle.
Desktop publishing	Transforms a computer into a desktop publishing workstation. Leading packages include Adobe FrameMaker, Adobe PageMaker, and QuarkXpress.
Email	Provides email services for computer users, including receiving mail, sending mail, and storing messages. Leading email software includes Microsoft Outlook, Microsoft Outlook Express, and Eudora.
Groupware	Increases the cooperation and joint productivity of small groups of co-workers.
Presentation graphics	Creates and enhances charts and graphs so that they are visually appealing and easily understood by an audience. A full-features presentation graphics package such as Lotus Freelance Graphics or Microsoft PowerPoint includes facilities for making a wide variety of charts and graphs and for adding titles, legends, and explanatory text anywhere in the chart or graph.
Programming	Possesses an artificial language consisting of a fixed vocabulary and a set of rules (called syntax) that programmers use to write computer programs. Leading programming languages include Java, C ++, C#, and .NET.
Spreadsheet	Simulates an accountant's worksheet onscreen and lets users embed hidden formulas that perform calculations on the visible data. Many spreadsheet programs also include powerful graphics and presentation capabilities to create attractive products. The leading spreadsheet application is Microsoft Excel.
Word processing	Transforms a computer into a tool for creating, editing, proofreading, formatting, and printing documents. Leading word processing applications include Microsoft Word and WordPerfect.

Key Terms

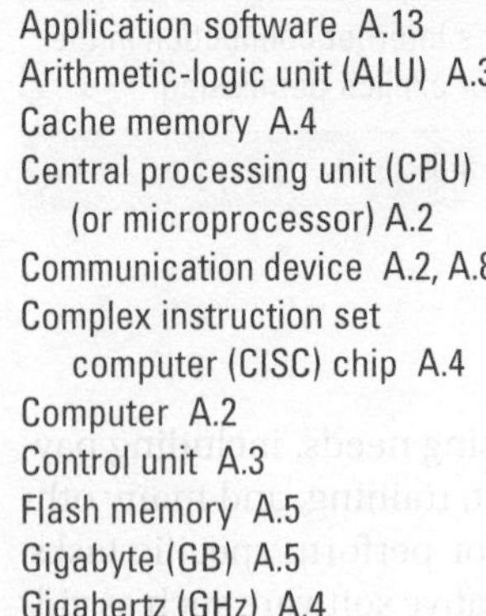

- Application software A.13
- Arithmetic-logic unit (ALU) A.3
- Cache memory A.4
- Central processing unit (CPU) (or microprocessor) A.2
- Communication device A.2, A.8
- Complex instruction set computer (CISC) chip A.4
- Computer A.2
- Control unit A.3
- Flash memory A.5
- Gigabyte (GB) A.5
- Gigahertz (GHz) A.4
- Hard drive A.6
- Hardware A.1
- Input device A.2, A.6
- Magnetic medium A.6
- Magnetic tape A.6
- Megabyte (MB, M, or Meg) A.5
- Megahertz (MHz) A.4
- Memory card A.5
- Memory stick A.5
- Multitasking A.12
- Operating system software A.12
- Output device A.2, A.7
- Primary storage A.2, A.4
- Random access memory (RAM) A.4
- Read-only memory (ROM) A.5
- Reduced instruction set computer (RISC) chip A.4
- Secondary storage A.2, A.5
- Software A.1
- System software A.11
- Terabyte (TB) A.5
- Utility software A.12
- Volatility A.4

Apply Your Knowledge

1. A Computer

Dell is considered the fastest company on Earth and specializes in computer customization. Connect to Dell's website at www.dell.com. Go to the portion of Dell's site that allows you to customize either a laptop or a desktop computer. First, choose an already prepared system and note its price and capability in terms of CPU speed, RAM size, monitor quality, and storage capacity. Now, customize that system to increase CPU speed, add more RAM, increase monitor size and quality, and add more storage capacity. What is the difference in price between the two? Which system is more in your price range? Which system has the speed and capacity you need?

2. Web-Enabled Cell Phones

When categorizing computers by size for personal needs, we focused on PDAs, laptops, and desktop computers. Other variations include Web-enabled cell phones that include instant text messaging and Web computers. For this project, you will need a group of four people, which you will then split into two groups of two. Have the first group research Web-enabled cell phones, their capabilities and costs. Have that group make a purchase recommendation based on price and capability. Have the second group do the same for Web computers. What is your vision of the future? Will we ever get rid of clunky laptops and desktops in favor of more portable and cheaper devices such as Web-enabled cell phones and Web computers? Why or why not?

3. Small Business Computers

Many different types of computers are available for small businesses. Use the Internet to find three different vendors of laptops or notebooks that are good for small businesses. Find the most expensive and the least expensive that the vendor offers and create a table comparing the different computers based on the following:

- CPU
- Memory
- Hard drive
- Optical drive
- Operating system
- Utility software
- Application software
- Support plan

Determine which computer you would recommend for a small business looking for an inexpensive laptop. Determine which computer you would recommend for a small business looking for an expensive laptop.

Networks and Telecommunications

B

Introduction

Change is everywhere in the information technology domain, but nowhere is change more evident and more dramatic than the realm of networks and telecommunications. Most management information systems today rely on digital networks to communicate information in the form of data, graphics, video, and voice. Companies large and small from all over the world are using networks and the Internet to locate suppliers and buyers, to negotiate contracts with them, and to provide bigger, better, and faster services than ever before. ***Telecommunication systems*** enable the transmission of data over public or private networks. A ***network*** is a communications system created by linking two or more devices and establishing a standard methodology by which they can communicate. The world's largest and most widely used network is the Internet. The Internet is a global "network of networks" that uses universal standards to connect millions of different networks around the world. Telecommunication systems and networks are traditionally complicated and historically inefficient. However, businesses can benefit from today's network infrastructures that provide reliable global reach to employees and customers.

LEARNING OUTCOMES

B.1. Compare LANs, WANs, and MANs.

B.2. List and describe the four components that differentiate networks.

B.3. Compare the two types of network architectures.

B.4. Explain topology and the different types found in networks.

B.5. Describe TCP/IP along with its primary purpose.

B.6. Identify the different media types found in networks.

Network Basics

Networks range from small two-computer networks to the biggest network of all, the Internet. A network provides two principle benefits: the ability to communicate and the ability to share.

Today's corporate digital networks include a combination of local area networks, wide area networks, and metropolitan area networks. A ***local area network (LAN)*** is designed to connect a group of computers in close proximity to each other such as in an office building, a school, or a home. A LAN is useful for sharing resources like files, printers, games, or other applications. A LAN in turn often connects to other LANs, and to the Internet or wide area networks. A ***wide area network (WAN)*** spans a large geographic area, such as a state, province or country. WANs often connect multiple smaller networks, such as local area networks or metropolitan area networks. The world's most popular WAN is the Internet. A ***metropolitan area network (MAN)*** is a large computer network usually spanning a city. Figure B.1 highlights the three different types of networks, and Figure B.2 illustrates each network type.

Direct data communication links between a company and its suppliers or customers, or both, have been successfully used to give the company a strategic advantage. The SABRE airline reservation system is a classic example of a strategic management information system that depends upon communication provided through a network. SABRE Airline Solutions pioneered technological advances for the industry in areas such as revenue management, pricing, flight scheduling, cargo, flight operations, and crew scheduling. In addition, not only did SABRE help invent ecommerce for the travel industry, the company holds claim to progressive solutions that defined—and continue to revolutionize—the travel and transportation marketplace.

A network typically includes four things (besides the computers themselves):

1. **Protocol**—a set of communication rules to make sure that everyone speaks the same language.
2. **Network interface card (NIC)**—card that plugs into the back (or side) of your computers and lets them send and receive messages from other computers.
3. **Cable**—the medium to connect all of the computers together.
4. **Hub (switch or router)**—hardware to perform traffic control.

We will continue to define many of these terms and concepts in the sections that follow.

Networks are differentiated by the following:

- Architecture—peer-to-peer, client/server.
- Topology—bus, star, ring, hybrid, wireless.
- Protocols—Ethernet, transmission control protocol/Internet protocol (TCP/IP).
- Media—coaxial, twisted-pair, fiber-optic.

figure B.1
Network Types

Network Types	
Local area network (LAN)	Designed to connect a group of computers in close proximity to each other such as in an office building, a school, or a home. A LAN is useful for sharing resources like files, printers, games, or other applications. A LAN in turn often connects to other LANs, and to the Internet or wide area networks.
Wide area network (WAN)	Spans a large geographic area, such as a state, province, or country. WANs often connect multiple smaller networks, such as local area networks (LANs) or metropolitan area networks (MANs).
Metropolitan area network (MAN)	A large computer network usually spanning a city. Most colleges, universities, and large companies that span a campus use an infrastructure supported by a MAN.

figure B.2 LAN, WAN, and MAN

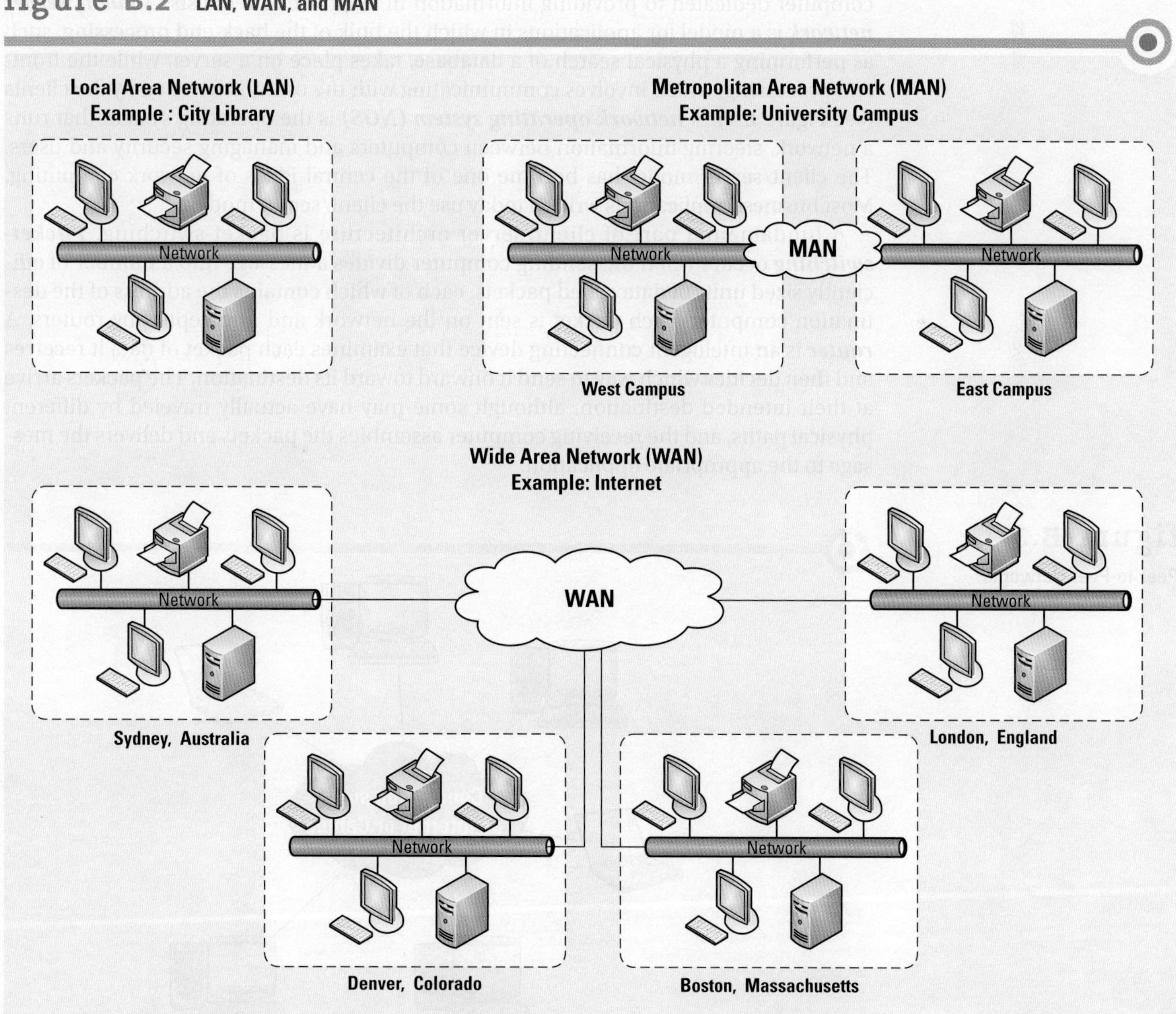

Architecture

The two primary types of network architectures are peer-to-peer networks and client/server networks.

PEER-TO-PEER NETWORKS

A ***peer-to-peer (P2P) network*** is a computer network that relies on the computing power and bandwidth of the participants in the network rather than a centralized server, as illustrated in Figure B.3. Each networked computer can allow other computers to access its files and use connected printers while it is in use as a workstation without the aid of a server.

While Napster may be the most widely known example of a P2P implementation, it may also be one of the most narrowly focused since the Napster model takes advantage of only one of the many capabilities of P2P computing: file sharing. The technology has far broader capabilities, including the sharing of processing, memory, and storage, and the supporting of collaboration among vast numbers of distributed computers such as grid computing described in Chapter 5. Peer-to-peer computing enables immediate interaction among people and computer systems.[1]

CLIENT/SERVER NETWORKS

A ***client*** is a computer designed to request information from a server. A ***server*** is a computer dedicated to providing information in response to requests. A ***client/server network*** is a model for applications in which the bulk of the back-end processing, such as performing a physical search of a database, takes place on a server, while the front-end processing, which involves communicating with the users, is handled by the clients (see Figure B.4). A ***network operating system (NOS)*** is the operating system that runs a network, steering information between computers and managing security and users. The client/server model has become one of the central ideas of network computing. Most business applications written today use the client/server model.

A fundamental part of client/server architecture is packet-switching. ***Packet-switching*** occurs when the sending computer divides a message into a number of efficiently sized units of data called packets, each of which contains the address of the destination computer. Each packet is sent on the network and intercepted by routers. A ***router*** is an intelligent connecting device that examines each packet of data it receives and then decides which way to send it onward toward its destination. The packets arrive at their intended destination, although some may have actually traveled by different physical paths, and the receiving computer assembles the packets and delivers the message to the appropriate application.

figure B.3
Peer-to-Peer Networks

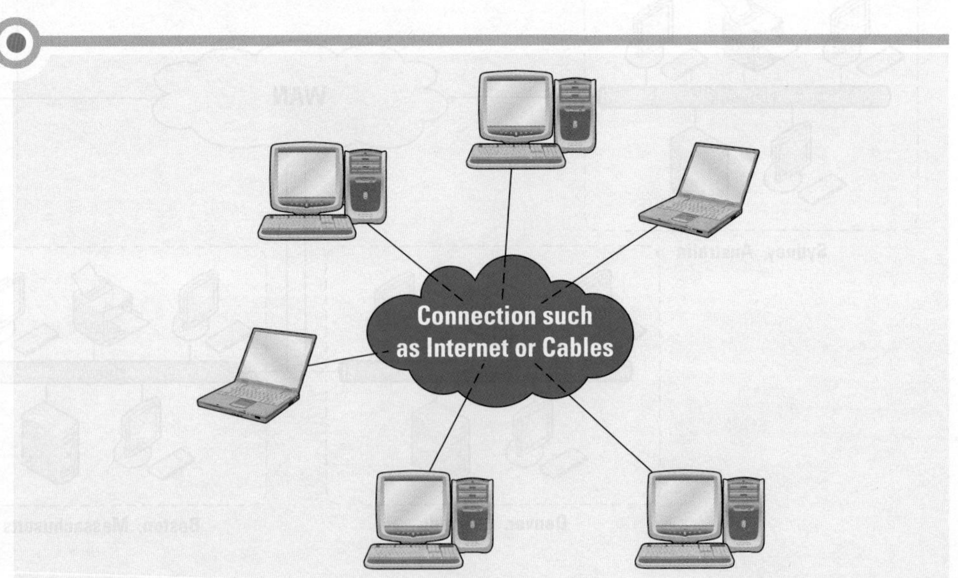

figure B.4 Client/Server Network

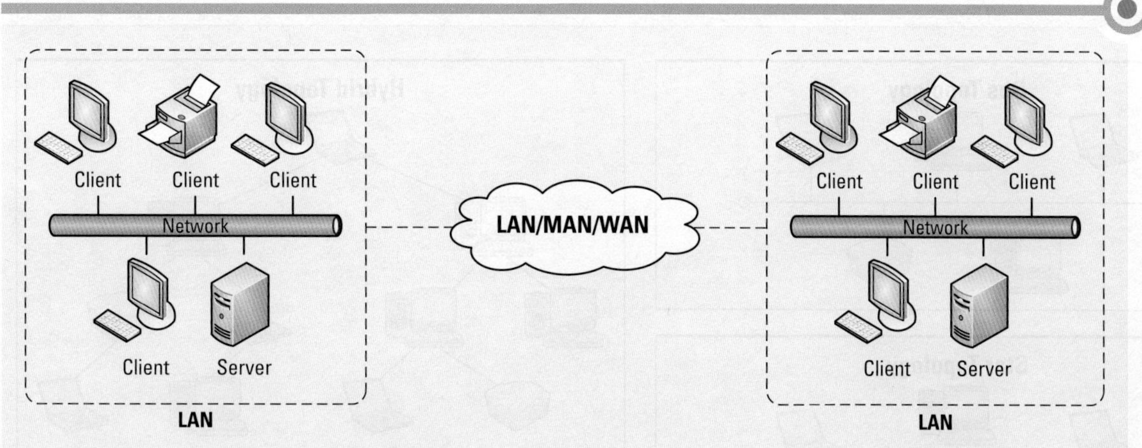

Topology

Networks are assembled according to certain rules. Cables, for example, have to be a certain length; each cable strand can support only a certain amount of network traffic. A ***network topology*** refers to the geometric arrangement of the actual physical organization of the computers (and other network devices) in a network. Topologies vary depending on cost and functionality. Figure B.5 highlights the five common topologies used in networks, and Figure B.6 displays each topology.

Protocols

A ***protocol*** is a standard that specifies the format of data as well as the rules to be followed during transmission. Simply put, for one computer (or computer program) to talk to another computer (or computer program) they must both be talking the same language, and this language is called a protocol.

A protocol is based on an agreed-upon and established standard, and this way all manufacturers of hardware and software that are using the protocol do so in a similar fashion to allow for interoperability. ***Interoperability*** is the capability of two or more computer systems to share data and resources, even though they are made by different

figure B.5
Five Network Topologies

Network Topologies

Bus	All devices are connected to a central cable, called the bus or backbone. Bus networks are relatively inexpensive and easy to install for small networks.
Star	All devices are connected to a central device, called a hub. Star networks are relatively easy to install and manage, but bottlenecks can occur because all data must pass through a hub.
Ring	All devices are connected to one another in the shape of a closed loop, so that each device is connected directly to two other devices, one on either side of it. Ring topologies are relatively expensive and difficult to install, but they offer high speed and can span large distances.
Hybrid	Groups of star-configured workstations are connected to a linear bus backbone cable, combining the characteristics of the bus and star topologies.
Wireless	Devices are connected by signals between access points and wireless transmitters within a limited range.

figure B.6 Network Topologies

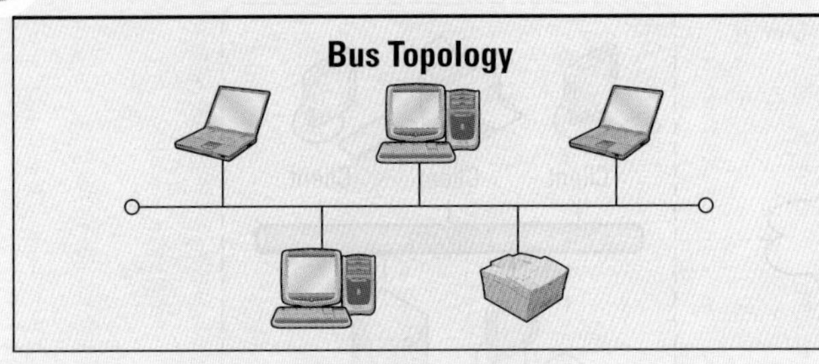

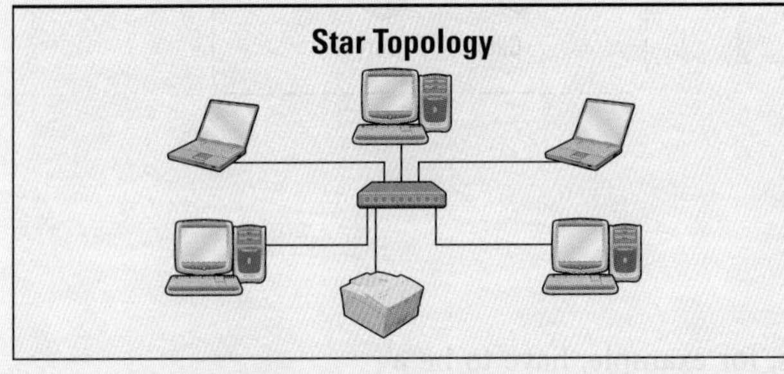

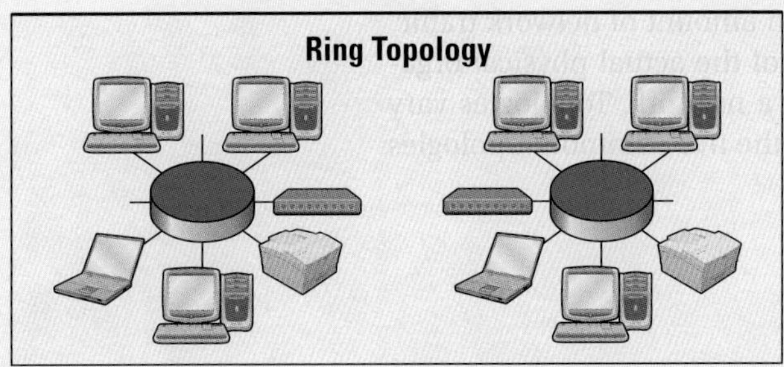

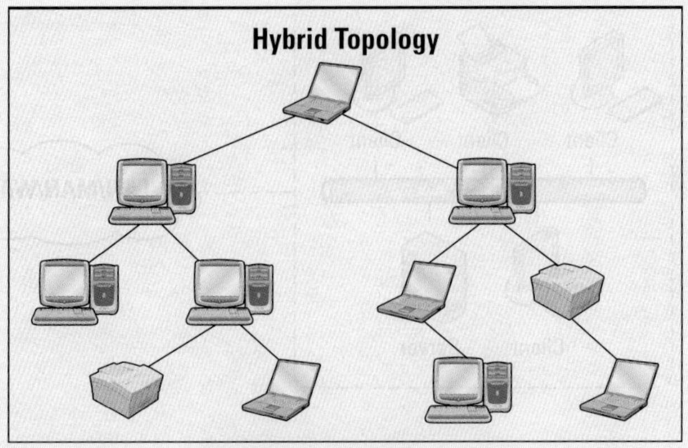

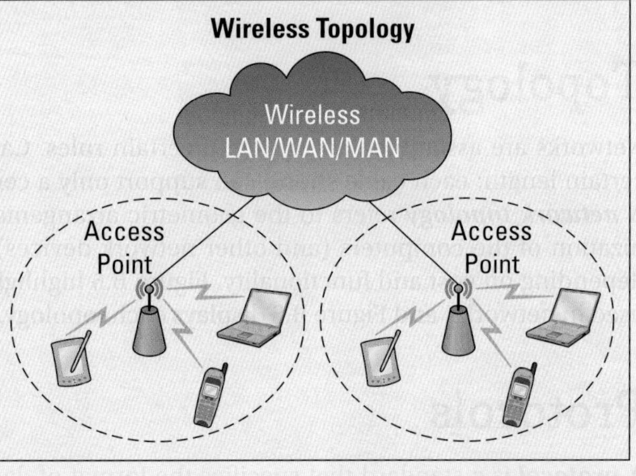

manufacturers. The most popular network protocols used are Ethernet and transmission control protocol/Internet protocol (TCP/IP).

ETHERNET

Ethernet is a physical and data layer technology for LAN networking (see Figure B.7). Ethernet is the most widely installed LAN access method, originally developed by Xerox and then developed further by Xerox, Digital Equipment Corporation, and Intel. When it first began to be widely deployed in the 1980s, Ethernet supported a maximum theoretical data transfer rate of 10 megabits per second (Mbps). More recently, Fast Ethernet has extended traditional Ethernet technology to 100 Mbps peak, and Gigabit Ethernet technology extends performance up to 1,000 Mbps.

Ethernet is one of the most popular LAN technologies for the following reasons:

- Is easy to implement, manage, and maintain.
- Allows low-cost network implementations.
- Provides extensive flexibility for network installation.
- Guarantees interoperability of standards-compliant products, regardless of manufacturer.[2]

TRANSMISSION CONTROL PROTOCOL/ INTERNET PROTOCOL

The most common telecommunication protocol is transmission control protocol/ Internet protocol (TCP/IP), which was originally developed by the Department of Defense to connect a system of computer networks that became known as the Internet.

figure B.7 Ethernet Protocols

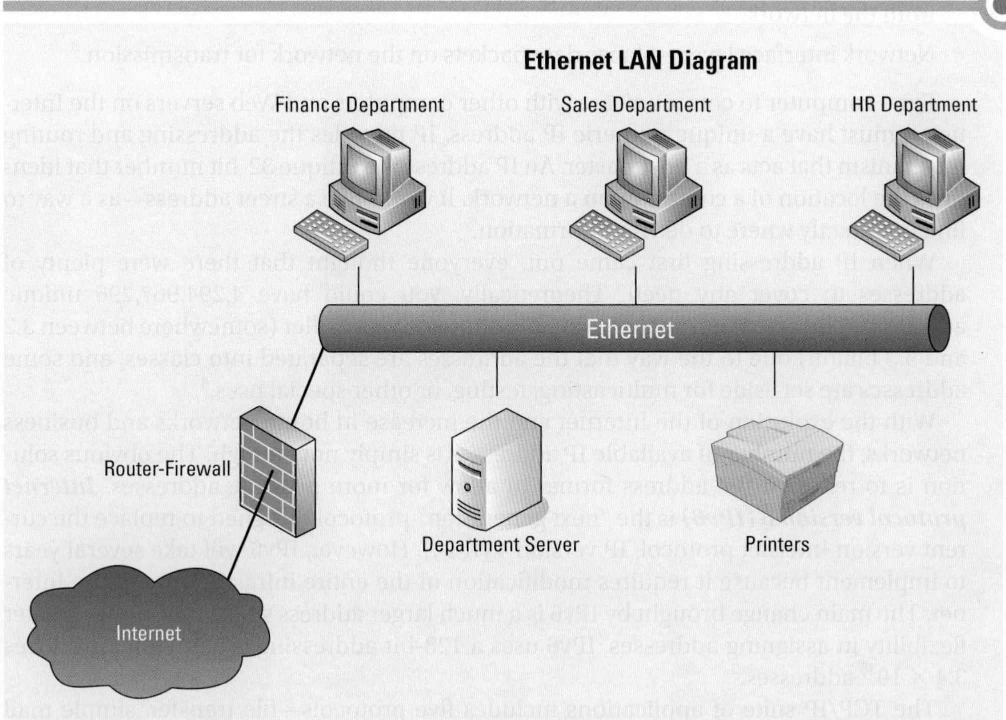

Transmission control protocol/Internet protocol (TCP/IP) provides the technical foundation for the public Internet as well as for large numbers of private networks. The key achievement of TCP/IP is its flexibility with respect to lower-level protocols. TCP/IP uses a special transmission method that maximizes data transfer and automatically adjusts to slower devices and other delays encountered on a network. Although more than 100 protocols make up the entire TCP/IP protocol suite, the two most important of these are TCP and IP. **TCP** provides transport functions, ensuring, among other things, that the amount of data received is the same as the amount transmitted. **IP** provides the addressing and routing mechanism that acts as a postmaster. Figure B.8 displays TCP/IP's four-layer reference model:

- Application layer—serves as the window for users and application processes to access network services.
- Transport layer—handles end-to-end packet transportation.

figure B.8 TCP/IP Four-Layer Reference Model

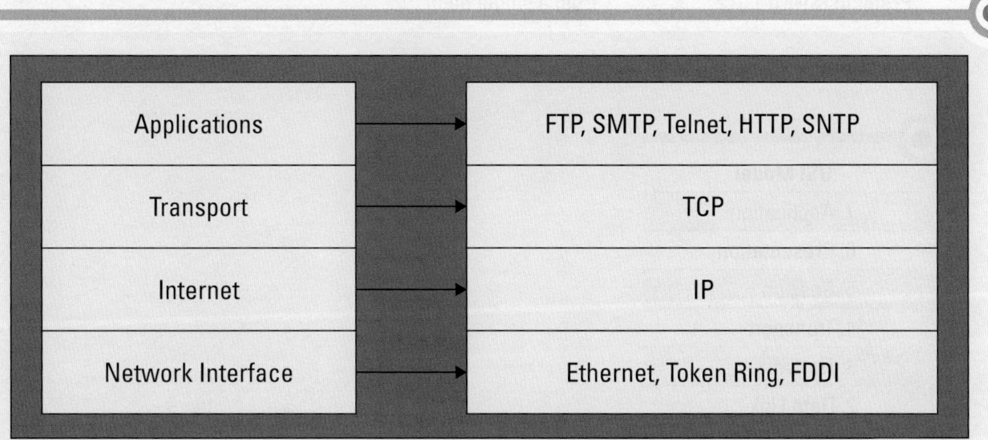

- Internet layer—formats the data into packets, adds a header containing the packet sequence and the address of the receiving device, and specifies the services required from the network.
- Network interface layer—places data packets on the network for transmission.[3]

For a computer to communicate with other computers and Web servers on the Internet, it must have a unique numeric IP address. IP provides the addressing and routing mechanism that acts as a postmaster. An IP address is a unique 32-bit number that identifies the location of a computer on a network. It works like a street address—as a way to find out exactly where to deliver information.

When IP addressing first came out, everyone thought that there were plenty of addresses to cover any need. Theoretically, you could have 4,294,967,296 unique addresses. The actual number of available addresses is smaller (somewhere between 3.2 and 3.3 billion) due to the way that the addresses are separated into classes, and some addresses are set aside for multicasting, testing, or other special uses.[4]

With the explosion of the Internet and the increase in home networks and business networks, the number of available IP addresses is simply not enough. The obvious solution is to redesign the address format to allow for more possible addresses. ***Internet protocol version 6 (IPv6)*** is the "next generation" protocol designed to replace the current version Internet protocol, IP version 4 (IPv4). However, IPv6 will take several years to implement because it requires modification of the entire infrastructure of the Internet. The main change brought by IPv6 is a much larger address space that allows greater flexibility in assigning addresses. IPv6 uses a 128-bit addressing scheme that produces 3.4×10^{38} addresses.[5]

The TCP/IP suite of applications includes five protocols—file transfer, simple mail transfer, telnet, hypertext transfer, and simple network management (see Figures B.9 and B.10).[6]

figure B.9
TCP/IP Applications

TCP/IP Applications	
File Transfer Protocol (FTP)	Allows files containing text, programs, graphics, numerical data, and so on to be downloaded off or uploaded onto a network.
Simple Mail Transfer Protocol (SMTP)	TCP/IP's own messaging system for email.
Telnet Protocol	Provides terminal emulation that allows a personal computer or workstation to act as a terminal, or access device, for a server.
Hypertext Transfer Protocol (HTTP)	Allows Web browsers and servers to send and receive Web pages.
Simple Network Management Protocol (SNMP)	Allows the management of networked nodes to be managed from a single point.

figure B.10
Open System Interconnection Model

OSI Model
7. Application
6. Presentation
5. Session
4. Transport
3. Network
2. Data Link
1. Physical

Media

Network transmission media refers to the various types of media used to carry the signal between computers. When information is sent across the network, it is converted into electrical signals. These signals are generated as electromagnetic waves (analog signaling) or as a sequence of voltage pulses (digital signaling). To be sent from one location to another, a signal must travel along a physical path. The physical path that is used to carry a signal between a signal transmitter and a signal receiver is called the transmission media. The two types of transmission media are wire (guided) and wireless (unguided).

WIRE MEDIA

Wire media are transmission material manufactured so that signals will be confined to a narrow path and will behave predictably. The three most commonly used types of guided media are (see Figure B.11):

- Twisted-pair cable
- Coaxial cable
- Fiber-optic cable

Twisted-Pair Cable ***Twisted-pair cable*** refers to a type of cable composed of four (or more) copper wires twisted around each other within a plastic sheath. The wires are twisted to reduce outside electrical interference. Twisted-pair cables come in shielded and unshielded varieties. Shielded cables have a metal shield encasing the wires that acts as a ground for electromagnetic interference. Unshielded twisted-pair (UTP) is the most popular and is generally the best option for LAN networks. The quality of UTP may vary from telephone-grade wire to high-speed cable. The cable has four pairs of wires inside the jacket. Each pair is twisted with a different number of twists per inch to help eliminate interference from adjacent pairs and other electrical devices. The connectors (called RF-45) on twisted-pair cables resemble large telephone connectors.[7]

Coaxial Cable ***Coaxial cable*** is cable that can carry a wide range of frequencies with low signal loss. It consists of a metallic shield with a single wire placed along the center of a shield and isolated from the shield by an insulator. Coaxial cable is similar to that used for cable television. This type of cable is referred to as coaxial because it contains one copper wire (or physical data channel) that carries the signal and is surrounded by another concentric physical channel consisting of a wire mesh. The outer channel serves as a ground for electrical interference. Because of this grounding feature, several coaxial cables can be placed within a single conduit or sheath without significant loss of data integrity.[8]

Fiber-Optic Cable ***Fiber optic*** (or ***optical fiber***) refers to the technology associated with the transmission of information as light impulses along a glass wire or fiber. Fiber-optic cable is the same type used by most telephone companies for long-distance service. Fiber-optic cable can transmit data over long distances with little loss in data integrity. In addition, because data are transferred as a pulse of light, fiber optical is not subject to interference. The light pulses travel through a glass wire or fiber encased in an insulating sheath.[9]

Fiber optic's increased maximum effective distance comes at a price. Optical fiber is more fragile than wire, difficult to split, and labor intensive to install. For these reasons, fiber optics is used primarily to transmit data over extended distances where the hardware required to relay the data signal on less expensive media would exceed the cost of fiber-optic installation. It is also used where large amounts of data need to be transmitted on a regular basis.

WIRELESS MEDIA

Wireless media are natural parts of the Earth's environment that can be used as physical paths to carry electrical signals. The atmosphere and outer space are examples of wireless media that are commonly used to carry these signals. Today, technologies for

figure B.11 Twisted-Pair, Coaxial Cable, and Fiber-Optic

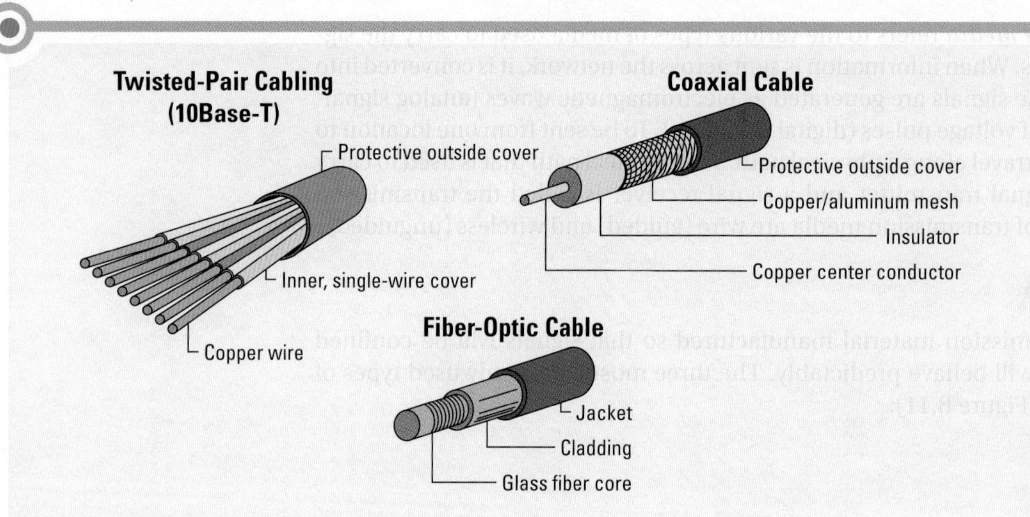

figure B.12 Communication Satellite Example

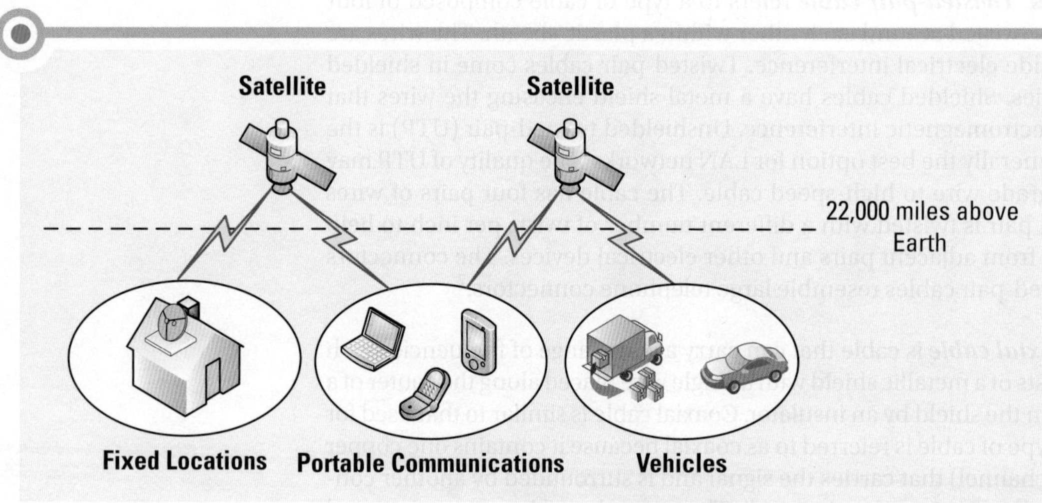

wireless data transmission include microwave transmission, communication satellites, (see Figure B.12) mobile phones, personal digital assistants (PDAs), personal computers (e.g., laptops), and mobile data networks.

Network signals are transmitted through all media as a type of waveform. When transmitted through wire and cable, the signal is an electrical waveform. When transmitted through fiber-optic cable, the signal is a light wave, either visible or infrared light. When transmitted through the Earth's atmosphere, the signal can take the form of waves in the radio spectrum, including microwaves, infrared, or visible light.

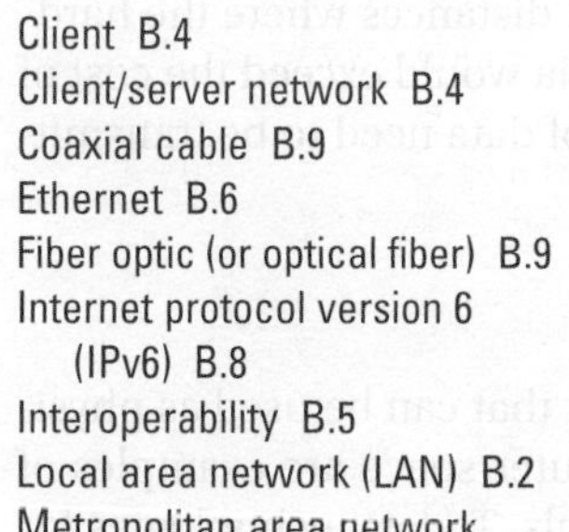

Key Terms

Client B.4
Client/server network B.4
Coaxial cable B.9
Ethernet B.6
Fiber optic (or optical fiber) B.9
Internet protocol version 6 (IPv6) B.8
Interoperability B.5
Local area network (LAN) B.2
Metropolitan area network (MAN) B.2
Network B.1
Network operating system (NOS) B.4
Network topology B.5
Network transmission media B.9
Packet-switching B.4
Peer-to-peer (P2P) network B.4
Protocol B.5
Router B.4
Server B.4
Telecommunication system B.1
Transmission control protocol/Internet protocol (TCP/IP) B.7
Twisted-pair cable B.9
Wide area network (WAN) B.2
Wire media B.9
Wireless media B.9

Apply Your Knowledge

1. Network Analysis

Global Manufacturing is considering a new technology application. The company wants to process orders in a central location and then assign production to different plants. Each plant will operate its own production scheduling and control system. Data on work in process and completed assemblies will be transmitted back to the central location that processes orders. At each plant, Global uses personal computers that perform routine tasks such as payroll and accounting. The production scheduling and control systems will be a package program running on a new computer dedicated to this application.

The MIS personnel at Global have retained you as a consultant to help with further analysis. What kind of network configuration seems most appropriate? How much bandwidth is needed? What data should be collected? Prepare a plan showing the information Global must develop to establish this network system. Should Global use a private network or can it accomplish its objectives through the Internet?

2. Secure Access

Organizations that have traditionally maintained private, closed systems have begun to look at the potential of the Internet as a ready-made network resource. The Internet is inexpensive and globally pervasive: Every phone jack is a potential connection. However, the Internet lacks security. What obstacles must organizations overcome to allow secure network connections?

3. Telecommunications Options

Research the telecommunications options that currently exist for you to link to the Internet from where you live. Prepare a list of criteria on which to compare the different technologies, such as price (is there tiered pricing depending on speed and amount you can download?), start-up cost (do you need to buy a special modem, or is there an installation fee), maximum data transfer rate, and so on. Compare your responses with several classmates, and then develop a summary of all telecommunications options that you identified, including the criteria and your group comparison based on the criteria.

4. Frying Your Brains?

Radio waves, microwaves, and infrared all belong to the electromagnetic radiation spectrum used. These terms reference ranges of radiation frequencies we use every day in our wireless networking environments. However, the very word *radiation* strikes fear in many people. Cell towers have sprouted from fields all along highways. Tall rooftops harbor many more cell stations in cities. Millions of cell phone users place microwave transmitters/receivers next to their heads each time they make a call. With all this radiation zapping around, should we be concerned? Research the Internet to find out what the World Health Organization (WHO) has had to say about this.

5. Home Network Experience

If you maintain a home computer network (or have set one up in the past), create a document that describes the benefits that the network provides along with the difficulties that you have experienced. Include in your document a network topology, a detailed description of the type of network you have and the equipment you use. If you have no experience with home networking, interview someone who does, and write up his or her comments. Compare this with several classmates, and discuss the benefits and challenges.

6. The Internet Is Almost Full

IPv4 has given us a little more than 4 billion possible IP addresses. Although 4 billion may sound like a lot, the number of devices connecting to the Internet is exploding! Internet access is now built into smart phones, tablets, televisions, DVD players, video game consoles, utility meters, thermostats, appliances, and more. There is another problem—large masses of existing addresses were not allocated efficiently, and these cannot be easily reclaimed from the corporations, universities, and other organizations that initially received them. This means that we are running out of IP addresses.

Research the Internet to identify just when IPv6 will roll out. Who is leading the charge for IPv6 rollout? What are the main issues for deploying IPv6? Is it backward-compatible with IPv4?

Designing Databases

Introduction

Businesses rely on databases for accurate, up-to-date information. Without access to mission critical data, most businesses are unable to perform their normal daily functions, much less create queries and reports that help make strategic decisions. For those decisions to be useful, the database must have data that are accurate, complete, consistent, timely, and unique. However, without a good underlying database design, decisions will be inaccurate and inconstant.

A ***database*** maintains information about various types of objects (inventory), events (transactions), people (employees), and places (warehouses). A ***database management system (DBMS)*** creates, reads, updates, and deletes data in a database while controlling access and security. A DBMS provides a way to create, update, delete, store, and retrieve data in the database.

Using a data model offers a method for designing a database correctly that will help in meeting the needs of the users in a DBMS environment.

LEARNING OUTCOMES

C.1 Describe the purpose of the relational database model in a database management system.

C.2 List the relational database model's basic components.

C.3 Describe why entities and attributes are organized into tables and fields.

C.4 Describe how data redundancy is handled in the relational database model.

C.5 Explain the need for an entity-relationship diagram in a database management system.

C.6 Describe the Chen model symbols used in entity-relationship modeling.

The Relational Database Model

Numerous elements in a business environment need to store data, and those elements are related to one another in a variety of ways. In fact, a database must contain not only the data but also information about the relationships between those data. Designing a database properly is fundamental to establishing a solid foundation in which to base business decisions. This is done by using a ***data model,*** or the logical data structures that detail the relationships among data elements using graphics or pictures. A ***relational database model*** stores information in the form of logically related two-dimensional tables. Tables, or entities as they are formally referred to, will be discussed later.

In developing the relational database model to design a database, an entity-relationship diagram is used. An ***entity-relationship diagram (ERD)*** is a technique for documenting the entities and relationships in a database environment. Before describing the notation used for developing an ERD, it is important to understand what entities and attributes are.

ENTITIES AND ATTRIBUTES

An ***entity*** stores information about a person, place, thing, transaction, or event. A customer is an entity, as is a product and an appointment. An ***attribute*** is the data elements associated with an entity. For example, consider Mega-Video, a physical and online retail store that sells movie DVDs. The company would need to store information on its customers (especially for online purchases) by creating an entity called *CUSTOMER* that contained many attributes such as *Customer Number, First Name, Last Name, Street, City, State, Zip Code, Phone Number,* and *Email* (refer to Figure C.1).

figure C.1 **Entities and Attributes Examples**

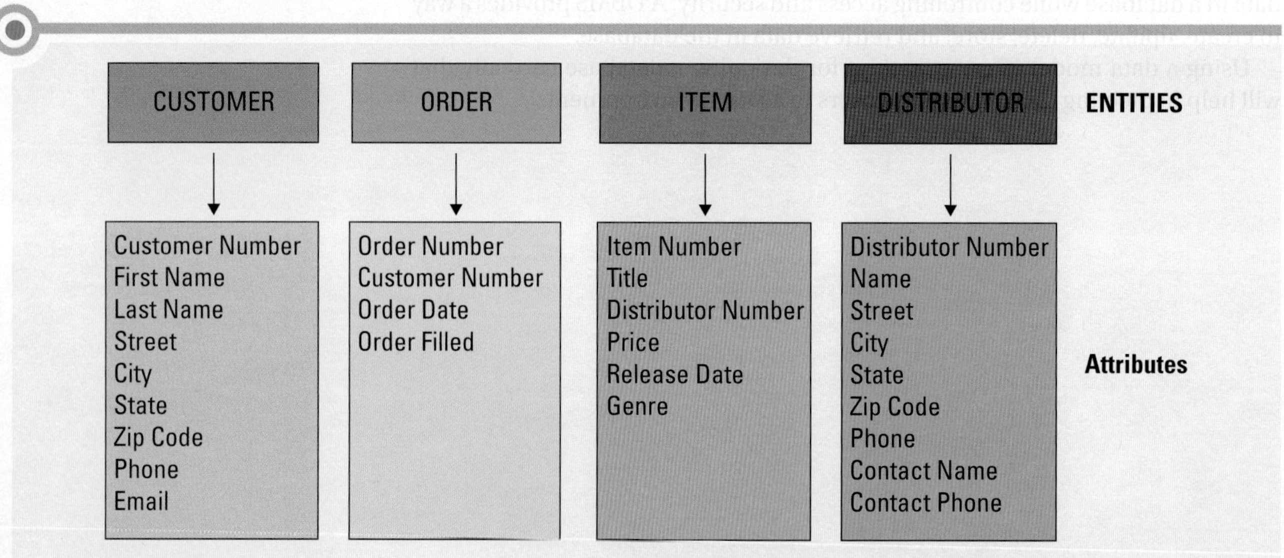

figure C.2 **Composite Attributes**

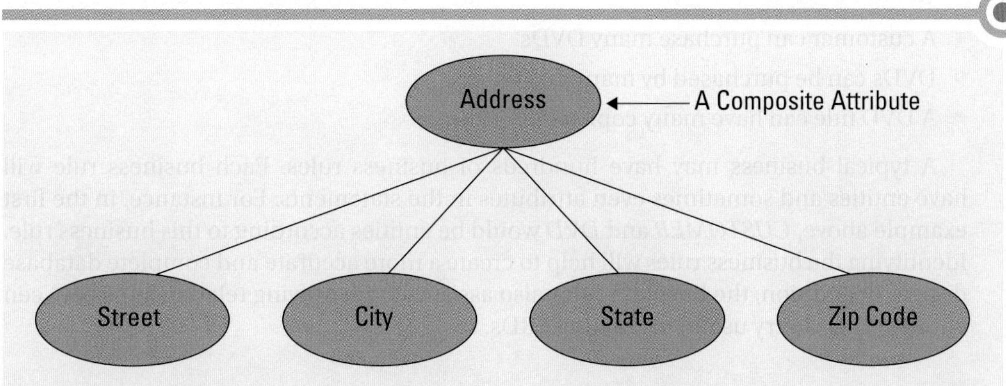

Type of Attributes There are several types of attributes, including:

- **Simple versus composite.** A simple attribute cannot be broken down into a smaller component. For example, a customer's first name and last name are simple. A composite attribute can be divided into smaller components, which represent more basic attributes that have their own meanings. A common example of a composite attribute is *Address* (see Figure C.2). *Address* can be broken down into a number of subparts, such as *Street, City, State, Zip Code.*
- **Single-valued versus multi-valued.** When creating a relational database, the attributes in the data model must be single-valued. ***Single-valued attribute*** means having only a single value of each attribute of an entity. A person's age is an example of a single-valued attribute because a person cannot have more than one age. ***Multi-valued attribute*** means having the potential to contain more than one value for an attribute. For example, an educational degree of a person is a multi-valued attribute because a person can have more than one degree. An entity in a relational database cannot have multi-valued attributes; those attributes must be handled by creating another entity to hold them. Therefore, in the example given previously, in designing the database there would be two entities, one called *PERSON* (or something similar) and one called *DEGREE.* If a multi-valued attribute has been identified, it typically is a clue that another entity is needed.
- **Stored versus derived.** If an attribute can be calculated using the value of another attribute, it is called a derived attribute. The attribute that is used to derive the attribute is called a stored attribute. Derived attributes are not stored in the file, but can be derived when needed from the stored attributes. One example of a derived and stored attribute is a person's age. If the database has a stored attribute such as the person's *Date of Birth,* then a derived attribute called *Age* can be created from taking the *Current Date* (this is retrieved from the DBMS) and subtracting the *Date of Birth* to get the age.
- **Null-valued.** There are cases where an attribute does not have an applicable value for an attribute. For these situations, the null-valued attribute is created. ***Null-valued attribute*** is assigned to an attribute when no other value applies or when a value is unknown. A person who does not have a mobile phone would have null stored for the value for the *Mobile Phone Number* attribute. Null can also be used in situations where the attribute value is unknown such as *Hair Color.* Every person has a hair color, but the information may be missing.

Business Rules

The "correct" design for a specific business depends on the business rules; what is correct for one organization may not be correct for another. A ***business rule*** is a statement that defines an aspect of a business. It is intended to convey the behavior and rules of a business. The following statements are examples of possible business rules for Mega-Video:

- A customer can purchase many DVDs.
- DVDs can be purchased by many customers.
- A DVD title can have many copies.

A typical business may have hundreds of business rules. Each business rule will have entities and sometimes even attributes in the statements. For instance, in the first example above, *CUSTOMER* and *DVD* would be entities according to this business rule. Identifying the business rules will help to create a more accurate and complete database design. In addition, the business rules also assist with identifying relationships between entities. This is very useful in creating ERDs.

Documenting Entity Relationship Diagrams

Once entities, attributes, and business rules have been identified, the ERD can be documented. The two most commonly used models of ERD documentation are Chen, named after the originator of entity-relationship modeling, Dr. Peter Chen, and information engineering, which grew out of work by James Martin and Clive Finkelstein. It does not matter which is used, as long as everyone who is using the diagram understands the notation. For purposes of simplicity, only the Chen model will be described here.

The Chen model notation uses very specific symbols in representing entities and attributes. Rectangles are used to represent entities. Each entity's name appears in the rectangle, is expressed in the singular, and is capitalized, as in *CUSTOMER*. Originally, attributes were not part of the Chen model; however, many database designers have extended it to include the attributes in ovals as illustrated in Figure C.3.

BASIC ENTITY RELATIONSHIPS

One of the main reasons for creating an ERD is to identify and represent the relationships between entities. If the business rules for Mega-Video state that a customer can order many videos (in this case, an item), then a relationship needs to be created between *CUSTOMER, ORDER,* and *ITEM*. This is a purely conceptual representation of what the database will look like and is completely unrelated to the physical storage of the data. Again, what the ERD is doing is creating a model in which to design the database.

figure C.3
Chen Model with Attributes

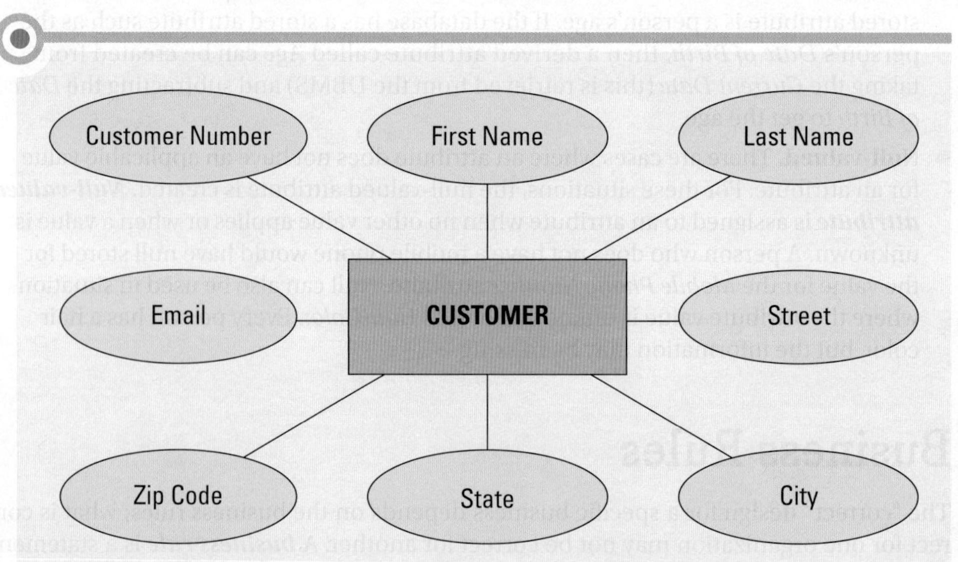

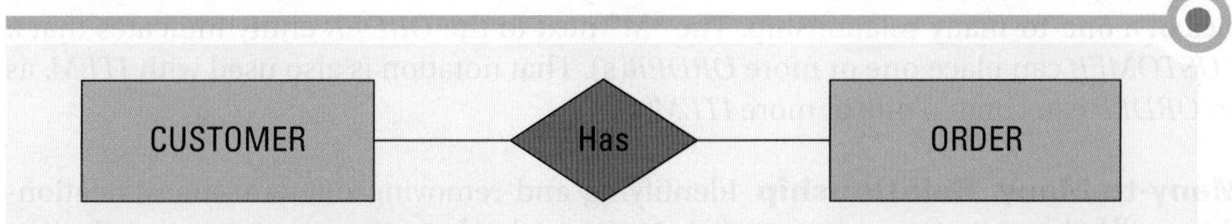

figure C.4
Chen Method with Relationship

The Chen model uses diamonds for relationships and lines to connect relationships between entities. Figure C.4 displays the relationship between a Mega-Video *CUSTOMER* and *ORDER* using this notation. The word within the relationship gives some indication of the meaning of the relationship.

Once the basic entities and their attributes have been defined, the next task is to identify the relationships among those entities. There are three basic types of relationships: (1) one-to-one, (2) one-to-many, and (3) many-to-many.

One-to-One Relationship A ***one-to-one relationship (1:1)*** is between two entities in which an instance of one entity can be related to only one instance of a related entity. Consider Mega-Video, which has many different stores with several employees and one manager. According to the company's business rules, the manager, who is an employee, can manage only one store. The relationship then becomes 1:1 between *EMPLOYEE* and *STORE.* Using the Chen model notation, as shown in Figure C.5, the relationships between the two instances can then be expressed as "An employee can manage one store and one store has one manager." The number "1" next to the *EMPLOYEE* and *STORE* entities indicates that only one *EMPLOYEE* manages one *STORE.*

One-to-Many Relationship Most relational databases are constructed from one-to-many relationships. A ***one-to-many relationship (1:M)*** is between two entities in which an instance of one entity can be related to many instances of a related entity. For example, Mega-Video receives many *ITEM*(s) from one *DISTRIBUTOR* and each *DISTRIBUTOR* supplies many *ITEM*(s) as Figure C.6 illustrates. Similarly, a *CUSTOMER* can

figure C.5
A One-to-One Relationship

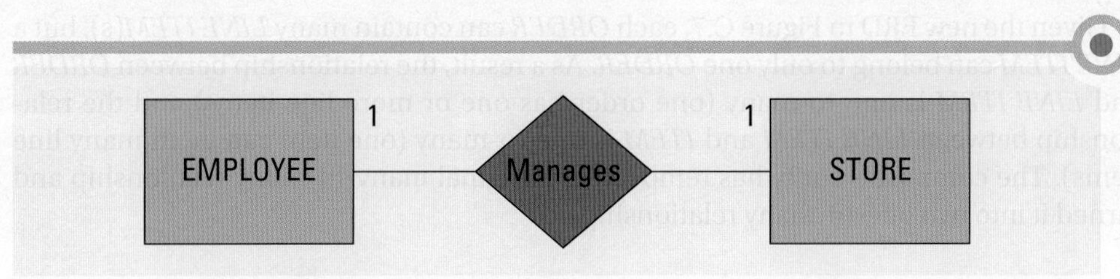

figure C.6 A One-to-Many Relationship

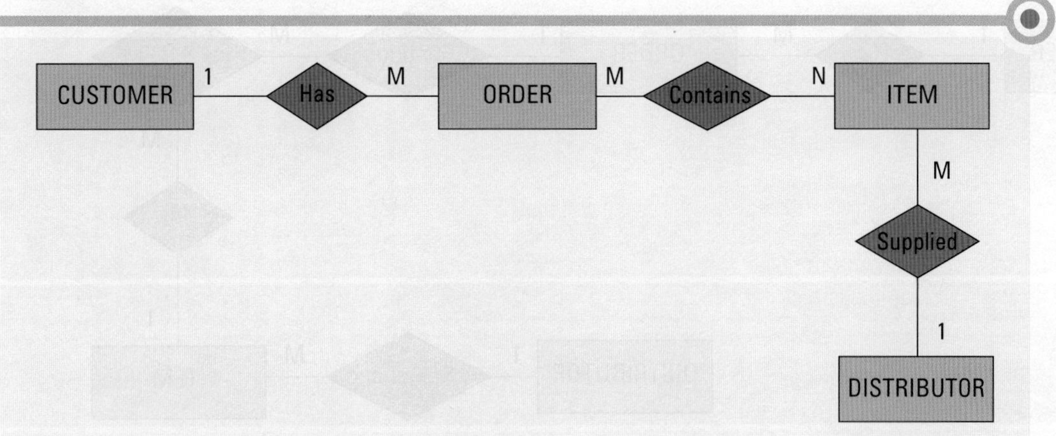

have many *ORDER*(s), but an *ORDER* has only one *CUSTOMER.* These are both examples of a one-to-many relationship. The "M" next to the *ORDER* entity indicates that a *CUSTOMER* can place one or more *ORDER*(s). That notation is also used with *ITEM,* as an *ORDER* can contain one or more *ITEM*(s).

Many-to-Many Relationship Identifying and removing many-to-many relationships will help to create an accurate and consistent database. A ***many-to-many relationship (M:N)*** is between two entities in which an instance of one entity is related to many instances of another and one instance of the other can be related to many instances of the first entity. There is a many-to-many relationship between a Mega-Video *ORDER* and *ITEM* (refer back to Figure C.6). An *ORDER* can contain many *ITEM*(s) and each *ITEM* can be on many *ORDER*(s). The letter "N" next to *ITEM* in Figure C.6 indicates the many-to-many relationship between *ORDER* and *ITEM.*

However, there are problems with many-to-many relationships. First, the relational data model was not designed to handle many-to-many relationships. This means they need to be replaced with a one-to-many relationship to be used in a relational DBMS. Second, many-to-many relationships will create redundancy in the data that are stored. This then has a negative impact on the accuracy and consistency that a database needs. To better understand this problem, consider the relationship between *ITEM* and *ORDER.* There is a many-to-many relationship between the *ORDER* and the *ITEM* because each *ORDER* can contain many *ITEM*(s) and, over time, each *ITEM* will be on many *ORDER*(s). Whenever a *CUSTOMER* places an *ORDER* for an *ITEM,* the number of *ITEM*(s) varies, depending on how many DVDs the *CUSTOMER* is buying. To break the many-to-many relationship, a composite entity is needed.

Entities that exist to represent the relationship between two other entities are known as ***composite entities.*** Our above example needs another entity that breaks up the many-to-many relationship between *ORDER* and *ITEM.* Figure C.7 displays the new relationship.

Creating a composite entity called *LINE ITEM* (think of it as a line item on an invoice slip) breaks up the many-to-many relationship between *ORDER* and *ITEM,* which then eliminates redundancy and other anomalies when deleting or updating information. Using the Chen model, composite entities are documented with a combination of a rectangle and a diamond.

Given the new ERD in Figure C.7, each *ORDER* can contain many *LINE ITEM*(s), but a *LINE ITEM* can belong to only one *ORDER.* As a result, the relationship between *ORDER* and *LINE ITEM* is one-to-many (one order has one or more line items) and the relationship between *LINE ITEM* and *ITEM* is one-to-many (one item can be in many line items). The composite entity has removed the original many-to-many relationship and turned it into two one-to-many relationships.

figure C.7 **A Composite Entity**

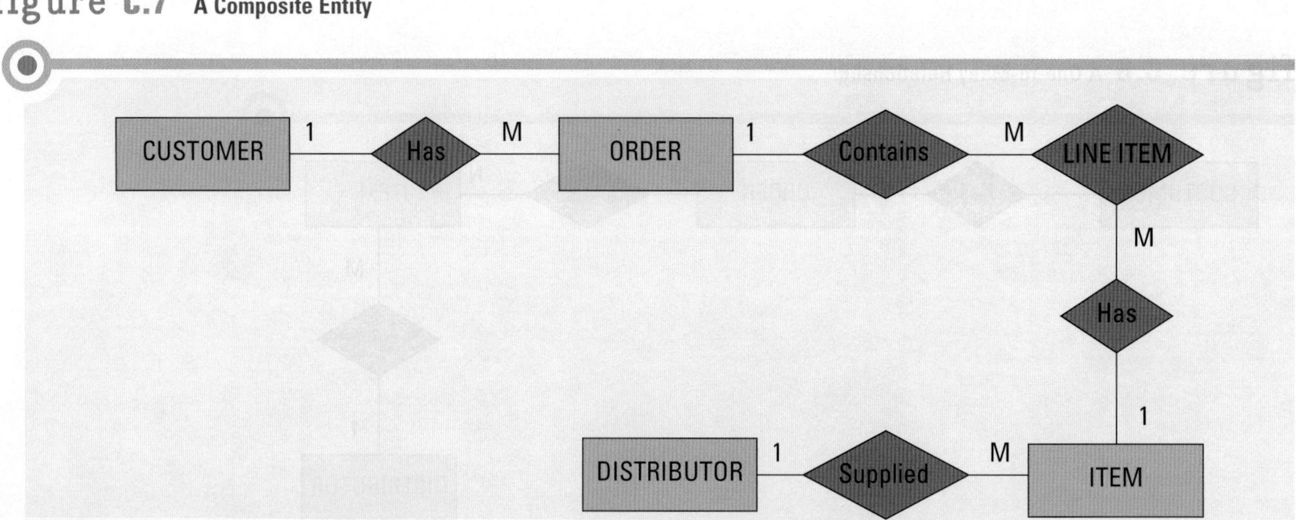

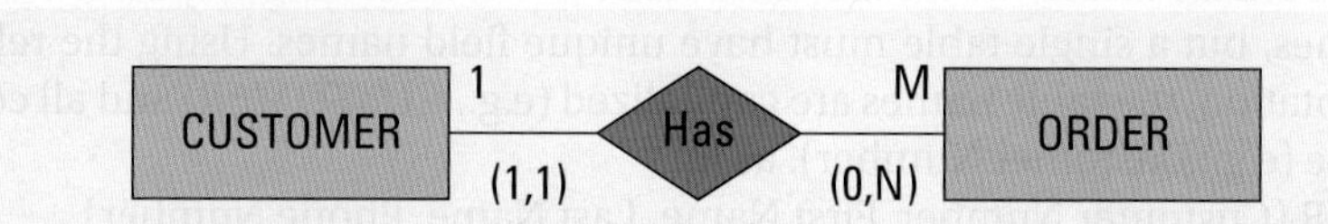

figure C.8
Example of Cardinalities

RELATIONSHIP CARDINALITY

Cardinality expresses the specific number of instances in an entity. In the Chen model, the cardinality is indicated by placing numbers beside the entities in the format of (x, y). The first number in the cardinality represents the minimum value and the second number is for the maximum value.

Mega-Video can store data about a *CUSTOMER* in its database before the *CUSTOMER* places an *ORDER*. An instance of the *CUSTOMER* entity does not have to be related to any instance of the *ORDER* entity, meaning there is an optional cardinality.

However, the reverse is not true for the Mega-Video database, an *ORDER must* be related to a *CUSTOMER*. Without a *CUSTOMER*, an *ORDER* cannot exist. An instance of the *CUSTOMER* entity can be related to zero, one, or more *ORDER*(s) using the cardinality notation (0,N). An instance of the *ORDER* entity must be related to one and only one *CUSTOMER*, having a cardinality of (1,1). The relationship between an instance of *ORDER* and *CUSTOMER* is a mandatory relationship. Figure C.8 illustrates these cardinalities.

Relational Data Model and the Database

Once the ERD is completed, it can be translated from a conceptual logical model into the formal data model required by the DBMS. The relational data model is the result of the work of Edgar (E. F.) Codd, a mathematician. During the 1960s, Dr. Codd was working with existing data models when he noticed that data relationships were very inefficient. Using his experience and knowledge in mathematics, he created the relational data model. Most databases, such as Access 2010 and SQL Server 2010, are based on the relational data model.

FROM ENTITIES TO TABLES

In creating an ERD for the conceptual model, the focus was on identifying entities and attributes. For the logical relational data model, the attention is on tables and fields. Using the ERD the entities become tables and attributes turn into fields. A ***table*** is composed of rows and columns that represent an entity. A ***field*** is a characteristic of a table. A ***record*** is a collection of related data elements. The columns in the table definition represent the field, while a row is a record.

At first glance, a table along with the fields and records looks much like information in a spreadsheet, such as that displayed in Figure C.9 of a *CUSTOMER* table.

figure C.9
A Sample Customer Table

CUSTOMER

Customer Number	First Name	Last Name	Phone Number
0001	Bill	Miller	777-777-7777
0505	Jane	Cook	444-444-4444
1111	Sam	Smith	555-555-5555
1212	John	Doe	666-666-6666

Fields Figure C.9 has four fields, *Customer Number, First Name, Last Name,* and *Phone Number.* Two or more tables within the same relational data model may have fields with the same names, but a single table must have unique field names. Using the relational data model notation, the table names are capitalized (e.g., *CUSTOMER*) and all columns are in title case (e.g., Customer Number), as in:

CUSTOMER (Customer Number, First Name, Last Name, Phone Number)

Records A record in a table has the following properties:

- A table cannot have multi-valued attributes (as mentioned previously); therefore, only one value is allowed at the intersection of a field and record.
- Each record needs to be unique; there are no duplicate records in a table.
- A record must have an entity identifier, or ***primary key,*** which is a field (or group of fields), that uniquely identifies a given record in a table.

Primary Key A primary key makes it possible to uniquely identify every record in a table. The primary key is important to retrieve data accurately from the database.

Using a *Customer Number* as a primary key states that no two customers will ever have the same number. The primary key will be used to identify records associated with it. For example, if someone was searching the Mega-Video database for all the *ITEMS* that a *CUSTOMER* with a *Customer Number* of "112299" bought, he would retrieve only those records and not those associated with another customer.

Along with being unique, a primary key must not contain the value *null.* Recall that null is a special value meaning unknown; however, it is not the same as a field being blank or set to the value of zero. If one record has a null primary key, then the data structure is not in violation. But once a second null value for another record is introduced, the uniqueness of the primary key is lost. Therefore, nulls are forbidden when establishing primary keys.

The proper notation to use when documenting the primary key is to underline it, such as:

CUSTOMER (<u>Customer Number</u>, First Name, Last Name, Phone Number)

LOGICALLY RELATING TABLES

Once the primary key has been defined, tables can be logically related. Each table in Figure C.10 is directly analogous to the entities of the same name in the Mega-Video ERD presented in Figure C.8, excluding the *DISTRIBUTOR.* The *CUSTOMER* table is identified by a Customer Number, a randomly generated unique primary key. The *ORDER* table is identified by an Order Number, another arbitrary unique primary key assigned by Mega-Video. The table *ORDER LINE* tells the company which *ITEM*(s) are part of which *ORDER.* This table requires a concatenated primary key (that is to say, joining two fields that act as one primary key) because multiple *ITEM*(s) can appear on multiple *ORDER*(s). The selection of this primary key, however, has more significance than simply identifying each record; it also represents a relationship between the *ORDER LINES,* the *ORDER* on which they appear, and the *ITEM*(s) being ordered. The primary key for the *ITEM* table is identified by the *Item Number.*

The *Item Number* field in the *ORDER LINE* table is the same as the primary key in the *ITEM* table. This indicates a one-to-many relationship between the two tables. Similarly, there is also a one-to-many relationship between the *ORDER* and *ORDER LINE* tables because the *Order Number* column in the *ORDER LINE* table is the same as the primary key of the *ORDER* table.

When a table contains a field that is the same as the primary key of another table, it is called a foreign key. A ***foreign key*** is a primary key of one table that appears as an attribute in another table and acts to provide a logical relationship between the two tables. The matching of foreign keys to primary keys represents data relationships in a relational database.

figure C.10 Logically Relating Tables

CUSTOMER			
Customer Number	First Name	Last Name	Phone
1111	Sam	Smith	555-555-5555
0505	Jane	Cook	444-444-4444

ORDER		
Order Number	Customer Number	Order Date
1000	1111	11/1/2011
1001	1111	11/10/2011
1002	0505	12/11/2011

LINE ITEM			
Order Number	Item Number	Quantity	Shipped?
1000	9244	1	Y
1001	9244	1	Y
1002	9250	1	Y
1002	9255	1	Y

ITEM			
Item Number	Title	Distributor Number	Price
9244	Iron Man 2	002	4.95
9250	Twilight Zone	002	4.95
9255	Avatar	004	5.95

Foreign keys may be a part of a concatenated primary key, as is the case in the *LINE ITEM* table in Figure C.10. By concatenating, or combining, both *Order Number* and *Item Number* in the *LINE ITEM* table as foreign keys, they then become primary keys. However, most foreign keys are not part of the table's primary key. Consider the relation between Mega-Video's *CUSTOMER* and *ORDER* in Figure C.10. The *Customer Number* field in the *ORDER* table is a foreign key that matches the primary key of the *CUSTOMER* table. It represents the one-to-many relationship between *CUSTOMER* and *ORDER*. However, the *Customer Number* is not part of the primary key of the *ORDER* table; it is simply used to create a relationship between the two tables, *CUSTOMER* and *ORDER*.

A relational database uses the relationships indicated by matching data between primary and foreign keys. Assume that a Mega-Video employee wanted to see what *Titles* had been ordered with *Order Number* 1002. First, the database identifies the records in the *LINE ITEM* table that contain an *Order Number* of 1002. Then, it matches them to the *Item Number*(s) in the *ITEM* table. The results are those that match the records from each table.

Key Terms

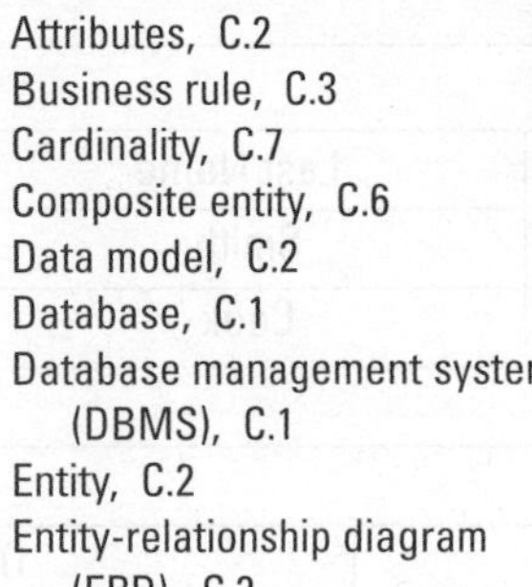

Attributes, C.2
Business rule, C.3
Cardinality, C.7
Composite entity, C.6
Data model, C.2
Database, C.1
Database management system (DBMS), C.1
Entity, C.2
Entity-relationship diagram (ERD), C.2
Field, C.7
Foreign key, C.8
Many-to-many relationship (M:N), C.6
Multi-valued attribute, C.3
Null-valued attribute, C.3
One-to-many relationship (1:M), C.5
One-to-one relationship (1:1), C.5
Primary key, C.8
Record, C.7
Relational database model, C.2
Single-valued attribute, C.3
Table, C.7

Apply Your Knowledge

1. SportTech Events

SportTech Events puts on athletic events for local high school athletes. The company needs a database designed to keep track of the sponsor for the event and where the event is located. Each event needs a description, date, and cost. Separate costs are negotiated for each event. The company would also like to have a list of potential sponsors that includes each sponsor's contact information, such as the name, phone number, and address.

Each event will have a single sponsor, but a particular sponsor may sponsor more than one event. Each location will need an ID, contact person, and phone number. A particular event will use only one location, but a location may be used for multiple events. SportTech asks you to create an ERD from the information described here.

2. Course and Student Schedules

Paul Bauer, the chair for the information technology (IT) department at the University of Denver, needs to create a database to keep track of all the courses offered by the department. In addition to the course information, Bauer would like the database to include each instructor's basic contact information, such as ID number, name, office location, and phone number. Currently, the department has nine instructors (seven full-time faculty and two adjuncts). For each course, Bauer would like to keep track of the course ID, title, and number of credit hours. When courses are offered, the section of the course receives an ID number, and with that number, the department keeps track of which instructor is teaching the course. There is only one instructor per course.

Finally, Bauer needs to be able to keep track of the IT students and to know which courses each student has taken. The information he would like to know about each student includes ID number, name, and phone number. He also needs to know what grade the student receives in each course.

He has asked you to create an ERD from the information described here using the Chen model.

3. Foothills Athletics

Foothills Athletics is an athletic facility offering services in Highlands Ranch, Colorado. All property owners living in Highlands Ranch are members of the Highlands Ranch Community Association (HRCA), which has partnered with Foothills Athletics to provide recreation facilities for its residents. Foothills Athletics has been using a spreadsheet to keep track of its personnel, facilities, equipment, and the HRCA members. The spreadsheet has created many redundancies along with several anomalies in adding, modifying, and deleting information. One of the HRCA members has suggested that the athletic facility should create a database to improve data collection that will also remove many of the difficulties that the spreadsheet is creating.

Foothills Athletics primary business operations are based on the following:

- **Personnel:** Foothills Athletics has a number of employees, primarily fitness instructors and administrative personnel. Records are kept on each employee, detailing employee name, address, phone number, data of hire, position, and status as either a current or former employee. Employees are assigned a unique four-digit employee ID number when they are hired.

- **Members:** When joining Foothills Athletics, HRCA members are assigned a unique four-digit member ID number. This information along with their name, address, phone number, gender, birth date, and date of membership are recorded. At the time of enrollment, each member decides on one of three available membership types along with a fixed membership fee: Platinum ($400), Gold ($300), and Silver ($200). This is a one-time fee that establishes a lifetime membership.
- **Facilities and equipment:** Foothills Athletics has a variety of facilities and equipment choices. Each facility has a unique room number and a size limitation associated with it. Some of the rooms contain a variety of exercise equipment; all have a serial number that is used for inventory and maintenance purposes. In addition, for each piece of equipment, the purchase date and the date of its last maintenance are recorded. Each piece of equipment belongs to a specific equipment type, such as elliptical machine, and is assigned a unique three-digit identification number. The description, the manufacturer's model number, and the recommended maintenance interval for that model of equipment are also kept on file. Each equipment type is associated with a single manufacturer that is referenced by a unique two-digit manufacturer ID number.

Project Focus:

You have been hired to assist Foothills Athletics to create an ERD from the information described here using the Chen model.

4. Slopeside Ski Rentals

Vail Resort in Vail, Colorado, is internationally known as one of the best places in North America for skiing. Since 1973, Slopeside Ski Rentals has been a tradition in the area. At Slopeside Ski Rentals, customers will find the largest selection of skis, boots, snowboards, clothing, helmets, eyewear, and a variety of other accessories needed for the slopes.

You have been employed for the past three winters by the company. Recently, there has been a surge in business, and the owners need a more accurate way to manage the rental business. You have decided to create a database to help the owners keep track of the ski rentals, who the customers are, amount paid, and any damage to the skis when they are rented. The skis and snowboards vary in type, size, and bindings. When customers rent equipment, they are required to leave their driver's license number and to give a home address, phone number, and credit card number.

A few business rules that you are aware of include:

- A customer can rent one or more skis or snowboards at one time.
- Skis and snowboards can be rented by many customers.
- A ski or snowboard need not be assigned to any customer.

Project Focus:

Your job is to develop an ERD from the business rules mentioned here.

THE TECHNOLOGY PLUG-INS

The overall goal of the Technology Plug-Ins is to provide additional information not covered in the text such as personal productivity using information technology, problem solving using Excel, and decision making using Access. These plug-ins also offer an all-in-one text to faculty, avoiding need to purchase an extra book to support Microsoft Office. These plug-ins offer integration with the core chapters and provide critical knowledge using essential business applications, such as Microsoft Excel, Microsoft Access, and Microsoft Project with hands-on tutorials for comprehension and mastery. Plug-Ins T1 to T12 are located on this textbook's website at www.mhhe.com/baltzan.

Plug-In	Description
T1. Personal Productivity Using IT	This plug-in covers a number of things to do to keep a personal computer running effectively and efficiently. The 12 topics covered in this plug-in are: ■ Creating strong passwords. ■ Performing good file management. ■ Implementing effective backup and recovery strategies. ■ Using zip files. ■ Writing professional emails. ■ Stopping spam. ■ Preventing phishing. ■ Detecting spyware. ■ Threads to instant messaging. ■ Increasing PC performance. ■ Using anti-virus software. ■ Installing a personal firewall.
T2. Basic Skills Using Excel	This plug-in introduces the basics of using Microsoft Excel, a spreadsheet program for data analysis, along with a few fancy features. The six topics covered in this plug-in are: ■ Workbooks and worksheets. ■ Working with cells and cell data. ■ Printing worksheets. ■ Formatting worksheets. ■ Formulas. ■ Working with charts and graphics.
T3. Problem Solving Using Excel	This plug-in provides a comprehensive tutorial on how to use a variety of Microsoft Excel functions and features for problem solving. The five areas covered in this plug-in are: ■ Lists ■ Conditional Formatting ■ AutoFilter ■ Subtotals ■ PivotTables
T4. Decision Making Using Excel	This plug-in examines a few of the advanced business analysis tools used in Microsoft Excel that have the capability to identify patterns, trends, and rules, and create "what-if" models. The four topics covered in this plug-in are: ■ IF ■ Goal Seek ■ Solver ■ Scenario Manager

(continued)

T5. Designing Database Applications	This plug-in provides specific details on how to design relational database applications. One of the most efficient and powerful information management computer-based applications is the relational database. The four topics covered in this plug-in are: ■ Entities and data relationships. ■ Documenting logical data relationships. ■ The relational data model. ■ Normalization.
T6. Basic Skills Using Access	This plug-in focuses on creating a Microsoft Access database file. One of the most efficient information management computer-based applications is Microsoft Access. Access provides a powerful set of tools for creating and maintaining a relational database. The two topics covered in this plug-in are: ■ Create a new database file. ■ Create and modify tables.
T7. Problem Solving Using Access	This plug-in provides a comprehensive tutorial on how to query a database in Microsoft Access. Queries are essential for problem solving, allowing a user to sort information, summarize data (display totals, averages, counts, and so on), display the results of calculations on data, and choose exactly which fields are shown. The three topics in this plug-in are: ■ Create simple queries using the simple query wizard. ■ Create advanced queries using calculated fields. ■ Format results displayed in calculated fields.
T8. Decision Making Using Access	This plug-in provides a comprehensive tutorial on entering data in a well-designed form and creating functional reports using Microsoft Access. A form is essential to use for data entry and a report is an effective way to present data in a printed format. The two topics in this plug-in are: ■ Creating, modifying, and running forms. ■ Creating, modifying, and running reports.
T9. Designing Web Pages	This plug-in provides a comprehensive assessment into the functional aspects of Web design. Websites are beginning to look more alike and to employ the same metaphors and conventions. The Web has now become an everyday thing whose design should not make users think. The six topics in this plug-in are: ■ The World Wide Web. ■ The unknown(s). ■ The process of Web design. ■ HTML basics. ■ Web fonts. ■ Web graphics.
T10. Creating Web Pages Using HTML	This plug-in provides an overview of creating Web pages using the HTML language. HTML is a system of codes that you use to create interactive Web pages. It provides a means to describe the structure of text-based information in a document—by denoting certain text as headings, paragraphs, lists, and so on. The five topics in this plug-in are: ■ HTML (an introduction). ■ Creating, saving, and viewing HTML documents. ■ Applying style tags and attributes. ■ Using fancier formatting. ■ Creating hyperlinks. ■ Displaying graphics.

(continued)

T11. Creating Web Pages Using Dreamweaver	This plug-in provides a tour of using Dreamweaver to create Web pages. Dreamweaver allows anyone with limited Web page design experience to create, modify, and maintain full-featured, professional-looking pages without having to learn how to code all the functions and features from scratch. The five topics in this plug-in are: ■ Navigation in Dreamweaver. ■ Adding content. ■ Formatting content. ■ Developing style sheets. ■ Creating tables.
T12. Creating Gantt Charts with Excel and Microsoft Project	This plug-in offers a quick and efficient way to manage projects. Excel and Microsoft Project are great for managing all phases of a project, creating templates, collaborating on planning processes, tracking project progress, and sharing information with all interested parties. The two topics in this plug-in are: ■ Creating Gantt Charts with Excel. ■ Creating Gantt Charts with Microsoft Project.

APPLY YOUR KNOWLEDGE

Apply Your Knowledge Project Overview

Project Number	Project Name	Project Type	Plug-In	Focus Area	Project Level	Skill Set	Page Number
1	Financial Destiny	Excel	T2	Personal Budget	Introductory	Formulas	AYK.4
2	Cash Flow	Excel	T2	Cash Flow	Introductory	Formulas	AYK.4
3	Technology Budget	Excel	T1, T2	Hardware and Software	Introductory	Formulas	AYK.4
4	Tracking Donations	Excel	T2	Employee Relationships	Introductory	Formulas	AYK.4
5	Convert Currency	Excel	T2	Global Commerce	Introductory	Formulas	AYK.5
6	Cost Comparison	Excel	T2	Total Cost of Ownership	Introductory	Formulas	AYK.5
7	Time Management	Excel or Project	T12	Project Management	Introductory	Gantt Charts	AYK.6
8	Maximize Profit	Excel	T2, T4	Strategic Analysis	Intermediate	Formulas or Solver	AYK.6
9	Security Analysis	Excel	T3	Filtering Data	Intermediate	Conditional Formatting, Autofilter, Subtotal	AYK.7
10	Gathering Data	Excel	T3	Data Analysis	Intermediate	Conditional Formatting	AYK.8
11	Scanner System	Excel	T2	Strategic Analysis	Intermediate	Formulas	AYK.8
12	Competitive Pricing	Excel	T2	Profit Maximization	Intermediate	Formulas	AYK.9
13	Adequate Acquisitions	Excel	T2	Break-Even Analysis	Intermediate	Formulas	AYK.9
14	Customer Relations	Excel	T3	CRM	Intermediate	PivotTable	AYK.9
15	Assessing the Value of Information	Excel	T3	Data Analysis	Intermediate	PivotTable	AYK.10
16	Growth, Trends, and Forecasts	Excel	T2, T3	Data Forecasting	Advanced	Average, Trend, Growth	AYK.11
17	Shipping Costs	Excel	T4	SCM	Advanced	Solver	AYK.12
18	Formatting Grades	Excel	T3	Data Analysis	Advanced	If, LookUp	AYK.12

(Continued)

Project Number	Project Name	Project Type	Plug-In	Focus Area	Project Level	Skill Set	Page Number
19	Moving Dilemma	Excel	T2, T3	SCM	Advanced	Absolute vs. Relative Values	AYK.13
20	Operational Efficiencies	Excel	T3	SCM	Advanced	PivotTable	AYK.14
21	Too Much Information	Excel	T3	CRM	Advanced	PivotTable	AYK.14
22	Turnover Rates	Excel	T3	Data Mining	Advanced	PivotTable	AYK.15
23	Vital Information	Excel	T3	Data Mining	Advanced	PivotTable	AYK.15
24	Breaking Even	Excel	T4	Business Analysis	Advanced	Goal Seek	AYK.16
25	Profit Scenario	Excel	T4	Sales Analysis	Advanced	Scenario Manager	AYK.16
26	Electronic Résumés	HTML	T9, T10, T11	Electronic Personal Marketing	Introductory	Structural Tags	AYK.17
27	Gathering Feedback	Dreamweaver	T9, T10, T11	Data Collection	Intermediate	Organization of Information	AYK.17
28	Daily Invoice	Access	T5, T6, T7, T8	Business Analysis	Introductory	Entities, Relationships, and Databases	AYK.17
29	Billing Data	Access	T5, T6, T7, T8	Business Intelligence	Introductory	Entities, Relationships, and Databases	AYK.19
30	Inventory Data	Access	T5, T6, T7, T8	SCM	Intermediate	Entities, Relationships, and Databases	AYK.20
31	Call Center	Access	T5, T6, T7, T8	CRM	Intermediate Entities, Relationships, and	Databases	AYK.21
32	Sales Pipeline	Access	T5, T6, T7, T8	Business Intelligence	Advanced	Entities, Relationships, and Databases	AYK.23
33	Online Classified Ads	Access	T5, T6, T7, T8	Ecommerce	Advanced	Entities, Relationships, and Databases	AYK.23

NOTE: Many of the Excel projects support multiple data files. Therefore the naming convention that you see in the text may not be the same as what you see in a data folder. As an example, in the text we reference data files as AYK1_Data.xlsx; however, you may see a file named AYK1_Data_Version_1.xlsx, or AYK1_Data_Version_2.xlsx.

Project 1:
Financial Destiny

You have been introduced to Microsoft Excel and are ready to begin using it to help track your monthly expenses and take charge of your financial destiny. The first step is to create a personal budget so you can see where you are spending money and if you need to decrease your monthly expenses or increase your monthly income.

Project Focus

Create a template for a monthly budget of your income and expenditures, with some money set aside for savings (or you can use the data file, AYK1_Data.xlsx, we created). Create variations of this budget to show how much you could save if you cut back on certain expenses, found a roommate, or got a part-time job. Compare the costs of a meal plan to costs of groceries. Consider how much interest would be earned if you saved $100 a month, or how much debt paid on student loans or credit card bills. To expand your data set, make a fantasy budget for 10 years from now, when you might own a home, have student loan payments, and have a good salary.

Data File: AYK1_Data.xlsx

Project 2:
Cash Flow

Gears is a five-year-old company that specializes in bike components. The company is having trouble paying for its monthly supplies and would like to perform a cash flow analysis so it can understand its financial position. Cash flow represents the money an investment produces after subtracting cash expenses from income. The statement of cash flows summarizes sources and uses of cash, indicates whether enough cash is available to carry on routine operations, and offers an analysis of all business transactions, reporting where the firm obtained its cash and how it chose to allocate the cash. The cash flow statement shows where money comes from, how the company is going to spend it, and when the company will require additional cash. Gears would like to project a cash flow statement for the next month.

Project Focus

Using the data file AYK2_Data.xlsx complete the cash flow statement for Gears using Excel. Be sure to create formulas so the company can simply input numbers in the future to determine cash flow.

Data File: AYK2_Data.xlsx

Project 3:
Technology Budget

Tally is a start-up website development company located in Seattle, Washington. The company currently has seven employees and is looking to hire six new employees in the next month.

Project Focus

You are in charge of purchasing for Tally. Your first task is to purchase computers for the new employees. Your budget is $250,000 to buy the best computer systems with a scanner, three color printers, and business software. Use the Web to research various products and calculate the costs of different systems using Excel. Use a variety of Excel formulas as you analyze costs and compare prices. Use the data file AYK3_Data.xlsx as a template.

Data File: AYK3_Data.xlsx

Project 4:
Tracking Donations

Lazarus Consulting is a large computer consulting company in New York. Pete Lazarus, the CEO and founder, is well known for his philanthropic efforts. Pete knows that most of his employees contribute to nonprofit organizations and wants to reward them for their efforts while encouraging others to contribute to charities. Pete began a program that matches 50 percent of each employee donation. The only stipulations are that the charity must be a nonprofit organization and the company will match only up to $2,000 per year per employee.

Project Focus

Open the data file AYK4_Data.xlsx and determine the following:

- What was the total donation amount per organization?
- What were the average donations per organization?

Data File: AYK4_Data.xlsx

Project 5: Convert Currency

You have decided to spend the summer traveling abroad with your friends. Your trip is going to take you to France, England, Italy, Switzerland, Germany, Norway, and Ireland. You want to use Excel to convert currencies as you travel around the world.

Project Focus

Locate one of the exchange rate calculators on the Internet (www.xe.com or www.x-rates.com). Find the exchange rates for each of the countries listed above and create formulas in Excel to convert $100, $500, and $1,000. Use the data file AYK5_Data.xlsx as a template.

Data File: AYK5_Data.xls

Project 6: Cost Comparison

You are thinking about purchasing a new computer since the machine you are using now is four years old, slow, not always reliable, and does not support the latest operating system. Your needs for the new computer are simple: anti-virus software, email, Web browsing, word processing, spreadsheet, database, iTunes, and some lightweight graphical tools. Your concern is what the total cost of ownership will be for the next three years. You have to factor in a few added costs beyond just the initial purchase price for the computer itself, such as: added hardware (this could include a new printer, docking station, or scanner), software (purchase of a new operating system), training (you're thinking about pursuing Web training to get an internship next term), subsequent software upgrades, and maintenance.

Project Focus

- It is useful to think about costs over time—both direct as well as indirect costs. Part of the reason this distinction is important is that a decision should rest not on the nominal sum of the purchase, but rather on the present value of the purchase.

	A	B	C	D	E	F
1	COST OF NEW COMPUTER					
2	Discount Rate	1	0.9325	0.9109	0.7051	
3		Time 0	Year 1	Year 2	Year 3	Present Value Costs
4	Computer					
5	Software					
6	Additional Hardware					
7	Training					
8	Software upgrades					
9	Maintenance					
10						
11	Total Costs					
12						

FIGURE AYK.1
Sample Layout of New Computer Spreadsheet

- A dollar today is worth more than a dollar one year from now.
- The relevant discount rate (interest rate) is your marginal cost of capital corresponding to a level of risk equal with the purchase.
- Use the data file AYK6_Data.xlsx as a template.

Data File: AYK6_Data.xlsx

Project 7: Time Management

You have just been hired as a business analyst by a new start-up company called Multi-Media. Multi-Media is an interactive agency that constructs phased and affordable website marketing, providing its clients with real and measurable solutions that are supported by easy-to-use tools. Since the company is very new to the business arena, it needs help in creating a project management plan for developing its own website. The major tasks for the development team have been identified but you need to create the timeline.

Project Focus

1. The task names, durations, and any prerequisites are:
    - Analyze and plan—two weeks. Cannot start anything else until done.
    - Create and organize content—four weeks. Can start to develop "look and feel" before this is done.
    - Develop the "look and feel"—four weeks. Start working on graphics and HTML at the same time.
    - Produce graphics and HTML documents—two weeks. Create working prototype after the first week.
    - Create a working prototype—two weeks. Give to test team when complete.
    - Test, test, test—four weeks.
    - Upload to a Web server and test again—one week.
    - Maintain.
2. Using Microsoft Excel or Microsoft Project, create a Gantt chart using the information provided above.

Project 8: Maximize Profit

Books, Books, Books is a wholesale distributor of popular books. The business buys overstocked books and sells them for a discount of more than 50 percent to local area bookstores. The owner of the company, BK Kane, would like to determine the best approach to boxing books so he can make the most profit possible. The local bookstores accept all shipments from Books, Books, Books because of BK's incredibly low prices. BK can order as many overstocked books as he requires, and this week's options include:

Title	Weight	Cost	Sale Price
Harry Potter and the Deathly Hallows, J. K. Rowling	5 lb	$9	$17
The Children of Húrin, J. R. R. Tolkien	4 lb	$8	$13
The Time Traveler's Wife, Audrey Niffenegger	3.5 lb	$7	$11
The Dark River, John Twelve Hawks	3 lb	$6	$ 9
The Road, Cormac McCarthy	2.5 lb	$5	$ 7
Slaughterhouse-Five, Kurt Vonnegut	1 lb	$4	$ 5

Project Focus

When packing a single box, BK must adhere to the following:

- 20 books or less.
- Books by three different authors.
- Between four and eight books from each author.
- Weight equal to or less than 50 pounds.

BK has come to you to help him determine which books he should order to maximize his profit based on the above information. Using the data file AYK8_Data.xlsx, determine the optimal book order for a single box of books.

Data File: AYK8_Data.xlsx

Project 9: Security Analysis

SecureWorks, Inc., is a small computer security contractor that provides computer security analysis, design, and software implementation for the U.S. government and commercial clients. SecureWorks competes for both private and U.S. government computer security contract work by submitting detailed bids outlining the work the company will perform if awarded the contracts. Because all of the work involves computer security, a highly sensitive area, almost all of SecureWorks tasks require access to classified material or company confidential documents. Consequently, all of the security engineers (simply known as "engineers" within the company) have U.S. government clearances of either Secret or Top Secret. Some have even higher clearances for the 2 percent of SecureWorks work that involves so-called "black box" security work. Most of the employees also hold clearances because they must handle classified documents.

Leslie Mamalis is SecureWorks' human resources (HR) manager. She maintains all employee records and is responsible for semiannual review reports, payroll processing, personnel records, recruiting data, employee training, and pension option information. At the heart of an HR system are personnel records. Personnel record maintenance includes activities such as maintaining employee records, tracking cost center data, recording and maintaining pension information, and absence and sick leave record keeping. While most of this information resides in sophisticated database systems, Leslie maintains a basic employee worksheet for quick calculations and ad hoc report generation. Because SecureWorks is a small company, Leslie can take advantage of Excel's excellent list management capabilities to satisfy many of her personnel information management needs.

Project Focus

Leslie has asked you to assist with a number of functions (she has provided you with a copy of her "trusted" personnel data file, AYK9_Data.xlsx):

1. Copy the worksheet Data to a new worksheet called Sort. Sort the employee list in ascending order by department, then by last name, then by first name.
2. Copy the worksheet Data to a new worksheet called Autofilter. Using the Autofilter feature, create a custom filter that will display employees whose birth date is greater than or equal to 1/1/1965 and less than or equal to 12/31/1975.
3. Copy the worksheet Data to a new worksheet called Subtotal. Using the subtotal feature create a sum of the salary for each department.
4. Copy the worksheet Data to a new worksheet called Formatting. Using the salary column, change the font color to red if the cell value is greater than or equal to 55000. You must use the conditional formatting feature to complete this step.

Data File: AYK9_Data.xlsx

Project 10:

Gathering Data

You have just accepted a new job offer from a firm that has offices in San Diego, Los Angeles, and San Francisco. You need to decide which location to move to. Because you have not visited any of these three cities and want to get in a lot of golf time, you determine that the main factor that will affect your decision is weather.

Go to www.weather.com and locate the box in which you can enter the city or zip code for which you want information. Enter San Diego, CA, and when the data appear, click the Averages and Records tab. Print this page and repeat this for Los Angeles and San Francisco. You will want to focus on the Monthly Average and Records section on the top of the page.

Project Focus

1. Create a spreadsheet to summarize the information you find.
2. Record the temperature and rainfall in columns, and group the cities into four groups of rows labeled Average High, Average Low, Mean, and Average Precipitation.
3. Fill in the appropriate data for each city and month.
4. Because rain is your greatest concern, use conditional formatting to display the months with an average precipitation below 2.5 inches in blue and apply boldface.
5. You also want to be in the warmest weather possible while in California. Use conditional formatting to display the months with average high temperatures above 65 degrees in green and apply an italic font face.
6. Looking at the average high temperatures above 65 degrees and average precipitation below two inches, to which city do you think you should relocate? Explain your answer.

Project 11:

Scanner System

FunTown is a popular amusement park filled with roller coasters, games, and water features. Boasting 24 roller coasters, 10 of which exceed 200 feet and 70 miles per hour, and five water parks, the park's attendance remains steady throughout the season. Due to the park's popularity, it is not uncommon for entrance lines to exceed one hour on busy days. FunTown would like your help to find a solution to decrease park entrance lines.

Project Focus

FunTown would like to implement a handheld scanner system that can allow employees to walk around the front gates and accept credit card purchases and print tickets on the spot. The park anticipates an overall increase in sales of 4 percent per year with online ticketing, with an expense of 6 percent of total sales for the scanning equipment. FunTown has created a data file for you to use, AYK11_Data.xlsx, that compares scanning sales and traditional sales. You will need to create the necessary formulas to calculate all the assumptions including:

- Tickets sold at the booth.
- Tickets sold by the scanner.
- Revenues generated by booth sales.
- Revenues generated by scanner sales.
- Scanner ticket expense.
- Revenue with and without scanner sales.
- Three year row totals.

Data File: AYK11_Data.xlsx

Project 12:
Competitive Pricing

Bill Schultz is thinking of starting a store that specializes in handmade cowboy boots. Bill is a longtime rancher in the town of Taos, New Mexico. Bill's reputation for honesty and integrity is well-known around town, and he is positive that his new store will be highly successful.

Project Focus

Before opening his store, Bill is curious about how his profit, revenue, and variable costs will change depending on the amount he charges for his boots. Bill would like you to perform the work required for this analysis and has given you the data file AYK12_Data.xlsx. Here are a few things to consider while you perform your analysis:

- Current competitive prices for custom cowboy boots are between $225 and $275 a pair.
- Variable costs will be either $100 or $150 a pair depending on the types of material Bill chooses to use.
- Fixed costs are $10,000 a month.

Data File: AYK12_Data.xlsx

Project 13:
Adequate Acquisitions

XMark.com is a major Internet company specializing in organic food. XMark.com is thinking of purchasing GoodGrow, another organic food Internet company. GoodGrow has current revenues of $100 million, with expenses of $150 million. Current projections indicate that GoodGrow's revenues are increasing at 35 percent per year and its expenses are increasing by 10 percent per year. XMark.com understands that projections can be erroneous, however; the company must determine the number of years before GoodGrow will return a profit.

Project Focus

You need to help XMark.com determine the number of years required to break even, using annual growth rates in revenue between 20 percent and 60 percent and annual expense growth rates between 10 percent and 30 percent. You have been provided with a template, AYK13_Data.xlsx, to assist with your analysis.

Data File: AYK13_Data.xlsx

Project 14:
Customer Relations

Schweizer Distribution specializes in distributing fresh produce to local restaurants in the Chicago area. The company currently sells 12 different products through the efforts of three sales representatives to 10 restaurants. The company, like all small businesses, is always interested in finding ways to increase revenues and decrease expenses.

The company's founder, Bob Schweizer, has recently hired you as a new business analyst. You have just graduated from college with a degree in marketing and a specialization in customer relationship management. Bob is eager to hear your thoughts and ideas on how to improve the business and help the company build strong lasting relationships with its customers.

Project Focus

Bob has provided you with last year's sales information in the data file AYK14_Data.xlsx. Help Bob analyze his distribution company by using a PivotTable to determine the following:

1. Who is Bob's best customer by total sales?
2. Who is Bob's worst customer by total sales?

3. Who is Bob's best customer by total profit?
4. Who is Bob's worst customer by total profit?
5. What is Bob's best-selling product by total sales?
6. What is Bob's worst-selling product by total sales?
7. What is Bob's best-selling product by total profit?
8. What is Bob's worst-selling product by total profit?
9. Who is Bob's best sales representative by total profit?
10. Who is Bob's worst sales representative by total profit?
11. What is the best sales representative's best-selling product (by total profit)?
12. Who is the best sales representative's best customer (by total profit)?
13. What is the best sales representative's worst-selling product (by total profit)?
14. Who is the best sales representative's worst customer (by total profit)?

Data File: AYK14_Data.xlsx

Project 15:

Assessing the Value of Information

Recently Santa Fe, New Mexico, was named one of the safest places to live in the United States. Since then housing development projects have been springing up all around Santa Fe. Six housing development projects are currently dominating the local market—Pinon Pine, Rancho Hondo, Creek Side, Vista Del Monte, Forest View, and Santa Fe South. These six projects each started with 100 homes, have sold all of them, and are currently developing phase two.

As one of the three partners and real estate agents of Affordable Homes Real Estate, it is your responsibility to analyze the information concerning the past 600 home sales and choose which development project to focus on for selling homes in phase two. Because your real estate firm is so small, you and your partners have decided that the firm should focus on selling homes in only one of the development projects.

From the New Mexico Real Estate Association you have obtained a spreadsheet file that contains information concerning each of the sales for the first 600 homes. It contains the following fields:

Column	Name	Description
A	LOT #	The number assigned to a specific home within each project.
B	PROJECT #	A unique number assigned to each of the six housing development projects (see table on the next page).
C	ASK PRICE	The initial posted asking price for the home.
D	SELL PRICE	The actual price for which the home was sold.
E	LIST DATE	The date the home was listed for sale.
F	SALE DATE	The date on which the final contract closed and the home was sold.
G	SQ. FT.	The total square footage for the home.
H	# BATH.	The number of bathrooms in the home.
I	# BDRMS	The numb er of bedrooms in the home.

The following numbers have been assigned to each of the housing development projects:

Project Number	Project Name
23	Pinon Pine
47	Rancho Hondo
61	Creek Side
78	Vista Del Monte
92	Forest View
97	Santa Fe South

It is your responsibility to analyze the sales list and prepare a report that details which housing development project your real estate firm should focus on. Your analysis should be from as many angles as possible.

Project Focus

1. You do not know how many other real estate firms will also be competing for sales in each of the housing development projects.
2. Phase two for each housing development project will develop homes similar in style, price, and square footage to their respective first phases.
3. As you consider the information provided to you, think in terms of what information is important and what information is not important. Be prepared to justify how you went about your analysis.
4. Upon completing your analysis, please provide concise, yet detailed and thorough, documentation (in narrative, numeric, and graphic forms) that justifies your decision.

   Data file: AYK15_Data.xlsx

Project 16: Growth, Trends, and Forecasts

Founded in 2002, Analytics Software provides innovative search software, website accessibility testing software, and usability testing software. All serve as part of its desktop and enterprise content management solutions for government, corporate, educational, and consumer markets. The company's solutions are used by website publishers, digital media publishers, content managers, document managers, business users, consumers, software companies, and consulting services companies. Analytics Software solutions help organizations develop long-term strategies to achieve Web content accessibility, enhance usability, and comply with U.S. and international accessibility and search standards.

You manage the customer service group for the company and have just received an email from CIO Sue Downs that the number of phone calls from customers having problems with one of your newer applications is on the increase. This company has a 10-year history of approximately 1 percent in turnover a year, and its focus had always been on customer service. With the informal motto of "Grow big, but stay small," it takes pride in 100 percent callbacks in customer care, knowing that its personal service was one thing that made it outstanding.

The rapid growth to six times its original customer-base size has forced the company to deal with difficult questions for the first time, such as, "How do we serve this many customers?"

One option might be for the company to outsource its customer service department. Before deciding to do that, Analytics Software needs to create a growth, trend, forecast analysis for future predictions.

Project Focus

1. Create a weekly analysis from the data provided in AYK16_Data.xlsx.
2. The price of the products, the actual product type, and any warrantee information is irrelevant.
3. Develop a growth, trend, and forecast analysis. You should use a three-day moving average; a shorter moving average might not display the trend well, and a much longer moving average would shorten the trend too much.
4. Upon completing your analysis, please provide concise yet detailed and thorough documentation (in narrative, numeric, and graphic forms) that justifies your recommendations.

Data File: AYK16_Data.xlsx

Project 17: Shipping Costs

One of the main products of the Fairway Woods Company is custom-made golf clubs. The clubs are manufactured at three plants (Denver, Colorado; Phoenix, Arizona; and Dallas, Texas) and are then shipped by truck to five distribution warehouses in Sacramento, California; Salt Lake City, Utah; Chicago, Illinois; Albuquerque, New Mexico; and New York City, New York. Since shipping costs are a major expense, management has begun an analysis to determine ways to reduce them. For the upcoming golf season, the output from each manufacturing plant and how much each warehouse will require to satisfy its customers have been estimated.

The CIO from Fairway Woods Company has created a data file for you, AYK17_Data.xlsx, of the shipping costs from each manufacturing plant to each warehouse as a baseline analysis. Some business rules and requirements you should be aware of include:

- The problem presented involves the shipment of goods from three plants to five regional warehouses.
- Goods can be shipped from any plant to any warehouse, but it costs more to ship goods over long distances than over short distances.

Project Focus

1. Your goal is to minimize the costs of shipping goods from production plants to warehouses, thereby meeting the demand from each metropolitan area while not exceeding the supply available from each plant. To complete this project it is recommended that you use the Solver function in Excel to assist with the analysis.
2. Specifically you want to focus on:
   - Minimizing the total shipping costs.
   - Total shipped must be less than or equal to supply at a plant.
   - Total shipped to warehouses must be greater than or equal to the warehouse demand.
   - Number to ship must be greater than or equal to 0.

Data File: AYK17_Data.xlsx

Project 18: Formatting Grades

Professor Streterstein is a bit absentminded. His instructor's grade book is a mess, and he would like your help cleaning it up and making it easier to use. In Professor Streterstein's course, the maximum possible points a student can earn is 750. The following table displays the grade equivalent to total points for the course.

Total Points	Calculated Grade
675	A
635	A–
600	B
560	B–
535	C
490	C–
450	D
0	F

Project Focus

Help Professor Streterstein rework his grade book. Open the data file AYK18_Data.xlsx and perform the following:

1. Reformat the workbook so it is readable, understandable, and consistent. Replace column labels, format and align the headings, add borders and shading as appropriate.
2. Add a column in the grade book for final grade next to the total points earned column.
3. Use the VLookup Function to automatically assess final grades based on the total points column.
4. Using the If Function, format the workbook so each student's grade shows a pass or fail—P for pass, F for fail—based on the total points.

Data File: AYK18_Data.xlsx

Project 19:

Moving Dilemma

Pony Espresso is a small business that sells specialty coffee drinks at office buildings. Each morning and afternoon, trucks arrive at offices' front entrances, and the office employees purchase various beverages such as Java du Jour and Café de Colombia. The business is profitable. Pony Espresso offices, however, are located north of town, where lease rates are less expensive, and the principal sales area is south of town. This means the trucks must drive across town four times each day.

The cost of transportation to and from the sales area plus the power demands of the trucks' coffee brewing equipment are a significant portion of variable costs. Pony Espresso could reduce the amount of driving and, therefore, the variable costs, if it moved the offices closer to the sales area.

Pony Espresso presently has fixed costs of $10,000 per month. The lease of a new office, closer to the sales area, would cost an additional $2,200 per month. This would increase the fixed costs to $12,200 per month.

Although the lease of new offices would increase the fixed costs, a careful estimate of the potential savings in gasoline and vehicle maintenance indicates that Pony Espresso could reduce the variable costs from $0.60 per unit to $0.35 per unit. Total sales are unlikely to increase as a result of the move, but the savings in variable costs should increase the annual profit.

Project Focus

Consider the information provided to you from the owner in the data file AYK19_Data.xlsx. Especially look at the change in the variability of the profit from month to month. From

November through January, when it is much more difficult to lure office workers out into the cold to purchase coffee, Pony Espresso barely breaks even. In fact, in December, the business lost money.

1. Develop the cost analysis on the existing lease information using the monthly sales figures provided to you in the data file.
2. Develop the cost analysis from the new lease information provided above.
3. Calculate the variability that is reflected in the month-to-month standard deviation of earnings for the current cost structure and the projected cost structure.
4. Do not consider any association with downsizing such as overhead—simply focus on the information provided to you.
5. You will need to calculate the EBIT (earnings before interest and taxes).

Data File: AYK19_Data.xlsx

Project 20:

Operational Efficiencies

Hoover Transportation, Inc., is a large distribution company located in Denver, Colorado. The company is currently seeking to gain operational efficiencies in its supply chain by reducing the number of transportation carriers that it is using to outsource. Operational efficiencies for Hoover Transportation, Inc., suggest that reducing the number of carriers from the Denver distribution center to warehouses in the selected states will lead to reduced costs. Brian Hoover, the CEO of Hoover Transportation, requests that the number of carriers transporting products from its Denver distribution center to wholesalers in Arizona, Arkansas, Iowa, Missouri, Montana, Oklahoma, Oregon, and Washington be reduced from the current five carriers to two carriers.

Project Focus

Carrier selection should be based on the assumptions that all environmental factors are equal and historical cost trends will continue. Review the historical data from the past several years to determine your recommendation for the top two carriers that Hoover Transportation should continue to use.

1. Analyze the last 24 months of Hoover's Transportation carrier transactions found in the data file AYK20_Data.xlsx.
2. Create a report detailing your recommendation for the top two carriers with which Hoover Transportation should continue to do business. Be sure to use PivotTables and PivotCharts in your report. A few questions to get you started include:
   - Calculate the average cost per carrier.
   - Calculate the total shipping costs per state.
   - Calculate the total shipping weights per state.
   - Calculate the average shipping costs per pound.
   - Calculate the average cost per carrier.

Data File: AYK20_Data.xlsx

Project 21:

Too Much Information

You have just landed the job of vice president of operations for The Pitt Stop Restaurants, a national chain of full-service, casual-themed restaurants. During your first week on the job, Suzanne Graham, your boss and CEO of the company, has asked you to provide an analysis of how well the company's restaurants are performing. Specifically, she would like to know which units and regions are performing extremely well, which are performing moderately well, and which are underperforming. Her goal is to identify where to spend time and focus efforts to improve the overall health of the company.

Project Focus

Review the data file AYK21_Data.xlsx and determine how best to analyze and interpret the data. Create a formal presentation of your findings. A few things to consider include:

- Should underperforming restaurants be closed or sold?
- Should high-performing restaurants be expanded to accommodate more seats?
- Should the company spend more or less on advertising?
- In which markets should the advertising budget be adjusted?
- How are The Pitt Stop Restaurants performing compared to the competition?
- How are units of like size performing relative to each other?

Data File: AYK21_Data.xlsx

Project 22:

Turnover Rates

Employee turnover rates are at an all-time high at Gizmo's Manufacturing plants. The company is experiencing severe worker retention issues, which are leading to productivity and quality control problems. The majority of the company's workers perform a variety of tasks and are paid by the hour. The company currently tests potential applicants to ensure they have the skills necessary for the intense mental concentration and dexterity required to fill the positions. Since significant costs are associated with employee turnover, Gizmo Manufacturing wants to find a way to predict which applicants have the characteristics of being a short-term versus a long-term employee.

Project Focus

1. Review the information that Gizmo Manufacturing has collected from two of its different data sources. The first data file, AYK22_Data_A.xlsx, contains information regarding employee wages. The second data file, AYK22_Data_B.xlsx, contains information regarding employee retention.
2. Using Excel analysis functions, determine the employee characteristics that you would recommend Gizmo Manufacturing look for when hiring new personnel. It is highly recommended that you use PivotTables as part of your analysis.
3. Prepare a report based on your findings (which should include several forms of graphical representation) for your recommendations.

Data Files: AYK22_Data_A.xlsx and AYK22_Data_B.xlsx

Project 23:

Vital Information

Martin Resorts, Inc., owns and operates four Spa and Golf resorts in Colorado. The company has five traditional lines of business: (1) golf sales; (2) golf lessons; (3) restaurants; (4) retail and rentals; and (5) hotels. David Logan, director of marketing technology at Martin Resorts, Inc., and Donald Mayer, the lead strategic analyst for Martin Resorts, are soliciting your input for their CRM strategic initiative.

Martin Resorts' IT infrastructure is pieced together with various systems and applications. Currently, the company has a difficult time with CRM because its systems are not integrated. The company cannot determine vital information such as which customers are golfing and staying at the hotel or which customers are staying at the hotel and not golfing.

For example, the three details that the customer Diego Titus (1) stayed four nights at a Martin Resorts' managed hotel, (2) golfed three days, and (3) took an all-day spa treatment the first day are discrete facts housed in separate systems. Martin Resorts hopes that by using data warehousing technology to integrate its data, the next time Diego reserves lodging for another trip, sales associates may ask him if he would like to book a spa treatment as well, and even if he would like the same masseuse that he had on his prior trip.

Martin Resorts is excited about the possibility of taking advantage of customer segmentation and CRM strategies to help increase its business.

Project Focus

The company wants to use CRM and data warehouse technologies to improve service and personalization at each customer touch point. Using a data warehousing tool, important customer information can be accessed from all of its systems either daily, weekly, monthly, or once or twice per year. Analyze the sample data in AYK23_Data.xlsx for the following:

1. Currently, the quality of the data within the above disparate systems is low. Develop a report for David and Donald discussing the importance of high-quality information and how low-quality information can affect Martin Resorts' business.
2. Review the data that David and Donald are working with from the data warehouse in the data file AYK23_Data.xlsx.
   a. Give examples from the data showing the kind of information Martin Resorts might be able to use to gain a better understanding of its customers. Include the types of data quality issues the company can anticipate and the strategies it can use to help avoid such issues.
   b. Determine who are Martin Resorts' best customers, and provide examples of the types of marketing campaigns the company should offer these valuable customers.
   c. Prepare a report that summarizes the benefits Martin Resorts can receive from using business intelligence to mine the data warehouse. Include a financial analysis of the costs and benefits.

Data File: AYK23_Data.xlsx

Project 24: Breaking Even

Mountain Cycle specializes in making custom mountain bikes. The company founder, PJ Steffan, is having a hard time making the business profitable. Knowing that you have great business knowledge and solid financial sense, PJ has come to you for advice.

Project Focus

PJ would like you to determine how many bikes Mountain Cycle needs to sell per year to break even. Using Goal Seek in Excel solve using the following:

- Fixed cost equals $65,000
- Variable cost equals $1,575
- Bike price equals $2,500

Project 25: Profit Scenario

Murry Lutz owns a small shop, Lutz Motors, that sells and services vintage motorcycles. Murry is curious how his profit will be affected by his sales over the next year.

Project Focus

Murry would like your help creating best, worst, and most-likely scenarios for his motorcycle sales over the next year. Using Scenario Manager, help Murry analyze the information in the data file AYK25_Data.xlsx.

Data File: AYK25_Data.xlsx

Project 26:
Electronic Résumés

Résumés are the currency of the recruitment industry. They are the cornerstone of communication between candidates, recruiters, and employers. Technology is automating elements of the recruitment process, but a complete solution requires proper handling of the actual development of all the pieces and parts that comprise not just a résumé, but also an erésumé. Electronic résumés, or erésumés, have moved into the mainstream of today's job market at lightning speed. Erésumés have stepped up the efficiency of job placement to such a point that you could get a call from a recruiter just hours after submitting your erésumé. With this kind of opportunity, you cannot afford to be left in the dark ages of using only a paper résumé.

Project Focus

In the text or HTML editor of your choice, write your erésumé as though you were really putting it online and inviting prospective employers to see it. We recommend typing in all the text and then later adding the HTML tags (rather than trying to type in the tags as you go).

Use the following checklist to make sure you're covering the basics. You do not need to match it exactly; it just shows what can be done.

- Add structural tags.
- Add paragraphs and headings.
- Find an opportunity to include a list.
- Add inline styles.
- Play with the alignment of elements.
- Add appropriate font selection, font size, and color.

Project 27:
Gathering Feedback

Gathering feedback from website's visitors can be a valuable way of assessing a site's success, and it can help build a customer or subscriber database. For example, a business could collect the addresses of people who are interested in receiving product samples, email newsletters, or notifications of special offers.

Project Focus

Adding form elements to a Web page is simple: They are created using a set of HTML form tags that define menus, text fields, buttons, and so on. Form elements are generally used to collect information from a Web page.

In the text or HTML editor of your choice, create a Web page form that would collect information for a customer ordering a customized bicycle. Use proper Web page design and HTML tools to understand the process and function of form elements. Be sure to pay attention to:

- Form layout and design.
- Visual elements, including labels, alignment, font selection, font size, color.
- Required versus nonrequired fields.
- Drop-down boxes, text fields, and radio buttons.

Project 28:
Daily Invoice

Foothills Animal Hospital is a full-service small animal veterinary hospital located in Morrison, Colorado, specializing in routine medical care, vaccinations, laboratory testing, and surgery. The hospital has experienced tremendous growth over the past six months due to customer referrals. While Foothills Animal Hospital has typically kept its daily service records in a workbook format, it feels the need to expand its reporting capabilities to develop a relational database as a more functional structure.

Foothills Animal Hospital needs help developing a database, specifically:

- Create a customer table—name, address, phone, and date of entrance.
- Create a pet table—pet name, type of animal, breed, gender, color, neutered/spayed, weight, and comments.
- Create a medications table—medication code, name of medication, and cost of medication.
- Create a visit table—details of treatments performed, medications dispensed, and date of the visit.
- Produce a daily invoice report.

Figure AYK.2 displays a sample daily invoice report that the Foothills Animal Hospital accountants have requested. Foothills Animal Hospital organizes its treatments using the codes displayed in Figure AYK.3. The entities and primary keys for the database have been identified in Figure AYK.4.

The following business rules have been identified:

1. A customer can have many pets but must have at least one.
2. A pet must be assigned to one and only one customer.
3. A pet can have one or more treatments per visit but must have at least one.
4. A pet can have one or more medications but need not have any.

Project Focus

Your job is to complete the following tasks:

1. Develop and describe the entity-relationship diagram.
2. Use normalization to assure the correctness of the tables (relations).

FIGURE AYK.2

Foothills Animal Hospital Daily Invoice Report

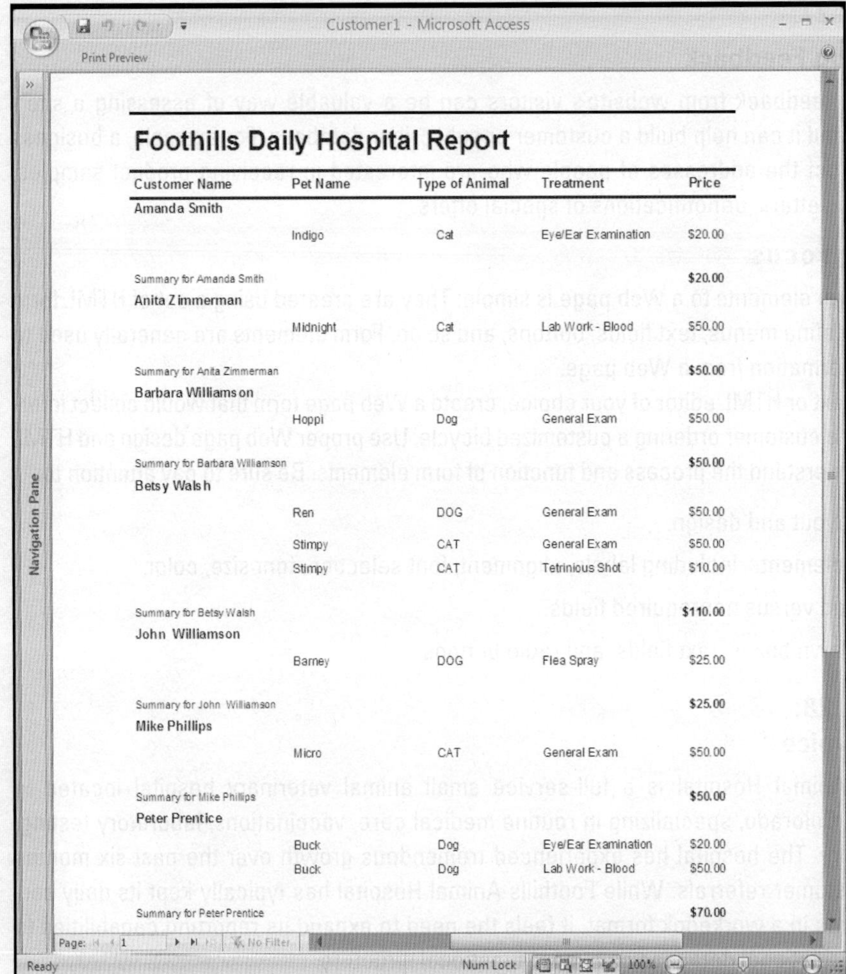

Customer1 - Microsoft Access

Print Preview

Foothills Daily Hospital Report

Customer Name	Pet Name	Type of Animal	Treatment	Price
Amanda Smith				
	Indigo	Cat	Eye/Ear Examination	$20.00
Summary for Amanda Smith				$20.00
Anita Zimmerman				
	Midnight	Cat	Lab Work - Blood	$50.00
Summary for Anita Zimmerman				$50.00
Barbara Williamson				
	Hoppi	Dog	General Exam	$50.00
Summary for Barbara Williamson				$50.00
Betsy Walsh				
	Ren	DOG	General Exam	$50.00
	Stimpy	CAT	General Exam	$50.00
	Stimpy	CAT	Tetrinious Shot	$10.00
Summary for Betsy Walsh				$110.00
John Williamson				
	Barney	DOG	Flea Spray	$25.00
Summary for John Williamson				$25.00
Mike Phillips				
	Micro	CAT	General Exam	$50.00
Summary for Mike Phillips				$50.00
Peter Prentice				
	Buck	Dog	Eye/Ear Examination	$20.00
	Buck	Dog	Lab Work - Blood	$50.00
Summary for Peter Prentice				$70.00

Navigation Pane

Page: 1 No Filter

Ready Num Lock 100%

Treatment Code	Treatment	Price
0100	Tetrinious Shot	$10.00
0201	Rabonius Shot	$20.00
0300	General Exam	$50.00
0303	Eye/Ear Examination	$20.00
0400	Spay/Neuter	$225.00
0405	Reset Dislocation	$165.00
0406	Amputation of Limb	$450.00
0407	Wrap Affected Area	$15.00
0408	Cast Affected Area	$120.00
1000	Lab Work—Blood	$50.00
1003	Lab Work—Misc	$35.00
2003	Flea Spray	$25.00
9999	Other Not Listed	$10.00

FIGURE AYK.3

Treatment Codes, Treatments, and Price Descriptions

FIGURE AYK.4

Entity Names and Primary Keys Foothills Animal Hospital

Entity	Primary Key
CUSTOMER	Customer Number
PET	Pet Number
VISIT	Visit Number
VISIT DETAIL	Visit Number and Line Number (a composite key)
TREATMENT	Treatment Code
MEDICATION	Medication Code

3. Create the database using a personal DBMS package (preferably Microsoft Access).
4. Use the data in Figure AYK.3 to populate your tables. Feel free to enter your own personal information.
5. Use the DBMS package to create the basic report in Figure AYK.2.

Project 29: Billing Data

On-The-Level Construction Company is a Denver-based construction company that specializes in subcontracting the development of single-family homes. In business since 1998, On-The-Level Construction has maintained a talented pool of certified staff and independent consultants providing the flexibility and combined experience required to meet the needs of its nearly 300 completed projects in the Denver metropolitan area. The field of operation methods that On-The-Level Construction is responsible for includes structural development, heating and cooling, plumbing, and electricity.

The company charges its clients by billing the hours spent on each contract. The hourly billing rate is dependent on the employee's position according to the field of operations (as noted above). Figure AYK.5 shows a basic report that On-The-Level Construction foremen would like to see every week concerning what projects are being assigned, the overall assignment hours, and the charges for the assignment. On-The-Level Construction organizes its internal structure in four different operations—Structure (500), Plumbing (501), Electrical (502), and Heating and Ventilation (503). Each of these operational departments can and should have many subcontractors who specialize in that area. On-The-Level Construction has decided to implement a relational database model to track project details according to project name, hours assigned, and charges per hour for each job description. Originally, On-The-Level Construction decided to let one of its employees handle the construction of the database. However, that employee has not had the time to completely implement the project. On-The-Level Construction has asked you to take over and complete the development of the database.

The entities and primary keys for the database have been identified in Figure AYK.6.

The following business rules have been identified:

1. A job can have many employees assigned but must have at least one.
2. An employee must be assigned to one and only one job number.

FIGURE AYK.5

On-The-Level-Construction Detail Report

ON-THE-LEVEL CONSTRUCTION PROJECT DETAIL

PROJECT NAME	ASSIGN DATE	EMPLOYEE LAST NAME	FIRST NAME	JOB DESCRIPTION	ASSIGN HOUR	CHARGE/HOUR
Chatfield						
	6/10/2011	Olenkoski	Glenn	Structure	2.1	$35.75
	6/10/2011	Sullivan	David	Electrical	1.2	$105.00
	6/10/2011	Ramora	Anne	Plumbing	2.6	$96.75
	6/11/2011	Frommer	Matt	Plumbing	1.4	$96.75
Summary of Assignment Hours and Charges					7.30	$588.08
Evergreen						
	6/10/2011	Sullivan	David	Electrical	1.8	$105.00
	6/10/2011	Jones	Anne	Heating and Ventalation	3.4	$84.50
	6/11/2011	Frommer	Matt	Plumbing	4.1	$96.75
	6/16/2011	Bawangi	Terry	Plumbing	4.1	$96.75
	6/16/2011	Newman	John	Electrical	1.7	$105.00
Summary of Assignment Hours and Charges					15.10	$1,448.15
Roxborough						
	6/10/2011	Washberg	Jeff	Plumbing	3.9	$96.75
	6/10/2011	Ramora	Anne	Plumbing	2.6	$96.75
	6/11/2011	Smithfield	William	Structure	2.4	$35.75
	6/11/2011	Bawangi	Terry	Plumbing	2.7	$96.75
	6/16/2011	Johnson	Peter	Electrical	5.2	$105.00
	6/16/2011	Joen	Denise	Plumbing	2.5	$96.75
Summary of Assignment Hours and Charges					19.30	$1,763.78

FIGURE AYK.6

Entity Classes and Primary Keys for On-The-Level Construction

Entity	Primary Key
PROJECT	Project Number
EMPLOYEE	Employee Number
JOB	Job Number
ASSIGNMENT	Assignment Number

3. An employee can be assigned to work on one or more projects.
4. A project can be assigned to only one employee but need not be assigned to any employee.

Project Focus

Your job is to complete the following tasks:

1. Develop and describe the entity relationship diagram.
2. Use normalization to assure the correctness of the tables (relations).
3. Create the database using a personal DBMS package (preferably Microsoft Access).
4. Use the DBMS package to create the basic report in Figure AYK.5.
5. You may not be able to develop a report that looks exactly like the one in Figure AYK.5. However, your report should include the same information.
6. Complete personnel information is tracked by another database. For this application, include only the minimum: employee number, last name, and first name.
7. Information concerning all projects, employees, and jobs is not readily available. You should create information for several fictitious projects, employees, and jobs to include in your database.

Project 30: Inventory Data

An independent retailer of mobile entertainment and wireless phones, iToys.com has built its business on offering the widest selection, expert advice, and outstanding customer service. However, iToys.com does not use a formal, consistent inventory tracking system. Periodically, an iToys.com employee visually checks to see what items are in stock. Although iToys.com does try to keep a certain level of each "top seller" in stock, the lack of a formal inventory tracking system has led to the overstocking of some items and understocking of other items. On occasion, a customer will request a hot item, and it is only then that iToys.com realizes that the item is out of stock. If an item is not available, iToys.com risks losing a customer to a competitor.

Lately, iToys.com has become concerned with its inventory management methods. The owner of iToys.com, Dan Connolly, wants to better manage his inventory. The company receives orders by mail, by telephone, or through its website. Regardless of how the orders are received, Dan needs a database to automate the inventory checking and ordering process.

Project Focus

Dan has provided you with a simplified version of the company's current system (an Excel workbook) for recording inventory and orders in an Excel spreadsheet data file AYK30_Data.xlsx.

1. Develop an ERD diagram before you begin to create the database. You will need to use the information provided here as well as the data given in the Excel workbook.
2. Create the database using a personal DBMS package (preferably Microsoft Access) that will track items (i.e., products), orders, order details, categories, suppliers, and shipping methods.
3. In addition to what is mentioned above, the database needs to track the inventory levels for each product, according to a reorder level and lead time.
4. At this time, Dan does not need information stored about the customer; he simply needs you to focus on the inventory structure.
5. Develop a query that will display the products that need to be ordered from their supplier. To complete this, you will want to compare a reorder level with how many units are in stock.
6. Develop several reports that display:
   a. Each product ordered by its supplier. The report should include the product name, quantity on hand, and reorder level.
   b. Each supplier ordered by shipping method.
   c. Each product that requires more than five days lead time. (Hint: You will want to create a query for this first).
   d. Each product ordered by category.
7. Here are some additional business rules to assist you in completing this task:
   a. An order must have at least one product, but can contain more than one product.
   b. A product can have one or more orders, but need not have any orders.
   c. A product must belong to one and only one category, but a category may contain many different products.
   d. A product can only be stocked by one supplier, but a supplier can provide more than one product.
   e. A supplier will use one type of shipping method, but shipping methods can be used by more than one supplier.

   Data File: AYK30_Data.xlsx

Project 31:

Call Center

A manufacturing company, Teleworks, has been a market leader in the wireless telephone business for the past 10 years. Other firms have imitated its product with some degree of success, but Teleworks occupies a dominant position in the marketplace because it has a first-mover advantage with a quality product.

Recently Teleworks began selling a new, enhanced wireless phone. This new phone does not replace its current product, but offers additional features, greater durability, and better performance for a somewhat higher price. Offering this enhanced phone has established a new revenue stream for the company.

Many sales executives at Teleworks seem to subscribe to the-more-you-have, the-more-you-want theory of managing customer data. That is, they believe they can never accumulate too much information about their customers, and that they can do their jobs more effectively by collecting infinite amounts of customer details. Having a firm grasp on a wide range of customer-focused details—specifically reports summarizing call center information—can be critical in enabling your company to successfully manage a customer relationship management (CRM) solution that creates a positive impact.

To continue to provide excellent customer support, and in anticipation of increased calls due to the release of its new product, Teleworks needs a database that it can use to record, track, and query call center information. Teleworks CIO KED Davisson has hired you to develop this database.

Project Focus

1. Teleworks has provided you with a data file AYK31_Data.xlsx; its current approach for recording cell center information is a spreadsheet file.
2. Develop an ERD diagram before you begin to create the database.
3. Create the database using a personal DBMS package (preferably Microsoft Access) that will allow data analysts to enter call center data according to the type of issue and the customer, assign each call to a consultant, and prioritize the call.
4. Develop a query that will display all issues that are "open."
5. Develop a screen form to browse all issues.
6. Develop several reports that display:
   a. All closed issues.
   b. Each issue in detail ordered by issue ID.
   c. Each issue in detail ordered by consultant.
   d. Each issue in detail ordered by category.
   e. Each issue in detail ordered by status.
7. Here are some additional business rules to assist you in completing this task:
   a. An issue must have at least one customer.
   b. A customer can have more than one issue.
   c. Each issue must be assigned to one consultant.
   d. Each consultant can be assigned to more than one issue.
   e. An issue can only belong to one category.
   f. An issue must be assigned only one status code.
   g. An issue must be assigned a priority code.
8. Priorities are assigned accordingly:

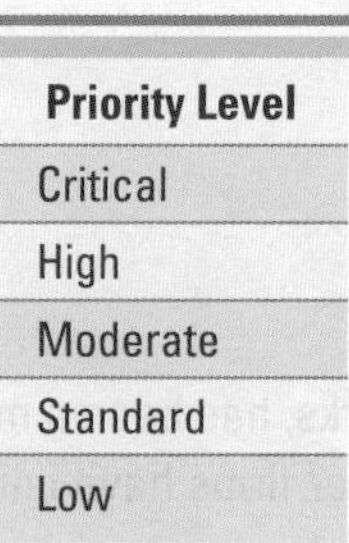

Priority Level
Critical
High
Moderate
Standard
Low

9. Status is recorded as either open or closed.
10. The categories of each issue need to be recorded as:

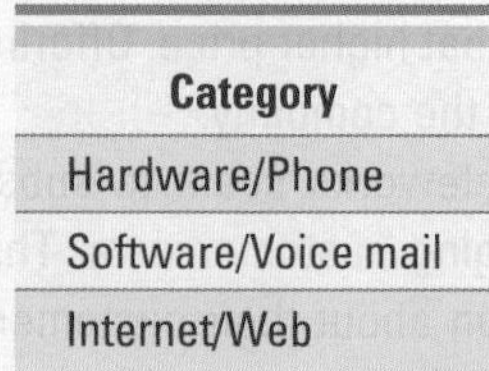

Category
Hardware/Phone
Software/Voice mail
Internet/Web

Data File: AYK31_Data.xlsx

Project 32:
Sales Pipeline

Sales drive any organization. This is true for every for-profit business irrespective of size or industry type. If customers are not buying your goods or services, you run the risk of not having a business. This is when tough decisions have to be made like whether to slash budgets, lay off staff, or seek additional financing.

Unfortunately, you do not wield ultimate power over your customers' buying habits. While you can attempt to influence buying behavior through strategic marketing, smart businesses remain one step ahead by collecting and analyzing historical and current customer information from a range of internal and external sources to forecast future sales. In other words, managing the sales pipeline is an essential ingredient to business success.

You have recently been hired by RealTime Solutions, a new company that collects information to understand, manage, and predict specific sales cycle (including the supply chain and lead times) in the automobile business. Having an accurate forecast of future sales will allow the company to increase or decrease the production cycle as required and manage personnel levels, inventory, and cash flow.

Project Focus

Using a personal DBMS package (preferably Microsoft Access) create a sales pipeline database that will:

1. Track opportunities from employees to customers.
   - Opportunities should have a ranking, category, source of opportunity, open date, closed date, description.
2. Create a form for inputting customer, employee, and opportunity data.
3. Create a few reports that display:
   - All open opportunities, including relevant customer and employee information.
   - Closed opportunities, including relevant customer and employee information.
   - All customers.
4. Create your own data to test the integrity of the relationships. Use approximately 10 records per table.

Project 33:
Online Classified Ads

With the emergence of the Internet as a worldwide standard for communicating information, *The Morrison Post,* a medium-size community newspaper in central Colorado, is creating an electronic version of its paper-based classified ads.

Advertisers can place a small ad that lists items that they wish to sell and provide a means (e.g., telephone number and email) by which prospective buyers can contact them. The nature of a sale via the newspaper's classified system goes as follows:

- During the course of the sale, the information flows in different directions at different stages.
- First, there is a downstream flow of information (from seller to buyer): the listing in print in the newspaper. (Thus, the classified ad listing is just a way of bringing a buyer and seller together.)
- When a potential purchaser's interest has been raised, then that interest must be relayed upstream, usually by telephone or by email.
- Finally, a meeting should result that uses face-to-face negotiation to finalize the sale, if the sale can be agreed.

By placing the entire system on the Internet, the upstream and downstream communications are accomplished using a Web browser. The sale becomes more of an auction, because many potential buyers, all with equal status, can bid for the same item. So it is fairer for all purchasers and gets a better deal for the seller.

Any user who is trying to buy an item can:

- View items for sale.
- Bid on an item they wish to purchase.

Any user who is trying to sell an item can:

- Place a new item for sale.
- Browse a list of the items that he or she is trying to sell, and examine the bids that have been made on each of those items.
- Accept a bid on an item that he or she is selling.

Your job is to complete the following:

1. Develop and describe the entity-relationship diagram for the database that will support the listed activities.
2. Use normalization to ensure the correctness of the tables.
3. Create the database using a personal DBMS package.
4. Use Figure AYK.7 as a baseline for your database design.

Data File: AYK33_Data.xlsx

FIGURE AYK.7

The Morrison Post Classified Section
New User Registration

In order to bid on existing "for-sale" items, or sell your own items, you need to register first. Once you have done that, you will have full access to the system.

E-Mail Address:
First Name:
Last Name:
Address:

City:
State:
Postal Code:
Country:
Password:
Verify Password:

Submit | Reset

GLOSSARY

802.11 A set of standards carrying out wireless local area network communication.

3G A service that brings wireless broadband to mobile phones.

A

acceptable use policy (AUP) A policy that a user must agree to follow to be provided access to corporate email, information systems, and the Internet.

accessibility Refers to the varying levels that define what a user can access, view, or perform when operating a system.

accounting and finance ERP component Manages accounting data and financial processes within the enterprise with functions such as general ledger, accounts payable, accounts receivable, budgeting, and asset management.

administrator access Unrestricted access to the entire system.

adware Software, while purporting to serve some useful function and often fulfilling that function, also allows Internet advertisers to display advertisements without the consent of the computer user.

agile methodology Aims for customer satisfaction through early and continuous delivery of useful software components developed by an iterative process using the bare minimum requirements.

agile MIS infrastructure Includes the hardware, software, and telecommunications equipment that, when combined, provides the underlying foundation to support the organization's goals.

analysis phase The firm analyzes its end-user business requirements and refines project goals into defined functions and operations of the intended system.

analytical CRM Supports back-office operations and strategic analysis and includes all systems that do not deal directly with the customers.

analytical information Encompasses all organizational information, and its primary purpose is to support the performing of managerial analysis or semistructured decisions.

anti-spam policy Simply states that email users will not send unsolicited emails (or spam).

antivirus software Scans and searches hard drives to prevent, detect, and remove known viruses, adware, and spyware.

application programming interface (API) A set of routines, protocols, and tools for building software applications.

application software Used for specific information processing needs, including payroll, customer relationship management, project management, training, and many others.

arithmetic-logic unit (ALU) Performs all arithmetic operations (for example, addition and subtraction) and all logic operations (such as sorting and comparing numbers).

artificial intelligence (AI) Simulates human thinking and behavior such as the ability to reason and learn.

as-is process model Represents the current state of the operation that has been mapped, without any specific improvements or changes to existing processes.

association detection Reveals the relationship between variables along with the nature and frequency of the relationships.

asynchronous communication Communication such as email in which the message and the response do not occur at the same time.

attribute The data elements associated with an entity.

authentication A method for confirming users' identities.

authorization The process of providing a user with permission including access levels and abilities such as file access, hours of access, and amount of allocated storage space.

automation Involves computerizing manual tasks making them more efficient and effective and dramatically lowering operational costs.

availability Refers to the time frames when the system is operational.

B

backup An exact copy of a system's information.

backward integration Takes information entered into a given system and sends it automatically to all upstream systems and processes.

balanced scorecard A management system, as well as a measurement system, that a firm uses to translate business strategies into executable tasks.

bandwidth The maximum amount of data that can pass from one point to another in a unit of time.

benchmark Baseline values the system seeks to attain.

benchmarking A process of continuously measuring system results, comparing those results to optimal system performance (benchmark values), and identifying steps and procedures to improve system performance.

biometrics The identification of a user based on a physical characteristic, such as a fingerprint, iris, face, voice, or handwriting.

bit The smallest element of data and has a value of either 0 or 1.

bit rate The number of bits transferred or received per unit of time.

black-hat hacker Breaks into other people's computer systems and may just look around or may steal and destroy information.

blog, or Web log An online journal that allows users to post their own comments, graphics, and video.

bluetooth Wireless PAN technology that transmits signals over short distances between cell phones, computers, and other devices.

bottleneck Occurs when resources reach full capacity and cannot handle any additional demands; they limit throughput and impede operations.

broadband A high-speed Internet connection that is always connected.

bullwhip effect Occurs when distorted product-demand information ripples from one partner to the next throughout the supply chain.

business continuity planning (BCP) Details how a company recovers and restores critical business operations and systems after a disaster or extended disruption.

business facing process Invisible to the external customer but essential to the effective management of the business; they include goal setting, day-to-day planning, giving performance feedback and rewards, and allocating resources.

business intelligence (BI) Information collected from multiple sources such as suppliers, customers, competitors, partners, and industries that analyze patterns, trends, and relationships for strategic decision making.

business model A plan that details how a company creates, delivers, and generates revenues.

business process Standardized set of activities that accomplish a specific task.

business process improvement Attempts to understand and measure the current process and make performance improvements accordingly.

business process management (BPM) system Focus on evaluating and improving processes that include both person-to-person work flow and system-to-system communications.

business process model A graphic description of a process, showing the sequence of process tasks, which is developed for a specific purpose and from a selected viewpoint.

business process modeling (or mapping) The activity of creating a detailed flowchart or process map of a work process that shows its inputs, tasks, and activities in a structured sequence.

business process reengineering (BPR) The analysis and redesign of workflow within and between enterprises.

business requirement The specific business requests the system must meet to be successful.

business rule A statement that defines an aspect of a business.

business strategy A leadership plan that achieves a specific set of goals or objectives.

business-critical integrity constraint Enforces business rules vital to an organization's success and often requires more insight and knowledge than relational integrity constraints.

business-to-business (B2B) Applies to businesses buying from and selling to each other over the Internet.

business-to-consumer (B2C) Applies to any business that sells its products or services directly to consumers online.

buyer power One of Porter's five forces; measures the ability of buyers to directly affect the price they are willing to pay for an item.

C

cache memory A small unit of ultra-fast memory that is used to store recently accessed or frequently accessed data so that the CPU does not have to retrieve this data from slower memory circuits such as RAM.

call scripting system Gathers product details and issue resolution information that can be automatically generated into a script for the representative to read to the customer.

campaign management system Guides users through marketing campaigns by performing such tasks as campaign definition, planning, scheduling, segmentation, and success analysis

capacity planning Determines future environmental infrastructure requirements to ensure high-quality system performance.

cardinality Expresses the specific number of instances in an entity.

central processing unit (CPU) The actual hardware that interprets and executes the program (software) instructions and coordinates how all the other hardware devices work together.

certificate authority A trusted third party, such as VeriSign, that validates user identities by means of digital certificates.

change control board (CCB) Responsible for approving or rejecting all change requests.

change management Offers procedures and policies managers can use to help manage change during system development.

change management system Includes a collection of procedures to document a change request and identifies the expected impact associated with the change.

chief information officer (CIO) Responsible for (1) overseeing all uses of MIS and (2) ensuring that MIS strategically aligns with business goals and objectives.

chief knowledge officer (CKO) Responsible for collecting, maintaining, and distributing company knowledge.

chief privacy officer (CPO) Responsible for ensuring the ethical and legal use of information within a company.

chief security officer (CSO) Responsible for ensuring the security of business systems and developing strategies and safeguards against attacks from hackers and viruses.

chief technology officer (CTO) Responsible for ensuring the speed, accuracy, availability, and reliability for MIS.

clickstream data Exact pattern of a consumer's navigation through a site.

click-to-talk Allows customers to click on a button and talk with a representative via the Internet.

client A computer designed to request information from a server.

client/server network A model for applications in which the bulk of the back-end processing, such as performing a physical search of a database, takes place on a server, while the front-end processing, which involves communicating with the users, is handled by the clients.

cloud computing Refers to the use of resources and applications hosted remotely on the Internet.

cluster analysis A technique used to divide information sets into mutually exclusive groups such that the members of each group are as close together as possible to one another and the different groups are as far apart as possible.

coaxial cable Cable that can carry a wide range of frequencies with low signal loss.

cold site A separate facility that does not have any computer equipment but is a place where employees can move after a disaster.

collaboration system A set of tools that supports the work of teams or groups by facilitating the sharing and flow of information.

collective intelligence Collaborating and tapping into the core knowledge of all employees, partners, and customers.

communication device Equipment used to send information and receive it from one location to another.

competitive advantage A feature of a product or service on which customers place a greater value than on similar offerings from competitors.

competitive intelligence The process of gathering information about the competitive environment, including competitors' plans, activities, and products, to improve a company's ability to succeed.

complex instruction set computer (CISC) chips Type of CPU that can recognize as many as 100 or more instructions, enough to carry out most computations directly.

composite entities Entities that exist to represent the relationship between two other entities.

computer An electronic device operating under the control of instructions stored in its own memory that can accept, manipulate, and store data.

confidentiality The assurance that messages and information remain available only to those authorized to view them.

consolidation The aggregation of data from simple roll-ups to complex groupings of interrelated information.

consumer-to-business (C2B) Applies to any consumer who sells a product or service to a business on the Internet.

consumer-to-consumer (C2C) Applies to customers offering goods and services to each other on the Internet.

contact center or call center Where customer service representatives answer customer inquiries and solve problems, usually by email, chat, or phone.

contact management CRM system Maintains customer contact information and identifies prospective customers for future sales, using tools such as organizational charts, detailed customer notes, and supplemental sales information.

content filtering Occurs when organizations use software that filters content, such as emails, to prevent the accidental or malicious transmission of unauthorized information.

content management system (CMS) Helps companies manage the creation, storage, editing, and publication of their website content.

control unit Interprets software instructions and literally tells the other hardware devices what to do, based on the software instructions.

copyright The legal protection afforded an expression of an idea, such as a song, book, or video game.

core ERP component The traditional components included in most ERP systems and primarily focus on internal operations.

corporate social responsibility Companies' acknowledged responsibility to society.

counterfeit software Software that is manufactured to look like the real thing and sold as such.

cracker A hacker with criminal intent.

critical path Estimates the shortest path through the project ensuring all critical tasks are completed from start to finish.

critical success factors (CSFs) Crucial steps companies perform to achieve their goals and objectives and implement their strategies.

CRM analysis technologies Help organizations segment their customers into categories such as best and worst customers.

CRM predicting technologies Help organizations predict customer behavior, such as which customers are at risk of leaving.

CRM reporting technologies Help organizations identify their customers across other applications.

cross-selling Selling additional products or services to an existing customer.

crowdsourcing Refers to the wisdom of the crowd.

cube The common term for the representation of multidimensional information.

customer facing process Results in a product or service that is received by an organization's external customer.

customer relationship management (CRM) A means of managing all aspects of a customer's relationship with an organization to increase customer loyalty and retention and an organization's profitability.

cybermediation Refers to the creation of new kinds of intermediaries that simply could not have existed before the advent of ebusiness.

cyberterrorists Seek to cause harm to people or to destroy critical systems or information and use the Internet as a weapon of mass destruction.

cycle time The time required to process an order.

D

data Raw facts that describe the characteristics of an event or object.

data center A facility used to house management information systems and associated components, such as telecommunications and storage systems.

data dictionary Compiles all of the metadata about the data elements in the data model.

data element (or data field) The smallest or basic unit of information.

data governance The overall management of the availability, usability, integrity, and security of company data.

data inconsistency Occurs when the same data element has different values.

data integrity issue Occurs when a system produces incorrect, inconsistent, or duplicate data.

data mart Contains a subset of data warehouse information.

data mining The process of analyzing data to extract information not offered by the raw data alone.

data-mining tool Uses a variety of techniques to find patterns and relationships in large volumes of information that predict future behavior and guide decision making.

data model Logical data structures that detail the relationships among data elements using graphics or pictures.

data quality audit Determines the accuracy and completeness of its data.

data redundancy The duplication of data, or the storage of the same data in multiple places.

data warehouse A logical collection of information, gathered from many different operational databases, that supports business analysis activities and decision-making tasks.

database Maintains information about various types of objects (inventory), events (transactions), people (employees), and places (warehouses).

database management system (DBMS) Creates, reads, updates, and deletes data in a database while controlling access and security.

data-driven website An interactive website kept constantly updated and relevant to the needs of its customers using a database.

decision support system (DSS) Model information using OLAP, which provides assistance in evaluating and choosing among different courses of action.

demand planning system Generates demand forecasts using statistical tools and forecasting techniques, so companies can respond faster and more effectively to consumer demands through supply chain enhancements.

dependency A logical relationship that exists between the project tasks, or between a project task and a milestone.

design phase Establishes descriptions of the desired features and operations of the system including screen layouts, business rules, process diagrams, pseudo code, and other documentation.

development phase Takes all the detailed design documents from the design phase and transforms them into the actual system.

digital certificate A data file that identifies individuals or organizations online and is comparable to a digital signature.

digital Darwinism Implies that organizations that cannot adapt to the new demands placed on them for surviving in the information age are doomed to extinction.

digital dashboard Tracks KPIs and CSFs by compiling information from multiple sources and tailoring it to meet user needs.

digital divide A worldwide gap giving advantage to those with access to technology.

digital subscriber line (DSL) Allows high-speed digital data transmission over standard telephone lines.

disaster recovery cost curve Charts (1) the cost to the company of the unavailability of information and technology and (2) the cost to the company of recovering from a disaster over time.

disaster recovery plan A detailed process for recovering information or a system in the event of a catastrophic disaster.

disintermediation Occurs when a business sells direct to the customer online and cuts out the intermediary.

disruptive technology A new way of doing things that initially does not meet the needs of existing customers.

domain name system (DNS) Converts IP address into domains, or identifying labels that use a variety of recognizable naming conventions.

downtime Refers to a period of time when a system is unavailable.

drill-down Enables users to view details, and details of details, of information.

dumpster diving Looking through people's trash, another way hackers obtain information.

dynamic scaling Means that the MIS infrastructure can be automatically scaled up or down based on needed requirements.

E

ebusiness Includes ecommerce along with all activities related to internal and external business operations such as servicing customer accounts, collaborating with partners, and exchanging real-time information.

ebusiness model A plan that details how a company creates, delivers, and generates revenues on the Internet.

ecommerce The buying and selling of goods and services over the Internet.

ediscovery (or electronic discovery) Refers to the ability of a company to identify, search, gather, seize, or export digital information in responding to a litigation, audit, investigation, or information inquiry.

effectiveness MIS metrics Measure the impact MIS has on business processes and activities including customer satisfaction and customer conversion rates.

efficiency MIS metrics Measure the performance of MIS itself such as throughput, transaction speed, and system availability.

egovernment Involves the use of strategies and technologies to transform government(s) by improving the delivery of services and enhancing the quality of interaction between the citizen-consumer within all branches of government.

electronic data interchange (EDI) A standard format for the electronic exchange of information between supply chain participants.

elogistics Manages the transportation and storage of goods.

email privacy policy Details the extent to which email messages may be read by others.

emergency notification service An infrastructure built for notifying people in the event of an emergency.

employee monitoring policy States explicitly how, when, and where the company monitors its employees.

employee relationship management (ERM) Provides Web-based self-service tools that streamline and automate the human resource department.

encryption Scrambles information into an alternative form that requires a key or password to decrypt.

enterprise application integration (EAI) Connects the plans, methods, and tools aimed at integrating separate enterprise systems.

enterprise application integration (EAI) middleware Takes a new approach to middleware by packaging commonly used applications together, reducing the time needed to integrate applications from multiple vendors.

enterprise architect A person grounded in technology, fluent in business, and able to provide the important bridge between MIS and the business.

enterprise resource planning (ERP) Integrates all departments and functions throughout an organization into a single IT system (or integrated set of IT systems) so employees can make decisions by viewing enterprisewide information about all business operations.

enterprise system Provides enterprisewide support and data access for a firm's operations and business processes.

entity Stores information about a person, place, thing, transaction, or event.

entity-relationship diagram (ERD) A technique for documenting the entities and relationships in a database environment.

entry barrier A feature of a product or service that customers have come to expect and entering competitors must offer the same for survival.

epolicies Policies and procedures that address information management along with the ethical use of computers and the Internet in the business environment.

eprocurement The business-to-business (B2B) online purchase and sale of supplies and services.

eshop (estore or etailer) An online version of a retail store where customers can shop at any hour.

ethernet A physical and data layer technology for LAN networking.

ethical computer use policy Contains general principles to guide computer user behavior.

ethics The principles and standards that guide our behavior toward other people.

ewaste Refers to discarded, obsolete, or broken electronic devices.

executive information system (EIS) A specialized DSS that supports senior-level executives and unstructured, long-term, nonroutine decisions requiring judgment, evaluation, and insight.

executive sponsor The person or group who provides the financial resources for the project.

expert system Computerized advisory programs that imitate the reasoning processes of experts in solving difficult problems.

explicit knowledge Consists of anything that can be documented, archived, and codified, often with the help of IT.

extended ERP component The extra components that meet organizational needs not covered by the core components and primarily focus on external operations.

extraction, transformation, and loading (ETL) A process that extracts information from internal and external databases, transforms it using a common set of enterprise definitions, and loads it into a data warehouse.

extranet An extension of an intranet that is only available to authorized outsiders, such as customers, partners, and suppliers.

extreme programming (XP) methodology Breaks a project into four phases, and developers cannot continue to the next phase until the previous phase is complete.

F

fact The confirmation or validation of an event or object.

failback Occurs when the primary machine recovers and resumes operations, taking over from the secondary server.

failover A specific type of fault tolerance, occurs when a redundant storage server offers an exact replica of the real-time data, and if the primary server crashes the users are automatically directed to the secondary server or backup server.

fault tolerance A general concept that a system has the ability to respond to unexpected failures or system crashes as the backup system immediately and automatically takes over with no loss of service.

feedback Information that returns to its original transmitter (input, transform, or output) and modifies the transmitter's actions.

fiber optic (or optical fiber) Refers to the technology associated with the transmission of information as light impulses along a glass wire or fiber.

field A characteristic of a table.

firewall Hardware and/or software that guard a private network by analyzing incoming and outgoing information for the correct markings.

first-mover advantage An advantage that occurs when a company can significantly increase its market share by being first to market with a competitive advantage.

flash memory A special type of rewritable read-only memory (ROM) that is compact and portable.

folksonomy Similar to taxonomy except that crowdsourcing determines the tags or keyword-based classification system.

forecasts Predictions based on time-series information.

foreign key A primary key of one table that appears as an attribute in another table and acts to provide a logical relationship between the two tables.

forward integration Takes information entered into a given system and sends it automatically to all downstream systems and processes.

fuzzy logic A mathematical method of handling imprecise or subjective information.

G

Gantt chart A simple bar chart that lists project tasks vertically against the project's time frame, listed horizontally.

genetic algorithm An artificial intelligence system that mimics the evolutionary, survival-of-the-fittest process to generate increasingly better solutions to a problem.

geographic information system (GIS) Consists of hardware, software, and data that provide location information for display on a multidimensional map.

gigabyte (GB) Roughly 1 billion bytes.

gigahertz (GHz) The number of billions of CPU cycles per second.

global positioning system (GPS) A satellite-based navigation system providing extremely accurate position, time, and speed information.

goal-seeking analysis Finds the inputs necessary to achieve a goal such as a desired level of output.

granularity Refers to the level of detail in the model or the decision-making process.

grid computing A collection of computers, often geographically dispersed, that are coordinated to solve a common problem.

H

hackers Experts in technology who use their knowledge to break into computers and computer networks, either for profit or motivated by the challenge.

hactivists Have philosophical and political reasons for breaking into systems and will often deface the website as a protest.

hard drive A secondary storage medium that uses several rigid disks coated with a magnetically sensitive material and housed together with the recording heads in a hermetically sealed mechanism.

hardware Consists of the physical devices associated with a computer system

high availability Occurs when a system is continuously operational at all times.

hot site A separate and fully equipped facility where the company can move immediately after a disaster and resume business.

human resources ERP component Tracks employee information including payroll, benefits, compensation, and performance assessment and ensures compliance with all laws.

hypertext markup language (HTML) Links documents allowing users to move from one to another simply by clicking on a hot spot or link.

hypertext transport protocol (HTTP) The Internet protocol Web browsers use to request and display Web pages using universal resource locators.

I

identity theft The forging of someone's identity for the purpose of fraud.

implementation phase The organization places the system into production so users can begin to perform actual business operations with it.

information Data converted into a meaningful and useful context.

information age The present time, during which infinite quantities of facts are widely available to anyone who can use a computer.

information architecture The set of ideas about how all information in a given context should be organized.

information cleansing or scrubbing A process that weeds out and fixes or discards inconsistent, incorrect, or incomplete information.

information compliance The act of conforming, acquiescing, or yielding information.

information ethics Govern the ethical and moral issues arising from the development and use of information technologies, as well as the creation, collection, duplication, distribution, and processing of information itself (with or without the aid of computer technologies).

information governance A method or system of government for information management or control.

information granularity The extent of detail within the information (fine and detailed or coarse and abstract).

information integrity A measure of the quality of information.

information management Examines the organizational resource of information and regulates its definitions, uses, value, and distribution ensuring it has the types of data/information required to function and grow effectively.

information MIS infrastructure Identifies where and how important information, such as customer records, is maintained and secured.

information privacy policy Contains general principles regarding information privacy.

information reach Measures the number of people a firm can communicate with all over the world.

information richness Refers to the depth and breadth of details contained in a piece of textual, graphic, audio, or video information.

information security A broad term encompassing the protection of information from accidental or intentional misuse by persons inside or outside an organization.

information security plan Details how an organization will implement the information security policies.

information security policies Identify the rules required to maintain information security, such as requiring users to logoff before leaving for lunch or meetings, never sharing passwords with anyone, and changing passwords every 30 days.

information technology monitoring Tracks people's activities by such measures as number of keystrokes, error rate, and number of transactions processed.

infrastructure as a service (IaaS) A service that delivers hardware networking capabilities, including the use of servers, networking, and storage over the cloud using a pay-per-use revenue model.

input device Equipment used to capture information and commands.

insiders Legitimate users who purposely or accidentally misuse their access to the environment and cause some kind of business-affecting incident.

in-sourcing (in-house development) Uses the professional expertise within an organization to develop and maintain its information technology systems.

instant messaging (sometimes called IM or IMing) A service that enables "instant" or real-time communication between people.

integration Allows separate systems to communicate directly with each other, eliminating the need for manual entry into multiple systems.

integrity constraint Rules that help ensure the quality of information.

intellectual property Intangible creative work that is embodied in physical form and includes copyrights, trademarks, and patents.

intelligent agent A special-purpose knowledge-based information system that accomplishes specific tasks on behalf of its users.

intelligent system Various commercial applications of artificial intelligence.

interactivity Measures advertising effectiveness by counting visitor interactions with the target ad, including time spent viewing the ad, number of pages viewed, and number of repeat visits to the advertisement.

intermediaries Agents, software, or businesses that provide a trading infrastructure to bring buyers and sellers together.

Internet A massive network that connects computers all over the world and allows them to communicate with one another.

Internet cable connection Provides Internet access using a cable television company's infrastructure and a special cable modem.

Internet protocol TV (IPTV) Distributes digital video content using IP across the Internet and private IP networks.

Internet protocol version 6 (IPv6) The "next generation" protocol designed to replace the current version Internet protocol, IP version 4 (IPv4)

Internet service provider (ISP) A company that provides access to the Internet for a monthly fee.

Internet use policy Contains general principles to guide the proper use of the Internet.

interoperability The capability of two or more computer systems to share data and resources, even though they are made by different manufacturers.

intranet A restricted network that relies on Internet technologies to provide an Internet-like environment within the company for information sharing, communications, collaboration, Web publishing, and the support of business process.

intrusion detection software (IDS) Features full-time monitoring tools that search for patterns in network traffic to identify intruders.

iterative development Consists of a series of tiny projects.

K

key performance indicators (KPIs) Quantifiable metrics a company uses to evaluate progress towards critical success factors.

kill switch A trigger that enables a project manager to close the project before completion.

knowledge Skills, experience, and expertise coupled with information and intelligence that creates a person's intellectual resources.

knowledge management (KM) Involves capturing, classifying, evaluating, retrieving, and sharing information assets in a way that provides context for effective decisions and actions.

knowledge management system (KMS) Supports the capturing, organization, and dissemination of knowledge (i.e., know-how) throughout an organization.

knowledge worker Individuals valued for their ability to interpret and analyze information.

L

legacy system A current or existing system that will become the base for upgrading or integrating with a new system.

list generator Compiles customer information from a variety of sources and segments it for different marketing campaigns.

local area network (LAN) Connects a group of computers in proximity, such as in an office building, school, or home.

location-based services (LBS) Applications that use location information to provide a service.

logical view Shows how individual users logically access information to meet their own particular business needs.

long tail Referring to the tail of a typical sales curve.

loyalty program A program to reward customers based on spending.

M

magnetic medium A secondary storage medium that uses magnetic techniques to store and retrieve data on disks or tapes coated with magnetically sensitive materials.

magnetic tape An older secondary storage medium that uses a strip of thin plastic coated with a magnetically sensitive recording medium.

mail bomb Sends a massive amount of email to a specific person or system that can cause that user's server to stop functioning.

maintainability (or flexibility) Refers to how quickly a system can transform to support environmental changes.

maintenance phase The organization performs changes, corrections, additions, and upgrades to ensure the system continues to meet its business goals.

management information systems A business function, like accounting and human resources, which moves information about people, products, and processes across the company to facilitate decision making and problem solving.

many-to-many relationship (M:N) Between two entities in which an instance of one entity is related to many instances of another and one instance of the other can be related to many instances of the first entity.

market basket analysis Analyzes such items as websites and checkout scanner information to detect customers' buying behavior and predict future behavior by identifying affinities among customers' choices of products and services.

market share The proportion of the market that a firm captures.

mashup A website or Web application that uses content from more than one source to create a completely new product or service.

mashup editor WYSIWYGs or What You See Is What You Get tools.

mass customization The ability of an organization to tailor its products or services to the customers' specifications.

megabyte (MB or M or Meg) Roughly 1 million bytes.

megahertz (MHz) The number of millions of CPU cycles per second.

memory cards Contain high-capacity storage that holds data such as captured images, music, or text files.

memory sticks Provide nonvolatile memory for a range of portable devices including computers, digital cameras, MP3 players, and PDAs.

metadata Details about data.

Metcalfe's Law The value of a network increases as its number of users grows.

methodology A set of policies, procedures, standards, processes, practices, tools, techniques, and tasks that people apply to technical and management challenges.

metrics Measurements that evaluate results to determine wheather a project is meeting its goals.

metropolitan area network (MAN) A large computer network usually spanning a city.

microblogging The practice of sending brief posts (140 to 200 characters) to a personal blog, either publicly or to a private group of subscribers who can read the posts as IMs or as text messages.

middleware Several different types of software that sit between and provide connectivity for two or more software applications.

MIS infrastructure Includes the plans for how a firm will build, deploy, use, and share its data, processes, and MIS assets.

mobile business (or mbusiness, mcommerce) The ability to purchase goods and services through a wireless Internet-enabled device.

model A simplified representation or abstraction of reality.

modem A device that enables a computer to transmit and receive data.

Moore's Law Refers to the computer chip performance per dollar doubling every 18 months.

multitasking Allows more than one piece of software to be used at a time.

multi-valued attribute Having the potential to contain more than one value for an attribute.

N

national service providers (NSPs) Private companies that own and maintain the worldwide backbone that supports the Internet.

nearshore outsourcing Contracting an outsourcing arrangement with a company in a nearby country.

network A communications system created by linking two or more devices and establishing a standard methodology in which they can communicate.

network access points (NAPs) Traffic exchange points in the routing hierarchy of the Internet that connects NSPs.

network convergence The efficient coexistence of telephone, video, and data communication within a single network, offering convenience and flexibility not possible with separate infrastructures.

network effect Describes how products in a network increase in value to users as the number of users increases.

network operating system (NOS) Operating system that runs a network, steering information between computers and managing security and users.

network topology Refers to the geometric arrangement of the actual physical organization of the computers (and other network devices) in a network.

network transmission media Refers to the various types of media used to carry the signal between computers.

neural network A category of AI that attempts to emulate the way the human brain works.

nonrepudiation A contractual stipulation to ensure that ebusiness participants do not deny (repudiate) their online actions.

null-valued attribute Assigned to an attribute when no other value applies or when a value is unknown.

O

offshore outsourcing Using organizations from developing countries to write code and develop systems.

one-to-many relationship (1:M) A relationship between two entities in which an instance of one entity can be related to many instances of a related entity.

one-to-one relationship (1:1) A relationship between two entities in which an instance of one entity can be related to only one instance of a related entity.

online analytical processing (OLAP) The manipulation of information to create business intelligence in support of strategic decision making.

online transaction processing (OLTP) The capturing of transaction and event information using technology to (1) process the information according to defined business rules, (2) store the information, and (3) update existing information to reflect the new information.

onshore outsourcing Engaging another company within the same country for services.

open source Refers to any software whose source code is made available free for any third party to review and modify.

open system Consists of non-proprietary hardware and software based on publicly known standards that allows third parties to create add-on products to plug into or interoperate with the system.

operating system software Controls the application software and manages how the hardware devices work together.

operational CRM Supports traditional transactional processing for day-to-day front-office operations or systems that deal directly with the customers.

opportunity management CRM system Targets sales opportunities by finding new customers or companies for future sales.

optimization analysis An extension of goal-seeking analysis, finds the optimum value for a target variable by repeatedly changing other variables, subject to specified constraints.

output device Equipment used to see, hear, or otherwise accept the results of information processing requests

outsourcing An arrangement by which one organization provides a service or services for another organization that chooses not to perform them in-house.

P

packet-switching Occurs when the sending computer divides a message into a number of efficiently sized units of data called packets, each of which contains the address of the destination computer.

paradigm shift Occurs when a new radical form of business enters the market that reshapes the way companies and organizations behave.

partner relationship management (PRM) Discovers optimal sales channels by selecting the right partners and identifying mutual customers.

peer-to-peer (P2P) A computer network that relies on the computing power and bandwidth of the participants in the network rather than a centralized server.

performance Measures how quickly a system performs a process or transaction.

personal area networks (PAN) Provide communication over a short distance that is intended for use with devices that are owned and operated by a single user.

personalization Occurs when a company knows enough about a customer's likes and dislikes that it can fashion offers more likely to appeal to that person, say by tailoring its website to individuals or groups based on profile information, demographics, or prior transactions.

PERT (Program Evaluation and Review Technique) chart A graphical network model that depicts a project's tasks and the relationships between them.

pharming Reroutes requests for legitimate websites to false websites.

phishing A technique to gain personal information for the purpose of identity theft, usually by means of fraudulent emails that look as though they came from legitimate sources.

physical view The physical storage of information on a storage device.

pirated software The unauthorized use, duplication, distribution, or sale of copyrighted software.

planning phase Establishes a high-level plan of the intended project and determines project goals.

platform as a service (PaaS) Supports the deployment of entire systems including hardware, networking, and applications using a pay-per-use revenue model.

podcasting Converts an audio broadcast to a digital music player.

portability Refers to the ability of an application to operate on different devices or software platforms, such as different operating systems.

Porter's Five Forces Model A model for analyzing the competitive forces within the environment in which a company operates, to assess the potential for profitability in an industry.

primary key A field (or group of fields) that uniquely identifies a given record in a table.

primary storage Computer's main memory, which consists of the random access memory (RAM), cache memory, and read-only memory (ROM) that is directly accessible to the CPU.

primary value activities Found at the bottom of the value chain, these include business processes that acquire raw materials and manufacture, deliver, market, sell, and provide after-sales services.

privacy The right to be left alone when you want to be, to have control over your personal possessions, and not to be observed without your consent.

product differentiation An advantage that occurs when a company develops unique differences in its products with the intent to influence demand.

production and materials management ERP component Handles production planning and execution tasks such as demand forecasting, production scheduling, job cost accounting, and quality control.

project Temporary activity a company undertakes to create a unique product, service, or result.

project assumption Factors considered to be true, real, or certain without proof or demonstration.

project charter A document issued by the project initiator or sponsor that formally authorizes the start of a project and provides the project manager with the authority to apply organizational resources to project activities.

project constraint Specific factors that can limit options.

project deliverable Any measurable, tangible, verifiable outcome, result, or item that is produced to complete a project or part of a project.

project management The application of knowledge, skills, tools, and techniques to project activities to meet project requirements.

Project Management Institute (PMI) Develops procedures and concepts necessary to support the profession of project management.

project management office (PMO) An internal department that oversees all organizational projects.

project manager An individual who is an expert in project planning and management, defines and develops the project plan, and tracks the plan to ensure the project is completed on time and on budget.

project milestones Represent key dates when a certain group of activities must be performed.

project objective Quantifiable criteria that must be met for the project to be considered a success.

project plan A formal, approved document that manages and controls project execution.

project scope statement Links the project to the organization's overall business goals.

project stakeholder Individuals and organizations actively involved in the project or whose interests might be affected as a result of project execution or project completion.

protocol A standard that specifies the format of data as well as the rules to be followed during transmission.

prototype A smaller-scale representation or working model of the users' requirements or the proposed design for an information system.

public key encryption (PKE) Uses two keys: a public key that everyone can have and a private key for only the recipient.

Q

query-by-example (QBE) tool Helps users graphically design the answer to a question against a database.

R

radio-frequency identification (RFID) Uses electronic tags and labels to identify objects wirelessly over short distances.

random access memory (RAM) The computer's primary working memory, in which program instructions and data are stored so that they can be accessed directly by the CPU via the processor's high-speed external data bus.

rapid application development (RAD) methodology (also called rapid prototyping) Emphasizes extensive user involvement in the rapid and evolutionary construction of working prototypes of a system, to accelerate the systems development process.

rational unified process (RUP) methodology Provides a framework for breaking down the development of software into four "gates."

read-only memory (ROM) The portion of a computer's primary storage that does not lose its contents when one switches off the power.

real simple syndication (RSS) A Web format used to publish frequently updated works, such as blogs, news headlines, audio, and video in a standardized format.

real-time communication Occurs when a system updates information at the same rate it receives it.

real-time information Immediate, up-to-date information.

real-time system Provides real-time information in response to requests.

record A collection of related data elements.

recovery The ability to get a system up and running in the event of a system crash or failure that includes restoring the information backup.

reduced instruction set computer (RISC) chips Limits the number of instructions the CPU can execute to increase processing speed.

redundancy Occurs when a task or activity is unnecessarily repeated.

regional service providers (RSPs) Offer Internet service by connecting to NSPs, but they also can connect directly to each other.

reintermediation Steps are added to the value chain as new players find ways to add value to the business process.

relational database management system Allows users to create, read, update, and delete data in a relational database.

relational database model Stores information in the form of logically related two-dimensional tables.

relational integrity constraint Rules that enforce basic and fundamental information-based constraints.

reliability (or accuracy) Ensures a system is functioning correctly and providing accurate information.

reputation system Where buyers post feedback on sellers.

return on investment (ROI) Indicates the earning power of a project.

rivalry among existing competitors One of Porter's five forces; high when competition is fierce in a market and low when competitors are more complacent.

router An intelligent connecting device that examines each packet of data it receives and then decides which way to send it toward its destination.

S

sales force automation (SFA) Automatically tracks all the steps in the sales process.

sales management CRM system Automates each phase of the sales process, helping individual sales representatives coordinate and organize all their accounts.

satellite A space station that orbits the Earth receiving and transmitting signals from Earth-based stations over a wide area.

scalability Describes how well a system can scale up or adapt to the increased demands of growth.

script kiddies or script bunnies Find hacking code on the Internet and click-and-point their way into systems to cause damage or spread viruses.

scrum methodology Uses small teams to produce small pieces of software using a series of "sprints," or 30-day intervals, to achieve an appointed goal.

secondary storage Consists of equipment designed to store large volumes of data for long-term storage.

secure hypertext transfer protocol (SHTTP or HTTPS) A combination of HTTP and SSL to provide encryption and secure identification of an Internet server.

secure sockets layer (SSL) A standard security technology for establishing an encrypted link between a Web server and a browser, ensuring that all data passed between them remains private.

semantic Web A component of Web 3.0 that describes things in a way that computers can understand.

semistructured decision Occurs in situations in which a few established processes help to evaluate potential solutions, but not enough to lead to a definite recommended decision.

sensitivity analysis A special case of what-if analysis, is the study of the impact on other variables when one variable is changed repeatedly.

server A computer dedicated to providing information in response to requests.

shopping bot Software that will search several retailer websites and provide a comparison of each retailer's offerings including price and availability.

single-valued attribute Having only a single value of each attribute of an entity.

slice-and-dice The ability to look at information from different perspectives.

smart card A device about the size of a credit card, containing embedded technologies that can store information and small amounts of software to perform some limited pro

smart grid Delivers electricity using two-way digital technology.

smart phones Offer more advanced computing ability and connectivity than basic cell phones.

social bookmarking Allows users to share, organize, search, and manage bookmarks.

social engineering Hackers use their social skills to trick people into revealing access credentials or other valuable information.

social media Refers to websites that rely on user participation and user-contributed content.

social media policy Outlines the corporate guidelines or principles governing employee online communications.

social network An application that connects people by matching profile information

social networking The practice of expanding your business and/or social contacts by constructing a personal network.

social networking analysis (SNA) Maps group contacts identifying who knows each other and who works together.

social tagging Describes the collaborative activity of marking shared online content with keywords or tags as a way to organize it for future navigation, filtering, or search.

software The set of instructions the hardware executes to carry out specific tasks.

software as a service (SaaS) Delivers applications over the cloud using a pay-per-use revenue model.

source code Contains instructions written by a programmer specifying the actions to be performed by computer software.

source document The original transaction record.

spam Unsolicited email.

spyware A special class of adware that collects data about the user and transmits it over the Internet without the user's knowledge or permission.

SSL Certificate An electronic document that confirms the identity of a website or server and verifies that a public key belongs to a trustworthy individual or company.

statistical analysis Performs such functions as information correlations, distributions, calculations, and variance analysis.

streaming A method of sending audio and video files over the Internet in such a way that the user can view the file while it is being transferred.

streamlining Improves business process efficiencies simplifying or eliminating unnecessary steps.

structured data Data already in a database or a spreadsheet.

structured decision Involves situations where established processes offer potential solutions.

structured query language (SQL) Users write lines of code to answer questions against a database.

supplier power One of Porter's five forces; measures the suppliers' ability to influence the prices they charge for supplies (including materials, labor, and services).

supplier relationship management (SRM) Focuses on keeping suppliers satisfied by evaluating and categorizing suppliers for different projects.

supply chain All parties involved, directly or indirectly, in obtaining raw materials or a product.

supply chain execution system Ensures supply chain cohesion by automating the different activities of the supply chain.

supply chain management (SCM) The management of information flows between and among activities in a supply chain to maximize total supply chain effectiveness and corporate profitability.

supply chain planning system Uses advanced mathematical algorithms to improve the flow and efficiency of the supply chain while reducing inventory.

supply chain visibility The ability to view all areas up and down the supply chain in real time.

support value activities Found along the top of the value chain and includes business processes, such as firm infrastructure, human resource management, technology development, and procurement, that support the primary value activities.

sustainable MIS disposal Refers to the safe disposal of MIS assets at the end of their life cycle.

sustainable MIS infrastructure Identifies ways that a company can grow in terms of computing resources while simultaneously becoming less dependent on hardware and energy consumption.

sustainable, or "green," MIS Describes the production, management, use, and disposal of technology in a way that minimizes damage to the environment.

sustaining technology Produces an improved product customers are eager to buy, such as a faster car or larger hard drive.

swim lane Layout arranges the steps of a business process into a set of rows depicting the various elements.

switching costs Costs that make customers reluctant to switch to another product or service.

synchronous communication Communications that occur at the same time such as IM or chat.

system A collection of parts that link to achieve a common purpose.

system software Controls how the various technology tools work together along with the application software.

systems development life cycle (SDLC) The overall process for developing information systems, from planning and analysis through implementation and maintenance.

systems thinking A way of monitoring the entire system by viewing multiple inputs being processed or transformed to produce outputs while continuously gathering feedback on each part.

T

T1 line A type of data connection able to transmit a digital signal at 1.544 Mpbs.

table Composed of rows and columns that represent an entity.

tacit knowledge The knowledge contained in people's heads.

tag Specific keywords or phrases incorporated into website content for means of classification or taxonomy.

taxonomy The scientific classification of organisms into groups based on similarities of structure or origin.

telecommunication system Enables the transmission of data over public or private networks.

terabyte (TB) Roughly 1 trillion bytes.

testing phase Brings all the project pieces together into a special testing environment to eliminate errors and bugs, and verify that the system meets all the business requirements defined in the analysis phase.

text mining Analyzes unstructured data to find trends and patterns in words and sentences.

threat of new entrants One of Porter's five forces, high when it is easy for new competitors to enter a market and low when there are significant entry barriers to joining a market.

threat of substitute products or services One of Porter's five forces, high when there are many alternatives to a product or service and low when there are few alternatives from which to choose.

time-series information Time-stamped information collected at a particular frequency.

to-be process model Shows the results of applying change improvement opportunities to the current (As-Is) process model.

tokens Small electronic devices that change user passwords automatically.

transaction processing system (TPS) The basic business system that serves the operational level (analysts) and assists in making structured decisions.

transactional information Encompasses all of the information contained within a single business process or unit of work, and its primary purpose is to support the performing of daily operational or structured decisions.

transmission control protocol/Internet protocol (TCP/IP) Provides the technical foundation for the public Internet as well as for large numbers of private networks.

twisted-pair cable Refers to a type of cable composed of four (or more) copper wires twisted around each other within a plastic sheath.

U

unavailable When a system is not operating or cannot be used.

unified communications (UC) The integration of communication channels into a single service.

universal resource locator (URL) The address of a file or resource on the Web such as www.apple.com.

unstructured data Data that do not exist in a fixed location and can include text documents, PDFs, voice messages, emails, etc.

unstructured decision Occurs in situations in which no procedures or rules exist to guide decision makers toward the correct choice.

up-selling Increasing the value of the sale.

usability The degree to which a system is easy to learn and efficient and satisfying to use.

user contributed content (also referred to as user generated content) Content created and updated by many users for many users.

utility computing Offers a pay-per-use revenue model similar to a metered service such as gas or electricity.

utility software Provides additional functionality to the operating system.

V

value chain analysis Views a firm as a series of business processes that each add value to the product or service.

variable A data characteristic that stands for a value that changes or varies over time.

virtual private network (VPN) Companies can establish direct private network links among themselves or create private, secure Internet access, in effect a "private tunnel" within the Internet.

virtual reality A computer-simulated environment that can be a simulation of the real world or an imaginary world.

virtualization Creates multiple "virtual" machines on a single computing device.

visualization Produces graphical displays of patterns and complex relationships in large amounts of data.

virus Software written with malicious intent to cause annoyance or damage.

voice over IP (VoIP) Uses IP technology to transmit telephone calls.

volatility Refers to RAM's complete loss of stored information if power is interrupted.

W

warm site A separate facility with computer equipment that requires installation and configuration.

waterfall methodology A sequence of phases in which the output of each phase becomes the input for the next.

Web 1.0 Refers to the World Wide Web during its first few years of operation between 1991 and 2003.

Web 2.0 The next generation of Internet use—a more mature, distinctive communications platform characterized by new qualities such as collaboration, sharing, and free.

Web browser Allow users to access the WWW.

Web conferencing Blends videoconferencing with document-sharing and allows the user to deliver a presentation over the Web to a group of geographically dispersed participants.

Web mining Analyzes unstructured data associated with websites to identify consumer behavior and website navigation.

Web-based self-service system Allows customers to use the Web to find answers to their questions or solutions to their problems.

website bookmark A locally stored URL or the address of a file or Internet page saved as a shortcut.

website personalization Occurs when a website has stored enough data about a person's likes and dislikes to fashion offers more likely to appeal to that person.

what-if analysis Checks the impact of a change in a variable or assumption on the model.

white-hat hackers Work at the request of the system owners to find system vulnerabilities and plug the holes.

wide area network (WAN) Spans a large geographic area such as a state, province, or country.

Wi-Fi protected access (WPA) A wireless security protocol to protect Wi-Fi networks.

wiki A type of collaborative Web page that allows users to add, remove, and change content, which can be easily organized and reorganized as required.

wire media Transmission material manufactured so that signals will be confined to a narrow path and will behave predictably.

wireless fidelity (Wi-Fi) A means by which portable devices can connect wirelessly to a local area network, using access points that send and receive data via radio waves.

wireless LAN (WLAN) A local area network that uses radio signals to transmit and receive data over distances of a few hundred feet.

wireless MAN (WMAN) A metropolitan area network that uses radio signals to transmit and receive data.

wireless media Natural parts of the Earth's environment that can be used as physical paths to carry electrical signals.

wireless WAN (WWAN) A wide area network that uses radio signals to transmit and receive data.

workflow Includes the tasks, activities, and responsibilities required to execute each step in a business process.

World Wide Web (WWW) Provides access to Internet information through documents including text, graphics, audio, and video files that use a special formatting language called HTML.

Worldwide Interoperability for Microwave Access (WiMAX) A communications technology aimed at providing high-speed wireless data over metropolitan area networks.

Chapter 1

1. Thomas L. Friedman, *The World is Flat,* New York: Farrar, Straus & Giroux, 2005 Thomas Friedman, "The World is Flat," www.thomaslfriedman.com, accessed June, 2010. Thomas L. Friedman, "The Opinion Pages," *The New York Times,* topics.nytimes.com/top/opinion/editorialsandoped/oped/columnists/thomaslfriedman, accessed June, 2010.
2. Interesting Facts, www.interestingfacts.org, accessed June 15, 2010.
3. Robert Lenzer, "Bernie Madoff's $50 Billion Ponzi Scheme," *Forbes,* December, 12, 2008 http://www.forbes.com/2008/12/12/madoff-ponzi-hedge-pf-ii-in_rl_1212croesus_inl.html.
4. Thompson, Clive; "Do You Speak Statistics?" *Wired,* pp 36; May 2010.
5. Blade Staff, "Identity theft risk: BGSU notifies past, current students about loss of personal information" *The Toledo Blade;* June 27, 2007 http://toledoblade.com/apps/pbcs.dll/article?AID=/20070627/NEWS08/70627020; accessed June 26, 2010.
6. Ina Fried, "Apple Earnings Top Estimates," *CNET News,* October 11, 2005, http://news.cnet.com/Apple-earnings-top-estimates/2100-1041_3-5893289.html?tag=lia;rcol accessed January 18, 2010.
7. Michael Arndt, Bruce Einhorn, "The 50 Most Innovative Companies," *Bloomberg Businessweek,* April 15, 2010 http://www.businessweek.com/magazine/content/10_17/b4175034779697.htm.
8. Jon Surmacz, "By the Numbers," *CIO Magazine,* October 2009.
9. Michael E. Porter, "The Five Competitive Forces that Shape Strategy," The Harvard Business Review Book Series, *Harvard Business Review,* January, 2008 Michael E. Porter, *Competitive Strategy: Techniques for Analyzing Industries and Competitors,* Harvard Business Review, January, 2002.

   Michael E. Porter, *On Competition,* The Harvard Business Review Book Series, 1985.

   Harvard Institute for Strategy and Competitiveness, http://www.isc.hbs.edu/, accessed June 10, 2010.
10. Thru 17 Ibid.
18. The Associated Press, "Postal Service Facing Losses of Historic Proportion," *USA Today,* March 25, 2009, http://www.usatoday.com/news/washington/2009-03-25-postal-woes_N.htm.
19. Michael E. Porter, "The Five Competitive Forces that Shape Strategy," The Harvard Business Review Book Series, *Harvard Business Review,* January, 2008 Michael E. Porter, *Competitive Strategy: Techniques for Analyzing Industries and Competitors,* Harvard Business Review, January, 2002.

    Michael E. Porter, *On Competition,* The Harvard Business Review Book Series, 1985.

    Harvard Institute for Strategy and Competitiveness, http://www.isc.hbs.edu/, accessed June 10, 2010.
20. Yukari Iwatani Kane, "First-Day Sales of Apple's iPad Fall Short of Sky-High Hopes."," The Wall Street Journal, April 6, 2010 http://online.wsj.com/article/SB10001424052702304017404575165621713345324.html.
21. Michael E. Porter, "The Five Competitive Forces that Shape Strategy," The Harvard Business Review Book Series, *Harvard Business Review,* January, 2008 Michael E. Porter, *Competitive Strategy: Techniques for Analyzing Industries and Competitors,* Harvard Business Review, January, 2002.

    Michael E. Porter, *On Competition,* The Harvard Business Review Book Series, 1985.

    Harvard Institute for Strategy and Competitiveness, http://www.isc.hbs.edu/, accessed June 10, 2010.
22. Ibid.
23. Joel Holland, "What's Your Problem?," *Entrepreneur,* May 2010, http://www.entrepreneur.com/magazine/entrepreneur/2010/may/206150.html.
24. "Apple Profit Surges 95 Percent on iPod Sales," Yahoo! News, http://news.yahoo.com/s/afp/20060118/bs_afp/uscompanyearningsit_060118225009, accessed January 18, 2005; "Apple's IPod Success Isn't Sweet Music for Record Company Sales," Bloomberg.com, http://quote.bloomberg.com/apps/news?pid=nifea&&sid=aHP5Ko1 pozM0, accessed November 2, 2005; Peter Burrows, "How Apple Could Mess Up Again," Businessweek online, http://yahoo.businessweek.com/technology/content/jan2006/tc20060109_432937.htm, accessed January 9, 2006; www.apple.com/iphone, accessed June 7, 2007; news.com.com/NikeiPod+raises+RFID+privacy+concerns/2100-1029_3-6143606.html, accessed June 7, 2007.
25. *Reprinted with special permission from MLB's Real Competitive Advantage, by Jay Yarow, Bloomberg BusinessWeek, August 2008.*
26. Thomas L. Friedman, "Hot, Flat, and Crowded: Why We Need a Green Revolution—and How It Can Renew America," Farrar, Straus, Giroux, New York, New York, 2008.
27. Salary Survey 2009 Special Report Staff and Entry Level Salary Comparision, *ComputerWorld Magazine,* http://www.computerworld.com/s/salary-survey/breakdown/2009/job_level/3; accessed 6/27/2010.
28. Ina Fried, "Adobe to Buy Omniture for $1.8 Billion, *CNET News,* September 15, 2009 http://news.cnet.com/8301-13860_3-10353733-56.html.
29. Seidell, Streeter, "10 Best Things We'll Say to Our Grandkids," *Wired Magazine,* September, 21, 2009, www.wired.com/culture/culturereviews/magazine/17-10/st_best#ixzz0s65fFq1t.
30. Thomas L. Friedman, *The World is Flat,* New York: Farrar, Straus & Giroux, 2005 Thomas Friedman, "The World is Flat," www.thomaslfriedman.com, accessed June, 2010. Thomas L. Friedman, "The Opinion Pages," *The New York Times,* topics.nytimes.com/top/opinion/editorialsandoped/oped/columnists/thomaslfriedman, accessed June, 2010.
31. JR Raphel, "The 15 Biggest Wiki Blunders," *PC World,* August 26, 2009, http://www.pcworld.com/article/170874/the_15_biggest_wikipedia_blunders.html.
32. Peter S. Green, "Merrill's Thain Said to Pay $1.2 Million to Decorator," *Bloomberg Businessweek,* http://www.bloomberg.com/apps/news?sid=aFcrG8er4FRw&pid=newsarchive January 23, 2009, accessed April 17 2010.

33. TED: Ideas Worth Spreading, http://www.ted.com/pages/view/id/5 accessed June 21, 2010.

Chapter 2

1. Stephen Baker, "What Data Crunchers Did for Obama," *Bloomberg Businessweek,* January 23, 2009, http://www.businessweek.com/technology/content/jan2009/tc20090123_026100.htm?chan=top+news_top+news+index+-+temp_top+story.
2. Tom Davenport, "Tom Davenport: Back to Decision-Making Basics," *Bloomberg Businessweek,* March 11, 2008 http://www.businessweek.com/managing/content/mar2008/ca20080311_211319.htm.
3. Jeff Voth, "Texting and other Bad Driving Decisions," http://ca.autos.yahoo.com/p/1960/texting-and-other-bad-driving-decisions.

   "Breastfeeding While Driving," *The New York Times,* March 2, 2009, http://parenting.blogs.nytimes.com/2009/03/02/breastfeeding-while-driving/.
4. Ken Blanchard, "Effectiveness vs. Efficiency," Wachovia Small Business, www.wachovia.com, accessed October 14, 2009.
5. Rich Jaroslovsky, "Your Own Private Help Desk," *Bloomberg Businessweek,* March 11, 2010.
6. "What is Systems Thinking," SearchCIO.com, http://searchcio.techtarget.com/definition/systems-thinking accessed March 13, 2010.
7. "French trader in scandal ordered behind bars," MSNBC, February 8, 2008 http://www.msnbc.msn.com/id/23065812/.
8. Leigh Buchanan, "Letting Employees Battle it Out," Inc. October 1, 2009 http://www.inc.com/magazine/20091001/letting-employees-battle-it-out.html.
9. "Put Better, Faster Decision-Making in Your Sights," www.teradata.com; "Neural Network Examples and Definitions," ece-www.colorado.edu/~ecen4831/lectures/NNdemo.html, accessed June 24, 2007.
10. Begley, "Software au Natural" McManus, "Robots at Your Service" Santa Fe Institute, www.dis.anl.gov/abms/, accessed June 24, 2007; Michael A. Arbib, (ed. 1995). *The Handbook of Brain Theory and Neural Networks L. Biacino and G. Gerla, "Fuzzy logic, continuity and effectiveness," Archive for Mathematical Logic.*
11. Rachel King, "Soon that Nearby Worker might be a Robot," *Bloomberg Businessweek,* June 1, 2010 http://www.businessweek.com/technology/content/jun2010/tc2010061_798891.htm.
12. Business Process Reengineering Six Sigma, www.isixsigma.com/me/bpr/, accessed May 10, 2010.
13. Michael Hammer, *Beyond Reengineering: How the Process-Centered Organization Is Changing Our Work and Our Lives* (New York: HarperCollins Publishers, 1996).

    Richard Chang, "Process Reengineering in Action: A Practical Guide to Achieving Breakthrough Results (Quality Improvement Series)," 1996.
14. Michael Hammer, *Beyond Reengineering: How the Process-Centered Organization Is Changing Our Work and Our Lives* (New York: HarperCollins Publishers, 1996).

    Richard Chang, "Process Reengineering in Action: A Practical Guide to Achieving Breakthrough Results (Quality Improvement Series)," 1996.
15. Michael Hammer, *Beyond Reengineering: How the Process-Centered Organization Is Changing Our Work and Our Lives* (New York: HarperCollins Publishers, 1996).

    Richard Chang, "Process Reengineering in Action: A Practical Guide to Achieving Breakthrough Results (Quality Improvement Series)," 1996.
16. Business Process Reengineering Six Sigma, www.isixsigma.com/me/bpr/, accessed May 10, 2010.

    SmartDraw.com, www.smartdraw.com/, accessed May 11, 2010.
17. H. James Harrington, *Business Process Improvement Workbook: Documentation, Analysis, Design, and Management of Business Process Improvement* (New York: McGraw-Hill, 1997).

    Hammer, *Beyond Reengineering;* Michael Hammer and James, Champy, "Reengineering the Corporation: A Manifest for Business Revolution," 1993.
18. H. James Harrington, *Business Process Improvement Workbook: Documentation, Analysis, Design, and Management of Business Process Improvement* (New York: McGraw-Hill, 1997).

    Hammer, *Beyond Reengineering;* Michael Hammer and James, Champy, "Reengineering the Corporation: A Manifest for Business Revolution," 1993.
19. Stever Robbins, "Tips for Mastering E-mail Overload," Harvard Business School, October 25, 2009 http://hbswk.hbs.edu/archive/4438.html.
20. H. James Harrington, *Business Process Improvement Workbook: Documentation, Analysis, Design, and Management of Business Process Improvement* (New York: McGraw-Hill, 1997).

    Hammer, *Beyond Reengineering;* Michael Hammer and James, Champy, "Reengineering the Corporation: A Manifest for Business Revolution," 1993.
21. H. James Harrington, *Business Process Improvement Workbook: Documentation, Analysis, Design, and Management of Business Process Improvement* (New York: McGraw-Hill, 1997).

    Hammer, *Beyond Reengineering;* Michael Hammer and James, Champy, "Reengineering the Corporation: A Manifest for Business Revolution," 1993.
22. Phil Mansfield, "Bronx graduate Trina Thompson sues Monroe College for $70,000 over unemployment," *NY Daily News,* August 3, 2009 http://www.nydailynews.com/ny_local/2009/08/03/2009-08-03_student_.html#ixzz1174LU5KS.
23. "Darpa Grand Challenge," www.darpa.mil/grandchallenge/, accessed September 1, 2005.
24. Secondlife.com, accessed May 28, 2007; "Linden Lab to Open Source Second Life Software, Linden Lab (January 8, 2007)," secondlife.com/community/land-islands.php, accessed May 22, 2010; Irene Sege, "Leading a Double Life," *The Boston Globe,* October 25, 200, accessed June 22, 2010; and James Harkin, "Get a (Second) Life," *Financial Times,* November, 17 2006, accessed June 15, 2010.

Chapter 3

1. Douglas MacMillan "Social Media: The Ashton Kutcher Effect," BloombergBusinessweek, May 3, 2009, http://www.businessweek.com/technology/content/may2009/tc2009053_934757.htm.
2. Adam Lashinsky, "Kodak's Developing Situation," *Fortune,* January 20, 2003, p. 176.
3. Clayton Christensen, *The Innovator's Dilemma* (Boston: Harvard Business School, 1997).
4. Clayton Christensen, *The Innovator's Dilemma* (Boston: Harvard Business School, 1997).
5. Clayton Christensen, *The Innovator's Dilemma* (Boston: Harvard Business School, 1997).

6. Internet World Statistics, www.internetworldstats.com, January 2010.
7. info.cern.ch, accessed March 1, 2005.
8. Brier Dudley "Changes in Technology Almost Too Fast To Follow," *The Seattle Times,* October 13, 2005.
9. Max Chafkin, "Good Domain Names Grow Scarce," *Inc.* July 1, 2009 http://www.inc.com/magazine/20090701/good-domain-names-grow-scarce.html.
10. Chris Anderson, Editor-in-Chief of *Wired* Magazine, The Long Tail: Why The Future of Business is Selling Less of More, http://www.longtail.com/ 2006.
11. Disintermediation, TechTarget, http://whatis.techtarget.com/definition/0,,sid9_gci211962,00.html accessed April 4, 2010.
12. Reintermediation, www.pcmag.com, http://www.pcmag.com/encyclopedia_term/0,2542,t=reintermediation&i=50364,00.asp accessed April 4, 2010.
13. Scott McCartney, "You Paid What for That Flight?," *The Wall Street Journal,* August 26, http://online.wsj.com/article/SB10001424052748704540904575451653489562606.html 2010.
14. "The Complete Web 2.0 Directory," www.go2web20.net/, accessed June 24, 2007, and "Web 2.0 for CIOs," www.cio.com/article/16807. www.emarketer.com, accessed January 2006.
15. "The Complete Web 2.0 Directory," www.go2web20.net/, accessed June 24, 2007, and "Web 2.0 for CIOs," www.cio.com/article/16807. www.emarketer.com, accessed January 2006.
16. Tim O'Reilly, "What Is Web 2.0: Design Patterns and Business Models for the Next Generation of Software," www.oreillynet.com/pub/a/oreilly/tim/news/2005/09/30/what-is-web-20.html, accessed June 25, 2007; and "Web 2.0 for CIOs," www.cio.com/article/16807, *CIO Magazine,* accessed June 24, 2007.
17. Tim O'Reilly, "What Is Web 2.0: Design Patterns and Business Models for the Next Generation of Software," www.oreillynet.com/pub/a/oreilly/tim/news/2005/09/30/what-is-web-20.html, accessed June 25, 2007; and "Web 2.0 for CIOs," www.cio.com/article/16807, *CIO Magazine,* accessed June 24, 2007.
18. Tim O'Reilly, "What Is Web 2.0: Design Patterns and Business Models for the Next Generation of Software," www.oreillynet.com/pub/a/oreilly/tim/news/2005/09/30/what-is-web-20.html, accessed June 25, 2007; and "Web 2.0 for CIOs," www.cio.com/article/16807, *CIO Magazine,* accessed June 24, 2007.
19. Joel Holland, "Risk It When You Are Young," *Entrepreneur Magazine,* July, 2010 http://www.entrepreneur.com/magazine/entrepreneur/2010/july/207174.html.
20. Tim O'Reilly, "What Is Web 2.0: Design Patterns and Business Models for the Next Generation of Software," www.oreillynet.com/pub/a/oreilly/tim/news/2005/09/30/what-is-web-20.html, accessed June 25, 2007; and "Web 2.0 for CIOs," www.cio.com/article/16807, *CIO Magazine,* accessed June 24, 2007.
21. "Kiva – Loans that Change Lives," www.kiva.org, accessed April 10, 2010.
22. Tim O'Reilly, "What Is Web 2.0: Design Patterns and Business Models for the Next Generation of Software," www.oreillynet.com/pub/a/oreilly/tim/news/2005/09/30/what-is-web-20.html, accessed June 25, 2007; and "Web 2.0 for CIOs," www.cio.com/article/16807, *CIO Magazine,* accessed June 24, 2007.
23. Tony Bradley, "Firefox 3.6 Becomes Number Two Browser as IE6 Declines," www.pcworld.com, September 1, 2010 http://www.pcworld.com/businesscenter/article/204698/firefox_36_becomes_number_two_browser_as_ie6_declines.html.
24. Tim O'Reilly, "What Is Web 2.0: Design Patterns and Business Models for the Next Generation of Software," www.oreillynet.com/pub/a/oreilly/tim/news/2005/09/30/what-is-web-20.html, accessed June 25, 2007; and "Web 2.0 for CIOs," www.cio.com/article/16807, *CIO Magazine,* accessed June 24, 2007.
25. Google Images, http://www.google.com/images?hl=en&q=social+network+image&wrapid=tlif12858857906612&um=1&ie=UTF-8&source=univ&ei=Yg-lTJyNJYn6sAP0l9H-Dg&sa=X&oi=image_result_group&ct=title&resnum=1&ved=0CCIQsAQwAA&biw=1362&bih=530.
26. About Us, "LinkedIn," http://press.linkedin.com/, accessed April 3, 2010.
27. Daniel Pink, "Folksonomy," *The New York Times,* December 11, 2005 http://www.nytimes.com/2005/12/11/magazine/11ideas1-21.html.
28. Daniel Nations, "What is Social Bookmarking," About.com: Web Trends, http://webtrends.about.com/od/socialbookmarking101/p/aboutsocialtags.htm, accessed April 5, 2010.
29. Gary Matuszak, "Enterprise 2.0: Fad or Future," KPMG International, www.kpmg.com/Global/en/.../Enterprise.../Enterprise-2-Fad-or-Future.pdf accessed April 10, 2010.
30. Rachel Metz, "Changing at the Push of a Button," *Wired,* September 27, 2004.
31. Wikipedia Statistics, http://en.wikipedia.org/wiki/Statistics Accessed April 15, 2010.
32. Wikipedia: The Free Encyclopedia, http://en.wikipedia.org/wiki/Wikipedia:About accessed April 15, 2010.
33. "Banana Code Connects Consumers and Farm," DoleOrganic.com, http://www.dole.com/NutritionInstituteLanding/NI_Articles/NI_DoleDiet/NI_DoleDiet_Detail/tabid/1058/Default.aspx?contentid=6328, accessed April 19, 2010.
34. Caroline McCarthy, "Bloomberg Mistakenly Publishes Steve Jobs Obituary," *CNET News,* August 28, 2008 http://news.cnet.com/8301-13579_3-10027886-37.html Accessed April 19, 2010.
35. John Seigenthaler, "A False Wikipedia Biography," USA Today, November 29, 2005 http://www.usatoday.com/news/opinion/editorials/2005-11-29-wikipedia-edit_x.htm.
36. Tim Berners-Lee, "Semantic Web Road map," October 14, 1998, http://www.w3.org/DesignIssues/Semantic.html Accessed April 12, 2010.
37. *Reprinted with special permission from BBC Taps Web 3.0 for New Music Site, by Tim Ferguson, Bloomberg BusinessWeek, April 7, 2009.*
38. Beth Bacheldor, "From Scratch: Amazon Keeps Moving," *Information Week,* March 5, 2004; Gary Wolf, "The Great Library of Amazonia," *Wired,* October 23, 2003; "Amazon Company Information," *Forbes,* www.forbes.com, September 2005; and Rob Hof, "Amazon's Newest Product: Storage," *BusinessWeek,* March 13, 2006.
39. Eric Goldman, "Technology & Marketing Law Blog," December 5, 2005, http://blog.ericgoldman.org/archives/2005/12/wikipedia_will.htm accessed April 15, 2010.
40. Kit Eaton, "Is Facebook Becoming the Whole World's Social Network?," Fast Company, April 7, 2010, http://www.fastcompany.com/1609312/facebook-global-expansion-social-networking-privacy-world-phone-book-users.
41. Jenna Ross, "Toughest college test: No cell phone, No Facebook," *Star Tribune,* March 13, 2010, http://www.startribune.com/entertainment/tv/87598062.html.

42. Larry Greenemeier, "Sun's Diffie: Second Life To Become Prime Source Of Intelligence," *InformationWeek,* May 17, 2007 http://www.informationweek.com/news/internet/showArticle.jhtml?articleID=199601513.
43. Neil Vidyarthi, "City Council Member Booted For Playing Farmville," *Social Times,* March 30, 2010 http://www.socialtimes.com/2010/03/fired-playing-farmville/.
44. Alissa Walker, "Theme Announced for 48 Hour Magazine, Over 6,000 Contributors Have Two Days to "Hustle" ," *Fast Company,* May 7, 2010, http://www.fastcompany.com/1640042/theme-is-announced-for-48-hour-magazine?partner=rss.
45. Brian Eisenberg, "What is Bubblegum Marketing?," *Beneath The Cover,* May 15, 2007, http://www.beneaththecover.com/2007/05/15/what-is-bubblegum-marketing/.
46. Gita Chandra, "14th Annual Webby Awards," http://www.webbyawards.com/press/press-release.php?id=189 accessed July 15, 2007.

Chapter 4

1. *Reprinted with special permission from The New E-spionage Threat, by Brian Gow, Keith Epstein and Chi-Chu Tschang, Bloomberg BusinessWeek, April 10, 2008.*
2. Michael Schrage, "Build the Business Case," *CIO Magazine,* http://www.cio.com/article/31780/Build_the_Business_Case_Extracting_Value_from_the_Customer, March 15, 2003, accessed April 17, 2010.
3. Scott Berinato, "The CIO Code of Ethical Data Management," *CIO Magazine,* www.cio.com, July 1, 2002, accessed April 17, 2010.
4. Peter S. Green, "Take the Data Pledge," *Bloomberg Businessweek,* April 23, 2009, accessed May 27 2010.
5. Richard Mason, "Four Ethical Issues of the Information Age," *Management Information Systems Quarterly,* Volume 10, Number 1, March, 1986 http://www.misq.org/archivist/vol/no10/issue1/vol10no1mason.html, accessed April 15, 2010.
6. Mike Brunker, "Online Poker Cheating Blamed on Employee," MSNBC.com, http://www.msnbc.msn.com/id/21381022/, October 19, 2007, accessed April 15, 2010.
7. Brian Womack, "Google Ends Self-Censorship, Defies China Government (Update4)," *Bloomberg Businessweek,* March 23, 2010, *http://www.bloomberg.com/apps/news?pid=newsarchive&sid=aaE9Owm3d5Bg.*
8. Raymund Flandez "Domino's Response Offers Lessons in Crisis Management," *The Wall Street Journal,* April 20, 2009 *http://blogs.wsj.com/independentstreet/2009/04/20/dominos-response-offers-lessons-in-crisis-management/.*
9. "CBC Tells Journalists How to Behave on Facebook," *ReportR.net,* August 3, 2007, http://www.reportr.net/2007/08/03/cbc-tells-journalists-how-to-behave-on-facebook/.
10. Andy McCue, "Bank Boss Quits after Porn Found on PC," www.businessweek.com, accessed June 2004.
11. Daniel Schorn "Whose Life is it Anyway?," CBS News – 60 Minutes, July 16, 2006 http://www.cbsnews.com/stories/2005/10/28/60minutes/main990617.shtml.
12. "Planned and Unplanned Downtime," SAP, http://help.sap.com/saphelp_nw72/helpdata/en/45/17396792ef5d79e10000000a11466f/content.htm.
13. AMA Research, "Workplace Monitoring and Surveillance," www.amanet.org, accessed March 1, 2004.
"2005 CSI/FBI Computer Crime and Security Survey," www.gocsi.com, accessed February 20, 2006.
14. Thomas Claburn, "Web 2.0. Internet Too Dangerous for Normal People," *InformationWeek,* April 1, 2009 http://www.informationweek.com/news/internet/web2.0/showArticle.jhtml?articleID=216402352&queryText=web%202.0%20security%20concerns.
15. Paige Baltzan, email received Friday, May 21, 2010.
16. Newcastle University, "Improving Password Protection With Easy To Remember Drawings." ScienceDaily. November 1, 2007, accessed April 15, 2010, from http://www.sciencedaily.com-/releases/2007/10/071030091438.htm.
17. Kim Zetter, "Lifelock's CEO Identity Stolen 13 Times," *Wired,* May 28, 2010, http://www.wired.com/threatlevel/2010/05/lifelock-identity-theft.
18. Barclays, "Online Fraud," www.barclays.com, http://www.barclays.co.uk/Helpsupport/Onlinefraud/P1242560035928.
www.norcrossgroup.com/casestudies.html , accessed October 2004.
19. Brian Grow, "Hacker Hunters," *BusinessWeek,* May 30, 2005. http://www.businessweek.com/magazine/content/05_22/b3935001_mz001.htm.
20. David Kravets, "Former Teen Cheerleader Dinged $27,750 for File Sharing 37 Songs," *Wired,* February 26, 2010, http://www.wired.com/threatlevel/2010/02/former-teen-cheerleader-dinged-27750-for-infringing-37-songs/.
21. Armen Keteyian "Digital Photocopier Loaded with Secrets," *CBSnews.com,* April 15, 2010 http://www.cbsnews.com/stories/2010/04/19/eveningnews/main6412439.shtml.

Chapter 5

1. Om Malik, "Pandora: Streaming Everywhere on Everything," *Bloomberg Businessweek,* January 12, 2010 http://www.businessweek.com/technology/content/jan2010/tc20100112_584610.htm.
2. "The Great 1906 San Francisco Earthquake," USGS, http://earthquake.usgs.gov/regional/nca/1906/18april/index.php accessed July 14, 2010.
3. "Moore's Law," www.intel.com/technology/mooreslaw, accessed April 2, 2010.
Electronics TakeBack Coalition, "Facts and Figures on E-Waste and Recycling," www.electronicstakeback.com, accessed April 3, 2010.
"EPA Report to Congress on Server and Data Center Energy Efficiency," www.energystar.gov/ia/partners/prod_development/downloads/EPA_Report_Exec_Summary_Final.pdf, accessed January 23, 2008.
4. Ibid.
5. Ibid.
6. "Switch on the Benefits of Grid Computing," h20338.www2.hp.com/enterprise/downloads/7_Benefits%20of%20grid%20computing.pdf, accessed on April 2, 2010.
"Talking to the Grid," www.technologyreview.com/energy/23706/, accessed April 3, 2010.
"Tech Update: What's All The Smart Grid Buzz About?," www.fieldtechnologiesonline.com/download.mvc/Whats-All-The-Smart-Grid-Buzz-About-0001, accessed April 3, 2010.
7. Ibid.
8. Ibid.
9. Ibid.

10. "VMware-History of Virtualization," www.virtualizationworks.com/Virtualization-History.asp, accessed January 23, 2008.
11. Rich Miller, "Google Data Center FAQ," www.datacenterknowledge.com/archives/2008/03/27/google-data-center-faq/, accessed April 1, 2010.
12. "VMware-History of Virtualization," www.virtualizationworks.com/Virtualization-History.asp, accessed January 23, 2008.
13. Rich Miller, "Google Data Center FAQ," www.datacenterknowledge.com/archives/2008/03/27/google-data-center-faq/, accessed April 1, 2010.
14. Rich Miller, "Google Data Center FAQ," www.datacenterknowledge.com/archives/2008/03/27/google-data-center-faq/, accessed April 1, 2010.
15. *UPS Invests $1 Billion in Technology to Cut Costs, by Agam Shah, IDG News Service, © 2010 IDG News Service. Reprinted with permission.*
16. "Olympic Medals Made from E-Waste," news.discovery.com/tech/olympic-medals-made-from-e-waste.html, accessed April 4, 2010.

    Rob Delaney, Olympic Champs Wear Old Trinitrons as Teck Turns Junk to Medals," *Bloomberg Businessweek,* February 3, 2010, http://www.bloomberg.com/apps/news?pid=newsarchive&sid=az0yJ8scpCqQ.
17. Google Docs, docs.google.com accessed June 4, 2010.
18. Martin LaMonica, "The Journey of Juice, Inside The Electric Grid," *CNET News,* August 24, 2010, http://news.cnet.com/8301-11128_3-20014393-54.html.
19. www.box.net, accessed April 2, 2010.
20. Goodwill Industries International, "Dell and Goodwill®Expand Free Recycling Program to Include Microsoft Product," April 21, 2010, http://www.goodwill.org/press-releases/dell-goodwill-expand-free-consumer-recycling-program-to-include-microsoft-products/ accessed June 3, 2010.
21. One Laptop Per Child, http://laptop.org/en/, accessed June 5, 2010.

Chapter 6

1. *Reprinted with special permission from Business Intelligence Software's Time Is Now, by Rachael King, Bloomberg BusinessWeek, March 2, 2009.*
2. Julia Kiling, "OLAP Gains Fans among Data-Hungry Firms," *ComputerWorld,* January 8, 2001, p. 54.
3. Allan Homes, "The TJX Security Breach. This One's Different. Way Different.," *CIO Magazine,* February 1, 2007, advice.cio.com/the-tjx-security-breach-this-ones-different-way-different.
4. "America's College College Startups: 2010," *Inc. Magazine,* 2010 http://www.inc.com/ss/cool-college-start-ups-2010.
5. Mitch Betts, "Unexpected Insights," *ComputerWorld,* April 14, 2003, www.computerworld.com, accessed September 4, 2003.
6. Jim Giles, "Data sifted from Facebook wiped after legal threats," *NewScientist,* March 31, 2010, www.newscientist.com/article/dn18721-data-sifted-from-facebook-wiped-after-legal-threats.html.
7. www.zappos.com, accessed on April 9, 2010.
8. "Data, Data Everywhere," *The Economist,* www.economist.com/specialreports/displayStory.cfm?story_id=15557443.
9. Julia Kiling, "OLAP Gains Fans among Data-Hungry Firms," *ComputerWorld,* January 8, 2001, p. 54.
10. Timothy Mullaney, "Netflix," *Bloomberg Businessweek,* May 25, 2006, www.businessweek.com/smallbiz/content/may2006/sb20060525_268860.htm.
11. www.google.com, accessed September 13, 2003.
12. Chris Wilson, "News Dots: The Day's Events as a Social Network," http://labs.slate.com/articles/slate-news-dots/, accessed on March 29, 2010.
13. *Reprinted with special permission from Data Visualization: Stories for the Information Age, by Maria Popova, Bloomberg Businessweek, August 12, 2009..*
14. Prashant Gopal "Zillow Opens Online Mortgage Marketplace," *Bloomberg Businessweek,* April 3, 2008, http://www.businessweek.com/lifestyle/content/apr2008/bw2008043_948040.htm.
15. Katie Cassidy "Barack Obama: "iPad Distracts from the Message," *Sky News,* May 10, 2010.
16. Ericka Chickowski "Goldman Sacs Sued for Illegal Database Access, *Security Darkreading.com,* May 11, 2010 http://www.darkreading.com/database_security/security/attacks/showArticle.jhtml?articleID=224701564&cid=nl_DR_DAILY_2010-05-12_h.

Chapter 7

1. www.ironman.com, accessed January 14, 2008.
2. "Top 23 U.S. ISPs by Subscriber: Q3 2010," *ISP Planet* http://www.isp-planet.com/research/rankings/usa.html.
3. Ibid.
4. "Bandwidth Meter Online Speed Test," CNET Reviews, http://reviews.cnet.com/internet-speed-test/ accessed June 2010.

    "Broadband Technology Overview," www.corning.com/docs/opticalfiber/wp6321.pdf, accessed February 1, 2008.
5. Ibid.
6. Ibid.
7. Ibid.
8. Ibid.
9. http://www.savetheinternet.com/, accessed May 15, 2010.
10. http://www.networksolutions.com/ accessed May 16, 2010.
11. www.godaddy.com, accessed May 16, 2010.
12. "IP Telephony/Voice over IP (VoIP): An Introduction," Cisco, http://www.cisco.com/en/US/tech/tk652/tk701/tsd_technology_support_protocol_home.html, accessed April 24, 2010.

    "VoIP Business Solutions," www.vocalocity.com, accessed January 21, 2008.
13. Ibid.
14. Ibid.
15. Ibid.
16. http://www.google.com/tv/, accessed April 30, 2010.
17. Internet 101, http://www.internet101.org/, accessed April 5, 2010.
18. ViVu: Better Than Being There, http://vivu.tv/vivuweb/, accessed May 4, 2010.
19. Boston Digital Bridge Foundation, http://www.digitalbridgefoundation.org/, accessed May 18, 2010.
20. The Liberty Coalition, :Carnivore – DCS 1000," July 27, 2006, http://www.libertycoalition.net/node/247.
21. "A Science Odyssey," *PBS,* http://www.pbs.org/wgbh/aso/databank/entries/btmarc.html.
22. "Rip Curl Turns to Skype for Global Communications," www.voipinbusiness.co.uk/rip_curl_turns_to_skype_for_gl.asp July 07, 2006, accessed January 21, 2008.

    "Navigating the Mobility Wave," www.busmanagement.com, accessed February 2, 2008.

"Sprint Plans Launch of Commercial WiMAX Service in Q2 2008," www.intomobile.com, accessed February 10, 2008. Deepak Pareek, "WiMAX: Taking Wireless to the MAX," CRC Press, 2006, pp. 150–wimax.com, accessed February 9, 2008.

23. Thru 32.
33. "Upward Mobility in Africa," *Bloomberg Businessweek,* September 24, 2007 http://www.businessweek.com/magazine/content/07_39/b4051054.htm.
34. V. C. Gungor, F. C. Lambert, "A Survey on Communication Networks for Electric System Automation, Computer Networks," *The International Journal of Computer and Telecommunications Networking,* May 15, 2006, pp. 877–897.
35. Mohsen Attaran, "RFID: an Enabler of Supply Chain Operations," *Supply Chain Management: An International Journal* 12 (2007), pp. 249–57.
Michael Dortch, "Winning RFID Strategies for 2008," *Benchmark Report,* December 31, 2007.
36. Damian Joseph, "The GPS Revolution," *Bloomberg Businessweek,* May 27, 2009 http://www.businessweek.com/innovate/content/may2009/id20090526_735316.htm.
37. Natasha Lomas, "Location Based Services to Boom in 2008," *Bloomberg Businessweek,* February 11, 2008, http://www.businessweek.com/globalbiz/content/feb2008/gb20080211_420894.htm.
38. Ibid.
39. Chris Silva, Benjamin Gray, "Key Wireless Trends That Will Shape Enterprise Mobility in 2008," www.forrester.com, accessed February 12, 2008.
40. Julia Layton, "How Cell Phone Viruses Work," *How Stuff Works,* http://electronics.howstuffworks.com/cell-phone-virus.htm/printable.
41. Michael Copeland, "Let the Helmet Make the Call," *Fortune,* February 4, 2010 http://money.cnn.com/galleries/2010/technology/1002/gallery.football_helmets_sensors.fortune/index.html.
42. Google Earth, "Jane Goodall Institute-Gombe Chimpanzee Blog," http://earth.google.com/outreach/cs_jgi_blog.html accessed April 3, 2010.
43. RFID Security Alliance, http://www.rfidsa.com/, accessed June 15, 2010.
44. Ibid.
45. Ibid.
46. Alissa Walker, "The Technology Driving Denver's B-cycle Bike Sharing System," *Fast Company,* June 3, 2010 http://www.fastcompany.com/1656160/the-technology-driving-denvers-new-b-cycle-bike-sharing-system?partner=rss.
47. Noam Cohen, "In Allowing Ad Blockers, a Test for Google," *The New York Times,* January 3, 2010 http://www.nytimes.com/2010/01/04/business/media/04link.html.
48. Julius Genachowski, "America's 2020 Broadband Vision," *The Official Blog of The Federal Communication Commission,* February 17th, 2010 http://reboot.fcc.gov/blog/?entryId=172819.
49. Al Sacco, " Foursquare Addresses Cheating Issue, Frustrates Legit Users," CIO Magazine, April 8, 2010 http://advice.cio.com/al_sacco/10000/foursquare_addresses_cheating_issue_frustrates_legit_users.
50. Ryan Singel, "FYI, Pandora Makes Your Music Public," *Wired Magazine,* May 14, 2010 http://www.wired.com/epicenter/2010/05/pandora-privacy/#ixzz118uMDaUa Wired Magazine.
51. Rob Flickenger, "Antenna On The Cheap," O'reilly Wireless DevCenter, July 2001, http://www.oreillynet.com/cs/weblog/view/wlg/448.
52. Hugo Miller, "AT&T Sparks User Backlash With End to Unlimited Plans," June 04, 2010, *Bloomberg Businessweek,* http://www.businessweek.com/news/2010-06-04/at-t-sparks-user-backlash-with-end-to-unlimited-plans-update2-.html.
53. Robert McMillian, "Domain Name Record Altered to Hack Comcast.net," *PC World,* May 28, 2009, http://www.pcworld.com/businesscenter/article/146461/domain_name_record_altered_to_hack_comcastnet.html.
54. Clint Boulton, "Google Street View Accidentally Collected User Data via WiFi," *eWeek,* May 16, 2010.
http://www.eweek.com/c/a/Search-Engines/Google-Street-View-Accidentally-Violates-User-Privacy-Via-WiFi-290159/.
55. http://top10.com/broadband/news/2010/02/top_10_broadband_gadgets/, accessed June 2010.
56. C.G. Lynch, "GPS Innovation Gives Weather Bots a New Ride," *CIO Magazine,* May 09, 2007 http://www.cio.com/article/108500/GPS_Innovation_Gives_Weather_Bots_a_New_Ride.
57. Austin Carr, "Kayak.com Cofounder Paul English Plans to Blanket Africa in Free Wireless Internet," *Fast Company,* May 12, 2010 http://www.fastcompany.com/1645485/kayak-co-founder-starting-initative-to-blanket-africa-in-free-wireless-internet.
58. Chris Matyszczyk "Marathon winner disqualified for wearing iPod," *CNET News,* October 11, 2009, http://news.cnet.com/8301-17852_3-10372586-71.html.
59. Bob Sullivan, "Ding A Ling Took my $400," MSNBC.com, October 2, 2009, http://redtape.msnbc.com/2009/10/mary-coxs-consumer-nightmare-began-with-poor-satellite-television-reception-but-ended-up-costing-her-a-430-early-terminatio/comments/page/2/.
60. Associated Press, "Woman has 911 meltdown over McNuggets," *MSNBC.com,* March 4, 2009, http://www.msnbc.msn.com/id/29498350/.
61. http://www.citysense.net/, accessed June 2010.

Chapter 8

1. Carmine Gallo, "Delivering Happiness the Zappos Way," *Bloomberg Businessweek,* May 12, 2009 http://www.businessweek.com/smallbiz/content/may2009/sb20090512_831040.htm.
2. James P. Womack, Daniel Jones, and Daniel Roos, *The Machine That Changed the World* (New York, Harper Perennial, 1991).
3. www.kiva.com, accessed April 10, 2010.
4. "Post Office Losses Reach $4.7B for Year," *CBS News,* August 5, 2009 http://www.cbsnews.com/stories/2009/08/05/national/main5216012.shtml.
5. "Harley-Davidson on the Path to Success," www.peoplesoft.com/media/success, accessed October 12, 2003.
6. "Integrated Solutions—The ABCs of CRM," www.integratedsolutionsmag.com, accessed November 12, 2003.
7. "Barclays, Giving Voice to Customer-Centricity," crm.insightexec.com, accessed July 15, 2003.
8. "Nice Emotions," http://www.nice.com/smartcenter-suitexs, accessed March 10, 2010.
9. "Customer Success," www.rackspace.com, accessed June 2005.
10. The Balanced Scorecard, www.balancedscorecard.org, accessed February 2008.
11. *Reprinted with special permission from When Customer Loyalty Is a Bad Thing," by Timothy Keiningham and Lerzan Aksoy, Bloomberg Businessweek, May 8, 2009.*

12. *Reprinted with special permission from Contaminated Milk Sours China's Dairy Business by Chi-Chu Tschang, Bloomberg BusinessWeek, Sept. 26, 2008.*
13. Quinn, "The Payoff Potential," and William Copacino, "How to Become a Supply Chain Master," *Supply Chain Management Review,* September 1, 2001, www.manufacturing.net, accessed June 12, 2003.
14. "Bridgestone/Firestone Tire Recall." *About.com,* August 9, 2000, http://usgovinfo.about.com/blfirestone.htm.
15. http://www.walmart.com/cp/An-Introduction-to-Walmart.com/542413, accessed May 2010.

Chapter 9

1. *Reprinted with special permission from Four Steps to Getting Things On Track, Bloomberg BusinessWeek, July 7, 2010.*
2. "Overcoming Software Development Problems," www.samspublishing.com, accessed October 2005.
3. www.ted.com, accessed June 15, 2010.
4. Antony Savvas, "Oklahoma Department of Corrections leaks personal data from website," *ComputerWeekly.com,* April 2008, http://www.computerweekly.com/Articles/2008/04/18/230353/Oklahoma-Department-of-Corrections-leaks-personal-data-from.htm.
5. *CIO Magazine,* June 1, 2006; "The Project Manager in the IT Industry" www.standishgroup.com; Johnson, "My Life Is Failure" and McGraw, "Making Essential Software Work."
6. Agile Alliance Manifesto, www.agile.com, accessed November 1, 2003.
7. "Building Software That Works," www.compaq.com, accessed November 14, 2003.
8. "Software Costs," *CIO Magazine,* www.cio.com, accessed December 5, 2003.
9. IBM Rational Unified Process, http://www-01.ibm.com/software/awdtools/rup/, accessed January 2010.
10. The Project Management Institute, www.pmi,org, accessed June 2010.
11. Ibid.
12. Ibid.
13. http://books.google.com/googlebooks/library.html, accessed March 15, 2010.
14. The Project Management Institute, www.pmi,org, accessed June 2010.
15. Jose Martinez, "Lesson In Fraud: NYU Employee Submitted $409K In Fake Expenses Using Receipts From Garbage," New York Daily News, December 23, 2009.
16. *CIO Magazine,* June 1, 2006; "The Project Manager in the IT Industry" www.standishgroup.com; Johnson, "My Life Is Failure" and McGraw, "Making Essential Software Work."
17. Karl Ritter, "Bill Murray faces DUI after golf-cart escapade in Sweden," *The Seattle Times,* August 22, 2007, http://seattletimes.nwsource.com/html/entertainment/2003848077_webmurray22.html.
18. Edward Yourdon, *Death March: The Complete Software Developer's Guide to Surviving "Mission Impossible" Projects* (Pearson Education).
19. "Baggage Handling System Errors," www.flavors.com, accessed November 16, 20.
20. "Overcoming Software Development Problems," www.samspublishing.com, accessed October 2005.

Appendix A

1. "Electronic Breaking Points," *PC World,* August 2005.
2. Tom Davenport, "Playing Catch-Up," *CIO Magazine,* May 1, 2001.
3. "Hector Ruiz, Advanced Micro Devices," *BusinessWeek,* January 10, 2005.
4. www.powergridfitness.com, accessed October 2005.
5. Denise Brehm, "Sloan Students Pedal Exercise," www.mit.edu, accessed May 5, 2003.
6. Margaret Locher, "Hands That Speak," *CIO Magazine,* June 1, 2005.
7. www.needapresent.com, accessed October 2005.
8. Aaron Ricadela, "Seismic Shift," *Information Week,* March 14, 2005.
9. www.mit.com, accessed October 2005.
10. "The Linux Counter," counter.li.org, accessed October 2005.

Appendix B

1. Andy Patrizio. Peer-to-Peer Goes Beyond Napster, *Wired*, http://www.wired.com/science/discoveries/news/2001/02/41768 accessed January, 2009.
2. Intel in Communications, "10 Gigabit Ethernet Technology Overview," http://www.intel.com/network/connectivity/resources/doc_library/white_papers/pro10gbe_lr_sa_wp.pdf accessed January, 2009.
3. Cisco, "TCP/IP Overview," http://www.cisco.com/en/US/tech/tk365/technologies_white_paper09186a008014f8a9.shtml accessed January, 2009.
4. Ibid.
5. IPv6, HYPERLINK "http://www.ipv6.org" www.ipv6.org, acessed January, 2009.
6. Cisco, "TCP/IP Overview," http://www.cisco.com/en/US/tech/tk365/technologies_white_paper09186a008014f8a9.shtml accessed January, 2009.
7. Cisco, "Network Media Types," http://www.ciscopress.com/articles.asp?p=31276 accessed January, 2009.
8. Ibid.
9. Ibid.

PHOTO CREDITS

Chapter 1

Page 3 left, © Digital Vision/Getty Images/DAL.

Page 3 center, © Digital Vision/Getty Images/DAL.

Page 3 right, © Masterfile (Royalty-Free Division)/DAL.

Chapter 2

Page 41 left, © The McGraw-Hill Companies, Inc./DAL.

Page 41 center, © Jack Star/PhotoLink/Getty Images/DAL.

Page 41 right, © Steve Cole/Getty Images/DAL.

Chapter 3

Page 88 left, © ThinkStock/SuperStock/DAL.

Page 88 center, © Getty Images/Blend Images/DAL.

Page 88 right, © BananaStock/PictureQuest/DAL.

Figure 3.18, page 107, © Punchstock/Digital Vision/DAL.

Figure 3.20, page 110 top, © Radius Images/Corbis/RF.

Chapter 4

Page 132 left, © 2007 Getty Images, Inc.

Page 132 center, © Simon Jarratt/Corbis/DAL.

Page 132 right, © Royalty-Free/Corbis/DAL.

Chapter 5

Page 167 left, © AP Photo/Jeff Chiu.

Page 167 center, © Mike Margol/PhotoEdit.

Page 167 right, Courtesy of Pandora Media, Inc.

Chapter 6

Page 202 left, © Image Source/SuperStock/DAL.

Page 202 center, © Steve Cole/Getty Images/DAL.

Page 202 right, © Imagestate Media (John Foxx)/DAL.

Chapter 7

Page 242 left, © Corbis - All Rights Reserved/DAL.

Page 242 center, © Corbis - All Rights Reserved/DAL.

Page 242 right, © Corbis - All Rights Reserved/DAL.

Chapter 8

Page 287 left, © Ethan Miller/Getty Images.

Page 287 center, © BananaStock/PunchStock/DAL.

Page 287 right, © Noah Berger/Bloomberg via Getty Images.

Chapter 9

Page 332 left, © Jason Reed/Ryan McVay/Getty Images/DAL.

Page 332 center, © BananaStock/Jupiterimages/DAL.

Page 332 right, © Janis Christie/Getty Images/DAL.

Appendix A

Figure A.2 clockwise from top left, page A.3, © Royalty-Free/Corbis/DAL, © Stockbyte/PunchStock Images/DAL, © Nick Rowe/Getty Images/DAL, © Digital Vision/Getty Images/DAL, © Image Club/DAL, © Royalty-Free/Corbis/DAL, © Getty Images/Photodisc/DAL, © Daisuke Morita/Getty Images/DAL, © Don Bishop/Photodisc/Getty Images/RF, © Stockbyte/PunchStock Images/DAL, © Stockbyte/PunchStock Images/DAL.

Page A.3 bottom left, © Royalty-Free/Corbis/DAL.

Page A.3 bottom right, © Stockbyte/PunchStock Images/DAL.

Page A.4, © Nick Rowe/Getty Images/DAL.

Page A.5, © Don Bishop/Photodisc/Getty Images/RF.

Page A.6 top, © Daisuke Morita/Getty Images/DAL.

Page A.6 bottom left, © Stockbyte/PunchStock Images/DAL.

Page A.6 bottom right, © Stockbyte/PunchStock Images/DAL.

Page A.8 left, © Digital Vision/Getty Images/DAL.

Page A.8 right, © Image Club/DAL.

Page A.9 left, © Getty Images/Photodisc/DAL.

Page A.9 right, © Royalty-Free/Corbis/DAL.

Page A.10, © Digital Vision/Getty Images/DAL.

INDEX

A

B

C

D

E

M

N

T

U

V

W

X

Z